Springer Series in Su[

MW01286232

Volume 4

Series Editor
Christopher S. Tang
University of California
Los Angeles, CA, USA

More information about this series at http://www.springer.com/series/13081

Yann Bouchery • Charles J. Corbett
Jan C. Fransoo • Tarkan Tan

Editors

Sustainable Supply Chains

A Research-Based Textbook on Operations and Strategy

 Springer

Editors
Yann Bouchery
Axe Logistique Terre Mer Risque
Ecole de Management de Normandie
Le Havre, France

Charles J. Corbett
Anderson School of Management
University of California Los Angeles
Los Angeles, CA, USA

Jan C. Fransoo
School of Industrial Engineering
Eindhoven University of Technology
Eindhoven, The Netherlands

Tarkan Tan
School of Industrial Engineering
Eindhoven University of Technology
Eindhoven, The Netherlands

ISSN 2365-6395   ISSN 2365-6409   (electronic)
Springer Series in Supply Chain Management
ISBN 978-3-319-80655-6   ISBN 978-3-319-29791-0   (eBook)
DOI 10.1007/978-3-319-29791-0

Printed on acid-free paper

This Springer imprint is published by Springer Nature
The registered company is Springer International Publishing AG Switzerland

Preface: About This Book

Objectives and Intended Audience

Who is this book for? In this Preface we give a quick introduction to the objectives and intended audience of the book, the guiding principles we adopted in assembling it, and its structure. In the Introduction (Chap. 1, by Bouchery et al. 2017), we offer some more broader perspectives on the current and future state of sustainability in supply chains.

Sustainability is increasingly seen as a supply chain issue, not something that a single firm can deal with effectively. Several authors have produced review articles on sustainable supply chains, as well as special issues of journals, including Linton et al. (2007), Srivastava (2007), and Seuring and Müller (2008). Reviews on sustainable operations, often including some discussion of supply chains, include Angell and Klassen (1999), Kleindorfer et al. (2005), and Corbett and Klassen (2006). Several books with similar titles have also appeared, each with their own focus. Some are aimed primarily at practitioners, such as *Greening the Supply Chain*, edited by Sarkis (2006); *Sustainable Supply Chains: Models, Methods, and Public Policy Implications*, edited by Boone et al. (2012); *Sustainable Supply Chain Management: Practical Ideas for Moving Towards Best Practice*, edited by Cetinkaya et al. (2010); *Green Supply Chains: An Action Manifesto* by Emmett and Sood (2010); and *Green Supply Chain Management: Product Life Cycle Approach* by Wang and Gupta (2011). The book on *Green Logistics: Improving the Environmental Sustainability of Logistics*, edited by McKinnon et al. (2010), focuses more in depth on logistics rather than on supply chains in the broader sense of the word.

Each of these reviews and books has their place, but none of them were produced with more technical graduate-level courses on sustainable supply chains in mind. That is our objective, to provide a textbook that can be used in M.Sc. or relatively technical M.B.A. courses (or advanced undergraduate courses) in this area. We have observed an increase in the number of such courses being offered, but without a corresponding increase in teaching materials. This book aims to draw on the latest research to support courses on sustainable supply chains for graduate programs such as business, management, industrial engineering, and industrial ecology.

Rather than write a mediocre book ourselves, we turned to leading experts to provide overviews of their respective fields. We asked them to describe the current state of affairs, and to identify future needs and trends, rather than presenting new results not yet published elsewhere. Nevertheless, we anticipate that the book should also be of interest for researchers in the broader sustainable supply chain space, whether from the operations management and industrial engineering side or more from the industrial ecology and life-cycle assessment side, as a vehicle to learn from another community and to identify new research opportunities.

Philosophy Behind This Book

In assembling this book, we followed a few key principles (discussed at more length in the Introduction). First, we use the term "sustainable" in a loose sense, meaning that one considers the triple bottom line in making decisions, i.e., taking into account economic, environmental, and social aspects. Second, we emphasize that sustainability is multidimensional and that measurement is key, which is why the book starts with several chapters on measurement. Third, we recognize the need to address a wide range of aspects of "sustainability" in the book, but do not necessarily aim to cover them all in every chapter. Fourth, and most importantly, we decided to let the experts who contributed these chapters speak: it is more important for readers to be exposed to a wide view of experts than just to hear our opinions. As a result, some topics may be covered in multiple chapters, while other topics are not covered at all.

Structure of This Book

The structure of the book is straightforward. Part I starts with several chapters on measurement and reporting. Separate chapters provide introductions to LCA, carbon footprinting, water footprinting, nonrenewable materials management, and reporting. Part II covers core operational aspects of sustainable supply chains, with separate chapters devoted to green logistics, green inventory management, green facility location, operational implications of environmental regulation, responsible purchasing, green technology choice, and principles of eco-design. Part III revolves around issues related to business models and strategy in sustainable supply chains, with chapters on the stock market value implications of environmental initiatives and business implications of sustainability practices, moving from a product-based to a service-based economy, and a strategic overview of closed-loop supply chains, design of sustainable food supply chains, and managing risk and uncertainty in sustainable supply chains. Part IV focuses more on the social dimension of sustainability, with chapters on how to improve social and environmental performance in global supply chains, perspectives on social responsibility in supply chains, and how to manage cross-sector partnerships with NGOs in sustainable supply chains. Inevitably, some chapters could have been arranged differently, and they can be read in any sequence. All chapters are also available from the publisher separately.

Le Havre, France	Yann Bouchery
Los Angeles, CA	Charles J. Corbett
Eindhoven, The Netherlands	Jan C. Fransoo
Eindhoven, The Netherlands	Tarkan Tan

Acknowledgments

We are deeply grateful to each and every author who contributed to this book, many of whom are leading authorities in their fields and none of whom were lacking in other opportunities. We worked closely with the authors, suggesting revisions here and there to enhance consistency between the chapters; despite their busy schedules, the authors were very gracious and patient with our requests. Without them, there would be no book. Naturally, it is difficult—no, impossible—to include in a single book every aspect of sustainable supply chains or to invite all the leading authorities in the field. Unsurprisingly, we failed on both fronts, and the resulting omission of some relevant topics and leading authorities can be chalked up to the space restrictions and time pressures we faced.

Between the four of us, we have too many parents, spouses, partners, children, colleagues, friends, and others to whom we are deeply indebted for their support (voluntary or involuntary, knowing, or otherwise) to name them all individually. We wish we could promise that with the completion of this book, we will have more time for all of you, but we cannot rule out that something else will come along to preoccupy us.

Contents

About the Editors

Yann Bouchery is an assistant professor at EM Normandie (France). Dr. Bouchery received a master's degree in industrial engineering and management from Lund University (Sweden) as well as a master's degree in industrial management and logistics from Ecole Centrale Lille (France). He obtained a Ph.D. in operations management from Ecole Centrale Paris (France) in 2012. His Ph.D. research dealt with sustainable supply chain optimization with a special focus on inventory models. He spent 2 years at Eindhoven University of Technology (the Netherlands) as a postdoc researcher. His research mainly focused on a Dinalog project called "Cargo driven intermodal transportation." This project aimed at studying container flow management at the cargo level and focused on both economic and environmental performance optimization. His main research interest is on sustainable operations and logistics. He has published articles in academic journals such as *International Journal of Production Economics* and *European Journal of Operational Research.*

Charles J. Corbett, Ph.D. is professor of operations management and sustainability at the UCLA Anderson School of Management, where he holds the IBM chair in management. He served as chairman and deputy dean of academic affairs from 2009 to 2012 and previously as associate dean of the M.B.A. program. His research and teaching focus on sustainable operations and operations of entrepreneurs and small business; he has published extensively in leading academic and business journals. Dr. Corbett has held various editorial positions in leading management journals as well as at the *Journal of Industrial Ecology* and currently serves as editor in chief for *Foundations and Trends in Technology, Information and Operations Management.* He was named an AT&T Faculty Fellow in Industrial Ecology in 1997, and in 2013 he was elected a lifetime fellow of the Production and Operations Management Society. He has received several teaching awards, in addition to the UCLA Staff Assembly's Faculty/Staff Partnership Award and the Anderson School's J. Clayburn LaForce Faculty Leadership Award. He founded and codirected the award-winning UCLA Leaders in Sustainability graduate certificate program and the Easton Technology Leadership Program. He has given (semi-)plenary and keynote lectures at conferences in Bali, Istanbul, Lima, Mexico City, Paris, Sao Paulo,

Salvador (Brazil), Shanghai, Tainan and Taipei (Taiwan), and Wroclaw (Poland). Professor Corbett holds a Ph.D. in production and operations management from INSEAD in Fontainbleau, France, and a drs. in operations research from Erasmus University Rotterdam (the Netherlands).

Jan C. Fransoo is a professor of Operations Management and Logistics in the School of Industrial Engineering at Eindhoven University of Technology in the Netherlands. He holds an M.Sc. in Industrial Engineering and a Ph.D. in Operations Management & Logistics from Eindhoven University of Technology. He also serves as Dean of the Graduate School of Eindhoven University of Technology. He is co-founder and member of the supervisory board of TKI Dinalog (Dutch Institute for Advanced Logistics), a Netherlands center of excellence in the area of supply chain management. Professor Fransoo held visiting appointments at Clemson University, the University of California at Los Angeles, Stanford University, and MIT. He serves as senior editor of *Production and Operations Management*, as associate editor of *Operations Research*, and holds advisory editorial positions at seven other academic journals in the fields of operations and supply chain management. He has published over 90 academic journal papers and book chapters and presented at many academic and industry conferences, on topics such as production planning, supply chain and inventory management, and sustainable logistics. His most recent work is addressing issues such as synchromodal transportation, retail distribution in megacities, and carbon-efficient supply chain management. As part from his academic activities, Professor Fransoo has conducted dozens of projects with industry, and has consulted with the World Bank and various national governments in developed and developing countries.

Tarkan Tan is an associate professor of sustainable operations management in the School of Industrial Engineering at Eindhoven University of Technology, the Netherlands. Dr. Tan received his Ph.D. in industrial engineering from the Middle East Technical University, Ankara, Turkey, in 2002. He spent one year at Columbia University, Graduate School of Business, Management Science/Operations Research Division, New York, as a Fulbright scholar. He joined Eindhoven University of Technology as a postdoc researcher in 2003 and started working as an assistant professor the same year in the Operations, Planning, Accounting, and Control group. He is currently the director of the operations management and logistics M.Sc. program at this university. In 2010 he spent an academic term at the University of California, Los Angeles, as a visiting scholar. Dr. Tan has been elected twice as the best lecturer in operations management and logistics M.Sc. program, by "Industria," the organization of the industrial engineering students of Eindhoven University of Technology. He is an executive board member of the European Supply Chain Forum. His research interests include inventory theory, capacity management, spare parts management, and supply chain management with a particular focus on the effects of carbon emissions. He served as guest editor for *International Journal of Production Economics* and currently serves as associate editor for *Mathematical Methods of Operations Research*. He has published articles in academic journals such as *Manufacturing & Service Operations Management*, *Transportation Science, IIE Transactions, Naval Research Logistics, Operations Research Letters*, and *European Journal of Operational Research*.

Chapter 1
Sustainable Supply Chains: Introduction

Yann Bouchery, Charles J. Corbett, Jan C. Fransoo, and Tarkan Tan

1.1 Sustainable Supply Chains: What's New?

Are supply chains becoming more or less sustainable over time? The answer is not obvious. In the 1960s, we became aware of the dangers inherent in various chemicals including those used in pesticides, specifically DDT. Some would point to Rachel Carson's 1962 book *Silent Spring* as a defining moment in the history of the environmental movement, contributing to the creation of the environmental movement and the Environmental Protection Agency in the USA. In the 1970s, we started to learn that seemingly innocent aerosols in spray cans were eating a hole in the ozone layer, removing a crucial protection against being toasted and eventually burned by the sun. Various regulatory and voluntary actions followed, and depletion of the ozone layer seems to have slowed down recently. In the 1980s, we found out that acid rain was killing our lakes and eating our cities. Various regulatory responses have since helped to reduce emissions of chemicals leading to acidification. During the 1990s, we heard horror stories of how workers in sweatshops in China, Vietnam, and elsewhere were treated. Firms such as Nike initially responded that they did not own the factories, and hence it was not their problem, but by the 2000s, at least some firms (including Nike) had completely changed their tone. Throughout these

Y. Bouchery (✉)
Axe Logistique Terre Mer Risque, Ecole de Management de Normandie, Le Havre, France
e-mail: ybouchery@em-normandie.fr

C.J. Corbett
Anderson School of Management, University of California Los Angeles,
Los Angeles, CA, USA
e-mail: charles.corbett@anderson.ucla.edu

J.C. Fransoo • T. Tan
School of Industrial Engineering, Eindhoven University of Technology, Eindhoven,
The Netherlands
e-mail: j.c.fransoo@tue.nl; t.tan@tue.nl

© Yann Bouchery, Charles J. Corbett, Jan C. Fransoo, and Tarkan Tan 2017
Y. Bouchery et al. (eds.), *Sustainable Supply Chains*, Springer Series in Supply
Chain Management 4, DOI 10.1007/978-3-319-29791-0_1

decades, it transpired increasingly clearly that anthropogenic emissions were likely contributing to rising levels of greenhouse gases in the atmosphere, with a variety of effects on sea level and climate. A plethora of regulatory and voluntary responses is underway to mitigate climate change, with decidedly mixed results so far.

But how much of all this is new? Insecticides have been regulated in the USA as far back as 1910, though what is now the UK already passed a rule in about 1236 AD that "forbade the addition of anything to the food supply which was 'not wholesome'" (Aspelin 2003, Chap. 2: 10–11). The ozone layer was discovered in 1913, and its properties and thickness were already increasingly measured during the subsequent decades (e.g., Solomon 1999). The link between acid rain and atmospheric pollution was established in 1852, with the term "acid rain" appearing in 1872; damaging effects of pollution had been observed even earlier (see, e.g., Cowling 1982). Early anti-sweatshop movements gave rise to the Factory Act in the UK in 1833 (Nardinelli 1980) and more recently to the Fair Labor Standards Act in the USA in 1938 (Samuel 2000).

Climate change is no different. Arrhenius (1896) already reported on the connection between atmospheric carbon dioxide concentrations and global temperature, predicting that a doubling of the CO_2 concentration would lead to a temperature increase of 4.9–6.1 °C (depending on the latitude). This estimate is remarkably close to more recent ones by the IPCC, who report a range of predicted temperature rises between 1.5–4.5 °C (Houghton et al. 1995). Arrhenius was keenly aware of the geological importance of his calculations, writing (p. 267) "I should certainly not have undertaken these tedious calculations if an extraordinary interest had not been connected with them." His primary motivation, however, was explaining the Ice Age, rather than predicting future global warming.

These timelines have a clear implication for any book on "sustainable supply chains": scientists of all kinds are undoubtedly already making observations and constructing theories of environmental and social aspects that we are blissfully unaware of today but that will come to haunt us in the decades to come. In other words, there can be no such thing as a "sustainable supply chain," as we do not and cannot know today what will be critical elements of "sustainability" tomorrow.

Even if we limit ourselves to the environmental and social factors that we are already aware of, a truly "sustainable" supply chain is difficult to envision. This is certainly true when one adopts a strong sustainability perspective, which does not allow manufactured capital to substitute for natural capital. Almost any supply chain, at some level, converts natural capital into manufactured capital, rendering them inherently unsustainable under that perspective. In the weak sustainability view, it is acceptable to deplete natural resources, as long as there is a corresponding increase in manufactured capital. Deforestation is acceptable as long as technological progress delivers substitutes for wood. Increasing water pollution is acceptable as long as decontamination technology advances in parallel. In this perspective, a supply chain could be sustainable if its "net" impact on people and planet is neutral, still a tall order. As Pagell and Wu argue in Chap. 15, sustainability in supply chains should be thought of in terms of trajectories, rather than absolute states.

Our quick historical sketches above underline that such trajectories can never have a well-defined endpoint. Instead, a more sustainable supply chain is one that is better at identifying current and future environmental and social impacts and finding ways to mitigate those. That is the, admittedly very loose, definition we use in this book for "sustainable." We take no position on weak vs. strong sustainability, on whether one should be more concerned about climate change, water availability, or social impacts. We do take the position that for a firm to thrive, it is increasingly imperative that it be aware of economic, environmental, and social dimensions of the entire supply chain it belongs to and that it proactively monitor and manage those.

The arguments so far might point towards the need for a firm to engage with its economic, environmental, and social impacts. But why would it need to do so for the entire supply chain within which it operates? As firms become progressively more tightly coupled in global supply chains, rather than being large vertically integrated monoliths, risks and opportunities associated with activities upstream or downstream will increasingly impinge upon their own well-being. Referring to "risks and opportunities associated with activities upstream or downstream" clearly signifies an equally broad and loose definition of "supply chains": we will not attempt to draw a clear boundary of what we do and do not consider part of a supply chain, but in this book, we do include not just suppliers and customers but also consumers, society, employees, communities, NGO partners, and others who in one way or another participate in the "activities upstream or downstream." For many firms, some of the main risks and opportunities do lie outside their own boundaries, hence necessitating this broader supply chain perspective.

To summarize, this book should not be called "Sustainable Supply Chains," but rather something like "Gradual but Never-Ending Paths Towards Less Unsustainable Global Value Networks."

1.2 Sustainable Supply Chains: What's Really New?

Having argued that in some sense "sustainability" is not new, one might still ask what *is* new? Why assemble this book at this particular point in time?

First, the scientific understanding of many aspects of sustainability is advancing faster than ever before. In the past, many environmental and social issues were largely treated independently from one another, but we are increasingly understanding that climate change interacts heavily with health and poverty. The links between energy, food, and water are sinking in. Climate change threatens biodiversity which in turn endangers continuity of supply of various crops, putting already poor constituencies at further risk, etc.

Second, the political landscape is evolving in parallel. While there is a wide variation in regulation and enforcement across countries, and even across cities or regions within countries, the global trend is undeniably towards more and more comprehensive environmental and social regulation.

Third, the landscape within which business operates is undergoing similar evolution. Firms no longer treat environmental concerns as single-issue one-off distractions, but are increasingly taking a comprehensive approach to managing their full spectrum of environmental and social (as well as economic) impacts. That is triggered in part by the evolution in scientific understanding and political agendas, but presumably most of all by the maturing realization that, done judiciously, a proactive approach to sustainability can go hand in hand with increased profitability (more on which below). This is the result of market forces, the changing regulatory environment, employee engagement, investor action, and more.

Finally, and perhaps most importantly in terms of this book, we have noticed a recent surge in the number of courses on "sustainable supply chain management" or related topics, but a relative lack of corresponding teaching materials. While sustainability has been widely studied at the level of company strategy and extensive pedagogical materials exist at that more strategic level, there is still a relative lack of materials on sustainability with a supply chain management perspective.

Taken together, we hope that these observations jointly indicate that the time is ripe for a book of this nature. At the same time, these observations point to some principles that we adopted in assembling this book, outlined in the next section.

1.3   Principles Underlying This Book

Having established that neither "sustainability" nor "supply chains" are necessarily new in themselves, we made a number of deliberate choices in designing this book, each of which we discuss in more detail below.

1. There are economic reasons for firms to adopt a proactive approach to sustainability (but not every sustainability initiative is necessarily profitable).
2. Merely measuring environmental and social impacts is often already enough to bring about improvements in performance.
3. Supply chain operations are key to boosting sustainability performance.
4. Sustainability is not a state, but (at best) a direction.
5. Sustainability involves engaging with a range of stakeholders, not limited to the traditional supply chain partners.

1.3.1   Economic Drivers of Sustainability

There is clearly a strong ethical dimension to sustainability. However, in this book we emphasize the economic side. Many studies seek to determine whether firms that are more sustainable are also more profitable. That question, as stated, is probably unanswerable, as "more sustainable" can mean too many different things, and even for any specific dimension of sustainability the answer will depend on too many conditions, such as geography, industry, market conditions, timing, and more. There are some meta-analyses of this literature that generally do point towards a positive link between sustainability and profitability; see for instance Orlitzky et al. (2003) for a meta-analysis of the link between corporate social performance and financial outcomes and Horváthová (2010) for the link between financial and environmental performance. This link need not always be direct; for instance, in Chap. 19, Scholten and Fynes (2017) discuss how sustainability can lead to greater resilience. Moreover, the fact that the weight of the evidence tilts towards a positive link does not mean that every sustainability initiative will be profitable by every metric. For instance, in Chap. 14, Jacobs et al. (2017) report that the US stock market responded negatively to firms' announcements of GHG and especially non-GHG emissions reductions, though they also point out that those emissions reductions may have other indirect benefits not immediately captured by the stock market reaction. Their findings should not be taken as implying that sustainability is not profitable; they do highlight that practitioners should not naively assume that every sustainability-related initiative will be immediately profitable or rewarded by the stock market.

This discussion might suggest that becoming more sustainable is optional. Sometimes, it is not: firms are facing increasing pressure to become more sustainable and to take their supply chains with them. That pressure comes from customers, both from individual consumers (especially in developed countries) and from organizations in the B2B context. Regulations continue to target larger segments of the supply chain and on more dimensions. Governments are moving more and more to a cradle-to-grave (or even cradle-to-cradle) perspective in designing regulation, which makes the supply chain the inevitable unit of analysis. In addition, non-governmental organizations (NGOs) find various ways to encourage or pressure firms to adopt more sustainable behavior, whether related to labor practices, eliminating various ingredients in food, reducing emissions, or otherwise. Add to this pressure from investors, banks, insurance companies, employees, and more, and it is clear that sustainability is often an imperative more than a luxury.

1.3.2 What You Measure Is What You Get

There are good reasons to believe that the mere act of measuring something triggers ways to improve it. The fact that Walmart, of all firms, was able to find ways to reduce both GHG emissions and costs by installing auxiliary power units in their trucks once they started taking a close look at their carbon footprint is a prime example of this. That is one reason why this book contains several chapters on measurement. Moreover, measurement is not at all straightforward and inherently requires a supply chain perspective. A firm seeking to reduce its "own" emissions faces two big challenges. First, it is practically impossible to unambiguously measure or even closely estimate a firm's responsibility for the emissions associated with a final product or service. A typical product goes through numerous manufacturing and transportation activities, often jointly operated by a number of companies in a supply chain. Second, the direct emissions that a firm might abate typically constitute a small part of the supply chain emissions. Matthews et al. (2008) report that across all industries, companies' direct emissions average only 14 % of their supply chain emissions *prior to* use and disposal. Therefore, sustainability measurement should take a supply chain perspective, rather than limiting itself to the firm's own emissions and impacts.

In Chap. 2, Guinée and Heijungs (2017) provide an introduction to life cycle assessment, which can be thought of as the overarching framework for measurement of environmental (and perhaps in future also social) impacts. Of all the environmental impacts, those related to climate change currently receive the most attention. Therefore, Chap. 3, by Boukherroub et al. (2017), focuses on measurement of carbon footprints specifically. Water is increasingly recognized as another key resource that is under threat, due to overuse, climate change, and pollution. Although the term "water footprint" insinuates a parallel with "carbon footprint," the measurement issues are in fact quite different, among others due to water not being time and space invariant the way that GHG emissions are. Hoekstra (2017) delves deeper into this in Chap. 4. There are numerous other raw materials that can be sources of concern, as outlined by Blass et al. (2017) in Chap. 5. Finally, Bateman et al. (2017) link these various measurement paradigms to reporting and disclosure programs in Chap. 6.

This series of chapters highlights that measurement, although highly valuable, is often not trivial. Challenges include the multiple dimensions of impacts that need to be consolidated, the appropriate acknowledgment of how impacts differ across space and time, the challenge of setting appropriate boundaries, how to deal with variation and uncertainty, and more. Many of these questions are the topic of ongoing research and unresolved. Nevertheless, we believe that the most frequent sustainability-related tasks which students will find themselves confronted with revolve around measurement.

1.3.3 Supply Chain Operations Are Key to Sustainability

One could argue that there are two broad domains within which one can strive for more sustainable outcomes. One is consumer behavior: this can be getting consumers to launder their clothes at lower temperatures and less frequently, or to consume less goods and services in the first place. That is largely outside the scope of this book. The other domain is the supply chain leading up to the consumer. Here, we contend, genuine improvements in sustainability outcomes ultimately require changes in the supply chain's operations, broadly defined. Operations form the core of every organization, whether in manufacturing, service, or nonprofit industries. In the past few decades, firms have experienced increasing globalization and a shifting focus to competition among networks of firms. Due to these trends, the field of supply chain management has become an increasingly central domain within operations. This can refer to greener logistics (Chap. 7 by Blanco and Sheffi 2017), inventory management (Chap. 8 by Marklund and Berling 2017), or facility location (Chap. 9 by Velázquez-Martínez and Fransoo 2017). The specific challenges and opportunities vary by industry, as Bloemhof and Soysal (2017, Chap. 18) discuss in the context of the food supply chain. Operations can involve adopting greener technologies (Ovchinnikov 2017, Chap. 12), rethinking product design (Luttropp 2017, Chap. 13), or developing closed-loop supply chains (Abbey and Guide 2017, Chap. 17).

Although inevitably these topics are discussed in separate chapters, one of the challenges in practice is that they are all interrelated. For example, a product or component design that serves the same functionality with less material use will not just help the manufacturer due to a cut down in the material costs, but it will also decrease all transport and storage related requirements downstream in the supply chain and hence also the related costs and environmental burden (such as emissions due to transport) in the supply chain. Similarly, developing technologies that increase fuel efficiency of vehicles or use renewable energy sources benefits also supply chain actors through decreased fuel usage.

Sometimes these operational changes are driven by changes in business model, by shifting the emphasis from products to services, as outlined in Bellos and Ferguson (2017, Chap. 16). In other instances, they result from regulation. Huang and Atasu (2017, Chap. 10) point out that even well-intended regulations can have adverse consequences, as the devil is often in the detail; an immediate consequence is that regulators also need a deeper understanding of the operations of the firms they are trying to regulate and that firms need a more nuanced understanding of the exact effect certain regulations will have on their supply chains.

1.3.4 Sustainability as a Direction, Not a State

As noted above, a supply chain is unlikely to ever be "sustainable" (even by the weak definition). It is nevertheless a worthwhile goal to constantly strive for, as some firms are aggressively doing. Dole's operating subsidiary Standard Fruit de Costa Rica will develop a carbon-neutral supply chain for bananas and pineapples from Costa Rica to North America and Europe[1] in keeping with Costa Rica's goal to become the first carbon-neutral country by 2030. Finsbury Green in Australia sells carbon-neutral paper under its FreshZero brand, offsetting all supply chain emissions. Tesco aims to be a zero-carbon business by 2050. Brazil's Natura Cosméticos offsets not only its own emissions but those of its entire supply chain, which is all the more noteworthy given that the supply chain accounts for 95 % of those emissions. As of 2015, Apple does not allow suppliers to use bonded labor. Other examples abound. In order to determine whether a firm or supply chain is making progress towards that goal, one has to have the right measures in place, hence our focus on measurement at the beginning of this book.

---

[1] http://www.doleorganic.com/index.php?option=com_content&view=article&id=158, last accessed October 1, 2015

Recognizing that sustainability is a path, not a state, it is helpful to analyze the stages that firms go through on that path. Pagell and Wu (2017, Chap. 15) outline three main trajectories that firms can follow and point out that choices firms make today determine the options available to them in future. This notion of path dependency, while well known in itself, is often neglected in the literature on sustainable supply chains. As a firm embarks on a path towards becoming more sustainable, that also changes the way they interact with their suppliers, as van Weele and van Tubergen (2017, Chap. 11) illustrate in more detail.

1.3.5 Sustainability Involves Wider Range of Stakeholders

An inescapable consequence of the rising expectations firms face related to sustainability is the expanding set of stakeholders they have to interact with and the more complex ways in which they have to interact with each of them. Keeping shareholders happy has long been a prime objective, but that now requires far more extensive reporting than ever before. This trend is further encouraged by an emerging set of NGOs who are, depending on one's perspective, either representing investors by asking these wide-ranging questions, or using investors to exert pressure on firms to expand their reporting. Customers, employees, and regulators are expecting more from firms. At the same time, firms are expected to be aware of environmental and social issues faced by communities around the world that are (positively or negatively) affected by their supply chains, whether directly or through local regulators and NGOs. Lee and Rammohan (2017, Chap. 20) explain the importance of sensing and responding to social and environmental problems in global supply chains. Sodhi and Tang (2017, Chap. 21) ask what social responsibility firms bear and argue that firms can and should take the utilities of a wide range of stakeholders into account when making decisions. Sometimes firms choose to partner proactively with NGOs to address environmental or social problems in their supply chains; Balaisyte et al. (2017, Chap. 22) discuss factors that contribute to the success of such partnerships.

1.4 The Future of Sustainable Supply Chains

We started this chapter by arguing that, in many ways, the themes currently being discussed under the heading "sustainability" are not new. Therefore, one easy prediction about what the future holds for sustainable supply chains is "more of the same." At the same time, it is certain that the future will bring new challenges and opportunities, some of which may already be visible today even if not yet recognized as major issues. Here, we first elaborate on what "more of the same" will look like and then speculate about what else may be around the corner.

1.4.1 More of the Same

We are convinced that "sustainability" will continue to become a larger part of the conversation between supply chain partners worldwide. These conversations will be increasingly wide ranging, moving from focusing on a single issue (such as carbon, child labor, or fire safety) to a more systematic multidimensional view. The emphasis may shift over time from one set of issues to another, depending on (unpredictable) world events, but we would be surprised if the overall emphasis on sustainability did not increase.

As a result of this, and of the constant expansion of resources dedicated to measuring and reporting sustainability performance, this will become an increasingly quantitative and standardized affair, ever more tightly integrated within firms' decision processes. This will enable firms to make more analytical, proactive, and long-term decisions related to sustainability, rather than (often) having to respond to "the issue of the day." Accounting as an organized profession emerged in the nineteenth century, and hence financial accounting has a head start of at least 100 years over sustainability accounting; one could use the advances that have occurred in financial accounting since the 1900s as a guideline for predicting what might happen with sustainability accounting and reporting over the coming 100 years. Despite those advances in financial accounting, the profession still faces challenges that are relevant for operations and supply chains.

One is that the data that are generated for financial accounting purposes are often unsuitable for operational decision-making, but nevertheless widely used for precisely that as there is no other easy substitute available. One can anticipate the same happening with sustainability-related information: data on social impacts that is collected for the firm's annual sustainability report may not be suitable to support day-to-day decisions on how to operate a supply chain, but unfortunately it is likely that the errors that currently exist in how financial accounting information is used will be replicated in sustainability accounting.

A second challenge is that financial accounting data are still subject to various degrees of manipulation, ranging from mild and innocent to outright fraud. As sustainability reporting gains importance, the stakes become higher, and hence the likelihood of biases and actual fraud increases. The fact that sustainability-related information may be even harder to audit than financial information further exacerbates this.

1.4.2 What's Around the Corner

Climate change may be the most-discussed environmental (and social) issue facing the world today. However, some might argue that availability of freshwater may overtake climate change as the dominant topic, either because society tires of climate change or because it genuinely becomes a more imminent threat. Even if, as seems very unlikely today, renewable energy grows fast enough to prevent dangerous climate change, will we discover negative unintended consequences of photovoltaic panels, solar farms, and wind turbines? Some are already known, and as adoption becomes more widespread, others will inevitable crop up.

As our historical analogies at the beginning of this chapter point out, there are undoubtedly chemicals being used today, or even new materials being introduced today, that, at some point in future, will turn out to have been mistakes. The continued opposition to genetically modified organisms (GMOs), especially in Europe, suggest that many fear they will fall into this category. Nanomaterials have great promise, but their properties are far from fully understood.

Improving working and living conditions for employees and local communities in faraway countries upstream in a global supply chain seems very noble (and should be encouraged). Is there a risk that firms, in doing so, contribute to creating a population that is more educated and less despondent, more prone to travel or migrate around the globe, and therefore less accepting of local governments, democratic or otherwise? Will firms that find ways to reduce poverty end up contributing to increasing inequality and hence fomenting social problems that do not currently exist?

None of these questions have easy answers. The fact that there may be unintended negative consequences of well-intended actions today does not mean that we should not take those well-intended actions, quite the contrary. But it does mean that we should constantly be vigilant, looking for what new issues may emerge, recognizing that more sustainable supply chains can be a force for good but that they will never be truly sustainable. We hope that this book will contribute to educating future supply chain managers and business leaders about many of the issues they will face today and tomorrow and equip them with the tools and frameworks that will help them on this journey.

References

Abbey JD, Guide VDR Jr (2017) Closed-loop supply chains: a strategic overview. In: Bouchery Y, Corbett CJ, Fransoo JC, Tan T (eds) Sustainable supply chains: a research-based textbook on operations and strategy. Springer, New York

Arrhenius S (1896) On the influence of carbonic acid in the air upon the temperature of the ground. Philos Mag J Sci 41(251):237–276, Series 5

Aspelin AL (2003) Pesticide usage in the United States: trends during the 20th Century. Center for Integrated Pest Management, North Carolina State University, Raleigh. Technical Bulletin 105. http://nifa.usda.gov/sites/default/files/resources/Pesticide%20Trends.pdf. Accessed 3 Nov 2015.

Balaisyte J, Besiou M, Van Wassenhove LN (2017) Cross-sector partnerships for sustainable supply chains. In: Bouchery Y, Corbett CJ, Fransoo JC, Tan T (eds) Sustainable supply chains: a research-based textbook on operations and strategy. Springer, New York

Bateman AH, Blanco EE, Sheffi Y (2017) Disclosing and reporting environmental sustainability of supply chains. In: Bouchery Y, Corbett CJ, Fransoo JC, Tan T (eds) Sustainable supply chains: a research-based textbook on operations and strategy. Springer, New York

Bellos J, Ferguson M (2017) Moving from a product-based economy to a service-based economy for a more sustainable future. In: Bouchery Y, Corbett CJ, Fransoo JC, Tan T (eds) Sustainable supply chains: a research-based textbook on operations and strategy. Springer, New York

Blanco EE, Sheffi Y (2017) Green logistics. In: Bouchery Y, Corbett CJ, Fransoo JC, Tan T (eds) Sustainable supply chains: a research-based textbook on operations and strategy. Springer, New York

Blass V, Chebach TC, Ashkenazy A (2017) Sustainable non-renewable materials management. In: Bouchery Y, Corbett CJ, Fransoo JC, Tan T (eds) Sustainable supply chains: a research-based textbook on operations and strategy. Springer, New York

Bloemhof JM, Soysal M (2017) Sustainable food supply chain design. In: Bouchery Y, Corbett CJ, Fransoo JC, Tan T (eds) Sustainable supply chains: a research-based textbook on operations and strategy. Springer, New York

Boukherroub T, Bouchery Y, Corbett CJ, Fransoo JC, Tan T (2017) Carbon footprinting in supply chains. In: Bouchery Y, Corbett CJ, Fransoo JC, Tan T (eds) Sustainable supply chains: a research-based textbook on operations and strategy. Springer, New York

Cowling EB (1982) Acid precipitation in historical perspective. Environ Sci Technol 16(2):110A–123A

Guinée J, Heijungs R (2017) Introduction to life cycle assessment. In: Bouchery Y, Corbett CJ, Fransoo JC, Tan T (eds) Sustainable supply chains: a research-based textbook on operations and strategy. Springer, New York

Hoekstra AY (2017) Water footprint assessment in supply chains. In: Bouchery Y, Corbett CJ, Fransoo JC, Tan T (eds) Sustainable supply chains: a research-based textbook on operations and strategy. Springer, New York

Horváthová E (2010) Does environmental performance affect financial performance? A meta-analysis. Ecol Econ 70:52–59

Houghton JT et al (eds) (1995) Climate change 1994: radiative forcing of climate change and an evaluation of the IPCC IS92 emission scenarios. Cambridge University Press, Cambridge

Huang X, Atasu A (2017) Operational implications of environmental regulation. In: Bouchery Y, Corbett CJ, Fransoo JC, Tan T (eds) Sustainable supply chains: a research-based textbook on operations and strategy. Springer, New York

Jacobs B, Subramanian R, Hora M, Singhal V (2017) Market value implications of voluntary corporate environmental initiatives. In: Bouchery Y, Corbett CJ, Fransoo JC, Tan T (eds) Sustainable supply chains: a research-based textbook on operations and strategy. Springer, New York

Lee HL, Rammohan SV (2017) Improving social and environmental performance in global supply chains. In: Bouchery Y, Corbett CJ, Fransoo JC, Tan T (eds) Sustainable supply chains: a research-based textbook on operations and strategy. Springer, New York

Luttropp C (2017) Principles of EcoDesign in sustainable supply chains. In: Bouchery Y, Corbett CJ, Fransoo JC, Tan T (eds) Sustainable supply chains: a research-based textbook on operations and strategy. Springer, New York

Marklund J, Berling P (2017) Green inventory management. In: Bouchery Y, Corbett CJ, Fransoo JC, Tan T (eds) Sustainable supply chains: a research-based textbook on operations and strategy. Springer, New York

Matthews HS, Hendrickson CT, Weber CL (2008) The importance of carbon footprint estimation boundaries. Environ Sci Technol 42:5839–5842

Nardinelli C (1980) Child labor and the factory acts. J Econ Hist 40(4):739–755

Orlitzky M, Schmidt FL, Rynes SL (2003) Corporate social and financial performance: a meta-analysis. Organ Stud 24(3):403–441

Ovchinnikov A (2017) Green technology choice. In: Bouchery Y, Corbett CJ, Fransoo JC, Tan T (eds) Sustainable supply chains: a research-based textbook on operations and strategy. Springer, New York

Pagell M, Wu Z (2017) Business implications of sustainability practices in supply chains. In: Bouchery Y, Corbett CJ, Fransoo JC, Tan T (eds) Sustainable supply chains: a research-based textbook on operations and strategy. Springer, New York

Samuel HD (2000) Troubled passage: the labor movement and the fair labor standards act. Mon Labor Rev 123(12):32–37

Scholten K, Fynes B (2017) Risk and uncertainty management for sustainable supply chains. In: Bouchery Y, Corbett CJ, Fransoo JC, Tan T (eds) Sustainable supply chains: a research-based textbook on operations and strategy. Springer, New York

Sodhi MS, Tang CS (2017) Social responsibility in supply chains: a research-based textbook on operations and strategy. In: Bouchery Y, Corbett CJ, Fransoo JC, Tan T (eds) Sustainable supply chains: a research-based textbook on operations and strategy. Springer, New York

Solomon S (1999) Stratospheric ozone depletion: a review of concepts and history. Rev Geophys 37(3):275–316

Velázquez-Martínez JC, Fransoo JC (2017) Green facility location. In: Bouchery Y, Corbett CJ, Fransoo JC, Tan T (eds) Sustainable supply chains: a research-based textbook on operations and strategy. Springer, New York

Weele AV, van Tubergen K (2017) Responsible purchasing: moving from compliance to value creation in supplier relationships. In: Bouchery Y, Corbett CJ, Fransoo JC, Tan T (eds) Sustainable supply chains: a research-based textbook on operations and strategy. Springer, New York

Part I
Measuring Environmental Impacts in Supply Chains

Chapter 2
Introduction to Life Cycle Assessment

Jeroen Guinée and Reinout Heijungs

This chapter[1] gives an overview of the mainstream method of life cycle assessment (LCA) on the basis of the generally accepted principles as laid down in International Organization for Standardization (ISO) series of Standards on LCA. The first part is devoted to the key questions addressed by LCA and sketches the historical development towards that method. The second part provides an overview of the LCA method itself, while the third part discusses some examples of LCA applications. Finally, the fourth part discusses some of the future challenges to LCA including life cycle sustainability assessment (LCSA) and streamlined LCA techniques.

2.1 LCA: What Does It Address and How Has It Developed?

Today's society is highly consumption based. Through advertisements and marketing campaigns, we are stimulated on a daily basis to consume products, services and, if possible, more and more. Products and services are the key selling items of our economic system. At the same time we are facing huge sustainability challenges with respect to, e.g. climate change, land use change, water shortages, toxic pollution and resource scarcity. Products and services are key concepts in addressing these sustainability challenges. Refrain from any consumption is not an option, so we have to strive for a more sustainable production and consumption pattern. Environmental

---

[1] This chapter is partly based on Heijungs, R. & Guinée, J.B. (2012). An Overview of the Life Cycle Assessment Method—Past, Present, and Future. In: Curran, M.A. (Ed.), Life Cycle Assessment Handbook: A Guide for Environmentally Sustainable Products, pp. 15–42. Beverly: Scrivener Publishing.

J. Guinée (✉) • R. Heijungs
Leiden University, Leiden, Netherlands
e-mail: guinee@cml.leidenuniv.nl; heijungs@cml.leidenuniv.nl

© Yann Bouchery, Charles J. Corbett, Jan C. Fransoo, and Tarkan Tan 2017
Y. Bouchery et al. (eds.), *Sustainable Supply Chains*, Springer Series in Supply
Chain Management 4, DOI 10.1007/978-3-319-29791-0_2

policy today focuses at the transition to such sustainable production and consumption patterns. This is taking place in various ways and at various levels.

For this purpose we often will have to compare the sustainability of products against each other. We then first need a few definitions: what is sustainability, what are comparable products and what exactly are products?

- Sustainability has at least three dimensions: the economic, the environmental and the social dimensions; LCA focuses on the environmental dimensions only.
- Products fulfil functions or services. We buy a car, motor or bike to travel from A to B; we eat and drink to satisfy our nutritional needs; etc. We generally have different alternative products to fulfil these functions.
- We are not so much looking into products as such but rather at a system of economic or industrial processes needed for the functioning of that product. Here the term "product system" (or even better "function system") enters the arena. A product system refers to the entire life cycle of a product, from extraction of natural resources to final waste management of the disposed product, from "cradle to grave". We don't just look at driving a car, but we include the total system of industrial/economic processes needed for constructing all components of the car, the maintenance of the car, the use of the car including the total life cycle of the fuels needed to drive the car, the roads needed, etc. until the final disposal of the car at the end of its life which may include recycling.

Knowledge of the environmental impacts of such product systems is indispensable if we are aiming for improving the environmental performance of these systems. We preferably need numbers for all relevant environmental impacts of product systems, from the cradle to the grave (whole life cycle), in order to find best solutions for their improvement without shifting impacts to other fields or to other phases of the life cycle (trade-offs). One of the assessment methods widely used for this is environmental life cycle assessment, abbreviated LCA.

Do we really need a potentially complex method as LCA? Isn't driving an electric vehicle simply better than driving a gasoline-based vehicle? If it was as simple as that, we wouldn't need LCA but unfortunately the reality is much more complex if we take a systems approach mapping the whole life cycle and all potentially relevant environmental impacts. Electric vehicles need a lot of batteries to store electricity, and these batteries need a lot of scarce resources that may potentially leak to the environment as hazardous substances, but depending on the source of electricity, they may perform better in the use phase compared to gasoline-based cars. Only by analysing the full life cycle of these two functionally equivalent "car driving systems", we can determine which one is environmentally better performing. But even then, it's often not possible to simply conclude that one option is better than the other as it may still depend on consumer's behaviour or on the source of electricity (e.g. renewables or fossil fuels) as in the case of the electric car (Hawkins et al. 2012). The same ratio can be applied to comparing plastic and carton disposable mugs with porcelain mugs for drinking coffee, disposable diapers versus cotton diapers, biofuel- versus fossil fuel-based electricity systems, etc.

2.1.1   *LCA in a Nutshell*

LCA offers a method for quantitatively compiling and evaluating the inputs, outputs and the potential environmental impacts of a product system throughout its life cycle (ISO 1996), and its results may be used to support decision-making in this area. LCA refers to a method, but it also refers to the result of this method. In this chapter, we will mainly focus on the method that is used to obtain an "LCA result".

LCA has made a long way, and it is still changing. But since a decade or so, there is a broadly accepted set of principles that can claim to be the present-day LCA framework based on a series of standards and technical reports issued by the ISO, the 14040 series (ISO 1996, 1998, 2000, 2000a, b, 2002, 2003, 2006, 2012, 2012a, b). This series consists of the documents listed in Table 2.1.

The standards are organized into the different phases of an LCA study. These are:

- Goal and scope definition
- Inventory analysis
- Life cycle impact assessment
- Life cycle interpretation

The relations between these phases have been illustrated in a figure, and this figure has become a sort of logo of LCA (Fig. 2.1).

Table 2.1 ISO documents on LCA

Number	Type	Title	Year
14040	International Standard	Principles and framework	1996, 2006
14041	International Standard	Goal and scope definition and inventory analysis	1998[a]
14042	International Standard	Life cycle impact assessment	2000a[a]
14043	International Standard	Life cycle interpretations	2000b[a]
14044	International Standard	Requirements and guidelines	2006[b]
14047	Technical report	Examples of application of ISO 14042	2003
14047	Technical report	Examples of ISO 14044 impact assessment application	2012a
14048	Technical specification	Data documentation format	2002
14049	Technical report	Examples of application of ISO 14041	2000
14049	Technical report	Examples of ISO 14044 goal and scope definition and inventory analysis application	2012b
14067	Technical report	Carbon footprint of products; requirements and guidelines	2012

[a]Updated in 2006 and merged into 14044
[b]Replaces 14041, 14042 and 14043

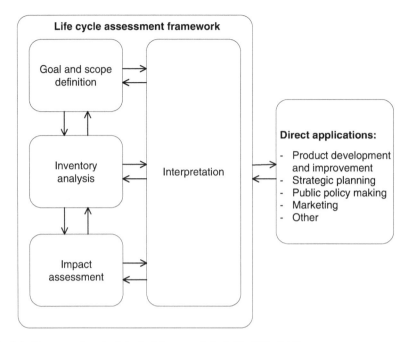

Fig. 2.1 The general methodological framework for LCA (ISO 1996)

2.1.2 History of LCA

As mentioned, LCA has made a long way. This section discusses the historical development of LCA in terms of its past and present. The text is largely based on Guinée et al. (2011).

2.1.2.1 The Past of LCA (1970–2000)

Firstly, we will briefly discuss and evaluate LCA as developed and applied in the past while distinguishing two periods: (1) 1970–1990 and (2) 1990–2000.

1970–1990: Decades of Conception

The first studies that are now recognized as (partial) LCAs date from the late 1960s and early 1970s, a period in which environmental issues like resource and energy efficiency, pollution control and solid waste became issues of broad public concern (Assies 1992). One of the first (unfortunately unpublished) studies quantifying the resource requirements, emission loadings and waste flows of different beverage containers was conducted by Midwest Research Institute (MRI) for the Coca Cola Company in 1969. Together with several follow-ups, this marked the beginning of the development of LCA as we know it today. After a period of diminishing public interest in LCA and a number of unpublished studies, there has been rapidly growing interest in the subject from the early 1980s on. In 1984 the Swiss published a report (BUS 1984) that presented a comprehensive list of the data needed for LCA studies, thus catalysing a broader application of LCA.

The period 1970–1990 comprised the decades of conception of LCA with widely diverging approaches, terminologies and results. There was a clear lack of international scientific discussion and exchange platforms for LCA. During the 1970s and the 1980s, LCAs were performed using different methods and without a common theoretical framework. LCA was repeatedly applied by firms to substantiate market claims. The obtained results differed greatly, even when the objects of the study were the same, which prevented LCA from becoming a more generally accepted and applied analytical tool (Guinée et al. 1993).

1990–2000: Decade of Standardization

The 1990s saw a remarkable growth of scientific and coordination activities worldwide. Also the first scientific journal papers started to appear in the *Journal of Cleaner Production*, in *Resources, Conservation and Recycling*, in the *International Journal of LCA*, in *Environmental Science & Technology*, in the *Journal of Industrial Ecology* and in other journals.

The Society of Environmental Toxicology and Chemistry (SETAC) started playing a leading and coordinating role in bringing LCA practitioners, users and scientists together to collaborate on the continuous improvement and harmonization of LCA framework, terminology and methodology. Next to SETAC, the ISO has been involved in LCA since 1994. Whereas SETAC working groups focused at development and harmonization of methods, ISO adopted the formal task of standardization of methods and procedures.

The period of 1990–2000 can therefore be characterized as a period of *convergence* through SETAC's coordination and ISO's standardization activities, providing a standardized framework and terminology, and platform for debate and harmonization of LCA methods. In other words, the 1990s was a decade of standardization. During this period, LCA also became part of policy documents and legislation. The main focus was on packaging legislation.

Although this decade is mainly one of convergence, it is also the stage of scientific scrutiny, research into the foundations of LCA, and exploring the connections with existing disciplines. For instance, we observe sprouting ideas on consequential LCA and related allocation methods (Weidema 2000, Ekvall 2000) marking the transition to the present decade of LCA.

2.1.2.2   2000–Present: The Era of Elaboration

The first decade of the twenty-first century has shown an ever increasing attention to LCA. In 2002, the United Nations Environment Programme (UNEP) and the Society for Environmental Toxicology and Chemistry (SETAC) launched an International Life Cycle Partnership, known as the Life Cycle Initiative (http://www.lifecycleinitiative.org/). In 2005 the European Platform on Life Cycle Assessment (http://eplca.jrc.ec.europa.eu/) was established to promote the availability, exchange and use of quality-assured life cycle data, methods and studies for reliable decision support in (EU) public policy and in business. In the USA, the US Environmental Protection Agency started promoting the use of LCA (http://www.epa.gov/nrmrl/std/lca/lca.html), and also US environmental policy got increasingly life cycle based all over the world (e.g. http://www.gpo.gov/fdsys/pkg/BILLS-110hr6enr/pdf/BILLS-110hr6enr.pdf).

In this same period, several life cycle-based carbon footprint standards have been, or are being, established (http://www.lcacenter.org/LCA9/special/Carbon-footprint.html). Although the footprint concept is broader than LCA (it, for instance, includes organization footprints and national footprints as well), a rich literature has spawned around the product environmental footprint (PEF; http://ec.europa.eu/environment/eussd/smgp/product_footprint.htm), which basically is an LCA, and in addition carbon footprints (CF), which are LCAs focusing on greenhouse gases only. CF is now often associated with consumer products, and in an increasing number of cases, we find the CF score on the packaging or the label. The introduction of carbon footprint standards for supporting policies and (bioenergy) performance-based regulation raised some severe problems, which have often not yet been solved adequately (Matthews et al. 2008). Life cycle-based carbon footprint results need to be robust and "lawsuit-proof". This implies that the freedom of methodological choices for the handling of, e.g., biogenic carbon balances and allocation should be reduced to an absolute minimum and that uncertainties are dealt with appropriately, which is unfortunately not yet common practice. Another issue is the limited scope of carbon footprints towards climate change impacts neglecting the possible trade-off to other impact. Finally, we reiterate that the term footprint not necessarily refers to a functional unit-based LCA; see also Hoekstra's (2017), Chap. 4 in this volume.

The period 2000–present can be characterized as the decade of elaboration. While the demand on LCA increases, the period is characterized by a *divergence* in methods again. As ISO never aimed to standardize LCA methods in detail and as there is no common agreement on how to interpret some of the ISO requirements, diverging approaches have been developed with respect to system boundaries and allocation methods, dynamic LCA, spatially differentiated LCA, environmental input–output-based LCA (EIO-LCA) and hybrid LCA, which combines the strengths of classical LCA and environmentally extended input–output analysis (EE-IOA). On top of this, various life cycle costing (LCC; cf. Hunkeler et al. 2008) and social life cycle assessment (S-LCA; cf. Benoît and Mazijn 2009) approaches have been proposed and/or developed.

2.2   Overview of LCA

Typically, LCA starts by defining goal and scope, then proceeds to the inventory analysis, then optionally continues to impact assessment and ends with the interpretation. However, as indicated in Fig. 2.1, an LCA study is a highly iterative process, so that the LCA practitioner may need to go back to goal and scope after the preliminary inventory work, to move back from impact assessment to inventory analysis, to have a look at the interpretation in an early stage, etc.

Below, we will discuss the main idea and content of the four phases distinguished in Fig. 2.1 in separate subsections. All quotations are taken from the ISO documents, unless otherwise indicated.

2.2.1   Goal and Scope Definition

There is no explicit ISO definition of the first phase of LCA. However, it obviously centres around formulating the question and stating the context of answering this question. In the goal and scope definition, no data is collected and no results are calculated. Rather, it is a place where the plan of the LCA study is defined as clearly and unambiguously as possible. Likewise, in an LCA report, it should help the reader to quickly find out the precise question addressed and main principles chosen.

The goal of the LCA should deal with the following topics:

- The intended application
- The reasons for carrying out the study
- The intended audience
- Whether the results are to be used in comparative assertions disclosed to the public

The choices made here have an influence on the rest of the LCA procedure. For instance, depending on the intended audience, a critical review may be needed, and it may be important that an external expert takes this task.

In the scope definition, a number of major choices are made. First of all, the product system or systems to be studied and the function the system delivers (or in case of a comparative LCA, the functions the systems deliver). For instance, one might be interested in the product systems' incandescent light bulb versus the LED bulb, with the function of lighting a room.

An important aspect of the scope definition is the functional unit. It is obviously pointless to compare an incandescent bulb with a LED bulb: the life spans and performances differ considerably, and the function is not having a light bulb but having light of a certain quality. The functional unit expresses the function of the products and thereby offers a way to equalize differences in performance. A functional unit for analysing lighting systems could thus better be phrased in terms of the function, for instance "lighting a standard room of 15 m² with 1000 lm for 1 h". As LCA employs mathematically a linear calculation rule, the results will scale by choosing a numerically different functional unit (say, "lighting a standard room of 20 m² with 800 lm for 3 h"), but the alternatives considered will scale up or down consistently, so this will not affect the conclusions. A consequence is, however, that LCA cannot tell if a product is "sustainable" or "environmentally friendly"; LCA can only indicate if product X is "more sustainable" or "more environmentally friendly" than product Y or that the use phase is the "least sustainable" or "least environmentally friendly" part of the life cycle for product Z.

The scope definition further sets the main outline on a number of subjects that are discussed and further refined in more detail in the later phases. These include, amongst others:

• System boundaries
• Impact categories
• Treatment of uncertainty

The ISO standard and some other texts at places suggest that these topics are implemented in detail in the scope definition. This is wrong: the goal and scope definition is not concerned with collecting data or calculating results, so no concrete details on such topics can be specified at this phase.

2.2.2 Inventory Analysis

ISO defines inventory analysis (LCI) as the "phase of life cycle assessment involving the compilation and quantification of inputs and outputs for a product throughout its life cycle". It will be clear that quantification is an important aspect here, and numbers, in terms of data and calculations, are of central concern in the inventory analysis.

The LCI is built up on the basis of the unit process. A unit process is the "smallest element considered in the life cycle inventory analysis for which input and output data are quantified". Examples of unit process are coal mining, steel production, refining of oil, production of furniture, use of a TV, recycling of wastepaper and transport by lorry. Each of these processes is described in quantitative terms as having inputs and outputs. As a matter of fact, a unit process is in LCA considered as a black box that converts a bundle of inputs into a bundle of outputs. Inputs come in several types: products (including components, materials and services), waste for treatment and natural resources (including fossils, ores, biotic resources and land). Outputs come in several types as well: again products (including components, materials and services), waste for treatment and residuals to the environment (including pollutants to air, water and soil, waste heat and noise); see Fig. 2.2.

Unit processes form the building blocks of an LCA. This is because products are not harmful for the environment as such, except for the processes involved in

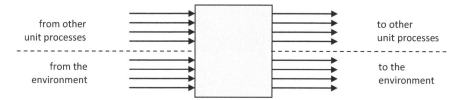

Fig. 2.2 General template of a unit process. The process (*grey rectangle*) is considered as a *black box*, having inputs (*left-hand side*) and outputs (*right-hand side*) from and to other unit process (*top lines*) and from and to the environment (*bottom lines*)

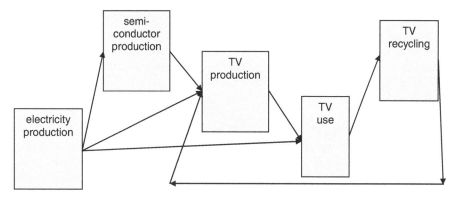

Fig. 2.3 Fragment of a simplified flow diagram for an LCA on television sets. Because the purpose is to show how unit process are connected, only the flows from and to other unit processes are displayed, and flows from and to the environment are hidden. All transport, packaging, etc. have been left out as well

products. Producing, using and disposing products create the burden to the environment. Therefore, these processes assume a central position in LCA.

The essential feature of LCA in which it distinguishes itself from the analysis of an industrial or agricultural process is that it connects different unit process into a system. A flow diagram is a graphical representation of the system of connected unit processes. Figure 2.3 shows a fragment of such a flow diagram.

As we can see, some unit processes are connected with one another in simple upstream–downstream connections, e.g. TV production is upstream connected to semiconductor production. But there are also more complicated connections, e.g. electricity linking to different parts of the system and recycling feeding back to production. Flow diagrams are in fact huge webs of interconnected unit processes. In the present era of digital databases, LCA studies can easily comprise several thousands of unit processes.

LCA is primarily a quantitative model. In the LCI, all unit processes included have to be quantified. This means that we have to specify the sizes of the inflows and outflows, per unit process. As an example, let us take the unit process of aluminium production.

Table 2.2 Example of a unit process specification

Type of flow	Name	Amount	Unit
Inputs from other unit processes	Aluminium oxide	2	kg
Inputs from other unit processes	Electricity	20	kWh
Outputs to other unit processes	Aluminium	1	kg
Outputs to the environment	CO_2	0.2	kg

An aluminium plant may specify their technology in terms of inputs and outputs by stating input requirements (e.g. 2 kg aluminium oxide and 20 kWh electricity per kg produced aluminium) and emissions (e.g. 200 g CO_2 per kg produced aluminium). We must translate this into our template for unit processes; see Table 2.2.

For each of the unit processes included, quantitative data should be collected. Moreover, in order to be able to process the data and perform the calculations automatically, a clear and unambiguous representation is needed. This implies, amongst others, harmonization of nomenclature (e.g. not using "carbon dioxide" for one unit process and "CO_2" for another one) and harmonization of units (e.g. not mixing up kg and lbs).

In Table 2.2, the unit process data is given per unit of output, here per kg of aluminium. In an LCA, we must next find out how much we need. For instance, the product may need 3 kg of aluminium, not 1 kg. The basic assumption of the LCA model is that technologies are linear. This means that we can scale the data of a unit process by a simple multiplication. In the example, 3 kg of aluminium would require 6 kg of aluminium oxide and 60 kWh of electricity, while it would release 600 g of CO_2. The assumption of linear technology is an important restriction of LCA; yet it is an important step in making the calculation and data collection feasible.

In scaling the unit processes, the web-like nature of the system quickly creates complications, as everything depends upon everything. The calculation of the scaling factors, and with that of the emissions to and extraction from the environment, is greatly simplified by considering the problem as a system of linear equations: one unknown (the scaling factor) for every unit process and one equation (a balance) for every flow. Thus, solutions may be obtained by matrix algebra. The details of this are not discussed here; see (Heijungs and Suh 2002) for a detailed exposition.

The approach mentioned above may fail in a number of cases. We mention two complications:

- For some products, upstream production processes or downstream disposal process may be difficult to quantify.
- For some unit processes, the balance equations become impossible due to the fact that these processes produce not just one product but several products.

The first issue can be solved by a procedure known as cut-off, the second one by allocation.

Cut-off is a solution to the problem that the system is theoretically infinitely large. To produce a TV, we need machines, and these machines are produced by machines, and these machines in turn need machines, etc. But of course we have an intuitive idea that some very distant upstream processes will be quite unimportant. This means that we will cut off certain inputs: although we know that something is needed, and we sometimes even know how much is needed, we do not go into the trouble of specifying how these inputs are produced. It turns out to be difficult to specify reliable criteria when cut-off is allowed or to estimate how large the error is when a cut-off is made. Criteria on the basis of negligible contribution to mass or cost (e.g. smaller than 1 %) often work pretty well but occasionally have been shown to yield large errors. Alternatively, estimates of missing parts by means of similar processes (e.g. estimating production of a freezer by production of a fridge) or by economic input–output tables may be helpful. Another approach is to do a difference analysis: in comparing a CRT and an LCD TV, we may leave out the broadcasting processes.

The second problem has given rise to one of the biggest controversies in LCA theory. The problem can be stated simply: if a transportation process needs gasoline, the upstream unit process is a refinery that produced not only gasoline but also diesel, kerosene, heavy oils and some more. The direct impacts (from pollutants like CO_2), but also the flows to and from other processes that may lead to impacts (e.g. from oil drilling), may be argued not to be attributed to gasoline only but in need to be distributed over gasoline, diesel and all other coproducts. This is hardly contested, but the debate focuses on how to do this. To make it more concrete: how much of the CO_2 from a refinery is allocated to the gasoline? Different schools have provided different arguments, and none of these have been completely compelling so far. Some solutions lead to strange results, other solutions may be very difficult to carry out (e.g. for lack of data or appropriate software), and still others are rejected by a large number experts. To complicate the issue, the problem does not only occur in unit processes that produce several coproducts but also in unit processes that treat more than one type of waste or that recycle a waste into a good. It is even not agreed if the multi-output case, the multi-input case and the recycling case must be treated in the same way or not.

Within ISO, a preference order for solving the multifunctionality problem has been designed. It distinguishes several solutions (dividing the unit process into two or more subprocesses, expanding the system to include the additional functions, partitioning on the basis of a physical parameter, partitioning on the basis of an economic parameter) separated by clauses like "wherever possible" and "where ... cannot be established". This stepwise procedure is a clear comprise, and in practice it leaves so much freedom that LCA studies that are according to the ISO standard can give conflicting results. One peculiarity deserves to be mentioned: besides the ISO-based "expanding the system to include the additional functions", we often see a method that is best described as "subtracting the avoided impacts from additional functions" but that is more commonly known as the substitution method or the avoided burdens method. For instance, when a waste treatment activity co-produces electricity, the emissions from the regular way of producing the same amount of electricity are subtracted. This method has similarities with that of system expansion, but of course it is not identical. Many LCA studies employing the substitution method claim to be ISO compliant, even though strictly speaking

ISO 14044 does not mention this method, let alone recommend it. That does not necessarily mean that these studies are incorrect, of course. Compliance with ISO is not a sufficient quality guarantee but also not a necessary one.

After appropriate cut-off and allocation steps, the final inventory results can be calculated. Typically, this is a table with the quantified inputs from and outputs to the environment, for each of the alternative systems considered, expressed in relation to the functional unit. With the present-day software and databases, this inventory table may be 1000 lines long or more. It contains not only the familiar pollutants and resources, such as CO_2, NO_x and crude oil, but also more exotic items, such as 1-pentanol, cyprodinil and dolomite. Typically, these so-called elementary flows are aggregated over the entire system, so that the CO_2 number is the life cycle emission of CO_2.

2.2.3   Impact Assessment

Life cycle impact assessment (LCIA), or impact assessment in short, is the "phase of life cycle assessment aimed at understanding and evaluating the magnitude and significance of the potential environmental impacts for a product system throughout the life cycle of the product". Its motivation comes from two observations:

- The final result of the inventory analysis, the inventory table, is too long (e.g. 1000 different items) to handle.
- The inventory table contains many items that require expert knowledge (such as 2-methyl-2-butene) to understand in terms of importance.

Impact assessment, and in particular the characterization step, solves both issues: it "involves the conversion of LCI results to common units and the aggregation of the converted results within the same impact category".

While the unit process is the central element of the inventory analysis, the central element in impact assessment is the impact category. ISO defines it as a "class representing environmental issues of concern to which life cycle inventory analysis results may be assigned". Perhaps more helpful are some examples: climate change, toxicity and depletion of fossil energy carriers.

As climate change (often used interchangeable with global warming) is a well-known issue, we will illustrate the main ideas of impact assessment with this case. The inventory table contains a number of greenhouse gases: CO_2, CH_4, N_2O, etc. These are known to contribute all to the phenomenon of climate change. Climate change involves long sequence of causal mechanisms: emissions of greenhouse gases lead to changes in the composition of the atmosphere, which lead to a change in the radiation balance, which in turn leads to a change in the temperature distribution, which leads to changes in climate, which leads to changes in ecosystems and human activities, etc. The further we proceed in this causal chain, the more uncertain and speculative our knowledge becomes. While quite some scientific evidence is available with respect to the composition of the atmosphere, the impacts on biodiversity are debated. Many of these later impacts are even conditional on our future activities, including future emission scenarios and mitigating actions. To be able to quantitatively model the emissions of different greenhouse gases into an impact indicator for climate change, we must do several things.

First, we must choose a certain point in the causal mechanism. This can be at the front end (change in radiation balance), at the back end (change of biodiversity) or somewhere in between (change in temperature). In LCA, two main schools have emerged:

- Those that focus on the front end, the so-called midpoint approach.
- Those that focus on the back end, the so-called end-point approach.

The midpoint approach has the advantage that it includes fewer debatable assumptions and less-established facts; the end-point approach has the advantage that it provides more intuitive metrics (like loss of life years instead of kg CO_2 equivalent). Regardless of the choice between midpoint and end point, the indicator chosen is referred to as the impact category indicator or category indicator in short.

Second, a way must be found to convert the emission data into the chosen impact indicator. Scientists in chemistry, meteorology, ecology, etc. have developed model fragments to estimate the atmospheric lifetimes of greenhouse gases, their effect on the radiation balance and the formation of clouds, the effects of temperature on the distribution of species, etc. These fragments have been combined by workgroups from the UN-based Intergovernmental Panel on Climate Change (IPCC) into quantitative models of the impacts of greenhouse gas emissions. Part of this are the global warming potentials (GWPs), which are quantitative measures of the strength of different greenhouse gases. Many midpoint LCIA methods apply GWPs for climate change. We will illustrate their usage below. For now, it suffices to mention that GWPs provide one example of a set of characterization factors and that the IPCC model from which they are derived is an example of a characterization model. Note, by the way, that IPCC has not developed this model as a characterization model for LCIA but that the LCA community has adopted this model as such and its derived GWPs as characterization factors. Also note that the characterization model itself is not used by LCA practitioners; only the characterization factors that have been derived from it as a one-time exercise are used. Characterization factors are often tabulated in LCA guidebooks and are implemented in many LCA software packages, while the characterization models often require supercomputers and expert knowledge.

In fact, there is one element before one can select a category indicator and a characterization model with associated characterization factors. It is the selection of impact categories to be addressed. Some LCA studies concentrate on just one impact category. For instance, the carbon footprint (of a product, not of a company or country) is a form of LCA that addresses just climate change at the midpoint level through GWPs. (Some chapters in this book go into more depth on a single impact category: see Chap. 3 by Boukherroub et al. (2017) for more on carbon footprinting, Chap. 4 by Hoekstra (2017) for more on water footprinting and Chap. 5 by Blass et al. (2017) for more on depletion of material resources.) At the other extreme, some LCA studies incorporate 15 or more impact categories. For consistency

Table 2.3 Overview of widely used impact categories with examples of category indicators at midpoint and end-point levels

Impact category	Midpoint category indicator	End-point category indicator
Climate change	Infrared radiative forcing	Loss of life years, fraction of disappeared species
Ozone layer depletion	Change in tropospheric ozone concentration	Loss of life years
Acidification	H^+ concentration	Fraction of disappeared species
Eutrophication	Biomass potential	Fraction of disappeared species
Human toxicity (sometimes split into carcinogens, noncarcinogens, respiratory effects, etc.)	Time-integrated exposure, corrected for hazard	Loss of life years
Ecotoxicity (sometimes split into aquatic toxicity, terrestrial toxicity, marine toxicity, etc.)	Time-integrated exposure, corrected for hazard	Fraction of disappeared species
Depletion of energy carriers	Primary energy requirement	Decreased availability
Depletion of material resources	Amount of material used, corrected for availability and/ or importance	Decreased availability
Land use impacts	Amount of land occupied or transformed	Fraction of disappeared species
Water use impacts	Amount of water used or displaced	Decreased availability

reasons, the choice of impact categories is often made on the basis of a recommended impact assessment guidebook or its implementation in software. Thus, in practice one often sees LCA studies reporting the use of "IMPACT2002+", "TRACI", "CML-IA", "ReCiPe", "ILCD", etc. All these methods comprise a recommended set of impact categories with a category indicator and set of characterization factors. ISO does not specify any choice in these matters. Table 2.3 gives an overview of some often-used impact categories and category indicators. We see that the column with end-point indicators contains many times the same term (e.g. "loss of life years"). This suggests that impact categories can be aggregated into fewer end-point indicators than midpoint indicators.

As a concrete example of how characterization works, let us study a fragment of a hypothetical inventory table, containing the following information: emission of CO_2 100 kg, emission of CH_4 1 kg and emission of SO_2 1 kg. Characterizing greenhouse gases with GWPs requires a table with GWPs. In such a table, one can find that the GWP of CO_2 is 1 (by definition) and that the GWP of CH_4 is 25 (kg CO_2 equivalent/ kg CH_4). SO_2 has no GWP; it is assumed not to contribute to climate change. Characterization now proceeds in the case of climate change by calculating

$$1 \times 100 + 25 \times 10 = 350 \, \text{kg CO}_2 \text{ equivalent}$$

For the more general case, this can be written as

$$GW = \sum_s GWP_s \times m_s$$

where GW is the global warming score, s the substance (the different greenhouse gases), GWP_s the GWP of substance s and m_s the emitted amount of substance s in kg. This may be further generalized as

$$I_c = \sum_s CF_{c,s} \times m_s$$

where c codes for the impact category, I_c represents the indicator result for category c and $CF_{c,s}$ is the characterization that links substance s to impact category c. This formula is the operational formula for characterization. With a table of characterization factors specified, it makes clear:

- That LCIA builds on the results of LCI (as is clear from the term m_s)
- That characterization converts the results of LCI into a common metric (as is clear from the multiplication by CF)
- That characterization aggregates the converted LCI results (as is clear from the summation symbol)

The results from characterization are a list of numbers, for instance, a score for climate change, a score for toxicity, etc. ISO refers to such numbers as "category indicator results", but most LCA practitioners prefer names like "score", sometimes expanded with the name of the impact (like in "toxicity score"). The complete list is known by names like "LCIA profile", "characterization table", etc.

An optional next step is normalization referring to calculating "the magnitude of the category indicator results relative to some reference information". It is an optional step for ISO, and indeed, many LCIA studies stop at the characterization. The reference information is in most cases that total impact in a certain region in a certain time period, e.g. in the country of decision in 1 year. Normalization is done "to understand better the relative magnitude for each indicator result". Without normalization, the indicator results are in quite different units, e.g. kg CO_2 equivalent for climate change and MJ primary energy for fossil energy depletion. To put these results in perspective, the normalization expresses them as a share of the total impact size in the region. Arbitrary differences due to a choice of units disappear, and it becomes clear to which impact category a product contributes relatively much. The units of the normalize indicator results are equal; nevertheless such numbers cannot meaningfully be added because the severity of the different impact categories has not yet been accounted for. This can be done in the weighting step; see below. Normalization fulfils several functions: it provides insight into the meaning of the impact indicator results, it helps to check for errors, and it prepares for a possible weighting step.

Weighting is a final step of the impact assessment phase. Weighting, like characterization, converts and aggregates, but while characterization does so for the LCI results, weighting starts with the characterization (or normalization) results. Typically, weighting factors are applied, either to the characterization indicator results or to their normalized version. The weighting factors themselves are supposed to reflect value judgements, such as social and political priorities. Weighting typically produces one final number, by means of

$$W = \sum_c WF_c \times I_c$$

where I_c again symbolizes the impact score (or normalized impact score) for impact category c, WF_c the weighting factor for this impact category and W the weighted result. Well-known examples of such weighted results are the eco-indicator and the ELU (environmental load unit).

2.2.4 Interpretation

ISO defines the interpretation as the "phase of life cycle assessment in which the findings of either the inventory analysis or the impact assessment, or both, are evaluated in relation to the defined goal and scope in order to reach conclusions and recommendations". Several elements are mentioned by ISO:

- Identification of significant issues
- An evaluation that considers completeness, sensitivity and consistency checks
- Conclusions, limitations and recommendations
- Appropriateness of the definitions of the system functions, the functional unit and system boundary
- Limitations identified by the data quality assessment and the sensitivity analysis

The text of ISO on interpretation is very concise, and no details are given on procedures and techniques to be employed. The same applies to most guidebooks on LCA. They mention carrying out an uncertainty analysis but give no clear guidance on how this should be done.

In another context, we have introduced the distinction between procedural and numerical approaches (Heijungs and Kleijn 2001):

- Procedural approaches include all types of analyses that deal with the data and results in relation to other sources of information, like expert judgements, reports on similar products, intuition, reputation of data suppliers and so on.
- Numerical approaches include those approaches that somehow deal with the data that is used during the calculations, without reference to those other sources of information, but as algorithms that use and process the data in different ways, so

as to produce different types of "smart" data reduction that provide an indication of reliability, key issues, discernibility, robustness and so on.

This distinction helps to understand some important roles of interpretation. On the one hand, it is about comparing the data and results with previous findings and to put the results in the context of decision-making and limitations. On the other hand, it is devoted to a systematic analysis with the help of statistical and other decision-analytic techniques. The latter type may be incorporated in software, and indeed, an increasing number of software packages contain options for running Monte Carlo analysis, doing sensitivity analysis, carrying out statistical significance tests, etc. For instance, in the CMLCA software, we have implemented, amongst others:

- Contribution analysis
- Comparative analysis
- Uncertainty analysis
- Perturbation analysis
- Key issue analysis
- Discernibility analysis

The iterative nature of the ISO framework (Fig. 2.1) shows up in this context. Whenever the uncertainties are too high, we may go back to collect better data. Whenever sensitivity analysis shows that some decisions are crucial, we may go back and do a more refined analysis. In this way, the interpretation helps to prepare for a balanced decision but also helps to improve the LCA.

The development of methods in this area is booming (see Henriksson et al. 2013; Henriksson et al. 2015), but current practice is quite meagre, unfortunately. We still see many LCA studies without uncertainty or sensitivity analysis, even though methods and software increasingly facilitate this. There is of course a psychological argument that a contractor pays for finding out something, not for increasing the doubt. And as many LCA practitioners spend several months on collecting data, it is never a nice thing to waste this effort in a last-minute uncertainty analysis. But decision-making obviously means also taking into account the limits of knowledge. Moreover, as discussed before, a proper analysis of uncertainties and sensitivities helps to prioritize the steps earlier on in the framework: collecting data, setting boundaries and making choices.

2.2.5 LCA in Practice

In the text above, the emphasis has been on the generally accepted practice. This is a mix of the ISO standards and a not precisely defined set of guidebooks (e.g. Wenzel et al. 1997; Guinée et al. 2002; Baumann and Tillman 2004; ILCD 2010; Curran 2012; Klöpffer and Grahl 2014). All these texts interpret, add, refine or modify the ISO standards. As has been indicated at a few places, the practice in LCA is sometimes different from what the ISO standards prescribe. There are differences in terminology (e.g. one seldom sees the term intermediate products), in method (cf. the frequent use of the substitution method), in quality control (judged by frequent absence of uncertainty analyses), etc.

There are also de facto additional standards, dictated by the use of software (for an overview, see http://eplca.jrc.ec.europa.eu/ResourceDirectory/toolList.vm) and databases (for an overview, see http://eplca.jrc.ec.europa.eu/ResourceDirectory/databaseList.vm). Many software packages for LCA have built-in options for impact assessment and uncertainty analysis, but nearly always in a restricted form, allowing some variants and prohibiting other variants. LCI databases are often constructed with predefined allocation methods and cut-off rules, so the user cannot choose otherwise and cannot carry out sensitivity analyses.

2.3   Examples of LCA Applications

LCA has been applied to a wide range of products and services. Until the late 1990s, bibliographies of LCA case studies performed were kept up to date (Grotz and Rubik 1997) on a continuous basis. Using Internet search machines results in a list of hundreds of LCA case studies documented in scientific papers or reports. Even more studies have been made for company-internal purposes, without publication in the scientific literature or on the web. LCA has been applied to simple products as shopping bags and packaging to more complex products such as mobile phones, PCs, cars and buildings. Studies may involve both an environmental comparison between existing products but also the development of new products (ecodesign). LCA has also been applied to services such as LCAs on hazardous waste site cleanup options, on waste management strategies and on different modes of freight transport (road, rail, water). As in the case of product LCAs, it is the function provided which is the core object of these service LCAs, but in this case the function is cleaning up a hazardous waste site, waste management or freight transport.

The results of these case studies were often in line with general expectations, but there were also numerous counter-intuitive results. We randomly provide a selection of examples of the latter below.

Fargione et al. (2008) stirred the biofuel debate by introducing the concept of "biofuel carbon debt". The increasing demand for biofuels was initially increasing the production of biofuels from food crops such as corn, sugarcane, soybeans and palms. As a result, land in undisturbed ecosystems, especially in the Americas and Southeast Asia, was being converted to biofuel production as well as to crop production (indirect land use change) when existing agricultural land was diverted to biofuel production (direct land use change). This land clearing releases huge amounts of CO_2 as a result of burning or microbial decomposition of organic carbon stored in plant biomass and soils over a long time. Fargione et al. (2008) called the amount of CO_2 released during the first 50 years of this process the "carbon debt" of land conversion. Over time, biofuels can afterwards repay this carbon debt if their production and combustion have less net GHG emissions compared to the life cycle emissions of the fossil fuels they displace. Their conclusion was that "converting rainforests, peatlands, savannas, or grasslands to produce food crop–based biofuels in Brazil, Southeast Asia, and the United States creates a 'biofuel carbon debt' by releasing 17–420 times more CO_2 than the annual greenhouse gas (GHG) reductions that these biofuels would provide by displacing fossil fuels. In contrast, biofuels made from waste biomass or from biomass grown on degraded and abandoned agricultural lands planted with perennials incur little or no carbon debt and can offer immediate and sustained GHG advantages". As policies throughout the world were increasingly promoting biofuels, this publication significantly influenced reconsidering these policies.

Bovea et al. (2010) compared the environmental life cycle performance of different alternatives for the management of municipal solid. They analysed and evaluated 24 different waste management scenarios. They concluded that "fuel consumed during the collection, transport and waste sorting stages makes a contribution to the impact in all the categories that were analyzed, since there is not any avoided environmental burden attributable to those processes". Moreover they conclude that "recycling allows the pollution burden to be avoided for all impact categories, since it avoids the consumption of virgin material according to the substitution rate of 1:1; the contribution made by landfilling depends on whether it is carried out with or without energy recovery [...]". This study shows the dependency of results of methodological choices such as the choice of allocation approach, which is particularly a problem in waste management studies (see also Ekvall et al. 2007).

Hawkins et al. (2012) developed a very comprehensive and transparent LCA study comparing the life cycle environmental performance of conventional and electric vehicles. They found that "EVs powered by the present European electricity mix offer a 10–24 % decrease in global warming results relative to conventional diesel or gasoline vehicles assuming lifetimes of 150,000 km. However, EVs exhibit the potential for significant increases in human toxicity, freshwater eco-toxicity, freshwater eutrophication, and metal depletion impacts, largely emanating from the vehicle supply chain. Results are sensitive to assumptions regarding electricity source, use phase energy consumption, vehicle lifetime, and battery replacement schedules". For EVs production impacts thus become more important, while for conventional cars the use phase is by far the most important phase. The environmental performance of the EV can be improved by extending the lifetime of the EV, reducing the impacts of the EV production supply chain and by wider adoption of cleaner electricity sources.

Gregory et al. (2013) evaluated and compared the environmental impact (focusing on climate change) of five hand-drying systems: hands-under dryers, high-speed hands-under dryers, high-speed hands-in dryers, cotton roll towels and paper towels. They also developed a method for incorporating uncertainty in the comparison of these hand-drying systems to understand the statistical robustness of the difference between the environmental impacts of the five hand-drying systems. They conclude "with a high degree of confidence that the high-speed dryers have a lower impact than paper towels and cotton roll towels".

van der Giesen et al. (2014) recently published an LCA study focusing on global warming impacts on a subject that receives increasing interest as part of the discussion on the transition towards renewable energy sources: using CO_2 as a resource to produce sustainable liquid hydrocarbon fuels. Producing these fuels by only using solar energy labels them as solar fuels. Today, new technologies for energy production are often claimed to be "sustainable" before they have been developed properly and/or subjected to any kind of sustainability assessment. Therefore, van der Giesen et al. (2014) performed a quantitative LCA "to investigate some of the claims made in this discussion". They concluded "that producing liquid hydrocarbon fuels starting from CO_2 by using existing technologies requires much more energy than existing fuels. An improvement in life cycle CO_2 emissions is only found when solar energy and atmospheric CO_2 are used. Producing fuels from CO_2 is a very long-term niche at best, not the panacea suggested in the recent public discourse".

2.4   Developments in and Challenges to LCA

LCA is an active research area in terms of methodology as well as in practical aspects. Methodology developers are working hard on further improving different parts of the LCA method while also putting efforts in keeping the methods practically feasible. We here briefly discuss a subjective selection of ongoing developments and challenges that LCA is facing:

1. Development of consequential LCA
2. Broadening LCA to LCSA
3. Dealing with uncertainty in LCA
4. Streamlining LCA and LCA for ecodesign
5. Standardization of LCA methods beyond ISO

2.4.1   Development of Consequential LCA

Since the beginning of the present century, consequential LCA has significantly grown in terms of the number of case study applications (Zamagni et al. 2012; Guinée and Heijungs 2011). Consequential LCA is a modelling approach that aims to describe the consequences of a decision and often models various scenarios to examine possible consequences. Consequential LCAs include unit processes in the product system to the extent that they are expected to change as a consequence of a change in the demand for the product (Weidema et al. 2009). Attributional—as opposed to consequential—LCA aims to describe the environmentally relevant physical flows to and from a life cycle and its subsystems as they are, were or are expected to be. According to Schmidt (2010) and Weidema (2003), the core differences between CLCA and attributional LCA (ALCA) are that (1) consequential LCA includes the suppliers actually affected by a change in demand instead of averages as in ALCA and (2) co-product allocation is avoided by system expansion instead of applying allocation factors. This change is modelled not over time but as a comparison of the situation with and without a specific demand; various product-related future scenarios are actually modelled. Future scenarios imply forecasting of future technologies, affluence and consumer behaviour and thus include large uncertainties, which increase as the term of the forecast becomes longer and the scope of the change becomes larger. Such uncertainties are inherent in modelling the future and thus also apply to an ALCA of a future system (Guinée and Heijungs 2011). However, due to the higher ambition of modelling how the world will look like, consequential LCA studies may have much bigger challenges in terms of data demand and models.

The modelling principles of ALCA and CLCA are the same; what distinguishes the two modes of LCA is the choice of the processes to be included in the system (Zamagni et al. 2012). Although the differences seem small, the application of the two modes to one case study (which can actually not be done, because they basically address different questions) may give significantly different results, not only between CLCA and ALCA but also between different (scenario) assumptions within CLCA (see Schmidt 2010). Bearing in mind that ALCA and CLCA can result in potentially significant differences, Plevin et al. (2014a) recently argued that "using ALCA to estimate climate-change mitigation benefits misleads policy-makers" basically claiming that CLCA is conceptually superior to ALCA for supporting robust decision-making. Plevin et al. received a lot of criticism (Anex and Lifset 2014; Brandão et al. 2014; Dale and Kim 2014; Hertwich 2014; Plevin et al. 2014b; Suh and Yang 2014; Plevin et al. 2014c), but the debate has not been cleared yet, if ever.

2.4.2 Broadening LCA to Life Cycle Sustainability Assessment

As disclosed in Sect. 2.1.2, environmental life cycle assessment (LCA) has developed fast over the last three decades. LCA developed from merely energy analysis to a comprehensive environmental burden analysis in the 1970s; full-fledged life cycle impact assessment and life cycle costing (LCC) models were introduced in the 1980s and 1990s, and—amongst many other things—social LCA (S-LCA) and particularly consequential LCA gained ground in the first decade of the twenty-first century. With these latter developments, LCA broadened itself from a merely environmental LCA into a more comprehensive life cycle sustainability analysis (LCSA). Based on definitions by Klöpffer and Renner (2007; see also Klöpffer 2008) and Guinée et al. (2011), we can distinguish three dimensions along which LCSA expanded or may expand when compared to environmental LCA:

1. *Broadening* the scope of current LCA from mainly environmental *impacts* only to covering all three dimensions of sustainability (people, planet and prosperity): LCSA=LCA+LCC+S-LCA.

2. *Broadening* the scope from predominantly product-related *questions* (product level) to questions related to sector (sector level) or even economy-wide levels (economy level).
3. *Deepening* current LCA *methods* to also include other than just technological relations, e.g. physical relations (including limitations in available resources and land), economic and behavioural relations (including rebound effects), etc.

LCSA is still a rather new area of research and needs a lot of further research, particularly in designing practical methods. Nevertheless, several articles on LCSA have already been published in international journals, professional sections have been established such as the ISIE-LCSA section (http://www.is4ie.org/sections#LCSA), and LCSA has become a subject area in, for example, the *International Journal of LCA* (http://www.springer.com/environment/journal/11367).

2.4.3   Dealing with Uncertainty in LCA

A huge challenge for environmental LCA, and even huger for LCSA and CLCA, is how to deal with the many uncertainties related to LCA and LCA results. Until today, this issue was largely underexposed by methodology developers, practitioners, databases and software.

LCA is an integral method, bringing together data on many processes, data and models on impacts, assumptions on functional unit, system boundaries, allocation, etc. All of these data and (impact) models already bring many uncertainties with them, and in LCA we lump these uncertainties. LCA practitioners are usually already happy when they get the main part of the data they need. Getting a grip on the uncertainties related to these data and to the models they apply is generally a bridge too far, let alone to also quantify the influence on the results of different methodological choices and different assumptions. However, work on this is progressing as shown above in the chapter on Interpretation. Recently, Henriksson et al. (2015) even showed that statistically testing a hypothesis—requiring a predefined null hypothesis and quantification of uncertainties—is practically feasible (and, as a matter of fact, indispensable) for LCA-based product carbon footprints and provides more robust decision support. Main challenges now are to harmonize methods developed, to consistently elaborate and apply them over all sources of uncertainties throughout the whole LCA method and to collect the relevant input uncertainty data. Particularly the latter requires substantial efforts and can only be achieved by reporting LCA data comprehensively, transparently and in a publicly accessible way.

2.4.4   Simplifying and Streamlining LCA

Improving the LCA method is one thing, but keeping it practically feasible for users is another. Options for simplifying and streamlining LCA have been reviewed by Zamagni et al. (2008) and Pesonen and Horn (2013). They distinguished three different types of simplified approaches: qualitative (e.g. qualitative matrices, checklists, expert panels), semi-quantitative (e.g. partly quantified matrices) and quantitative (simplified LCA). For all three categories practical methods have been developed. There is unfortunately no "one size fits all" solution for streamlining and simplification, and streamlined methods generally don't produce conclusions similar to those reached through full LCAs (Hunt et al. 1998). Zamagni et al. (2008) conclude that "the choice of the most suitable simplified method, or combination of simplified methods, depends on the type of results users are looking for". For a study "aiming at supporting a choice between several alternatives and a study aimed at identifying critical aspects and suggesting mitigation strategies different methods may be suitable. In the first case, it is much more important to have quantitative data than in the second case. In fact, in the first case the lack of a quantitative dimension would hinder the comparison and make it difficult to differentiate between products. On the other hand, problems could arise when in quantitative LCA, aspects that are difficult to quantify are handled qualitatively, because this qualitative information is often overlooked" (Hoschorner and Finnveden 2003; Zamagni et al. 2008). For this first type of question, the challenge is to simplified LCA models based on detailed LCA experiences for specific product (categories). The EU 5th framework project OMNIITOX developed models calculating characterization factors for assessing the potential toxic impacts of chemicals within the framework of LCA. The project developed two interrelated models in order to be able to provide LCA impact assessment characterization factors for toxic releases for as broad a range of chemicals as possible: (1) a base model representing a state-of-the-art multimedia model and (2) a simple model derived from the base model using statistical tools. Most simplified LCA models up till now have been developed in a rather "isolated" way, independent from detailed LCAs. The experiences in OMNIITOX (Birkved and Heijungs 2011) and reported by Huijbregts et al. (2006) seem useful to copy to simplified LCA models based on detailed LCAs for specific products. However, in some cases simplification may be much simpler than this. In the 1990s LCAs were performed on light bulbs, and the results were clearly dominated by the electricity needed for using the bulb. That steered all new bulb designs later on.

Simplification and streamlining are particularly relevant for ecodesigners. Ecodesign and LCA have always had a natural connection as they both strive to improve the environmental performance of product systems. Although the natural connection between the two seems obvious, there is also a natural tension between them. Whereas product designers in early stages often only have limited ideas—and thus data—on the eventual material and chemical composition of the product, an LCA study needs this information in order to produce useful supporting environmental information for the designer at stake. Designers' rules of thumb should be based on LCAs. The recent interest in meta-analysis of LCA (JIE 2012) is an interesting development in that respect. However, rules of thumb always have the danger of being wrong. In particular, they may turn out to be self-denying in the long run. For TV sets with a cathode ray tube, energy use was the most successful predictor of overall life cycle impact. With the development of flat screens, the value of this rule of thumb has decreased dramatically. Now the presence of the rare metals may be a better predictor.

2.4.5 Standardization of LCA Methods Beyond ISO

As disclosed in Sect. 2.1.2, the past first decade of the twenty-first century showed basically divergence in LCA methods again. On top of this LCA started increasingly supporting policies and (bioenergy) performance-based regulations. For that LCA results needed to be robust and reliable. Both robustness and reliability can be challenged. For example, some of these performance-based regulations in the field of bioenergy adopted ALCA, others consequential LCA and others a hybrid of these approaches, resulting in different ratings and even altering preference orders for transportation fuels that were the subject of these regulations. In addition, most regulations lack reporting requirements on the uncertainty of the LCA results and subjective choices by the LCA practitioner, which can result in LCA results seeming more certain and scientifically objective than they really are. It became clear that ISO standards were not sufficient to tackle these problems, and thus product carbon footprint standards were developed all around the world, and for EU policy applications, the *International Reference Life Cycle Data System (ILCD) Handbook* was developed (ILCD 2010).

Standardizing and harmonizing methods for supporting policies and performance-based regulations is of utmost importance, but it will remain a challenge to properly balance this need with the equally justified need of science to progress and improve itself. It may thus make sense to distinguish between LCAs for science and LCAs for policy. "Whereas the former aims for completeness, the latter aims for robustness. The use of LCA in the policy context will benefit largely from the acceptance of this difference and by drawing up a guideline that is based on the aim of robustness" (Wardenaar et al. 2012) with an update every now and then to include progresses in science, the balance could be established. Eventually, also here there will be no "one size fits all" solution, and we will have to accept that different questions require different approaches.

A complication that is getting more and more pervasive is that software and databases de facto dictate the methodology. For instance, if scientists prove that one method for uncertainty calculations is superior to another but the available software continues to offer only the inferior method, practice will not change. Similarly, scientists may develop noise impact methods, but if unit process databases do not offer information on sound emissions, such developments will remain within the academic domain only.

References

Anex R, Lifset R (2014) Life cycle assessment—different models for different purposes. J Ind Ecol 18(3):321–323

Assies JA (1992) Introduction paper to SETAC-Europe workshop on environmental life cycle analysis of products. In life-cycle assessment, Proceedings of a SETAC-Europe workshop on

Environmental Life Cycle Assessment of Products. December 2–3 1991, Leiden. SETAC-Europe, Brussels

Baumann H, Tillman A-M (2004) The hitch hiker's guide to LCA. Studentlitteratur, Lund

Benoît C, Mazijn B (eds) (2009) Guidelines for social life cycle assessment of products; UNEP/SETAC Life Cycle Initiative, Paris. http://www.estis.net/includes/file.asp?site=lcinit&file=524CEB61-779C-4610-8D5B-8D3B6B336463

Birkved M, Heijungs R (2011) Simplified fate modelling in respect to ecotoxicological and human toxicological characterisation of emissions of chemical compounds. Int J Life Cycle Assess 16(8):739–747

Blass V, Chebach TC, Ashkenazy A (2017) Sustainable non-renewable materials management. In: Bouchery Y, Corbett CJ, Fransoo J, Tan T (eds) Sustainable supply chains: a research-based textbook on operations and strategy. Springer, New York

Boukherroub T, Bouchery Y, Corbett CJ, Fransoo J, Tan T (2017) Carbon footprinting in supply chains. In: Bouchery Y, Corbett CJ, Fransoo J, Tan T (eds) Sustainable supply chains: a research-based textbook on operations and strategy. Springer, New York

Bovea MD, Ibáñez-Forés V, Gallardo A, Colomer-Mendoza FJ (2010) Environmental assessment of alternative municipal solid waste management strategies: a Spanish case study. Waste Manag 30(11):2383–2395

Brandão M, Clift R, Cowie A, Greenhalgh S (2014) The use of LCA in the support of robust (climate) policy-making: comment on "Using attributional life cycle assessment to estimate climate-change mitigation …". J Ind Ecol 18(3):461–463

Curran MA (ed) (2012) Life cycle assessment handbook: a guide for environmentally sustainable products. Scrivener Publishing, Beverly

Dale B, Kim S (2014) Can the predictions of consequential life cycle assessment be tested in the real world? Comment on "Using attributional life cycle assessment to estimate climate-change mitigation …". J Ind Ecol 18(3):466–467

Ekvall T (2000) A market-based approach to allocation at open-loop recycling. Resour Conserv Recycl 29(1–2):93–111

Ekvall T, Assefa G, Björklund A, Eriksson O, Finnveden G (2007) What life-cycle assessment does and does not do in assessments of waste management. Waste Manag 27(8):989–996

Fargione J, Hill J, Tilman D, Polasky S, Hawthorne P (2008) Land clearing and the biofuel carbon debt. Science 319(5867):1235–1238

Gregory JR, Montalbo TM, Kirchain RE (2013) Analyzing uncertainty in a comparative life cycle assessment of hand drying systems. Int J Life Cycle Assess 18(8):1605–1617. doi:10.1007/s11367-013-0606-0

Grotz S, Rubik F (1997) Bibliographie Produktbilanzen. Publication series of the Institut für ökologische Wirtschaftsforschung, Berlin, No. 92/97

Guinée JB (ed), Gorrée M, Heijungs R, Huppes G, Kleijn R, de Koning A, van Oers L, Wegener Sleeswijk A, Suh S, Udo de Haes HA, de Bruijn JA, van Duin R, Huijbregts MAJ (2002) Handbook on life cycle assessment: operational guide to the ISO standards. Eco-Efficiency in industry and science, vol 7. Springer, Dordrecht

Guinée JB, Heijungs R (2011) Life cycle sustainability analysis: framing questions to approaches. J Ind Ecol 15(5):656–658. doi:10.1111/j.1530-9290.2011.00398.x

Guinée JB, Udo de Haes HA, Huppes G (1993) Quantitative life cycle assessment of products 1: goal definition and inventory. J Clean Prod 1(1):3–13

Guinée JB, Heijungs R, Huppes G, Zamagni A, Masoni P, Buonamici R, Ekvall T, Rydberg T (2011) Life cycle assessment: past, present and future. Environ Sci Technol 45(1):90–96. doi:10.1021/es101316v

ILCD Handbook (2010) General guide for life cycle assessment—provisions and action steps. European Commission, JRC-IES, Ispra. http://lct.jrc.ec.europa.eu/pdfdirectory/ILCD-Handbook-General-guide-for-LCA-ROVISIONSonline-12March2010.pdf. Accessed 29 Mar 2010

Hawkins TR, Singh B, Majeau-Bettez G, Strømman AH (2012) Comparative environmental life cycle assessment of conventional and electric vehicles. J Ind Ecol 17(1):53–64

Heijungs R, Guinée JB (2012) An overview of the life cycle assessment method—past, present, and future. In: Curran MA (ed) Life cycle assessment handbook: a guide for environmentally sustainable products. Scrivener Publishing, Beverly, pp 15–42

Heijungs R, Kleijn R (2001) Numerical approaches to life-cycle interpretation. Five examples. Int J Life Cycle Assess 6(3):141–148

Heijungs R, Suh S (2002) The computational structure of life cycle assessment. Kluwer Academic Publishers, Dordrecht

Henriksson PJG, Guinée JB, Heijungs R, de Koning A, Green DM (2013) A protocol for horizontal averaging of unit process data—including estimates for uncertainty. Int J Life Cycle Assess 19(2):429–436

Henriksson PJG, Heijungs R, Dao HM, Phan LT, de Snoo GR, Guinée JB (2015) Product carbon footprints and their uncertainties in comparative decision contexts. PLoS One 10(3), e0121221

Hertwich E (2014) Understanding the climate mitigation benefits of product systems: comment on "Using attributional life cycle assessment to estimate climate-change mitigation …". J Ind Ecol 18(3):464–465

Hoekstra AY (2017) Water footprint assessment in supply chains. In: Bouchery Y, Corbett CJ, Fransoo J, Tan T (eds) Sustainable supply chains: a research-based textbook on operations and strategy. Springer, New York

Hoschorner E, Finnveden G (2003) Evaluation of two simplified life cycle assessment methods. Int J Life Cycle Assess 8(3):119–128

Huijbregts MAJ, Rombouts LJ, Hellweg S, Frischknecht R, Hendriks AJ, van de Meent D, Ragas AM, Reijnders L, Struijs J (2006) Is cumulative fossil energy demand a useful indicator for the environmental performance of products? Environ Sci Technol 40(3):641–648

Hunkeler D, Lichtenvort K, Rebitzer G (eds) (2008) Environmental life cycle costing. CRC Press, New York

Hunt RG, Boguski TK, Weitz K, Sharma A (1998) Case studies examining LCA streamlining techniques. Int J Life Cycle Assess 3(1):36–42

ISO International Standard 14040 (1996) Environmental management—life cycle assessment—principles and framework. International Organisation for Standardisation (ISO), Geneva

ISO International Standard 14041 (1998) Environmental management—life cycle assessment—goal and scope definition and Inventory analysis. International Organisation for Standardisation (ISO), Geneva

ISO International Standard 14042 (2000a) Environmental management—life cycle assessment—life cycle Impact assessment. International Organisation for Standardisation (ISO), Geneva

ISO International Standard 14043 (2000b) Environmental management—life cycle assessment—life cycle Interpretation. International Organisation for Standardisation (ISO), Geneva

ISO International Standard 14044 (2006) Environmental management—life cycle assessment—requirements and guidelines. International Organization for Standardization, Geneva

ISO International Standard 14067 (2012) Greenhouse gases—carbon footprint of products—requirements and guidelines for quantification and communication. Geneva

ISO Technical Report 14047 (2003) Environmental management—life cycle impact assessment—examples of application of ISO 14042. International Organisation for Standardisation (ISO), Geneva

ISO Technical Report 14047 (2012a) Environmental management—life cycle assessment—illustrative examples on how to apply ISO 14044 to impact assessment situations. International Organisation for Standardisation (ISO), Geneva

ISO Technical Report 14049 (2000) Environmental management—life cycle assessment—illustrative examples on how to apply ISO 14041—LCA—goal and scope definition and Inventory analysis (draft). International Organisation for Standardisation (ISO), Geneva

ISO Technical Report 14049 (2012b) Environmental management—life cycle assessment—illustrative examples on how to apply ISO 14044 to goal and scope definition and inventory analysis. International Organisation for Standardisation (ISO), Geneva

ISO Technical Specification 14048 (2002) Environmental management—life cycle assessment—data documentation format. International Organisation for Standardisation (ISO), Geneva

Journal of Industrial Ecology (JIE) (2012) Special issue: meta-analysis of life cycle assessments, April 2012, vol 16, Issue Supplement s1, pp S1–S205. Wiley

Klöpffer W (2008) Life cycle sustainability assessment of products. Int J Life Cycle Assess 13(2):89–95

Klöpffer W, Grahl B (eds) (2014) Life cycle assessment (LCA): a guide to best practice. Wiley-VCH Verlag GmbH & Co. KGaA, Weinheim

Klöpffer W, Renner I (2007) Lebenszyklusbasierte Nachhaltigkeitsbewertung von Produkten. Technikfolgenabschätzung — Theorie und Praxis (TATuP) 16:32–38

Matthews SH, Hendrickson C, Weber CL (2008) The importance of carbon footprint estimation boundaries. Environ Sci Technol 42(16):5839–5842

Pesonen H-L, Horn S (2013) Evaluating the Sustainability SWOT as a streamlined tool for life cycle sustainability assessment. Int J Life Cycle Assess 18(9):1780–1792. doi:10.1007/s11367-012-0456-1

Plevin RJ, Delucchi MA, Creutzig F (2014a) Using attributional life cycle assessment to estimate climate-change mitigation benefits misleads policy makers. J Ind Ecol 18(1):73–83

Plevin RJ, Delucchi MA, Creutzig F (2014b) Response to comments on "Using attributional life cycle assessment to estimate climate-change mitigation …". J Ind Ecol 18(3):468–470

Plevin RJ, Delucchi MA, Creutzig F (2014c) Response to "On the uncanny capabilities of consequential LCA" by Sangwon Suh and Yi Yang (Int J Life Cycle Assess, doi:10.1007/s11367-014-0739-9). Int J Life Cycle Assess 19(8):1559–1560

Schmidt JH (2010) Comparative life cycle assessment of rapeseed oil and palm oil. Int J Life Cycle Assess 15(2):183–197

Suh S, Yang Y (2014) On the uncanny capabilities of consequential LCA. Int J Life Cycle Assess 19(6):1179–1184

BUS (Bundesamt für Umweltschutz) (1984) Ökobilanzen von Packstoffen. Schriftenreihe Umweltschutz no. 24. Bern, Switzerland

van der Giesen C, Kleijn R, Kramer GJ (2014) Energy and climate impacts of producing synthetic hydrocarbon fuels from CO_2. Environ Sci Technol 48(12):7111–7121

Wardenaar T, van Ruijven T, Beltran AM, Vad K, Guinée J, Heijungs R (2012) Differences between LCA for analysis and LCA for policy: a case study on the consequences of allocation choices in bio-energy policies. Int J Life Cycle Assess 17(8):1059–1067. doi:10.1007/s11367-012-0431-x

Weidema B (2000) Avoiding co-product allocation in life-cycle assessment. J Ind Ecol 4(3):11–33

Weidema BP (2003) Market information in life cycle assessment. Environmental Project no. 863. Danish Environmental Protection Agency. Copenhagen

Weidema BP, Ekvall T, Heijungs R (2009) Guidelines for application of deepened and broadened LCA. Technical Report of CALCAS project. http://www.calcasproject.net

Wenzel H, Hauschild M, Alting L (1997) Methodology, tools and case studies in product development, vol 1, Environmental assessment of products. Chapman & Hall, London

Zamagni A, Buttol P, Porta PL, Buonamici R, Masoni P, Guinée JB, Heijungs R, Ekvall T, Bersani R, Bieńkowska A, Pretato U (2008). Critical review of the current research needs and limitations related to ISO-LCA practice. Deliverable 7 of the CALCAS project (http://www.estis.net/sites/calcas/)

Zamagni A, Guinée J, Heijungs R, Masoni P, Raggi A (2012) Lights and shadows in consequential LCA. Int J Life Cycle Assess 17(7):904–918. doi:10.1007/s11367-012-0423-x

Chapter 3
Carbon Footprinting in Supply Chains

Tasseda Boukherroub, Yann Bouchery, Charles J. Corbett, Jan C. Fransoo, and Tarkan Tan

3.1 Introduction

Climate change is a key issue in sustainability, as it may lead to dangerous increases in temperature and sea level, flooding, droughts, etc. (WRI and WBCSD 2004). Scientists all over the world are providing information supporting the fact that the climate is changing and that this change is partly due to human activities through the release of greenhouse gases (GHGs). "Carbon" is often used as a shorthand for GHGs, as carbon dioxide is the main GHG released by human activities. As a consequence, the activity of measuring GHG emissions is often referred to as carbon footprinting, the term we use in the reminder of this chapter.

A carbon footprint may concern an organization, a value chain, or a product (Carbon Trust 2014). The organizational carbon footprint accounts for emissions from all activities across an organization (including building energy use, industrial processes, and the company's vehicles). The value chain carbon footprint includes also emissions outside the organization's own operations (i.e., emissions from both suppliers and consumers, including product use and end-of-life emissions). Finally,

T. Boukherroub (✉)
Laval University, Leiden, Netherlands
e-mail: tasseda.boukherroub@cirrelt.ca

Y. Bouchery
Axe Logistique Terre Mer Risque, Ecole de Management de Normandie, Le Havre, France
e-mail: ybouchery@em-normandie.fr

C.J. Corbett
Anderson School of Management, University of California Los Angeles, Los Angeles, CA, USA
e-mail: charles.corbett@anderson.ucla.edu

J.C. Fransoo • T. Tan
School of Industrial Engineering, Eindhoven University of Technology,
Eindhoven, The Netherlands
e-mail: j.c.fransoo@tue.nl; t.tan@tue.nl

© Yann Bouchery, Charles J. Corbett, Jan C. Fransoo, and Tarkan Tan 2017 43
Y. Bouchery et al. (eds.), *Sustainable Supply Chains*, Springer Series in Supply
Chain Management 4, DOI 10.1007/978-3-319-29791-0_3

the product carbon footprint includes emissions over the whole life cycle of a given unit of product or service, from the extraction of raw materials and manufacturing to its use and final reuse, recycling, or disposal. This chapter focuses on the organization and value chain footprints; product-level carbon footprinting is more closely related to life-cycle assessment (LCA), which is covered in Chap. 2 by Guinée and Heijungs (2017).

This chapter is organized into four sections. Section 3.1 provides a brief scientific background on climate change, to the extent necessary to understand the methodology behind carbon footprinting. It also introduces the main motivations for carbon footprinting. Section 3.2 explains how carbon footprints can be measured and describes several carbon accounting methodologies. Section 3.3 focuses on supply chain carbon footprinting and provides an example from the automobile industry. Finally, Section 3.4 provides some challenges related to supply chain carbon footprinting in practice.

3.1.1   The Science of Climate Change

According to the Intergovernmental Panel on Climate Change (IPCC),[1] climate change refers to any change in climate over time due to natural variability or as a result of human activity (IPCC 2007). The scientific community has collected substantial evidence that the climate is changing (IPCC 2013a), as a result of the increased concentration of GHGs in the atmosphere, which is due in part to human activity. The main greenhouse gases are water vapor, carbon dioxide, methane, nitrous oxide, hydrofluorocarbons, perfluorocarbons, and sulfur hexafluoride. Some of these GHGs are naturally present in the atmosphere and are responsible for the greenhouse effect, a natural phenomenon responsible for warming the atmosphere and allowing life on Earth. However, in recent times, GHG emissions have increased, among others, due to industrialization and changes in agriculture and land use. Carbon dioxide, for example, is emitted by the combustion of fossil fuels such as coal, oil, and gas. Methane mainly comes from agriculture, livestock, and landfills. Nitrous oxide is found in large quantities in nitrogen fertilizer and chemical processes. These human-made GHGs known as "anthropogenic GHGs" intensify the greenhouse effect.

In order to measure the climate impact of GHG emissions, the life-cycle assessment (LCA) community (see Chap. 2 by Guinée and Heijungs (2017) for more detail) has developed an impact category called the global warming potential (GWP). GWP is the recommended metric to compare future climate impacts of emissions (IPCC 2007). It refers to the heat trapped in the atmosphere by a given amount of GHG over a given time period, relative to that trapped by an equivalent amount of CO_2 during the same period. Table 3.1 shows the GWP of some GHGs over 100-year and 20-year periods, respectively. For example, the GWP of methane (CH_4) over a 100-year period is 28. This means that 1 metric ton (referred to as ton

---

[1] IPCC is the leading international body for the assessment of climate change (http://www.ipcc.ch/).

Table 3.1 Atmospheric lifetime and global warming potentials of some GHGs

Gas	Atmospheric lifetime	100-year GWP	20-year GWP
CH_4 (methane)	12.4	28	84
HFC-134a (hydrofluorocarbon-134a)	13.4	1,300	3,710
CFC-11 (trichlorofluoromethane)	45	4,660	6,900
N_2O (nitrous oxide)	121	265	264
CF_4 (tetrafluoromethane)	50,000	6,630	4,880

Source: IPCC 2013b, Table 8.7

in what follows) of methane in the atmosphere over 100 years traps the same amount of heat as 28 t of carbon dioxide over 100 years. Carbon dioxide is taken as a reference for evaluating global warming as this is the most important anthropogenic GHG in quantity and in total impact (based on 100-year GWP calculations). Consequently, GHG emissions are often referred to as carbon emissions.

Table 3.1 shows that the GWP and the atmospheric lifetime vary widely between GHGs. The variation in atmospheric lifetimes means that the time period chosen to calculate the GWP may lead to significant differences. For instance, the atmospheric lifetime of methane is about 12 years, much lower than that of carbon dioxide. Consequently, the 20-year GWP of methane is much higher than the 100-year GWP. The opposite effect occurs when the atmospheric lifetime of a GHG is much higher than the lifetime of carbon dioxide, as is the case for CF_4. The 100-year GWP is used by convention in practice. However, the IPCC (2007) highlights that the proper time horizon for evaluating dangerous anthropogenic interference in the climate system has not been determined, neither scientifically, economically, nor politically. We refer to Dyckhoff and Kasah (2014) for more details on the effect of time horizons on LCA.

Using the GWP enables us to aggregate GHG emissions into a single metric commonly expressed in carbon dioxide equivalent (CO_2e) or in carbon equivalent. These two metrics should not be confused: 3 million tons of carbon equivalent is equal to 11 million tons of CO_2e. The conversion between carbon equivalent and CO_2e is related to the ratio of the atomic mass of a carbon dioxide molecule to the atomic mass of a carbon atom, i.e., 44/12 (EPA 2005).

Carbon emissions expressed in CO_2e (or in carbon equivalent) are often thought of as an unambiguous measure of the effect of GHGs on global warming. However, this measure is based on various assumptions and imperfect models. Any recommendation based on carbon dioxide equivalent calculations needs to acknowledge that the results are subject to some scientific uncertainty. For instance, the GWPs are revised periodically as the models used in the calculations evolve (Carbon Trust 2014). This can be observed in Table 3.2, which shows three different estimates for methane.

This has immediate implications for carbon footprinting and reporting as the carbon footprints for different companies and especially at different points in time may be based on different GWPs. An analogy in financial accounting is the effect of currency exchange rates: financial statements are published in a single currency, using whatever collection of exchange rates is appropriate at that time, but changes

Table 3.2 Changes in global warming potential estimates for methane for three IPCC reports

Methane (CH$_4$)		Global warming potential (GWP) Time horizon		
IPCC report:	Lifetime years	20 years	100 years	500 years
SAR 1995	12	56	21	6.5
TAR 2001	12	62	23	7
AR4 2007	12	72	25	7.6

Source: IPCC (1996, 2002, 2007)

in reported financial metrics may result in part from changes in exchange rates rather than in actual performance. Even though one may not expect GWPs to be as volatile as currency exchange rates, Table 3.2 shows that the 20-year GWP for methane has changed by about 29 % between the 1995 and 2007 IPCC reports. Despite these shortcomings, using the GWP to aggregate different GHGs into a single metric expressed in CO$_2$e is the most common approach to carbon footprinting.

3.1.2 Motivations for Carbon Footprinting and Reporting

Carbon footprinting has become more widely used (see, e.g., Minx et al. 2009) than other environmental footprints, such as the ecological footprint, land footprint, water footprint, etc. (see Chap. 4 by Hoekstra (2017) for more on water footprinting). The main reasons for this can be linked to legislation around carbon emissions, public awareness of climate change risks, and investors' expectations for carbon emission reporting. Consequently, some companies ask their suppliers and subcontractors to provide data on their emissions. For instance, DHL requires all its carriers to enter data on vehicles used, distance traveled, fuel efficiency, etc., not only to calculate total carbon emissions but also to screen the carriers for environmental performance (WRI and WBCSD 2004). Reducing carbon emissions can also lead to lower costs. For instance, a survey of the Consumer Electronics Association (CEA) found that companies measuring their carbon footprint were able to reduce their electricity consumption by 5–25 % per million dollars of revenue (Vasan et al. 2014).

Regarding regulations on carbon emissions, many governments require carbon emitters to report their emissions annually on a mandatory basis. Other countries have established carbon and energy taxes (e.g., the CRC Energy Efficiency Scheme in the UK) under which financial penalties are associated with carbon emissions. In addition, most countries have signed the Kyoto Protocol[2] that entered into force in 2005; discussions on a follow-up agreement are taking place in Paris in 2016.

---

[2] The Kyoto Protocol commits its parties by setting internationally binding carbon emission reduction targets (UNFCCC, 2014): 5 % against 1990 levels during the first commitment period (2008–2012) and at least 18 % below 1990 levels during the second commitment period (2013–2020).

As a result, many governments are taking steps to reduce carbon emissions through regional or national policies including the introduction of emission trading programs (e.g., the European Union Emission Trading Scheme or ETS). Under a trading system, permits are required for a given company to be allowed to emit GHGs, and the number of available permits in the market (regional, national, or international) is limited. European companies such as Lafarge and Rockwool International which are covered by the EU ETS report their carbon emissions on a mandatory basis (CDP 2014a). Other companies report their emissions in order to be prepared for future regional, national, or international climate policies (Carbon Trust 2014; CDP 2014a). According to the CDP (formerly the "Carbon Disclosure Project"),[3] despite having no federal regulations on carbon in the USA, 69 US companies disclosed that they are already participating in the EU ETS (CDP 2014a). Moreover, global companies doing business in China and South Korea such as Alstom, Bayer, and Canadian Tire Corporation are closely monitoring emerging Chinese emission trading systems that will soon put a price on carbon (CDP 2014a).

Another incentive for carbon footprinting emanates from the pressure exerted by the public, which is more and more aware of the risks of climate change. Several reports demonstrate that climate change and global warming are nowadays considered among the risks of highest concerns worldwide. For instance, in a global survey, DHL (2010) states that 60 % of all respondents identified climate change as being among the top three most serious current world problems. In the ninth global risks assessment report released by the World Economic Forum in 2014 (WEF 2014), "Failure of climate change mitigation and adaptation" and "Greater incidence of extreme weather events (e.g. floods, storms, fires)" were ranked fifth and sixth, respectively, among the top 10 global risks. In 2014, the European Commission performed its second survey on climate change. The results reveal that climate change is perceived as the third most serious issue worldwide, after "poverty, hunger and lack of drinking water" and "the economic situation" (EC 2014).

Investors also require that the long-term risks related to environmental externalities are managed in order to protect their long-term investments. For instance, the CDP Investor Initiatives, backed in 2015 by more than 822 institutional investors representing over US$95 trillion in assets[4], provide investors with a global source of annual information to support long-term objective analysis, including evidence and insight into companies' carbon footprint and strategies for managing climate change. The CDP's Carbon Action initiative (backed by 190 investors) asks companies in heavy emitting industries to take actions on carbon emission reduction every year, by setting emission targets and making reductions while generating return on investment (CDP 2014b).

---

[3] The CDP is an international organization that holds the largest collection of climate change-, water-, and forestry-related data reported by companies (https://www.cdp.net/). More than 5 000 companies report to CDP every year. For instance, in 2013, 334 firms in the S&P 500 index have disclosed their emissions to CDP (CDP 2015).

[4] See https://www.cdp.net/en-US/WhatWeDo/Pages/investors.aspx, last accessed December 2, 2015.

To conclude, the first step toward managing carbon emissions is to measure the carbon footprint because "if you can't measure it, you can't manage it" (Kaplan and Norton 1992). The next section is devoted to this question.

3.2 How Can a Carbon Footprint Be Measured?

This section is divided into two parts. The first presents the GHG Protocol, the most used framework to account for carbon emissions. The second part highlights the main methods used for carbon footprinting.

3.2.1 The GHG Protocol

The GHG Protocol[5] (www.ghgprotocol.org/) is the guideline for many existing methodologies for carbon footprint measurement. It is developed by the World Resources Institute (WRI) and the World Business Council for Sustainable Development (WBCSD). The first version "The Greenhouse Gas Protocol: A Corporate Accounting and Reporting Standard" was released in 2001. This is the main framework for carbon emissions accounting worldwide. It is used by government and business leaders to understand, quantify, and manage their carbon footprint. The GHG Protocol also serves as the foundation for nearly every GHG standard and program in the world as well as hundreds of GHG inventories prepared by individual companies (WRI and WBCSD 2004). As an example, the corporate standard serves as the basis for international standards such as ISO 14064-1 (EPA 2014).

The GHG Protocol is now composed of seven standards (corporate standard, project protocol, product life-cycle standard, corporate value chain standard, GHG Protocol for cities, mitigation goal standard, and policy and action standard). At the time of writing, WRI and WBCSD have been scoping the need for a new standard on product innovation. Among these standards, we briefly introduce the two that are directly related to supply chains: the corporate and corporate value chain standards.

The corporate standard, released in 2001 and most recently amended in 2013, provides guidance for companies in preparing a carbon emission inventory. It was designed with the following objectives in mind (WRI and WBCSD 2004):

– "To help companies prepare a carbon inventory that represents a true and fair account of their emissions, through the use of standardized approaches and principles.

---

[5] Where appropriate, we quote extensively directly from the GHG Protocol throughout this chapter.

- To simplify and reduce the costs of compiling a carbon inventory.
- To provide business with information that can be used to build an effective strategy to manage and reduce carbon emissions.
- To increase consistency and transparency in carbon emission accounting and reporting among various companies and GHG programs."[6]

The corporate value chain standard (also referred to as Scope 3 standard), released in 2011, allows companies to assess their entire value chain emission impact and identify the most effective ways to reduce emissions. The standard was developed with the following objectives (WRI and WBCSD 2011a: 4):

- "To help companies prepare a true and fair scope 3 GHG inventory in a cost-effective manner, through the use of standardized approaches and principles.
- To help companies develop effective strategies for managing and reducing their Scope 3 emissions through an understanding of value chain emissions and associated risks and opportunities.
- To support consistent and transparent public reporting of corporate value chain emissions according to a standardized set of reporting requirements."

These two standards are built on the same underlying principles. In both cases, setting clear boundaries is of crucial importance. The GHG Protocol recommends setting organizational boundaries and operational boundaries.

- *Organizational boundaries*
  Two distinct approaches can be used: the *equity share* and the *control* approaches. Following equity share, a company accounts for carbon emissions from operations according to its share of equity in the operation (i.e., economic interest). Typically, the share of economic risks and rewards in an operation is aligned with the company's percentage ownership of that operation, and equity share will be the same as the ownership percentage. With the control approach, the company accounts for 100 % of the carbon emissions from operations over which it has control. Control can be defined in either financial terms (ability to direct the financial and operating policies) or operational ones (full authority to introduce and implement operating policies at the operation).
- *Operational boundaries*
  This involves identifying carbon emissions associated with a company's operations, categorizing them as direct or indirect emissions, and choosing the scope of accounting and reporting for indirect emissions. The GHG Protocol distinguishes three "scopes" (see Fig. 3.1):

  - *Scope 1: Direct carbon emissions*
    Direct carbon emissions occur from sources that are owned or controlled by the company, for example, emissions from combustion in owned or controlled

---

[6] See http://www.ghgprotocol.org/standards/corporate-standard, last accessed December 1, 2015.

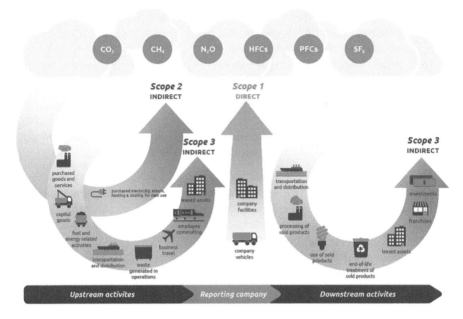

Fig. 3.1 Overview of scopes and emissions across a value chain (*Source*: Fig. 1.1 in WRI and WBCSD, 2011a)

boilers, furnaces, vehicles, etc., or emissions from chemical production in owned or controlled process equipment.

– *Scope 2*: *Purchased energy indirect carbon emissions*
Scope 2 accounts for carbon emissions from the generation of purchased or acquired electricity, steam, heating, or cooling consumed by the reporting company. Scope 2 emissions physically occur at a facility outside the organizational boundary of the reporting company.

– *Scope 3*: *Other indirect carbon emissions*
Scope 3 allows for the treatment of all other indirect emissions. Scope 3 emissions are a consequence of the activities of the company, but occur from sources owned or controlled by other entities in the value chain (e.g., materials suppliers, third-party logistics providers, waste management suppliers, travel suppliers, lessees and lessors, franchisees, retailers, employees, and customers). Scope 3 emissions are all indirect emissions including both upstream (e.g., purchased products or purchased products transportation) and downstream emissions (e.g., use of sold products or disposal of sold products).

These three scopes are mutually exclusive for the reporting company. Scope 3 emissions do not include any emissions already accounted for as Scope 1 or Scope 2 by the same company. They enable clarifying the distinction between corporate and value chain standards. Under the corporate standard, companies are required to report all Scope 1 and Scope 2 emissions, while reporting Scope 3 emissions is optional. The corporate value chain standard is designed to create further consistency in Scope 3 inventories through additional requirements and guidance for Scope 3 accounting and reporting (WRI and WBCSD 2011a).

Once the organizational and operational boundaries are defined, the carbon footprint can be measured. The next section gives an overview of the main methodologies used to measure the carbon footprint.

3.2.2   *Methodologies for Measuring the Carbon Footprint*

Various methods for measuring carbon emissions have been proposed. We classify them by the level of extrapolation involved, from the most direct measurement methodology to the one relying most heavily on extrapolation:

– Direct measurement
– Energy-based calculations
– Activity-based calculations
– Economic input–output life-cycle assessment (EIO-LCA)

• *Direct measurement*
  The direct measurement methodology is usually applied to production sites. The measurement of emissions is achieved by continuously measuring the pollutants emitted into the atmosphere in exhaust gases from combustion or industrial processes, often via the use of continuous emission monitoring systems (EPA 2008). Due to their high cost, continuous emission monitoring systems are mainly installed in production sites subject to environmental regulations and process monitoring applications such as the US EPA 40 CFR Part 75 and 40 CFR Part 60. Apart from these sites under regulation, direct measurement of carbon emissions by monitoring concentration and flow rate is not common in supply chains. Direct measurement is generally only applicable for a share of Scope 1 emissions.
• *Energy-based calculations*
  Energy-based calculations determine carbon emissions based on mass balance or theoretical combustion specific to a facility or a process. This methodology applies mainly to fuel consumption, both at production sites and for transportation. Several levels of analysis may be conducted, depending on the information available. Indeed, the amount of fuel combusted is generally not directly monitored, and extrapolation based on the amount of fuel consumed is commonplace. In addition, the carbon content of a given combusted fuel is often estimated based on average values. Energy-based calculations may also be applied for indirect emissions from electricity consumption, as many providers release the average level of carbon emissions per unit of electricity produced. Energy-based calculations require information that is generally available for a share of Scope 1

and Scope 2 emissions. This is most applicable to process-related emissions such as those from cement, aluminum, and waste processing (DEFRA 2009) and to transportation-related emissions.

- *Activity-based calculations*

  An activity-based calculation method aims at deriving the carbon emissions from activity information by using conversion factors. These factors are calculated ratios relating carbon emissions to a proxy measure of activity at an emissions source. They are often referred to as emission factors. Activity-based calculation is the most common approach used to calculate carbon emissions (DEFRA 2009). The available activity-based methods differ in their level of aggregation, some of them requiring more detailed information than other (Velazquez-Martinez et al. 2014). As an example, consider a reporting company that uses truck transportation for inbound deliveries. Assume that transportation is outsourced to a third-party logistics provider and are therefore Scope 3 emissions. Data on fuel consumption (required for energy-based calculation) are generally not shared by third-party logistics providers, as fuel consumption is a key element in the cost structure of truck transportation and the carrier is usually not willing to share information about his cost structure with the customer. In this case, the reporting company can apply activity-based calculation, by converting the weight transported over a given distance and using a given type of truck to estimate average carbon emissions by using emission factors. Several initiatives provide such type of emission factors for the main supply chain activities. Chapter 7 by Blanco and Sheffi (2017) provides more detail in the context of logistics.

- *Economic input–output life-cycle assessment (EIO-LCA)*

  EIO-LCA enables converting the expenditures by a company in a given industry sector into an average amount of carbon emissions. For instance, \$X spent in the transport industry sector leads on average to Y tons of CO_2e. We refer to Hendrickson et al. (2010) for a detailed exposition of the approach and to Huang et al. (2009) for an application of EIO-LCA to estimate that the carbon footprint of all economic sectors in the US. EIO-LCA is relatively widespread, especially in the USA, due to its ease of use. However, one limitation of EIO-LCA is that it exclusively accounts for upstream emissions.

  Methodologies relying less on extrapolation will provide more accurate estimation of the true carbon footprint of operations. For example, Matthews et al. (2008) state that firm-level data such as electricity and energy use will produce more accurate footprint results than EIO-LCA. On the other hand, the data required to apply a methodology that relies less on extrapolation may be harder to gather or simply not available. O'Rourke (2014) mentions that accessing data from full supply chains can be expensive, time consuming, and, sometimes, impossible. There is an inherent trade-off between the scope of measurement chosen (and consequently the portion of the total footprint analyzed) and the accuracy of the estimation made. (We return to the issue of accuracy in Sect. 3.4.2.) Consequently, defining the right scope for carbon emission measurement is of crucial importance as this decision will have strong implications for the type of measurement methods that can be implemented. One of the key questions here consists in assessing the importance of Scope 3 emissions for the reporting company. If Scope 3 emissions represent a small share of total supply chain emissions for the company, it may make more sense to focus on Scope 1 and Scope 2 emissions and to apply a more direct methodology. However, Scope 3 emissions can be of high importance when it represents a large share of a company's carbon footprint, as is true for most firms. We discuss the importance of Scope 3 emissions in more depth below.

3.3 Supply Chain Carbon Footprinting

This section is divided into four parts. First, the importance of Scope 3 emissions in supply chain carbon footprinting is analyzed. Second, the process of supply chain carbon footprinting is presented. Then, the process of carbon footprinting in a supply chain is illustrated by referring to the process followed by Hyundai Motor Company (HMC) (as described in Lee (2011)). Finally, some issues related to carbon footprint allocation among different supply chain partners are discussed.

3.3.1 *Importance of Scope 3 Emissions*

Matthews et al. (2008) estimated that on average 74 % of an industry sector's carbon footprint is attributed to upstream Scope 3 emissions (without accounting for downstream Scope 3 emissions). This average value gives an idea of the importance of accounting for carbon emissions through the supply chain. Huang et al. (2009) focused on upstream emissions of US economic sectors and provided a sector-specific repartition of emissions from Scope 1 to Scope 3.

Huang et al. show that the impact of upstream Scope 3 emissions is substantial for most of the US industry sectors. Moreover, a large share of US companies' upstream Scope 3 emissions can be attributed to their top-10 suppliers. This result may help a company to understand which upstream Scope 3 category contributes most to its total carbon footprint and thus help it focus its measurement efforts on relevant suppliers. In practice, companies often focus on measuring the portion of their Scope 3 emissions related to employee commuting and business travel. However, CDP (2013a) indicates that 72 % of the global 500 companies reporting to CDP report emissions from business travel even if these emissions account for only 0.2 % of total reported Scope 3 emissions. CDP (2013a) concludes that "instead of measuring carbon-intensive activities in their supply chain, companies often focus on relatively insignificant opportunities for carbon reduction."

Huang et al. (2009) also show that the portion of Scope 3 emissions widely varies from one industry sector to another. This explains why it is difficult to provide generic guidance on which emissions of Scope 3 to include in the inventory (see Sect. 3.3.2 for more details), leading Huang et al. (2009) to recommend that protocol organizations develop sector-specific Scope 3 guidelines.

Even companies that voluntarily disclose Scope 3 emissions are under no obligation to be comprehensive. To estimate how (in)complete current Scope 3 emissions reports are, Blanco et al. (2014) compare CDP disclosures by US firms to the predicted breakdown of emissions in Huang et al. (2009). They estimate that US firms that disclose any Scope 3 emissions in 2013 only reported 22 % of their full upstream supply chain emissions to CDP. Scope 3 reporting is generally underdeveloped even though companies are progressively improving. The next section provides some general guidelines on how to perform supply chain carbon footprinting.

3.3.2   The Process of Supply Chain Carbon Footprinting

The supply chain carbon footprint corresponds to Scope 1, 2, and 3 emissions. Accounting for Scope 3 emissions, and therefore the value chain carbon footprint, need not involve a full-blown inventory of all products and operations, which would generally be infeasible. Usually it is most valuable to focus on the major GHG-generating activities. As mentioned above, the structure of Scope 3 emissions varies from one industry sector to another, and consequently, it is difficult to provide generic guidance on which Scope 3 emissions to include in an inventory. However, some general steps can be articulated (WRI and WBCSD 2011a):

1. *Describe the value chain.* It is important, for the sake of transparency, to provide a general description of the value chain and the associated carbon emission sources.
2. *Determine which Scope 3 categories are relevant.* Only some types of upstream or downstream emission categories might be relevant to the reporting company. They may be relevant, for example, because they are large (or believed to be large) relative to the company's Scope 1 and Scope 2 emissions, they contribute to the company's carbon risk exposure, they are deemed critical by key stakeholders (e.g., feedback from customers, suppliers, investors, or civil society), etc.
3. *Identify partners along the value chain,* e.g., customers or users, product designers, manufacturers, energy providers, etc. This is important when trying to identify sources, obtain relevant data, and calculate emissions.
4. *Quantify Scope 3 emissions.* While data availability and reliability may influence which Scope 3 activities are included in the inventory, it is accepted that data accuracy may be lower. It may be more important to understand the relative

magnitude of and possible changes to Scope 3 activities. Emission estimates are acceptable as long as there is transparency with regard to the estimation approach, and the data used for the analysis are adequate to support the objectives of the inventory. Verification of Scope 3 emissions will often be difficult and may only be considered if data is of reliable quality.

3.3.3   An Example from the Automobile Industry

To better understand how carbon footprinting might work in practice, we briefly summarize Lee (2011), who describes a three-step process that HMC took jointly with its ten-key 1st-tier suppliers in a pilot study, to measure carbon emissions in the upstream supply chain. The study focused on Avante passenger car model manufacturing. Lee mentioned that one of the most difficult challenges that HMC faced was determining the emission boundary. Based on the GHG Protocol, direct (in-house) and limited indirect carbon emission boundaries were considered, while downstream stages of distribution, consumers, disposal, and recycling were excluded (Lee 2011). The first step is to identify the key suppliers' carbon footprint. HMC set up guidelines and provided measurement manuals to key suppliers. Based on this, each supplier conducted Scope 1 and 2 emission measurement and reporting, using a direct measurement methodology. The scope of the guidelines prepared by HMC includes raw material suppliers, manufacturers, and distributors. In the second step, a carbon process map was established to identify each component and part at each stage of the simplified supply chain. This process helped HMC and its suppliers to calculate the carbon footprint of each component and part. The carbon process map also helped HMC and its suppliers to identify components and parts with high carbon burdens. Finally, in the third step, HMC and its suppliers calculated the products' carbon footprint by adding the carbon emissions of the supply chain stages. Regarding the front bumper product, for example, it was found that through the simplified supply chain, the raw material stage accounts for 18 % of the carbon emissions, the manufacturing stage accounts for 70 %, and the distribution accounts around 12 % (Lee 2011).

Although reporting Scope 3 emissions is optional and might be difficult (data availability, data reliability, supplier capability, etc.), a supply chain carbon footprint that includes these emissions is very important from a decision-making perspective, as discussed in Sect. 3.3.1. As stated by Lee (2011), reducing the supply chain carbon emissions may be more cost effective for companies than reducing direct or purchased electricity-related emissions (Scopes 1 and 2). Indeed, accounting for carbon emissions along the value chain can help companies to identify where to allocate limited resources in a way that maximizes carbon emission reduction while possibly lowering costs at the same time. For instance, a senior manager of one of HMC's suppliers stated that "we didn't realize how much electricity we wasted during the production stage and the importance of efficient energy management from raw materials to distribution. We learned that carbon footprint identification and measurement practice brought cost savings, and we also began to re-examine our products design to minimize carbon footprint in our products and their supply chain" (Lee 2011: 1221).

3.3.4 Emission Allocation in Supply Chains[7]

In determining the carbon footprint for an organization, value chain, or product, it is generally necessary to allocate shared emissions to separate units. For instance, emissions of a truck need to be allocated to all the products transported on that truck. Emissions caused by heating, cooling, and lighting in a plant need to be allocated to the range of products and customers that it serves. Allocation is a thorny issue in LCA in general (see also Chap. 2 by Guinée and Heijungs, 2017) and hence also for carbon footprinting.

Chapter 8 in "The GHG Protocol Corporate Value Chain (Scope 3) Accounting and Reporting Standard" (WRI and WBCSD 2011a) provides guidance on allocating emissions. Accordingly, allocation should be avoided or minimized when possible, by collecting more detailed data through (1) obtaining product-level GHG data from value chain partners, (2) separately submetering energy use and other activity data (e.g., at the production line level), and (3) using engineering models to separately estimate emissions related to each product produced.

When allocation is inevitable, companies should select the allocation approach that (1) best reflects the causal relationship between the production of the outputs and the resulting emissions, (2) results in the most accurate and credible emission estimates, (3) best supports effective decision-making and GHG reduction activities, and (4) otherwise adheres to the principles of relevance, accuracy, completeness, consistency, and transparency (WRI and WBCSD 2011a). It is preferable to use a physical relationship between the multiple inputs/outputs and the quantity of emissions generated, through allocation factors such as mass, volume, energy, chemical, number of units, or others (e.g., protein content of food coproducts or floor space occupied by products); otherwise the remaining options are to use economic factors (by value) or other relationships. This is because physical factors are expected to best reflect the causal relationship between the production of the outputs and the resulting emissions. Clearly, different allocation methods are prone to yielding significantly different results.

The general method proposed by WRI and WBCSD (2011a) to allocate emissions from a facility is to multiply total facility emissions by the reporting company's purchases as a fraction of total production. For example, using mass as the allocation factor:

---

[7]This section draws on "The GHG Protocol Corporate Value Chain (Scope 3) Accounting and Reporting Standard" (WRI and WBCSD 2011a) and on Caro et al. (2013), both of which sources we cite at various points throughout this section.

$$\text{Allocated facility emissions} = \frac{\text{Mass of Products Purchased}}{\text{Total Mass of Products Produced}} \times \text{Total Emissions}.$$

As for collecting and allocating GHG emissions from suppliers, two basic approaches are suggested:

- Supplier allocation. Individual suppliers report preallocated emission data to the reporting company and disclose the allocation metric used.
- Reporting company allocation. The reporting company allocates supplier emissions by obtaining two types of data from individual suppliers: (1) total supplier GHG emission data (e.g., at the facility or business unit level) and (2) the reporting company's share of the supplier's total production, based on either physical factors (e.g., units of production, mass, volume, or other metrics) or economic factors (e.g., revenue, spend).

It is argued that reporting company allocation is likely to ensure more consistency in methodologies for the reporting company, while the supplier allocation approach may be more practical by avoiding the need for suppliers to report confidential business information. Finally, examples and guidance for determining the most appropriate allocation method to use are also provided by WRI and WBCSD (2011a).

Many GHG emissions are the result of joint processes by multiple parties in a supply chain (Caro et al. 2013). A typical product goes through numerous manufacturing and transportation stages operated by a number of companies in a supply chain. Although joint production can occur anywhere, it is likely to be particularly common in indirect goods and services, which do not become part of the final product or service. Consequently, further reductions in emissions—in addition to those of a firm's own operations—can be achieved by joint effort of multiple parties in a supply chain through collaboration, coordination, or information sharing. This brings in also additional cost-saving opportunities. The CDP 2015 supply chain report notes that companies that engage with one or more of their suppliers, consumers, or other partners are more than twice as likely to see a financial return from their emission reduction investments and almost twice as likely to reduce emissions, as those who do not engage with their value chain (CDP 2015). Nevertheless, when a number of firms jointly affect total emissions, they face a critical and nontrivial challenge in measuring their share of the responsibility for emissions (or that of the emission reductions): How should the emissions be allocated to the various value chains, organizations, final products, or services? The CDP 2011 supply chain report found that 86 % of respondents have a collaborative process in place to jointly reduce carbon footprints with suppliers (up from 49 % the year before), but suppliers face difficulties in allocating their emissions to their multiple customers (CDP 2011).

In the LCA and carbon footprinting literatures, various guidelines exist on how to allocate shared emissions. A common attribute in those guidelines—including that of the GHG Protocol covered in this section—is that the sum of the allocated emissions for each output of a system should equal 100 % of emissions from the system. Given that LCA is aimed at making product and process design decisions based on an accurate inventory of environmental impacts, it is natural that the LCA literature seeks to avoid over-allocation, i.e., "double counting," of impacts (see, e.g., Lenzen 2008). Similarly, in trading schemes, avoiding double counting of GHG emissions is crucial due to the financial consequences involved. More recently the LCA literature has started investigating how to reconcile allocating responsibility for impacts while avoiding double counting. Lenzen et al. (2007), building on Gallego and Lenzen (2005), propose a scheme by which producers and consumers share responsibility for emissions in such a way that adding total emissions across all producers and consumers yields the correct economy-wide emissions. Nevertheless, Caro et al. (2013) argue that whenever emissions (or reduction in emissions) result from multiple parties, double counting is necessary to induce the optimal level of abatement effort among the supply chain members. Accordingly, even if the true social cost of carbon emissions is internalized (e.g., by applying a carbon tax to all supply chain members), the abatement efforts implemented would be less than the optimal level when double counting is avoided. Even in the absence of an optimal allocation rule (which would require double counting), firms with an interest in overall supply chain efficiency should at a minimum include the full cost of all GHG emissions that they can influence when they decide where to focus their efforts. The fact that double counting is unlikely to be implemented on a large scale in practice should not preclude firms from identifying where their efforts may have the greatest effect. If the greatest return on firm 1's effort is on emissions currently allocated to firm 2, then firm 1 could explore mechanisms to share the costs and benefits of reducing emissions with firm 2. Without at least allowing double counting in a pro forma fashion, many valuable opportunities for joint improvement will go unexploited.

3.4 Discussion

This section discusses several issues related to supply chain carbon footprinting. We first introduce the challenges related to gathering information necessary to calculate a carbon footprint. Second, we discuss the issue of accuracy. Third, we highlight the need to extend the horizon of sustainable supply chains beyond carbon emissions.

3.4.1 How to Get Information in Practice?

The amount of data required to calculate the carbon footprint of a company is substantial, and the data are often difficult to gather, especially when performing a value chain carbon footprint. For instance, when Fujitsu carried out a carbon footprint analysis on its desktop PC and servers to show customers its product's superiority through reduced carbon emissions, it faced some challenges to gather data in the use and disposal phases and had to make numerous assumptions to be able to conduct a cradle-to-grave LCA (Vasan et al. 2014).

Even when the data exist, most companies are not organized to systematically and automatically collect these data, although ERP systems are progressively including information on carbon footprint and other sustainability metrics. In this regard, SAP, IBM, SAS, and other software vendors have built tools to extract energy data from supply chain procurement systems (O'Rourke 2014). Some companies have also developed their own software. For instance, in the energy sector, an Excel-based data management information system called SANGEA™ Energy and Greenhouse Gas Emissions Estimating System has been implemented by Chevron Corporation in 2002 to gather carbon emissions and energy usage data from energy operations (exploration and production, refining and marketing, petrochemicals, transportation, electricity generation, manufacturing, real estate, and coal activities) at its facilities worldwide. The company used the software to compile its first corporate-wide carbon inventory (Chevron 2002). SANGEA™ streamlines corporate-level data consolidation by allowing the inventory coordinator at each facility to configure a spreadsheet, enter monthly data, and send quarterly reports to a centralized database (WRI and WBCSD 2004). The software, which was available free of charge for other companies in the oil and gas sector, has been donated to the American Petroleum Institute (API). More recently, Chevron developed in 2009 its GHG and Energy Reporting System CGERS™ to align with existing and emerging regulatory requirements (Chevron 2009). In 2010, the company completed enterprise-wide deployment of the software and improved it in 2012 by incorporating mechanisms to facilitate electronic reporting to the US Environmental Protection Agency (CDP 2013b).

However, currently most companies need to manually combine data from disparate sources to compile the carbon footprint, often in spreadsheets. As data collection and compilation is not standardized, the process is reiterated every year. This is often a time-consuming task, subject to errors and/or approximations. Thus, DEFRA (2009) recommends that companies include carbon emissions reporting into existing reporting tools and processes of the organization. Interface, Inc., the world's largest manufacturer of carpet tiles, has developed an environmental data system based on its corporate financial data reporting. This system provides activity and material flow data from the company's business units (the USA, Canada, Australia, Europe, etc.) and metrics (the Interface's EcoMetrics) for measuring progress on environmental issues including carbon emissions. The data are reported to a central database each quarter and made available for establishing Interface's annual inventory and enabling data comparison over time (WRI and WBCSD 2004).

The manual, time-consuming compilation of data from separate sources also causes a transparency issue. Indeed, it is very hard to keep all the calculations transparent and it is quite easy to introduce mistakes. Several organizations propose expertise and data to support companies in the process of carbon footprint measurement. For instance, in the transportation sector, DHL, through its GREEN SERVICES portfolio, offers a suite of tools such as Track and Trace, Carbon Report, and Carbon Dashboard to assist companies in reporting their carbon emissions and identifying reduction opportunities. The Carbon Dashboard (a web-based version of the Carbon Report) allows companies to access statistics on the carbon emissions generated by the transport of their freight, and based on this information, they can consider scenarios to reduce their carbon footprint.[8]

Some other organizations have also developed carbon footprint certification programs to enable companies to report a verified carbon footprint. For example, DHL states that the reporting methodologies and calculation tools used in its express and air, ocean, and road freight divisions have been verified by the Swiss-based Société Générale de Surveillance (SGS) since 2011 (DHL 2015). However, even third-party audits may miss errors by focusing more on whether correct conversion factors were used than on whether the input data are correct and complete. The question of how to collect and organize verifiable information in an efficient way, without having to redo it every year, is of crucial importance for companies and deserves particular attention.

3.4.2 How Accurate Is Accurate Enough?

Carbon footprinting is always associated with a certain level of uncertainty. More particularly, as Scope 3 covers activities that are not under the reporting company's ownership or control, companies are likely to face additional challenges that contribute to uncertainty in Scope 3 accounting (WRI and WBCSD 2011a). Lee (2011) reports that one senior manager from HMC stated: "we had some difficulties in terms of scopes and measurement of carbon footprint. In our case, Scope 1 and 2 carbon footprint measurements are completed with over 95 % confidence. But Scope 3 CO_2 measurement is still limited with regard to the supply chain network. We should explore further feasible methods and practices to track CO_2 emissions from the supply chain."

Uncertainties related to carbon inventories can be categorized into scientific uncertainty and estimation uncertainty (WRI and WBCSD 2004). Scientific uncertainty arises when the science of the actual emission is not completely understood. For example, many direct and indirect factors associated with GWP values involve significant scientific uncertainty (IPCC 2000). The evolution of the 100-year GWP of methane from 21 in the second IPCC report in 2005 (see Table 3.2) to 28 in the fifth IPCC report in 2013 (see Table 3.1) is an example of scientific uncertainty. Analyzing and quantifying scientific uncertainty is challenging and best addressed by the scientific community rather than by companies (IPCC 2000).

Estimation uncertainty occurs any time carbon emissions are quantified. Therefore each carbon footprint is associated with estimation uncertainty. Estimation uncertainty can be further classified into two types: model uncertainty and parameter

---

[8] See for instance http://www.dhl.com/en/logistics/green_logistics_solutions.html, last accessed December 2, 2015.

uncertainty (IPCC 2000). Model uncertainty occurs when the emissions are not directly measured (i.e., under energy-based calculations, activity-based calculations, and EIO-LCA). In this case, a model translates a given input into a certain amount of carbon emissions. The way this translation is handled is subject to uncertainty referred to as model uncertainty. For instance, estimating emissions from truck transportation under an energy-based calculation methodology would lead to uncertainty in the precise amount of carbon emissions released by the motor, as this depends on the quality of the combustion and thus on the operating conditions of the vehicle.

Parameter uncertainty refers to the uncertainty associated with quantifying the parameters used as inputs into estimation models (IPCC 2000), for instance, the amount of fuel consumed by the truck.

Given that uncertainty is an intrinsic part of any carbon footprint assessment, an immediate question is what level of uncertainty is acceptable. On the one hand, high-quality information has greater value and more uses, and even if a company does not anticipate future regulatory mechanisms, internal and external stakeholders may demand high-quality inventory information (WRI and WBCSD 2004). On the other hand, in the context of carbon emission regulations, low-quality information may have little or no value and may even incur penalties. Defining the level of accuracy depends on the carbon footprinting analysis objective, as well as on the capability of the company. However, this decision may greatly influence the estimated carbon footprint of a company. This decision is referred to as the application of a cutoff threshold in the LCA literature.

Once the desired level of accuracy has been determined, the next question is how to report uncertainties in carbon footprints. Given that only parameter uncertainties are within the feasible scope of most companies, uncertainty estimates for carbon inventories will necessarily be imperfect (IPCC 2000). Parameter uncertainties can be evaluated through statistical analysis, measurement equipment precision determinations, and expert judgment (IPCC 2000). Statistical analysis may be difficult due to a lack of complete and robust sample data. Most of the time, a single data point is available (e.g., liters of fuel for truck transportation). In case the data is obtained from an instrument, precision and/or calibration information may be used. However, IPCC (2000) states that expert judgment is often the only possibility for companies. Experts can either be the source of the necessary data, or they can help identify and explain uncertainties. The problem with expert judgment is that it is difficult to obtain in a comparable and consistent manner across parameters, source categories, or companies (WRI and WBCSD 2004).

The GHG Protocol Corporate Standard has developed a supplementary guidance document on uncertainty assessments along with an uncertainty calculation tool (WRI and WBCSD 2011b). The guidance document describes how to use the calculation tool in aggregating uncertainties. It also discusses in more depth different types of uncertainties, the limitations of quantitative uncertainty assessment, and how uncertainty estimates should be properly interpreted. Additional guidance and information on assessing uncertainty can also be found in EPA (1999) and in IPCC (2000).

3.4.3 How to Extend the Horizons Beyond Carbon?

We highlighted in Sect. 3.1.2 some of the reasons explaining why there is nowadays a strong focus on carbon emissions. However, sustainability cannot be reduced to carbon emissions. For example, water scarcity, its quality, and the regulations affecting it are a growing business problem (The Economist 2014). Other environmental dimensions of sustainability as well as social impacts should not be overlooked because of too much focus on carbon emissions. We refer to Chap. 4 by Hoekstra (2017) for more on water footprinting, to Chap. 5 by Blass et al. (2017) for more on managing nonrenewable materials, and to Chaps. 20 and 21 by Lee and Rammohan (2017) and Sodhi and Tang (2017) for more on socially responsible supply chains.

The strong current focus on carbon emissions may be an opportunity for other environmental indicators to be developed and adopted, in the sense that platforms and accumulated experience related to carbon footprinting can be beneficial. For example, once acquainted with environmental reporting through carbon emissions, a company may be more prone and able to develop an overall sustainability assessment. This trend is also reflected by CDP's commitment to use the experience and reputation obtained from carbon footprinting to develop new initiatives related to water use and forest management.

One important observation here is that the capability developed through carbon footprinting may not necessarily be directly transposed to other sustainability aspects. Indeed, companies, non-governmental organizations, and governments need to take into account that the other sustainability aspects might have different characteristics than carbon emissions. For example, location and timing play a major role in water footprinting, but not in carbon footprinting. Extending the capabilities being built up for carbon footprinting to other dimensions of sustainability presents an exciting opportunity but one that should be approached thoughtfully.

References

Blanco EE, Sheffi Y (2017) Green logistics. In: Bouchery Y, Corbett CJ, Fransoo J, Tan T (eds) Sustainable supply chains: a research-based textbook on operations and strategy. Springer, New York

Blanco C, Caro F, Corbett C (2014) The state of Scope 3 carbon emissions reporting in supply chains. Working paper, UCLA

Blass V, Chebach TC, Ashkenazy A (2017) Sustainable non-renewable materials management. In: Bouchery Y, Corbett CJ, Fransoo J, Tan T (eds) Sustainable supply chains: a research-based textbook on operations and strategy. Springer, New York

Carbon Trust (2014) http://www.carbontrust.com

Caro F, Corbett CJ, Tan T, Zuidwijk R (2013) Double counting in supply chain carbon footprinting. Manuf Serv Oper Manag 15(4):545–558

CDP (2011) Carbon Disclosure Project supply chain report 2011. https://www.cdp.net/CDPResults/CDP-2011-Supply-Chain-Report.pdf. Accessed 10 Dec 2015

CDP (2013a) Sector insights: what is driving climate change action in the world's largest companies? Global 500 Climate Change Report 2013. Carbon Disclosure Project

CDP (2013b) Investor CDP Information request. Chevron Corporation

CDP (2014a) Global corporate use of carbon pricing. Disclosures to investors

CDP (2014b) Lower emissions, higher ROI: the rewards of low carbon investment

CDP (2015) CDP supply chain report 2014–15. Supply chain sustainability revealed: a country comparison. https://www.cdp.net/CDPResults/CDP-Supply-Chain-Report-2015.pdf. Accessed 10 Dec 2015

Chevron (2002) ChevronTexaco corporate responsibility report: integrity and learning in an evolving world

Chevron (2009) ChevronTexaco corporate responsibility report: the value of partnership.

DEFRA (2009) Guidance on how to measure and report your greenhouse gas emissions. Department for Environment, Food and Rural Affairs

DHL (2010) Delivering tomorrow: towards sustainable logistics. Deutsche Post DHL

DHL (2015) http://www.dhl.com/

Dyckhoff H, Kasah T (2014) Time horizon and dominance in dynamic life cycle assessment. J Ind Ecol 18(6):799–808

EC (2014) European special survey on climate change, 2nd edn. Eurobarometer 409, European Commission

EPA (1999) Emission inventory improvement program, vol VI: Quality Assurance/Quality Control. US Environmental Protection Agency

EPA (2005) Metrics for Expressing greenhouse gas emissions: carbon equivalents and carbon dioxide equivalents. Environmental protection Agency

EPA (2008) Direct emissions from stationary combustion sources. Environmental protection Agency

EPA (2014) Environmental footprint analysis. Environmental protection Agency

Gallego B, Lenzen M (2005) A consistent input-output formulation of shared producer and consumer responsibility. Econ Syst Res 17(4):365–391

Guinée J, Heijungs R (2017) Introduction to life cycle assessment. In: Bouchery Y, Corbett CJ, Fransoo J, Tan T (eds) Sustainable supply chains: a research-based textbook on operations and strategy. Springer, New York

Hendrickson CT, Lave LB, Matthews HS (2010) Environmental life cycle assessment of goods and services: an input-output approach. Routledge, London

Hoekstra AY (2017) Water footprint assessment in supply chains. In: Bouchery Y, Corbett CJ, Fransoo J, Tan T (eds) Sustainable supply chains: a research-based textbook on operations and strategy. Springer, New York

Huang YA, Weber CL, Matthews HS (2009) Categorization of Scope 3 emissions for streamlined enterprise carbon footprinting. Environ Sci Technol 43(22):8509–8515

IPCC (1996) Climate change 1995: the science of climate change. Contribution of WGI to the Second Assessment Report of the Intergovernmental Panel on Climate Change

IPCC (2000) Good practice guidance and uncertainty management in national greenhouse gas inventories. Intergovernmental Panel on Climate Change

IPCC (2002) Climate change 2001: the scientific basis. Contribution of working group I to the third assessment report of the Intergovernmental Panel on Climate Change. Weather 57(8):267–269

IPCC (2007) Contribution of working groups I, II and III to the fourth assessment report of the intergovernmental panel on climate change. Intergovernmental Panel on Climate Change report

IPCC (2013a) IPCC fifth assessment report: summary for policymakers. Intergovernmental Panel on Climate Change report

IPCC (2013b) Climate change 2013: the physical science basis. IPCC Working Group I

Kaplan RS, Norton DP (1992) The balanced scorecard—measures that drive performance. Harvard Business Review, Jan–Feb, pp 71–79

Lee K-H (2011) Integrating carbon footprint into supply chain management: the case of Hyundai Motor Company (HMC) in the automobile industry. J Clean Prod 19:1216–1223

Lee HL, Rammohan SV (2017) Improving social and environmental performance in global supply chains. In: Bouchery Y, Corbett CJ, Fransoo J, Tan T (eds) Sustainable supply chains: a research-based textbook on operations and strategy. Springer, New York

Lenzen M (2008) Double-counting in life cycle calculations. J Ind Ecol 12(4):583–599

Lenzen M, Murray J, Sack F, Wiedmann T (2007) Shared producer and consumer responsibility— theory and practice. Ecol Econ 61(1):27–42

Matthews HS, Hendrickson CT, Weber CL (2008) The importance of carbon footprint estimation boundaries. Environ Sci Technol 42(16):5839–5842

Minx JC, Wiedmann T, Wood R, Peters GP, Lenzen M, Owen A, Scott K, Barrett J, Hubacek K, Baiocchi G, Paul A, Dawkins E, Briggs J, Guan D, Suh S, Ackerman F (2009) Input–output analysis and carbon footprinting: an overview of applications. Econ Syst Res 21(3):187–216

O'Rourke D (2014) The science of sustainable supply chains. Science 344(6188):1124–1127

Sodhi MS, Tang CS (2017) Social responsibility in supply chains. In: Bouchery Y, Corbett CJ, Fransoo J, Tan T (eds) Sustainable supply chains: a research-based textbook on operations and strategy. Springer, New York

The Economist (2014) http://www.economist.com/news/business/21631047-water-growing-business-problem-many-companies-havent-noticed-value-diluted

United Nations Framework Convention on Climate Change (UNFCCC) (2014) Parties to the convention and observer states. http://unfccc.int/parties_and_observers/parties/items/2352.php. Accessed 22 Mar 2016

Vasan V, Sood B, Pecht M (2014) Carbon footprinting of electronic products. Appl Energy 136:636–648

Velazquez-Martinez JC, Fransoo JC, Blanco EE, Mora-Vargas J (2014) The impact of carbon footprinting aggregation on realizing emission reduction targets. Flex Serv Manuf J 26(1-2): 196–220

WEF (2014) Global risks 2014, 9th edn. World Economic Forum

WRI and WBCSD (2004) The greenhouse protocol: a corporate accounting and reporting standard, revised edition. World Resources Institute and World Business Council for Sustainable Development

WRI and WBCSD (2011a) Corporate value chain (Scope 3) accounting and reporting standard. World Resources Institute and World Business Council for Sustainable Development

WRI and WBCSD (2011b) GHG Protocol guidance on uncertainty assessment in GHG inventories and calculating statistical parameter uncertainty. World Resources Institute and World Business Council for Sustainable Development

Chapter 4
Water Footprint Assessment in Supply Chains

Arjen Y. Hoekstra

4.1 Introduction

The World Economic Forum has listed water scarcity as one of the three global systemic risks of highest concern, an assessment based on a broad global survey on risk perception among representatives from business, academia, civil society, governments and international organisations (WEF 2014). Freshwater scarcity manifests itself in the form of declining groundwater tables, reduced river flows, shrinking lakes and heavily polluted waters, but also in increasing costs of supply and treatment, intermittent supplies and conflicts over water (Hoekstra 2014a). Future water scarcity will grow as a result of various drivers: population and economic growth, increased demands for animal products and biofuels and climate change (Ercin and Hoekstra 2014). The private sector is becoming aware of the problem of freshwater scarcity but is facing the challenge of formulating effective responses. Even companies operating in water-abundant regions can be vulnerable to water scarcity, because the supply chains of most companies stretch across the globe. An estimated 22 % of global water consumption and pollution relates to the production of export commodities (Hoekstra and Mekonnen 2012). Countries such as the USA, Brazil, Argentina, Australia, India and China are big virtual water exporters, which means that they intensively use domestic water resources for producing export commodities. In contrast, countries in Europe, North Africa and the Middle East as well as Mexico and Japan are dominated by virtual water import, which means that they rely on import goods produced with water resources elsewhere. The water use behind those imported goods is often not sustainable, because many of the export regions overexploit their resources.

A.Y. Hoekstra (✉)
University of Twente, Enschede, The Netherlands
e-mail: a.y.hoekstra@utwente.nl

© Yann Bouchery, Charles J. Corbett, Jan C. Fransoo, and Tarkan Tan 2017
Y. Bouchery et al. (eds.), *Sustainable Supply Chains*, Springer Series in Supply
Chain Management 4, DOI 10.1007/978-3-319-29791-0_4

Increasingly, companies start exploring their water footprint, thereby looking at both their operations and supply chain. Key questions that industry leaders pose themselves are as follows: where is my water footprint located, what risks does water scarcity impose to my business, how sustainable is the water footprint in the catchments where my operations and supply-chain processes are located, where and how can water use efficiency be increased and what is good water stewardship? The demand for new sorts of data emerges, types of data that were usually not collected. The focus shifts from relatively simple questions—whether the company has got sufficient water abstraction permits and whether wastewater disposal standards are met—to the more pressing question: how the company actually contributes to the overexploitation and pollution of water resources, not only through its own facilities but through its supply chain as well. Having permits and meeting standards do not imply sustainability. Most experience with collecting the new sorts of data required and with addressing questions about good water stewardship is within the food and beverage sector, which depends most clearly on water. In other industries, the connection with water is not always clear, because it is indirect and mostly through the supply chain. The aim of this chapter is to introduce the water footprint concept, review experiences with water footprint assessment and reflect on future challenges.

In the next section, I will start with discussing and comparing three methods to trace resource use and pollution over supply chains: environmental footprint assessment (EFA), life cycle assessment (LCA) and environmentally extended input–output analysis. Next, I will discuss what new perspective the water footprint concept brings to the table, compared to the traditional way of looking at water use. In the third section, I will reflect on direct and indirect water footprints of the different sectors of the economy, with examples for two specific sectors: food and beverage and transport. In the last section, I will discuss future challenges, such as the issue of data gathering and reporting, the demand for water stewardship and greater product transparency and the need to establish water footprint benchmarks.

4.2   Footprints, Life Cycle Assessment and Input–Output Modelling

4.2.1   Methods to Trace Natural Resource Use and Pollution Over Supply Chains

Three different methods have been developed to analyse direct and indirect natural resource use and emissions in relation to products or economic sectors: EFA, LCA and environmentally extended input–output analysis (EE-IOA). All three methods have been applied also in the field of water, to trace direct and indirect water use and pollution over supply chains. Each of the three methods has its specific goal, approach and focus, but there are commonalities across the methods as well. They all focus on understanding natural resource use and emissions along supply or value chains. EFA focuses on macro-questions on resource use sustainability, efficiency, equitability and security. LCA concentrates on the comparative analysis of environmental impacts of products. EE-IOA focuses on understanding how natural resource use and environmental impacts can be traced throughout the economy.

The field of EFA comprises methods to quantity and map land, water, material, carbon and other environmental footprints and assess the sustainability of these footprints as well as the efficiency, equitability and security of resource use (Hoekstra and Wiedmann 2014). Water footprint assessment (WFA) can be regarded as a specific branch of this field and refers to the full range of activities to quantify and locate the water footprint of a process, product, producer or consumer or to quantify in space and time the water footprint in a specified geographic area; assess the environmental sustainability, economic efficiency and social equitability of water footprints; and formulate a response strategy (Hoekstra et al. 2011). Broadly speaking, the goal of assessing water footprints is to analyse how human activities or specific products relate to issues of water scarcity and pollution and to see how consumption, production, trade and specific products can become more sustainable from a water perspective.

LCA is a method for estimating and assessing the environmental impacts attributable to the life cycle of a product, such as climate change; stratospheric ozone depletion; tropospheric ozone (smog) creation; eutrophication; acidification; toxicological stress on human health and ecosystems; the depletion of resources, water use, land use and noise; and others (Rebitzer et al. 2004). The assessment includes all stages of the life cycle of a product, from cradle to grave (from material extraction to returning of wastes to nature). An LCA study includes four phases: setting goal and scope, inventory accounting, impact assessment and interpretation. Water use and pollution can be considered as specific impact categories within LCA (Kounina et al. 2013). LCA focuses on *comparing* the environmental impacts of alternative processes, materials, products or designs. (See Chap. 2 by Guinée and Heijungs (2017) for more on LCA.)

Environmentally extended input–output analysis (EE-IOA) is a method for studying the relation between different sectors of the economy and indirect natural resource use and environmental impacts. It combines the classical monetary input–output formalism with satellite accounts containing data on resource use and emissions into the environment. Over the past decade, we have seen quite a number of applications of EE-IOA to analyse 'embodied' water flows through the economy (Daniels et al. 2011). Applications have been carried out, for example, for Australia (Lenzen and Foran 2001), Spain (Duarte et al. 2002; Cazcarro et al. 2013), the UK (Yu et al. 2010; Feng et al. 2011a), China (Zhao et al. 2009; Zhang and Anadon 2014) and the city of Beijing (Zhang et al. 2011). Input–output models basically show monetary flows between sectors within the economy; environmentally extended input–output models usually express water use in terms of litre per dollar (or other currencies). Most environmentally extended input–output models also have some form of accounting of product flows in physical units, but due to the aggregation of specific economic activities into sectors, it remains difficult to reach the same high level of detail as achieved in a process-based WFA or LCA. Both WFA and LCA enable an analysis of water use in all processes of the value chain and attribution of the water use along value chains to specific products. A promising path in this respect is the method of so-called *hybrid* environmentally extended input–output modelling, in which physical flows are integrated into the model (Ewing et al. 2012; Steen-Olsen et al. 2012).

Process-based WFA and LCA are generally constrained by the fact that parts of the value chain have to be left out from the analysis for practical reasons. This problem does not occur in input–output modelling. Therefore, there is a development to enhance process-based WFA and LCA with the advantage of input–output modelling. In the case of LCA, this results in the so-called hybrid LCA approach (Finnveden et al. 2009). In hybrid LCA, the environmental impacts of flows that were not included in the process-based LCA are estimated with an environmentally extended input–output model. This hybrid approach is also called environmental input–output-based LCA (EIO-LCA). In the case of WFA, a similar development can be expected (Feng et al. 2011b).

The difference between EFA and LCA is the focus on sustainability of production and consumption at macro-level of the former and the focus on comparing environmental impact at process and product level of the latter (Hoekstra 2015b). This is explained in Box 4.1 for the example of cutting trees. Typical questions in EFA studies relate to how different processes and products contribute to the overall footprints at larger scales, how different consumption patterns influence the overall footprint, whether footprints at the larger scales remain within their maximum sustainable levels, how footprints can be reduced by better technology, whether different people have equitable shares in the total footprint of humanity and what externalisation of footprints may imply for resource security (Hoekstra and Wiedmann 2014). LCA is designed to compare the environmental impact of one product over its full value chain with the overall impact of another product or to compare the differences in environmental impact between different product designs or alternative production processes.

Box 4.1 The Sustainability of Cutting Trees: The Fundamental Difference Between LCA and EFA

Is it sustainable to cut a tree? Although a relevant question, it is impossible to answer this question in isolated form. On the one hand, it is hard to argue that cutting just one tree is not sustainable. After a tree has been cut, a new one will grow, so that is sustainable. On the other hand, if one takes this insight on the sustainability of cutting one tree to conclude that one can cut all forests, one cannot maintain that this is sustainable. The reason why answering a simple question like this tree-cutting question causes a fundamental problem is that sustainability is a concept that cannot be applied at the level of single

(continued)

Box 4.1 (continued)

activities, but only at the level of a system as a whole. Still, there is a strong wish among people to measure the sustainability of single activities, because individuals undertake single activities and consume goods and services that relate to series of single activities to produce them. The methods of LCA and EFA deal with this problem in fundamentally different ways. In LCA, the approach is to leave the larger question on sustainability and look at *comparative* contributions of different activities to natural resource appropriation, emissions and potential impacts at the larger scale. In other words, LCA addresses the question how cutting one tree compares to cutting two trees, a question that is not hard to answer. In EFA, the approach is to estimate humanity's total natural resource appropriation and emissions and compare that to the Earth's carrying or assimilation capacity. Both methods struggle in a similar way with how to compare apples and pears, for example, how to compare cutting trees with polluting water. The approach in LCA is to *weigh* different types of primary resource use or emissions according to their potential final impact on human health and ecosystem health. The approach in EFA is to compare the different types of resource use and pollution to their respective maximum sustainable levels. The great similarity between LCA and EFA is that resource use and emissions are analysed per process (activity) and per product (by analysing the processes along supply chains). The difference comes when LCA starts weighing different types of resource use and emissions based on their potential impact and comparing alternative processes or products according to their overall potential environmental impact. In contrast, EFA adds the resource use and emissions of different activities in order to get a complete picture, analyse the sustainability of the whole and study the relative contribution of different processes, products and consumers to the total. In many applications, though, the difference between LCA and EFA is not so clear. By comparing the footprints of two different processes or products, EFA also allows for comparative analysis. However, the comparative analysis is partial in this case, because different footprints are not weighted and added to get a measure of 'overall potential environmental impact'. On the other hand, one can also extend an LCA from comparing products to comparing consumption patterns, which is at the larger scale typically for EFA. The fundamental difference between LCA and EFA in the way they treat the tree-cutting question, however, remains.

At the level of basic data, EFA and LCA require similar data. The data collection and analysis required in the accounting stage of a product-focused WFA (as opposed to a geographic- or consumption-focused WFA) are very much similar to what is needed in the inventory stage of a water-focused LCA (Boulay et al. 2013).

EFA, LCA and EE-IOA are not static analytical methods, but still young fields under development. We can observe a development in the past few years in which a fruitful exchange between the three fields leads to the adoption of approaches from one field into the other. In EFA studies we have seen the adoption of life cycle accounting procedures from LCA and the exploration of using input–output models to calculate national and sector footprints, in addition to the already existing bottom-up and top-down trade-balance approaches. In LCA we recently observe, fed by experiences in EFA, an interest to develop methods to carry out an LCA for a whole organisation instead of for a product and to carry out LCAs for consumer lifestyles or for national consumption as a whole (Hellweg and Milà i Canals 2014). Additionally, based on experiences in EE-IOA, the LCA community is exploring hybrid LCA methods as already mentioned above. The EE-IOA practice improves in the direction of hybrid methods that include physical accounting and have greater granularity in the analysis, fed by the practices in the EFA and LCA fields. This mutual enrichment and to some extent convergence of approaches do not imply that the three methods will grow into one. They may develop into a more consistent framework of coherent methods, but the fact that different sorts of questions will remain implies that different approaches will continue to be necessary.

All three methods—EFA, LCA and EE-IOA—have a focus on environmental issues, leaving out social issues (like labour conditions, human rights). Principally, though, there is nothing that necessarily restricts the methods to environmental issues. Broadly speaking, one can trace all sorts of process characteristics along supply chains. The oldest forms of accounting along supply chains are the accounting of monetary added value and the accounting of material flows and energy use along supply chains. Material flow analysis (MFA) or substance flow analysis (SFA) aims at the quantification of stocks and flows of materials or substances in a well-defined system, drawing mass balances for each subsystem and the system as a whole. Energy flow analysis aims at quantifying the energy content of flows within an economy. The innovation of EFA, LCA and EE-IOA lies in the attribution of resource use, emissions or impacts along supply chains to products and final consumption. In this context, one speaks about the embodied, embedded, indirect or virtual land, water and energy in a product or consumption pattern, the indirect emissions, etc. When doing so, the method of EE-IOA is linked to traditional economic accounting, which is a strong point of this method. The methods of EFA and LCA are rather linked to physical accounting, which is their strength. In all three fields, we observe efforts to enhance the methods and broaden the scope, with an increasing number of hybrid approaches.

4.2.2   The Water Footprint Concept

The water footprint (WF) is a measure of freshwater appropriation underlying a certain product or consumption pattern. Three components are distinguished: the blue, green and grey WF (Hoekstra et al. 2011). The blue WF measures the volume of water abstracted from the ground or surface water system minus the volume of water returned to the system. It thus refers to the sum of the water flow that evaporates during the process of production, the water incorporated into a product and the water released in another catchment. The blue WF differs from the conventional way of measuring freshwater use by looking at net rather than gross water withdrawal. This is done because it makes more sense to look at net water withdrawal if one is interested in the effect of water use on water scarcity within a catchment. Return flows can be reused within the catchment, unlike the water flow that evaporates or is captured within a product. The green WF refers to the volume of rainwater consumed in a production process. This is particularly relevant in agriculture and forestry, where it refers to the total rainwater evapotranspiration (from fields and plantations) plus the water incorporated into the harvested crop or wood. The grey WF is an indicator of freshwater pollution and defined as the volume of freshwater required to assimilate a load of pollutants based on natural background concentrations and existing ambient water quality standards. The advantage of expressing water pollution in terms of the water volume required for assimilating the pollutants, rather than in terms of concentrations of contaminants, is that this brings water pollution into the same unit as consumptive use. In this way, the use of water as a drain and the use of water as a resource, two competing uses, become comparable. The WF refers thus to both consumptive water use (of rainwater—the green WF—and of surface and groundwater—the blue WF) and degenerative or degradative water use (the grey WF).

As a measure of freshwater use, the WF differs from the classical measure of 'water withdrawal' in several ways. The term 'water withdrawal'—also called 'water abstraction' or often simply 'water use'—refers to the extraction of water from the groundwater or a surface water body like a river, lake or artificial storage reservoir. It thus refers to what we call *blue* water use. The WF is not restricted to measuring blue water use, but also measures the use of green water resources (the green WF) and the volume of pollution (the grey WF). Another difference between the WF and the classical way of measuring water use was mentioned already above: the classical measure of 'water use' always refers to gross blue water abstraction, while the blue WF refers to net blue water abstraction. Another difference between the classical way of measuring water use and the WF is that the latter concept can be used to measure water use over supply chains. When we talk about the WF of a product, we refer to the water consumption and pollution in all stages of the supply chain of the product. When we speak about the WF of a producer or a consumer, we refer to the full WF of all the products produced or consumed.

The WF thus offers a wider perspective on how a product, producer or consumer relates to the use of freshwater systems. It is a volumetric measure of water consumption and pollution. WF accounts give spatiotemporally explicit information on how water is appropriated for various human purposes. The local environmental impact of a certain amount of water consumption and pollution depends on the vulnerability of the local water system and the number of water consumers and polluters that make use of the same system. The WF within a catchment needs to be compared to the maximum sustainable WF in the catchment in order to understand the sustainability of water use. The WF of a specific process or product needs to be compared to a WF benchmark based on best available technology and practice in

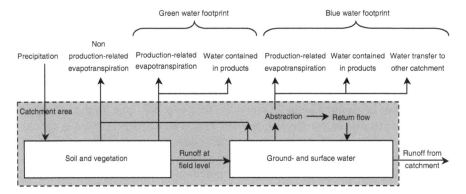

Fig. 4.1 Definition of the green and blue water footprint in relation to the water balance of a catchment area. *Source*: Hoekstra et al. (2011)

order to understand the efficiency of water use. The WF per capita for a community can be compared to the WF of other communities to understand the degree of equitable sharing of limited water resources. WF accounts can thus feed the discussion about the sustainability, efficiency and equitability of water use and allocation (Hoekstra 2013, 2014b).

The definition of the green and blue WF can best be understood by considering the water balance of a river basin (Fig. 4.1). The total annual water availability in a catchment area is given by the annual volume of precipitation, which will leave the basin partly through evapotranspiration and partly through runoff to the sea. Both the evaporative flow and the runoff can be appropriated by humans. The green WF refers to the human use of the evaporative flow from the land surface, mostly for growing crops or production forest. The blue WF refers to the consumptive use of the runoff flow, i.e. the net abstraction of runoff from the catchment. The term 'water consumption' can be confusing, because many people — particularly those not aware of the big difference between gross and net water abstraction — use the term for gross water abstraction. Specialists, though, define water consumption as net blue water abstraction (gross abstraction minus return flow). Evaporation is generally considered as a loss to the catchment. Even though evaporated water will always return in the form of precipitation at global scale, this will not alleviate the water scarcity in the catchment in the period that the river is emptied due to net water abstractions. Moisture recycling at smaller spatial scales is generally only modest.

The definition of the grey WF is clarified in Fig. 4.2. The basis for the calculation is the anthropogenic load of a substance into a freshwater body (groundwater, river, lake), that is, the additional load caused by a human activity (e.g. a production process). We should acknowledge that the effluent from an industry might contain certain amounts of chemicals that were already in the water abstracted. Therefore, we should look at the *additional* load to a freshwater body as a result of a certain activity. Furthermore, we should look at the load of a substance that really enters the river, lake or groundwater, which means that, if an effluent is treated before disposal, we have to consider the load of chemicals in the effluent that remains *after* treatment.

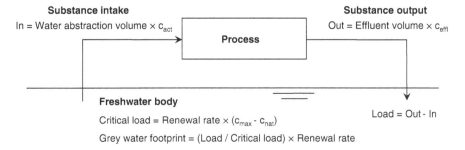

Fig. 4.2 Definition of the grey water footprint based on the load of a chemical into a freshwater body. The symbols c_{act}, c_{nat} and c_{max} refer to the actual, natural and maximum allowable concentration of the chemical in the freshwater body; c_{effl} refers to the concentration of the chemical in the effluent

The critical load in a freshwater body is defined as the difference between the maximum acceptable and natural concentration of a chemical for the receiving water body times the renewal rate of the freshwater body. Note that as for the maximum allowable concentration, we have to take the ambient water quality standard for the receiving freshwater body, not the effluent standard (Franke et al. 2013). In a river, the renewal rate is equal to runoff; in a groundwater reservoir, the renewal rate is equal to groundwater recharge, which (over the longer term) is the same as groundwater runoff. In a lake, the renewal rate equals the flow through the lake. The grey WF is calculated as the pollutant load to a freshwater body divided by the critical load, times the renewal rate of that freshwater body. Defined in this way, it means that when the grey WF onto a freshwater body becomes as big as the renewal rate of this freshwater body, the assimilation capacity has been fully used. When the size of the grey WF in a catchment exceeds the size of runoff from this catchment, pollution is bigger than the assimilation capacity, resulting in a violation of the maximum acceptable concentration. When an effluent contains different sorts of pollutants, as is usually the case, the grey WF is determined by the pollutant that is most critical, that is the one that gives the largest pollutant-specific grey WF. Thermal pollution can be dealt with in a similar way as pollutants, whereby the load consists of heat and the assimilation capacity depends on the accepted temperature increase of the receiving water body (Hoekstra et al. 2011).

4.3   Direct and Indirect Water Footprints of Different Sectors of the Economy

4.3.1   The Importance of Water Use in the Primary Sector

Usually, economic activities are categorised into three different sectors. The primary sector of the economy, the sector that extracts or harvests products from the earth, has the largest water footprint on Earth. This sector includes activities like

Table 4.1 Global water footprint within different water-using categories (period: 1996–2005)

Economic sector	Water use category	Global water footprint (10^9 m³/year)					Remark
		Green	Blue	Grey	Total	%	
Primary sector	Crop farming	5771	899	733	7404	81.5	
	Pasture	913	–	–	913	10.0	
	Animal farming	–	46	–	46	0.5	Water for drinking and cleaning
	Agriculture total	6684	945	733	8363	92.0	
	Aquaculture	?	?	?	?	?	No global data
	Forestry	?	?	?	?	?	No global data
	Mining, quarrying	?	?	?	?	?	No global data
Secondary sector	Industry (self-supply)	–	38	363	400	4.4	Water use in manufacturing, electricity supply and construction
	Municipal water supply	–	42	282	324	3.6	Water supply to households and (small) users in primary, secondary and tertiary sector
Tertiary sector	Self-supply	?	?	?	?	?	No global data
Households	Self-supply	?	?	?	?	?	No global data
Total		6684	1025	1378	9087	100	

Data sources: Mekonnen and Hoekstra (2011) for crop farming; Mekonnen and Hoekstra (2012) for pasture and animal farming; Hoekstra and Mekonnen (2012) for industry and municipal water supply

Note that the blue WF figure for crop farming relates to evapotranspiration of irrigation water at field level; it excludes losses from storage reservoirs and irrigation canals

The blue WF figure for 'industry' presented here includes water use in mining, which is part of the primary sector

The figure excludes water lost from reservoirs for hydroelectric generation

All grey WF figures are conservative estimates

Forestry is not included as a water use sector because of a lack of data

agriculture, forestry, fishing, aquaculture, mining and quarrying. The green WF of humanity is nearly entirely concentrated within the primary sector. It has been estimated that about 92 % of the blue WF of humanity is just in agriculture alone (Table 4.1).

The secondary sector covers the manufacturing of goods in the economy, including the processing of materials produced by the primary sector. It also includes construction and the public utility industries of electricity, gas and water. Sometimes, the public utility industries are also mentioned under the tertiary (service) sector, because they do not only produce something (electricity, gas, purified water), but also supply it to customers (as a service). Water utilities could even partly fall under the primary sector, because part of the activity is the abstraction of water from the environment (rivers, lakes, groundwater). The work of water utilities comprises water collection, purification, distribution and supply, wastewater collection (sewerage), wastewater treatment, material recovery and wastewater disposal. It's rather common to categorise the whole water utility sector under the secondary sector. The tertiary industry is the service industry and covers services to both businesses and final consumers. This sector includes activities like retail and wholesale sales, transportation and distribution, entertainment, restaurants, clerical services, media, tourism, insurance, banking, healthcare, defence and law. Even though sometimes categorised into another, quaternary sector, one can also list here activities related to government, culture, libraries, scientific research, education and information technology. The secondary and tertiary sectors have much smaller WFs than the primary sector.

The contribution of agriculture to water scarcity is underestimated by conventional water use statistics, which show gross blue water abstractions. In agriculture, most of the gross water use will evaporate from storage reservoirs, irrigations canals or finally from the field. The water abstracted for irrigation in agriculture is thus largely unavailable for reuse within the basin. In industrial water use, the ratio of net to gross abstraction is estimated at less than 5 %. In municipal water use, this ratio varies from 5 to 15 % in urban areas and from 10 to 50 % in rural areas (FAO 2014). Water that returns to the catchment after use can be reused. Presenting gross or net water abstractions thus makes a huge difference for industries and households and less in agriculture.

Even though the primary sector is the largest water user, governmental programmes to create public awareness of water scarcity often focus on public campaigns calling for water saving at home. This is little effective at large given the fact that the major share of water use in most places relates to agriculture and in second instance to industry. Water scarcity is thus generally caused mostly by excessive water use in agriculture. Installing water-saving showerheads and dual-flush toilets in households will have hardly any impact in mitigating water scarcity at all, but still this is what most water-saving campaigns advocate for. It would be more useful to make people aware of the water use and pollution underlying the food items and other products they buy and to advocate for product labels that show the sustainability of the WF of a product.

4.3.2 Food and Beverage Products

The food and beverage sector is the manufacturing sector with the largest WF, maybe not the largest operational WF, but definitely the largest supply-chain WF. (Chap. 18 by Bloemhof and Soysal (2017) focuses on designing sustainable food supply chains.) The reason is that the food and beverage sector is the largest client of the agricultural sector, which is responsible for the largest share in global water consumption (Table 4.1). Interesting WF studies carried out in the beverage sector are, for example, the studies carried out by SABMiller (SABMiller and WWF-UK 2009; SABMiller et al. 2010), Coca-Cola (TCCC and TNC 2010; Coca-Cola

Europe 2011) and the Beverage Industry Environmental Roundtable (BIER 2011). Some nice examples of WF studies in the food sector come from Unilever (Jefferies et al. 2012), Dole (Sikirica 2011), Mars (Ridoutt et al. 2009) and Barilla (Ruini et al. 2013).

Traditionally, the beverage industry focuses on the so-called water use ratio (WUR), which is defined as the total water use divided by the total production at a bottling facility, expressed in terms of litre of water used per litre of beverage produced. Water use stands here for gross blue water abstraction, not net blue water abstraction (blue WF). In a global benchmarking study for the period 2009–2011, BIER (2012) reports a WUR of 1.2–2.2 L/L (with an average of 1.5) for bottled water, a WUR of 1.5–4.0 (average 2.1) for carbonated soft drinks, a WUR of 3.2–6.6 (average 4.3) for beer breweries, a WUR of 8–126 (average 36) for distilleries and a WUR of 2.0–18.5 (average 4.4) for wineries. The WUR is of limited value, because the operational WF of bottling factories is very small when compared to the full WF of a beverage, as shown by Ercin et al. (2011) for a carbonated soft drink. They show that the WF of a half-litre bottle of soft drink resembling cola can range between 150 and 300 L, of which 99.7–99.8 % refers to the supply chain.

4.3.3 Transport

Transport is always considered as an important sector in carbon footprint assessment, since transport can significantly contribute to the overall carbon footprint of a final product, measured over its full supply chain. In the case of the WF of a final product, the contribution of transport will generally be relatively small, because not much freshwater is being consumed or polluted during transport. It is worth considering the indirect WF of transport related to materials (trucks, trains, boats, airplanes) and energy used, but particularly materials will generally contribute very little, due to the fact that the WF of transport vehicles can be distributed over all goods transported over the lifetime of a vehicle. The WF of energy may be more relevant, but even that can be small compared to the other components of the WF of goods, particularly in the case of agricultural goods. The key determinant in the WF of transport is probably the energy source (Gerbens-Leenes et al. 2009a; King and Webber 2008). The WF of bioenergy in terms of cubic metre per GJ is generally two to three orders of magnitude larger than that for energy from fossil fuels or wind or solar power. However, in all energy categories, WFs per unit of energy can widely vary, depending on the precise source and production technology. The technique of hydraulic fracturing (fracking) to mine natural gas or petroleum reserves, for example, has a larger blue and grey WF than when mining reserves that are easier accessible using more conventional techniques. In the case of bioenergy, it matters greatly whether one speaks about biodiesel from oil crops, bioethanol from sugar or starch crops (Gerbens-Leenes et al. 2009b; Dominguez-Faus et al. 2009), biofuel from cellulosic fractions of crops or waste materials (Chiu and Wu 2012), biofuel from algae (Gerbens-Leenes et al. 2014) or about bioelectricity. In the latter case,

Table 4.2 The water footprint of different modes of passenger and freight transport when based on first-generation biofuel produced in the European Union

Transport mode	Energy source	Green + blue water footprint of passenger transport (L per passenger km)	Green + blue water footprint of freight transport (L per 1000 kg of freight per km)
Airplane	Biodiesel from rapeseed	142–403	576–1023
	Bioethanol from sugar beet	42–89	169–471
Car (large)	Biodiesel from rapeseed	214–291	–
	Bioethanol from sugar beet	138–289	–
Car (small)	Biodiesel from rapeseed	65–89	–
	Bioethanol from sugar beet	24–50	–
Bus/lorry	Biodiesel from rapeseed	67–126	142–330
	Bioethanol from sugar beet	20–58	–
Train	Biodiesel from rapeseed	15–40	15–40
Ship (inland)	Biodiesel from rapeseed	–	36–68
Ship (sea, bulk)	Biodiesel from rapeseed	–	8–11
Electric train	Bioelectricity from maize	3–12	2–7
Electric car	Bioelectricity from maize	4–7	–
Walking	Sugar from sugar beet	3–6	–
Bike	Sugar from sugar beet	1–2	–

Source of data: Gerbens-Leenes and Hoekstra (2011)
The total water footprint of transport based on first-generation biofuel mainly relates to the water volumes consumed in growing the crop

it makes a large difference what is burnt: biomass grown for the purpose or organic waste. As an illustration of the large differences between different bioenergy forms, Table 4.2 shows the WF of different modes of passenger and freight transport when based on first-generation biofuel produced in the European Union. Governmental policies to replace substantial percentages of fossil fuels by biofuels will lead to a rapid growth of the WF of the transport sector (Gerbens-Leenes et al. 2012).

4.4 Challenges

4.4.1 The Need to Take a Supply-Chain Perspective

The supply-chain WF of most companies is many times greater than their operational footprint, but most companies restrict their efforts to reducing the latter, leaving the supply-chain WF out of scope. Studies carried out by companies like Coca-Cola, PepsiCo, SABMiller and Heineken have shown that the supply-chain WF for beverage companies can easily be over 99 % of their total WF. Nevertheless, all these companies apply a 'key performance indicator' for water that refers to the water use in their own operations only. Common reduction targets in the beverage industry, such as going from 2 to 1.5 L of water use in the bottling plant per litre of beverage, have little effect on the larger scale given that the supply-chain WF of most beverages is of the order of 100 L of water per litre of beverage or even more (Hoekstra 2013). Water-sustainability investments by beverage companies are geared to better perform in their own operations, which means that investments are made that aim to reduce that one per cent of their total WF. It is difficult to imagine that these investments will be most cost effective if really sustainability is the goal. Incorporating sustainability principles into a company's business model would include the adoption of mechanisms to secure sustainable water use in the supply chain. For companies, moving towards a sustainable supply chain is a much bigger challenge than greening their own operations, because the WF of the supply chain can be influenced only indirectly. Mechanisms to reduce the supply-chain WF are, for example, the application of water criteria for sustainable procurement and reaching agreements with suppliers about footprint reduction over time.

4.4.2 The Need to Incorporate Temporal and Spatial Variability in Water Footprint Assessment

When formulating WF reduction targets for processes in their operations or supply chain, companies should not only look at the numbers but also at the geographic locations where their WF is sited. Priority is to be given to WF reduction in catchments in which the overall footprint exceeds the carrying capacity or assimilation capacity of the catchment. It has been argued that reduction in water-abundant catchments does not even make sense (Pfister and Hellweg 2009), but this is based on a misunderstanding. Since the WF (m³/product unit) is simply a reverse of water productivity (product units per m³), it is difficult to see why one would not set targets regarding the reduction of the WF of a product, which is the same as setting targets regarding the increase of water productivity. The relevance of increased water productivities worldwide, also in water-abundant places, can be illustrated with the following example (Hoekstra 2013). Suppose the hypothetical case of two river basins, with the same surface (Table 4.3). Basin A is relatively dry and has, on

Table 4.3 Example of how overexploitation in a water-stressed river basin (A) can be solved by increasing water productivity in a water-abundant basin (B)

Parameter	Unit	Current situation		Possible solution	
		Basin A	Basin B	Basin A	Basin B
Max. sustainable water footprint	Water units/unit of time	50	250	50	250
Water footprint	Water units/unit of time	100	200	50	200
Production	Product units/unit of time	100	100	50	200
Water footprint per product unit	Water units/product unit	1	2	1	1
Water productivity	Product units/water unit	1	0.5	1	1

Source: *Hoekstra* (2013)

an annual basis, 50 water units available, the maximum sustainable WF. The maximum level, however, is exceeded by a factor of two. Farmers in the basin consume 100 water units per year to produce 100 crop units. Basin B has more water available, 250 water units per year. Water is more abundant than in the first basin, but water is used less efficiently. Farmers in the basin consume 200 water units per year, to produce 100 crop units, the same amount as in the first basin, but using two times more water per crop unit. A geographic analysis shows that in basin B, the WF (200) remains below the maximum level (250), so this is sustainable. In basin A, however, the WF (100) by far exceeds the maximum sustainable level (50), so this is clearly unsustainable. The question is now: should we categorise the crops originating from basin A as unsustainable and the crops from basin B as sustainable? From a geographic perspective, the answer is affirmative. In basin A, the WF of crop production needs to be reduced that seems to be the crux. However, when we take a product perspective, we observe that the WF per crop unit in basin B is two times larger than in basin A. If the farmers in basin B would use their water more productively and reach the same water productivity as in basin A, they would produce twice as many crops without increasing the total WF in the basin. It may well be that farmers in basin A cannot easily further increase their water productivity, so that—if the aim is to keep global production at the same level—the only solution is to bring down the WF in basin A to a sustainable level by cutting production by half, while enlarging production in basin B by increasing the water productivity. If basin B manages to achieve the same water productivity level as in basin A, the two basins together could even increase global production while halving the total WF in basin A and keeping it at the same level in basin B.

4.4.3   Measuring and Reporting

It is difficult to get water use statistics organised along the same structure of economic sector classifications. Many countries and regions have their own classification of economic activities, distinguishing main sectors, subsectors, etc. One of the international standard classifications is the Industrial Classification of All Economic Activities of the United Nations (UN 2008). Conventional water use statistics mostly show gross blue water withdrawals and distinguish three main categories: agricultural, industrial and municipal water use (FAO 2014). Also WF statistics distinguish between the agricultural, industrial and municipal sector. These three sectors cannot be mapped one to one onto the primary, secondary and tertiary sector. 'Agricultural water use' obviously is about water use in the primary sector, while 'industrial water use' is about water use in the secondary sector. However, water use in mining—part of the primary sector—will generally be categorised under 'industrial water use' as well. Industrial water use refers to self-supplied industries not connected to the public distribution network. It includes water for the cooling of thermoelectric plants, but it does not include hydropower (which is often left out of the water use accounts altogether). Municipal water use—often alternatively called domestic water use or public water supply—refers to the water use by water utilities and distributed through the public water distribution network. Water utilities provide water directly to households, but also to water users in the primary, secondary and tertiary sector.

The mismatch between the three main categories in water use statistics and the different sectors as usually distinguished in the economy can be quite confusing. The 'water supply sector' as distinguished in economic classifications refers to water utilities delivering municipal water to households and others connected to the public water supply system. Unfortunately, the category of municipal water use lumps water use for a great variety of water users: final consumers (households) and users in all economic sectors. Specifications by type of user are not always available. Additionally confusing is that, even though the 'water supply sector' serves all sorts of users, the sector refers to only a minor fraction of total water use. Most of the water use in agriculture, the largest water user, is not part of the 'water supply sector'. Furthermore, water self-supply by industries does not fall within this sector and neither does self-supply in the tertiary sector and self-supply by final consumers. Given that only an estimated 3.6 % of the total WF of humanity relates to what we call the 'water supply sector' (Hoekstra and Mekonnen 2012), the sector receives disproportionate attention in public debates about water use and scarcity, diverting the necessary attention on water use in agriculture and industry.

For companies, much confusion exists as to what needs to be measured and reported. Traditionally, companies have focused on monitoring gross water abstractions and compliance with legal standards. However, net water abstractions are more relevant than gross abstractions, and meeting wastewater quality standards is not enough to discard the contribution to water pollution made by a company. Regarding terminology and calculation standards, the Water Footprint Network—a global network of universities, nongovernmental organisations, companies, investors and international organisations—developed the global water footprint standard (Hoekstra et al. 2011). The International Organization for Standardization developed a reporting standard based on LCA (ISO 2014). Both standards emphasise the need to incorporate the temporal and spatial variability in WFs and the need to consider the WF in the context of local water scarcity and water productivity. In practice, companies face a huge challenge in tracing their supply chain. Apparel companies, for example, have generally little idea about where their cotton is grown or processed, yet both cotton growing and processing are notorious water consumers and polluters. It is difficult to see quick progress in the field of supply-chain reporting if governments don't force companies to do it.

4.4.4 Water Stewardship and Transparency

There is an increasing call for good water stewardship and transparency in the private sector, driven by increased public awareness, demands from investors and perceived water risks by the sector itself. Water stewardship is a comprehensive concept that includes the evaluation of the sustainability of water use across the entire value chain, the formulation of water consumption and pollution reduction targets for both the company's operations and supply chain, the implementation of a plan to achieve these targets and proper reporting on all of this (Hoekstra 2014a). In priority catchments, it requires the pursuit of collective action and community engagement (Sarni 2011). Large priority river basins are, for example, the Colorado and San Antonio basins in North America; the Lake Chad, Limpopo and Orange basins in Africa; the basins of the Jordan, Tigris, Euphrates, Indus, Ganges, Krishna, Cauvery, Tarim and Yellow rivers; the Yongding River basins in Asia; and the Murray–Darling basin in Australia (Hoekstra et al. 2012).

The increasing interest in how companies relate to unsustainable water use calls for greater transparency on water consumption and pollution. Openness is required at different levels: the company, product and facility level. Driven by environmental organisations and the investment community, businesses are increasingly urged to disclose relevant data at company level on how they relate to water risks (Deloitte 2013). Simultaneously, there is an increasing demand for product transparency through labelling or certification. Despite the plethora of existing product labels related to environmental sustainability, none of these includes criteria on sustainable water use. Finally, there is a movement to develop principles and certification schemes for sustainable site or facility management, such as the initiatives of the European Water Partnership and the Alliance for Water Stewardship. But despite progress in awareness, still hardly any companies in the world report on water consumption and pollution in their supply chain or reveal information about the sustainability of the WF of their products.

Another concern regarding good water stewardship is the extent to which a company pays for the full cost of its water use. Water use is subsidised in many countries, either through direct governmental investments in water supply infrastructure or indirectly by agricultural subsidies, promotion of crops for bioenergy or fossil-energy subsidies to pump water. Besides, water scarcity and pollution remain unpriced (Hoekstra 2013). In order to give the right price signal, users should pay for their pollution and consumptive water use, with a differentiated price in time and space based on water vulnerability and scarcity.

4.4.5   The Need to Establish WF Benchmarks

WFs per unit of product strongly vary across different production locations and production systems. Therefore we need to establish WF benchmarks for water-intensive products such as food and beverages, cotton, flowers and biofuels. The benchmark for a product will depend on the maximum reasonable water consumption in each step of the product's supply chain, based on best available technology and practice. Benchmarks for the various water-using processes along the supply chain of a product, can be taken together to formulate a WF benchmark for the final product. An end-product point of view is particularly relevant for the companies, retailers and consumers who are not directly involved in the water-using processes in the early steps of the supply chains of the products they are manufacturing, selling or consuming, but still interested in the water performance of the product over the chain as a whole. WF benchmarks will offer a reference for companies to work towards and a reference for governments in allocating WF permits to users. Besides, manufacturers, retailers and final consumers in the lower end of the supply chain get an instrument to compare the actual WF of a product to a certain reference level. Business associations within the different sectors of economy can develop their own regional or global WF benchmarks, though governments can take initiatives in this area as well, including the development of regulations or legislation. The latter will be most relevant to completely ban worst practices.

4.4.6 Water Footprint Reduction Goals and Possible Trade-Offs

Companies should strive towards zero WF in industrial operations, which can be achieved through nullifying evaporation losses, full water recycling and recapturing chemicals and heat from used water flows. The problem is not the fact that water is being used, but that it is not fully returned to the environment or not returned clean. The WF measures exactly that: the consumptive water use and the volume of water polluted. As the last steps towards zero WF may require more energy, the challenge will be to find a balance between reducing the water and the carbon footprint. Furthermore, companies should set reduction targets regarding the WF of their supply chain, particularly in areas of great water scarcity and in cases of low water productivity. In agriculture and mining, achieving a zero WF will generally be impossible, but in many cases the water consumption and pollution per unit of production can be reduced easily and substantially (Brauman et al. 2013).

4.5 Conclusion

Spatial patterns of water depletion and contamination are closely tied to the structure of the global economy. As currently organised, the economic system lacks incentives that promote producers and consumers to move towards wise use of our limited freshwater resources. In order to achieve sustainable, efficient and equitable water use worldwide, we need greater product transparency, international cooperation, water footprint ceilings per river basin, water footprint benchmarks for water-intensive commodities, water pricing schemes that reflect local water scarcity and some agreement about equitable sharing of the limited available global water resources among different communities and nations.

Acknowledgement This chapter is abridged and adapted from Hoekstra (2015a).

References

BIER (2011) A practical perspective on water accounting in the beverage sector. Beverage Industry Environmental Roundtable. www.waterfootprint.org/Reports/BIER-2011-WaterAccounting SectorPerspective.pdf. Accessed 4 Aug 2014

BIER (2012) Water use benchmarking in the beverage industry: trends and observations 2012. Beverage Industry Environmental Roundtable, Anteagroup, St. Paul

Bloemhof JM, Soysal M (2017) Sustainable food supply chain design. In: Bouchery Y, Corbett CJ, Fransoo J, Tan T (eds) Sustainable supply chains: a research-based textbook on operations and strategy. Springer, New York

Boulay AM, Hoekstra AY, Vionnet S (2013) Complementarities of water-focused Life Cycle Assessment and Water Footprint Assessment. Environ Sci Tech 47(21):11926–11927

Brauman KA, Siebert S, Foley JA (2013) Improvements in crop water productivity increase water sustainability and food security: A global analysis. Environ Res Lett 8(2):024030

Cazcarro I, Duarte R, Sánchez Chóliz J (2013) Multiregional input-output model for the evaluation of Spanish water flows. Environ Sci Tech 47(21):12275–12283

Chiu YW, Wu M (2012) Assessing county-level water footprints of different cellulosic-biofuel feedstock pathways. Environ Sci Tech 46:9155–9162

Coca-Cola Europe (2011) Water footprint sustainability assessment: towards sustainable sugar sourcing in Europe, Brussels

Daniels PL, Lenzen M, Kenway SJ (2011) The ins and outs of water use—a review of multi-region input-output analysis and water footprints for regional sustainability analysis and policy. Econ Syst Res 23(4):353–370

Deloitte (2013) Moving beyond business as usual: a need for a step change in water risk management, CDP Global Water Report 2013, CDP, London

Dominguez-Faus R, Powers SE, Burken JG, Alvarez PJ (2009) The water footprint of biofuels: a drink or drive issue? Environ Sci Tech 43(9):3005–3010

Duarte R, Sánchez-Chóliz J, Bielsa J (2002) Water use in the Spanish economy: An input-output approach. Ecol Econ 43(1):71–85

Ercin AE, Hoekstra AY (2014) Water footprint scenarios for 2050: A global analysis. Environ Int 64:71–82

Ercin AE, Aldaya MM, Hoekstra AY (2011) Corporate water footprint accounting and impact assessment: The case of the water footprint of a sugar-containing carbonated beverage. Water Resour Manag 25(2):721–741

Ewing BR, Hawkins TR, Wiedmann TO, Galli A, Ercin AE, Weinzettel J, Steen-Olsen K (2012) Integrating ecological and water footprint accounting in a multi-regional input-output framework. Ecol Indic 23:1–8

FAO (2014) Aquastat database, food and agriculture organization of the United Nations, Rome, Italy. www.fao.org/nr/aquastat. Accessed 4 Aug 2014

Feng K, Hubacek K, Minx J, Siu YL, Chapagain A, Yu Y, Guan D, Barrett J (2011a) Spatially explicit analysis of water footprints in the UK. Water 3(1):47–63

Feng K, Chapagain A, Suh S, Pfister S, Hubacek K (2011b) Comparison of bottom-up and top-down approaches to calculating the water footprints of nations. Econ Syst Res 23(4):371–385

Finnveden G, Hauschild MZ, Ekvall T, Guinée J, Heijungs R, Hellweg S, Koehler A, Pennington D, Suh S (2009) Recent developments in Life Cycle Assessment. J Environ Manage 91(1):1–21

Franke NA, Boyacioglu H, Hoekstra AY (2013) Grey water footprint accounting: Tier 1 supporting guidelines. Value of Water Research Report Series No. 65, UNESCO-IHE, Delft

Gerbens-Leenes W, Hoekstra AY (2011) The water footprint of biofuel-based transport. Energy Environ Sci 4(8):2658–2668

Gerbens-Leenes PW, Hoekstra AY, Van der Meer T (2009a) The water footprint of energy from biomass: A quantitative assessment and consequences of an increasing share of bio-energy in energy supply. Ecol Econ 68(4):1052–1060

Gerbens-Leenes W, Hoekstra AY, Van der Meer TH (2009b) The water footprint of bioenergy. Proc Natl Acad Sci U S A 106(25):10219–10223

Gerbens-Leenes PW, Van Lienden AR, Hoekstra AY, Van der Meer TH (2012) Biofuel scenarios in a water perspective: The global blue and green water footprint of road transport in 2030. Glob Environ Chang 22:764–775

Gerbens-Leenes PW, Xu L, De Vries GJ, Hoekstra AY (2014) The blue water footprint and land use of biofuels from algae. Water Resour Res 50(11):8549–8563

Guinée J, Heijungs R (2017) Introduction to life cycle assessment. In: Bouchery Y, Corbett CJ, Fransoo J, Tan T (eds) Sustainable supply chains: a research-based textbook on operations and strategy. Springer, New York

Hellweg S, Milà i Canals L (2014) Emerging approaches, challenges and opportunities in life cycle assessment. Science 344(6188):1109–1113

Hoekstra AY (2013) The water footprint of modern consumer society. Routledge, London

Hoekstra AY (2014a) Water scarcity challenges to business. Nat Clim Chang 4(5):318–320

Hoekstra AY (2014b) Sustainable, efficient and equitable water use: The three pillars under wise freshwater allocation. WIREs Water 1(1):31–40

Hoekstra AY (2015a) The water footprint of industry. In: Klemeš JJ (ed) Assessing and measuring environmental impact and sustainability. Butterworth-Heinemann, Oxford, pp 219–252

Hoekstra AY (2015b) The sustainability of a single activity, production process or product. Ecol Indic 57:82–84

Hoekstra AY, Mekonnen MM (2012) The water footprint of humanity. Proc Natl Acad Sci 109(9):3232–3237

Hoekstra AY, Wiedmann TO (2014) Humanity's unsustainable environmental footprint. Science 344(6188):1114–1117

Hoekstra AY, Chapagain AK, Aldaya MM, Mekonnen MM (2011) The water footprint assessment manual: Setting the global standard. Earthscan, London

Hoekstra AY, Mekonnen MM, Chapagain AK, Mathews RE, Richter BD (2012) Global monthly water scarcity: Blue water footprints versus blue water availability. PLoS One 7(2), e32688

ISO (2014) ISO 14046: Environmental Management — Water Footprint — Principles, Requirements and Guidelines. International Organization for Standardization, Geneva

Jefferies D, Muñoz I, Hodges J, King VJ, Aldaya M, Ercin AE, Milà i Canals L, Hoekstra AY (2012) Water footprint and life cycle assessment as approaches to assess potential impacts of products on water consumption: key learning points from pilot studies on tea and margarine. J Clean Prod 33:155–166

King CW, Webber M (2008) Water intensity of transportation. Environ Sci Tech 42(21):7866–7872

Kounina A, Margni M, Bayart J-B, Boulay A-M, Berger M, Bulle C, Frischknecht R, Koehler A, Milà I, Canals L, Motoshita M, Núñez M, Peters G, Pfister S, Ridoutt B, Van Zelm R, Verones F, Humbert S (2013) Review of methods addressing freshwater use in life cycle inventory and impact assessment. Int J Life Cycle Assess 18(3):707–721

Lenzen M, Foran B (2001) An input-output analysis of Australian water usage. Water Policy 3(4):321–340

Mekonnen MM, Hoekstra AY (2011) The green, blue and grey water footprint of crops and derived crop products. Hydrol Earth Syst Sci 15(5):1577–1600

Mekonnen MM, Hoekstra AY (2012) A global assessment of the water footprint of farm animal products. Ecosystems 15(3):401–415

Pfister S, Hellweg S (2009) The water "shoesize" vs. footprint of bioenergy. Proc Natl Acad Sci 106(35):E93–E94

Rebitzer G, Ekvall T, Frischknecht R, Hunkeler D, Norris G, Rydberg T, Schmidt WP, Suh S, Weidema BP, Pennington DW (2004) Life cycle assessment Part 1: Framework, goal and scope definition, inventory analysis, and applications. Environ Int 30:701–720

Ridoutt BG, Eady SJ, Sellahewa J, Simons L, Bektash R (2009) Water footprinting at the product brand level: case study and future challenges. J Clean Prod 17:1228–1235

Ruini L, Marino M, Pignatelli S, Laio F, Ridolfi L (2013) Water footprint of a large-sized food company: The case of Barilla pasta production. Water Res Ind 1–2:7–24

SABMiller and WWF-UK (2009) Water footprinting: identifying & addressing water risks in the value chain, SABMiller, Woking, UK/WWF-UK, Godalming

SABMiller, GTZ and WWF (2010) Water futures: working together for a secure water future, SABMiller, Woking, UK/WWF-UK, Godalming

Sarni W (2011) Corporate water strategies. Earthscan, London

Sikirica N (2011) Water footprint assessment bananas and pineapples. Dole Food Company, Soil & More International, Driebergen

Steen-Olsen K, Weinzettel J, Cranston G, Ercin AE, Hertwich EG (2012) Carbon, land, and water footprint accounts for the European Union: Consumption, production, and displacements through international trade. Environ Sci Tech 46(20):10883–10891

TCCC and TNC (2010) Product water footprint assessments: practical application in corporate water stewardship, The Coca-Cola Company, Atlanta, USA/The Nature Conservancy, Arlington

UN (2008) International standard industrial classification of all economic activities, Revision 4. Statistics Division, Department of Economic and Social Affairs, United Nations, New York

WEF (2014) Global risks 2014. World Economic Forum, Geneva

Yu Y, Hubacek K, Feng K, Guan D (2010) Assessing regional and global water footprints for the UK. Ecol Econ 69(5):1140–1147

Zhang C, Anadon LD (2014) A multi-regional input-output analysis of domestic virtual water trade and provincial water footprint in China. Ecol Econ 100:159–172

Zhang Z, Shi M, Yang H, Chapagain A (2011) An input-output analysis of trends in virtual water trade and the impact on water resources and uses in China. Econ Syst Res 23(4):431–446

Zhao X, Chen B, Yang ZF (2009) National water footprint in an input-output framework-A case study of China 2002. Ecol Model 220(2):245–253

Chapter 5
Sustainable Non-Renewable Materials Management

Vered Blass, Tzruya Calvão Chebach, and Amit Ashkenazy

5.1 Introduction

Natural resources are the basis for many economic activities that support human wellbeing. Over the last 30 years, global material consumption has increased by 80 % in absolute terms, and forecasts suggest that by 2050, human beings will consume about 180 billion tons of different materials. This represents growth by a factor of 2.7 compared to today's levels, leading to increased competition for resource extraction (Dittrich et al. 2012). Therefore, policy makers and firms, especially manufacturers that are highly dependent on natural resources, are increasingly interested in sustainable raw materials management.

Natural resources refer to a large set of resources such as water, land, and materials. In general, while the non-metallic resources (e.g., sand and gravel, aggregates, and energy resources), which are mainly required to satisfy the basic needs for housing, heating, and transportation are more widely available, the metallic resources are becoming more problematic. Although there are many sustainability issues related to renewable resources, in this chapter is focus on management aspects related to non-renewable materials such as metal ores and construction materials (see Fig. 5.1, shaded boxes).

The ability of firms to deliver value depends on a consistent supply of material inputs. A particular industry could be more or less resource-intensive, requiring a certain material more than others. Sustainable raw materials management refers to the

V. Blass (✉) • T.C. Chebach
Tel Aviv University, Tel Aviv, Israel
e-mail: vblass@post.tau.ac.il; tzruyac@post.tau.ac.il

A. Ashkenazy
TU Delft, Delft, The Netherlands
e-mail:a.ashkenazy@tudelft.nl

© Yann Bouchery, Charles J. Corbett, Jan C. Fransoo, and Tarkan Tan 2017
Y. Bouchery et al. (eds.), *Sustainable Supply Chains*, Springer Series in Supply
Chain Management 4, DOI 10.1007/978-3-319-29791-0_5

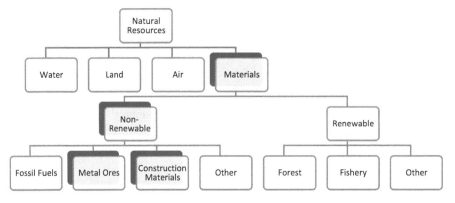

Fig. 5.1 Natural resources chart (Adapted from UN SEEA Group)

way nations and firms manage the natural resources they own and use in production and consumption systems from economic, social, and environmental perspectives.

From the firm perspective, the stability of raw material availability and supply is a key element for supply chain management and forecasting (Xiao and Yu 2006). However, several global trends raise concerns including: (a) rapid depletion of the stocks of certain raw materials which results in higher effort during extraction and possibly also higher environmental impacts during extraction and more expansive operations; (b) increasing prices of certain global commodities and resources; and (c) a geographic distribution of materials that may signify concentrated control by some countries (such as China) over certain materials, turning them into what is often described as critical materials, vital for various industries such as the clean-tech industry in different countries, yet originating from only a few source countries (McKinsey, 2012).

These global trends have the potential to affect the very core of a firm's production activity with the implication that firms can benefit from raw materials management and from active engagement in more sustainable practices and resource management. This approach goes beyond the traditional concept of material costs or inventory management.

The production and operations management literature has touched on the implications of sustainable management of raw materials from several perspectives: Galbreth et al. (2013) modelled the optimal material strategy for firms, based on potential benefit, required rate of innovation, and actual environmental impact of more sustainable material use strategies, such as integration of product reuse. Pil and Rothenberg (2003) demonstrated that environmental improvements have reciprocal effects on manufacturing quality. Others looked at the role of sustainability in supply chain management and at inspiring new tools and strategies firms can use to improve their decision making (Kleindorfer et al. 2005). For example, Jacobs and Subramanian (2012) show how sharing responsibility for sustainable materials management along the supply chain can affect environmental performance and social welfare in product recovery schemes.

Finally, policy makers have demonstrated the central role of policy in materials management and its implications at all levels, from national to firm level. National policies directly affect the availability and secured supply of natural resources for industry. The uneven geographical distribution of resources between countries around the world and the decisions by policy makers within countries on exploration and production may render a resource scarce for a particular country while at a lesser supply risk for another. In addition, some resources may be scarce and their global allocation may be affected by geopolitical challenges, protectionism, and other aspects controlled at the policy level. For example, the ability of firms to secure access to resources may affect their choice of manufacturing location, and the national risk of scarcity of certain resources may potentially affect the design of a product and the preference of a substitute material.

In this chapter we first discuss key aspects that are important for understanding raw materials management issues related to sustainability at the firm and supply chain levels. We then elaborate on the management of material flows using tools such as Material Flow Analysis (MFA) and Material Flow Cost Accounting (MFCA) methods, describing them and providing examples of their use. We continue with a summary of other practical tools and approaches that can be used to enhance sustainable materials management and we conclude with future questions and discussion.

5.2   How Changes in Global Production and Consumption Affect Supply Chain Material Management?

Raw materials management requires both macro- and microscale understanding. In this section we describe the main aspects that are relevant to the bigger picture in the context of raw materials management in order to provide the reader with the relevant background on this topic.

5.2.1   What Is the Trend in Price, Availability, and Recycling Rates of Metallic Resources?

Demand for raw materials has soared since the beginning of the twenty-first century. Growing quality of life in emerging economies and industrial expansion there have maintained high levels of pressure on the resource base. At the same time, many emerging economies have deployed strategies to maintain raw materials, especially metallic resources, within the country in order to ensure their continued ability to expand production and meet local demand. For example, China has introduced export restrictions on yellow phosphorous, bauxite, coke, fluorspar, magnesium, manganese, silicon metal, silicon carbide, and zinc. (EU Commission 2010). Furthermore, the prices of metals and other commodities have increased since the 1970s. Raw materials are reported to be between 5 and 55 % of the product's total cost, depending on the industry, region, and product category (PBL 2014; Vogel 2009). Therefore, their prices are critical for product planning and development. Prices are usually affected by demand (which increases every year) as well as by the availability and effort required to produce these metals.

The concentration of the metals in the ore decreases over time (International Resource Panel 2011) so that mining companies are required to expend more effort in achieving the same yield per every square meter of excavation. As a result, the environmental impacts of mining actions also increase over time (International Resource Panel 2014). Technically, some of the metals exist together in ores and therefore not extracted separately. If the demand or supply for a certain metal changes sharply, the entire value-added and price structure of the different main and co-materials might change. For example, copper ores commonly include six different elements including copper, silver, gold, arsenic, selenium, and tellurium (Graedel et al. 2015). A review of recent trends of metal mining sites suggests a shift in the areas where mining companies choose to operate. For example, while in the 1990s South Africa, the USA and Australia produced together more than 50 % of the world's gold, in 2012, this accounted for less than 25 % of the production. Other countries that now produce gold include Mexico, Russia, Peru, Ghana, and China (Scott Wright 2013, based on USGS production data, Zeal website). The reasons for such a shift include lower concentration in existing mining sites, increasing environmental regulation of the mining sector in some countries, and overall cost of labor and operation in the more developed countries. The emergence of concepts such as urban mining, referring to mining elements in old landfills and in discarded products also suggest that with the reduction in concentration of the metals in the ore overtime, alternatives are needed.

On the other side of the equation, it is important to look at trends in the recycling rates of different materials. Graedel et al. (2011) reported recycling rates for about 60 metals worldwide and suggested that for many elements, less than 1 % is currently recycled. While 18 elements had recycling rates higher than 50 %, most were under 25 %. It was also evident that for many of the elements there is insufficient data for reporting and, therefore, a great deal of important information about end-of-life recycling and technologies for many materials is missing. Furthermore, Reck and Graedel (2012) make the distinction between end-of-life recycling rates for "base metals", reaching 50 % and or more, and "specialty elements" which are hardly ever recycled.

Base metals are elements that are commonly used in large quantities and relatively pure forms, making them easier to re-smelt, and in products with longer life spans for which suitable recycling infrastructure is already in place. On the other hand, specialty metals are used in small quantities, mixed with other elements which are hard to separate, and in products with much shorter life spans (such as electronic devices) which require extensive collection and recycling operations to economically justify their extraction at the product's end of life. They suggest that three main improvements have to occur in order for society to reap the environmental benefits embodied in metals recycling: (1) extended collection efforts, (2) better design of products for recycling, and (3) new and better recycling technologies.

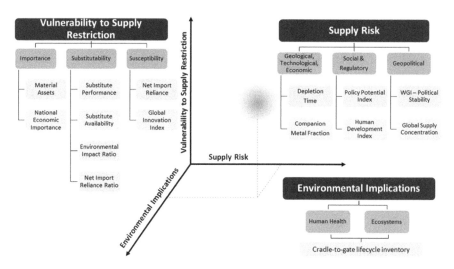

Fig. 5.2 Criticality assessment framework (*Source*: Graedel et al. 2013)

Based on all of the above parameters, one can start asking questions about the criticality of some materials for everyday economic activities or for specific applications and industries. Graedel et al. (2015) suggested a methodology to assess the criticality of materials at the national level. Figure 5.2 explains their framework for looking at criticality in three dimensions: supply risk, environmental implications, and vulnerability to supply restriction. Several indicators on each axis are aggregated to arrive at a criticality assessment, as indicated on the diagram. Data sources for such criticality assessment could be the following: (a) metal in-use stock determinations, (b) material flow analysis, (c) metal substitution potential, (d) country-level information, and (e) environmental lifecycle assessment results. Firms can use this framework in order to assess criticality of specific elements they use in their products.

5.2.2 *What Are the Environmental Impacts of Raw Materials Extraction?*

Raw materials extraction results in different environmental impacts created by the mining equipment, the digging, the chemicals used for extraction, and the transportation activities in and out of the mine area. In the extraction phase, the "Ecological Rucksack" or Material Intensity (in kilograms) has become a common unit of measure. This unit of measure (factor), developed by the Wuppertal Institute in Germany, refers to the amount of materials moved to obtain 1 kg of the resource, also known as Material Input per Service Unit (MIPS) (Wuppertal Institute 2015).

The MIPS index is published for a variety of materials and provides a quick and good reference to demonstrate the effort and impacts associated with the extraction of different materials.

Raw materials extraction also creates a set of impacts that includes air pollution, soil contamination, water pollution due to energy and water use, as well as waste and emissions emitted in the different processes. The mining industry is considered a very energy-intensive sector (Lusty and Gunn 2014) and is therefore associated with a variety of environmental impacts. Table 5.1 provides examples of the MIPS factors and a range of primary energy consumption numbers based on a full Lifecycle Assessment (LCA) approach, from extraction of raw materials to the end of the useful life of a product. This LCA approach is used to demonstrate the differences among several materials and takes into account the full impacts. (See Chap. 2 by Guinée and Heijungs (2017) for more on LCA.) Several databases and software tools allow companies and researchers to conduct LCA (for example, Ecoinvnet LCI database; GaBi 6. LCA software). Energy and MIPS factors are available for a variety of mineral fertilizers, resins, construction materials, plastics, chemicals, metals, etc. In order to illustrate this factor, several commonly used materials as well as more rare materials with very high energy and waste intensity are listed in Table 5.1.

The table suggests that some rare materials such as precious metals (i.e., gold and platinum) and diamonds are very resource- and energy-intensive at the extraction and production stages, thousands or even hundreds of thousands times more than more common and abundant materials such as aluminum, lead, etc.

Different LCA studies which take into account the environmental impacts of products across their different lifecycle stages reveal that a significant share of the environmental impacts of production actually originate in the raw materials extraction and production phases. Therefore, these stages show great potential for increased eco-efficiency. Due to the high environmental and social impacts of raw materials extraction, more and more countries tighten their environmental regulations in the extraction sector.

Table 5.1 Materials environmental impact: MIPS and energy consumption

Material (primary)	Rucksack waste factor MIPS[a]	Primary energy range (MJ/Kg)[b]
Aluminum	37	2.6–5.3
Copper	348.5	0.7–1.78
Gold	540,000	2267–4612
Lead	18	0.4–0.7
Platinum	320,301	4827–6658
Silver	7500	5–227
Diamond	5,260,000	168,000–1,445,400
Sand	1.42	0.0008–0.001

Data Sources: Material intensity data sheet by the Wuppertal Institute for Climate, Environment and Energy (Dated February 3, 2014), GaBi 6 LCI database, and Ali 2011
[a]http://wupperinst.org/uploads/tx_wupperinst/MIT_2014.pdf
[b]Range is based on different available production processes in different countries, data from GaBi 6 database except for diamonds, which are based on Ali 2011

5.2.3   How Does Raw Material Extraction Affect Different Sectors of the Economy?

Despite the evident role of materials management and the potential for resource efficiency, scarcity of resources and susceptibility to supply risk are perceived differently in different sectors. In this section we introduce the different approaches and point to the sectors most susceptible.

5.2.3.1   Sector-Level Impact

Materials scarcity is presumed to affect different sectors in different ways. A survey of senior executives of leading global companies on the impact of minerals and metals scarcity on business, conducted by PricewaterhouseCoopers (PWC 2011), illustrates how some sectors may be perceived to be more susceptible to scarcity. In the survey, 69 senior executives from leading companies were interviewed on different aspects related to scarcity, including awareness, preparedness, impact, causes, risks, and opportunities, and responses to mineral and metal scarcity. The executives interviewed were from seven different sectors including aviation, automotive, chemicals, energy and utilities, high-tech, infrastructure and renewable energy. Key actors in these sectors were surveyed, with revenues of 84 % of the companies exceeding $10 billion and revenues of the remaining 16 % ranging from $2–10 billion. The respondents included directors, vice-presidents, and other senior executives. According to the PwC survey, certain sectors perceived the scarcity of minerals and metals to be a more pressing issue than others. For example, 82 % of respondents in the infrastructure sector considered the issue to be pressing and 78 % considered it to be so in the high- tech sector. In the aviation and energy and utilities sectors, only about 50 % considered the issue to be pressing. Key insights that emerged from the report included lack of awareness of the issue of scarcity amongst stakeholders. The scarcity risk was perceived to be rising in a 5-year projection, with the expectation that the impact will be felt throughout the entire supply chain. Moreover, it was found that the leading driver of scarcity apart from demand (65 %) was geopolitics (54 %) while the exhaustion of reserves rated less highly (30 %). In addition, low substitution was also perceived as a major driver of scarcity, particularly for renewable energy (89 %), energy and utilities (79 %) and chemical (78 %) industries. Companies singled out resource efficiency as the key response to the rising scarcity challenge (75 %) and also highlighted the importance of collaboration, such as strategic alliances along the supply chain to tackle the challenge. A high level of cooperation with first-tier suppliers was particularly evident in certain sectors. According to the survey, the level of preparedness at the time the survey was conducted varied according to sectors. For example, 67 % of respondents in the renewable energy sector and 64 % of respondents in the automotive sector felt prepared, while only 33 % in the high-tech and chemical industry felt prepared.

Angerer et al. (2009) emphasizes that from a statistical standpoint—it is not depletion of natural resources that is affecting the supply of raw materials, but rather the imbalance between supply and demand. This imbalance was caused by an inability to predict two major variables—the first is technological developments that exert unexpected pressures on specific materials. For example the report points to gallium, used for production of thin-layer photovoltaics and high-speed, integrated circuits, which is expected to cause a sixfold increase in demand by 2030. The second variable is the challenge posed by China's economic growth and that of the world economy at large. As the gap between rich and poor nations diminishes, consumption increases and with it the world's economic output, which relies on an ever-growing stream of materials for production.

5.2.3.2 Who Is More Susceptible?

Clean-tech companies are particularly susceptible to scarcity and criticality of raw materials. First, many of the technologies are emerging technologies with an ever increasing number of materials in each product. Second, many of the technologies already rely on critical materials. When it comes to the energy clean-tech cases of wind, vehicles, PV cells, lighting and fuel cells, all these technologies rely on critical minerals for their components. Thin film PV panels require tellurium, gallium germanium, indium, selenium, silver, and cadmium. Wind energy generators require neodymium, and dysprosium, and lithium–ion batteries in electric vehicles require lithium and cobalt.[1] Platinum and palladium are used for technologies related to emissions prevention. Silver and REEs are used for emissions purification (European Commission 2008). Surveys and interviews conducted with industry illustrate the importance given to scarcity. Table 5.2 summarizes the main materials used for emerging technologies and the forecasted shortage in supply for 2030.

Note: the indicators calculate the share of demand for those materials from emerging technologies, out of the total world production in 2006. If the ratio is higher than one, it means there is not enough supply.

The table suggests that for many materials, if world production will not increase substantially, the demands will be a few times higher than the available supply.

5.2.4 What Is the Environmental Impact Versus Economic Added Value along the Value Chain?

The link between economic and environmental parameters on the value chain can be constructed using measures that take into account the eco-efficiency of the lifecycle stages of the different products as presented in Fig. 5.3 for mobile phone manufacturing as an example (Clift and Wright 2000). The figure describes

---

[1] The Resnick Institute 2011 http://resnick.caltech.edu/docs/R_Critical.pdf & EU report: http://ec.europa.eu/enterprise/sectors/metals-minerals/files/sec_2741_en.pdf#page=6

Table 5.2 Selected materials and their use applications in emerging technologies 2006–2030

Raw material	Emerging technologies	Demand (2006) share out of world production (2006)	Forecasted demand (2030) share out of world production (2006)
Gallium	Thin-layer photovoltaics, IC, WLED	0.28	6.09
Neodymium	Permanent magnets, laser technology	0.55	3.82
Indium	Displays, thin-layer photovoltaics	0.4	3.29
Germanium	Fiber optic cable, IR optical technologies	0.31	2.44
Platinum	Fuel cells, catalysts	Low	1.56
Tantalum	Micro capacitors, medical technology	0.39	1.01
Silver	RFID, lead-free soft solder	0.26	0.78
Cobalt	Lithium–ion batteries, synthetic fuel	0.19	0.40
Palladium	Catalysts, seawater desalination	0.10	0.34
Titanium	Seawater desalination, implants	0.08	0.29
Copper	Efficient electric motors, RFID	0.09	0.24
Niobium	Micro capacitors, ferroalloys	0.01	0.03

Source: Critical raw materials for the EU, Report of the Ad-hoc Working Group on defining critical raw materials, 2010, page 43, and from Angerer et al. 2009

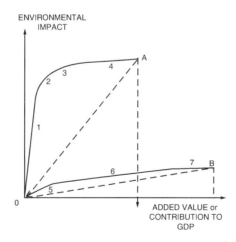

1: Resource extraction
2: Processing & Refining
3: Manufacturing
4: Retail and distribution
5: Recovery
6: Dismantling
7: Remanufacturing

www.surrey.ac.uk
Prof Roland Clift Centre for Environmental Strategy (CES)

Fig. 5.3 Environmental and economic added value graph (*Source*: Clift and Wright 2000)

the scale of the environmental impact on the Y axis and the economic added value on the X axis, and numbers the different stages of the lifecycle of phone production beginning with the extraction of raw materials. As the figure illustrates, in the first stages the environmental impact is highest while the contribution to the economic added value is lowest; therefore, the slope of the chart at that stage is very steep. This observation is relevant to different industries. In addition, various end-of-life scenarios can be integrated into the analysis, especially important in products with high refurbishing and recycling rates of products, parts, and materials. In the case of mobile phones, as presented in the figure for stage 5 and onwards, remanufacturing captures added value, with much lower environmental impact because the raw materials extraction and phone manufacturing stages are avoided.

It is also important to note that in many cases, the product's lifecycle spans across different countries. For example, a country where the environmental impact is potentially the highest may see little added value in contributing to the environmental degradation caused by the extraction of raw materials. Moreover, materials may not necessarily be available in the country in which the stage in the supply chain occurs, thus further contributing to environmental impact as is the case, for example, in transportation.

Added value analysis using combined economic and environmental parameters is becoming a more common tool in different sectors. The automobile and textiles industries are good examples of industries where added value is not well distributed. Most of the environmental impacts are attributed to the early stages of raw materials extraction and production, while most of the economic added values occur at the later stages of sales in the case of textiles and sales and service in the case of cars. Furthermore, there is also an end-of-life dismantling value for cars as recycling becomes mandatory in many countries.

5.2.4.1 Production Side: Mining Companies

The market structure of the mining industry is highly concentrated. According to the Raw Material Group quoted in an EU report, less than 4% of mining companies (149 out of 4173 companies) controlled 83% of the metal mining market (European Commission 2008). Such a centralized market structure is prone to risks emanating from unexpected problems to the stability of these companies and from possible illegal coordination between them to influence market prices. Tackling price volatility, fraud, regulatory uncertainty, mounting government hostility to the mining sector, water/energy availability, worker safety and a talent gap are all key priority areas presenting major challenges to the mining industry. According to a recent report, in order to address these challenges and manage global trends, the mining industry's previous focus on volume has to be replaced with more strategic scenario planning as well as innovative new approaches for dealing with supply chain stakeholders. Media and civil society scrutiny of the local environmental impacts of mining companies has expanded in scale and scope and includes monitoring and standard setting bodies. Mounting hostility to the mining industry has also proliferated, highlighting the unsustainability of current management of stakeholders in the supply chain.

Some countries have reconsidered their resource management resulting in demand for new royalty regimes, concessions and even expropriation. Examples mainly relate to developing countries, but also to some developed countries, such as the new mining royalty regime introduced in Québec in 2013 (Deloitte 2013).

5.2.4.2 Downstream Firm Level Perspective

There are several reasons and motivations for firms to be aware and better informed about their raw materials management, especially critical materials. These include:

- Supply chain disruption—Rare earth minerals and critical materials are unevenly distributed throughout the world. Companies reliant on them could suffer operationally and financially if a certain government decides to stop export in order to increase the resource price, or if a natural phenomenon hinders material extraction and logistics.
- Resource risk—As extraction companies exhaust their efforts to reach readily available materials, they will have to extend their operations into more expansive and environmentally impactful territory. This could affect manufacturers' cost analysis and their accountability to local communities as well as their clients in ensuring supplier sustainability.
- Reliance on China as supplier and market—China produces 90% of the global supply of rare earth minerals. Its monopoly on these essential resources allows it to control prices and flows by restricting export. In 2014, the World Trade Organization upheld a ruling that China had violated international trade rules in these restrictions, specifically through tariffs and export quotas. While the WTO decision could facilitate export, illegal mining is still a matter of conflict between local and national government (Shen 2014). Furthermore, within a growing global demand for rare earth, China's own demand exceeds the rest of the world's (de Boer and Lammertsma 2012).
- Regulation in different countries—While some countries have set concrete policies to identify critical materials, assess their risk of depletion, and put in place measures to reduce it, they vary in scope of materials and extent of solutions. For example, while the USA has a holistic approach to determine material criticality, its strategy focuses on the energy sector (DEFRA 2012).
- Price volatility—Commodity prices have not remained stable over the past two decades, with growing demand from emerging economic centers such as China and India pushing prices up, followed by falling prices in the wake of the financial crisis of 2008. Changes in oil prices have been particularly volatile, making it harder for companies to predict their long-term costs and revenues (Lin 2009).
- Availability of alternative materials—Some of the world's most widely used metals have no easily available substitutes for their current major uses, including, for example, copper, chromium, manganese and lead (Graedel et al. 2015). Thus, finding design solutions ahead of diminishing supply, or alternatively finding new sources of supply from existing stocks becomes a critical task for companies' long-term planning efforts.

- Size of business—Small- and medium-sized enterprises (SMEs) are particularly vulnerable to disruptions in the supply of raw materials, as they are often less aware and less equipped to find alternatives when these problems arise. Higher material costs can also negatively affect their competitive positions, unless the government takes action to ensure their survival by, for example, ensuring national material reserves (de Boer and Lammertsma 2012). However, SMEs can also become part of the solution through technological and design innovation, or taking part in national research programs (DEFRA 2012).
- Low stakeholder awareness of scarcity—Research has found distinct differences between economic sectors in their awareness of natural resources scarcity and its possible effects on their prosperity. For example, the infrastructure, high-tech and automotive industries showed a high level of concern when asked if minerals and metals scarcity is a pressing issue for the firm, in contrast to only half of the respondents in the aviation industry (PWC 2011).

5.2.4.3 Downstream Consumers Level Perspective

One of the inevitable forces driving resource scarcity is the growing demand for new products and technology by a rapidly urbanizing world that is expected to see three billion new consumers entering the middle class by 2050, most of them in emerging markets (World Economic Forum 2013). During the twentieth century, resource use per capita globally doubled while income increased by a factor of seven, reflecting a relative decoupling of economic growth and resource use (UNEP 2012). However, the International Resource Panel warns that current consumption rates are unsustainable and will lead to accelerated resource depletion and further shocks to the economic system. The panel urged governments and companies to act rapidly to increase resource productivity, mentioning in its 2014 report that some forecasts caution that certain rare earth metals will run out in two decades unless recycling rates dramatically improve (International Resource Panel 2014). That said, cities are already moving toward a zero waste vision, adopting the waste hierarchy, trying to eliminate resources from ending up in landfills, and engaging in urban mining that captures the full potential of material stocks in the city (UNEP 2012). Overall consumption plays an important role in the demand upstream of raw materials, and firms may conclude that their strategy must change and they may need to take an active part in decreasing the rate of product replacements and technology cycles.

5.3 How Can Industry Better Understand Material Flows?

In previous sections we highlighted the risks involved with production of certain materials, especially metals, due to unexpected changes in demand, technology, or even states' willingness to allow trade that might undermine their material resource base. These risks require firms as well as governments to evaluate their current and future needs. It also requires assessing how these materials accumulate and move throughout the economy, supply chains, or within their borders as stocks and flows. In this section we review several tools to conduct these assessments, focusing on the MFA methodology. We introduce the concepts and uses of MFA studies as a generic tool that can be used at different levels and continue with the more specific firm level tool of MFCA while providing some concrete examples.

5.3.1 *Introduction to Material Flow Analysis*

Industrial ecology is a growing discipline of research that aims to understand the structure and function of industrial or societal metabolism, or how materials move and transform in different systems and processes across space and time (Ayres and Ayres 2002). For example, how does a certain country use fossil fuels? What happens to paper globally in different phases of its lifecycle? In order to answer such questions industrial ecologists have created different quantitative methodologies. For example, LCA allows us to measure and compare the different impacts that certain products or services have on the environment in each of the phases of their lifecycle—from raw materials extraction, to production and use, to end of life, such as landfilling or recycling—based on a detailed account of the inputs and outputs invested and created in the system (see also Chap. 2 by Guinée and Heijungs (2017) on LCA and Chap. 4 by Hoekstra on water footprinting).

A complementary tool that concentrates on the material flow side is MFA, which studies the flows and stocks of materials across a defined system, with explicit boundaries in a given timeframe. It is the main quantitative tool available today to assess and map the use of raw materials by type, quantity and location across supply chains, economic sectors, regions, nations, or the economy at large. It can point to potential depletion in specific raw materials and gaps in recycling rates, and can provide useful predictions that may affect decisions regarding future developments and operations. Most MFA studies in recent years were done at the region and country level, although some aimed at worldwide assessment (see Box 5.1 and Behrens et al., 2007).

The immediate geographical location of companies also affects their performance and decisions in multiple fields—city zoning codes, available resources for production, regulation on waste and energy management, transportation costs, and so on. Thus, learning about the city's and the region's material flows can heavily influence companies' strategies and operational management. Describing the way cities mobilize, use and discard materials has been instrumental in understanding cities as systems since the 1960s. Researchers conducting MFAs believe they can improve both regional and corporate materials management, optimizing resource extraction and use, and ensuring proper environmental protection best fitted for the region in question. MFAs can also serve as indicators, or as the basis for a monitoring program to evaluate companies' actions and regional or municipal policy mea-

Box 5.1 The Yale Stocks and Flows (STAF) Project By Thomas Graedel and Barbara Reck, Yale University

Modern society is made possible by the use of metals, and metals have historically been supplied from virgin stocks (ore bodies, mineral deposits, and the like). Other reservoirs exist, however, a principal one being materials or products in use, stored, or discarded over the years by corporations and individuals. These reservoirs might become very important in the next few decades of rapid population growth and resource and energy use. There are also concerns about the use of energy in the extraction and processing of metals, and realization that the loss of resources by dissipation or landfilling can sometimes be problematic from an environmental standpoint, and concerns over the short and long-term "criticality" of metals.

The STAF project evaluates current and historical flows of specific technologically significant materials, determining the stocks available in different types of reservoirs and the flows among the reservoirs, developing scenarios of possible futures of metal use, and assessing metal supply and demand. Between 2002 and 2010, the group completed the characterization and quantification of the material flow cycles of copper, zinc, chromium, lead, iron, nickel, silver, and stainless steel, comprising complete cycle characterizations for all countries using significant amounts of these materials (more than 50), nine world regions including Europe, North America and Asia, and the planet as a whole. Figure 5.4 is an example of this work. Targeted studies of a few states and cities have also been accomplished. Specialized studies on tin, cobalt, tungsten, aluminum, and ten of the rare earths have been done as well, and additional studies are under way.

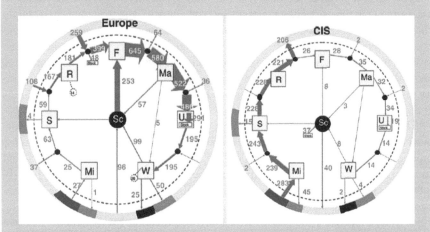

Fig. 5.4 Nickel material flow analyses for year 2000 for Europe and CIS regions. The units are Gg (thousand metric tons) of nickel per year (adapted from Reck et al. 2008). In this example, the charts demonstrate how mining and production happens in CIS but are not largely consumed locally and therefore leave the region while the fabrication and consumption quantities in EU are much larger than locally extracted and therefore flows enter the system

sures and to identify future problems related to scarcity, waste and emissions (Binder et al. 2009). Examples of regional and urban scale MFAs include, among others, Vienna and its hinterlands, Basque Country, London, Hamburg, Singapore and Lisbon. (See Kennedy et al., 2007, providing examples from different metropolitan regions around the globe.)

Doing an MFA study can be a lengthy process, mainly due to data availability challenges. Although interest in MFA studies is increasing, it is still not a common tool used by nations and firms. In the practical implications section, we review MFA studies, how they can be used at firm level and for what purposes.

5.3.2 How Can MFA be Utilized in Strategic and Operational Planning?

Firms have different opportunities to use resources more efficiently. MFA provides an excellent tool for companies to track and manage their materials management. Tracking the type, quantities, origin and transformation of materials along the supply chain enables companies to identify opportunities for sustainable materials management and possible hotspots along the flow of materials. Depending on the question or challenge at hand, an MFA can be conducted on different levels. The first step in identifying the opportunities of firms to become more sustainable in their raw materials management is a review of the actual materials the firm uses, where they come from and how they transform along the supply chain. In other words, this means performing an MFA at different levels, depending on the system in which the firm operates, or the problem the analyst is trying to solve—from a single product to whole supply chains, from factory and neighborhood to city, national and even global analyses. Furthermore, MFA is becoming a customary tool in policy analysis and design. Thus, it may help firms anticipate and prepare for regulatory changes that would mandate a change in operations and strategy. Following are several examples of MFA studies used at different scales along with the risks and opportunities they expose and their possible uses for companies.

5.3.2.1 Using MFA to Optimize Production Processes

Industry has successfully used MFA insights to adjust material flows and waste streams in production processes in order to maximize both economic and environmental gains (Binder 2007). Analyzing the material flows in industrial parks offers an especially salient opportunity to identify opportunities for greater efficiency, as well as possible beneficial use of by-products created by different entities within the park (Sendra et al. 2007). MFA can reflect potential gains in material efficiency at a single factory level as well, disaggregating production into different stages and processes.

Looking at a particular substance flow through the economy can also help identify potential improvements for specific industries and systems. For example,

Kowalski and Mazanek (1998) analyzed the flow of sodium chromate in Poland. Their analysis indicated that by technologically modernizing chromium production and using various chromium compounds, industry can improve its chromium waste management solutions so that imported raw materials are reduced, storage fees are reduced and productivity is improved.

5.3.2.2   Using MFA to Identify and Weigh Pollution Sources

Finding the causes of pollution and its detrimental effects can often be an intricate endeavor. Regulators, courts and communities, as well as firms aiming to diminish their impact on the environment may need to contend with multiple possible sources of pollution in different locations, perhaps even in different times, with multiple materials intertwining downstream. MFA can help identify, classify and weigh the relative contribution each source and each material may have in creating environmental harm, and thus lead the way in its solution.

For example, Cadmium (Cd) is a dangerous substance known to cause human kidney disease and other physical illnesses through chronic exposure. It is easily absorbed into the body through food, smoking and contaminated air and water, and has a slow rate of excretion. One of the known sources of Cd is agricultural fertilizers, as Cd is present in relatively high concentrations in the phosphate rocks and acid used in their manufacturing. Kwonpongsagoon et al. (2007) used MFA to examine how Cd is used in the Australian economy and how it dissipates into the environment. By conducting a thorough substance flow analysis, which tracks a single substance, Cd, researchers can find hidden and expected flows of Cd. For example, construction materials were found to be an important Cd sink in Australia in addition to non-ferrous metal production and electricity generation, which are the main sources of Cd emissions. These results suggested that the National Cadmium Minimization Strategy, which focused on crops and soils, should pay greater attention to intentional use of Cd products and to wastes containing Cd. If a change in regulation occurs, firms in these industries would need to take into account the possibility of stricter substance control, which would require a change in their production methods and in their end-of pipe solutions.

5.3.2.3   Using MFA to Analyze Products and Identify Hidden Trade-Offs

When a particular product or material is found to have harmful effects on the environment or on public health (or both), one of the solutions may be to substitute this material or product for another, more benign alternative. That is also one of the theoretical solutions for dealing with resource depletion or scarcity. MFA can help identify potential problems associated with substitution. For example, in a study of the shift to a lead-free economy, an MFA conduced on the Japanese market, and on solders in particular, found that while the shift to lead-free solders has progressed rapidly with the substitution of silver and copper for lead, it slows down in the products' late lifecycle stages, due to the long life spans of electronic products. Thus, not only do emissions still contain lead, but they now also contain silver with its possible impacts on air and water quality. One of the beneficial ways to decrease these emissions could be higher circuit board recycling rates (Fuse and Tsunemi 2012).

Lam et al. (2013) combined environmental impact assessment with dynamic MFA in order to predict the timing of product substitution, the changing quantities of e-waste generation, and the environmental burden the electronic products market may create in coming years. Based on their analysis they proposed a consideration of e-waste pollution prevention measures, targeting specific materials with high toxicity rates taking in mind their model's estimated timing of disposal.

Looking at a specific market, MFA is particularly useful in calculating available stocks and forecasting needs for a specific material in different timeframes. Bergsdal et al. (2007) integrated scenarios about population, persons per dwelling, and floor area per dwelling, with data regarding the Norwegian housing stock to infer wood and concrete demand over the coming century. They found that despite decreasing growth in concrete density, its total use is expected to increase due to continued increase in housing stock. The outgoing flow of concrete is delayed, due to its late introduction as a building material and low renovation rate. Wood, on the other hand, has always been a prominent building material in Norway and undergoes renovation much more frequently, thus creating more output from renovation and demolition.

5.3.2.4 Using MFA to Design a More Efficient and Effective Recycling Scheme

MFA is also useful in looking at waste patterns and designing effective recycling schemes. In Beijing, for example, MFA was used to prepare for upcoming recycling schemes in the electronic appliances sector. Researchers used surveys and existing data to project the amount of electronic units to be discarded in recycling centers versus other end-of-life options. Thus, it allowed a more informed planning process, both by companies expected to take part in the recycling scheme, by recyclers that are dependent on the inflow of end-of-life electronic appliances and by local government, which needs to build proper recycling infrastructure and reshape its waste policies accordingly (Liu et al. 2006).

In Denmark, MFA of NdFeB permanent magnets, which are used in telecommunication products, electronic appliances and energy technology, revealed that focusing recycling efforts on household consumers could yield minimal results in terms of actual supply of rare earth minerals such as neodymium, a key element in the magnets. The study showed that despite the fact that IT applications comprise 60 % of the maximum theoretical recovery potential, overall potential recovery rates of neodymium and dysprosium from NdFeB in Denmark were equivalent to the amount found in five 3 MW direct-drive wind turbines. Thus, it is much more economically sensible and practical to focus efforts on major end users such as wind turbines, rather than hundreds of thousands of decentralized sources (Habib et al. 2014).

One of the most important utilizations of MFA in improving recycling schemes lies in enabling the process of urban mining—the systematic reuse of materials originating in human use in urban areas. Tapping existing stocks of resources, whether in infrastructure, houses or landfills, requires the preservation of information regarding available materials from production through recovery, and the location of recycling facilities in or close to cities so that they remain both economic and environmentally beneficial (Brunner 2011).

5.3.3   How Could Firms Integrate MFA with Cost Analysis?

The concept of MFA described in the previous section has been further developed into a practical tool for firms, linking the flow of materials to actual costs through MFCA. MFCA, developed in the late 1990s, is a tool for improving material productivity in order to optimize the relative consumption of materials, energy and water in the production process. It measures the flow and stock of materials in both monetary and physical units such as weight and volume, facilitating the understanding of the interconnectedness of environmental factors such as material use and emissions to economic considerations. Under this approach, the full economic cost of waste is made tangible by examining the cost of waste in the purchase, production and disposal stages instead of simply calculating the cost of the disposal stage.

Experience demonstrates that material purchase costs and materials lost as waste and emissions may account for significant, and at times, the most significant cost drivers in different organizations. This may be particularly evident in countries where other cost drivers such as labor costs are low. The MFCA captures all input and output materials in the MFA. Input materials include raw materials, auxiliary materials, merchandise, packaging, operating materials, water, and energy. Outputs are divided into product outputs that go into the final product and non-product outputs (waste, wastewater, and emissions). Successful implementation of MFCA depends on inputs from both accounting and production, two parts of the organization which do not necessarily share a synchronized information system. Total environmental costs include environmental protection expenditure (end-of-pipe emissions treatment and waste prevention) as well as material flow costs. Together these two account for the total corporate environmental costs (Jasch 2008).

The integrated analysis of costs and the flows and stocks of materials in an organization has proven to yield opportunities for economic and environmental savings through resource efficiency. The ISO 14051 standard published in 2011 was designed as an internal environmental management accounting tool for organizations (ISO 14051 standard). It provides a general framework for MFCA on an organization level through a common terminology, principles, objectives, fundamental elements and implementation steps. The ISO framework tracks and quantifies in physical units the flows and stocks of materials within an organization and their associated internal costs. External costs are outside the scope of the MFCA but can be included if desired by the organization. It therefore promotes increased transparency of material use practices (Kokubu and Tachikawa 2013). Organizations can then use the information gathered to highlight opportunities to simultaneously generate financial benefits and reduce adverse environmental impacts such as waste production. The standard supports companies by providing a step by step guidance to the process through the different stages of an MFCA from guidance on building a materials and energy flow model to guidance on the communication of the MFCA results and the involvement of management. In addition, it includes some real examples to better illustrate the process.

Another ISO standard, the ISO 14052 titled "Environmental management— (MFCA)—Guidance for practical implementation in a supply chain" is currently being developed and planned to provide guidance on implementation of MFCA along the supply chain.

The framework is relevant to organizations regardless of their products, services, size, structure, location, and existing management and accounting systems. Moreover, it can be extended to other organizations in the supply chain, both upstream and downstream. The supply chain component can then inform the organization and support decisions on an integrated approach to improving material and energy efficiency in the supply chain. For example, waste generation in an organization is often determined by the nature or quality of materials provided by a supplier, or by the specification of the product requested by a customer.

Dedicated software tools were developed to support the use of the framework (e.g., Umberto®). Examples of the use of MFCA encompass the manufacturing and non-manufacturing industries and include opportunities in a multitude of processes, such textile manufacturing, construction, cleaning, recycling, surface treating and chemical reactions processes, machining and forming processes as well as logistics and distribution.

In order to demonstrate the use of this tool, two examples of firms that applied it in practice are provided. While the concept was first developed in Germany, both examples are from Japan, where the government has both actively promoted the development of the ISO standard and identified different case studies whose experience contributed to the process of developing and fine-tuning the standard.

5.3.3.1 Using MFCA to Identify Waste Hotspots in a Pharmaceutical Product

The first example, the Mitsubishi Tanabe Pharma Corporation, a manufacturer of medical products in Japan, selected the production of a medical product for MFCA analysis. The firm identified the processes that generated the key waste management cost and the material loss cost in its production process. The process which consists of the composition, refinement, bulk pharmaceuticals, weighing capacity, and formulation and packaging stages was outlined. Furthermore, the use of materials, auxiliary materials, reaction agents and solvents as well as packaging materials inputs into the process and all material losses were mapped for all production phases. Waste management costs incurred in the composition process amounted to 126 million yen, while the cost of material losses from the composition to the bulk pharmaceuticals processes amounted to 285 million yen. The identification of these waste hotspots led to changes in investment decisions and manufacturing operations, resulting in a reduction in waste, reduction in chloroform emissions, significant reduction in CO_2 emissions and annual economic savings (METI 2010, Mitsubishi Tanabe Pharma Corporation company website). The MFCA analysis can support evaluation practices at the design phase as well as providing for a common production indicator (METI 2010).

5.3.3.2 Using MFCA to Reduce Material Input Use through Collaboration with a Supplier

The second example relates to an MFCA conducted jointly by Canon Inc. and its glass material supplier. It highlighted the gap between input and output in the production process, indicating a much higher proportion of material loss rates than previously estimated. The company looked at the MFCA of the production of the lens used for a single-lens reflex camera and a broadcast camera produced in Japan. The process, including the stages of grinding, smoothing, polishing, centering and coating, was analyzed for input materials and material losses. The analysis revealed that material loss encompassed a third of the total material and that about 66 % of the material losses were generated in the grinding phase, mainly in the form of cost of the material and cost of disposal and treatment of liquid waste and sludge management. Canon closely analyzed this information, and instituted improvement initiatives for waste reduction in cooperation with the material supplier. Through collaboration with the glass material supplier, innovative new materials for lens production, known as "Near-shaping," were developed. Raw material input was reduced by a total of 85 % with a similar reduction in energy input. Waste volume was reduced by 92 % and sludge volume was reduced by 50 %. Additional savings were achieved through reduction in process costs (METI 2010). Changes due to the MFCA saved a total of about 5.1 billion yen between 2004 and 2012 (Schmidt and Michiyasu 2013). This example highlights the positive outcomes of applying this analysis upstream on the supply chain through cooperation with a supplier.

5.3.4 Additional Tools for Material Flows Management

5.3.4.1 Materials Substitutes

While substitution may present an opportunity for addressing the scarcity of certain materials, it can only provide such a solution, and an incomplete solution at that, in certain cases. A study of the substitution potential of different metals in their major uses around the globe highlighted that for 12 out of 62 different metals studied, the potential substitutes for their major uses are either inadequate or non-existent. The study also found that for none of the 62 metals does one single substitute accommodate all major uses (Graedel et al. 2015).

Finding substitutes is still a major challenge for industries, especially with regard to the different properties of certain materials as well as their pricing and availability. Concepts such as Design for the Environment and tools such as LCA can help R&D teams and new technology teams to assess the true meaning of new substitute options in terms of their cost and environmental perspectives and, in a more holistic approach, also in terms of their social aspects.

5.3.4.2 Servicizing Examples for Dematerialization

Certain business models present a potential for dematerialization, or the reduction of raw material use through a circular product lifecycle, which may include recycling, reuse, etc.[2] Servicizing presents one such example. Servicizing is a business model defined as "a transaction where value is provided through a combination of products and services and where satisfaction of customer needs is achieved by selling the product's function rather than product per se, and/or by increasing the service component of the offer" (SPREE Project 2012). Servicizing examples showing a reduction of material use include the shift from selling printers to selling documentation services by Xerox, which reduces material use for the production of printers, copiers, paper and toners while also reducing solid waste generation. Another example is the shift of Gage Products from selling chemical blends for automotive paint applications to providing an effective paint shop operation (i.e., providing the customer with a painted product). Material savings include lower use of paint, solvents and cleaners (Rothenberg 2012). (See also Chap. 16 by Bellos and Ferguson (2017) for more on servicizing.)

5.3.4.3 Increase Supply Chain Transparency and Accountability

Efforts have already been developed to increase supply chain transparency and accountability in conflict minerals through a process somewhat analogous to the Kimberly Process established for other, more famous, minerals- diamonds. The Kimberley Process was initiated in 2000 with the aim of stopping the trade in "conflict diamonds" and ensuring that diamond purchases were not financing the violation of human rights nor fueling rebel movements undermining governments in production and trade countries. By 2002 an international certification scheme, "the Kimberley Process Certification Scheme" was established and implemented as of 2003. The Kimberley Process (KP) was established through a multi-stakeholder

---

[2] Examples for circular business models can be found here: http://reports.weforum.org/toward-the-circular-economy-accelerating-the-scale-up-across-global-supply-chains/how-it-works-up-close-case-examples-of-circular-products/?doing_wp_cron=1420793342.83788108825683593759000.

process involving government, civil society and industry and currently has 54 members, representing 81 countries (EU countries count as one member) and covers 99.8 % of the global production of rough diamonds. The process works through an extensive list of requirements members have to meet to get certified that the diamonds are "conflict free" (KP website http://www.kimberleyprocess.com/en/about).

In order to assure due diligence along the supply chain of other minerals sources for its industry, the USA has issued a rule on conflict minerals in 2012. One of the specific specialized disclosure provisions included in Title XV of the Dodd-Frank Wall Street Reform and Consumer Protection Act is Section 1502 on conflict minerals, specifically tin, tantalum, tungsten and gold. It requires annual disclosure of whether any conflict minerals that are necessary to the functionality or production of a product manufactured by an issuer originated in the Democratic Republic of the Congo (DRC) or an adjoining country. In case the minerals originated in the DRC or an adjoining country, it requires a detailed report on measures taken to exercise due diligence upstream on the source and chain of custody of those minerals. At the international level, the OECD's Due Diligence Guidance for Responsible Supply Chains of Minerals from Conflict-Affected and High-Risk Areas provides guidelines to multinational organizations on sourcing minerals responsibly (OECD 2013).

The Extractive Industries Transparency Initiative (EITI) is another voluntary initiative promoting a global standard seeking to improve transparency and accountability in countries rich in oil, gas, and mineral resources. In each host country, the EITI is supported by a coalition of governments, companies and civil society working together. Once the EITI is endorsed in the country, its process becomes mandatory for all extractive industry operators, private or state-owned, which operate within that country. As of 2015, 31 countries have already become EITI compliant, and 17 countries are currently candidate countries (EITI 2014).

The European Union has also enacted new disclosure requirements in 2013 in order to improve the transparency of payments made to governments all over the world by the extractive and logging industries. The objective of the disclosure is to provide civil society in resource-rich countries with the necessary data and information required to assure governmental accountability for income made through the exploitation of natural resources. The requirements also aim to promote the adoption of the EITI in those countries (European Commission 2013). Chapter 6 by Bateman et al. (2017) provides more background on various disclosure requirements in supply chains.

5.4 How Do Countries Manage Material Flows at the Global Level?

In this section we outline additional tools that can help to manage and enhance sustainable raw materials management more broadly at the global level. We provide insights into more targeted policy aspects and international trade issues.

5.4.1   National Assessments and Policies

The EU has recognized the growth in the number of materials used in products and the need to reduce supply risk and strategically secure stable access to these raw materials and resources for manufacturers in Europe. Therefore, as part of its strategy, it initiated the Raw Materials Initiative which manages raw materials issues at an EU level. A subgroup of the Raw Materials Supply Group, specifically working on defining critical raw materials, published its first criticality analysis for raw materials in 2010. The report focused on non-energy and non-food materials and identified 14 critical raw materials out of a list of 41 materials.

The list has been formally adopted by the European Commission which continues to monitor criticality in order to determine priority actions. In a subsequent review published in 2013, the same methodology, indicators and thresholds were used to review a longer list of 54 raw materials in order to enable comparison of criticality over time and implications for economic importance and supply risk criteria. It identified 20 critical materials. Analysis of economic importance is conducted based on the proportion of each material associated with industrial mega-sectors at an EU level. The proportions are then combined with the mega-sectors' gross value-added (GVA) to the EU's GDP. Finally the total is scaled according to the total EU GDP so that an overall economic importance for a material can be defined. Supply risk of raw materials is based on the World Governance Indicator (WGI) which takes into account a variety of influences including voice and accountability, political stability and absence of violence, government effectiveness, and regulatory quality, rule of law or control of corruption.[3] Table 5.3 presents the different materials in the criticality reports of the EU (based on data from the 2010 and 2013 reports).

The European Union's Critical Material Studies guides decision makers on conflict minerals' policy and industry on scarcity and trade implications. Comparing the two reports can be instrumental in understanding what changes are taking place over even a short period of time of 3 years. In 2000 42 materials were reviewed, and in 2013 already 54. Tantalum, a critical mineral in 2010 was no longer in the same level of supply risk in 2013 and was removed from the list. Other minerals were added as the scope grew and changes in the market were occurring enlarging the list to also include Borates, Chromium, Coking Coal, Magnesite, Phosphate Rock and Silicon Metal. This comparison clearly indicates that the status of minerals and their criticality cannot be considered as a static status and must be reviewed periodically. It emphasizes the need for ongoing reviews both on a firm and a national level in order to assure risk and management of minerals is up to date with global fluctuations.

National level policy making can help to resolve some of the criticality challenges. Table 5.3 outlines several points that elucidate the important connection between companies and regulators in this policy arena. The table presents the different goals and strategies governments adopted to face possible resource scarcity

---

[3] http://ec.europa.eu/growth/sectors/raw-materials/

Table 5.3 National strategies

Country	Goal	Business policy	R&D policy	Materials of interest
Japan	Securing a stable supply of raw materials for Japanese industries	• Funding for international mineral exploration	• Substitution research funded through METI and MEXT	Ni, Mn, Co, W, Mo, V
		• Loan guarantees for high-risk mineral projects	• Exploration, excavation, refining and safety research funded through JOGMEC	
		• Stockpiling		
		• Information gathering		
Netherlands	Reducing material consumption to prevent global shortages by employing "managed austerity"	Government–industry collaboration on material policy through the M2i Institute	• Substitutes for abundant or renewable materials	Ag, As, Au, Be, Bi, Cd, Co, Ga, Ge, Hg, In, Li, Mo, Nb, Nd, Ni, Pb, Pd, PGMs, REEs, Re, Ru, Sb, Sc, Se, Sn, Sr, Ta, Te, Ti, V, W, Y, Zn, Zr
			• Processes for recycling depleting materials	
			• Study of consumption patterns as a result of policy	
China	Maintaining a stable supply of raw materials for domestic use through industry consolidation, mitigating overproduction and reducing illegal trade	• Taxes and quotas on REE exports	• Rare earth separation techniques and exploration of new rare earth functional materials	Sb, Sn, W, Fe, Hg, Al, Zn, V, Mo, REEs
		• Prohibition of foreign companies in REE mining	• Rare earth metallurgy; optical, electrical, and magnetic properties of rare earths; basic chemical sciences of rare earths	
		• Industry consolidation		
		• Unified pricing mechanisms		
		• Production quotas		
		• Moratorium on new mining permits until mid-2011		
South Korea	Ensuring a reliable supply of materials critical to Korean mainstay industries	• Financial support for Korean firms at overseas mines	• Recycling of end-use products	As, Ti, Co, In, Mo, Mn, Ta, Ga, V, W, Li and REEs
		• Free Trade Agreements and MOUs with resource-rich nations	• Designing for recyclability	
		• Stockpiling	• Substitute materials	
			• Production efficiency	

Country				Minerals
Australia	Maintaining investment in the mining industry while fairly taxing the depletion of national resources	• Low tax on the value of extracted resources • High tax on mine profits • Tax rebates for mineral exploration • Fast turnaround for land permit applications	• Promoting sustainable development practices in mining	Al, Ag, Au, Fe, Ni, Cu, Pb, Mo
Canada	Promoting sustainable development and use of mineral and metal resources, protecting the environment and public health, and ensuring an attractive investment climate	• Promoting a recycling industry and incorporating recycling as part of product design • Requiring accountability in environmental performance and mineral stewardship • Using a lifecycle-based approach to mineral management and use	• Providing comprehensive geosciences information infrastructure • Promoting technological innovation in mining processes • Developing value-added mineral and metal products	Al, Ag, Au, Fe, Ni, Cu, Pb, Mo
Germany[a]	Safeguarding a sustainable supply of non-energy mineral resources for Germany	• Supporting efficient production techniques	• Supporting the "Innovative SMEs: resource and energy-efficiency" initiative • Enhancing raw materials productivity in high-input industries	
United Kingdom		Reducing business risk from resource scarcity	Producing "Risk Lists" from 2011	"Risk list[b]": REEs, W, Sb, Bi, Mo, Sr, Hg, BA, C, Be, Ge, Nb, PGEs, Co, ThIn, Ga, As,
EU	Limiting impact of supply shortages on the European economy	Resource-efficient Europe as a flagship initiative for EU 2020	Resource efficiency in technology and business model innovation	Sb, Be, B, Cr, Co, Coking coal, CaF$_2$, Ga, Ge, In, Magnesite, Mg, Natural graphite, Nb, Phosphate rock, PMGs[c] REEs (Heavy, Light),[d] Si W[e]

Sources: Adapted and elaborated from United States DOE (2010); DEFRA (2012), EU criticality report (2014), Resnick Institute (2011)

[a]Plan: http://www.bmwi.de/English/Redaktion/Pdf/raw-materials-strategy.property=pdf,bereich=bmwi2012,sprache=en,rwb=true.pdf

[b]The British Geological Survey (BGS) Centre for Sustainable Mineral Development: http://www.bgs.ac.uk/mineralsuk/statistics/riskList.html

[c]Profiles: http://ec.europa.eu/enterprise/policies/raw-materials/files/docs/crm-critical-material-profiles_en.pdf

[d]The term "rare earth elements" (REEs) is a collective name for the 15 elements in the lanthanide group: lanthanum, cerium, praseodymium, neodymium, promethium, samarium, europium, gadolinium, terbium, dysprosium, holmium, erbium, thulium, ytterbium, and lutetium

[e]The Platinum Group Metals (PGMs) consist of six precious metals, (platinum (Pt), palladium (Pd), rhodium (Rh), ruthenium (Ru), iridium (Ir), and osmium (Os))

in specific materials of interest. It is clear that some materials are of interest to many countries, however others are endemic to particular needs and expected demand. This represents the importance for national analysis of the existing stock for each material, its future use and possible barriers to its production and import, and ways the government can overcome these challenges through substitution, recycling and excavation, or through changes in consumption. Second, this table demonstrates the need to align business policies and R&D policies, within the government and through collaboration between supply chain managers, the academia, and government officials. For example, trade agreements may pose problems or opportunities for supply of materials that companies rely on for their future production processes or upcoming technologies.

5.4.2   International Trade

International trade restrictions may present a major challenge for firms as they may create supply risk for manufacturers in one country and may secure preferential use of the materials for manufacturers in another country. In 2012, the USA requested a consultation through the World Trade Organization[4] with the People's Republic of China regarding China's restrictions on rare earths, tungsten and molybdenum, which are raw materials used in the production of various kinds of electronic goods (WTO 2014). The following countries were third parties to the request: Brazil, Canada, Colombia, European Union, India, Japan, Korea, Norway, Oman, Saudi Arabia, Chinese Taipei, Viet Nam, Argentina, Australia, Indonesia, Turkey, Peru and the Russian Federation. The listed restrictions included export duties, export quotas, minimum export price requirements, export licensing requirements and additional requirements and procedures in connection with the administration of the quantitative restrictions. In 2014, the appellate body found that key measures were inconsistent with WTO obligations. In December 2014, China and the USA agreed that China would implement the recommendations and rulings of the Dispute Settlement Body by May 2015 based on the argument that the restrictions were designed to provide Chinese industries that produce downstream goods with protected access to the subject materials.

International trade is also relevant in the case of waste streams and recycling activities. For example, in 2013 China announced that it would tighten the enforcement of its recycling criteria for products and would no longer accept poorly sorted or dirty shipments of recyclable waste from other countries around the world (Green Fence Policy). The customs initiative does not present new legislation but rather better enforcement to assure that the country will not continue to import harmful waste products. China's initiative immediately provoked a strong reaction within the country and abroad as it reshuffled the global recycling market by putting up a

---

[4]The World Trade Organization (WTO) deals with the global rules of trade between nations. Its main function is to ensure that trade flows as smoothly, predictably and freely as possible.

metaphorical fence in order to reject past practices of sending such harmful materials to China. The initiative disrupted existing waste streams flows and has already required other countries to reconsider their waste export strategy and shift scrap waste to destinations other than China (Bureau of International Recycling 2013).

5.5 What's Next?

Based on this chapter review, and looking forward to the topic of sustainable materials management, we outline in this summary section topics that require further thinking, research, and practical solutions as the next step for advancing raw materials management for sustainable supply chains.

We start with a few questions that are relevant to the firm perspective, as the user of the raw materials:

- *How can firms internalize material issues*: Many of the issues discussed in this chapter are still not common knowledge for procurement managers, designers, and supply chain managers. In order to understand the local and global trends and take actions, firms need simple tools that will help them assess their situation and act on it in the most relevant way, both internally within the firm and externally to it.
- *Practical use of MFA at the firm and supply chain levels*: As presented, there is already a vast body of research and findings on the use of MFA methodology, and firms can use these studies in various ways. However, thus far, MFAs have mainly been conducted at the national and regional levels. Much less work has been done at the firm level. Further work that concentrates on the supply chain level and the firm level will give higher value to firms and will increase their understanding of the importance of this tool for decision making. It will help them to better understand such questions as: "what are the specific implications and concerns with regards to the materials I use in my products."
- *Questions for firms to ask*: Firms that are newly introduced to this topic should ask some guiding questions to help those set priorities and better understand their pathways. We outline below some of these main questions and thoughts (partially adopted from DEFRA 2012).

  - Are we relying on domestic or imported materials? Domestic supply offers greater security, while imported resources may be at risk due to geopolitical issues, or protectionist policies from key supplying countries.
  - Can the government help us secure the availability of some materials? Regulatory and government policy may have resource availability implications as it may impact on supply or increase demand for particular resources.
  - Can we change our products and use material substitutes? Businesses will need to identify alternative sources domestically and/or internationally, while

also bearing in mind issues relating to the time lag of developing a new mine, for example.

– Are we innovative enough? Businesses may need to invest further in process or production innovation and recycling technologies of materials.

At a higher level, some actions require attention:

- *Integration of data on raw materials*: Currently very little is known about materials in large scales, especially the environmental and social impacts nexus. Integration of data and information regarding material flows, consumption rates, technological cycles, availability, criticality, etc., sorted by materials, by industries, and by nations, would require meta-level coordination between different organizations. However, since the body of knowledge in this area is still concentrated, this could provide an opportunity for reorganizing the data and collecting it in ways that are more accessible to the different stakeholders involved in collecting and using the data.
- *What innovation is needed more specifically*? Three forms of innovation should be encouraged by nations and by industrial associations:

  - New recycling technologies for materials currently not recycled.
  - Small-scale recycling operations that will be economic and will help countries that are poor in local resources to maintain the materials within the country at the end-of-life stage.
  - New substitutes for existing and new industries.

- *Needed collaboration*: Since some material issues are global, some regional, and some sector-specific, sector level "think-tank" groups could be very effective in reaching a solution (for example, the process of finding substitutes for the ROHS banned materials in the electronics sector was a collaborative action in some cases).
- *Needed research*: Empirical work on material flows and risks at the firm and supply chain levels is currently fairy limited. It is necessary to extend this body of work and to include more disciplines (such as policy, law, international trade, economics, etc.) in order to better research this topic in collaboration with industry and governmental organizations.
- *Urban mining is not just a buzz word*: The concept of urban mining is becoming much more relevant, especially within regions poor in local resources. At one end, new collection and recycling schemes for different product waste streams must be developed on a large scale. At the other end, new technologies for mining landfills must be developed and deployed. Landfill sites can become a major source of materials and employment.

This chapter provides an overview of the main topics related to sustainable management of non-renewable materials such as metallic elements. It starts with reviewing the main trends in global supply and demand as well as providing some insights for the economic and environmental impact of using those materials within the economy. It talks in length on tools available for firms in order to better understand their material flows (with special attention to MFA) and provides examples of how to use such tools and for what purposes. This chapter is designed to provide basic information about the main issues reacted to this topic and we highly encourage the readers of this book to further examine those issues by looking in more detailed into the many references we provide.

References

Ali SH (2011) ecological comparison of synthetic versus mined diamonds. Working Paper, Institute for Environmental Diplomacy and Security. http://www.uvm.edu/~shali/Synthetic_Diamonds_Mined_Diamonds.pdf. Accessed 15 Jan 2015

Angerer G, Marscheider-Weidemann F, Erdmann ML et al. (2009) Raw materials for emerging technologies. The influence of sector-specific feedstock demand on future raw materials consumption in material-intensive emerging technologies

Ayres RU, Ayres L (eds) (2002) A handbook of industrial ecology. Edward Elgar, Cheltenham

Bateman AH, Blanco EE, Sheffi Y (2017) Disclosing and reporting environmental sustainability of supply chains. In: Bouchery Y, Corbett CJ, Fransoo J, Tan T (eds) Sustainable supply chains: a research-based textbook on operations and strategy. Springer, New York

Behrens A, Giljum S, Kovanda J, Niza S (2007) The material basis of the global economy: worldwide patterns of natural resource extraction and their implications for sustainable resource use policies. Ecol Econ 64(2):444–453

Bellos J, Ferguson M (2017) Moving from a product-based economy to a service-based economy for a more sustainable future. In: Bouchery Y, Corbett CJ, Fransoo J, Tan T (eds) Sustainable supply chains: a research-based textbook on operations and strategy. Springer, New York

Bergsdal H, Brattebø H, Bohne RA, Müller DB (2007) Dynamic material flow analysis for Norway's dwelling stock. Build Res Inf 35(5):557–570

Binder CR (2007) From material flow analysis to material flow management Part I: social sciences modeling approaches coupled to MFA. J Clean Prod 15(17):1596–1604

Binder CR, Van Der Voet E, Rosselot KS (2009) Implementing the results of material flow analysis. J Ind Ecol 13(5):643–649

Brunner PH (2011) Urban mining. J Ind Ecol 15(3):S-339

Bureau of International Recycling (2013) 'Green Fence' alters plastic scrap flows. http://www.bir.org/assets/conventions/warsaw2013/Press/RI-9-BIR-plastics-tyres.pdf. Accessed 26 November 2014

Clift R, Wright L (2000) Relationships between environmental impacts and added value along the supply chain. Technol Forecast Soc Chang 65(3):281–295

de Boer MA, Lammertsma K (2012) Scarcity of rare earth elements, a review commissioned by the Royal Netherlands Chemical Society. http://www.kncv.nl/Uploads/2012/7/SREE-KNCV-rapport-02.07.pdf. Accessed 21 Dec 2014

DEFRA (UK Department for Food, Environment and Rural Affairs) (2012) A review of National Resource Strategies and Research. https://www.gov.uk/government/uploads/system/uploads/attachment_data/file/69526/pb13722-national-resource-strategies-review.pdf. Accessed 22 Dec 2014

Deloitte (2013) Tracking the trends 2014 the top 10 issues mining companies will face in the coming year. https://www2.deloitte.com/content/dam/Deloitte/global/Documents/Energy-and-Resources/dttl-er-Tracking-the-trends-2014_EN_final.pdf. Accessed Dec 2014

Dittrich M, Giljum S, Lutter S, Polzin C (2012) Green economies around the world? implications of resource use for development and the environment. Published by the Sustainable Europe Research Institute (SERI), Vienna. http://seri.at/wp-content/uploads/2012/06/green_economies_around_the_world.pdf. Accessed 12 Feb 2015

European Commission (2008) Communication from the Commission the European Parliament and the Council: the raw materials initiative—meeting our critical needs for growth and jobs in

Europe. http://ec.europa.eu/enterprise/sectors/metals-minerals/files/sec_2741_en.pdf#page=10. Accessed 2 Oct 2014

European Commission (2010) Critical raw materials for the EU, Report of the Ad-hoc Working Group on defining critical raw materials. http://ec.europa.eu/enterprise/policies/raw-materials/files/docs/report-b_en.pdf. Accessed 30 Oct 2014

European Commission (2013) New disclosure requirements for the extractive industry and loggers of primary forests in the Accounting (and Transparency) Directives (Country by Country Reporting)—frequently asked questions. http://europa.eu/rapid/press-release_MEMO-13-541_en.htm. Accessed 10 Nov 2014

European Commission (2014) Critical raw materials, for the EU, Report of the Ad-hoc Working Group on raw materials. http://ec.europa.eu/enterprise/policies/raw-materials/files/docs/crm-report-on-critical-raw-materials_en.pdf. Accessed Dec 2014

Extractive Industries Transparency Initiative (2014) What is the EITI? https://eiti.org/eiti. Accessed 10 Dec 2014

Frischknecht R, Jungbluth N, Althaus H-J, Doka G, Dones R, Heck T, Hellweg S, Hischier R, Nemecek T, Rebitzer G, Spielmann M (2005) The ecoinvent database version 2.2.: overview and methodological framework. Int J Life Cycle Assess 10:3–9

Fuse M, Tsunemi K (2012) Assessment of the effects of the Japanese shift to lead-free solders and its impact on material substitution and environmental emissions by a dynamic material flow analysis. Sci Total Environ 438:49–58

GaBi 6. LCA software. PE International (2012) Professional database. http://www.gabisoftware.com/databases/gabi-databases/professional/. Accessed 15 Jan 2015

Galbreth MR, Boyacı T, Verter V (2013) Product reuse in innovative industries. Prod Oper Manag 22(4):1011–1033

Graedel TE, Allwood J, Birat JP, Buchert M, Hagelüken C, Reck BK, Sibley SF, Sonnemann G (2011) What do we know about metal recycling rates? J Ind Ecol 15(3):355–366

Graedel TE, Harper EM, Nassar NT, Reck BK (2015) On the materials basis of modern society. Proc Natl Acad Sci U S A 112(20):6295–6300

Guinée J, Heijungs R (2017) Introduction to life cycle assessment. In: Bouchery Y, Corbett CJ, Fransoo J, Tan T (eds) Sustainable supply chains: a research-based textbook on operations and strategy. Springer, New York

Habib K, Schibye PK, Vestbø AP, Dall O, Wenzel H (2014) Material flow analysis of NdFeB magnets for Denmark: a comprehensive waste flow sampling and analysis approach. Environ Sci Technol 48(20):12229–12237

International Resource Panel (2011) Decoupling natural resource use and environmental impacts from economic growth. http://www.unep.org/resourcepanel/decoupling/files/pdf/Decoupling_Report_English.pdf. Accessed 30 Nov 2014

International Resource Panel (2014) Decoupling 2 technologies, opportunities and policy options. http://www.unep.org/resourcepanel/Portals/24102/PDFs/IRP_DECOUPLING_2_REPORT.pdf. Accessed 30 Nov 2014

ISO 14051:2011. Environmental management—material flow cost accounting—general framework. International Organization for Standardization, Geneva, Switzerland. http://www.iso.org/iso/catalogue_detail.htm?csnumber=50986. Accessed 25 Nov 2014

Jacobs BW, Subramanian R (2012) Sharing responsibility for product recovery across the supply chain. Prod Oper Manag 21(1):85–100

Jasch Christine M (2008) Environmental and material flow cost accounting: principles and procedures, vol 25. Springer, Heidelberg

Kennedy C, Cuddihy J, Engel-Yan J (2007) The changing metabolism of cities. J Ind Ecol 11(2):43–59

Kimberley Process website. http://www.kimberleyprocess.com/en/about. Accessed 15 Sept 2015

Kleindorfer PR, Singhal K, Wassenhove LN (2005) Sustainable operations management. Prod Oper Manag 14(4):482–492

Kokubu K, Tachikawa H (2013) Material flow cost accounting: significance and practical approach. In: Kauffman J, Lee K-M (eds) Handbook of Sustainable Engineering. Springer, Dordrecht, pp 351–369

Kowalski Z, Mazanek C (1998) Sodium chromate—material flow analysis and technology assessment. J Clean Prod 6(2):135–142

Kwonpongsagoon S, Waite DT, Moore SJ, Brunner PH (2007) A substance flow analysis in the southern hemisphere: cadmium in the Australian economy. Clean Techn Environ Policy 9(3):175–187

Lam CW, Lim SR, Schoenung JM (2013) Linking material flow analysis with environmental impact potential. J Ind Ecol 17(2):299–309

Lin JY (2009) Natural resources, economic growth and future generations: how to create a win-win outcome for everyone? Global Development Network: Tenth Annual Conference on "Natural Resources and Development". http://web.worldbank.org/WBSITE/EXTERNAL/NEWS/0,contentMDK:22058269~menuPK:34472~pagePK:34370~piPK:34424~theSitePK:4607,00.html. Accessed 3 Jan 2015

Liu X, Tanaka M, Matsui Y (2006) Generation amount prediction and material flow analysis of electronic waste: a case study in Beijing, China. Waste Manag Res 24(5):434–445

Lusty PAJ, Gunn AG (2014) Challenges to global mineral resource security and options for future supply. Geological Society, London, Special Publications 393: SP393-12. http://nora.nerc.ac.uk/508092/1/SP393.13.full.pdf

McKinsey (2012) Resource revolution report. http://eco-efficiency-action-project.com/2012/02/02/mckinsey-resource-revolution-report/. Accessed 1 Dec 2014

METI (2010) http://www.jmac.co.jp/mfca/thinking/data/MFCA_Case_example_e.pdf. Accessed 12 Feb 2015

Mitsubishi Tanabe Pharma Corporation company website. http://www.mt-pharma.co.jp/shared/show.php?url=../e/company/csr-report/2008/report25.html. Accessed 10 Apr 2015

PBL Netherlands Environmental Assessment Agency (2014) PBL note: share of raw material costs in total production costs. http://www.pbl.nl/sites/default/files/cms/publicaties/pbl-2014-share-of-raw-material-costs-in-total-production-costs_01506.pdf. Accessed 20 Nov 2014

OECD (2000) Special session on material flow accounting. http://www.oecd.org/env/indicators-modelling-outlooks/4425421.pdf. Accessed 12 Feb 2015

OECD (2013) Guidelines to multinational organization responsible supply chains of minerals from conflict-affected and high-risk areas. http://www.oecd.org/daf/inv/mne/GuidanceEdition2.pdf. Accessed 12 Feb 2015

Pil FK, Rothenberg S (2003) Environmental performance as a driver of superior quality. Prod Oper Manag 12(3):404–415

PWC (2011) Minerals and metals scarcity in manufacturing: the ticking time bomb. http://www.pwc.com/en_GX/gx/sustainability/researchinsights/assets/impact-of-minerals-metals-scarcity-on-business.pdf. Accessed 10 Nov 2014

SPREE Project (2012) A glance at servicizing. www.spreeproject.com. Accessed 15 Dec 2014

Reck BK, Graedel TE (2012) Challenges in metal recycling. Science 337(6095):690–695

Reck BK, Müller DB, Rostkowski K, Graedel TE (2008) Anthropogenic nickel cycle: insights into use, trade, and recycling. Environ Sci Technol 42(9):3394–3400

Resnick Institute (2011) Critical materials for sustainable energy applications. http://resnick.caltech.edu/docs/R_Critical.pdf. Accessed 15 Dec 2014

Rothenberg S (2012) Sustainability through servicizing. MIT Sloan Manag Rev. 48(2)

Schmidt M, Michiyasu N (2013) Material flow cost accounting as an approach to improve resource efficiency in manufacturing companies. Resources 2(3):358–369

Sendra C, Gabarrell X, Vicent T (2007) Material flow analysis adapted to an industrial area. J Clean Prod 15(17):1706–1715

Shen H (2014) WTO's ruling on the 'rampant illegal rare earth production' in China force rapid regulation changes. Investor Intel. http://investorintel.com/rare-earth-intel/china-currently-sits-difficult-inflection-point-wtos-final-ruling-rare-earth/#sthash.lw4YhZLn.dpuf. Accessed 15 Dec 2014

UNEP (United Nations Environmental Program) (2012) Global environmental outlook 5. http://www.unep.org/geo/geo5.asp. Accessed 15 Nov 2014

US DOE (2010) Critical materials strategy. http://energy.gov/sites/prod/files/edg/news/documents/criticalmaterialsstrategy.pdf. Accessed 15 Nov 2014

Vogel D (2009) Trading up: consumer and environmental regulation in a global economy. Harvard University Press, Cambridge

World Economic Forum (2013) Engaging tomorrow's consumer. http://www3.weforum.org/docs/WEF_RC_EngagingTomorrowsConsumer_Report_2013.pdf. Accessed 2 Jan 2015

WTO (2014) Dispute settlement: dispute DS431; China—measures related to the exportation of rare earths, Tungsten and Molybdenum. http://www.wto.org/english/tratop_e/dispu_e/cases_e/ds431_e.htm. Accessed 25 Nov 2014

Wuppertal institute (2015) MIPS online. http://wupperinst.org/en/projects/topics-online/mips/. Accessed 2 Jan 2015

Xiao T, Yu G (2006) Supply chain disruption management and evolutionarily stable strategies of retailers in the quantity-setting duopoly situation with homogeneous goods. Eur J Oper Res 173(2):648–668

Zeal Speculation and Investment website, Scott Wright Analysis (2013) http://www.zealllc.com/2013/ggmt3.htm. Accessed 15 Dec 2014

Chapter 6
Disclosing and Reporting Environmental Sustainability of Supply Chains

Alexis H. Bateman, Edgar E. Blanco, and Yossi Sheffi

6.1 Why Do Firms Disclose?

Environmental disclosure and reporting can be broadly defined as the various methods that businesses use to communicate their environmental impacts, responsibilities, and mitigation activities to stakeholders. Although practitioners often use the words "disclosure" and "reporting" interchangeably, they can be distinguished in terms of "what" is communicated versus "how" it is communicated. *Disclosure* involves previously unknown, secret, or proprietary information. In contrast, *reporting* is the communication process—often structured—by which the disclosed information is transmitted to the public, shareholders, stakeholders, or governments. The decision of what and when to disclose is specific to each setting; companies make disclosure decisions while considering internal objectives, external pressure, and regulatory requirements. And the decision of how to report these disclosures is similarly a function of internal and external forces.

Non-financial reporting largely started in Europe in 1970s Germany with social reporting and the Organisation for Economic Co-operation and Development's (OECD) Social Indicators reporting program. Regulatory disclosure gained momentum in the United States during the 1980s with the "right to know" legislation set forth in the Superfund Amendments and Reauthorization Act. This legislation established the Toxic Release Inventory, wherein companies were asked to disclose the production and release of toxic chemicals (EPA 2015). Then, in 1989, voluntary reporting further came into focus in the United States following the massive oil spill by Exxon Valdez. The Valdez Principles were introduced by the Coalition for Environmentally Responsible Economies (CERES), which outlined the first major environmental conduct and reporting practices specifically for companies (Sanyal and Neves 1991).

A.H. Bateman (✉) • E.E. Blanco • Y. Sheffi
MIT, Cambridge, MA, USA
e-mail: hickmana@mit.edu; eblanco@mit.edu; sheffi@mit.edu

© Yann Bouchery, Charles J. Corbett, Jan C. Fransoo, and Tarkan Tan 2017
Y. Bouchery et al. (eds.), *Sustainable Supply Chains*, Springer Series in Supply Chain Management 4, DOI 10.1007/978-3-319-29791-0_6

At the international level, the United Nations Rio Earth Summit in 1992 and the Rio+20 Summit in 2012 have encouraged companies to act and be accountable through reporting on social and environmental responsibility (UNEP 2014).

The driving forces for environmental sustainability reporting and corporate disclosure of other types of information are not different. However, unlike other information disclosed by companies, stakeholder pressure and brand positioning have been the dominant forces for environmental sustainability disclosure. Environmental reporting is a relatively recent practice that is often complex and hard to verify, requiring data from multiple supply chain partners. Often, it is difficult for an organization to navigate the increasing number of reporting and disclosure alternatives available.

Private firms are used to disclosing information on their activities. Companies disclose for four primary reasons: (1) to satisfy requirements imposed by governments and regulators; (2) to satisfy requirements from shareholders; (3) to communicate attributes of the brand, products or services to current and future customers and consumers; and (4) to mitigate reputational risks with other stakeholders such as NGOs, the communities in which they operate, their own employees, and the public at large.

In general, environmental disclosure and reporting rates are high in the developed world. According to the consulting firm KPMG, companies reported at rates of 86 % in the United States and 91 % in the United Kingdom in 2013 (KPMG 2013). Even more promising is the rapid growth of companies reporting in the developing areas of the world, such as Asia Pacific. For example, rates of companies reporting in China increased from 59 % in 2011 to 75 % in 2013. While the growing global rates of environmental reporting are encouraging, they largely represent reporting limited to the company level without addressing the impacts of the supply chain.

6.1.1   Regulatory Disclosures

Although many companies are choosing to report voluntarily or due to pressure from external stakeholders, there are governmental policies that force companies to report on specific environmental practices or impacts. If a company is found to be in noncompliance, it can, in some cases, be penalized. Most existing policies require disclosure only on the company's own internal practices, not on the practices of external partners along the supply chain. However, the requirement to disclose internal practices forces companies to reevaluate processes that may be substandard, and may force them to look into those same practices in their supply chains. Furthermore, regulation can vary across cities, states, and countries; this variability holds multinational companies to a multiplicity of regulatory mandates. Some examples of this include the European Union's Registration, Evaluation, Authorization, and Restriction of Chemicals Act (REACH), France's Grenelle II Act, the United States' Dodd-Frank Act, and California's AB 32 Global Warming Solutions Act.

As an example of basic disclosure policies, the REACH Act requires companies to report their use of specific chemicals and the measures in place to handle them safely. The requirements of this act are based on the quantity of the chemical used and the risk associated with the chemical (Europa 2014). Companies are required to report this information; the information is then included in a public repository managed by the European Union (EU). This repository includes information about quantity, use, and emergency management plans for chemicals used in European operations and products. In addition, if products contain one or more of the 161 chemicals that are classified as substances of very high concern (SVHC) at a quantity above a 0.1 % weight-by-weight threshold, this information must be communicated to the consumer. For example, because it sells its computers in Europe, Dell complied with this requirement by reporting on its website that none of its products contained any SVHC above the required threshold (DELL 2010). In addition to the reporting of chemicals used in operations and products, the REACH Act also includes in its Annex XVII a list of outlawed chemicals that include chemicals like mercury and chloroform (European Chemical Agency 2014).

Some governments have taken mandatory environmental disclosures a step further. Similar to the objective of reporting platforms like the Global Reporting Initiative (GRI) and the CDP (formerly the Carbon Disclosure Project), the French government made company-wide environmental reporting mandatory. Under President Nicolas Sarkozy, the French government created the Grenelle de l'environnement, a French roundtable on sustainable development, in 2007. Through this roundtable, a series of national environmental commitments was created. Released in 2012, Article 225 of the Grenelle II Act requires companies to report on their environmental practices (IRSE 2012). It mandates that French companies with 500 or more employees must produce an annual report that includes third-party vetted environmental, social, and governance indicators. Although many parts of the Grenelle regulation have yet to be enacted, the reporting component of the regulatory mandates was implemented and companies are complying.

The French government also proposed regulation to achieve higher levels of corporate transparency. Based on pilot projects in 2011, legislation was planned for a multi-criteria product label that would include information on carbon footprint, water use, and biodiversity impacts across the entire supply chain (Department of the Commissioner-General for Sustainable Development 2012). Given the rigorous, costly, and time-consuming nature of this data collection, this part of the legislation had not been put into place at the time of this writing (2015).

In the United States, the Dodd-Frank Act became one of the first regulatory mandates to (indirectly) require companies to deeply examine their supply chains. The act is actually a financial disclosure policy, but Section 1502 of the Act requires companies to report whether any of their products contain conflict minerals (GPO 2012). Conflict minerals include tantalum, tin, tungsten, and gold sourced from conflict regions in the Democratic Republic of Congo. These minerals are used to make anything from smartphones to jewelry. The main suppliers of these minerals are commonly four or five tiers deep in a brand owner's supply chain. Therefore, although the requirement sounds straightforward, it requires companies to conduct investigations into often highly complex and impermeable supply chains of smelters, primary metals processors, component makers, and interconnecting import/export firms. Moreover, even when a primary supplier of a mineral has been identified, the reporting company still may not know whether the mineral was sourced from a conflict region or not, due to the highly secretive and opaque nature of the industry (Businessweek 2014). Chapter 5 by Blass et al. (2017) discusses material flows and regulations surrounding such non-renewable materials in more detail.

Although the mandate only requires that companies establish whether or not they use any conflict minerals in their products, most companies also want to avoid the use of conflict minerals in their products. Phasing out sources of conflict minerals includes working with industry groups like the Electronics Industry Citizenship Council (EICC) to audit smelters (the linchpin in the conflict mineral supply chain) to provide transparency onto the source of minerals and allow companies to purchase conflict-free minerals (Businessweek 2014).

At the state level, the state of California enacted the California Global Warming Solutions Act, AB 32 (CARB 2014a, b), in 2006. This policy requires that all industrial facilities, fuel suppliers, and electricity importers report greenhouse gas emissions (GHG emissions) annually through the California Reporting System. The policy came into force in 2008 and remains a requirement. California then took the reporting requirement a step further, by requiring emissions reductions across the same sources through a cap-and-trade program.

California's cap-and-trade program requires that businesses and organizations comply with a reduction of GHGs to 1990 levels by the year 2020 (CARB 2014b). The requirement, which began in 2013 for electric utilities and industrial facilities, requires about a 3 % reduction annually through carbon pricing. The mandate to reduce annual levels will potentially lead to investment in clean technologies. In 2015, the policy will expand to distributors of transportation, natural gas and other fuels (CARB 2011). Policy frameworks such as AB 32 guide companies from mere disclosure toward substantive emissions reductions. This type of regulatory framework can be successful because it links reporting with management, as the reporting process itself reveals areas that need improvement. While findings on success are limited at this time, the system has been broadly adopted across the state.

6.1.2 Additional Pressure to Report

While regulations require companies to report on impacts of their operations, there are additional pressures that encourage companies to report voluntarily.

These include two main mechanisms: (a) multi-stakeholder public agreements and (b) shareholder engagement.

6.1.2.1 Multi-Stakeholder Public Agreements

Multi-stakeholder public agreements refer to environmental commitments by a firm through engagement of public, private, and nongovernmental actors' concerns. By bringing together a diverse group of key stakeholders, company leaders can argue a market interest, or at least mitigate any risks of being left behind, when explaining environmental commitments to shareholders and employees. By committing to a path of improvement, companies are implicitly committing to measure, disclose, and ultimately make progress—voluntarily—on well-defined environmental issues.

For instance, on January 31, 1999, Secretary-General Kofi Annan announced the United Nations Global Compact. The Compact is an initiative to encourage businesses and other organizations worldwide to both adopt sustainable and socially responsible policies and to report on their practices. The Compact is based on ten principles within the four major categories of human rights, labor, environment, and anti-corruption (UN Global Compact 2015). Under the environmental principles, the Global Compact suggests companies should report on their precautionary approach to environmental challenges, on initiatives to promote greater environmental responsibility, and on the diffusion of environmentally friendly technologies. Under each of these principles, companies should describe their assessment, policies and goals; implementation; and measurement of outcomes in their reports. By reporting on its four main categories and their ten sub-principles, an organization will be able to communicate progress to its stakeholders as well as maintain an Active Status under the Global Compact.

With 12,000 companies and organizations from over 145 countries as participants, the Compact represents the largest voluntary initiative established thus far. As a part of its framework, the Compact includes a policy called the Communication on Progress (COP). The COP requires participants to increase their transparency and disclose their progress towards achieving the framework principles. If a company does not report its progress, it will no longer be considered a participant in the Compact. This and similar global initiatives have led to increasing rates of corporate reporting globally.

6.1.2.2   Shareholder Pressure

A more direct way to establish pressure for companies to report environmental impacts and drive reductions is to engage shareholders. Managers in public and private companies have a fiduciary responsibility toward shareholders, both for the short- and long-term financial viability of the business. Whenever environmental concerns can be connected with the long-term viability of the business, and shareholders are also aligned with this view, managers will be required to start measuring and reporting their environmental impacts.

However, it remains highly unclear whether corporate environmental reporting has significant impact on consumer choice or investor practices. Examining a limited set of companies listed in the FTSE 250 of the London Stock Exchange, Haddock-Fraser and Fraser (2008) found that consumer-facing companies were more likely to report than those that operating in a business-to-business setting. Given their analysis of listed companies, the authors conclude that "higher-turnover, public-listed companies" include consumers in their decision to report environmental practices (Haddock-Fraser and Fraser 2008: 153).

In most cases, the shareholder perception of corporate social responsibility (CSR) and embedded activities, including reporting, is neutral as long as these principles and activities increase shareholder value. However, some studies find that a company's decision to report and pursue environmentally focused activities may be negatively interpreted by shareholders due to the perception that any dollar spent toward environmentally and socially responsible activities may be seen as decreasing shareholder profit (Barnea and Rubin 2010). In Chap. 14, Jacobs et al. (2017) also find mixed evidence for how the stock market responds to environmental initiatives.

In both the consumer and shareholder pressure driven cases, only limited research, and a company's perception of the issue, informs the decision of whether or not to report. This means that a company's decision is often based on anecdotal evidence and perceived pressures from different sources.

The Dow Jones Sustainability Indices

The Dow Jones Sustainability Indices (DJSI) is a group of sustainability performance indices that evaluate environmental performance of companies listed on the Dow Jones Global Total Stock Market Index (DJSI). Launched in 1999, the DJSI evaluates corporate environmental and social attributes in conjunction with economic performance (DJSI 2015). Focusing on shareholder interests, the DJSI is the first set of global indices to track sustainability in companies. Although financial performance is a big part of the index, issues assessed include, but are not limited to, supply chain standards, risk management, and climate change mitigation. The DJSI uses both general and industry-specific criteria for evaluation. In addition to the main index, DJSI also has several geographically focused indices including Asia Pacific, Emerging Markets, Europe, North America, Australia, Korea, and Nordic. In addition, it manages industry indices, also known as "blue chip indices."

In 2012, the Dow Jones merged with the S&P Indices to become the S&P Dow Jones Indices. Together with Robeco SAM, an investment specialist for sustainability, they created "objective benchmarks for managing sustainability investment portfolios" (DJSI 2014). The DJSI selects over 3000 publicly traded companies to report on their sustainability practices; 800 of these companies are located in emerging markets (DJSI 2013). The corporate sustainability assessment identifies leaders across 59 industry groups, based on methodology that includes both general and industry-specific sustainability trends. Selecting companies for the DJSI index involves rating companies on a Total Sustainability Score based on Robeco SAM's Corporate Sustainability Index. The annual process begins in March, and scores are released in September of the same year. In 2014, DJSI released the results of the assessment by announcing the top companies in 24 industry groups. Awardees included Siemens AG in Capital Goods; Unilever NV in Food, Beverage and Tobacco; and Kao Corporation in Household & Personal Products.

6.1.3   Report or Explain

In most cases, companies are faced with overlapping voluntary initiatives and mandatory regulations. For example, in India, government guidelines are designed to promote voluntary reporting and responsible business. However, Indian policy also dictates that the top one hundred publicly listed companies report their social and environmental impacts (UNEP 2014).

To promote compliance while allowing flexibility, an increasingly common practice in some parts of the world is the "report or explain" principle (GRI 2011). For example, this practice is included in Denmark's Financial Statements Act, which requires the largest companies to disclose sustainability information. The principle directs that companies should report where possible and explain if they are incapable of reporting on some issues. An inability to report may be due to limited capabilities or capacity to report at the time of compliance. However, the principle includes the expectation that reports will improve over time with increasing levels of disclosure through increased training and capacity in the area of reporting (GRI 2011). The practice became popular because of its flexibility and ability to allow companies to grow into high quality reporting practices, and it was highlighted at the Rio+20 United Nations Summit in 2012. However, allowing companies to "explain" can also be seen as a delaying tactic by which some companies can put off disclosing their impacts, especially if there are no penalties for non-reporting.

Businesses also receive pressure to report from stakeholders including consumers, investors, NGOs, or even their own employees. There is an increased awareness in civil society of the role of business in sustainability. Through social media and the Internet, environmental organizations have engaged consumers in their fight. Environmental NGOs push for transparency and accountability from companies (Buckley 2002). With both brand reputation and consumer loyalty at risk, companies (especially those that are consumer facing) are responding to this pressure.

In some countries, stock exchanges require companies to disclose environmental information. The Australian Securities Exchange (ASX) requires companies to disclose if they have environmental and/or social sustainability risks, while the Swedish OMX reserves the right to delist companies that have social and environmental violations (INI 2014). In addition, in cases where reporting is growing within an industry, a company may report to avoid being seen as a laggard (MacLean and Rebernak 2007). Whether companies are faced with some or all of these pressures, many are complying with requests to disclose and report their environmental impacts. However, these disclosures vary widely in breadth and quality.

6.1.4   Variability of Reporting

Reporting companies disclose environmental information in several different ways: by publishing quantitative metrics, by comparing performance with set targets, through third-party verification, and by means of environmental cost accounting (OECD 2003).

Table 6.1 Examples of major standards and reporting organizations

Standards and reporting orgs.
CDP
Water Disclosure Project
Connected Reporting Framework
Energy industry sustainability reporting guidelines
Forest Footprint Disclosure Project
Global reporting initiative's sustainability reporting guidelines
Greenhouse Gas Protocol
International integrated reporting committee's integrated reporting framework
International standards of accounting and reporting
UN Global Compact communication on progress
Environmental management and audit scheme
International finance corporation's policy and performance standards on social and environmental sustainability
International Organization for Standardization (ISO) 14000
OECD guidelines for multinational enterprises

In reporting, most companies only account for their own operations, not for the entire supply chain. Many critics of standard reporting suggest that assessments scoped at the company level misses far too much and does not account for the supply chain at all (Ethical Corporation 2013). Some suggest this oversight can be eliminated through full product transparency, which is often seen as the future of reporting. Using this method, a company must report the impacts at every phase of the supply chain for each product. Companies can account for the full life cycle of their product through a life cycle assessment (LCA), which is a methodology to meticulously enumerate and aggregate the various impacts of a product at each stage of its life cycle (see Sect. 6.2 for more on practices). Full transparency onto a product's life cycle would, in effect, achieve the highest level of transparency for reporting. However, many companies are reluctant to take on this challenge due to the significant time and expense of the analysis.

There is momentum toward global standardized reporting. Some barriers, however, exist to standardization. These barriers range from limited know-how, to data collection time constraints, to the multiplicity of standards and platforms. Additional staff or increased training may be required to take on the new task of collecting, analyzing, and reporting data. Even if there is support, appropriate systems may not be in place to collect the data. Executive support and time allocation to review and approve reports may be limited. Moreover, additional time and costs are also embedded in preparing the report and having it verified or audited for legitimacy.

The multiplicity of competing reporting standards and organizations also works against the goal of reporting (see Table 6.1 for a snapshot of some examples of this multiplicity). Different content, requirements, and audiences challenge businesses to select and commit to a reporting format. However, in recent years, some of the main reporting mechanisms—including the GRI, the CDP, and the United Nations Global Compact—have made efforts to align information required to facilitate translation between standards (UNEP 2014). Initiatives like these are contributing to better alignment for corporate standardized reporting.

6.2 Methods of Disclosing and Reporting

Companies can take a variety of routes to disclose and report their environmental impacts. The method for how to assess and what to report is based on a company's preferences. The most popular method is the CSR report as a supplement to the company's annual financial report. Some companies use general and area-specific protocols and guidelines to formulate their reports, including the GRI, the Greenhouse Gas Protocol, and the Water Footprint Network (WFN). Protocols guide how and what to assess and report. Once a company has assessed its impacts, corporate decision makers can then choose to report solely through their individual reports or to disclose their impacts through a variety of platforms. The GRI serves as both a set of guidelines and a reporting platform for general sustainability indicators. For carbon reporting, the CDP and SmartWay serve as reporting platforms. For water, the WFN serves as the protocol to assess water and wastewater, while the CDP serves as a platform for reporting.

6.2.1 Firm Reporting

CSR reports have been and are the traditional way for companies to voluntarily disclose information to a variety of stakeholders about their non-financial performance. CSR reports not only disclose social and environmental activities, they may also recognize achievements by employees beyond their day-to-day responsibilities. CSR reports are very often "free-form"; a company can choose to include any activity it considers worth sharing with external and internal stakeholders. CSR reports are also marketing-driven and not necessarily connected with firm operations or the corporate mission.

Most companies report some quantitative metrics that serve as indicators for their environmental impacts. These metrics may be potentially comparable across an industry if peer companies use the same metric. The metrics might cover CO_2 emissions, water usage, waste generation, and others. Companies may also create targets and goals. For example, Johnson and Johnson, a health products company, proposed to achieve a 20 % absolute reduction of facilities CO_2 emissions by 2020, from a baseline of 2010 (Johnson and Johnson 2014). This makes it easier for external stakeholders to gauge progress relative to the metrics the companies are reporting. In addition to the most common practices of environmental metrics and target setting, companies may also engage third parties to verify their reports and validate their accuracy with organizations such as Trucost (Trucost 2014).

A final method of reporting is environmental cost accounting. This means that the companies also include information on financial and non-financial costs and benefits of a company's environmental strategy (OECD 2013). For example, General Motors reported saving $1 billion a year through reuse and recycling of by-products through waste avoidance (Triple Pundit 2012).

The type and breadth of information shared in CSR reports varies widely. For example, Seventh Generation, an environmentally focused homecare company, includes information ranging from product formulas and data on environmentally sensitive materials sourcing to community engagement information (Seventh Generation 2013). The report covers goals set by the company, highlights its progress towards these goals, and provides qualitative coverage of environmental and social action throughout the company.

On the other hand, CSR reports can be quite limited, and their quality can vary greatly over time. In 2010, British Petroleum (BP) released a sustainability report that addressed its role in the Gulf of Mexico Oil Spill without reporting the extensive environmental consequences of the amount of oil spilled in the gulf. The report also failed to disclose the amount of CO_2 or methane released as a consequence of the spill, and it only set forth a single and vague environmental goal (BP 2010). Furthermore, the report included minimal stakeholder input. Although BP's report was considerably lacking, the oil and gas giant had actually been long considered a leader in reporting, releasing one of the first major sustainability reports in 1998. BP also received reporting awards in subsequent years (Triple 2015).

Other companies opt to commit to many different goals; for example, Marks and Spencer proposed 100 different commitments that it reports on annually. These commitments include, but are not limited to, improving building energy efficiency, reducing food waste, and achieving zero-carbon operations. The 2014 report highlighted company goals and the annual progress achieved on each. That report disclosed that 12 commitments were incomplete, 9 were fully achieved, and 79 were on track to be finished by the proposed deadline (Marks and Spencer 2014). For example, the goal that 50 % of cotton used would be sourced sustainably by 2020 had achieved a rate of 20 % by 2014. Marks and Spencer's UK emissions totaled 533,000 t of CO_2 in 2014, down from 698,000 t in 2006; this represents an overall reduction of 37 % with a final goal of carbon neutral operations in 2020. The company's zero-waste-to-landfill-in-operations goal was achieved and maintained through 2014 with 100 % of waste recycled, despite an 11 % increase in waste production that year.

While most companies release their own sustainability reports, they also participate in a variety of standardized reporting protocols and platforms to assess and communicate their practices. The GRI is the primary reporting initiative through which companies disclose social and environmental practices.

6.2.2 General Reporting Platforms

In an attempt to provide more structured guidance to CSR reporting, CERES launched the GRI in 1998. In 2001, GRI became a separate organization focusing on corporate social and environmental reporting. As of 2015, the GRI reported that 7546 organizations had a profile in its Sustainability Disclosure Database and that 18,744 GRI Reports had been filed (GRI 2014b).

As a part of its efforts, GRI defines metrics and provides guidance for reporting year to year. The GRI recommends a four-step process for defining report content (GRI 2013) that includes identification, prioritization, validation, and review. The identification process begins by considering the GRI aspect list, stakeholder concerns, and existing impacts. Following an analysis of these considerations, a company prioritizes these concerns by evaluating their individual significance to the organization and their influence on stakeholders; define thresholds of materiality to the company; and decide the coverage on the issue. The third step, validation, sets up the systems to collect and measure the information and translates internal data into digestible public disclosures. The final step is a review of the collected material, assessed with previously reported information, and preparation for the next round of reporting. This step-by-step process is detailed extensively in the GRI's "G4: Sustainability Reporting Guidelines," to help companies manage the process year to year (GRI 2013). However, it is largely up to each company itself to determine and implement strategies to improve its reported scores.

Unlike previous versions of the GRI's reporting guidelines, the G4 guidelines include supply chain disclosure as a major component. The boundary of what a company should report on is extended from just a company's individual operations to the full value chain to better understand where impacts occur both upstream and downstream. To visualize these impacts, the G4 guidelines recommend conducting a value-chain assessment to map some of the company's key products and/or services. During the mapping process, the company collects information about impacts at each stage of the supply chain. The data may be derived from the company itself or through the use of proxy data from life cycle management databases. To enable this increase in scope, the GRI initiated the Business Transparency Program that allows suppliers and smaller companies to report under the "umbrella" of a larger organization. The program supports the implementation of reporting within suppliers to manage risk and improve sustainability performance.

GRI facilitates comparison of corporate practices globally. The GRI's reporting framework outlines over 100 environmental, social, economic, and governance topics on which companies may report (See Table 6.2) (GRI 2013). Although the framework includes many topics from different focus areas, companies are encouraged to report only on those applicable to their business. Because of the framework's broader focus, companies often use their GRI report as a basis for their sustainability report. For example, Microsoft uses the 2013 GRI Sustainability Reporting Guidelines in the creation of its annual sustainability report (Microsoft 2014).

Table 6.2 GRI reporting framework topics (GRI)

Biodiversity
Location and size of land (owned, leased, managed) in or adjacent to protected areas and areas of high diversity value
Impacts of activities, products and services on biodiversity
Habitats protected or restored
Managing impacts on biodiversity
National conservation list species with habitats in areas affected by operations
Compliance
Monetary value of fines and total number of non-monetary sanctions for noncompliance to laws and regulations
Emissions, effluents, and waste
Total direct and indirect GHG emissions by weight
Other relevant indirect GHG emissions by weight
Reductions in GHGs achieved
Emissions of ozone-depleting substances by weight
No$_X$, So$_X$, and other air emissions by type and weight
Total water discharge by quality and destination
Total weight of waste by type and disposal method
And volume of spills
Weight of waste (transported, exported) deemed hazardous and percent of waste shipped internationally
Identity, size, protected status and biodiversity of water bodies and habitats affected by organization's discharges
Materials
Materials used by weight or volume
Percent of materials that are recycled
Energy
Direct energy consumption
Indirect energy consumption
Energy saved by conservation and efficiency
Provision of energy-efficient, renewable energy-based products and services; net energy reduction
Reducing indirect energy consumption; net energy reduction
Products and services
Mitigation of environmental impacts of products and services
Percent of products sold and packaging materials reclaimed by category
Transport
Environmental impacts of transporting goods and materials used for organization's operations and members of workforce
Overall
Total environmental protection expenditures by investment and type

6.2.3 Issue-Specific Reporting

Environmental disclosures via CSR reports, even when structured by GRI, are general in nature. When environmental topics gain prominence, specific guidelines that allow firms to perform more detailed reporting and disclosures and allow for benchmarking and credible target setting are often developed. These guidelines for reporting are commonly supported by reporting platforms that collect information and report it publicly in a centralized location. Although there are other competing protocols and platforms in the environmental reporting space, the following are those that have reached critical mass through the number of corporate users globally.

6.2.3.1 Carbon

Since the introduction of GHG emissions as a central component of the Kyoto Protocol of the United Nations Framework Convention on Climate Change, reporting of these emissions has become an increasingly common practice (United Nations 1998).

The Greenhouse Gas Protocol Corporate Standard is the main accounting tool for businesses to quantify their GHG emissions. Started as a partnership between the World Resources Institute and the World Business Council for Sustainable Development, the protocol divides emissions into three scopes (see Fig. 6.1) (Greenhouse Gas 2014). Scope 1 includes the emissions that come directly from company-owned operations. The second scope includes indirect emissions from the purchase of electricity, heat, or steam. The third scope includes all other indirect emissions including, but not limited to, activities that are not owned by the company—such as employee travel, waste disposal, outsourced activities, and production of purchased materials, customer impacts, and end-of-life product disposal. In many cases, about 80% of a business' emissions occur in Scope 3 (WRI and WBCSD 2011).

Most companies are able to report on Scope 1 because they have control over the emissions in question. However, emissions in the Scope 2 and Scope 3 categories are difficult for companies to account for, measure, and report because most of the activities are not under their direct control; this is especially true in the case of Scope 3 (Blanco et al. 2014). To identify Scope 2 and 3 emissions, companies must rely on upstream suppliers and/or downstream buyers to understand the full life cycle impacts of their practices and goods (Greenhouse Gas 2014).

To calculate the emissions at each scale, "emissions factors" (the amount of direct or indirect GHG emissions of a given practice), companies may collect data that is specific to their practices. Alternatively, they can use generalized values available from the GHG Protocol to calculate impacts. With the ability to use generalized values for emissions amounts for certain practices or processes, a company can assess its Scope 1 emissions simply by collecting basic data from its own operations. For example, a company can collect data on the distance traveled by its trucks and use

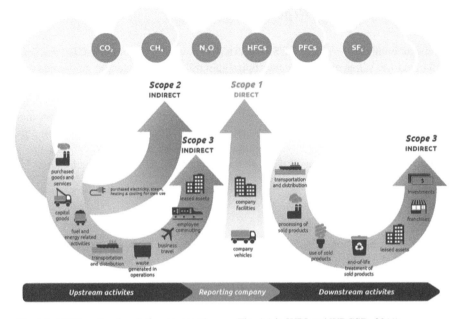

Fig. 6.1 GHG protocol emission scopes (*Source*: Fig. 1.1 in WRI and WBCSD, 2011)

this data to calculate emissions impacts using generalized values for vehicle emissions. The emissions factors are based on the best available data sets as determined by the GHG Protocol and are aligned with those used by the Intergovernmental Panel on Climate Change (IPCC), the internationally recognized body on climate change (Greenhouse Gas Protocol 2014). However, because practices can vary widely across time and region, the best emissions data is company-specific. Chapter 3 by Boukherroub et al. (2017) provides further background on carbon footprinting.

CDP

While the GHG Protocol serves as the reporting protocol, the CDP serves as a wider platform for emissions reporting. The CDP is a UK-based organization established in 2001 that enables large organizations to measure and report GHG. In 2002, the CDP sent out its first survey to engage companies in reporting; it received 221 responses from 500 surveyed companies (Winston 2010). Twelve years later, in 2014, the number of reporting companies had increased to 5003 (CDP 2015a, b, c).

For its reporting requirements, the CDP utilizes assessment guidelines and scope definitions outlined in the GHG Protocol. In recent years, it has expanded to include water, climate risk, and supply-chain wide reporting. The annual questionnaire includes over 100 questions spanning the range of emissions-producing activities. The findings are released every September along with two additional indices: the Carbon Disclosure Leadership Index and the Carbon Performance Leadership

Index, which acknowledge increasing levels of transparency and the greatest GHG reduction over previous years across reporting companies. Such reporting rankings may provide motivation for companies to continue to report and strive to match reductions of their peers.

An important feature of the CDP is that it contacts companies to report on behalf of investors. When a company reports to the CDP platform, it provides investors an annual resource of environmental impacts that "supports long-term objective analysis" (CDP 2015a). The CDP investor initiatives include 822 institutional investors with $95 trillion in assets under management (CDP 2015a). With pressure from investors, companies are encouraged to measure, disclose, and manage their emissions. In this way, investor pressure is playing a role in total emission reductions.

The CDP has also taken a step further into supply chain disclosure with its supply chain program. The program works with buyers and suppliers to collect GHG emissions data information from the suppliers. In Europe and North America, 64 companies currently participate in the program, and the CDP supply chain program facilitates reporting from 5600 of their suppliers (CDP 2014b). The CDP designs and circulates a survey to assess the practices of the suppliers. This survey includes a 17-page questionnaire with 86 questions on issues including climate change risks, management, strategy, and policy. In 2013, of the 5600 suppliers surveyed, 2869 responded (CDP 2014b). This initiative helps to expand the system boundary of environmental reporting from companies to their supply chains. In most cases, however, the survey only addresses Tier 1 suppliers, even though global supply chains tend to be at least five or six tiers deep.

EPA SmartWay Program

In the case of logistics, the U.S. EPA's SmartWay Program serves as the main reporting platform in the U.S. The SmartWay program was created in 2004 to reduce environmental impacts across the goods movement industry. As a collaborative initiative, it brings together shippers, carriers, logistics service providers, and governmental entities. Shippers range from food companies like Chiquita to retail stores like Whole Foods. The program started with 15 motor carriers but has grown to 3000 in 2014, with major carriers such as Ryder and C.H. Robinson reporting to SmartWay (SmartWay 2014).

SmartWay provides tools to measure and report the impact of logistics carriers over time. Shippers use the assessments to select high-achieving carriers and to gauge progress over time. To measure their impact, carriers collect data from their operations such as miles driven, fuel used, vehicle model year, and cargo payload (EPA 2013). Using the SmartWay-provided tools together with their activity specific data, carriers calculate their environmental performance in grams-per-ton-mile or gram-per-mile emissions. Following the assessment, the carrier's information is publicly reported and ranked within its sector. SmartWay conducts random quality checks on reporting carriers to encourage accuracy in reporting.

In recent years, shippers began to commit to increasing the share of their freight moved by carriers that are SmartWay certified. This emphasis on certification provides market incentive for carriers not only to measure and report, but to reduce their environmental impacts relative to their peers. SmartWay also offers tools for benchmarking, vehicle environmental rankings, and guidance on how to replicate a SmartWay-style program internationally (SmartWay 2014).

6.2.3.2 Water

The WFN serves as a framework to calculate an organization's water footprint across the supply chain in the production of its goods and services. The WFN defines a water footprint as the "volume of freshwater used to produce the product, measured over the full supply chain" (Hoekstra et al. 2011, also Chap. 4 by Hoekstra (2017)). A water footprint includes information about volumes of water by source geographically and temporally. It further distinguishes water consumption in terms of blue, green, and grey water, which are defined as surface and groundwater, rainwater, and polluted water, respectively. As with many assessments, the water footprint is based on a focus area the company selects. For example, an assessment can focus on a specific process step within the supply chain or on the total water footprint of a final product; it can also assess the footprint of a specific producer or an entire economic sector (Hoekstra et al. 2011).

In 2010, the Coca Cola Company released a report entitled, "Product Water Footprint Assessments" (The Coca Cola Company 2010). To inform its sustainability water use goals with a comprehensive water footprint analysis, the global beverage company assessed indirect water use in its supply chain by accounting for packaging and ingredients, while also assessing direct operational water use in its bottling plants. The analysis revealed that the water footprint associated with the production of a half-liter of Coca Cola in Dongen, the Netherlands, equated to 12 L of grey water, 15 L of green water, and 8 L of blue water. From this assessment, Coca Cola was able to determine that two-thirds of the water footprint for that particular product was related to using blue and green water to grow sugar beets for drink ingredients, while one-third of the footprint was related to grey water effluents from the supply chain, which included nitrogen in the fertilizer for the beet field and the cooling water for PET production (The Coca Cola Company 2010). This indicated the company that a greater focus on sugar beets was important to address impacts on its water footprint.

At the time of this writing (2015), most companies were reporting their water footprint individually through their own websites or corporate sustainability reports; for example, Coca-Cola's water footprint is presented on a sub-domain discussing its efforts within its corporate website. Given the absence of a neutral water reporting platform, the CDP, in addition to its role as a carbon reporting platform, initiated a program to serve as a central water impact repository.

While the CDP is most known and used for its carbon reporting platform, CDP's water program is becoming increasingly utilized by companies and organizations alike to report their water impacts. Similar to its carbon questionnaire, which assists companies to collect relevant carbon impact information, CDP's water questionnaire provides guidance for companies to consistently assess, report annually, and act on their water impact (CDP 2015b). This allows investors to include a company's annual water performance in their decision making.

6.2.4   Product Level

If a company is working to achieve higher levels of environmental sustainability in the production of a product, it may include a label with environmental information to inform its consumers of its activities. These labels are sometimes called eco-labels. Eco-labels range widely in the areas they address, rigor of certification, categories and issues covered, and region of applicability. These multiple factors increase the challenges for both the company and the consumer. Additional voluntary labels, such as the Rainforest Alliance Certification that identifies socially and environmentally conscious farming practices, are also used.

Other voluntary labels offered by environmental organizations require companies to provide information about the supply chain in order to receive certification. For example, the Rainforest Alliance Certified™ Seal indicates that products are made from ingredients sourced from farms using the standards of the Sustainable Agriculture Network (Rainforest Alliance 2014). These standards include practices that protect local environments, workers, wildlife, and the communities from which materials are supplied. The seal indicates that the company has traceability to ensure verified practices.

Once this information has been vetted by the Rainforest Alliance, the company can place the seal on its products to indicate that the products include ingredients that are made with superior environmental and social practices. Another example is the Forest Stewardship Council Certification (FSC). FSC-certified products are made from materials sourced from forests managed using FSC Principles and Criteria. These criteria include maintaining high conservation value forests (HCVF), conserving resources such as biological diversity and water, and promoting social principles such as the protection of indigenous people's rights (FSC 2014).

There are also government-mandated labels, such as the US EPA's vehicle MPG (miles per gallon) label that indicates fuel efficiency. A newly updated label released by the US EPA in 2011 requires that information to inform consumers about smog and greenhouse gas tailpipe emissions on a 1–10 scale appears on the label (US DOE 2011). In addition to environmental impact ratings, this label also provides an MPG rating for city and highway driving and estimates the fuel cost savings for cars with better MPG than the average-performing car. The objectives of this label are to increase consumer awareness and preference for cars with better environmental performance and encourage the car market to support this demand.

When deciding whether or not to pursue any type of labeling, a company must first decide whether it is worth the time, effort, and expense of obtaining some form of label. This question may arise because some consumers may have no knowledge of or interest in the label's disclosures. For example, a 2010 study by Delmas and Grant showed that wine producers featuring the USDA Organic label on their bottles actually had to reduce their selling prices to get consumers to buy their products (Delmas and Grant 2010). This may be due to a perception that organic wines are of lower quality. However, in other cases, the high recognition and regard for a label by local consumers may allow a company to gain a price premium for its products. For example, Bjørner et al. (2004) found that consumers in Denmark were willing to pay 10–17 % more for toilet paper labeled with the Nordic Swan certification, a local multi-criteria environmental label. This demonstrates that a company must think strategically about potential price and reputation benefits, if any, prior to obtaining a label.

A majority of labels represent sustainability at only one phase or dimension of the supply chain. For example, the MPG label only accounts for the environmental impact at the consumer use phase of driving the automobile but indicates nothing about the impact of the manufacturing processes or vehicle recycling. The USDA organic label informs the consumer that produce has been farmed organically but gives no information about the transportation impacts from farm to store or whether virgin forest was destroyed to make the farm. Some labels seek to inform the consumer about the full life cycle carbon, water use, or waste impacts of a product across the supply chain, from materials to manufacturing to transportation. The Carbon Trust is one organization offering a label of this type, called the Carbon Footprint Label (Carbon Trust 2015). The Carbon Footprint Label displays the total carbon impact of a product over its entire life cycle. The Carbon Trust also offers certification that discloses total water usage, management, and effluent, as well as waste management and disposal. A company can inform consumers about the total impact of a product, such as grams of CO_2 produced, with a measurement label. The company can also communicate to consumers that it has reduced the overall footprint of that product with a reduction label. To attain this level of disclosure, a company must assess the impact of its products through life cycle assessment.

6.2.4.1 Life Cycle Assessment

For companies that want to take disclosure a step further, a Life Cycle Assessment (LCA) offers deep insight into the environmental impacts of a company's products. (See Chap. 2 by Guinée and Heijungs (2017) for a comprehensive introduction to LCA.) This rigorous assessment tool accounts not only for the company's environmental impacts but also for those of its upstream suppliers and downstream buyers to provide the fullest depth of detail possible. LCAs became widely used in the 1970s and 1980s, during a period of growing environmental awareness and an energy crisis. However, when manufacturers began to calculate LCAs for their products, they often used varying methodologies that had not been scrutinized or validated, and assessments were often manipulated to support a preferred outcome. To overcome this, the International Organization for Standardization (ISO) introduced a standardized LCA methodology in 1997 (ISO 2006). The LCA methodology includes four steps that are designed to account for a product's total environmental impact.

The LCA's four steps include: goal and scope definition; inventory analysis; impact assessment; and interpretation. The Goal and Scope Definition element informs a company about the system boundary of its product. Inventory Analysis facilitates the collection of data for all inputs and outputs of a final product and its end of life. Impact Assessment uses the collected data to calculate the specified inputs and outputs, and Interpretation provides a discussion of the analysis results, highlighting limitations and recommendations as related to the original goal of the study (ISO 2006).

If a company wants faster results, software systems such as SimaPro (Pre Sustainability 2014) and GaBi (2014), which use databases that draw from generalizable data sets for specific activities such as Ecoinvent (2014), are often used to conduct an LCA. An LCA provides insight into the greatest sources of impact along the supply chain. However, the practice incorporates some sensitivity flaws when generalized data sets or incorrect assumptions are used.

Although the Life Cycle Assessment offers a more complete picture of a company's impacts across its supply chain, the findings go largely unreported. Many companies use the tool primarily to obtain information about which areas in their supply chain offer the greatest opportunities to reduce environmental impact. Companies also may not report their results because they believe that the complex nature of the information would not be generally understood by the public.

6.3 Environmental Reporting Strategy

The practice of reporting helps a business understand its impact and seek appropriate action to minimize this impact. To effectively manage impact reduction over time, companies must set up a regular reporting cycle, which includes collection of data, communication of results, and external feedback (GRI 2014a, b). If reporting is regular, then environmental actions are more closely monitored and evaluated, which can make them more successful. In addition, this process keeps all stakeholders, both internal and external, informed. Internal alignment with reporting can engage company executives to help align sustainability with company strategy.

6.3.1 Decision to Report

In many cases, companies are leading the way by reporting without the pressure of regulation. They report to contend with competitors or to satisfy stakeholder pressures. Although companies are proactively disclosing, internal practices are not always aligned to support robust sustainability reporting. Much data collection continues to be ad hoc, with a few individuals gathering necessary information from around the company through emails and Excel spreadsheets. Some software solutions are emerging through organizations like Enviance (2015) and Systems, Applications and Products in Data Processing (SAP). SAP is a German multinational software corporation that developed the Product Stewardship Network (2015) to assist corporations with their reporting. Intelex and the EHS Regulatory Documentation OnDemand offer similar software solutions (2015). These tools allow a company to track environmental data across the company or products; some also manage regulatory limits as applicable to the company. Although helpful, these software solutions have limitations in terms of supply chain scope, training requirements, compatibility with enterprise systems, and cost. The variability in data collection also influences the content of reports.

In addition, the scale of reporting does not always indicate quality or accuracy. For example, research commissioned by the European Union indicated that, although companies operating in Europe are releasing environmental reports, the information may be lacking in substance (Wensen et al. 2011). The information provided is incomplete and selective, designed only to show positive company practices, and the information provided may be skewed. The report goes on to say that regulation of sustainability reports may improve the content and accuracy of the reports and standardize reporting across companies (Wensen et al. 2011). In addition to the challenges of selective representation and accuracy, reports tend to have a limited focus. As previously noted, because a company only has direct control over and visibility into its own operations and little leverage to account for and manage upstream suppliers and downstream buyers, supply chain impacts are largely absent from the reports.

Companies are increasingly interested in understanding the impacts of their supply chains, either voluntarily or because they are required to evaluate them by pressure or mandate. However, the practice of supply chain assessment beyond a company's direct operations brings numerous additional challenges. In many cases, in order to obtain the information required to account for the full impact of the supply chain, companies send out questionnaires, surveys, or scorecards to their suppliers. These documents ask the suppliers to report their environmental impacts and to allow the requesting company to gauge their full impact. This initiates what is sometimes referred to as the "survey waterfall": when the initiating company requests information about a supplier's practices, it must also survey the supplier's suppliers, and so on. Often, suppliers may lack the knowledge or tools to conduct such an assessment. In some cases, the requesting company will support its suppliers in learning how to audit their practices. For example, when Siemens' started to assess its suppliers and their energy use in an attempt to reduce its total carbon footprint, it provided both training and a methodology for suppliers (Siemens 2012).

In other cases, specific industries have developed a standard questionnaire. For example, the electronics sector offers the Electronics Industry Citizenship Coalition Self-Assessment Questionnaire (EICC 2014). The pharmaceutical industry developed the Pharmaceutical Supply Chain Initiative Self-Assessment Questionnaire (Pharmaceutical Supply Chain Initiative 2013). These industry initiatives are beneficial because they reduce the burden on suppliers to respond to differing requests for information from various buyers; they also provide a clear standard and guidance for reporting and offer tools to address environmental challenges.

6.3.2 The Role of Third Parties in Reporting

In cases where there is no industry standard, or where a company has limited capacity to contact its supply chain partners, a third party may be engaged to conduct environmental data collection. Designed initially around risk management issues, organizations like EcoVadis now additionally focus on environmental reporting. EcoVadis' primary role is to collect information from suppliers on behalf of its customers. To do this, it sends a questionnaire to suppliers that includes questions on topics ranging from child labor to carbon emissions, as requested by the customer. EcoVadis then manages the entire information-gathering process—from crafting the questions to following up on non-responsive suppliers to obtain data a company needs to assess its supply chain impacts (EcoVadis 2014). It also asks for documentation from suppliers to support answers and data provided.

EcoVadis and other such companies serve as intermediaries between companies needing to collect relevant data and their suppliers through reporting platforms. Platforms of this type can be beneficial to both buyers and suppliers. Buyers have an organization collecting the necessary data for them, and suppliers have a repository for their information from which to draw for other requesting buyers. In addition, if they so choose, suppliers can make information about their environmental practices public so other buyers may source from them if their practices are better than those of their peers. However, when engaging a middleman like EcoVadis, suppliers are assessed a fee to use these services and maintain their relationship with their buyer.

6.4 Future of Reporting

Although many driving factors have led to increased environmental reporting from companies internationally, the business impact of disclosure is still unclear. The motivations that drive reporting are often regulatory compliance, risk mitigation, and brand positioning. However, if reporting can be linked to increasing corporate value, the case for more widely spread and higher quality reporting can be made. Existing challenges that continue to prevent greater adoption of reporting include the time, cost, and limited benefits associated with reporting (Wensen et al. 2011). Further identification of clear boundaries, areas of focus, quality, and value to the company will increase motivation to report for companies of all sizes and across jurisdictions.

6.4.1 Future Trends

Several trends can be seen in the future of reporting. The first is the consolidation and standardization of various disclosure paradigms and reporting schemes used by companies. Currently, companies face multiple mandatory and voluntary standards, and additional (often different) organizations exist to which companies report. Not only are standards sometimes unconnected to reporting mechanisms, but they also address different issues (carbon, water, deforestation, social). Furthermore, they may have different geographical scopes, such as state (California), national (United States), regional (European Union), or global. This multiplicity impedes high-quality reporting practices at companies, and it also confuses external readers of the reports: the different forms of reporting can overwhelm even the most conscientious environmentalist.

The next major trend is the shift from company-wide to supply chain-wide reporting. As previously discussed, upstream and downstream impacts are not currently included in most reports. Preliminary assessments are conducted on a limited and private scale; this includes the increasingly common practice of LCA to assess the full impact of a product. At this time, the disclosure of LCA findings is not common. Reporting institutions such as CDP are beginning to address the supply chain issue through supplier questionnaires and other programs (Jira and Toffel 2013), but these only address first-tier suppliers. Although this practice may be limited, the findings are promising. A report commissioned by CDP found that suppliers who had several buyers requesting information were more likely to report (CDP 2014b). The next major challenge will be for companies and reporting institutions to engage the deeper tiers to increase supply chain transparency.

An additional reporting trend can be observed in new platforms for reporting, such as social media and e-commerce. Digital communications in the form of social media have become the modern venue for information sharing. The platforms can serve to inform other businesses, the investing community, stakeholder groups, and customers. This trend can be seen in financial reporting, and it was addressed by the Securities and Exchange Commission (SEC) in 2013 through guidance for public companies on the use of social media. The SEC's intent was to align companies with obligations under the federal securities laws (U.S. Securities and Exchange Commission 2013). As companies find it more relevant to disclose financial events through social media, environmental disclosure may also follow this route.

In addition to disclosures through social media, e-commerce platforms such as online shopping and B2B marketplaces may be a new channel for environmental disclosures. As online marketplaces have proliferated and become mainstream with websites like Amazon, so has the engagement of the consumer with web-based information presented via those marketplaces. Consumer reviews and ingredient disclosures represent two forms of this type of data. To further inform consumers, companies may use e-commerce platforms as an additional opportunity to present environmental disclosures. For example, eBay Inc. created a supplemental website specifically to offer products with positive environmental attributes under green. eBay.com (eBay 2015). These products have better environmental attributes and more environmental disclosures than do their counterparts. This trend is likely to continue across other products.

The final major trend involves transitioning from merely reporting environmental impacts to also managing them. In many cases, companies are seeing reporting as a box to be checked. If they have reported their impacts and seen no major external feedback, their environmental engagement ends. If reporting is treated as a management tool, however, a business might be better equipped to identify key issues and to set appropriate goals backed by solid metrics (MacLean and Rebernak 2007). If reporting were linked with clear metrics to assess how company activities are creating environmental impacts, the rationale behind reporting could be strengthened.

References

Barnea A, Rubin A (2010) Corporate Social Responsibility as a Conflict Between Shareholders. J Business Ethics (97):71–86

Bjørner TB, Hansen LG, Russell CS (2004) Environmental labeling and consumers' choice—an empirical analysis of the effect of the Nordic Swan. J Environ Econ Manag 47(3):411–434

Blanco C, Caro F, Corbett C (2014) The state of Scope 3 carbon emissions reporting in supply chain, Working Paper

Blass V, Chebach TC, Ashkenazy A (2017) Sustainable non-renewable materials management. In: Bouchery Y, Corbett CJ, Fransoo J, Tan T (eds) Sustainable supply chains: a research-based textbook on operations and strategy. Springer, New York

Boukherroub T, Bouchery Y, Corbett CJ, Fransoo J, Tan T (2017) Carbon footprinting in supply chains. In: Bouchery Y, Corbett CJ, Fransoo J, Tan T (eds) Sustainable supply chains: a research-based textbook on operations and strategy. Springer, New York

British Petroleum (2010) Sustainability review. http://www.bp.com/content/dam/bp/pdf/sustainability/group-reports/bp_sustainability_review_2010.pdf. Accessed May 2015

Buckley PJ (2002) Is the international business research agenda running out of steam? J Int Bus Res 33(2):365–373

Businessweek (2014) The conflict over conflict-free minerals. http://www.businessweek.com/articles/2014-06-05/conflict-free-minerals-intel-apple-and-hp-struggle-to-comply. Accessed Sept 2014

CARB (2011) Overview of ARB emissions trading program. http://www.arb.ca.gov/newsrel/2011/cap_trade_overview.pdf. Accessed Dec 2014

CARB (2014a) Mandatory greenhouse gas emissions reporting. from: http://www.arb.ca.gov/cc/reporting/ghg-rep/ghg-rep.htm. Accessed Dec 2014

CARB (2014b) California air resources board: cap-and-trade-program. http://www.arb.ca.gov/cc/capandtrade/capandtrade.htm. Accessed Dec 2014

Carbon Trust (2015) Certification. http://www.carbontrust.com/client-services/footprinting/footprint-certification. Accessed June 2015

CDP (2014a) Reports and data. https://www.cdp.net/en-US/Results/Pages/overview.aspx. Accessed Sept 2014

CDP (2014b) Collaborative action on climate risk: supply chain report 2013–2014. https://www.cdp.net/CDPResults/CDP-Supply-Chain-Report-2014.pdf. Accessed November 2014

CDP (2015a) CDP investor initiatives. https://www.cdp.net/en-US/WhatWeDo/Pages/investors.aspx. Accessed Sept 2014

CDP (2015b) CDP water program. https://www.cdp.net/water. Accessed June 2015

CDP (2015c) Reports and data. https://www.cdp.net/en-US/Results/Pages/overview.aspx. Accessed June 2015

Dell (2010) EU REACH SVHC Disclosure on candidate list. http://i.dell.com/sites/doccontent/corporate/environment/en/Documents/earth-materials-REACH-tables-2010.pdf. Accessed Sept 2014

Delmas M, Grant L (2010) Eco-labeling strategies and price-premium: the wine industry puzzle. Bus Soc

Department of the Commissioner-General for Sustainable Development (2012) Display of the environmental footprint of products. No. 64, April 2012

Dow Jones Sustainability Indices (2013). Press release: results announced for 2013 Dow Jones sustainability indices review; 24 Sustainability Industry Group Leaders Named. S&P Dow Jones Indices and RobecoSAM. http://www.sustainability-indices.com/images/130912-djsi-review-2013-en-vdef.pdf. Accessed May 2015

Dow Jones Sustainability Indices (2014) Dow Jones sustainability indices: methodology. http://www.djindexes.com/mdsidx/downloads/meth_info/Dow_Jones_Sustainability_Indices_Methodology.pdf. Accessed May 2015

Dow Jones Sustainability Indices (2015) Dow Jones sustainability indices: overview. http://www.djindexes.com/sustainability/. Accessed May 2015

eBay (2015) Green products on eBay. http://pages.ebay.com/html/greenplan.html. Accessed May 2015

Ecoinvent (2014) Discover Ecoinvent 3. www.ecoinvent.org. Accessed Nov 2014

Ecovadis (2014) Supplier solutions. http://www.ecovadis.com/website/l-en/supplier-solutions.EcoVadis-41.aspx. Accessed Dec 2014

EICC (2014) EICC assessment tools help members meet our standards and drive continuous improvement. http://www.eiccoalition.org/standards/assessment/. Accessed Nov 2014

Enviance (2015) Environmental compliance and data management. http://www.enviance.com/solutions/environmental-compliance.aspx. Accessed June 2015

EPA (2013) SmartWay Transport partnership: driving data integrity in transportation supply chains. http://epa.gov/smartway/forpartners/documents/dataquality/420b13005.pdf. Accessed Dec 2014

EPA (2015) Toxics release inventory (TRI) program. http://www2.epa.gov/toxics-release-inventory-tri-program. Accessed May 2015

Ethical Corporation (2013) Full product transparency is the future of reporting. http://www.ethicalcorp.com/print/36497?utm_source=http%3A%2F%2Fuk...nsparency%20is%20the%20future%20of%20reporting&utm_content=321467. Accessed Sept 2014

Europa (2014) Summaries of EU legislation: regulatory framework for the management of chemicals (REACH), European Chemicals Agency. http://europa.eu/legislation_summaries/internal_market/single_market_for_goods/chemical_products/l21282_en.htm. Accessed Sept 2014

European Chemicals Agency (2014) List of restrictions table. http://echa.europa.eu/web/guest/addressing-chemicals-of-concern/restrictions/list-of-restrictions/list-of-restrictions-table. Accessed Sept 2014

FSC (2014) Forest management certification. https://us.fsc.org/forest-management-certification.225.htm. Accessed December 2014

GaBi (2014) GaBi sustainability software. http://www.gabi-software.com/america/index/. Accessed Nov 2014

GPO (2012). Dodd-Frank wall street reform and consumer protection act. H.R. 4173, United States, Securities and Exchange Commission

Greenhouse Gas Protocol (2014) GHG protocol website. http://www.ghgprotocol.org/calculation-tools/faq. Accessed Sept 2014

GRI (2011) Report or explain: why all big companies should report their sustainability performance, or explain why they don't. https://www.globalreporting.org/SiteCollectionDocuments/ReportOrExplainBrochure.pdf. Accessed Sept 2015

GRI (2013) G4: sustainability reporting guidelines. https://www.globalreporting.org/resourcelibrary/GRIG4-Part1-Reporting-Principles-and-Standard-Disclosures.pdf. Accessed May 2015

GRI (2014a) About GRI. https://www.globalreporting.org/information/about-gri/Pages/default.aspx. Accessed Sept 2014

GRI (2014b) Sustainability disclosure database. http://database.globalreporting.org. Accessed May 2015

Guinée J, Heijungs R (2017) Introduction to life cycle assessment. In: Bouchery Y, Corbett CJ, Fransoo J, Tan T (eds) Sustainable supply chains: a research-based textbook on operations and strategy. Springer, New York

Haddock-Fraser J, Fraser I (2008) Assessing corporate environmental reporting motivations: differences between 'Close-to-Market' and 'Business-to-Business' companies. Corp Soc Responsib Environ Manag 15:140–155

Hoekstra AY (2017) Water footprint assessment in supply chains. In: Bouchery Y, Corbett CJ, Fransoo J, Tan T (eds) Sustainable supply chains: a research-based textbook on operations and strategy. Springer, New York

Hoekstra AA, Chapagain M, Aldaya MM (2011) The water footprint assessment manual: setting the global standard. Earthscan, London

Intelex (2015) Environmental management system: the better way to manage environmental impacts and compliance. http://www.intelex.com/. Accessed June 2015

International Organization for Standardization (ISO) 14040 (2006) Environmental management—life cycle assessment—principles and framework. ISO, Geneva

IRSE (2012) The Grenelle II Act in France: a milestone towards integrated reporting. Institute RSE survey n7, June 2012. http://www.capitalinstitute.org/sites/capitalinstitute.org/files/docs/Institut%20RSE%20The%20grenelle%20II%20Act%20in%20France%20June%202012.pdf. Accessed December 2014

Jacobs B, Subramanian R, Hora M, Singhal V (2017) Market value implications of voluntary corporate environmental initiatives. In: Bouchery Y, Corbett CJ, Fransoo J, Tan T (eds) Sustainable supply chains: a research-based textbook on operations and strategy. Springer, New York

Jira C, Toffel M (2013) Engaging supply chains in climate change. Manuf Serv Oper Manag 15(4):559–577, Articles in Advance: 1–19

Johnson and Johnson (2014) Citizenship and Sustainability Report. http://www.jnj.com/sites/default/files/pdf/cs/2014-JNJ-Citizenship-Sustainability-Report.pdf. Accessed June 2015

KPMG (2013) International survey of corporate responsibility reporting 2013. http://www.kpmg.com/global/en/issuesandinsights/articlespublications/corporate-responsibility/pages/default.aspx. Accessed June 2015

MacLean R, Rebernak K (2007) Closing the credibility gap: the challenges of corporate responsibility reporting. Environ Qual Manag 16(4):1–6. doi:10.1002/tqem

Marks and Spencer (2014) M&S Annual Report 2014. http://annualreport.marksandspencer.com/?utm_source=Master+List&utm_campaign=3fe4407c54-Marks+&+Spencer+June+2014&utm_medium=email&utm_term=0_92af8574fc-3fe4407c54-. Accessed Sept 2014

Microsoft (2014) Global reporting initiative index. http://www.microsoft.com/about/corporatecitizenship/en-us/reporting/key-performance-indicators/. Accessed Dec 2014

OECD (2003) an overview of corporate environmental management practices. Joint Study by the OECD Secretariat and EIRIS. http://www.oecd.org/daf/inv/corporateresponsibility/18269204.pdf. Accessed Sept 2015

Pharmaceutical Supply Chain Initiative (2013) Supporting suppliers to operate consistent with industry expectations for ethics, labor, health and safety, environment and management systems. http://www.pharmaceuticalsupplychain.org. Accessed Sept 2014

Pre Sustainability (2014) SimaPro—world's leading LCA software. http://www.pre-sustainability.com/simapro. Accessed Sept 2014

Rainforest Alliance (2014) Agriculture certification. http://www.rainforest-alliance.org/agriculture/certification. Accessed Dec 2014

Sanyal J, Neves R (1991) The Valdez principles: implications for corporate social responsibility. J Bus Ethics 10:883–890

SAP (2015) SAP product stewardship network. http://www.sap.com/pc/tech/cloud/software/product-stewardship-network/overview/index.html. Accessed June 2015

Seventh Generation (2013) Future tense: 2012 corporate consciousness report. http://2013.7genreport.com/2012_Corporate_Responsibility_Report/#/1/. Accessed May 2015

Siemens (2012) CDP webinar—energy efficiency for customers. Munich June 27, 2012

SmartWay (2014) Partners and affiliate lists. http://www.epa.gov/smartway/about/partnerlists. htm. Accessed Sept 2014

The Coca Cola Company & The Nature Conservancy (2010) Product water footprint assessment: practical application in corporate water stewardship. http://assets.coca-colacompany.com/6f/6 1/43df76c8466d97c073675d1c5f65/TCCC_TNC_WaterFootprintAssessments.pdf. Accessed May 2015

Triple Pundit (2012) GM's recycling division now generates $1B annually. http://www.triplepundit.com/2012/10/gm-zero-waste/. Accessed Dec 2014

Triple Pundit (2015) BP: back in the picture. http://www.triplepundit.com/2015/01/bp-back-picture/. Accessed June 2015

Trucost (2014) Data validation & assurance. http://trucost.com/environmental-data-validation. Accessed Dec 2014

UNEP (2014) Corporate sustainability reporting. http://www.unep.org/resourceefficiency/ Business/SustainableandResponsibleBusiness/CorporateSustainabilityReporting/tabid/78907/ Default.aspx. Accessed Dec 2014

United Nations (1998) Kyoto protocol to the United Nations framework convention on climate change. United Nations International treaty

United Nations Global Compact (2015) Basic COP template. https://www.unglobalcompact.org/ docs/communication_on_progress/templates/Basic/Basic_COP_EN.pdf. Accessed May 2015

US DOE (2011) Gasoline vehicles: learn more about the new label. www.fueleconomy.gov/feg/ label/learn-more-gasoline-label.shtml. Accessed Sept 2014

US Securities and Exchange Commission (2013) SEC says social media OK for company announcements if investors are alerted. http://www.sec.gov/News/PressRelease/Detail/ PressRelease/1365171513574. Accessed May 2015

Wensen et al (2011) The state of play in sustainability reporting in the European Union. Report Commissioned by the European Union's Programme for Employment and Social Solidarity: PROGRESS (2007–2013)

Winston (2010) The most powerful green NGO you've never heard of. HBR blogs. http://blogs. hbr.org/winston/2010/10/the-most-powerful-green-ngo.html. Accessed Sept 2014

WRI and WBCSD (2011) Corporate value chain (Scope 3) accounting and reporting standard. World Resources Institute and World Business Council

Part II
Operational Aspects
of Sustainable Supply Chains

Chapter 7
Green Logistics

Edgar E. Blanco and Yossi Sheffi

7.1 Introduction

Logistics encompasses the business processes that plan, control, and implement the flow of goods and related information between points of origin and points of consumption to meet customer demand. It does so by managing transportation, warehousing, and inventory decisions across the company and, whenever possible, across its supply chain.

Traditionally, logistics decisions have been driven by minimizing cost, maximizing profitability, or achieving customer service targets. As companies have added sustainability goals to their business objectives, there has been an increased interest in mitigating the social and environmental impact of their products and operations. This new focus has also impacted the field of logistics: transportation providers are expected to reduce greenhouse gas emissions from their vehicles, warehouse managers have focused on waste and energy reduction strategies, and products are redesigned to increase recyclability and reuse, which require different inventory planning needs.

Green Logistics refers to the systematic measurement, analysis, and, ultimately, mitigation of the environmental impact of logistics activities. This effort to mitigate environmental externalities in logistics activities includes reducing of consumption of nonrenewable energy sources, air emissions (e.g., particulate matter), greenhouse gas emissions, and waste. Some of these efforts may be technological, such as

E.E. Blanco (✉)
MIT Center for Transportation & Logistics, Cambridge, MA, USA

Walmart Stores, San Bruno, CA, USA
e-mail: eblanco@mit.edu

Y. Sheffi
MIT Center for Transportation & Logistics, Cambridge, MA, USA
e-mail: sheffi@mit.edu

© Yann Bouchery, Charles J. Corbett, Jan C. Fransoo, and Tarkan Tan 2017   147
Y. Bouchery et al. (eds.), *Sustainable Supply Chains*, Springer Series in Supply
Chain Management 4, DOI 10.1007/978-3-319-29791-0_7

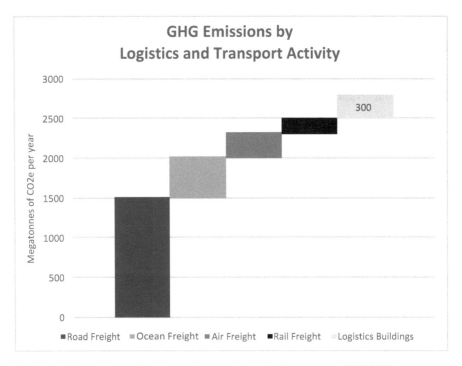

Fig. 7.1 GHG emissions of logistics and transport activity (*Data source*: WEF, 2009)

replacing vehicle fleets from diesel to hybrid or replacing cardboard boxes with returnable totes. Other strategies involve better ways to plan and execute the movement of goods, such as increasing the utilization of trucks while maintaining inventory levels under control; or using modes of transportation that have lower greenhouse gas emissions. Finally, some green logistics initiatives may be in support of larger business environmental goals, such as increasing reverse logistics activities to recover and reuse more of the products delivered to customers.

The International Energy Agency (IEA 2009) estimates that transport as a whole accounts for 19 % of global energy use and 23 % of energy-related carbon dioxide (CO_2) emission. Under current policies and technology trends, these emissions are expected to grow 50 % by 2030 and between 80 and 130 % by 2050 from 2007 levels. Within the transportation sector, freight, especially trucking, is expected to experience the fastest growth. In the USA, medium and heavy-duty freight trucks account for more than 60 % of the freight transportation emissions and are growing faster than any other mode (Greene and Plotkin 2001). Figure 7.1 provides an overall estimate of CO_2 emissions from freight transport and logistics activities. Transport is responsible for about 90 % of these emissions. The main focus of this chapter on green logistics consequently relates to freight transportation.

This chapter is organized as follows. Section 7.2 describes the main environmental impacts of logistic operations, namely greenhouse gases, pollution, noise, vibration, and packaging waste. Details on how these impacts could be estimated and their relative importance is discussed. Section 7.3 focuses on the importance and subtleties of measuring green logistics. Section 7.4 introduces the various green logistics strategies available to mitigate these impacts. These strategies are presented within a framework of decision-making, including a discussion on how to leverage two important modeling approaches to achieve green logistics: network design and vehicle routing. Using real-life success stories, Sect. 7.5 discusses how organizations collaborate to implement green logistics in practice. We conclude with a discussion on other strategies and relevant aspects of a sound green logistics strategy.

7.2   The Environmental Impact of Logistics

As goods flow from origins to destinations through the logistics network, they are moved in conveyances (e.g., planes, trucks, ships, motorcycles) powered by fossil fuels (e.g., diesel, petrol). During the engine combustion process, visible and invisible gasses are emitted through exhaust pipes that impact the local, regional, and global atmospheric composition, ranging from local air, water, or soil pollution to global climate change. Energy used during storage and handling of goods also impacts the atmosphere, albeit not always directly, but indirectly through nonrenewable energy use. The transport conveyances also generate noise and vibration as they navigate roads, highways, and waterways, thereby affecting human and wildlife quality of life. Finally, additional packaging and materials is used to preserve the integrity of products before they reach customers. Inadequate disposal or excess waste of this additional protective packaging is another potential environmental impact of logistics.

In this section we will describe the four main environmental impacts of transportation operations in logistics: Greenhouse gas (GHG) emissions that affect global climate, pollution of air quality and water ways, noise and vibration that affect human health, and packaging waste that increases pressure on landfills.

7.2.1   GHG Emissions

Greenhouse gases trap heat, making the planet warmer. The Intergovernmental Panel on Climate Change (IPCC) identifies transportation activities as producing three direct greenhouse gases: carbon dioxide (CO_2), methane (CH_4), and nitrous oxide (N_2O). The combustion of transport fuels produces relatively little carbon in non-CO_2 gases. The impact of each of these greenhouse gases is expressed in terms of carbon dioxide equivalents (CO_2e), a process commonly referred to as carbon footprinting. (For more on carbon footprinting, see also Chap. 3 by Boukherroub et al. (2017)).

As mentioned earlier, more than 90 % of the GHG emissions in logistics are due to freight transportation. For each mode of transportation in a logistics network (road, railways, water-borne navigation, aviation) the IPCC recommends a fuel-based approach to measuring emissions due to the fairly consistent estimates of the amount of greenhouse gases produced by combustion of each type of fuel. This approach is also known as energy-based calculation, and it is the most reliable for CO_2, the primary greenhouse gas from transportation, representing an estimated 97 % of GHG emissions from road (IPCC 2006) and 98 % from marine transportation (IMO 2009).

If total fuel consumption is known, CO_2 emissions can be computed as described in Eq. 7.1 by multiplying the total fuel used by the conveyance multiplied by the emissions factor for that fuel.

$$\text{Emission} = \sum_a \left[\text{Fuel}_a \times \text{EF}_a \right]$$

Where:

Emission = Emissions of CO_2 (7.1)

Fuel_a = fuel sold

EF_a = emission factor equal to carbon content of the fuel multiplied by 44/12

a = type of fuel

CH_4 and N_2O are best estimated using distance traveled plus emissions produced during cold start of the conveyance. It necessitates a more detailed breakdown of the data, requiring distance traveled and emissions factors by fuel type, vehicle type, emission control technology, and operating conditions such as road types. This is shown in Eq. 7.2.

$$\text{Emission} = \sum_{a,b,c,d} \left[\text{Distance}_{a,b,c,d} \times \text{EF}_{a,b,c,d} \right] + \sum_{a,b,c,d} C_{a,b,c,d}$$

Where:

Emission = emission of CH_4 or N_2O

$\text{EF}_{a,b,c,d}$ = emission factor

$\text{Distance}_{a,b,c,d}$ = distance travelled during thermally stabilized engine operation phase for a given mobile source activity

$C_{a,b,c,d}$ = emissions during warm-up phase

a = fuel type

b = vehicle type

c = emission control technology

d = operating conditions

(7.2)

Table 7.1 illustrates the resulting emissions for 1000 gal of fuel, using emission factors from various sources. Note that the resulting calculations are affected by the

Table 7.1 GHG emissions calculated for 1000 gal of fuel

Fuel	GHGs	Source	Emissions included	Results	Units
Diesel	CO_2	UK Defra	Pump-to-wheel	9998	kg CO_2
Diesel	CO_2	US EPA	Pump-to-wheel	10,150	kg CO_2
Diesel	CO_2, CH_4, N_2O	GHG Protocol (EPA)	Pump-to-wheel	10,159	kg CO_2e
Biodiesel	CO_2	GHG Protocol (EPA)	Pump-to-wheel	0	kg CO_2
Biodiesel	CO_2 (biomass)	GHG Protocol (EPA)	Pump-to-wheel	9460	kg CO_2
Diesel	CO_2, CH_4, N_2O	GREET	Well-to-wheel	12,933	kg CO_2e
Biodiesel	CO_2, CH_4, N_2O	GREET	Well-to-wheel	2964	kg CO_2e

Source: Craig et al. (2013)

type of GHG gas included, as well as the scope of emissions included in the calculation, from the pump-to-wheel or well-to-wheel/life-cycle (see Sect. 7.3.2 for a discussion on emission scopes).

7.2.1.1   Activity-Based Calculations

Equations 7.1 and 7.2 from the IPCC guidelines assume total fuel consumption numbers are readily available or easy to estimate. Although this may be the case at the national or regional level (e.g., total oil imports, total petrol sales) or to conveyance owners that keep track of fuel purchases, this data is often not accessible to third-party logistics providers, manufacturers or retailers who make logistics decisions. Moreover, logistics decisions are not made at the conveyance level (e.g., truck, vessel, locomotive) but rather at the shipment level (e.g., box, carton, pallet) or at another planning metric (e.g., kilogram, cubic feet, or tonne).

Activity-based methods work by estimating the fuel consumed during transportation based on vehicle characteristics, or combining fuel consumption data with activity data to calculate average efficiency numbers. Like fuel-based methods, these methods will be sensitive to the choice of fuel emissions factors.

Distance Based

The simplest approach to estimating emissions from activity data is to use the distance traveled multiplied by the average fuel consumption of the vehicle or conveyance. Together, these produce an estimate of the fuel consumed, which can then be used to estimate GHG emissions by choosing an appropriate factor, as discussed in the fuel-based methods. A number of different approaches are used in practice to estimate vehicle-distance emissions factors, generally varying in the level of precision they provide.

The GHG Protocol provides default emissions factors per mile for a number of vehicle types, using both US and UK numbers. The emissions factors for US vehicles are based on assumed average vehicle efficiency for a variety of vehicle types

(Heavy Duty, Light Duty, Passenger Cars, Motorbikes, etc.) to determine fuel consumption, and the standard factors for CO_2, CH_4, and N_2O from the US Environmental Protection Agency (EPA) discussed in the fuel-based section. Numbers in the UK are based on surveys of fuel consumption in vehicle fleets. The fuel consumption data is combined with the UK Department for Environment, Food & Rural Affairs (Defra) standard CO_2 factor to produce an emission factor considering only CO_2 on a per-kilometer basis.

Other sources have focused more on a single mode type to provide more precise levels of emissions factors. The EPA's SmartWay program (see Sect. 7.5.4) collects data from a number of different carriers. It employs a fuel-based methodology to calculate emissions from the carriers, and combines this with activity data supplied by the carriers to calculate distance-based emission factors at the individual carrier level. This is then used to create a hierarchy of emissions factors, from which a user can select emission factors for a mode (truck, rail, multi-modal, logistics), a category within the mode (such as package, truckload/dry van, refrigerated, and others within the truck category), and finally a specific carrier within that category. A single company may have a number of different emissions factors, one for each category of business for which it reported data.

The Network for Transport and Environment (NTM) program does not collect specific data from carriers, but rather uses the ARTEMIS simulation tool to calculate fuel consumption for a number of different scenarios (NTM 2010). These scenarios account for different sizes of vehicles, percent loaded, road type, and driving conditions. By using these scenarios and an associated fuel-based emissions factor, a range of emissions factors can be calculated. In each case, the emissions are calculated using a straightforward multiplication of the distance and the vehicle-specific emissions factor.

Table 7.2 shows a summary of the results of using a number of different types of factors to calculate the emissions from a 1000-mile trip.

Despite little variation between emissions factors for diesel fuel, the emissions estimated for a specific trip using activity-based distance methods can vary considerably. This is true even for vehicles in the same class, as the NTM factors shown for a truck + semi-trailer range from 1.6 to 2.3 depending on the load factor and road type. The EPA SmartWay factors illustrate the correlation of emissions by specific carrier and type of freight.

This demonstrates important points about the precision of the emissions factors used. Estimations of fuel consumed can vary considerably, and therefore even if consistent fuel-based factors are used, the results obtained from activity-based data are sensitive to the assumptions regarding vehicle operating conditions (e.g., terrain, amount of cargo, driver proficiency).

Weight-Distance Based

Despite the ease of using vehicle-distance factors and the availability of a wide range of emissions factors, it is still inadequate for logistics analysis when using shared modes of transportation or when only the bare minimum of information is

Table 7.2 Estimated emissions for a 1000 mile distance for various modes

Source	Emission factor	Value	Units	GHGs	Total	Units
GHG protocol	Heavy goods vehicle—articulated—diesel—year 1960-present (US EPA)	1.722	kg CO_2e/mile	CO_2, CH_4, N_2O	1722	kg CO_2e
GHG protocol	HGV—articulated—engine size Unknown (UK Defra)	1.560	kg CO_2/mile	CO_2	1560	kg CO_2
GHG protocol	HGV—rigid—engine size 7.5–17 t—50 % weight laden (UK Defra)	1.235	kg CO_2/mile	CO_2	1235	kg CO_2
SmartWay	Flatbed, carrier A[a]	1.700	kg CO_2/mile	CO_2	1700	kg CO_2
SmartWay	TL/dry van, carrier A[b]	1.750	kg CO_2/mile	CO_2	1750	kg CO_2
SmartWay	TL/dry van, carrier B[b]	1.550	kg CO_2/mile	CO_2	1550	kg CO_2
NTM	Small lorry/truck, motorway, 100 % loaded	0.583	kg CO_2/mile	CO_2	583	kg CO_2
NTM	Lorry/truck + semi-trailer, motorway, 100 % loaded	2.296	kg CO_2/mile	CO_2	2296	kg CO_2
NTM	Lorry/truck + semi-trailer, urban roads, 0 % loaded	1.569	kg CO_2/mile	CO_2	1569	kg CO_2

Source: Craig et al. (2013)
[a]Specific carrier names and factors are available for download
[b]Assumes default Defra factor for diesel fuel

known about the shipment. In the first case, the emissions of the vehicle as a whole are not of concern, rather the share of emissions related to a specific amount of goods shipped. In the second case, the logistics decision maker may not know the specific vehicle, the loading factors, or the exact route used.

In these situations, weight-distance methods are generally used, though in some cases a volume-distance method may be more appropriate. Emissions factors for weight-distance methods are generally expressed in terms of ton-miles of goods moved (or perhaps TEU-miles for ocean containers where volume may be more important than weight). These methods provide a quick and easy method of calculating emissions, relying only on the weight of the goods shipped, the distance, and a general knowledge of the mode of transport used. They are also useful in comparing between modes, when efficiency is measured not just in the amount of emissions produced but the total amount of goods moved.

The GHG Protocol provides emissions factors in terms of ton-miles for a variety of transportation modes, using factors derived from both the EPA and Defra. These factors introduce another layer of assumptions beyond those of fuel-based and vehicle-distance-based methods, as now the factors must include assumptions regarding the total amount of goods on the vehicle. This can lead to a wide range of emissions factors, depending on the assumptions used. This is illustrated in Table 7.3, where emissions factors for different modes and types of transportation are compared for a shipment consisting of 10,000 short ton-miles (equivalent to a 10-t shipment being moved 1000 miles).

Table 7.3 CO_2 emissions for a 10,000 short ton-mile shipment across multiple modes

Source	Emission factor	Value	Units	GHGs	Total (kg CO_2)
GHG protocol	Air—long haul (US EPA)	1.527	kg CO_2/t-mile	CO_2	15,270
GHG protocol	Air—long haul (UK Defra)	0.346	kg CO_2/t-mile	CO_2	3460
GHG protocol	Air—domestic (US EPA)	1.527	kg CO_2/t-mile	CO_2	15,270
GHG protocol	Air—domestic (UK Defra)	1.105	kg CO_2/t-mile	CO_2	11,050
GHG protocol	Watercraft—shipping—large container vessel (20,000 t deadweight) (US EPA)	0.048	kg CO_2/t-mile	CO_2	480
GHG protocol	Watercraft—shipping—large container vessel (20,000 t deadweight) (UK Defra)	0.007	kg CO_2/t-mile	CO_2	70
GHG protocol	Watercraft—shipping—small tanker (844 t deadweight) (US EPA)	0.048	kg CO_2/t-mile	CO_2	480
GHG protocol	Watercraft—shipping—small tanker (844 t deadweight) (UK Defra)	0.019	kg CO_2/t-mile	CO_2	190
GHG protocol	Road vehicle—HGV—articulated—engine size>33 t (US EPA)	0.297	kg CO_2/t-mile	CO_2	2970
GHG protocol	Road vehicle—HGV—articulated—engine size>33 t (UK Defra)	0.049	kg CO_2/t-mile	CO_2	490
GHG protocol	Road vehicle—light goods vehicle—petrol—engine size 1.305–1.74 t (US EPA)	0.297	kg CO_2/t-mile	CO_2	2970
GHG protocol	Road vehicle—light goods vehicle—petrol—engine size 1.305–1.74 t (UK Defra)	0.462	kg CO_2/t-mile	CO_2	4620
GHG protocol	Rail (US EPA)	0.025	kg CO_2/t-mile	CO_2	250
GHG protocol	Rail (UK Defra)	0.016	kg CO_2/t-mile	CO_2	160

Source: Craig et al. (2013)

Table 7.3 also shows the wide variation not just between modes, in which ocean shipping may be as much as 200 times more efficient than air transport, but also between sources. The EPA's numbers, for instance, are based on high-level data and do not distinguish between types of transport within a mode. Thus, there is no distinction between heavy-duty trucks or light-duty vehicles within road transport, or between large container ships and small tankers in watercraft. This is in contrast to the Defra numbers that are generated at a greater level of precision and show the range of values that can exist between different types of transport.

It is important to note that some organizations, such as NTM or EcoTransIT, provide calculators with the ability to adjust some of the assumptions behind weight-distance-based emission factors, such as vehicle loading factors, to provide more realistic estimates. This fine-tuning requires more data, which is not always available to logistics decision makers. The EPA SmartWay program also collects similar data by carrier, providing another layer of detail to emission factors. Finally, some logistics operators and transportation companies, such as DHL, FedEx, or Maersk, use their internal proprietary systems and their transportation network information (e.g., total weight or cube moved on a particular transportation lane during a year) and combine it with fuel consumption records of the vehicles or vessels, to provide lane-specific distance-weight emission factors, and in some cases, shipper-specific factors for dedicated customers. These factors are often updated annually, although there is a trend toward more frequent reporting. Even these organizations rely on emission factors like the ones listed in Table 7.3, because their shipments may move between trucks, ships, or airplanes for which fuel records are not available or that belong to third parties with less detailed information.

7.2.1.2   Mode-Specific Adjustments

All of the GHG calculation approaches and methods discussed above are applicable to all modes of transportation (road, rail, water-borne, and air). Most salient differences, besides variations in engine technology and type of fuels, are related to the GHG gases included, the quality of data, the allocation of emissions to freight due to capacity sharing (e.g., same vehicle moving people and boxes), and strategies to overcome data limitations.

Rail

The most important variation in rail has to do with the variability of the number of railcars (empty and full) being pulled by a single locomotive. In theory the amount of fuel consumed during any journey or leg can be tracked and allocated to the cargo being hauled on that specific leg, thereby creating movement-specific factors. In practice, however, rail operators plan their movements and balance on a network perspective. Thus, it only makes sense to look at emissions from a series of interconnected networks or services and to measure the total amount of fuel and cargo moved through that rail network, as opposed to individual legs. These calculations are often done annually but could also be done on a monthly or quarterly basis, aligned with rail operator planning cycles.

Water-Borne Navigation

Some water-borne navigation providers, such as barges, operate in a similar fashion as long-haul vehicles, albeit through a smaller transportation network: rivers and canals. For these providers, trip-based estimations are sensible: measuring the total fuel consumed between origin and destination and allocating the emissions to the amount of cargo loaded. Because adjustments for empty journeys need to be added and assigned to various trips, emission factors that span more than one journey over a time horizon are often needed.

For large ocean-going cargo ships, the situation is very different. Unlike river waterways, ocean shipping companies plan their transportation networks by trade lanes between continents and sub-continents, stringing together multiple trade lanes to provide regular service to various ports. Thus, similar to rail transportation, even though is mathematically possible, it doesn't make sense to compute GHG emissions by looking at port-to-port distances without full understanding of the overall trade-lane dynamics. In addition, given the size of the vessels and the relatively few number of carriers (compared to road transport) the industry has been developing joint efforts to calculate emission factors by trade-lane in a homogeneous way. The Clean Cargo Working Group has been collecting data in collaboration with major shipping companies to provide a homogeneous calculation approach of emissions by trade-lane and ship assignment, if possible.

An additional feature of some water-borne navigation has to do with the relevant unit of measures used by shipping companies to determine the amount of freight being transported: the container. After the invention and wide adoption of the container, water-borne navigation was transformed to leverage the economic and efficiency advantages of the container. As a consequence, all planning and pricing decisions are made in TEU or Twenty-Foot-Equivalent-Units, a volumetric unit of measure equivalent to the total cube of a standard twenty feet container. Although cargo owners may know the total weight inside a particular container, shipping companies often only know (and care) about the TEU. Thus, emission factors computed by water-borne transportation are often originally computed in kilograms of CO_2-e per TEU-kilometer and then converted into ton-kilometers by using a pre-agreed conversion factor.

Aviation

Sources of emissions for aviation are all civil commercial airplanes, including general aviation such as agricultural aircraft, private jets, and helicopters. The fuel-based methodology again uses only fuel consumption data and average emission factors to estimate emissions, and is suitable for aircraft using aviation gasoline or when operational data for jet-fueled vehicles are not available. A fuel-based approach can also be estimated by calculating emissions separately for the cruise phase of a flight and the landing/take-off (LTO) phase. This requires knowing the number of LTOs and separating the fuel consumed during this phase from the cruise phase, but it allows for using emissions factors that capture differences in emissions, specially CH_4 and N_2O, during these phases.

Distance-based methods can be based on origin-destination (OD) data or full flight trajectory information. The OD approach accounts for different flight distances, which changes the relative impact of the LTO phase compared to the cruise phase. The full flight trajectory model uses aircraft—and engine-specific performance information over the entire flight, requiring engine performance modeling.

An additional complexity in aviation has to do with the allocation of emissions between people and freight, because they share the same airplane when cargo is loaded onto commercial flights. The most accurate way to allocate emissions is to use the ratio of weight used by passengers (and their bags) vs. the weight of freight, because weight is what determines the amount of fuel consumed during the flight. However, airlines do not plan routes using this criteria; instead, they evaluate the economics of each flight and the revenue from the various services they offer. Thus, emissions could be allocated based on the revenue of passenger vs. freight as a proxy to the planning approach. Even this approach has further complications because first class, business, and economy fares are sold at different rates on every flight as part of yield management strategy, varying the revenue profile of each flight and "underutilizing" the maximum weight potential of a flight. A third approach would be to allocate a fixed share of emissions to freight on a flight, recognizing that airlines often plan and balance their network using revenue targets. The EN 16258 (see Sect. 7.3.3) has favored this latter approach, recommending a factor between 70 and 80 % of emissions to be allocated to freight on commercial flight, regardless of actual load capacity or revenue. This number, although arbitrary, is a result of a consultation process with experts from academia and industry trying to balance accuracy of emissions with practical business matters of data collection and consistency in reporting.

7.2.1.3 Carbon Footprint Calculations in Transportation: A Primer

As mentioned at the beginning of this section, the most accurate method for calculation carbon footprints of transportation emissions is to use fuel records of the conveyance (see Eq. 7.1).

However, since most transportation activities often involve multiple organizations (e.g., shipper and carrier) and may further involve other intermediaries such as freight forwarders or 3PLs, weight-distance activity-based calculations are more commonly used in practice (see Sect. 7.2.1.1). The carbon footprint calculation using this approach is often estimated as a function of the shipment weight (w) or volume (v), the distance (d), and a mode-specific emission factor (EF). The most basic relationship is multiplicative as follows:

$$e(d,w) = d \times w \times \mathrm{EF} \text{ or } e(d,v) = d \times v \times \mathrm{EF}$$

The shipment weight is the gross weight of the product being transported (including all primary and secondary packaging). This information is often well known by the shipper. The distance is the total over-the-road, over-the-air, over-the-track, or over-the-waterway distance traveled by the shipment. This number may not always be accurate or easily available for the shipper, but it is often known by the carrier or asset owner, or can be approximated by using over-the-air distances multiplied by an adjustment factor. Such approximations should be avoided (if possible) since they add another level of uncertainty to the calculation.

The final component, the emission factor EF, is the most critical element of this computation. As discussed earlier in this section, there are multiple sources that publish values that are commonly used by practitioners (see Table 7.3). Ideally, these emissions factors should be gathered directly from fuel consumption records from the carrier or vessel operator (see Sect. 7.5.4), but are most commonly a result of carrier surveys, econometric models or engine fuel consumption modeling. Fuel consumption models allow for more accurate functional forms of $e(d,w)$.

The modeling and data collection undertaken by NTM is one of the most comprehensive and detailed methodologies available to estimate emission factors of transportation. Based on the excellent summary by Hoen et al. (2014a) of NTM recommended calculations, the following sections summarize functional forms of carbon footprint calculations for different modes of transportation. For all calculations, the resulting calculation emissions are expressed in kilograms of CO_2. Distance d is expressed in kilometers, weight w in kilograms, and volume v in m^3.

Air Transport

Emissions of air transportation can be estimated as follows:

$$e_{air}(d,w) = (E_1 + \epsilon_1 \cdot d) * \frac{w}{(W_1 \cdot \lambda_1)}$$

where
W_1 is the aircraft maximum payload in kg
λ_1 is the aircraft payload utilization % for the specific trip
E_1 are the emissions (kg of CO_2) corresponding to take-off and landing. These emissions are a function of the actual aircraft payload $W_1 \cdot \lambda_1$
ϵ_1 kilograms of CO_2 per kilometer (kg of CO_2/km)

For a Boeing 757-200SF, the maximum payload is W_1 is 29,029 kg. When fully loaded (e.g., $\lambda_1 = 100$ %), $E_1 = 4531.182$ and $\epsilon_1 = 15.363$. For a payload of $\lambda_1 = 75$ % of maximum capacity, $E_1 = 4041.709$ and $\epsilon_1 = 15.351$. Thus, the share of emissions associated to moving a 500 kg shipment for 1000 km will be 342.66 kg CO_2 in a fully loaded Boeing 757-200SF and 445.36 kg CO_2 if the aircraft will be loaded at 75 % payload capacity.

As mentioned earlier, aircraft payload capacity between passenger and cargo needs to be adequately accounted for. Also, air shipments are often priced volumetrically. In that case $w = v \cdot \rho$, where ρ is the shipment density. This density will vary by product and may also be adjusted for pricing purposes.

Road Transport

Emissions of road transportation can be estimated as follows:

$$e_{road}(d,w) = \epsilon_2 \cdot d \cdot \frac{w}{(W_2 \cdot \lambda_2)}$$

where
W_2 is the vehicle maximum payload in kg
λ_2 is the vehicle payload utilization % for the specific trip
ϵ_2 kilograms of CO_2 per kilometer (kg of CO_2/km).

Commonly used transport vehicles (tractor+trailer) have a maximum payload W_2 of 26,000 kg. To estimate ϵ_2, NTM recommends taking into account fuel efficiency, type of road, load factor, and terrain slope. NTM estimates that diesel consumption for an unloaded freight vehicle with a payload capacity of 26,000 kg is 0.226, 0.230, and 0.288 L per km for highway, rural, and city environments, respectively. At the other extreme, a fully loaded vehicle consumes 0.360, 0.396, and 0.504 L per km in highway, rural, and city roads. Other load factors may be linearly interpolated between these numbers. Thus, for a load factor of 70 %, fuel consumption will be 0.3198, 0.3462, and 0.4392 L per km for highway, rural, and city roads, respectively. Assuming diesel emissions are 2.621 kg CO_2 per L, ϵ_2 for a $\lambda_2 = 70$ % loaded vehicle will be given by $2.621 \cdot 0.3198 = 0.8382$ kg CO_2 per km. An additional adjustment to fuel consumption may be applied to take into account the steepness of the terrain. For instance, Hoen et al. (2014a) estimate a European wide adjustment of an additional 5 % to account to terrain. Thus $\epsilon_2 = 0.8382 \cdot 1.05 = 0.8801$.

Therefore, the share of emissions associated to moving a 500 kg shipment for 1000 km will be 11.85 kg CO_2 in a 70 % utilized 26,000 kg diesel powered vehicle. Note that for road transport, the allocation of empty miles have a noticeable impact on final shipment emission calculations.

Rail Transport

Since only a handful of national rail operators provide rail transport service by country, it is often most reliable to obtain the emission factor directly from rail transport companies. These factors take into account overall locomotive efficiency, including electric and diesel powered technology, as well as required boxcar repositioning throughout the network. Thus, emissions can be simply calculated as follows:

$$e_{\mathrm{rail}}(d, w) = \epsilon_3 \cdot d \cdot w$$

where
ϵ_3 kilograms of CO_2 per kilometer (kg of CO_2/kg-km)

The EPA estimates this number to be $1.713 \cdot 10^{-5}$ kg of CO_2 per kg-km for the US rail network. Hoen et al. (2014a) present a detailed derivation of rail emission factor for Europe, that takes into account a combination of electric and diesel power distance and hilly terrain. The resulting value was $2.223 \cdot 10^{-5}$ kg of CO_2 per kg-km.

Water Transport

Emissions of inland water transportation can be estimated as follows:

$$e_{water}(d,w) = FC_4 \cdot FE_4 \cdot d \cdot \frac{w}{(W_4 \cdot \lambda_4)}$$

where
W_4 is the total vessel capacity in kg, TEU, or meters (for RORO vessels)
λ_4 is the vessel payload utilization % for the specific trip
FC_4 is the vehicle fuel consumption in L per km
FE_4 are the fuel emissions in kg of CO_2 per L

The cargo capacity of an inland cargo vessel is 3,840,000 kg. Inland cargo vessels often have low utilization levels, close to 50 %. Vessel fuel consumption is in the order of 0.007 t of diesel per km and diesel emissions of approximately 3178 kg of CO_2 per t of diesel. Using these parameters, the share of emissions associated to moving a 500 kg shipment for 1000 km via inland waterways will be 5.79 kg CO_2.

In the case of ocean shipping, it is often advised to use carrier-specific emission factors, such as the ones published by the Clean Cargo Working Group (CCWG), although similar calculations as the ones used above can be estimated by adjusting the fuel type used (often bunker fuel oil).

7.2.2   Pollution

Pollution is the introduction of a substance—solid, liquid, or gas—into a system that can have adverse consequences on humans or the natural ecosystem. In the case of logistics and transportation, the most important environmental impacts are due to air and water pollution generated during the operation of trucks, airplanes, locomotives, and vessels. Unlike GHG emissions that have global effects, pollution impacts tend to be local to cities, ports, trade lanes, or freight corridors, although pollutants can also travel long distances and have global effects.

7.2.2.1   Air Pollution

The use of internal combustion engines in trucks, airplanes, ships, and locomotive engines that move freight is the major source of air pollution. There are six common air pollutants, also known as "criteria pollutants" in combustion: particle pollution (often referred to as particulate matter), ground-level ozone, carbon monoxide, sulfur oxides, nitrogen oxides, and lead (EPA 2015a):

- Ground-level ozone is not emitted directly into the air, but it is created by chemical reactions between oxides of nitrogen (NO_x) and volatile organic compounds (VOC) in the presence of sunlight.

- Particulate matter (PM) is a mixture of extremely small particles and liquid droplets. PM is made up of a number of components, including acids (such as nitrates and sulfates), organic chemicals, metals, and soil or dust particles. The size of particles is directly linked to their potential for causing health problems. The EPA regulations focuses on particles that are 10 μm (PM10) in diameter or smaller because those generally pass through the throat and nose and enter the lungs.
- Carbon monoxide (CO) is a colorless, odorless gas emitted from combustion processes. Nationally, and particularly in urban areas, the majority of CO emissions to ambient air come from transportation activities (both passenger and freight). CO can cause harmful health effects by reducing oxygen delivery to the body's organs (like the heart and brain) and tissues. At extremely high levels, CO can cause death.
- Nitrogen Oxides—or NO_x—are a family of seven compounds, of which NO_2 is the most prevalent form. About 50 % of all NO_x come from mobile sources including automobiles, trucks, and vessels (EPA 2014). They are generated during the combustion process of engines as a function of the ratio of fuel and oxygen. In addition to contributing to the formation of ground-level ozone, and fine-particle pollution, NO_x are linked with a number of adverse effects on the respiratory system. The amount of NO_x can be controlled through several means: engine design, regulating the oxygen and fuel mix, maintaining optimal temperature levels within the engine, changing fuel types, or adding a catalytic converter. All of these actions have an impact on fuel economy, sometimes positive or negative, and they are very dependent on individual engine configurations (EPA 2014).
- Sulfur oxides—or SO_x—are highly reactive gases of which sulfur dioxide (SO_2) is the most prevalent form in transportation. SO_x is linked with a number of adverse effects on the respiratory system. The largest sources of SO_x emissions come from fossil fuel combustion at power plants (73 %) and other industrial facilities (20 %). Smaller sources of SO_x emissions include industrial processes such as extracting metal from ore, and the burning of high sulfur containing fuels by locomotives, large ships, and non-road equipment. Although maritime transportation represents a small share of global SO_x emissions, the emissions tend to accumulate in higher concentrations near ports and then travel to neighboring population centers. SO_x emissions are increasingly being regulated across Europe and are part of the focus areas of the maritime industry as whole (IMO 2015).
- Lead is a naturally occurring element that can be harmful to humans when ingested or inhaled. Lead poisoning is particularly detrimental to the neurological development of children. The major sources of lead emissions have historically been from fuels in on-road motor vehicles (such as cars and trucks) and industrial sources. As a result of US and EU regulatory efforts to remove lead from on-road motor vehicle gasoline, emissions of lead from the transportation sector dramatically declined by 95 % between 1980 and 1999, and levels of lead in the air decreased by 94 % between 1980 and 1999. The major sources of lead emissions to the air today are ore and metals processing and piston-engine aircraft operating on leaded aviation gasoline.

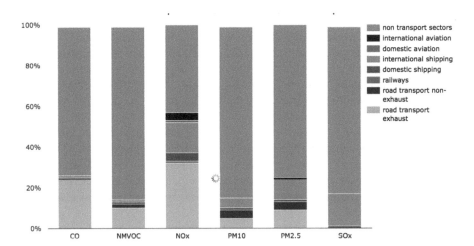

Fig. 7.2 Contribution of the transport sector to total air pollution (*Source*: European Environmental Agency 2015)

Table 7.4 Emission rates (grams per mile) for heavy-duty diesel trucks

Speed (mph)	NO_x	SO_x	PM_{10}
35	14.76	0.576	1.527
40	15.16	0.576	1.527
45	16.12	0.576	1.527
50	17.77	0.576	1.527
55	20.29	0.576	1.527

Source: Forkenbrock (1999)

Reliable global figures are not available, but the European Environment Agency (see Fig. 7.2) estimates that international shipping represents 16 % of SO_x emissions, 15 % of NO_x emissions, 10 % of PM2.5, and 5 % of PM10. Road transport (both passenger and freight) represents 32 % of NO_x emissions, 9 % of PM2.5, and 5 % PM10. Aviation mainly contributes to NO_x emissions (5 %), while railways have negligible emissions compared to other sources.

The levels of air pollution generated by engines are heavily dependent on the vehicle engine technology as well as operational conditions such as speed, road geometry, wind speeds, and altitude. Table 7.2 compares emission rates (grams per mile) of a diesel heavy-duty vehicle. PM and SO_x emissions don't vary by speed, but NO_x emissions increase significantly at higher speeds (Table 7.4).

It is important to highlight that noticeable progress has been made in reducing all sources of air pollutants in the transport sector since 1990 (see Fig. 7.3).

An important consideration related to air pollution is the trade-off between GHG emissions, fuel efficiency, and cost. A comprehensive field study commissioned by Defra in the UK illustrates this complexity. Figure 7.4 shows the overall progress achieved through legislation: a steady reduction of the ratio of NO_x vs. CO_2 emissions. Although diesel fuels have achieved significant reductions in absolute CO_2

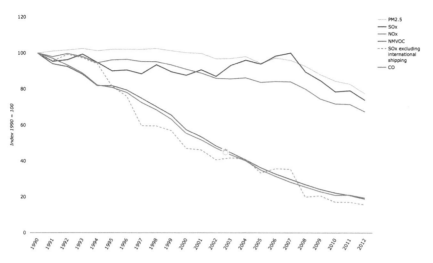

Note: PM₂.₅: particulate matter with aerodynamic diameter of 2.5 μm or less. NMVOC: non-methane volatile organic compounds; SOₓ: sulphur oxides. NOₓ: nitrogen oxides. CO: carbon monoxide.

Fig. 7.3 Trends in emissions of air pollutants (*Source*: European Environmental Agency 2015)

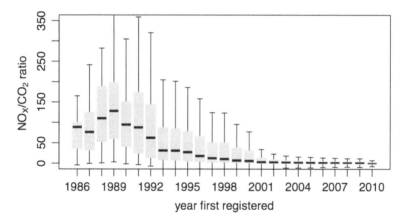

Fig. 7.4 Box plot of the volume ratio of NO_x/CO_2 for petrol cars (*Source*: Carslaw et al. 2011; https://uk-air.defra.gov.uk/assets/documents/reports/cat05/1108251149_110718_AQ0724_Final_report.pdf)

emissions and are considered a "greener" alternative, they have not improved at the same rate of NO_x reductions compared to petrol (Fig. 7.5).

7.2.2.2 Water Pollution

Water pollution occurs during water-borne transportation due to four main causes:

- Release of oil and chemicals through accidental spills and operational discharges

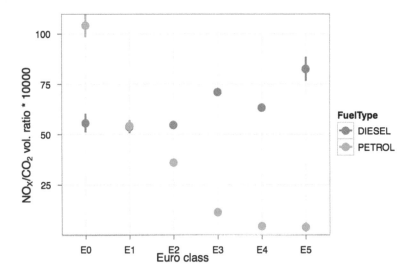

Fig. 7.5 Volume ratio of estimated NO_x/CO_2 for petrol and diesel cars by Euro classification. The *error bars* show the 95 % confidence intervals in the mean (*Source*: Carslaw et al. 2011; https://uk-air.defra.gov.uk/assets/documents/reports/cat05/1108251149_110718_AQ0724_Final_report.pdf)

Table 7.5 Distribution of pollution from seabed activities, 2011

Seabed activity	Tonnes/year	%
Ships	457,000	36.7 %
Offshore exploration and production	20,000	1.6 %
Coastal facilities	115,000	9.2 %
Small craft activity	53,000	4.3 %
Natural seeps	600,000	48.2 %
Unidentified sources	200	0.0 %
Total	**1,245,200**	**100 %**

Source: IMO (2012)

- Release of biocides from toxic chemicals used in antifouling paints. No estimates are available for the impact of these chemicals.
- Dumping of waste such as garbage and sewage
- Transfer of invasive aquatic species due to ballast water

Table 7.5 summarizes the total estimated water pollution (in tons per year) from seabed activities. Ships and small craft account for more than 40 % of seabed pollution while coastal facilities, including port activity, add another 9.2 % of pollution. Any efforts taken to reduce the amount of this pollution, often through better technology and environmentally aware operations, have a direct impact on these figures.

Given the economic and political importance of water-borne transportation—90 % of global trade is transport via international shipping (IMO 2015)—multi-stakeholder action is the main strategy to address water pollution. The MARPOL Convention signed in 1973 remains the most important international

Table 7.6 Noise levels of common activities

Activity	Noise level
Whisper	30 dB
Normal conversation/laughter	50–65 dB
Vacuum cleaner at 10 ft	70 dB
Washing machine/dishwasher	78 dB
Midtown Manhattan traffic noise	70–85 dB
Motorcycle	88 dB
Train	100 dB
Jackhammer/PowerSaw	85–90 dB
Thunderclap	110 dB
Stereo/boombox	110–120 dB
Nearby jet takeoff	130 dB

Source: NYCDEP (2008)

treaty instrument covering the prevention of pollution by ships. It sets out regulations dealing with pollution from ships by oil; by noxious liquid substances carried in bulk; by harmful substances carried by sea in packaged form; by sewage; by garbage; and with the prevention of air pollution from ships.

7.2.3   Noise and Vibration

The goal of establishing acceptable noise levels is to avoid hearing loss in people over their lifespan, as well as to allow for a comfortable environment to work and rest. In 1974, the EPA determined that a 24-h exposure level of 70 decibels (dB) to be the threshold that will prevent any measurable hearing loss over a lifetime. Levels of 55 dB outdoors and 45 dB indoors were considered as acceptable levels for normal activity. These levels are not peak levels, but 8–24-h averages.

Table 7.6 presents some reference activities and their noise levels.

Noise levels related to freight transportation activities (traffic 70 dB, trains 100 dB, and airplanes 130 dB) are above the recommended 70 dB threshold level. This limits the amount of time that freight activities should be allowed near heavily population centers. Localities often require stricter noise levels after 6 pm and before 6 am in residential areas, to further mitigate disruption to audible quality of life.

7.2.4   Packaging Waste

Packaging is used to sell, inform, contain, protect, preserve, and transport products (Soroka 1999). After product use, all packaging joins the waste stream.

There are three main types of packaging (Saphire 1994):

- *Manufacturer-provided packaging*. This is the primary packaging that protects and preserves the product. In some cases, this packaging also informs and helps

Table 7.7 Generation and recovery of containers and packaging

Container and packaging material	Weight generated (tons)	Weight recovered (tons)	Recovery as % of generation
Steel	2.74	1.89	69.0%
Aluminum	1.90	0.68	35.8%
Glass	9.36	3.13	33.4%
Paper and cardboard	37.68	26.85	71.3%
Plastics	13.68	1.85	13.5%
Wood	9.94	2.30	23.1%
Other materials	0.34	Negligible	Negligible
Total	**75.64**	**36.70**	**48.5%**

Source: US EPA (2015b)

to sell the product contained within. As a customer decides which product to purchase, the packaging has the ability to draw the customer in with its design, image, and attractiveness, regardless of the quality and necessity of a product (Paine 2002).

- *Transport packaging or secondary packaging.* This type of packaging is used for the sole purpose of moving product around. Most commonly, it is used for bulk handling of product, usually in pallet sizes to facilitate the easy transfer from warehouse to truck or container for shipment across land, air, or sea. Its main function is to protect the contents within from damage from the elements or rough handling.
- *Parcel packaging or tertiary packaging.* This is used mainly to group primary packages together. It is most frequently used in the retail delivery industry to aggregate customer orders into one box, to facilitate easy delivery through the fulfillment system.

Logistics and transportation activities have direct influence on the design, use, and disposal of secondary and tertiary packaging. Any unnecessary levels or inadequately disposed packaging is an additional source of waste.

Although detailed statistics are not available, product containers and packaging represent 29% of the 250 million tons of waste generated in 2010 (EPA 2015a). Approximately 49% of this waste is recovered (see Table 7.7), which leaves a 51% opportunity to either reduce packaging use or make sure that it reaches the right recycling facilities.

7.3 Measuring Green Logistics Impacts

Logistics decisions are metrics driven, which means that green logistics models and initiatives require having the right measurements of the various environmental impacts.

Pollution, noise, vibration, and waste measurements are technical in nature and can be estimated through specialized equipment. For example, the EPA or the European Union standards (see Table 7.1) are enforced by subjecting technologies to lab and road tests under standard conditions. Driving, weather, terrain, congestion, and operational conditions can dramatically change the actual environmental impact of freight operations. In a detailed study of drayage trucks in the port of Genoa, Zamboni et al. (2015) were able to observe differences of more than 50 % in total fuel consumption, NO_x and SO_x emissions under a variety of speeds and stop patterns. Environmental analysis of logistics operations needs to be very aware of the various assumptions underlying commonly used emission factors. This is particularly important when estimating GHG emissions.

7.3.1 GHG Emission Measurement in Logistics

As discussed in Sect. 7.2.1, there are important variations in emission factors across sources (see Table 7.3). For instance, depending on the assumed (or observed) utilization factor of the conveyance and the granularity of data available (e.g., surveys or fuel records), the average fuel consumption per ton of cargo transported will vary significantly. Table 7.8 includes some of the emission factors included in the GHG Protocol. Note that the EPA reference numbers are the same for trucks of various engine sizes, while the Defra numbers vary dramatically between large (over 33 t) and smaller trucks (1.3–1.7 t). This difference is due to the level of detail of data collected by these two agencies at the moment of publication of the GHG Protocol: the EPA was using sector-level aggregated data while Defra had access to vehicle-level surveys. Moreover, these numbers are regularly challenged and updated as more and better data becomes available across the logistics sector (Table 7.8).

Another complexity, especially relevant to GHGs measurements, is what is and what is not included in the emission factors and calculations.

7.3.2 GHG Standards and Scopes[1]

There are three types of standards that cover GHG impact estimations. If the intent of the measurement is an absolute quantity for a whole company, this is known as *Corporate Carbon Footprinting*. The most widely known and adopted standard is the GHG Protocol followed by the ISO 14064. If the intent is to measure the GHG impact of an individual product, often from cradle to grave, it is known as *Product*

---

[1] The GHG Protocol Corporate Standard also includes a scope definition. Although conceptually related, it does not correspond to the scope definition when applied to logistics activities. See Chap. 3 by Boukherroub et al. (2017) for an in-depth discussion of carbon footprinting, including more on the GHG Protocol Scope definitions.

Table 7.8 Selected emission factors from the GHG protocol

Emission factor	Value	Units
Road vehicle—HGV—articulated—engine size > 33 t (US EPA)	0.297	kg CO$_2$/t-mile
Road vehicle—HGV—articulated—engine size > 33 t (UK Defra)	0.049	kg CO$_2$/t-mile
Road vehicle—light goods vehicle—petrol—engine size 1.305–1.74 t (US EPA)	0.297	kg CO$_2$/t-mile
Road vehicle—light goods vehicle—petrol—engine size 1.305–1.74 t (UK Defra)	0.462	kg CO$_2$/t-mile

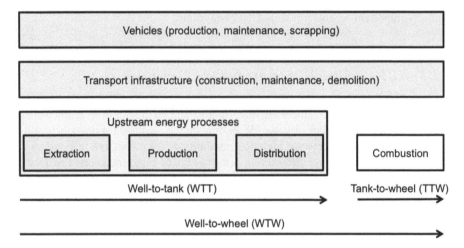

Fig. 7.6 Life-cycle phases of transport (*Source*: VTT as reported by COFRET 2012)

Carbon Footprinting. The PAS-2050, ISO 14040, and the GHG Protocol Life Cycle Accounting and Reporting Standards are well-known references. Finally, and most recently, the EN 16258 (VTT 2012) standard for quantifying greenhouse gas emissions from freight focus specifically on carbon footprinting in the transportation sector.

All of these standards use emission factors and variations of the equations presented in Sect. 7.2.1. One of the main differences, besides the goal itself, is the scope of the GHG calculations. Figure 7.6 shows all the life-cycle sources of GHG emissions of transportation services, from cradle to grave. These emissions are generated at different moments in time and points in space and allocated throughout the delivery of the service.

The first layer of emissions is all the GHG emissions generated during the manufacturing and maintenance of the trucks, airplanes, or boats. These emissions include the energy used in the assembly plants, the extraction of raw materials, and the operation of maintenance operations. Next are all the emissions related to the construction and maintenance of the transportation infrastructure, including roadways, ports, airports, and intermodal terminals. Some of this infrastructure is shared with other services (e.g., roads are shared with bicycles and personal vehicles, ports

Table 7.9 GHG emissions for various types of fuels (kg of CO_2 equivalents per L) in accordance with EN 16258

	TTW	WTW
	kg CO_2e/L	kg CO_2e/L
Petrol	2.42	2.88
Ethanol	0.00	1.24
Petrol E5 (5 vol.% Ethanol)	2.30	2.80
Petrol E10 (10 vol.% Ethanol)	2.18	2.72
Diesel	2.67	3.24
Biodiesel	0.00	1.92
Diesel D5 (5 vol.-% biofuel)	2.54	3.17
Diesel D7 (7 vol.-% biofuel)	2.48	3.15
Compressed natural gas	2.68*	3.07*
Liquefied petroleum gas	1.70	1.90
Jet kerosene	2.54	3.10
Heavy fuel oil (HFO)	3.05	3.31
Marine diesel oil (MDO)	2.92	3.53
Marine gas oil (MGO)	2.88	3.49

*Per Kg

are shared with government and military operations) and needs to be properly allocated.

In order to be able to do a complete calculation of the impact of freight transportation, some share of the vehicle and infrastructure emissions should be added to each logistic operation. This is a fairly complex and uncertain calculation that requires very large amounts of data and assumptions. With the exception of life-cycle analysis or product carbon footprint calculations, most of these emissions are not included in GHG calculations in the logistics sector.

This leaves emissions from "well-to-wheel" (WTW): these are all the emissions related to the extraction, production, and distribution of fuels used during transportation operations, up to point when the fuel is placed in the vehicle—"well-to-tank" (WTT)—plus all emissions generated during the combustion of this fuel during transport operations, "tank-to-wheel" (TTW). The EN 16258 explicitly requires that all transport GHG calculations include WTW emissions. Other standards, including the GHG corporate protocol, only required TTW emissions, although WTW were encouraged. Similarly, the EPA SmartWay program initially only required TTW emissions and is now expanding to WTW emissions. Table 7.9 shows the emission factor differences between TTW and WTW by fuel.

7.3.3   GHG Allocation

The other source of complexity is the allocation of the emissions from a corporate or individual route level to an individual shipment. The GHG Protocol and the EPA program favor "simple" activity-based approaches: first compute all the emissions of a company or service using, for instance, fuel records. Then calculate the total distance (including empty miles) and weight moved during the transportation activities. Once WTW or TTW emission factors are applied to fuel consumption data, they can be divided by the total ton-mile of the logistics or transportation provider to estimate an emission factor per ton-mile. This approach ignores the fact that individual routes or services may have different efficiency levels, or that specific vehicles may have different performance metrics, in favor of a simple and consistent calculation that can be easily adopted by many organizations. The EPA SmartWay program does allow for tracking emissions by type of fleet (e.g., flat bed trucks vs. drayage trucks), but it still recommends an aggregate approach for computing emission factors.

The EN 16258, on the other hand, favors a detailed approach. It recommends using the product of the weight of the consignment and the actual distance traveled—i.e., the transport capacity measured in tonne kilometers—as the allocation parameter. It aims at providing as accurate as possible assignment of emission factors to individual packages, taking into account logistics network configurations such as the relative location of the warehouse with respect to customers in a delivery route. Variations of this calculation are allowed in the standard, based on the quality of the information and type of service. An in-depth discussion of the EN 16258 standard is beyond this chapter, but this requires consistently collecting data across every transportation route, including shipment information, sequence, and distance. This is a gargantuan task, especially since logistics operations often include multiple providers with various levels of sophistication. Nevertheless, for large organizations like UPS, DHL, FedEx, or Maersk, the EN 16258 does provide a framework to develop information systems that can provide very accurate shipment level-allocation of GHG emissions.

7.3.4   GHG Metric Trade-Offs

As discussed on this section, GHG Metrics will vary due to assumptions, scope, or data availability. Standards can guide organizations' choices, but designing metrics that excel in all dimensions is not practically possible. Instead, firms must choose metrics that trade off between certain criteria. Two of the primary trade-offs are between integrative and useful metrics, and between robust and valid metrics (Caplice and Sheffi 1994) (Fig. 7.7).

Integrative metrics promote coordination across functions, while useful metrics are easily understood and provide managers with direct guidance. Providing managers with actionable guidance requires a level of specificity that makes promoting coordination across functions difficult. In this sense, measuring the carbon footprint of transportation is a useful metric, because it provides guidance on one specific aspect but not across functions. As such, it must be incorporated as one metric in an entire performance measurement system that covers both environmental and non-environmental aspects across the functions of the supply chain.

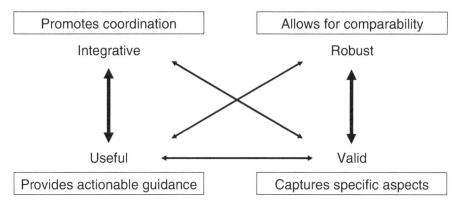

Fig. 7.7 Trade-offs between criteria (*Source*: Caplice and Sheffi 1994)

The other trade-off is between a robust metric that allows for comparability and a valid metric that captures specific aspects. A valid metric, such as the ones favored by the EN16258, provides help with making a specific decision but is less suitable to external uses where it might be compared with similar metrics for other organizations, unlike the GHG Protocol or EPA approaches.

7.4   Green Logistics Strategies

As discussed in the previous sections, logistics activities, though integral to the economic and social development, negatively impact the environment on multiple dimensions. The goal of *green logistics* is to mitigate the environmental impact of logistics—related activities.

As governments and companies have increased their focus on green logistics, numerous "best practices" and frameworks have been proposed (Craig et al. 2013). However, as the impacts outlined in the previous section show, there are five main logistics variables that, when combined, drive the environmental impact of logistics:

- *Distance*. How far are products being moved? Where are they loaded/unloaded?
- *Mode*. Which mode of transportation is being used?
- *Equipment*. What kind of equipment is being used for the logistics operation? What kind of fuel and how much fuel does it consume?
- *Load*. How much product is being loaded into the conveyance? How efficiently is it loaded?
- *Operation*. How skillful is the driver in operating the vehicle? How optimal is the logistics plan?

Each of these variables is a lever that can be used toward designing greener logistics systems: distance reduction, modal shift, cleaner equipment, better load planning, and operational excellence.

All business decisions, including logistics and transportation, are made at the strategic, tactical, or operational level (Stank and Goldsby 2000). Strategic decisions are revisited every 3–5 years, tactical decisions are often done with a 6-month to 2-year horizon in mind, and operational level decisions are made on a daily and weekly basis. Thus, decisions at strategic, tactical, and operational level are opportunities to mitigate the environmental impact of logistics by flexing one or more of the five green logistics levers.

Table 7.10 shows a non-exhaustive list of green logistics strategies for each of the five levers across the three decision levels. These strategies require a combination of business and analytical approaches in logistics. Some of these strategies may appear simplistic or obvious, but they matter in practice. For instance, everyone recognizes that idling vehicles consumes fuel unnecessarily. According to the EPA SmartWay program, long-duration idling of truck and locomotive engines consumes more than 1 billion gallons of diesel fuel per year, emits 11 million tons of carbon dioxide, 200,000 t of oxides of nitrogen, 5000 t of particulate matter, and elevates noise levels (EPA 2015a). But only when there is a managerial commitment to reduce these impacts are the required actions taken, even when they are economically sound. Walmart, for examples, outfitted its 7000-vehicle truck fleet with auxiliary power units (APUs). Walmart estimated an 18-month payback period through fuel and engine wear savings, in addition to all associated environmental benefits.

The next two sections will expand on two well-studied modeling approaches—network design and vehicle-routing—that are commonly used in logistics decision-making and that have direct applicability on all levers at the strategic, tactical, and operational level. Business-centric dimensions will be further explored in the case studies of Sect. 7.4, focusing on real-life implementation challenges.

7.4.1 Network Design

Logistics network design is a strategic decision that has direct impact on two of the most important levers for green logistics: distance reduction and mode shift. It includes decisions related to the location of manufacturing plants, assembly facilities and multiple tiers of warehouses, as well as deciding how products flow through the network from suppliers to customers.

As elegantly summarized by Magnanti and Wong (1984), the basic ingredients of all network design models are a set of nodes (N) and a set of directed arcs (A) that are available to design the network. There are two types of decisions in network design models: (a) discrete-choice decisions relating to selecting which nodes and which arcs should be included in the final network and (b) decisions about the flow of one or multiple commodities from supply to demand nodes along the selected network. To find the optimal solution, mathematical models trade-off a variety of fixed and variable costs, as well as minimum and maximum flows, through each arc and node.

Table 7.10 Green logistics strategies

	Strategic	Tactical	Operational
Reduce distances	• Include environmental impacts in network design	• Flexible territories/ service contracts that allow for increased density of pickup/ delivery networks	• Advanced vehicle routing that includes congestion, fuel consumption modeling, and flexible time windows
	• Local sourcing	• Identify cross-industry partnerships to reduce empty-miles	
Modal shift	• Evaluate network design incorporating facilities alongside intermodal terminals	• Collaborate with customers/suppliers to adjust order quantities, inventory levels, lead times and service levels to allow multiple modes in lanes	• Define a clear hierarchy of preferred modes by lane
	• Design networks to support flexible inventory and service levels to allow various network speeds	• Develop multi-modal third-party logistics providers	• Develop multimodal experience by operating lanes across multiple modes
Cleaner equipment	• Joint investment in cleaner technologies, including early-trials to foster equipment innovation	• Incentivize capital investments to regularly upgrade/ replace aging equipment	• Track equipment performance (fuel consumption, emissions, noise)
		• Pilot new technologies to obtain "real" operational environmental performance	• Develop environmentally aware preventive maintenance plans
Load planning	• Redesign product packaging to improve conveyance utilization	• Add environmental metrics to logistics planning reports	• Track & report the environmental impact of every move
		• Review "green scenarios" in load planning	• Optimize conveyance loading using analytical approaches (OR)
Operational excellence	• Develop an environmentally aware logistics culture	• Benchmark environmental operational performance	• Develop operational environmental dashboards (e.g., fuel consumption, idling)
		• Recognize top environmental performers regularly	• Establish targets and incentives

Network design models are widely used and studied in logistics planning decisions, ranging from global flows (see Goetschalckx et al. 2002) to locating single facilities (see Melo et al. 2009). These models often include cost and service trade-offs.

Adding environmental considerations can be achieved by augmenting a traditional network flow model with an environmental cost or an environmental constraint.

For instance, when deciding to open or close a facility in a network, there is often a fixed cost plus a variable cost driven by productivity, capacity, or labor choices. Because operating facilities may also generate environmental impacts that may vary by these same choices (e.g., pollution, GHG emissions), an "environmental cost" may be added to each candidate facility and then added as part of the objective function to minimize total emissions or as constraint to limit the total environmental impacts (see Chap. 9 by Velázquez and Fransoo (2017)).

Another common variation to network flow models to take into account green impacts, is related to the flows through the network. Since every arc in the network represents the movement of one or more commodities via a mode of transportation, the model could explicitly estimate the environmental impact of this move using mode-specific emission factors. For example, Table 7.3 includes the amount of CO_2 emitted per ton-mile for various modes. By multiplying these factors to the corresponding arc-flow variables, the model can estimate the total CO_2 emissions of a particular transportation network configuration. These total transportation emissions could also be added to an objective function or part of a constraint to limit total emission costs. Because different transportation modes have different speeds, they will also have inventory impacts. To fully capture the network environmental impact, factors that measure the increased in emissions due to extra holding inventory may also be needed (e.g., extra energy required to hold extra inventory, extra waste generated due to increase obsolescence).

Hoen et al. (2014b) conducted a comprehensive modeling and analysis of the economic and environmental impact of selecting various transportation modes to fulfill customer orders for Cargill. They modeled the impact on revenue, inventory, and costs, and traded it off with total CO_2 emissions. Figure 7.8 shows their results as a trade-off curve between reduction of emissions vs. cost increase.

Although the trade-off curve will vary depending on the specific network configuration, economics, and mode choices available, it often has a similar shape: it is possible to achieve noticeable environmental reductions without adding significant extra cost to the logistics network. In the case study analyzed by Hoen et al., 10 % CO_2 reductions can be achieved by adding less than 1 % in cost. Achieving higher CO_2 reductions (e.g., 25 %), however, will require a significant cost increase (e.g., 15 %).

In addition to the cost vs. environment trade-off analysis, analyzing various scenarios can yield important insights to the network topology. Figure 7.9 shows the different network configurations for an apparel manufacturer in the USA under different scenarios. In this case, the optimal cost scenario will open four warehouses,

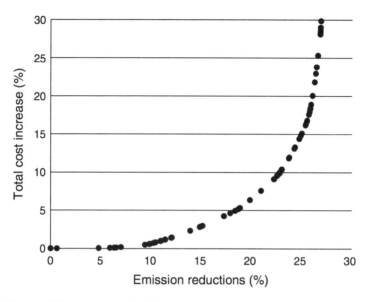

Fig. 7.8 Cost vs. CO_2 emissions trade-off curve (*Source*: Hoen et al. 2014b)

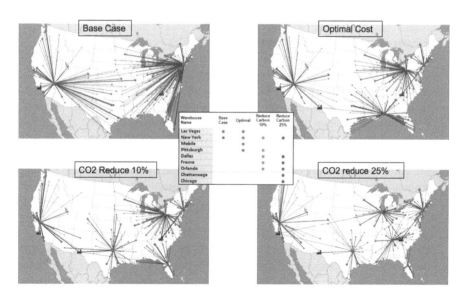

Fig. 7.9 Network variations under different CO_2 reductions (*Source*: Blanco and Simchi-Levi 2008)

compared to five or six facilities if the company would like to reduce 10 % and 25 % of total CO_2 emissions in the network, respectively. More importantly, by looking at which facilities are selected under each scenario, logistics planners may elect to evaluate hybrid solutions that balance economic and environmental objectives.

7.4.2 Vehicle Routing

At the other end of the spectrum of network design is the daily execution of logistics activities. This includes warehouse operations (e.g., receiving, unloading, loading, storing, picking, and packing) and distribution operations (e.g., load building, product delivery, and product collection).

The design of the network and customer requirements limit the mode choices available for distribution operations, but there are still several levers that could be influenced directly, such as distance, equipment, and load building. Vehicle routing and scheduling is often the most environmentally intensive activity (from an energy and GHG perspective) because it is during the physical delivery of products that fuel is consumed and that the majority of transport emissions are generated (see Fig. 7.1).

There is a large body of literature devoted to solving vehicle routing problems (VRP) (see Laporte 2009 for a comprehensive review). These models almost always focus on minimizing distance, time, or cost of the planned routes. Although highly correlated, solving for minimum distance does not always translate into minimizing environmental impacts (Bektaş and Laporte 2011).

A similar approach to add environmental measurements to network design problem, can be used to modify vehicle routing models: explicitly calculate the factors affecting fuel consumption and pollution such as equipment characteristics, customer time windows, product loaded during each leg of the route, speed of travel, slope of the road network, and congestion. These variations of VRP models are known as "pollution-routing problems" or PRP (Bektaş and Laporte 2011; Koç et al. 2014).

PRP problems explicitly capture the environmental impacts of vehicle routing operations. Assigning a vehicle to a route is one example. Besides differences in fuel consumption (that are part of the variable costs of operating a vehicle), different types of vehicle technologies have different environmental impacts (see Table 7.11).

Speed of travel is another dimension of vehicle operations that is relevant in PRP problems. Figure 7.10 shows fuel consumption by speed for a light-weight vehicle. We can notice the U-shape of the curve leading to an optimal speed at 40 km/h. As vehicles are assigned to various road segments in a network with varying speeds, the total emissions generated may vary (e.g., highways or local roads). For instance, Staples was able to achieve an increase in fuel efficiency from 8.5 to 10.4 miles per gallon by limiting driver speeds to 60 miles per hour without impacting delivery

Table 7.11 EU Emission standards for heavy-duty diesel engines (Steady-State Testing)

Stage	Date	CO	HC	NO$_x$	PM
		g/kWh			
Euro I	1992, ≤ 85 kW	4.5	1.1	8.0	0.612
	1992, > 85 kW	4.5	1.1	8.0	0.36
Euro II	1996.10	4.0	1.1	7.0	0.25
	1998.10	4.0	1.1	7.0	0.15
Euro III	1999.10 EEV only	1.5	0.25	2.0	0.02
	2000.10	2.1	0.66	5.0	0.10a
Euro IV	2005.10	1.5	0.46	3.5	0.02
Euro V	2008.10	1.5	0.46	2.0	0.02
Euro VI	2013.01	1.5	0.13	0.40	0.01

Source: https://www.dieselnet.com

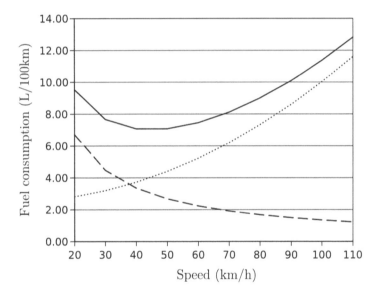

Fig. 7.10 Schematic fuel consumption rates by speed of travel (*Source*: Bektaş and Laporte 2011)

performance (Staples 2012). Also, for vehicle routing problems with time windows, tracking environmental impact at various speeds is more relevant due to the interaction with customer service expectations.

Although fuel efficiency equations by vehicle type and speed are already complex, they can also be augmented to add payload impacts: the amount of fuel consumed while traveling at a certain speed increases with the amount of cargo hauled (Barth and Boriboonsomsin 2009). Thus, it is theoretically possible to reduce environmental impacts on vehicle routes by giving priority to deliver large payloads early in the route, due to the potential to continue the route with a lighter load. Furthermore, by modeling road slopes or stop lights, one can further explore route variations that can further reduce fuel consumption and emissions. UPS delivery routes, for example, are designed to minimize left turns, which require vehicles to wait at an intersection for traffic to clear before making the turn. UPS has lowered CO_2 emissions by 100,000 metric tons (UPS 2015).

7.5   Case Studies: Implementing Green Logistics Strategies

The strategies included in Table 7.10 are known to reduce emissions and, in some cases, also drive cost savings. Nevertheless, companies often have trouble implementing them.

One of the challenges is focus: these initiatives are not always management priority. Another key obstacle is that they require internal and external collaboration. The logistics function interfaces with multiple business activities and supports a wide range of decisions. Client-supplier relationships, outsourcing arrangements, cost sharing, and coordination between trading partners are a few examples.

The following four case studies illustrate how, through collaboration, green logistics initiatives were put into practice.[2] The case studies focus on some of the unique business considerations and details required to make green logistics successful in practice. The first case study discusses how Boise was able to shift from truck to rail shipments and increase its load utilization by working with its customers on service and inventory impacts and through internal improvements of package design. The second case study also discusses modal shift, but this time achieved by two competitors sharing "empty miles" of a rail backhaul leg. The third case study is an example of a package redesign in Caterpillar's inbound network that that reduces shipment weight and thus consumes less transportation fuel. The section concludes by describing the EPA SmartWay program, a multi-stakeholder voluntary collaboration that has incentivized companies to prioritize green logistics efforts by providing the right incentives and transparency to the process.

---

[2] The first three cases studies in this section closely follow "Delivering on the Promise of Green Logistics," by Edgar Blanco and Ken Cotrill (Blanco and Cottrill 2013).

7.5.1 Customer Collaboration: OfficeMax and Boise, Inc.

Boise, Inc. manufactures a wide range of packaging and paper products, with reported earnings of $2.56 billion in 2012.[3] The company operates mainly in the USA and has long-term relationships with many customers, including retailer OfficeMax. Boise supplies the majority of OfficeMax's paper products due to a long tradition of business and commercial relationships.

Truck transportation offers Boise the flexibility and speed it needs to meet customer delivery promises. However, moving products by truck also accounts for the largest percentage of the CO_2 emissions associated with logistics operations. Rail transport is more cost effective and emits much less carbon per equivalent weight and distance, but it's also slower and less flexible than trucking.

As part of its cost and environmental efforts, Boise developed two initiatives. In the first one, called Carload Direct, Boise needed to coordinate with its long-time partner OfficeMax. Prior to the initiative, shipments from Boise were routinely moved by truck to the retailer's facilities, even when the destinations were accessible by rail. OfficeMax became a test case for switching to direct-by-rail shipments. The two companies' longstanding relationship helped Boise negotiate the change, but the Boise team was still tasked to make sure the transition did not disrupt OfficeMax's ordering process.

The benefits of the change, carbon-wise, were significant: a traditional truckload shipment comprises about 20 t of paper product, whereas a railcar carries around 70 t. The main drawback to the process is that a rail solution required customer orders to be warehoused until there was enough freight to fill a boxcar. This meant that the time from order placement to delivery was potentially extended, while running the risk that inventory needed by stores would be stuck in a warehouse. By coordinating the ordering process, the Boise team was able to determine when enough OfficeMax orders were available to "pool" into a Carload Direct shipment or when a regular truck shipment was the best option.

The solution may seem straightforward, but it required extensive cooperation between the transportation departments at Boise and OfficeMax. For example, ordering processes had to be adjusted and coordinated to take account of the change in product flows. Not every SKU was suitable for a Carload Direct shipment, so the teams had to select products that could be part of the pooling system. And the changes had to be made without altering the inventory positions or service levels of either enterprise, especially OfficeMax. The shift from using a mix of truck and rail to primarily rail between the major Boise and OfficeMax distribution centers eliminated more than 2600 t of CO_2, a 70 % reduction compared to truckload shipments, or the equivalent of saving over 264,000 gal of fuel consumed by road vehicles.

---

[3] The Boise organization described in this case study refers to Boise Cascade LLC, the paper and forest products. It should not be confused with Boise Cascade Corporation that is now OfficeMax Incorporated.

Both companies benefitted from this greener supply chain as the reduced transportation costs were shared between them.

For the second initiative, Boise looked at its packaging and loading processes. Paper products are often ordered in large quantities and shipped in full pallets. Boise field operations noticed that full pallets did not always maximize the space in the rail boxcars. Boise redesigned its pallets and loading procedures to accommodate a half-pallet, which allowed Boise to reorganize pallet stacking and maximize shipping capacities for its loads. Once the operational configuration was solved, Boise needed to work with its customers to allow orders that included a half-pallet size.

Boise created new SKUs and modified ordering and receiving systems to allow for the new half-pallet product configuration. The company realized that this was a win-win situation; the half-pallet solution was a perfect fit for companies that shipped seasonal and low-demand products. Using just 930 railcars in 2011, Boise reduced the company's CO_2 emissions by 190 t or 6.8 % of its annual rail shipment emissions without any extra cost. This is equal to the CO_2 emissions from 21,600 gal of fuel, or the annual GHG emissions from 38 passenger vehicles. In addition to improving the environmental performance of Boise and participating customers, the smaller, the half-pallet unit gave Boise and its customers more order flexibility.

7.5.2 Competitor Collaboration: Ocean Spray and Tropicana

Identifying opportunities for using intermodal can be challenging. The respective transportation services must mesh seamlessly in order to maintain service standards and avoid delays that could result in the costly build-up of inventory. Ocean Spray captured such an opportunity in an unconventional way: it collaborated with a competitor.

Ocean Spray is an agricultural cooperative owned by more than 700 cranberry growers in Massachusetts, Wisconsin, New Jersey, Oregon, Washington, Canada, and Chile, as well as 35 Florida grapefruit growers. The organization posted fiscal 2012 gross sales of $2.2 billion and net proceeds of $338 million.

One of Ocean Sprays' most significant logistics expenses—and a major contributor to its carbon footprint—was the need to ship product from its Bordentown, New Jersey, distribution center over 1000 miles to another distribution center in Lakeland, Florida. By coincidence, both of these distribution centers were located a short distance (60–65 miles) from rail yards used by a competitor, Tropicana, which shipped orange juice north from Florida in special refrigerated boxcars.

Tropicana also had a key difficulty when it came to logistics. Although it could send product direct from Florida up to the CSX rail terminal in New Jersey, once offloaded, the refrigerated rail boxcars were often traveling empty back to Florida.

Tropicana's third-party logistics (3PL) provider, Wheels Clipper, saw an opportunity to help its client while earning the trust of a new customer. The company approached Ocean Spray and proposed that they operate an intermodal lane from New Jersey to Florida that would put Tropicana's empty orange juice boxcars to use on Ocean Spray's behalf. The goal was to save Ocean Spray money (and reduce emissions) by allowing them to switch from trucking their cranberry juice to sending it more efficiently by rail, while also saving Tropicana the cost and emissions associated with empty cars returning south.

The plan provided environmental benefits and lowered costs for both companies. But there were potential downsides. To make the idea work, Ocean Spray would have to switch logistics providers and work with a new 3PL, transporting via a mode with which the company was unfamiliar. Even more challenging, the arrangement required Ocean Spray to collaborate with one of the company's strongest competitors in the beverage business, Tropicana.

Using the intermodal solution would save Ocean Spray over 40 % in transportation costs compared to the previous trucking method, and it would also reduce its GHG emissions by a 65 %. Meanwhile, Tropicana would eliminate most of the costs and GHG emissions of the boxcars' return trip from its ledger—a significant reduction in each metric, at the price of some (admittedly complex) process changes.

Ocean Spray accepted that the plan did make sense, and the company reconfigured its load planning processes to make shipments compatible with the rail mode. Tropicana and Wheels Clipper also needed to change their operating procedures to communicate railcar availability to Ocean Spray. To guarantee the on-time delivery of all shipments, all the participants worked to improve supply chain visibility. For example, they improved the flow of information between the parties on the status of shipments and potential delays. As the intermediary, Wheels Clipper helped to ensure that this information was delivered to the relevant parties in a timely fashion.

During several pilot runs, the companies were able to coordinate load pickup and delivery within required time windows, and to confirm that product was being handled properly. The trials also revealed potential problems. For example, the new intermodal solution added 1–2 days to transit times, and Ocean Spray had to adjust its logistics operations to avoid having a negative impact on customer service. Yet in the end, the fact that there was a clear ROI for both shippers gave incentives to the participants that helped them to move the project forward and make it successful.

7.5.3   Supplier Collaboration: Caterpillar and Part Suppliers

Caterpillar Global Mining Division makes specialized trucks for the mining industry. Over the past 30 years, Caterpillar has produced nearly three times as many trucks as its closest competitor. The company assembled its 50,000th rigid-frame construction and mining truck in 2009.

Caterpillar worked on an initiative focused on the North American inbound parts logistics for Caterpillar's manufacturing facility in Decatur, Illinois. The goal was to reduce the weight of the thousands of returnable packing containers that Caterpillar used to transport parts from suppliers. Replacing the heavy metal packing containers with light-weight plastic units cuts the weight of shipments, which translates into less fuel consumption and reduced carbon emissions.

However, the effort required Caterpillar to coordinate with multiple suppliers in different countries. It was a daunting challenge, particularly when long-established practices have to be changed. Some of these containers had been in circulation for more than 50 years.

Prior to the carbon footprint study, Caterpillar's internal analysis had determined that the fuel savings from light-weighting inbound containers would be significant. Yet Caterpillar had been slow to adopt the plastic containers because of several internal organizational and budgetary constraints.

The first step was to carry out a detailed analysis of the inbound flow of containers. In partnership with MIT, Caterpillar analyzed 16 weeks of transportation data that included detailed information about North American suppliers, number of parts shipped, and delivery dates for three of the flagship mining trucks. The data included more than 15,000 truck deliveries of 1400 different item numbers from more than 200 suppliers that ship directly to the Decatur manufacturing plant. The Caterpillar and MIT teams determined that 9.5 % of shipments were eligible for light-weight packaging.

By reducing the shipping containers from 130 to 200 lb each to 20–40 lb each, Caterpillar could reduce CO_2 emissions across the Caterpillar North American network by 130 t. Caterpillar could now present a strong environmental case, in addition to a 2-year ROI viable financial benefit to all internal and external stakeholders affected by the packaging changes.

7.5.4   The EPA SmartWay Program

The SmartWay Transport Partnership is an innovative voluntary collaborative program between the EPA and the freight industry designed to improve energy efficiency and to lower GHG emissions and air pollution. Started in February 2004, the partnership aims to create strong market-based incentives for companies shipping products, and for the truck and rail companies delivering those products, to improve the environmental performance of their freight operations.

7.5.4.1   History[4]

In 2003, staff at the EPA's Office of Transportation and Air Quality (OTAQ) developed an initial concept to build an innovative voluntary freight transportation program focused on energy savings and emission reductions. They worked for over a

---

[4] Based on interviews and research conducted by K. C. Tan and E. E. Blanco from the MIT Center for Transportation & Logistics in 2009.

year in collaboration with a group of public and private stakeholders to develop the foundation of the EPA SmartWay Transport Partnership. Members of the group included the American Trucking Association, Business for Social Responsibility, Canon USA, Coca Cola Enterprises, CSX, FedEx, H-E-B Grocery, Home Depot, IKEA, Interface, Nike, Norm Thompson Outfitters, Schneider National, Swift Transportation, UPS, and YRC Worldwide.

Together, these stakeholders and the EPA designed a freight transportation program that addressed the goals and needs of both the freight industry and the EPA. The freight industry was interested in an improved public image, recognition for its efforts, and fuel savings to help companies in an extremely competitive industry. The EPA was interested in reducing emissions from diesel engines and improving energy security in the freight industry. The companies provided critical operational and technical insight into freight management and supply chain logistics. Their input helped the EPA to identify appropriate fuel saving technologies for heavy trucks and to develop a fuel and emissions tracking tool that carriers and shippers could use to track their performance.

Because program enrollment was going to be on a voluntary basis, it was important to make it attractive for companies to participate and to motivate them toward a collaborative solution in addressing energy and environmental issues in the freight sector. After much planning, the EPA formally launched the program with the full support of the trucking industry at the American Trucking Association's annual conference on February 9, 2004, with 15 initial charter partners.

7.5.4.2 Program Structure

The SmartWay Transport Partnership is tailored to progressive corporations and organizations involved in shipping goods. Companies that provide and hire freight delivery services become SmartWay Transport Partners by committing to improve the environmental performance of their freight delivery operations. SmartWay Transport Carriers commit to integrate innovative cost saving strategies into their fleet operations. SmartWay Transport Shippers commit to ship the majority of their goods with SmartWay Transport Carriers. Companies that meet SmartWay Transport Partnership requirements benefit from reduced operating costs and enhanced recognition and visibility: partners that demonstrate superior performance earn the right to display the SmartWay Transport logo.

The SmartWay program also provides technical assistance to help partners benchmark and evaluate the effectiveness of a broad range of technology, equipment controls, and fuel-saving logistics management strategies. The SmartWay program has also established connections with financial institutions to provide flexible, reduced-interest loans to improve access to these fuel-saving technologies and pollution controls.

7.5.4.3 Impact

Since 2004, SmartWay partners have eliminated over 51 million metric tons of CO_2, saved over 120 million barrels of oil and $16 billion in fuel costs, and reduced 738,000 t of NO_x and 37,000 t of PM (EPA 2014).

The success of SmartWay in the USA has led to its adoption in Canada, where Natural Resources Canada now administers the program for Canadian firms, using the same tools methods and metrics for assessing freight efficiency. In addition, the SmartWay public–private partnership model is now being replicated in other countries in Latin America, Asia, and the European Union. SmartWay is also being used as a template to inform the development of freight sustainability programs under the United Nations Climate Environment Program's and Clean Air Coalition (EPA 2014).

7.6 Beyond Green Logistics

This chapter has presented various levers available to improve the environmental impact of logistics operations. Most of the approaches discussed are familiar to logisticians: optimize distance, maximize loads, assign the right equipment and resource, and avoid waste. These are themes that have been used for many years to reduce cost and improve service. The same systematic approach can be used to make logistics better for the environment.

Underlying all the success stories and approaches presented throughout the chapter—from network design, vehicle routing or multi-stakeholder collaboration—is the need for a solid measurement foundation of GHG, pollution, noise, and waste impacts. Unlike financial measurements that are common and well understood, environmental metrics are uncertain and continuously evolving. Green logistics is not only about finding the optimal solution to an environmental metric, but also to make sure that traditional strategies are reviewed with environmental lenses. New trade-offs may be uncovered, as well as new sources of value and cost reduction.

This chapter uses a narrow scope—just logistics activities—for all analyses of impacts and strategies for improving. In transport sustainability some cases, a broader scope of analysis, such as an end-to-end life-cycle analysis, will reveal trade-offs between the greenest choices in logistics and greenest choices in sourcing, manufacturing, returns, product design, and so forth. For example, differences in manufacturing efficiencies or the energy portfolios of different regions may mean that higher impacts in transportation permit much lower environmental impacts overall. Or, a slower mode of transport might reduce transportation emissions but increase the amount of waste due to spoilage, obsolescence, or excessive inventory.

Thus, the analyses and strategies in this chapter are an element of a broader process of analyzing and improving the sustainability of the business or supply chain at a more holistic level. As a consequence, there are more opportunities related to green logistics. Reverse logistics and closed loop supply chains (see Chap. 17 by Abbey and Guide (2017)) adds a new dimension to managing waste by focusing on how to recover products delivered to customers and extract new sources of value. Technological improvements that completely avoid emissions, such as solar energy, could completely avoid the need to reconfigure logistics networks. Advances in nanomaterials and biodegradable materials may make packaging waste a nonissue. And, in some cases, life-cycle thinking may challenge logistics operations to increase their impact to allow for a holistic reduction of the environmental impact of products: it may be sometimes better to import a product from the other side of the world if energy sources are cleaner there than to manufacture it locally.

A new generation of green logistics choices is quickly unfolding, and the concepts discussed in this chapter provide a foundation for the journey ahead.

References

Abbey JD, Guide VDR Jr (2017) Closed-loop supply chains: a strategic overview. In: Bouchery Y, Corbett CJ, Fransoo J, Tan T (eds) Sustainable supply chains: a research-based textbook on operations and strategy. Springer, New York

Barth M, Boriboonsomsin K (2009) Energy and emissions impacts of a freeway-based dynamic eco-driving system. Transp Res Part D: Transp Environ 14(6):400–410

Bektaş T, Laporte G (2011) The pollution-routing problem. Transp Res B Methodol 45(8):1232–1250

Blanco E, Cottrill K (2013) Delivering on the promise of green logistics. MIT Sloan Manag Rev. http://sloanreview.mit.edu/article/delivering-on-the-promise-of-green-logistics/. Accessed 16 Dec 2013

Blanco E, Simchi-Levi D (2008). Generating a sustainability scorecard: assessing your company's footprint. CSCMP annual conference

Boukherroub T, Bouchery Y, Corbett CJ, Fransoo J, Tan T (2017) Carbon footprinting in supply chains. In: Bouchery Y, Corbett CJ, Fransoo J, Tan T (eds) Sustainable supply chains: a research-based textbook on operations and strategy. Springer, New York

Caplice C, Sheffi Y (1994) A review and evaluation of logistics metrics. Int J Logist Manag 5(2):11–28

Carslaw D, et al. (2011) Trends in NOx and NO2 emissions and ambient measurements in the UK. DEFRA, London

Craig A.J., Blanco E.E., Caplice C.G. (2013). "Carbon Footprint of Supply Chains: A Scoping Study". Final Report for NCFRP Project 36 (04).

EPA (2014) Mobile source technical review subcommittee: SmartWay Legacy Fleet Workgroup. Recommendations and findings

EPA (2015a) SmartWay Technology. http://epa.gov/smartway/forpartners/technology.htm

EPA (2015b). Municipal solid waste generation, recycling, and disposal in the United States: facts and figures for 2010 (pp 1–12)

European Environmental Agency (2015). Emissions of air pollutants from transport. http://www.eea.europa.eu/data-and-maps/indicators/transport-emissions-of-air-pollutants-8/transport-emissions-of-air-pollutants-2

Forkenbrock DJ (1999) External costs of intercity truck freight transportation. Transp Res A Policy Pract 33(7):505–526

Goetschalckx M, Vidal CJ, Dogan K (2002) Modeling and design of global logistics systems: a review of integrated strategic and tactical models and design algorithms. Eur J Oper Res 143(1):1–18

Greene DL, Plotkin SE (2011) Reducing greenhouse gas emissions from US Transportation. Pew Center on Global Climate Change, Arlington

Hoen KMR, Tan T, Fransoo JC, van Houtum GJ (2014a) Effect of carbon emission regulations on transport mode selection under stochastic demand. Flex Serv Manuf J 26(1–2):170–195

Hoen KMR, Tan T, Fransoo JC, van Houtum GJ (2014b) Switching transport modes to meet voluntary carbon emission targets. Transp Sci 48(4):592–608

IEA (2009) Transport, energy and CO2. Technical report. OECD, Paris

IMO (2009) Second IMO GHG Study 2009. International Maritime Organization (IMO), London

IMO (2012). International shipping facts and figures. International Maritime Organization

IMO (2015). Introduction to the IMO. http://www.imo.or. Accessed Nov 2015

IPCC (2006). IPCC guidelines for national greenhouse gas inventories. In: Eggleston S, Buendia L, Miwa K, Ngara T, Tanabe K. IGES, Japan

Koç Ç et al (2014) The fleet size and mix pollution–routing problem. Transp Res B Methodol 70:239–254

Laporte G (2009) Fifty years of vehicle routing. Transp Sci 43(4):408–416

Liedtke G and Friedrich H (2012) Generation of logistics networks in freight transportation models. Transportation: 1–17

Magnanti TL, Wong RT (1984) Network design and transportation planning: models and algorithms. Transp Sci 18(1):1–55

Martin S and Wolfram K (2012) Calculating GHG emissions for freight forwarding and logistics services. European Association for Forwarding, Transport, Logistics and Customs Services (CLECAT)

Mathers J et al (2014) The green freight handbook. Environmental Defense Fund

Melo MT, Nickel S, Saldanha-da-Gama F (2009) Facility location and supply chain management–a review. Eur J Oper Res 196(2):401–412

NTM (2010). Road transport Europe. Network for Transport and Environment

New York City Department of Environmental Protection - NYCDEP (2008). A guide to New York City's Noise Code. http://www.nyc.gov/html/dep/pdf/noise_code_guide.pdf Paine F (2002) Packaging reminiscences: some thoughts on controversial matters. Packag Technol Sci 15(4):167–179

Richter A et al (2004) Satellite measurements of NO2 from international shipping emissions. Geophys Res Lett 31(23)

Saphire D (1994) Delivering the goods: benefits of reusable shipping containers. INFORM, New York

Sheffi Y, Daganzo C (1978) Hypernetworks and supply-demand equilibrium obtained with disaggregate demand models. Transp Res Rec 673

Soroka W (1999) Fundamentals of packaging technology, Vol 3. Institute of Packaging Professionals

Stank TP, Goldsby TJ (2000) A framework for transportation decision making in an integrated supply chain. Supply Chain Manag Int J 5(2):71–78

Staples (2012) Interview to Mike Payette. http://www.brightfleet.com/blog/2012/interview-with-mike-payette-at-staples-about-speed-limiters-fuel-economy-and-safety/

UPS Pressroom. https://www.pressroom.ups.com/pressroom/ContentDetailsViewer.page?ConceptType=FactSheets&id=1426321581228-233. Accessed 2015

Velázquez Martínez JC, Fransoo JC (2017) Green facility location. In: Bouchery Y, Corbett CJ, Fransoo J, Tan T (eds) Sustainable supply chains: a research-based textbook on operations and strategy. Springer, New York

VTT Technical Research Centre of Finland (2012). Methodologies for emission calculations—best practices, implications and future needs. COFRET

Wang H, Liu D, Dai G (2009) Review of maritime transportation air emission pollution and policy analysis. J Ocean Univ China 8(3):283–290

Winebrake JJ, Corbett JJ et al (2008) Assessing energy, environmental, and economic tradeoffs in intermodal freight transportation. J Air Waste Manage Assoc 58(8):1004–1013

World Economic Forum—WEF (2009) Supply chain decarbonization (pp 1–41)

Zamboni G et al (2015) Experimental evaluation of Heavy Duty Vehicle speed patterns in urban and port areas and estimation of their fuel consumption and exhaust emissions. Transp Res D Transp Environ 35:1–10

Chapter 8
Green Inventory Management

Johan Marklund and Peter Berling

8.1 Introduction

Managing inventories and thereby controlling the material flows through a facility, or network of facilities, is a matter of key importance in achieving efficient supply chains. Core issues in traditional inventory management are *how much to order when and where to satisfy the customers' service needs at minimum cost?* In this context, reasons for keeping inventory are economies of scale in batch ordering/production, and/or uncertainties in demand and supply. However, inventory management may also involve strategic decisions regarding design of distribution and production networks, facility location, procurement, supplier selection, choice of product range, etc. Many of these strategic issues are treated thoroughly in other chapters of this book, and will not be further discussed in this chapter. Instead, we will focus on the core operational issues and define inventory management in line with the operations research and management science (OR/MS) literature on inventory control and inventory modeling. It should be noted that closed loop systems encompassing reverse logistics flows, which is part of this literature, are treated separately in Chap. 17 by Abbey and Guide (2017).

In green (or sustainable) inventory management, the pure economic focus (traditionally measured in terms of costs) is complemented with an environmental perspective (typically measured in terms of emissions). This means that potential trade-offs need to be identified and resolved. Thus, green inventory management in the context of this chapter is concerned with the overarching question of how to

J. Marklund (✉)
Department of Industrial Management and Logistics, Lund University, Lund, Sweden
e-mail: johan.marklund@iml.lth.se

P. Berling
Department of Industrial Management and Logistics, Lund University, Lund, Sweden

Department of Accounting and Logistics, Linnaeus University, Vaxjo, Sweden
e-mail: Peter.Berling@iml.lth.se

© Yann Bouchery, Charles J. Corbett, Jan C. Fransoo, and Tarkan Tan 2017
Y. Bouchery et al. (eds.), *Sustainable Supply Chains*, Springer Series in Supply
Chain Management 4, DOI 10.1007/978-3-319-29791-0_8

efficiently manage inventories (and thereby material flows) with respect to both costs and emissions. An important insight is that inventory decisions are interlinked with production and transportation decisions that directly influence emissions. A total cost and emissions perspective is therefore important in green inventory management to avoid suboptimization and achieve cost-efficient emission reductions. Crudely speaking, emissions are often divided into three categories: Green House Gases (GHG), other harmful gases, and particles. Among these, GHG emissions (for convenience often measured in CO_2 equivalents) are getting most of the attention in media, and society at large, because of its impact on global warming. This is also reflected in the OR/MS literature on green inventory management and in the contents of this chapter. (Chap. 3 by Boukherroub et al. (2017) focuses entirely on carbon footprinting.) However, it is important not to forget that environmental consequences are not limited to (GHG) emissions and may, for example, include: noise, accidents, waste product accumulation in landfills and oceans, chemicals that pollute our air, ground, and water supply, deforestation and exploitation of natural resources that damage our ecological systems, etc. (Chap. 2 by Guinée and Heijungs (2017) introduces LCA and, in doing so, a full spectrum of environmental impact categories.)

Looking at how inventory management decisions may influence emissions, we first note that emissions are associated with energy consumption. Thus, decisions that affect the energy consumption of the supply chain will influence its emissions. With this in mind one may divide the emissions associated with operating an inventory system into three categories: *emissions associated with ordering (i.e., producing and transporting) items*, *emissions associated with holding items in stock*, and *emissions associated with not satisfying customer demand on time*. Note that this partition mirrors the cost components usually considered in inventory management: *costs for ordering/procuring items*, *costs for holding items in stock*, and *shortage costs for not satisfying customer demands on time*.

In the remainder of this introduction, we will take a closer look at these three categories of emissions and costs and use them as a basis for identifying key questions and challenges for green inventory management research. Basic inventory modeling structures, assumptions, and issues are also discussed. This is followed by an overview of the existing green inventory management literature in Sects. 8.2 and 8.3, which illustrate what issues and challenges have been addressed in the literature so far, and how. Section 8.2 considers deterministic demand models and Sect. 8.3 stochastic demand models. We also distinguish between single-echelon and multi-echelon inventory systems. Section 8.4 concludes with remarks about findings, practical implications, and what remains to be done in.

8.1.1 Emissions and Costs Associated with Ordering Items

The decision of when and how much to order is intricately connected to the issue of how ordered items should be produced and/or transported. For example, larger lot (or order) sizes in manufacturing, especially in energy-intensive process industries, may have a significant impact on the energy use and emissions. However, it also leads to more finished goods and work in process inventory. The importance of transportation from an emissions point of view is apparent. For example, by choosing a greener transport mode such as sea or rail instead of road or air, the transport emissions, and generally also the transportation costs, can be reduced. Similarly, by employing shipment consolidation strategies and shipping full truck-loads and containers less frequently, the transportation capacity is better utilized. This means fewer vehicles are needed to ship the same volume suggesting less transportation emissions, and typically lower transportation costs for operating the system. The problem is that these strategies, which appear attractive when transportation is considered in isolation, can have negative consequences for the system as a whole. For example, greener transportation modes are generally slower, and often associated with larger fixed costs, suggesting longer transportation lead times and larger order sizes/shipment quantities. This means more inventory, and thereby increasing costs and emissions for holding inventory. Similarly, shipment consolidation suggests larger, less frequent, and/or less flexible shipments, and thereby more inventories. It is also noteworthy that these strategies are at odds with general perceptions of Just In Time (JIT) and LEAN, where frequent shipments of small batches are often implied.

8.1.2   Emissions and Costs Associated with Holding Items in Stock

The fact that there are costs of holding items in stock is undisputed. How these costs should be determined in practice is often more of an issue. The norm is to assume that they are proportional to the number of items in stock. (As some of the cost components usually are fixed, or tend to increase stepwise with the number of units in stock, the appropriateness of assuming linear holding costs may sometimes be questioned). The holding cost per unit and time unit can be divided into two main components: cost of capital, and out-of-pocket holding costs. The former is generally determined as a holding cost rate multiplied by the monetary value of the item. It should reflect the opportunity cost of tying up capital in inventory instead of in other investment opportunities. Conversely, the out-of-pocket holding cost rate should reflect the costs of operating the inventory facilities (including energy costs), handling the items, and loosing items because they perish, are stolen, destroyed in accidents, misplaced, etc. The emissions associated with holding items in stock are clearly connected to the energy consumption of operating the inventory facilities and handling the items, but also to items that are discarded and wasted. An important example of the latter is food (often with high CO_2 content) that perishes and is thrown away. For instance, the Swedish Institute for Food and Biotechnology (SIK) 2011, reports that roughly one-third of the food produced for human consumption is lost or wasted globally. Furthermore, in high income countries, one of the main reasons for the waste is lack of coordination between demand and supply. For more in-depth discussions of challenges and issues in sustainable food supply chain design, we refer to Chap. 18 by Bloemhof and Soysal (2017). Another less obvious emission source can be leakage of pollutants. As an example, Walmart states that leakage of highly potent GHG refrigerants account for 13% of their total GHG footprint, which is almost twice as much as what the fuel to their trucks account for (Walmart Global Responsibility Report 2013). This emphasizes the fact that the emissions of operating inventory facilities and stock handling is case dependent, and very much affected by the type of products considered. If a temperature-controlled environment is needed, as is the case for frozen or refrigerated products, the energy consumption and thereby emissions of holding items in stock are much higher and more important to consider than if items are stored in a non-heated warehouse or outdoors. Another example, in contrast to refrigerated products, is that many chemical companies, such as Eastman, at least for limited periods, store products in molten form, which requires a lot of energy.

Generally speaking, more inventories suggest increased costs and emissions, although exactly how and to what extent is often more difficult to say without a careful analysis. Assuming a proportional relationship, which is often done, is convenient, but may not always be appropriate. Relating inventory holding costs and emissions to the strategies for reducing production and/or transport emissions and costs above (e.g., use of greener transport modes, and shipment consolidation) illustrates important trade-offs. Reducing transport emissions and costs may lead to more inventory suggesting increased emissions and costs for holding items in stock. Resolving trade-offs like this to minimize *total costs and emissions* for the system is a key challenge in green (or sustainable) inventory management.

8.1.3   Emissions and Costs Associated with Not Satisfying Customer Demand on Time

The purpose of the inventory system is to provide adequate service to its customers. Not satisfying customer demands on time have negative impact on the customers as they are not receiving the service they expect. This negative impact can be translated into shortage costs for the inventory system. The shortage cost may be a fixed cost per shortage or it may be dependent on the time a customer has to wait for an item (it is then often referred to as a backorder cost). The shortage cost can reflect concrete monetary reimbursements or price discounts in case of delayed deliveries. It should also reflect loss of goodwill in terms of foregone future sales and revenues. Some shortage cost components may be relatively easy to determine, such as downtime costs in a machine or in a production facility. Other shortage cost components, such as loss of goodwill and future revenues, are more difficult to ascertain. These difficulties explain why service (level) constraints are more popular in practice than shortage costs. On the other hand, shortage costs are the preferred choice in the research literature as measuring all performance aspects in monetary terms enables a total cost perspective. Thus making it less ambiguous to compare the performance of different policies where the exact same service cannot be achieved.

The negative consequences of not satisfying customer demands on time may also involve increased emissions. For example, consider a dairy where a machine breakdown halts the production process. If the necessary spare part is not available within hours, the semi-finished milk products in the process must be discarded, and the facility needs to be cleaned before it can be restarted. Clearly, the emissions associated with throwing away a production batch of dairy products, and steam-cleaning the process facility are significant. Another example of emissions associated with not satisfying customer demand on time is the transport emissions of a customer making an extra trip, e.g., to IKEA, because the product was stocked out when she initially went there to buy it. In situations like this when poor service generates emissions at a firm's customer (Scope 3 emissions) there is a problem of how to allocate the emissions between the two parties. The problem is especially difficult if the customer, as in the IKEA example, has a choice to make the extra trip or not. Emission allocation issues are briefly discussed in Chap. 3 (Boukherroub et al. 2017). A common situation not complicated by emission allocation issues between the firm and its customers is when the firm uses emergency shipments to deal with inventory shortages. The extra transportation emissions for these emergency shipments may be interpreted as emissions for not satisfying customer demand on time through the regular inventory system. The emergency shipments are often associated with higher emissions than regular deliveries due to lower load efficiency in vehicles and use of faster, more energy intensive, transportation modes.

Similarly to shortage costs, the emissions associated with not satisfying customer demand on time can be more or less difficult to determine: In the dairy example above and in terms of emergency shipments, it is relatively straightforward although not without practical challenges. However, in the IKEA example it is more difficult as the second trip to IKEA in some cases would have been made anyway because the customer was going there to buy other products. Also, the length of the trip, and thereby the emissions, are different across customers, making it difficult to estimate. Although the emissions and costs associated with not satisfying customer demand on time are sometimes challenging to determine, they can be very important to consider in green inventory management. Returning to the dairy example above, which stems from a real case, the spare parts provider initially had the ambition to eliminate air freight, and switch to road and sea freight to reduce transport emissions. However, after further analysis, they concluded that these reductions were minute in comparison to the increased risk of not delivering spare parts fast enough to avoid production losses.

From the discussion above we can conclude that key challenges in green inventory management are to understand how a decision impacts the costs and emissions for the inventory system, and how to leverage this understanding to make the "best" decisions. The overarching goal is to minimize both costs and emissions, but decisions that minimize the system's costs rarely minimize its emissions and vice versa. Thus a key question is how these potentially conflicting objectives may be reconciled, or in other words, to define what "best" decisions means in different contexts. The main approaches used are to: (1) translate emissions into environmental costs and minimize the total costs, (2) minimize the costs while restricting the total emissions to not exceed a given maximum value or cap, (3) minimize the costs under an emissions cap that can be traded on a market, and (4) use Multiple Criteria Decision Making (MCDM) techniques to combine the emission and cost perspectives. The latter may involve identifying efficient frontiers, Pareto optimal solutions, construction of utility functions etc. The former three reflects a hierarchical view where the main goal is cost minimization. From a company perspective, emission restrictions and environmental costs can reflect regulations and taxes imposed by society, or it may be based on voluntary commitments. Another form of the latter is investing in different types of carbon offsets (e.g., planting of trees).

An aspect worth noting is that depending on how the supply chained is organized, the types of emissions discussed above may (according to the GHG protocol) belong to Scope 1 (direct emissions, e.g., from company owned vehicles), Scope 2 (indirect emissions from electricity, heating, cooling, etc. purchased by the company) or Scope 3 (other indirect emissions, e.g., from customers and outsourced services, including transportation and warehousing). As outsourcing is very common in logistics (for example, companies today rarely have their own private transportation fleet), the Scope 3 emissions are significant. The challenges of measuring and allocating (Scope 3) emissions in supply chains are thoroughly discussed in Chap. 3 (Boukherroub et al. 2017) and will not be further discussed in this chapter.

Considering the relative size of the emissions discussed above, emissions for producing and transporting items are in general much larger than those for holding items in stock. For instance, the World Economic Forum (2009) estimates that about 90 % of the emissions (measured in CO_2 equivalents) for logistics and transport activities are due to freight transportation, and 10 % for operating logistics buildings. (Emissions associated with production, or not satisfying the customer on time, are not discussed in this report, which focuses on emission sources in logistics and transportation from a macroperspective). Moreover, the energy demand for freight transport is expected to continue to increase because of the globalization of trade and supply chains. The European Commission (2009) estimates a 60 % increase in this energy demand from 1990 to 2030 (1990–2009 the observed increase was 36 %). Thus from a climate perspective, reducing transport emissions is important. An obvious step in this direction is development of cleaner vehicle technologies, but the World Economic Forum (2009) also emphasizes several other important strategies including: despeeding the supply chain, optimizing transport networks, and switching of transport modes to greener alternatives. Important enablers for despeeding the supply chain, without significant cost increases due to prolonged lead times, are improved collaboration and information sharing between suppliers, customers, and other parties in the supply chain. With respect to optimized networks, the Word Economic Forum estimate that 24 % of the goods vehicle kilometers in the EU are associated with empty vehicles, and when carrying a load, vehicles are on average filled to 57 % of their maximum gross weight. Altogether this indicates a large potential for increasing the capacity utilization of vehicles, for example, through better shipment consolidation and multimodal transport solutions. From an inventory management perspective, all these strategies for greener transports (except perhaps cleaner vehicle technologies) suggests longer lead times, and thereby a need for more inventory, or a decline in customer service. Thus an important question in green inventory management is how to enable reduction in transport emissions without compromising customer service or increasing total costs and emissions. Here, green (or sustainable) management of multi-echelon (or multi-stage) inventory systems, with inventories upstream and downstream in the supply chain that jointly can compensate for lead time changes, offers interesting opportunities.

From a modeling perspective, the added complexity in green inventory management, compared to traditional cost-based inventory models, is to quantify also the emissions (or environmental consequences), and to find optimal decisions with respect to both costs and emissions. An important first step is then to be able to evaluate the expected emissions and costs associated with a decision. We note that in cases where the emissions accumulate in the same way as the costs, the expected costs and the expected emissions may be evaluated using the same method. Thus, if a traditional inventory management model already exists for evaluating the expected costs, the same model can be used also for determining the expected emissions. The remaining challenge is then to find the best joint decisions with regard to costs and emissions. Of course, if the emission and cost components cannot be modelled analogously, new evaluation methods are needed. Thus, an important question for green (or sustainable) inventory management modeling is to what extent it may be built on existing results. The fact that it requires careful balancing of costs against emissions emphasizes a need for precise models and evaluation methods in both dimensions. This means that traditional approximations and model assumptions, not least regarding costs, should be carefully analyzed before they are used.

8.2   Green Inventory Management Under Deterministic Demand

This section provides an overview of green inventory models that are based on the assumption that future demand is known with certainty. Such an assumption of deterministic demand can be appropriate in some situations, but clearly most often, future demand is uncertain. Still, deterministic models are often used with good results as heuristics for determining order quantities (or lot sizes) also when the demand is stochastic. Disregarding demand uncertainties simplifies the analysis. It is therefore a natural starting point for gaining some first insights of the cost and emission trade-offs that exist in green inventory management. An important aspect of this is the impact of different mechanisms for reducing emissions used by policy makers. Most of the literature on sustainable inventory control with deterministic demand is based on the well-known economic order quantity (EOQ) model for lot sizing published already in 1913 by Ford W. Harris, (Harris 1913). We first present some of these results and then discuss some more elaborate models that extend and confirm the main insights gained from the simpler EOQ-models.

8.2.1 The Single-Echelon EOQ-Model with Environmental Considerations

The traditional EOQ-model considers a single inventory location and a single product with a constant and continuous demand D per time unit. The lead-time is zero and no backorders or lost sales are allowed so each time the inventory level goes to zero a new order is placed. Stock keeping in this simple setting is motivated by economies of scale in batch ordering/production as reflected by the fixed cost per order. The aim is to minimize the average cost per time unit of ordering and keeping this product in stock. Extensions to discrete demand, a positive lead-time, planned backorders, and a volume-based price per unit are straightforward (see, for example, Axsäter 2006), but will not be further discussed in this chapter.

Each time an order is placed in the EOQ-model, the firm incurs a fixed cost A per order and a variable cost c per unit purchased. The cost for an order of Q units is thus $A + cQ$ and such an order will be placed every Q/D time unit. There is a holding cost h per unit and time unit for inventory kept in stock. The average amount of inventory if one orders Q will be $Q/2$. The total cost per time unit, $Z(Q)$, can be divided into two parts; the per unit purchase cost, cD, and the inventory-related cost, $Z'(Q)$,

$$Z(Q) = \frac{AD}{Q} + h\frac{Q}{2} + cD = Z'(Q) + cD.$$

The cost-minimizing solution, which does not involve any environmental considerations, is of the well-known square root form

$$\min_Q Z(Q) \Rightarrow Q_z^* = \sqrt{\frac{2AD}{h}} \Rightarrow Z'(Q_z^*) = \sqrt{2AhD}.$$

Emissions are incorporated into the model using an emissions structure that mirrors the cost structure. To do so we introduce the emission parameters $\hat{A}$, $\hat{c}$ and $\hat{h}$ denoting the emission per placed order, per unit ordered, and per unit kept in stock for one unit of time. The average emissions per time unit, $E(Q)$, can then be expressed as

$$E(Q) = \frac{\hat{A}D}{Q} + \hat{h}\frac{Q}{2} + \hat{c}D = E'(Q) + \hat{c}D.$$

The associated emission minimizing solution, $\min_Q E(Q)$, is analogously

$$Q_E^* = \sqrt{\frac{2\hat{A}D}{\hat{h}}} \Rightarrow E'(Q_E^*) = \sqrt{2\hat{A}\hat{h}D}.$$

It follows that a reduction in emissions by adjusting the order quantity from the cost-minimizing solution can only be attained if the relationship

$$\alpha = \frac{\hat{A}/\hat{h}}{A/h} \neq 1$$

Note that if $\alpha = 1$, the two solutions, Q_Z^* and Q_E^*, will coincide. In all other cases, i.e., $\alpha \neq 1$, a reduction in emissions implies a deviation from the cost-minimizing order quantity, Q_Z^*, and thus an increase in cost. The best ordering decision from a joint emission and cost perspective is the one that gives the lowest cost for a given amount of emission or vice versa, i.e., a solution that belongs to the efficient cost-emission frontier as depicted in Fig. 8.1. The properties of this frontier for the classical EOQ-problem are analyzed and discussed in Bouchery et al. (2012). Key results, illustrated in Fig. 8.1, are that the efficient frontier is convex, and that substantial emission reductions can be attained with only a modest increase in cost when the cost is close to optimal. The opposite holds when the inventory-related cost is far from optimal, that is, a large increase in cost is needed to attain a small emission reduction.

The behavior can be explained by the well-established fact that for the classic EOQ-problem, the total cost is fairly insensitive to changes in the order quantity around its optimum Q_Z^*. Conversely, the total cost is highly sensitive to such changes

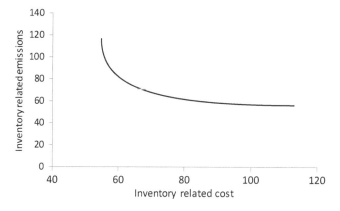

Fig. 8.1 Efficient cost-emission frontier for a single-echelon EOQ system (adapted from Bouchery et al. 2012)

when the order quantity is far from the optimum. This relationship between cost and emissions is formalized by Chen et al. (2013), which show that the relative reduction of the inventory-related emissions

$$\delta_{E'}\left(\delta_{Z'},\alpha\right)=\frac{E'\left(Q_Z^*\right)-E'\left(Q(\delta_{Z'},\alpha)\right)}{E'\left(Q_Z^*\right)}$$

as a function of the relative increase in inventory-related costs

$$\delta_{Z'}=\frac{Z'\left(Q(\delta_{Z'},\alpha)\right)-Z'\left(Q_Z^*\right)}{Z'\left(Q_Z^*\right)}$$

is,

$$\delta_{E'}\left(\delta_{Z'},\alpha\right)=\begin{cases}-\dfrac{\left(\delta_{Z'}-\sqrt{2\delta_{Z'}+\delta_{Z'}^{\,2}}\right)\left(1-\alpha+\delta_{Z'}-\sqrt{2\delta_{Z'}+\delta_{Z'}^{\,2}}\right)}{\left(1+\alpha\right)\left(1+\delta_{Z'}-\sqrt{2\delta_{Z'}+\delta_{Z'}^{\,2}}\right)},&if\ \alpha<1,\\[4mm]-\dfrac{\left(\delta_{Z'}+\sqrt{2\delta_{Z'}+\delta_{Z'}^{\,2}}\right)\left(1-\alpha+\delta_{Z'}+\sqrt{2\delta_{Z'}+\delta_{Z'}^{\,2}}\right)}{\left(1+\alpha\right)\left(1+\delta_{Z'}+\sqrt{2\delta_{Z'}+\delta_{Z'}^{\,2}}\right)},&if\ \alpha>1.\end{cases}$$

They also show that the maximum relative decrease in emissions compared to the cost-minimizing solution is $\delta_{E'}=\left(E'\left(Q_Z^*\right)-E'\left(Q_E^*\right)\right)/E'\left(Q_Z^*\right)=\left(1-\sqrt{\alpha}\right)^2/\left(1+\alpha\right)$ which is attained with a relative increase in the cost of $\delta_{Z'}=\left(Z'\left(Q_E^*\right)-Z'\left(Q_Z^*\right)\right)/Z\left(Q_Z^*\right)=\left(1-\sqrt{\alpha}\right)^2/2\sqrt{\alpha}$

As mentioned earlier, Multiple Criteria Decision Making techniques based on efficient frontier analyses and/or formulas as the ones above is one of several approaches used for combining emission and cost considerations in green inventory management. The other approaches, i.e., to translate the emission into an environmental cost (for example, in terms of an imposed carbon tax), to use an emission constraint with a fixed cap, or to operate under cap and trade or cap and offset systems, have all been studied in the literature on green EOQ-problems, for example, in Chen et al. (2013) and Hua et al. (2011). These findings are summarized below.

If a tax of t is imposed for each emission unit, the average inventory-related cost per time unit is

$$Z'_t(Q)=Z'(Q)+tE'(Q)=\frac{\left(A+t\hat{A}\right)D}{Q}+\left(h+t\hat{h}\right)\frac{Q}{2},$$

and the associated optimal (cost-minimizing) order quantity is

$$Q_t^*(t) = \sqrt{\frac{2\left[A+t\hat{A}\right]D}{h+t\hat{h}}} \Rightarrow Z_t'\left(Q_t^*(t)\right) = \sqrt{2\left[A+t\hat{A}\right]\left(h+t\hat{h}\right)D}.$$

The order quantity $Q_t^*(t)$ is equal to the traditional cost-minimizing order quantity, Q_Z^*, if $t=0$ (i.e., the tax rate is zero). Moreover, it approaches the emission minimizing order quantity, Q_E^*, as $t \to \infty$ (from above when $\alpha < 1$, and from below when $\alpha > 1$). With $u = \hat{A}/A$, and $v = \hat{h}/h$, the relative shift in inventory-related costs and emissions as a function of the tax rate is

$$\frac{Z_t'\left(Q_Z^*\right) - Z_t'\left(Q_t^*(t)\right)}{Z_t'\left(Q_Z^*\right)} = 1 - \frac{\sqrt{(1+ut)(1+vt)}}{1+(u+v)t/2}$$

$$\frac{E'\left(Q_Z^*\right) - E'\left(Q_t^*(t)\right)}{E'\left(Q_Z^*\right)} = 1 - \left(\frac{u}{u+v}\sqrt{\frac{1+vt}{1+ut}} + \frac{v}{u+v}\sqrt{\frac{1+ut}{1+vt}}\right)$$

Both of these relative changes are increasing in the tax rate with the limiting value $\left(1-\sqrt{\alpha}\right)^2 / (1+\alpha)$ as the tax rate goes to infinity (see Chen et al. 2013 for details). The relative cost increase compared to a system without any tax can be substantial, and are equal to

$$\delta_{z',t} = \frac{Z_t'(Q_t^*(t)) - Z'(Q_Z^*)}{Z'(Q_Z^*)} = \sqrt{\frac{(A+t\hat{A})(h+t\hat{h})}{Ah}} - 1.$$

However, most of this increase in cost is due to tax payments. The increase of the sum of holding and ordering costs is still limited to $(1-\sqrt{\alpha})^2 / 2\sqrt{\alpha}$ in accordance with the findings for the efficient frontier.

If a cap, C, is imposed on the average emissions per time unit we have

$$E'(Q) = \frac{\hat{A}D}{Q} + \hat{h}\frac{Q}{2} \leq C' = C - c'D.$$

This restricts the possible order quantities to

$$Q_L(C') \leq Q \leq Q_U(C')$$

where

$$Q_L(C') = \frac{C' - \sqrt{C'^2 - 2\hat{A}\hat{h}D}}{\hat{h}} \quad \text{and} \quad Q_U(C') = \frac{C' + \sqrt{C'^2 - 2\hat{A}\hat{h}D}}{\hat{h}}$$

As $Z(Q)$ is convex in Q, the optimal (cost-minimizing) order quantity under a carbon constraint is

$$
Q_C^*(C,) = \begin{cases} Q_L(C,) & Q_Z^* < Q_L(C,) \\ Q_Z^* & Q_L(C,) \le Q_Z^* \le Q_L(C,) \\ Q_U(C,) & Q_Z^* > Q_U(C,) \end{cases}
$$

The inventory policy and the inventory-related emissions, $E'(Q_C^*(C')) = \min(E'(Q_Z^*), C')$, is independent of the cap as long as the constraint is not violated by the traditional cost-minimizing policy, Q_Z^*.

If a cap and trade system is used for regulating emissions, it is possible to purchase emission rights to relax the constraint, or to sell unused emission rights if the firm's emissions are below the cap. If the buying and selling price of the emission rights, p, are the same, and potential revenue from trading is viewed as a negative cost, the average inventory-related cost under cap and trade is

$$
Z'(Q) = Z'(Q) + p(E'(Q) - C') = \frac{(A + p\hat{A})D}{Q} + (h + p\hat{h})\frac{Q}{2} - pC'.
$$

Comparing this cost expression with the one where an emission tax is applied, $Z_t'(Q)$, we can see that they are indeed very similar. The difference is that the price for emissions, p, has replaced the tax rate, t, and that an adjustment, pC', is made as one only pays for the emissions in excess of the cap. Consequently, the optimal solution is also similar

$$
Q_{C\&T}^*(p) = \sqrt{\frac{2(A + p\hat{A})D}{h + p\hat{h}}} \Rightarrow Z'_{C\&T}(Q_{C\&T}^*(p)) = \sqrt{2(A + p\hat{A})(h + p\hat{h})D} - pC'.
$$

In fact, the EOQ-model with an emission tax, can be viewed as a special case of the same model with a cap and trade mechanism, with the cap set to zero, and price of emission rights, p, set to the tax rate t. A major difference between a cap and trade system and tax system (also when $p = t$) is that the former implies less of a cost increase for the firms (except when $C' = 0$) as one gets a reimbursement equal to pC'. For some firms the revenue from selling emission rights might even exceed their increase in inventory-related cost. This means they are better off under a cap and trade system than without any regulations.

Interestingly, from the expression for $Q_{C\&T}^*(p)$ we can see that there is no direct connection between the cap, C, and the optimal inventory policy. There should be an indirect connection though, as reduced caps imply an increased demand for emission rights. This should increase the price p and push $Q_{C\&T}^*(p)$ towards the emission minimizing order quantity, Q_E^*. Some companies will benefit from a general reduction of the cap whereas others will lose money.

A cap and offset system is similar to a cap and trade system but it does not allow companies to sell emission rights. The optimal (cost-minimizing) policy in such a system is given by

$$Q^*_{C\&O}(p,C') = \begin{cases} Q^*_{C\&T}(p) & \text{if} Q^*_Z \le Q^*_{C\&T}(p) \le Q_L(C') \\ Q_L(C') & \text{if} Q^*_Z \le Q_L(C') \le Q^*_{C\&T}(p) \\ Q^*_Z & \text{if} Q_L(C') \le Q^*_Z \le Q_U(C') \\ Q_U(C') & \text{if} Q^*_{C\&T}(p) \le Q_U(C') \le Q^*_Z \\ Q^*_{C\&T}(p) & \text{if} Q_U(C') \le Q^*_{C\&T}(p) \le Q^*_Z \end{cases}$$

This means that the cost-minimizing order quantity, Q^*_Z, is chosen if possible. Otherwise, the optimal order quantity is determined by the cap, via $Q_L(C')$ and $Q_U(C')$, or by the optimal cap and trade solution, $Q^*_{C\&T}(p)$. Note that $Q^*_{C\&T}(p)$ implies that emission rights are sold if $Q_L(C') < Q^*_{C\&T}(p) < Q_U(C')$. Hence, $Q^*_{C\&T}(p)$ is not a viable solution in a cap and offset system in this interval. The cap and offset system can be viewed as a special case of a cap and trade system with buying price of emission rights, p, and selling price of zero. Any cap and trade system with a difference in buying and selling price of emission rights will exhibit similar structure. Albeit with seven possible order quantities as emission rights will be sold if the optimal order quantity when doing so falls between $Q_L(C')$ and $Q^*_{C\&T}(p)$, or $Q_U(C')$ and $Q^*_{C\&T}(p)$.

8.2.2   Extensions of the Single-Echelon EOQ-Model with Environmental Considerations

Extensions of the single-echelon EOQ-model with environmental considerations found in the literature include alternative cost/emission structures, non-stationary demand, and multi-echelon models.

Several authors, Battini et al. (2014), Bozorgi et al. (2014), and Konur and Schaefer (2014) consider non-linear (stepwise increasing) ordering costs and emissions to capture the limited capacity of trucks and similar transportation resources. Problems with non-linear ordering cost are not new but one can argue that they are of particular interest for environmental considerations as much of the transport emissions are due to the movement of the actual vehicle. Konur (2014) elaborates further on this problem by integrating the design of the transportation fleet into the inventory management decisions.

Toptal et al. (2014) consider the EOQ-model where there exists an alternative emission-reducing investment. In a cap and trade system, the optimal order quantity is still $Q^*_{C\&T}(p)$. The reason is that an emission reduction leads to the same saving or revenue no matter how it is achieved. In contrast, in a system with a fixed cap, the optimal ordering quantity and the alternative emission-reducing investment will be interdependent. To achieve an emission reduction, an adjustment of the order quantity will always be made. The alternative emission-reducing investment is used as a complement if the reduction required to reach the cap is substantial.

Inventory problems with deterministic non-stationary demand are considered in Benjaafar et al. (2013), Absi et al. (2013) and Helmrich et al. (2015) among others. Benjaafar et al. (2013) make a number of observations based on a series of numerical experiments that are in line with what can be deduced directly from the EOQ-model discussed above. In addition they point to the fact that if the emission cap is not based on the long-run average but is imposed on a given period, then a tighter cap might lead to higher total emissions (something that applies to the problem with stationary demand as well).

The literature on green inventory control in a multi-echelon setting with deterministic demand is more limited. Bouchery et al. (2012) extend the analysis of the efficient cost-emission frontier to a two stage serial system. For a single criteria problem, the optimal policy is a stationary nested policy, i.e., the higher echelon always order an integer multiple k of the lower echelon's order quantity. For a multi-criteria problem, the optimal policy is still nested but not necessarily stationary. This is illustrated in Fig. 8.2 that shows the frontier for the best combined policy as well as the efficient frontier of a number of stationary-nested policies.

The analysis in Bouchery et al. (2012) focuses on stationary policies arguing that such policies are easier to implement in practice. In the non-convex segments of the frontier of stationary policies, a better solution can be obtained using a linear combination of two nested policies, represented by the dotted straight line in Fig. 8.2. This renders the true cost/emission frontier. Thus, in contrast to a single-echelon system, the optimal policy in a serial system is not necessarily stationary even under constant demand.

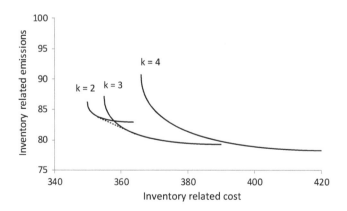

Fig. 8.2 Efficient cost-emission frontier in a serial system (adapted from Bouchery et al. 2012). The solid line depicts the efficient frontier for stationary nested policies with $k = 2, 3$, and 4 respectively. The efficient frontier for all policies is a combination of these and the dotted line which is a non-stationary policy

Benjaafar et al. (2013) investigates the cost benefit of collaborating in a supply chain in order to meet emission caps. They show numerically that the relative benefits can be substantial, particularly for mid-range emission caps. When the cap is high, it has little influence on the supply chain. If the cap is low, the cost for the supply chain to adhere to it will be very high, and the relative savings of collaborating to meet the cap will be low, even if they might be high in absolute values. They also show that as always, it is important that the benefits of collaboration are not distributed in a too unfair manner. If they are, some parties might prefer to not collaborate as this will increase their costs, even if the total cost for the supply chain decreases. Wahab et al. (2011) investigate supply-chain collaboration in an EOQ-setting considering imperfect items and environmental impact. The latter is captured as a tax on emissions, and they assume that there are no emissions linked to holding inventory. Their numerical examples show a reduction of the order-quantity when environmental considerations are taken. With a larger amount of emissions linked to holding inventory, the results could, of course, be reversed.

8.3   Green Inventory Management Under Stochastic Demand

In this section we extend the scope to green inventory management models that deals with demand uncertainty. In these models, the demand is represented by stochastic (or random) variables with known probability distributions. A stochastic variable can have many different outcomes, and the probability (or density, if it is a continuous variable) for each outcome is specified in a probability distribution. In practice, demand is almost always uncertain, and arguably one of the main reasons for stock keeping in practice is to buffer against this uncertainty, and maintain acceptable customer service. The importance of stochastic demand models in inventory management is therefore undisputed. In the following, we will consider a range of green inventory models available in the literature to illustrate and explain how the different challenges and trade-offs discussed in the beginning of this chapter are considered. We first focus on single-echelon models and then extend the scope to multi-echelon models involving networks of inventory locations. (We assume the locations as given; in Chap. 9, Velásquez Martínez and Fransoo examine green facility location.) For reasons of space, some models are treated more briefly than others. This does not mean that they are less important or interesting. Mathematical details of more complex models are omitted.

8.3.1   Single-Echelon Models for Green Inventory Management

A single-echelon inventory model considers a single stock-point in isolation. One of the simplest and most widely used single-echelon inventory models for stochastic demand is the newsvendor model. It considers a single product in a single period (or selling season) and may be appropriate for seasonal goods, fashion clothing, and high tech products with very short lifecycles. Our exposuré begins by considering green inventory management in newsvendor settings. The scope is then extended to more general inventory management situations with multiple periods and replenishment opportunities.

8.3.1.1   Green Inventory Management in Newsvendor Settings

The classical newsvendor model assumes that the demand during the selling period is stochastic, and at the end of the period there are overage (holding) costs associated with every unsold unit, and underage (shortage) costs associated with every unsatisfied demand. The focus is on the inventory management decision of how many units to order for the coming period, when the objective is to minimize the expected overage (holding) and underage (shortage) costs. An alternative objective is to maximize the expected profit for the considered period by also taking purchase and selling prices per unit into consideration.

To illustrate how the newsvendor framework can be used for green inventory management, we consider a dual sourcing model analyzed in Rosič and Jammernegg (2013), and Arıkan and Jammernegg (2014). Together these two papers consider costs and emissions associated with ordering, producing, and transporting items and with holding items in stock. They also consider different types of emission regulations and emission constraints for a profit maximizing firm. More precisely, Rosič and Jammernegg (2013) investigate the economic and environmental impact of dual sourcing for three scenarios of emission regulations: (1) no regulations, (2) an emission (or carbon) tax and (3) a cap and trade system with fixed price emission allowances. In their model a profit maximizing firm has the option to source from a low-cost offshore supplier before a given selling season starts, or to use a more expensive, fast, onshore supplier, when demand has been realized at the end of the selling season. Transporting goods from the offshore supplier is associated with transport emissions, while transport emissions from the onshore supplier are negligible. During the selling season there is a stochastic demand for X units, and the firm sells the product at unit price p. Unsold products (in inventory) at the end of the season has a per unit salvage value z, which includes the inventory holding costs. The firm procures q units from the offshore supplier at the unit price c before the season starts, and the rest from the onshore supplier at unit price $c+d$ at the end of the season when the demand is known. It is assumed that $p>c>z$, and $p>c+d$ so that the onshore supplier is an option to consider. Thus, if a demand of x units is realized max$(x-q, 0)=(x-q)^+$ units are purchased from the onshore supplier. This corresponds to the underage or lost sales in the classical newsvendor model. Moreover, the underage cost is d, the overage cost is $c-z$, and the firm's profit function, given q and x, is

$$P(q,x) = \begin{cases} (p-c)x - (c-z)(q-x) & \text{if } x \le q \\ (p-c)x - d(x-q) & \text{if } x > q \end{cases}$$

The expected profit, given the offshore order quantity q, is obtained by taking the expectation with respect to the demand X

$$P(q) = E\left[(p-c)X - (c-z)(q-X)^+ - d(X-q)^+\right].$$

Letting $F(x)$ denote the cumulative distribution function (cdf) of the continuous demand X, and $F^{-1}(.)$ its inverse, it follows from the classical newsvendor analysis that the optimal offshore order quantity is

$$q^* = F^{-1}\left(\frac{d}{d+c-z}\right).$$

Introducing a transportation emission tax, t, per unit shipped from the offshore supplier increases its per-unit costs to $c+t$. This decreases the optimal amount procured offshore, q^t, and thereby the transport emissions, but it also decreases the expected profit.

$$P(q) = E\left[(p-c-t)X - (c+t-z)(q-X)^+ - (d-t)(X-q)^+\right].$$

$$q^t = F^{-1}\left(\frac{d-t}{d+c-z}\right)$$

As an alternative to the linear emission tax, the authors also consider an emissions trading system, where the company, free of charge, receives emission allowances corresponding to an emission cap of L products transported from the offshore supplier. The firm can buy more emission allowances at the per unit price b, and sell allowances it does not use at the per unit price s ($b \geq s$). This means that the transport emission costs are $b(q-L)^+$, the revenue of selling unused emission allowances is $s(L-q)^+$, and the expected profit for emission cap L and offshore order quantity q is:

$$P_L(q) = \begin{cases} P_s(q) \text{ for } q \leq L \\ P_b(q) \text{ for } q > L \end{cases}, \text{ where } \begin{cases} P_s(q) = P(q) + s(L-q) \\ P_b(q) = P(q) - b(q-L) \end{cases}.$$

It is straightforward to show that the optimal offshore order quantity for an emission cap of L, q^L, is obtained as a two-sided control limit policy

$$q^L = \begin{cases} q^b & \text{for } L < q^b \\ L & \text{for } q \leq L < q^s \\ q^s & \text{for } L > q^s \end{cases}$$

Here q^b and q^s maximizes $P_b(q)$ and $P_s(q)$, respectively, and are easily obtained as

$$q^b = F^{-1}\left(\frac{d-b}{d+c-z}\right) \text{ and } q^s = F^{-1}\left(\frac{d-s}{d+c-z}\right)$$

Note that $b \geq s$ implies that $q^b \leq q^s$, and that $s = b = 0$ brings us back to the basic dual sourcing model without emission regulations. Moreover, $L = 0$ and $b = t$ renders the emission tax model.

From the above expressions one can conclude that $q^L < q^*$, meaning that the offshore order quantity, and thereby the emissions are reduced through the emission trading system. One can also see that the smallest offshore order quantity under the emission trading system is q^b. Thus, setting the cap, L, lower than this will not reduce the transport emissions further it will only decrease the firm's profit.

In a numerical study based on normally distributed demand, the authors illustrate that dual sourcing as described in this stylized model can reduce emissions and improve economic performance in comparison to single sourcing from an offshore supplier. By implementing environmental regulations in terms of a linear transport emission tax or a cap and trade system, the transport emissions can be further reduced. Both an emission tax and a cap and trade system are in the context of this model very effective tools to reduce emissions, but the emission tax tend to affect the firm's profit more severely. Under the cap and trade system profits can even increase, as the firm may generate extra revenues by selling emission allowances it has received for free but do not need. These results indicate that from the firm's perspective a cap and trade system is preferred over an emission tax.

Arıkan and Jammernegg (2014) consider the same dual sourcing model, but when a Product Carbon Footprint (PCF) constraint, set voluntarily or by regulators, is used to limit the emissions. Hence, the management objective is to maximize the profit, $P(q)$, subject to the PCF constraint. The carbon footprint may be used for differentiating the firm's products, for example, by displaying it on an eco-label. The emissions considered in the model are production, transportation, and warehousing activities. Emissions caused customers by usage and consumption are excluded. The emissions related to holding items in stock (overage), including disposal of products or shipping them to secondary markets, etc. are modelled explicitly by use of e_L, the per unit emissions for surplus inventory at the end of the period. Similarly, the target emissions per unit is denoted e, the per unit emissions from the first (offshore) and second supply options are denoted e_1 and e_2, respectively. Let $L(q)$ denote the expected overage given the offshore order quantity q, and $Q(q)$ the expected underage.

$$L(q) = E\left[(q - X)^+\right] = \int_0^q (q - x) f(x) dx,$$

$$Q(q) = E\left[(X - q)^+\right] = \int_q^\infty (x - q) f(x) dx$$

The expected total emissions given the offshore order quantity q, $E(q)$, is determined as

$$E(q) = e_1 q + e_2 Q(q) + e_L L(q)$$

Note that the model now considers emissions both from the first supply option, (the offshore supplier), the second supply option (which may be an onshore supplier), and from items in stock at the end of the selling period. The latter includes disposal of the unsold products.

The inventory management problem is to maximize the expected profit $P(q)$, defined as above, subject to the PCF constraint, $E(q) \leq B(q)$, where $B(q) = e(q + Q(q))$. Note that this PCF constraint concerns the expected emissions, and that the upper bound $B(q)$ is linear in the total order quantity $(q + Q(q))$ which corresponds to the total demand. (An alternative, for example, used in Song and Leng (2012) is to set a constant upper bound on the emissions independent of q, say, B. This is then analogous to a capacity constraint.) Under reasonable parameter values it is shown that the optimal offshore order quantity under the PCF constraint, q_{CF} is

$$q_{CF} = \begin{cases} q_{l1} & \text{if } q^* < q_{l1} \\ q_{l2} & \text{if } q^* > q_{l2} \\ q^* & \text{otherwise} \end{cases}$$

The lower and upper control limits, $q_{l1} < q_{l2}$, define the feasible region, and are obtained as the intersection points of $E(q)$ and $B(q)$. Note however that the lower limit q_{l1} might be non-existing, for example, if the condition $e_1 \leq e \leq e_2$ is not fulfilled. Recall that $q^* = F^{-1}(d/(d+c-z))$ is the unconstrained optimum to max $P(q)$ defined above.

Based on this analysis, Arıkan and Jammernegg (2014) consider two situations for the second supply option: (i) an environmentally friendly but expensive onshore supplier (similar to Rosič and Jammernegg (2013) above) and (ii) a fast emergency transport option from the offshore supplier. The onshore supplier is characterized by lower per unit emissions than the offshore alternative (motivated by less transport emissions), i.e., $e_2 < e_1$. Conversely, fast emergency shipments from the offshore supplier suggests higher per unit emissions (and costs) than its regular shipments (e.g., air vs. sea) with $e_2 > e_1$.

For the onshore option with $q_{CF} = \min\{q^*, q_{l2}\}$, one can conclude that q_{CF} decreases if the per unit emissions e_1, e_2, or e_L increases, or if e (the per unit emission target) decreases. Thus, if the per unit emissions increase, or if a tougher emission target is introduced, the firm buys less from the offshore supplier, and more from the environmentally friendly onshore supplier. Recall that the model presumes that all demand is satisfied.

For the fast emergency transport option from the offshore supplier, the behavior of q_{CF} with respect to e_1, e_2, e_L, and e is the same as long as e_2 is smaller than e (i.e., the per unit emissions for emergency shipments are below the per unit target). In case $e_2 > e$, the behavior depends on the critical ratio $d/(d+c-z)$, and q_{CF} may either decrease or increase.

From a numerical study the authors make a number of observations about trade-offs between the sourcing options, costs, and emissions. For example, within large ranges of the emission and cost parameters, the alternative with an onshore supplier offers significant reductions in emissions with only small reductions in expected profits. Moreover, if the onshore option offers lower per unit costs than the emergency shipment option, it is better both from environmental and economic perspectives. On the other hand, if the per unit cost for the onshore option is much higher than for the emergency shipment option, onshoring may lead to both higher costs and emissions. The latter is due to the model requirement of satisfying all demands. To avoid using the expensive onshore option (which must be used if there are shortages) q_{CF} is increased significantly, which leads to more emissions for producing and transporting ($e_1 q_{CF}$), but also for handling and disposing of more units that are left over in inventory ($e_L L(q_{CF})$).

Other green inventory management literature based on the newsvendor framework includes Song and Leng (2012). They consider the classical newsvendor model under three types of carbon emission regulations; a mandatory carbon emission constraint, a linear carbon emissions tax, and a cap and trade system.

Choi and Chiu (2012) consider a newsvendor model for a risk averse fashion retailer where any items in stock at the end of the selling period is obsolete and wasted. They establish mean-variance (MR), and mean-downside risk (MDR) models and compare their levels of sustainability to the classical risk neutral retailer, which maximizes the expected profit. The considered measures of sustainability are: expected number of unsold items in stock, expected sales to expected overage ratio, rate of return on investment, and the probability of achieving a predetermined profit target. They find that for these measures, the risk averse MR retailer is more green than a risk neutral retailer.

Choi (2013) considers a dual-supply model in a newsvendor framework for a fashion retailer employing a quick response system. In contrast to Rosič and Jammernegg (2013) above, both supply options (i.e., orders both to the offshore and onshore suppliers) occur before the selling season starts. Between the time of the first ordering opportunity (with the offshore supplier), O, and the time of second order opportunity (with the local supplier), L, it is assumed that the fashion retailer can improve its demand forecast. The analysis shows how a properly designed per unit tax can be used to enhance the environmental sustainability by sourcing more (or solely) from the local (onshore) supplier with less emissions. However, the emissions are not modelled explicitly.

8.3.1.2 Multi-period Single-Echelon Models Considering Modal Choice and Shipment Consolidation

The literature on inventory management of multi-period single-echelon inventory systems is very large. However, there are relatively few papers on green inventory management approaches that explicitly consider emissions or environmental concerns. Issues emphasized in this emerging literature, so far, are modal choice and shipment consolidation. This makes sense, as transportation is one of the major sources of emissions in logistics.

Hoen et al. (2014) consider a single item, single-echelon, infinite horizon, periodic review inventory model, where replenishments are made in the beginning of each period according to an order-up-to-S (or base-stock) policy. Demand is assumed to be continuous and stochastic, and all unsatisfied demand is backordered. In this basic modeling context the authors study how carbon emission regulations can affect a firm's choice of transportation mode for inbound deliveries. More precisely, the firm can choose between transport mode options with different constant lead-times (L_i, $i = 1, 2, \ldots I$), costs, and emission characteristics. The firm can only choose one option involving a single transport mode (i.e., terminal to terminal transport is assumed). The considered cost components for transport mode i are: a backorder cost per unit and time unit (p_i), a holding costs per unit and time unit (h_i), and purchase and transportation costs per unit (c_i). The holding and transportation costs depend on the emissions for transport mode i via an emission cost, c^e, per unit of emissions. This emission cost can reflect an emissions regulation, for example, in terms of a carbon tax. The emissions associated with shipping one unit on transport mode i, e_i, depend on the transportation distance, constant and variable emission factors, and load factors. The expected costs $C_i(S_i|c^e)$ for transport mode i, with base-stock level S_i, and emission cost c^e, can be expressed as

$$C_i(S_i \mid c^e) = h_i(c^e)[S_i - \mu(L_i + 1)] + (p + h_i(c^e))G_i(S_i) + c_i(c^e)\mu$$

where
$h_i(c^e) =$ holding cost per unit and time unit for transport mode i and emission cost c^e
$c_i(c^e) =$ transportation cost per unit for mode i and emission cost c^e
$f_i(x) =$ density function of the demand for $L_i + 1$ periods
$G_i(y) =$ loss function $= \int_y^\infty (x - y) f_i(x) dx$

μ $=$ expected demand per period

The optimal base-stock level, S_i, that minimizes $C_i(S_i|c^e)$ coincides with the solution to the traditional newsvendor problem (see, for example, Axsäter 2006). The transport mode that minimizes the expected costs for a given emission cost, c^e, are easily obtained by comparing the cost-minimizing solutions for each transport mode.

$$\min_{i \in I} \left\{ \min_{S_i} C_i(S_i \mid c^e) \right\}$$

The authors investigate how the choice of transportation mode depends on the emission cost by deriving intervals for c^e where different modes are preferred. These intervals indicate how high a carbon tax needs to be in order for a certain transport mode to be selected. From a small numerical study, based on realistic values for cost parameters and emissions, they conclude that the emission cost typically needs to increase drastically for a greener transport mode to be preferred. This suggests that emission taxes are blunt weapons for achieving emission reductions through modal shifts. On the other hand, introducing emission constraints that force a change may lead to significantly higher costs. However, the authors are careful to note that in practice many other issues outside their model may influence the choice of transportation mode.

Turning to issues of shipment consolidation and joint deliveries, Larsen and Turkensteen (2014) analyze a VMI (Vendor-Managed Inventory) system by jointly modeling shipment consolidation, routing, and retailer inventory decisions using a JRP (Joint Replenishment Problem) approach. A vendor with ample stock is supplying a product to a large number of geographically dispersed retailers. The objective is to minimize the total inventory and transportation costs. The retailers are assumed to be identical and uniformly distributed over a two-dimensional (circular) area, or a one dimensional line, for example, describing a transportation corridor. The retailers, experiencing Poisson-distributed demand, are grouped into zones, where each zone is replenished by joint deliveries on a single vehicle. Each retailer incurs holding and backorder costs and uses an order-up-to-S policy to replenish its inventory.

The replenishment orders from zone j accumulate at the vendor, and corresponding stock units are reserved and placed in a transportation bin. When the level V_j is reached (i.e., the bin is full) a dispatch is made (at the end of the considered time period). Hence, a quantity-based shipment release policy is used. The holding costs for units in the transportation bin are attributed to zone j. The transportation costs include a fixed cost per dispatch, a cost per distance unit traveled, and a fixed cost per retailer visited. As demand is stochastic, a shipment may contain replenishments to only a subset of the retailers in zone j. Because retailers are identical, it is easy to determine the probabilities for m retailers in zone j being replenished by a shipment. The expected length of a delivery route can then be estimated using continuous approximations. The detailed specification of the transportation costs enables an analysis of how the inventory decisions affect the vehicle utilization and transportation distances. Turkensteen and Larsen (2013) build on these results and in conjunction with an engine emission model they provide a method for evaluating the expected transport-related CO_2 emissions for the VMI system at hand. A numerical study illustrates that as the fixed dispatch costs increase, the CO_2 emissions decrease. This is a result of using shorter less frequent delivery routes (smaller zones) with increased load factor, and comes at the price of more inventory.

Shipment consolidation may be done in many different ways (the quantity-based policy above is just one example) and there is a large body of literature that focuses on inventory management of single-echelon systems using various types of shipment consolidation (or release) policies (e.g., Çetinkaya and Lee 2000; Axsäter 2001; Çetinkaya and Bookbinder 2003; Chen et al. 2005; Çetinkaya et al. 2006; Çetinkaya et al. 2008; Mutlu and Çetinkaya 2010; Mutlu et al. 2010; Kaya et al. 2012). These papers typically study inventory management at a vendor, which dispatches consolidated shipments to a number of retailers (the inventory management of these are not considered), with the objective to minimize holding and transportation costs. Emissions or environmental effects are in general not explicitly evaluated in this literature. An exception is Merrick and Bookbinder (2010) that use simulation to investigate how three commonly used shipment release policies can affect transport emissions. However, arguably, many of the cost models in this existing literature could be extended to include evaluations of expected emissions, particularly if the transport emissions can be modelled analogous to the transportation costs, i.e., by a fixed component per dispatch and a variable component proportional to the number of units on the shipment.

Another stream of literature of interest from a green inventory management perspective is the one focusing on inventory management of perishable products. Extensive reviews are provided in Nahmias (2011) and Karaesmen et al. (2011). A perishable item is characterized by having a limited life span during which it has a constant value (or utility). When that life span ends the item loses its value and needs to be disposed of. This may fit many different types of products, but from an environmental perspective, food and pharmaceuticals are important examples where the disposal of outdated and wasted products may have a big financial and environmental impact, not only in terms of GHG emissions. The existing models for inventory management of perishable items (excluding the trivial special case of the newsvendor model) focus on cost minimization or profit maximization and do not, to our knowledge, explicitly consider emissions or environmental consequences. However, it is easy to incorporate evaluation of these sustainability issues as the analysis generally renders the expected number of perished items associated with certain inventory policy decisions. The challenge to reconcile the economic and environmental objectives and determine the best decision from a sustainable inventory management perspective still remains though. The perishable item literature is because of its complexity focused on inventory management of single-echelon systems. However, considering multi-echelon systems, as in Olsson (2010), is an interesting venue for future research in green inventory management.

8.3.2   Green Multi-Echelon Inventory Management

In multi-echelon inventory management, the scope is extended from managing a single stock-point, to jointly managing a system of connected inventory locations, typically, upstream and downstream in a supply chain. The simplest multi-echelon structure is a serial system where each inventory location has exactly one predecessor and one successor. In distribution of finished goods, the divergent structure, where each inventory location has one predecessor but many successors, is very common. Conversely, in manufacturing, assembly systems, where each inventory location can have many predecessors but only one successor is commonly seen. Managing a network of connected inventory locations clearly increases the complexity, but also the degrees of freedom and potential for green supply-chain solutions. The substantial literature on stochastic multi-echelon inventory management still contains few models that explicitly incorporate emissions or environmental consequences, but the field is emerging.

Stenius et al. (2016) consider green inventory management of a distribution system with a central warehouse supplying goods to a number of retailers (in accordance with a VMI agreement) using a time-based shipment consolidation policy with periodic shipment intervals. The central warehouse has access to inventory and point of sale information for the entire system in real-time through an integrated IT system. The free flow of demand information means that there are no incentives for batch ordering at the retailers. However, fixed costs for handling and shipping, together with ambitions to reduce transport emissions, create strong incentives for shipment consolidation and joint deliveries to groups of retailers. The presented model extends the work in Marklund (2011) by enabling exact evaluation of load-dependent non-linear shipment costs and emissions. A key result is the derivation of the probability distribution for the number of units on each shipment. Based on these results, a setting emphasizing the model's usefulness from a sustainability perspective is further analyzed. It involves capacitated dual transport options from the central warehouse to the retailers, and is motivated by industry applications. Transportation capacity can be reserved in advance at an intermodal shuttle train solution (or alternatively at a fleet of modern low-emission trucks). If this capacity is insufficient when a shipment is to be dispatched, truck transports available on demand (typically a more emission-intensive option) are used as a complement. The analysis, assuming Poisson demand, shows how to jointly optimize the reorder levels (at the warehouse and all retailers), the shipment intervals (to all retailer groups), and the capacity reservation quantities (for all shipments) so as to minimize the total expected costs. Emissions are taken into consideration by use of a side constraint on the total expected emissions or alternatively by introducing emission costs. The analysis is applicable to both single- and multi-item systems. A numerical example, based on realistic cost and emission data illustrates how the model can be used for evaluating the cost impact of managerial decisions to reduce emissions. It indicates that relatively large reductions of the expected emissions can be achieved without severe cost increases. However, minimizing the emissions may increase the costs significantly. For instance, reducing the CO_2 emissions by 24 % compared to the cost optimal solution only increases the expected costs by 3.5 %. To achieve this, the shipment intervals (time between shipments) are increased, and more capacity is reserved on the train, resulting in an additional 10 % of the total shipment volume to be moved from truck to train. The inventory is also increased to compensate for the longer lead times. On the other hand, minimizing the expected emissions leads to a maximum reduction of 34.5 % compared to the cost optimal solution, while this causes the expected costs to increase by 17.5 %.

Berling and Martínez-de-Albéniz (2015) use a continuous serial system (i.e., a serial system with infinite number of stages) to investigate the economic and environmental benefits of adjusting the speed at which a unit is transported through the system, based on the current inventory situation. This can be interpreted as the value of slow steaming or despeeding of the supply chain when the situation allows it. Applying the model to a road transport case study illustrates that substantial savings in both cost and emissions can be attained by adjusting the speed to the inventory situation rather than using a fixed speed policy (savings of 7% and 20% respectively were recorded).

So far, there are few models that incorporate emissions associated with not satisfying customer demand on time, still in some cases these emissions may be quite significant and most relevant to consider. One area where the impact of insufficient service often is quite severe is in the distribution of spare parts. The parts are often quite small suggesting limited emissions associated with transportation, inventory holding, and warehousing. However, not delivering them promptly may have serious consequences on costs and emissions. The former is accentuated by an increasing use of service contracts with high penalty costs and liability clauses in case of insufficient service fulfillment. A related issue is the use of emergency shipments to reduce the impact of shortages and associated downtime costs commonly seen in practice.

Johansson and Olsson (2016) consider a model motivated by collaboration with a spare parts service provider in the dairy industry. In this case, failure to provide a spare part within a relatively short time limit after a machine breakdown leads to grave environmental and economic consequences. The reason is that the entire production batch, of, say, yogurt, must be discarded and the facility must be cleaned before production may be resumed. The analysis deals with a one-warehouse-N-retailer system and provides a method for evaluating and minimizing the expected costs by optimizing the base-stock levels at all facilities. The method also enables evaluation of the expected emissions associated with not satisfying the demand within the given time window.

As indicated above, when shortages occur it is often economically rational to use emergency shipments even though they are generally more expensive and emission-intensive than regular shipments. At least if they are supplied from the same location as regular orders. The increased emissions may be caused by use of faster and more emission-intensive modes of transportation (e.g., air instead of road or sea), or by reduced load efficiencies in vehicles used for emergency deliveries. One may interpret costs and emissions for emergency shipments as a consequence of not succeeding in satisfying customer demand on time through the regular system. Avoiding unnecessary use of emergency shipments is therefore a way towards green inventory management. A first step in this direction is to assure that the inventory control system provides the intended service. Berling and Marklund (2014b) use simulation to study this issue at a Scandinavian spare parts provider for agricultural machinery. The company's distribution system consists of a central warehouse (located in the south of Sweden) and a large number of retailers/dealers spread out across the Scandinavian countries. The objective is to investigate the potential of reducing total costs and transport emissions. This is done by simulating the system when applying the multi-echelon inventory control methods presented in Berling and Marklund (2013, 2014a) instead of the methods currently used by the company. The simulation study, encompassing a stratified sample of 106 representative items, shows that by using the reorder points obtained from the multi-echelon method, transport-related CO_2 emissions are reduced by 57%, the inventory holding costs are down by 18%, and the demand-weighted average fill-rate across retailers and items increased by 34%. These results illustrate that avoiding unnecessary shortages by implementing inventory control methods with better precision can be a first low hanging fruit in achieving more sustainable inventory management in practice.

Another aspect, discussed above, is that many existing models for evaluation and minimization of expected costs have a potential for incorporating evaluation of emissions or environmental aspects to some extent. We make no attempt to review the multi-echelon literature from this perspective, but we would like to highlight two areas with apparent sustainability potential: the use of advance demand information, and systems that allow for lateral transshipments and/or include emergency/quick response stocks.

Use of advance demand information essentially means that customers place (firm) orders before they need the products. The time between the order placement and demand realization represents a time buffer that offers possibilities to reduce inventories and/or use greener but slower transportation options. The use of different shipping alternatives by Amazon is one example motivating the work in Chen (2001). Other examples from the multi-echelon inventory literature on advance demand (or advance order) information include Özer (2003), Gallego and Özer (2003) and Marklund (2006). To our knowledge the literature does not yet contain any sustainable inventory management models that explicitly consider advance demand (or advance order) information in conjunction with emissions or environmental consequences.

Inventory systems with lateral transshipments (sometimes referred to as complete pooling models) are characterized by multiple retailers sharing their inventory by agreeing to transship stock between them when needed. For a recent literature overview we refer to Paterson et al. (2011). From an emissions point of view, lateral transshipment systems offer interesting opportunities to combine short distance transshipments by environmentally friendly electrical or biogas vehicles, with long-distance consolidated shipments by diesel truck, train, or ship to a geographical region. A related system structure seen in practice is one with partial pooling, where designated support warehouses with quick response stocks offer local warehouses fast emergency deliveries to avoid shortages (e.g., Kranenburg and van Houtum (2009), Axsäter et al. (2013) and Howard et al. (2015)). In principle they offer the same possibilities to combine consolidated deliveries to a region with fast short-distance emergency shipments. The managerial complexity to coordinate decisions is reduced in these systems at the expense of reduced potential for inventory pooling. To our knowledge, no complete or partial pooling models that explicitly consider emissions are yet available in the literature.

8.4 Concluding Remarks About Findings, Practical Implications, and What Remains to be Done

A recurring finding throughout this chapter is that sustainable inventory management can offer opportunities to reduce emissions quite substantially (from a cost-minimizing solution) with relatively small increases in total costs. However, attaining solutions that minimize emissions may be costly.

Several case studies have shown through simulation of real data that companies can improve the cost and service performance of the inventory management system by using better inventory control methods. More recent studies illustrate that this finding can carry over to the environmental aspect as well. A common problem in practice is that the inventory management system does not deliver the intended service. This leads to additional shortages and if these shortages give rise to e.g., emergency shipments or goods being wasted, the additional emissions can be significant. Examples from work cited above show reductions of expected costs of 18 % along with emission reductions of up to 57 % linked solely to improved inventory control and better fulfillment of target service levels. This without involving changes to order quantities, shipment frequencies, mode of transport, shipment consolidation policies, etc. This illustrates a promising improvement potential of inventory management practices to simultaneously reduce both costs and emissions.

With respect to the studied regulatory systems that policy makers may invoke to reduce emissions, the conclusion from several models is that a cap and trade system is more attractive from a company perspective (less costly) than carbon taxes or systems with fixed emission caps. Moreover, indications are that complete modal shifts to greener transportation alternatives are difficult to attain by use of carbon taxes alone, unless they are extremely high. At the same time, other results suggest that multimodal transport solutions or dual-supply options may offer attractive compromise solutions.

A noteworthy finding is that most of the existing literature on green (or sustainable) inventory management is based on very simple inventory models, particularly the EOQ-model and the newsvendor model. More general inventory models that incorporate emissions and other environmental consequences are needed in order to offer adequate tools for practical use. The literature is growing but much remains to be done. Existing inventory models with pure cost or profit focus can be a good starting point, if the emissions structure and cost structure coincide.

Finally, we note that the practical use of any green inventory management method requires access to accurate emissions (and cost) data at appropriate levels of detail. To avoid suboptimization and achieve reductions in total costs and emissions for a supply chain, inventory management decisions should be considered in conjunction with transportation and production planning decisions, and strategic decisions such as network-configuration, modal shifts, etc. To facilitate this, standardization of emission measurements and calculations across different industries, companies, and activities that cause emissions (production, transportation, warehousing, etc.) are important. Otherwise, evaluating trade-offs and total effects become ambiguous.

Refinement and more widespread use of common tools for environmental impact calculations such as NTM^{CALC} by the organization NTM (Network for Transport Measures) are promising developments in this area.

References

Abbey JD, Guide VDR Jr (2017) Closed-loop supply chains: a strategic overview. In: Bouchery Y, Corbett CJ, Fransoo J, Tan T (eds) Sustainable supply chains: a research-based textbook on operations and strategy. Springer, New York

Absi N, Dauzère-Pérès S, Kedad-Sidhoum S, Penz B, Rapine C (2013) Lot sizing with carbon emission constraints. Eur J Oper Res 227(1):55–61

Arıkan E, Jammernegg W (2014) The single period inventory model under dual sourcing and product carbon footprint constraint. Int J Prod Econ 157:15–23

Axsäter S (2001) A note on stock replenishment and shipment scheduling for vendor-managed inventory systems. Manag Sci 47(9):1306–1310

Axsäter S (2006) Inventory control. Kluwer, Boston

Axsäter S, Howard C, Marklund J (2013) A distribution inventory model with transshipments from a support warehouse. IIE Trans 45(3):309–322

Stenius O, Marklund J, Axsäter S (2016) Sustainable multi-echelon inventory control with shipment consolidation and volume dependent freight costs. in Stenius O, Exact methods for multi-echelon inventory control - Incorporating shipment decisions and detailed demand information, Doctoral Thesis Lund University, Lund, Working Paper

Battini D, Persona A, Sgarbossa F (2014) A sustainable EOQ model: theoretical formulation and applications. Int J Prod Econ 149:145–153

Benjaafar S, Li Y, Daskin M (2013) Carbon footprint and the management of supply chains: insights from simple models. IEEE Trans Autom Sci Eng 10(1):99–116

Berling P, Marklund J (2013) A model for heuristic coordination of real life distribution inventory systems with lumpy demand. Eur J Oper Res 230(3):515–526

Berling P, Marklund J (2014a) Multi-echelon inventory control—an adjusted normal demand model for implementation in practice. Int J Prod Res 52:3331–3347

Berling P, Marklund J (2014b) Reducing costs and emissions at a spare parts provider using multi-echelon inventory control. Proceedings to the 5th international conference on information systems, logistics and supply chain management, Breda

Berling P and Martínez-de-Albéniz V (2015) Dynamic speed optimization in supply chains with stochastic demand. Transp Sci, forthcoming http://dx.doi.org/10.1287/trsc.2014.0561

Bloemhof JM, Soysal M (2017) Sustainable food supply chain design. In: Bouchery Y, Corbett CJ, Fransoo J, Tan T (eds) Sustainable supply chains: a research-based textbook on operations and strategy. Springer, New York

Bouchery Y, Ghaffari A, Jemai Z, Dallery Y (2012) Including sustainability criteria into inventory models. Eur J Oper Res 222(2):229–240

Boukherroub T, Bouchery Y, Corbett CJ, Fransoo J, Tan T (2017) Carbon footprinting in supply chains. In: Bouchery Y, Corbett CJ, Fransoo J, Tan T (eds) Sustainable supply chains: a research-based textbook on operations and strategy. Springer, New York

Bozorgi A, Pazour J, Nazzal D (2014) A new inventory model for cold items that considers costs and emissions. Int J Prod Econ 155:114–125

Çetinkaya S, Bookbinder JH (2003) Stochastic models for the dispatch of consolidated shipments. Transp Res B Methodol 37(8):747–768

Çetinkaya S, Lee CY (2000) Stock replenishment and shipment scheduling for vendor-managed inventory systems. Manag Sci 46(2):217–232

Çetinkaya S, Mutlu F, Lee CY (2006) A comparison of outbound dispatch policies for integrated inventory and transportation decisions. Eur J Oper Res 171(3):1094–1112

Çetinkaya S, Tekin E, Lee CY (2008) A stochastic model for joint inventory and outbound shipment decisions. IIE Trans 40(3):324–340

Chen F (2001) Market segmentation, advanced demand information, and supply chain performance. Manuf Serv Oper Manage 3(1):53–67

Chen FY, Wang T, Xu TZ (2005) Integrated inventory replenishment and temporal shipment consolidation: a comparison of quantity-based and time-based models. Ann Oper Res 135(1):197–210

Chen X, Benjaafar S, Elomri A (2013) The carbon-constrained EOQ. Oper Res Lett 41(2):172–179

Choi TM (2013) Local sourcing and fashion quick response system: the impacts of carbon footprint tax. Transp Res E Logist Transp Rev 55:43–54

Choi TM, Chiu CH (2012) Mean-downside-risk and mean-variance newsvendor models: implications for sustainable fashion retailing. Int J Prod Econ 135(2):552–560

European Commission (2009) European energy and transport trends to 2030—Update 2009, Technical report. European Commission, Directorate-General for Energy and Transport

Gallego G, Özer Ö (2003) Optimal replenishment policies for multiechelon inventory problems under advance demand information. Manuf Serv Oper Manage 5(2):157–175

Guinée J, Heijungs R (2017) Introduction to life cycle assessment. In: Bouchery Y, Corbett CJ, Fransoo J, Tan T (eds) Sustainable supply chains: a research-based textbook on operations and strategy. Springer, New York

Harris WF (1913) How many parts to make at once. Mag Manage 10(2):135–136

Hoen KMR, Tan T, Fransoo JC, Van Houtum GJ (2014) Effect of carbon emission regulations on transport mode selection under stochastic demand. Flex Serv Manuf J 26(1–2):170–195

Howard C, Marklund J, Tan T, Reijnen I (2015) Inventory control in a spare parts distribution system with emergency stocks and pipeline information. Manuf Serv Oper Manage 17(2):142–156

Hua G, Cheng TCE, Wang S (2011) Managing carbon footprints in inventory management. Int J Prod Econ 132:178–185

Johansson L and Olsson F (2016) Quantifying sustainable control of inventory systems with demand non-linear backorder costs. Working paper, Lund University

Karaesmen IZ, Scheller-Wolf A, Borga D (2011) Managing perishable and aging inventories: review and future research directions. In: Kempf KG et al (eds) *Planning production and inventories in the extended enterprise*, vol 151, *International series in operations research & management science*. Springer, New York. doi:10.1007/978-1-4419-6485-4_15

Kranenburg, A. A., & Van Houtum, G. J. (2009). A new partial pooling structure for spare parts networks. European Journal of Operational Research, 199(3), 908-921.

Kaya O, Kubali D, Örmeci L (2012) Stochastic models for the coordinated production and shipment problem in a supply chain. Comput Ind Eng 64:838–849

Konur D (2014) Carbon constrained integrated inventory control and truckload transportation with heterogeneous freight trucks. Int J Prod Econ 153:268–279

Konur D, Schaefer B (2014) Integrated inventory control and transportation decisions under carbon emissions regulations: LTL vs. TL carriers. Transp Res E Logist Transp Rev 68:14–38

Larsen C, Turkensteen M (2014) A vendor managed inventory model using continuous approximations for route length estimates and Markov chain modeling for cost estimates. Int J Prod Econ 157:120–132

Marklund J (2006) Controlling inventories in divergent supply chains with advance-order information. Oper Res 54:988–1010

Marklund J (2011) Inventory control in divergent supply chains with time based dispatching and shipment consolidation. Nav Res Logist 58:59–71

Merrick RJ, Bookbinder JH (2010) Environmental assessment of shipment release policies. Int J Phys Distrib Logist Manag 40(10):748–762

Mutlu F, Çetinkaya S (2010) An integrated model for stock replenishment and shipment scheduling under common carrier dispatch costs. Transp Res E 46:844–854

Mutlu F, Çetinkaya S, Bookbinder JH (2010) An analytical model for computing the optimal time-and-quantity based policy for consolidated shipments. IIE Trans 42:367–377

Nahmias S (2011) Perishable inventory systems, vol 160, *International series in operations research & management science*. Springer, New York

NTM. http://www.transportmeasures.org/en/

Olsson F (2010) Modelling two-echelon serial inventory systems with perishable items. IMA Journal of Management Mathematics 21:1–17.

Özer Ö (2003) Replenishment strategies for distribution systems under advance demand information. Manage Sci 49:255–272

Paterson C, Kiesmueller G, Teunter RH, Glazebrook KD (2011) Inventory models with lateral transshipments: a review. Eur J Oper Res 210:125–136

Helmrich MJR, Jans R, van den Heuvel W, Wagelmans AP (2015) The economic lot-sizing problem with an emission capacity constraint. Eur J Oper Res 241(1):50–62

Rosič H, Jammernegg W (2013) The economic and environmental performance of dual sourcing: a newsvendor approach. Int J Prod Econ 143:109–119

Song J, Leng M (2012) Analysis of the single-period problem under carbon emissions policies. In: Choi T (ed) Handbook of newsvendor problems. Springer, NewYork, pp 297–313

Swedish Institute for Food and Biotechnology (SIK) (2011) Global food losses and food waste. http://www.fao.org/ag/ags/agsdivision/publications/publication/en/?dyna_fef[uid]=74045

Toptal A, Özlü H, Konur D (2014) Joint decisions on inventory replenishment and emission reduction investment under different emission regulations. Int J Prod Res 52(1):243–269

Turkensteen M, Larsen C (2013) Transport costs and carbon emissions in a vendor managed inventory situation. In: Huisman D et al (eds) *Operations research proceedings 2013*. Springer, Switzerland. doi:10.1007/978-3-319-07001-8_62

Wahab MIM, Mamun SMH, Ongkunaruk P (2011) EOQ models for a coordinated two-level international supply chain considering imperfect items and environmental impact. Int J Prod Econ 134(1):151–158

Walmart Global Responsibility Report 2013. http://corporate.walmart.com/microsites/global-responsibility-report-2013/greenhouseGas.html

World Economic Forum (2009) Supply chain decarbonization—the role of logistics and transport in reducing supply chain carbon emissions. Report World Economic Forum, Geneva, http://www3.weforum.org/docs/WEF_LT_SupplyChainDecarbonization_Report_2009.pdf

Chapter 9
Green Facility Location

Josué C. Velázquez Martínez and Jan C. Fransoo

9.1 Introduction

Transportation emissions comprise a large share of the world's overall emissions, and freight transport is responsible for a relatively large share of these emissions. Transportation emissions can be reduced by making different choices in logistics, such as in changing the mode of transport or changing routing or loading of the vehicles in the network (see Chap. 7 by Blanco and Sheffi (2017) for more on green logistics). These logistics choices are influenced significantly by the inventory policies that have been deployed in a company (see Chap. 8 by Marklund and Berling (2017) for more on green inventory management). For instance, allowing for a more carbon-friendly slow mode of transportation would typically require increasing or repositioning the inventory in the supply network.

Apart from logistics choices and inventory policies, the transportation performance in terms of costs and emissions is strongly determined by the design of the network. In distribution networks, this refers in particular to the location of distribution centers or other transport hubs such as factories or cross-docks. In this chapter, we will address the issue of locating such a transport hub.

The logistics problem that determines the configuration of a company's delivery of goods is the facility location problem. The facility location problem is to locate a set of facilities (e.g., factories, cross-docks, distribution centers) in a physical space, such that all the demands of the customers are assigned to at least one facility and

J.C.V. Martínez (✉)
Center for Transportation & Logistics, Massachusetts Institute of Technology, Cambridge, Massachusetts, United States
e-mail: josuevm@mit.edu

J.C. Fransoo
School of Industrial Engineering, Eindhoven University of Technology, Eindhoven, The Netherlands
e-mail: j.c.fransoo@tue.nl

© Yann Bouchery, Charles J. Corbett, Jan C. Fransoo, and Tarkan Tan 2017
Y. Bouchery et al. (eds.), *Sustainable Supply Chains*, Springer Series in Supply
Chain Management 4, DOI 10.1007/978-3-319-29791-0_9

the total transport cost is minimized. While the literature of facility location is well-established and large in size, in this chapter, we focus on a variant of this problem that specifically includes the transport carbon emissions in the formulation. We refer to location problems that aim at minimizing transportation CO_2 emissions as Green Facility Location problems.

By limiting the scope to emissions from *mobile* sources (i.e., transport), we obviously do not consider emissions from *stationary* sources that could be influenced by the location decision. Without being exhaustive, these may include:

- *Emissions at the distribution center.* These relate to the energy usage of the distribution center. In most cases this would be electricity for light and/or automation, and for refrigeration. Potentially economies of scale could exist that would be related to the design of the network. Industry data suggest that in most distribution networks, the emissions at the distribution center are less than 10 % of the total logistics-related emissions
- *Availability of local energy sources.* In particular for energy-intensive operations, the availability of renewable local energy may significantly impact the supply chain emissions. For instance, locating an aluminum plant in an area where geothermal electricity is available could reduce a supply chain's overall carbon emissions while still increasing its transport emissions.

Excluding the emissions from stationary sources from the models discussed in this chapter implies that effectively we are limiting ourselves to distribution networks and the location choice of distribution centers and cross-docks. However, in our discussion we use the more general term "facility."

Usually companies designing their distribution channels select the locations of warehouses and distribution centers with the objective to serve the demand of the customers while minimizing distance (or transport costs). In this chapter, we review some models that include the transportation CO_2 emissions in the uncapacitated facility location. We then discuss the solutions we may obtain when the number of facilities to be located is fixed by using the p-Median problem. We present discussions and managerial implications for the green facility location. We are interested in learning whether location decisions obtained by cost minimization are different from those obtained by the green facility location model.

9.1.1   Facility Location and Carbon Emissions

Typically, facility location decisions are made by considering the associated costs that include transportation (from the facilities to the customers) and the operation of the facility (production and storage). As discussed above, we may split the main sources of CO_2 emissions associated to the location of facilities in a similar way: emissions from mobile sources (transportation) and emissions from stationary sources (production, storage, and handling). Having more facilities reduce the CO_2 emissions from mobile sources due to the fact that the distance from the facility to the customer destinations decreases. Obviously, this increases emissions from stationary sources due to their larger number. Therefore, the challenge in green facility location is to define the proper number and position of the facilities that will serve a set of customers while minimizing the overall CO_2 emissions.

Many studies show that transportation and production may substantially contribute to CO_2 emissions. For example, the three main contributing sectors to emissions in the developed world are electricity production, energy-intensive manufacturing, and transportation (European Commission 2011). While production of electricity and energy-intensive manufacturing are considered within Scope 1 and 2 of the GHG inventory, transportation by service providers is considered within the Scope 3 emissions (see Chap. 3 by Boukherroub et al. (2017) for further detail). Scope 3 emissions often represent the largest source of GHG emissions and in some cases can account for up to 90 % of the total carbon impact (Carbon Trust 2013). In addition, when the facility location problem consists of locating distribution centers instead of manufacturing plants, typically the CO_2 emissions from mobile sources are much higher those of the stationary sources, as the latter then only include the emission at the distribution center. Storage and handling emissions are substantially smaller than transportation emissions, by a factor of 10 for some products (Cholette and Venkat 2009). Therefore, in this chapter, we will focus on studying the location of distribution centers with main emphasis on transportation carbon emissions.

Many practices exist in industry to reduce carbon emissions by implementing more efficient and sustainable practices into their logistics operations (e.g., Heineken Sustainability Report (2013), Groupe Danone (2014), MIT-EDF (2013)) However, very few have considered the location of distribution centers as an relevant alternative to reduce transportation CO_2 emissions. One of the exceptions may be Unilever, which increased the number of regional hubs and located these hubs closer to the customers (Unilever Press Release (2013)).

The location of facilities is critical to the efficient and effective operation of a supply chain; poorly placed plants can result in excessive costs and low service level no matter how well tactical decisions (e.g., vehicle routing, inventory management) are optimized (Daskin et al. 2005). In this chapter we demonstrate that facility location choice may significantly impact mobile CO_2 emissions in the supply chain. Note that the main drivers of transportation carbon emissions are distance, truck load (Greenhouse Gas Protocol Standard 2011), and the number of trips required to deliver demand to each customer. Changing the number and location of the facilities in the distribution network impacts all of these drivers.

9.1.2 Trade-Off Between Cost and Carbon Emissions in the Facility Location

Transportation costs (TC) in facility location problems typically take demand (w) and distance (d) into account. These costs are usually modeled as an objective function using the demand-weighted total distance ($TC = \alpha w d$), and assuming an α

constant cost per distance per unit (Revelle et al. 2008). Notice that this formulation finds optimal solutions where the facilities are closer to regions with high demand. However, for minimizing transportation CO_2 emissions, good solutions may require a different analysis.

Transportation CO_2 emissions are affected by a variety of conditions related to the type of vehicle (e.g., engine power, torque, fuel type, aerodynamic drag coefficient) and the characteristics of the delivery operation (e.g., road, slope, vehicle speed, load) (Akçelik and Besley 2003). Due to the lack of detailed information about the delivery operation (specific slopes, speed, aerodynamics, etc.) during the decision-making process, companies typically use more aggregate activity-based methods to estimate CO_2 emissions (see Chap. 3 by Boukherroub et al. (2017) for more background on carbon footprinting). Two of the most common activity-based methods are the GHG Protocol and the methodology developed by the Network for Transport and Environment (NTM). Because the GHG Protocol methodology typically uses an emission factor that is independent of the type of vehicle or type of road (United States Environmental Protection Agency 2011) (GHG Protocol Calculation Tools 2011), a facility location model minimizing CO_2 emission based on the GHG protocol would provide optimal locations that are identical to cost-minimization model solutions, i.e., optimal locations tend to be closer to regions with high demand. However, this does not hold necessary when a more detailed approach like the NTM methodology is used.

The NTM methodology requires more detailed parameters: fuel consumption, distance travelled, and weight per shipment (NTM Road 2010). The fuel consumption is a function of the type of truck, the load factor, and the type of road. NTM uses the European Assessment and Reliability of Transport Emission Models and Inventory Systems' database which developed a detailed emission model for all transport modes to provide consistent emission estimates at the national, international, and regional level (TRL 2010). The NTM estimation model is:

$$E = l\left[d\left(f^e + \left(f^f - f^e\right)\frac{w}{W}\right)\right],$$

where

E total emissions in grams of CO_2
l constant emission factor (2621 g of CO_2/L)
f^e fuel consumption of the empty vehicle (L/km)
f^f fuel consumption of the fully loaded vehicle (L/km)
W truck capacity

Comparing transport cost and CO_2 emissions, notice that the effect of distance is linear in both expressions. However, demand and truck capacity drive the transport cost in a different way from driving the CO_2 emissions. Figure 9.1 shows the comparison of transport costs and CO_2 emissions for different demand levels. For the example we use a 14-t truck for urban road type and we set 100 demand units equivalent to 1 t.

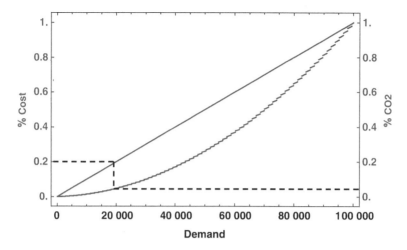

Fig. 9.1 Transport costs and CO_2 emissions over different demand levels

Note that the growth in demand does not translate into a linear increase in CO_2 emissions, as it is in cost. For example, a demand of 20,000 units increases the cost up to 20 % while the increase in CO_2 is approximately of 5 %. The chart also shows that an increase in demand has an impact on CO_2 emissions mainly when this growth implies more trips.

Because of these differences in the transport cost and CO_2 emission structures, intuitively we may conclude that facility location models with one or the other objective function may have different optimal solutions. While cost-minimization models find optimal locations closer to high-demand nodes, CO_2 minimization models may also consider optimal locations closer to demand nodes where a larger number of trips are required to serve the customer's demand. This characteristic of CO_2 minimization models may be observed in both the high-demand nodes and for restricted truck accessibility constraint in the nodes. Therefore, in facility location problems, solutions obtained by minimizing transportation cost are not necessarily equivalent to solutions obtained by minimizing transportation CO_2 emissions.

9.2   Green Facility Location Models

In this section we present some general facility location models that are commonly studied in the logistics literature, including both continuous and discrete models. We later discuss some extensions of these models that study CO_2 emissions in location decisions.

9.2.1 Traditional Facility Location Models

The facility location problem has a very long history. It was first introduced by Weber (1909) and a large number of extensions and applications can be found in the literature. For a basic explanation of the facility location problems we refer to (Daskin 2008) (Daskin et al. 2005) and for recent reviews we refer to (Melo et al. 2009) (Revelle et al. 2008). Typically, facility location problems are classified based on their solution space as *continuous* if the candidate locations can be located anywhere within the area or *discrete* if the candidate facilities are restricted to a finite set of locations (Daskin 2008). In addition, when continuous models assume that demands are distributed continuously across a service region, this approach is known as *analytical* location model.

The continuous and analytical approaches provide a general overview of the optimal locations, and are commonly used for researchers to provide guidelines or insights (Geofrion 1976). A variety of applications can be found in the literature related to extensions of location models, such as hub location problem (Saberi and Mahmassani 2013), freight transport network (Campbell 2013), and hub-and-spoke network design (Carlsson and Jia 2013). For analytical models, solution methods are derived by using mathematical analysis, while for continuous location models that are not analytically solveable, iterative numerical procedures ensure its convergence to optimal solutions, for example the Weiszfeld algorithm (Weiszfeld 1936) for the Weber problem.

For practical applications, discrete formulations are more realistic to provide feasible and optimal locations, but are more difficult to solve. For this type of models, candidate locations are pre-screened based on complementary information such as supplier's proximity, labor proximity, local regulations, and available physical space, among others. The basic model that locates the optimal facility among a set of candidate locations in a discrete space is known as the p-Median problem. The p-Median problem is defined as follows (Revelle and Swain 1970):

Let I be a set of demand nodes and J be a set of candidate locations.

Parameters:
h_i demand at node $i \in I$
d_{ij} distance between candidate facility site $j \in J$ and customer location $i \in I$

Decision variables:
X_j 1 if we locate at site $j \in J$, 0 otherwise.
Y_{ij} fraction of demand at customer location $i \in I$ that is served by facility at site $j \in J$.

The p-Median problem is then formulated as follows (P1):

$$\text{Min} \rightarrow \sum_{j \in J} \sum_{i \in I} h_i d_{ij} Y_{ij}$$

Subject to

$$\sum_{j \in J} Y_{ij} = 1 \quad \forall i \in I \tag{9.1}$$

$$\sum_{j \in J} X_j = p \tag{9.2}$$

$$Y_{ij} - X_j \le 0 \quad \forall i \in I \; \forall j \in J \tag{9.3}$$

$$X_j \in \{0,1\} \quad \forall j \in J \tag{9.4}$$

$$Y_{ij} \ge 0 \quad \forall i \in I, \forall j \in J \tag{9.5}$$

The objective function minimizes the demand-weighted total distance. Constraint (1) states that each demand node is covered. Constraint (2) establishes that p facilities are located. Constraint (3) states that the facility is opened when a demand node is assigned. Constraints (4) are the integrality constraints and (5) are the non-negative constraints. When applied to a general network, the p-Median problem can be difficult to solve. However, since the single sourcing condition holds in this formulation (i.e., Y_{ij} will naturally take values of zero or one), the property limits the potential facility locations to the network nodes, and therefore it reduces the number of possible location configurations to $n!/(n-p)!p!$, where n is the number of nodes (Owen and Daskin 1998). However, a total enumeration of all possible solutions may be computationally prohibited. Kariv and Hakimi (1979) showed that the p-Median problem is NP-hard.

The p-Median problem has been the basis of multiple extensions such as the fixed charge facility location problem, both uncapacitated and capacitated, and in other problems such as multi-item and multi-echelon (Geoffrion and Graves 1974) (Pirkul and Jayaraman 1996). It also has multiple real-world applications such as plant location-allocation (Daskin and Dean 2005), network design (Kalpakis et al. 2001), (Ruffolo et al. 2007), (Stephens et al. 1994), sensor deployment (Greco et al. 2010), and data mining (Christou 2011). Other applications are presented in ReVelle et al. (2008). The p-Median problem has also attracted much research attention in combinatorial optimization and many solution methods have been proposed to solve the problem. For instance, variable neighborhood search (Hansen and Mladenovi 1997), genetic algorithm (Hosage and Goodchild 1986), tabu search (Rolland et al. 1997), scatter search (García-López et al. 2003), ant colony optimization (Kochetov et al. 2005), and simulated annealing (Murray and Church 1996). Pullan (2008) finally presents a population-based hybrid search that was tested again in multiple instances from literature and the results show that the algorithm finds the optimal solutions for many problems, and for others it was capable of finding improvements on the best known solutions from literature.

A natural extension of the p-Median problem is to relax the number of facilities to be opened p and include a fixed location cost f_j. This problem is called the fixed charge facility location problem (P2) (Balinski 1965):

$$\text{Min} \rightarrow \sum_{j \in J} \sum_{i \in I} f_j X_j + \alpha \sum_{j \in J} \sum_{i \in I} h_i d_{ij} Y_{ij}$$

Subject to

(1)–(5)

When we also include a constraint (6) $\sum_{i \in I} h_i Y_{ij} - b_j X_j \leq 0, \ \forall j \in J$, that limits the assigned demand at facility $j \in J$ to a maximum of b_j, the resulting model (P3) is known as the capacitated facility location problem. Similar to the p-Median problem, the fixed charge facility location is also NP-hard. Previous approaches used to solve the p-Median problem may also be applicable in this case. Other solution heuristics methods are tabu search (Glover 1989; Glover and Laguna 1997) and the dual ascendant algorithm (Erlenkotter 1978), among others.

9.2.2   Carbon Emissions in Facility Location Models

We now discuss some models that include the estimation of CO_2 emissions in the facility location problem. As mentioned in Sect. 9.1, transportation CO_2 emissions in facility location models should be considered carefully, specifically because cost and CO_2 emissions structures do not typically share the same structures. However, some studies show that even when this is the case, still solutions obtained by minimizing transport cost are not necessarily equivalent to solutions obtained by minimizing CO_2 emissions.

9.2.2.1   Analytical and Continuous Models

We start by discussing the study of Bouchery and Fransoo (2015) on intermodal hinterland network design. The authors present an analytical model that aims at finding the optimal location of one facility (in their example an inland container terminal) with respect to cost, carbon emissions, and modal shift objectives. The demand is assumed to be uniform over a rectangle region representing the hinterland of the port under consideration. The density of the demand is equal to ρ containers per square kilometer and the origin of the flows (the port) is located at coordinates $(0, 0)$.

The model assumes that transport cost and carbon emissions have the same structure, and considers two transport mode options: direct shipment (shipment via truck directly from the origin to the customer) and intermodal transportation (shipment via rail to an intermodal terminal and subsequently from the terminal via truck to the customer). The cost and CO_2 emissions of serving a demand region i of size A_i by using direct shipment are expressed as follows: $Z_{0,i}^{DS} = \delta_{0,i} \rho A_i Z_1$ and $E_{0,i}^{DS} = \delta_{0,i} \rho A_i E_1$, respectively, where:

$\delta_{o,i}$ distance from the port to the gravity center of demand zone i (km)
Z_1 truck transportation cost per container-kilometer
E_1 carbon emissions from truck transportation (kg of CO_2 per container-km)

The cost and CO_2 emissions when using intermodal transportation are expressed as follows: $Z_{0,j}^{IT} = \delta_{0,T}\left(ZF_2 + \rho A_i Z_2\right) + \delta_{T,i}\rho A_i Z_1$ and $E_{0,i}^{IT} = \delta_{o,T}\left(EF_2 + \rho A_i E_2\right) + \delta_{T,i}\rho A_i E_1$, where:

$\delta_{0,T}$ distance from the port to the inland terminal (km)
$\delta_{T,i}$ distance from the terminal to the gravity center of demand zone i (km)
ZF_2 fixed train transportation cost per km
Z_2 linear train transportation cost per container-km
EF_2 fixed emissions associated to train transportation (kg of CO_2 per km)
E_2 linear train transportation emissions (kg of CO_2 per container-km)

The authors identify optimal solutions based on European data.

Their results show that the terminal is located closer to the port when optimizing cost and is located further away from the port when optimizing carbon emissions. This result shows that even when cost and CO_2 emissions have the same structure, there are significant differences in the optimal solutions for both formulations. This effect is clearly explained by the differences in the fixed train parameters, which is also consistent to the fact that train transportation under high utilization is more efficient from the emissions perspective than truck, but it is more expensive in terms of cost. For more details we refer to the full study (Bouchery and Fransoo 2015).

Although some other articles on continuous green facility location models can be found in the literature, the area is still very scarce. Buyuksaatci and Esnaf (2014) present a carbon emission-based facility location problem that considers the minimization of CO_2 emissions by using the gravitational center method. The study uses a formulation based on the GHG protocol, but it does not discuss any managerial insight or implication derived from the proposed formulation.

9.2.2.2   Discrete Models

We now discuss the studies on green facility location models with discrete formulations. Diabat and Simchi-Levi (2010) present a two-level multi-commodity facility location problem with a carbon constraint. Their problem is to decide the optimal location of plants and distribution centers and the assignment, in such a way that the total costs are minimized and the carbon emissions do not exceed a specific carbon cap. The model assumes carbon emissions from distributions by using a distance emission factor (tons of CO_2 per km), and thus neglecting the impact of the load on CO_2 emissions (see Chap. 7 Blanco and Sheffi (2017), that explains how transportation emissions are also affected by the load of the vehicles in the network). Despite this rather coarse assumption, the general conclusion seems in line with intuition: if carbon emission allowance decreases, supply chain cost increases

Elhedhli and Merrick (2012) study a supply chain network design problem that takes CO_2 emissions into account. The objective of the study is to simultaneously minimize logistics costs and the environmental costs of CO_2 emissions by strategically locating warehouses within the distribution network. This model considers the

GHG protocol estimation of CO_2 emissions and uses a scaling parameter to convert the CO_2 into cost. This approach allows inclusion of the cost of carbon emissions into supply chain network design. The experimental results show that the addition of carbon costs drives solutions with more distribution centers be opened to decrease CO_2 emissions in transportation.

Although the study provides interesting managerial insights, the model uses the most aggregate approaches to estimate CO_2 emissions in transportation (i.e., the GHG protocol with EPA emission factors). Velázquez-Martínez et al. (2014a) address the effects of using different aggregation levels to measure transport carbon emissions, and they show that errors associated with aggregation could be substantial and systematic. This suggests that increasing the level of detail in the facility location problem is necessary.

Cost may not necessarily be the only driver to reduce CO_2 emissions in transportation. For example, companies may be subject to a cap-and-trade system, or may use carbon emission reductions as a driver for brand management, product differentiation, or employee motivation (CDP 2011a, b). This suggests that a practical formulation of green facility location models should potentially take simultaneously cost and CO_2 objectives into account.

A possible alternative to consider both objectives (cost and CO_2 emissions) is to model the green facility location problem using a multi-objective setting. Most real-world problems naturally involve multiple objectives (minimizing cost, maximizing service level, minimizing CO_2 emissions, etc.) A Multi-objective approach allows to define a set of efficient solutions (or a Pareto frontier) which are defined as the set of solutions such that there is no other solution that dominates them, i.e., each solution of the set is strictly better than the rest of the solutions in at least one objective and is not worse than the rest of the solutions in all objectives (Coello 2009). These efficient solutions are often preferred to single solutions because they can be practical when considering real-life problems since the final solution of the decision maker is always a trade-off (Konak et al. 2006).

In line with this stream of research, Harris et al. (2014) present a formulation of the fixed charge facility location model (P3) with two objective functions: costs and CO_2 emissions. Their facility location model considers individual depots with capacities b_j, where each customer is served directly by a single depot, and thus, forcing the "single sourcing condition" to be held in the model. Therefore, it is possible to build a solution algorithm that first determines which facilities to open, and then to allocate the customers to the open facilities. The study proposes an expression to estimate transportation CO_2 emissions based on the GHG protocol, i.e., transportation CO_2 emissions are linearly dependent on the distance travelled and demand.

The study discusses a multi-objective optimization solution method for the cost and CO_2 facility location model, in which a decision maker can explore trade-off solutions for customer allocation based on the pre-selected facility location. Figure 9.2 (Harris et al. 2014) shows the different solutions of the location decision, and for each decision, the potential allocation assignment.

The article focuses on the solution methods and provides a framework to analyze trade-offs between cost and CO_2 emissions for location models.

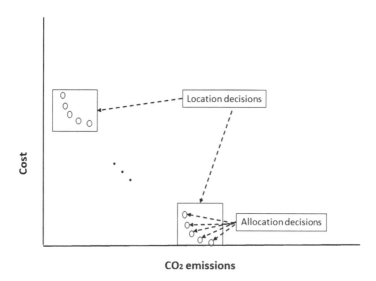

Fig. 9.2 Trade-off solutions for customer location—allocation decisions. Adapted from Harris et al. (2014)

Because we notice that all previous studies conclude that the increase in the number of open facilities implies a reduction on CO_2 emissions (and typically more facilities also imply higher costs), we may argue that a practical approach to analyze the trade-off between cost and CO_2 emissions in facility locations, is to simplify the formulation by not including the fixed emission per open facility. Therefore, we are interested in studying the effect of transportation cost versus transportation CO_2 emissions with a fixed amount of facilities previously defined (i.e., p-Median problem).

Vélazquez-Martínez et al. (2014b) study the trade-off between cost and CO_2 emissions by using a multi-objective approach for the facility location problem. The model corresponds to the p-Median problem with cost and CO_2 objective functions. The general assumptions of the p-Median problem are applicable to this model; that is, deterministic demand and the candidate locations are known in advance. In addition, the model also assumes that the company may manage multiple trucks with different capacities and the trucks are assigned according to demand node constraints (or company policy). These assumptions allow the model to include the possibility that certain customers are reachable only by certain types of trucks, with distinct cost structures.

To formulate the carbon emissions objective function, the authors include the NTM methodology in the objective function (Vélazquez-Martínez et al. 2014b). Note that $\left\lceil \dfrac{h_i}{W_i} \right\rceil$ represents the number of trips that are required to serve customer $i \in I$, and thus, affects the total distance travelled.

$$l\sum_{j\in J}\sum_{i\in I}d_{ij}\left[f_i^e+\left(f_i^f-f_i^e\right)\frac{h_i}{W_i}\right]\left\lceil\frac{h_i}{W_i}\right\rceil Y_{ij}$$

This formulation enables us to understand in more detail the trade-off between distance (d_{ij}) and utilization (h_i/W_i) while deciding the location-allocation decisions. For example, when serving customers with a homogeneous fleet (i.e., $W_i = W$ for all $i \in I$), the location solutions are the same as those that are obtained by P1, i.e., facilities are located closer to customers with the highest demand, and thus minimizing transport cost is equivalent to minimizing CO_2 emissions. However, when serving customers with a non-homogeneous fleet (e.g., caused by truck constraints due to regulations or transport infrastructure), facilities may be located closer to customers served by small trucks. This may be explained due to the fact that multiple trips are required and thus more distance is travelled to serve these customers.

9.3   Practical Implications of the Green Location Models

Transportation is one of the main contributing factors of global carbon emissions, and thus, when dealing with facility location models in a distribution context, transportation emissions may be substantially higher than the emissions due to production or storage. In addition, because facility location models define the configuration of deliveries, green location models become an important alternative to reduce CO_2 emissions in logistics. Because transportation usually is included in Scope 3 of the GHG inventory, and usually represents the highest source of emissions in a supply chain, companies may start focusing more on increasing the number of distribution centers while increasing the reachability to customers.

While cost-minimization solutions tend to locate facilities closer to high-demand customers, CO_2 emissions minimization solutions tend to locate facilities closer to customers that have truck accessibility constraints. This is explained because truck constraints drive the number of trips required to serve customers, and this factor is larger than the increase in demand and/or utilization. This may be particularly important for companies managing non-homogeneous vehicle fleet, or for policy makers in large dense areas where demand is high (based on the high density of inhabitants and small stores), but heavy-duty vehicles are not allowed. New regulations may be needed to balance the accessibility of big trucks in certain periods to increase logistics efficiency and to also reduce the number of small vehicle in those regions.

For some logistics problems, even when aggregate approaches are used to estimate transportation CO_2 emissions and thus this formulation shares the same structure with transportation cost, the location solutions may be substantially different. For companies that are interested in increasing modal shift or using more intermodal transport, these strategies may result in increase in CO_2 emissions. Particularly when different modes are used like in intermodal networks, the difference in parameters for transportation cost and CO_2 emissions can lead to a completely different set of solutions for both objective functions.

A multi-objective setting for the green facility location models may provide decision makers with a framework to analyze the trade-off between cost and CO_2 emissions. This approach may bring a new tool for companies to define better strategies to reduce CO_2 emissions. Because decision makers likely seek alternatives that reduce emissions but keep costs low, multi-objective modeling provides a set of trade-off solutions that were previously unknown in single objective modeling. This may imply that new solutions may appear with good offset of cost and CO_2 emissions. For example, locations where small increases in cost may imply high reductions of CO_2 emissions.

9.4   Directions for Future Work

The area of green facility location is still small in research. Because transportation cost and CO_2 emissions do not have the same structure, a specific formulation for CO_2 emissions minimization model for facility location should be considered. Unfortunately few studies consider the detailed expression to estimate transportation CO_2 emissions in location models, and most of them use GHG protocol, and thus, the complete effect has not been studied and understood.

In addition, only a few companies have implemented strategies using facility locations to reduce their environmental impact. Thus, more applications of the models in practical cases are needed so more understanding of the models and trade-off can be achieved and validated in practice. In addition, a few articles from prior literature include in their formulations the emissions generated by the facilities, and usually only the production of electricity. The models are mainly focus on the emissions causes by transportation, and specifically for the last-mile delivery. However, no research has been conducted to analyze the impact of transportation of raw materials in facility locations, and thus, more model formulations are needed to address this gap.

In addition, considering the different sources of energy for the facilities (wind, fuels, etc.) and to include them in the future green facility location models to understand the impact of energy source on plan locations, is a fruitful research avenue. Furthermore, including other type of pollutants—such as noise, particulate matter, CO, and NO_x—as possible objective functions in the green facility location models is a worthwhile research direction. For this problem, researchers may need to develop new heuristics strategies to accommodate the complexities.

In this chapter, we have limited our discussion on the impact of emissions from mobile sources, within which carbon and other pollutants are the most impactful. Inclusion of environmental effects of stationary sources has not yet been studied in the facility location problem. As discussed above, this could also relate to carbon emission, for instance due to local presence of renewable energy sources. However, also other effects could then be taken into account, such as the effect of the location choice on the water footprint.

References

Akçelik R, Besley M (2003) Operating cost, fuel consumption, and emission models in aaSIDRA and aaMOTION. In: 25th Conference of Australian Institutes of Transport Research (CAITR 2003). University of South Australia, Adelaide, Australia

Balinski ML (1965) Integer programming: methods, uses, computation. Manag Sci 12:253–313

Bouchery Y, Fransoo JC (2015) Cost, carbon emissions and modal shift in intermodal network design decisions. Int J Prod Econ 164:388–399

Boukherroub T, Bouchery Y, Corbett CJ, Fransoo J, Tan T (2017) Carbon footprinting in supply chains. In: Bouchery Y, Corbett CJ, Fransoo J, Tan T (eds) Sustainable supply chains: a research-based textbook on operations and strategy. Springer, New York

Blanco EE, Sheffi Y (2017) Green logistics. In: Bouchery Y, Corbett CJ, Fransoo J, Tan T (eds) Sustainable supply chains: a research-based textbook on operations and strategy. Springer, New York

Buyuksaatci S, Esnaf S (2014) Carbon emission based optimization approach for the facility location problem. J Sci Technol 4:1

Campbell JF (2013) A continuous approximation model for time definite many-to-many transportation. Transp Res B Methodol 54:100–112

Carbon Trust (2013) Make business sense of Scope 3. http://www.carbontrust.com/news/2013/04/make-business-sense-of-scope-3-carbon-emissions/. Accessed Aug 2015

Carlsson JG, Jia F (2013) Euclidean hub-and-spoke networks. Oper Res 61:1360–1382

CDP (2011a) Carbon disclosure project. www.cdproject.net/. Accessed 21 Mar 2011

CDP (2011b) Carbon disclosure project. Supply chain report: ATKearney. https://www.cdproject.net/CDPResults/CDP-2011-Supply-Chain-Report.pdf. Accessed 21 Mar 2011

Cholette S, Venkat K (2009) The energy and carbon intensity of wine distribution: a study of logistical options for delivering wine to consumers. J Cleaner Prod 17(16):1401–1413

Christou IT (2011) Coordination of cluster ensembles via exact methods. IEEE Trans Pattern Anal Mach Intell 2:279–293

Coello CA (2009) Evolutionary multi-objective optimization: some current research trends and topics that remain to be explored. Front Comput Sci China 3(1):18–30

Daskin MS (2008) What you should know about location modeling. Nav Res Logis 55(4):283–294

Daskin MS, Snyder LV, Berger RT (2005) Facility location in supply chain design. In: Langevin A, Riopel D (eds) Logistics systems design and optimization. Springer, New York

Daskin MS, Dean L (2005) Location of health care facilities. Oper Res Health Care J 70:43–76

Diabat A, Simchi-Levi D (2010) A carbon-capped supply chain network problem. In: IEEE International Conference on Industrial Engineering and Engineering Management, 2009. IEEE, New Jersey, pp 523–527

Elhedhli S, Merrick R (2012) Green supply chain network design to reduce carbon emissions. Transp Res D 17:370–379

Erlenkotter D (1978) A dual-based procedure for uncapacitated facility location. Oper Res 26:992–1009

US Environmental Protection Agency (2011). Environmental protection agency, metrics for expressing GHG emissions. http://www.epa.gov/autoemissions. Accessed 12 Apr 2011

European Commission (2011) Roadmap to a Single European transport area—towards a competitive and resource efficient transport system. http://ec.europa.eu/transport/index_en.htm. Accessed 27 May 2011

García-López F, Melián-Batista B, Moreno-Pérez JA, Marcos Moreno-Vega J (2003) Parallelization of the scatter search for the p-Median problem. Parallel Comput 29(5):575–589

Geoffrion AM, Graves GW (1974) Multicommodity distribution system design by Benders decomposition. Manag sci 20(5):822–844

Geofrion AM (1976) The purpose of mathematical programming is insight, not numbers. Interfaces 7:81–92

Glover F (1989) Tabu search—Part l. ORSA J Comput 1(3):190–206

Glover F, Laguna M (1997) Tabu Search. Kluwer, Boston

Greenhouse Gas Protocol Standard (2011) The greenhouse gas protocol. http://www.ghgprotocol. org/standards. Accessed 11 Mar 2011

GHG Protocol Calculation Tools (2011) GHG emissions from transport or mobile sources. http:// www.ghgprotocol.org/calculation-tools/all-tools. Accessed 11 Mar 2011

Greco L, Gaeta M, Piccoli B (2010) Sensor deployment for networklike environments. IEEE Trans Autom Control 11:2580–2585

Groupe Danone (2014) IUF Dairy Division. http://www.iuf.org/sites/cms.iuf.org/files/DANONE. pdf. Accessed 5 Feb 2015

Harris I, Mumford CL, Naim MM (2014) A hybrid multi-objective approach to capacitated facility location with flexible store allocation for green logistics modeling. Transp Res E 66:1–22

Heineken Sustainability Report 2013. Reducing CO2 emissions in distribution. http://www.sus- tainabilityreport.heineken.com/Reducing-CO2-emissions/Actions-and-results/Reducing- CO2-emissions-in-distribution/index.htm. Accessed 5 Feb 2015

Hansen P, Mladenovi N (1997) Variable neighborhood search for the p-median. Locat Sci J 4:207–226

Hosage CM, Goodchild MF (1986) Discrete space location-allocation solutions from genetic algo- rithms. Ann Oper Res 2:35–46

Kalpakis K, Dasgupta K, Wolfson O (2001) Optimal placement of replicas in trees with read, write, and storage costs. IEEE Trans Parallel Distrib Syst 12:628–637

Kariv O, Hakimi SL (1979) An algorithmic approach to network location problems, Part ll: the p-median. J SIAM Appl Math 37:539–560

Kochetov Y, Alekseeva E, Levanova T, Loresh M (2005) Large neighborhood local search for the p-median problem. Yugoslav J Oper Res 15(1):53–63

Konak A, Coit DW, Smith AE (2006) Multi-objective optimization using genetic algorithms: a tutorial. Reliab Eng Syst Saf 91:992–1007

Marklund J, Berling P (2017) Green inventory management. In: Bouchery Y, Corbett CJ, Fransoo J, Tan T (eds) Sustainable supply chains: a research-based textbook on operations and strategy. Springer, New York

Melo MT, Nickel A, Saldanha-da-Gama F (2009) Facility location and supply chain manage- ment—a review. Eur J Oper Res 196:401–412

MIT-EDF (2013) Ocean spray case study. http://business.edf.org/files/2014/03/OceanSpray_fact- sheet _02_01.pdf. Accessed 7 Oct 2015

Murray AT, Church RL (1996) Applying simulated annealing to location-planning models. J Heuristics 2(1):31–53

NTM Road (2010). Environmental data for international cargo transport-road transport. http:// www.ntmcalc.se/index.html. Accessed 13 Feb 2011

Owen SH, Daskin MS (1998) Strategic facility location: a review. Eur J Oper Res 111:423–447

Pirkul H, Jayaraman V (1996) Production, transportation and distribution planning in a multi- commodity tri-echelon system. Transp Sci 30:291–302

Pullan W (2008) A population based hybrid metaheuristic for the p-median problem. In: Evolutionary Computation. IEEE World Congress on Computational Intelligence. IEEE, Hong Kong, pp 75–82

Revelle CS, Eiselt HA, Daskin MS (2008) A bibliography for some fundamental problem catego- ries in discrete location science. Eur J Oper Res 184:817–848

ReVelle CS, Swain R (1970) Central facilities location. Geogr Anal 2:30–42

Rolland E, Schilling DA, Current JR (1997) An efficient tabu search procedure for the p-median problem. Eur J Oper Res 2:329–342

Ruffolo M, Daskin MS, Sahakian AV, Berry RA (2007) Design of a large network for radiological image data. IEEE Trans Inf Technol Biomed 11:25–39

Saberi M, Mahmassani HS (2013) Modeling the airline hub location and optimal market problems with continuous approximation techniques. Journal Transp Geogr 30:68–76

Stephens AB, Yesha Y, Humenik KE (1994) Optimal allocation for partially replicated database systems on ring networks. IEEE Trans Knowl Data Eng 6:975–982

TRL (2010) Information retrieved from ARTEMIS project web site. http://www.trl.co.uk/artemis/

Unilever Press Release (2013) Unilever factories and logistics reduce CO2 by 1 million tonnes. http://www.unilever.com/mediacentre/pressreleases/2013/Unileverfactoriesandlogistics reduceCO2by1milliontonnes.aspx. Accessed 3 Feb 2015

Velázquez-Martínez JC, Fransoo JC, Blanco EE, Mora-Vargas J (2014a). The impact of carbon footprinting aggregation on realizing emission reduction targets. Flex Serv Manuf J 1–25

Vélazquez-Martínez JC, Fransoo JC, Blanco EE, Mora-Vargas J (2014b) Transportation cost and CO2 emissions in location decision models. BETA working paper

Weber A (1909) Theory of the location of industries. University of Chicago Press, Chicago

Weiszfeld E (1936) Sur le point pour lequel la somme des distances de n points donnes est minimum. Tohoku Math J 43:355–386

Chapter 10
Operational Implications of Environmental Regulation

Ximin (Natalie) Huang and Atalay Atasu

10.1 Introduction and Motivation

Industrial production and consumption activities may have adverse environmental implications that lead to calls from the public, environmental groups, and non-governmental organizations (NGOs) for regulatory measures to promote sustainable practices in supply chains. As a result, many different forms of environmental regulations have been considered or enacted in the recent years, in many countries, and for various industries. Examples of those include the Restriction of Hazardous Substances (RoHS) (2002/95/EC) (Europa-Environment 2002), the End-of-Life Vehicle (ELV) (2000/53/EC) (Europa-Environment 2000), and the Waste Electrical and Electronic Equipment (WEEE) (2003/108/EC) (Europa-Environment 2003) Directives of the European Union, the Regional Greenhouse Gas Initiative in the US (RGGI 2013), and the new electronic waste (e-waste) regulation in China (State Council of China 2008).

Environmental regulation is inevitably an influential factor on different facets of firm operations. Nevertheless, implementation choices for environmental regulation are often made based on certain implicit assumptions that do not take into account firms' possible operational choices driven by such regulation or other dynamics on the implementation ground. Existing research in operations management has successfully demonstrated that this is indeed the case. In particular, recent operations management research has challenged numerous implicit assumptions made by high-impact regulations such as the WEEE Directive, identified the associated unintended consequences, and provided recommendations regarding the implications of different implementation choices for environmental regulation on the environment, supply chains, and the economy in general.

X. Huang (✉) • A. Atasu
Scheller College of Business, Georgia Institute of Technology, Atlanta, GA 30308, USA
e-mail: ximin.huang@scheller.gatech.edu; atalay.atasu@scheller.gatech.edu

© Yann Bouchery, Charles J. Corbett, Jan C. Fransoo, and Tarkan Tan 2017
Y. Bouchery et al. (eds.), *Sustainable Supply Chains*, Springer Series in Supply Chain Management 4, DOI 10.1007/978-3-319-29791-0_10

In this chapter, we review a number of research papers to highlight challenges associated with environmental regulation implementations, particularly in the context of take-back regulation, given its popularity in the last decade. These papers cover a broad spectrum of possible issues that may arise in the transposition of regulative principles into working systems. Some of them challenge the assumptions implicitly embedded in the forms or specifications of regulation; some of them point out possible loopholes of regulation; and others identify how differences across the regulated industries or the nature of products will necessitate different supply chain responses to environmental regulation. These papers collectively show that the devil is in the details and highlight the importance of an operational perspective in designing, implementing, and coping with environmental regulation.

Consequently, we posit that an operational lens is crucial for defining appropriate environmental regulation implementation models so that regulators can set proper boundaries and scope for environmental regulation. We further suggest that supply chain managers should have a clear understanding of the operational implications of different regulation implementations in order to maintain the environmental and economic sustainability of their supply chains. In what follows, we first provide a basic background on environmental regulation, followed by our unit of analysis, take-back regulation. We then take a deep dive into operational challenges associated with such regulation and conclude with insights for supply chains and regulators.

10.2   Some Background on Environmental Regulation

The environmental policy literature contains many different classifications of regulatory instruments (see Richards 1999, for a detailed discussion), which can differentiate environmental regulations in multiple dimensions: Some regulations are product-related (such as the WEEE and the RoHS Directives of the European Union) and others are facility-related (such as the Clean Water Act (EPA 2015)). Some regulations impose restrictions (e.g., the RoHS Directive) and others require only disclosures (such as the US Consumer Protection Act, see Kalkanci et al. 2015). Some regulations are international (such as the Basel Convention (BAN 2005) and the US Responsible Recycling Act (Kyle 2011) for waste export), some are national (such as the WEEE Directive), and some are local (such as the 26 state level e-waste recycling regulations in the US (ETBC 2013)).

Among those, classifications that focus on policy implementation choice differences are relevant from a supply chain perspective. In this context, Fullerton (2001) is a very useful reference that classifies environmental policy in two basic dimensions: with respect to the form of control imposed by regulation, and the type of incentives utilized by regulation. In the first classification dimension, one distinguishes between emission restrictions (sometimes called performance standards) and technology restrictions (sometimes referred to as design standards). Examples of the former include the greenhouse gas emission restrictions with cap-and-trade systems that can be found in different parts of the world including the US and the EU (Islegen et al. 2015). Examples of the latter include the RoHS Directive and the requirements to install flue-gas desulphurization in electric plants (Fullerton 2001). In the second classification dimension, one distinguishes between the types of incentives, i.e., taxes and subsidies. Examples of the former include the carbon taxes such as those used in Australia (Islegen et al. 2015) and examples of the latter include renewable energy credits (Ata et al. 2010). The unit of our analysis, e-waste take-back regulation, typically operates under a mix of these policy instruments. Some of these policies use performance standards such as collection and recycling targets imposed on producers (e.g., the WEEE Directive) and others charge unit disposal taxes to consumers or producers, as in California and Washington State, respectively (ETBC 2013). We provide a more detailed discussion on e-waste take-back regulation next.

The momentum for the recent rapid development of take-back regulation is driven by the urge to manage the growing volume of e-waste. The average lifespan of a computer has shrunk from 6 years in 1997 to just 2 years in 2005 (Greenpeace 2010). In 2010, 384 million units (2.4 million tons) of e-waste entered municipal waste streams in the US, with more than 142,000 computers and 416,000 mobile devices thrown away every day. Less than 20 % of those were recycled, and the rest were sent to landfills or incinerators (EPA 2011). Landfilling and incineration, however, can lead to release of hazardous substances such as dioxins, lead and mercury into the air, soil, or water, posing serious threats to the environment and public health. To deal with this problem, take-back regulation organizes proper treatment of e-waste, through environmentally friendly collection and recycling.

The majority of take-back regulation implementations utilize the Extended Producer Responsibility (EPR) principle, which directs the financial or physical responsibility of proper end-of-life product treatment to producers (see Walls 2006, for an extensive overview) via performance standards or disposal taxes as explained above. The rationale behind EPR is to have producers internalize the negative environmental impacts created by their products, so that they find incentives to redesign their products to overcome such externalities. As such, take-back regulation based on EPR aims to not only divert end-of-life products from landfills, but also create incentives for producers to embed environmentally superior attributes in their products (OECD 2001). This potential of EPR appears to explain its popularity across the globe. The WEEE Directive of the European Union, which probably has the largest scope in the world, is EPR-based. Moreover, despite the lack of federal level regulation in the US, 25 out of the 26 states (except for CA) that have passed state level e-waste bills stipulate producer responsibility (ETBC 2013).

It is important to note that successful implementation of and response to environmental regulation are challenging (Drake and Just 2015). Be it with respect to take-back, emissions control, or any other environmental objective, setting up the ground rules for regulatory objectives is a critical step and should not rely on basic convenient assumptions. Recent research has observed that efficient implementations of cap-and-trade or tax-based emission regulations need to carefully consider the incentives they create for carbon leakage (Islegen et al. 2015, Sunar 2015).

Likewise, it has been shown that environmental taxes can drive producers to invest in environmentally inferior technologies (Krass et al. 2015), and disclosure mandates can drive producers towards not learning their actual environmental impacts (Kalkanci et al. 2015). Similarly, in the context of take-back regulation—our unit of analysis—the landfill diversion and product redesign potentials of EPR heavily rely on certain premises, which, from a basic economic point of view may make sense. These basic premises include (1) that recycling end-of-life products (particularly electronics) must be costly and if left unregulated, hazardous waste will leak into the environment (see Sect. 10.3), (2) take-back regulation will create incentives to recycle only end-of-life products that can be considered as waste (see Sect. 10.4), (3) design incentives coming out of take-back regulation will mainly focus on designing more recyclable products (see Sect. 10.5), (4) such regulation is appropriate for most product categories including durables or consumables (see Sect. 10.6), (5) regulatory distortion of competitive markets is not a concern (see Sect. 10.7), (6) implementation details that relate to the existing reverse supply chain infrastructures (networks) will not matter (see Sect. 10.8), and that (7) take-back and recycling take place in the country where the regulation is enacted (see Sect. 10.9). While these assumptions may appear reasonable at the stage of designing and planning to cope with potential take-back regulation, they (or the invalidity of any of those) can be quite harmful in terms of the efficacy of the implementations on the ground and have important supply chain management implications, as we demonstrate in the following sections.

10.3 Trash or Treasure?

A fundamental assumption underlying take-back regulation is that environmentally sound treatment of end-of-life products is always costly. This also constitutes the reason why regulation is needed in the first place: to ensure that producers take the responsibility for proper collection and recycling. The thinking that logically follows is that increasing the stringency of requirements for regulatory compliance should strengthen incentives for landfill diversion and environmentally friendly design of products, which appears to underlie the 2012 Recast of the WEEE Directive (2012/19/EU) increasing the collection target to 45 % by 2016, and then to 65 % by 2019. However, in recent years, doubt has been cast on the assumption of costly recycling, especially with the roaring prices and scarcity of certain raw materials. For example, the amount of gold that can be recovered from 1 mt of computers is 17 times greater than that from a gold ore of equal weight (USGS 2001). In other words, recycling some of the e-waste can be more profitable than metal ore mining. Consequently, it appears that producers may be motivated to recycle some electronics voluntarily even in the absence of take-back regulation. At the same time, it is important to note that this opportunity presents itself to others as well, i.e., third party recyclers may also be attracted into the product recovery business, introducing competition in the market for end-of-life products with recoverable value.

These observations slightly contradict the costly recycling premise, and may imply challenges on the effectiveness of take-back regulation, which is explored by Esenduran et al. (2014).

In their paper, Esenduran et al. (2014) consider a stylized model of a recycling market in which producers and third party recyclers may compete for recycling valuable waste. They focus on a single product category. After reaching the end-of-life, products remain in the hands of a set of waste-holders that may be geographically dispersed. The recoverable value in each waste-holder's product may vary depending on its proximity to the producers and recyclers. Hence, producers and recyclers can extract different values from end-of-life products, and they compete on acquiring the e-waste from waste-holders by respectively offering recovery prices. Given the recovery prices and their respective value heterogeneity, waste-holders decide on whether and to whom to return their end-of-life products to maximize their utilities from waste recovery. In this context, the authors assume take-back regulation in the form of a collection and recycling target imposed only on the producers. They further assume that producers can enhance the product end-of-life value by increasing the recyclability at a cost.

The authors show the following: Even when waste has value, the existence of regulation may be necessary if the producers exhibit a strong position in terms of their access to the recoverable waste. The reason is that although the value of waste turns into some incentives for the producers to recycle, it is only limited to inducing recycling of the "low-hanging fruits" (i.e., easier or cheaper to access items). As a result, the recycling level chosen by the producers remains below the social optimum. In this case, enacting regulation is beneficial in several ways: It increases landfill diversion, encourages more recyclable product design, and also guarantees improvement of social welfare. However, in the presence of competition in the recycling market, regulation can lead to unintended consequences. First, more stringent regulation can reduce landfill diversion. This is because an increased collection and recycling target imposed only on the producers drives the producers to act more aggressively in acquiring the products from waste-holders. This may lead to very high prices paid to waste-holders, driving third party recyclers to hold back from the product recovery market. Effectively, this suggests that the overall collection and recycling volume in the end-of-life product market may suffer because the portion of volume contributed by the third party recyclers may go down. Furthermore, this may happen to an extent that the decrease in third party recycled volume actually offsets the increase in producer recycling induced by take-back regulation. Second, a higher collection and recycling target imposed on producers may discourage improvement on product design. This is because the spill-over of design benefits can be accentuated by competition, which makes design improvement a less appealing option for the producers. In turn, the authors suggest that more stringent regulation may not always be ideal, particularly when waste is valuable. Rather, reducing the stringency of collection and recycling targets imposed on producers, while regulating the third party recycling market in terms of the quality of recycling standards may be an ideal solution from both the economic and environmental points of view under such circumstances. The take-away from Esenduran et al. (2014) is that even the simplest and possibly the most reasonable assumption that underlies the need for environmental regulation may be challenged by market dynamics. When this happens, the solution may appear to be trivial, e.g., in the case of valuable e-waste one may argue that the more value in waste, the more producers (or the supply chain divisions that are responsible) will recycle. Yet, how the competition on the ground functions may completely change this perspective. As demonstrated by Esenduran et al. (2014), competing for geographically dispersed heterogeneous waste in the presence of design improvement options may imply the need for supply chain managers to think differently about how they cope with such regulation. In particular, reverse supply chain managers will play a key role in such compliance efforts, as they are the parties to see waste competition related issues and inform compliance departments about such challenges in advance. In sum, the operational considerations (i.e., devil in the detail) that matter in this case are the geographical dispersion of waste (see Dhanorkar et al. 2015; Sunar 2015 for similar observations in the waste exchange and emissions regulation contexts) and whether and how producers and their reverse supply chains can effectively access the waste under competition with third parties.

10.4   End-of-Life or Used Product Recycling?

Another basic assumption of take-back regulation is that in order to fulfill the EPR obligation, producers solely obtain end-of-life products from waste-holders such as municipal collection locations. Intuitively sound as it is, this assumption may not directly extend to durable goods. In particular, durable good producers can also acquire used (midlife) items from the secondary market for product recovery, despite the remaining lifespans these items have.

Producers may have incentives to pull used products off the secondary markets and use them as inputs for recycling due to two reasons. First, a secondary market offers used products as cheaper (although maybe inferior) alternatives to the new ones and hence potentially attracts consumers away from buying new products, i.e., cannibalizes the new product sales. In this case, reducing the cannibalization constitutes a motivation for producers to interfere with, or even suppress the secondary market. Second, acquiring used products also helps lower the need and cost of collecting end-of-life items to meet the collection target. In addition to being viable, this option is also feasible for producers: They can obtain used products through offering trade-ins or buyback programs.

However, from the environmental and regulatory standpoint, retiring used products before they reach the end-of-life can be unfavorable because this practice shortens the average useful life of products and increases the total waste volume. This leads to two critical questions: How will the producers' optimal strategies to interfere with the secondary market change when faced with regulation? Consequently, how will such interference influence the effectiveness of take-back regulation? Alev et al. (2014a) shed light on these questions.

Alev et al. (2014a) develop a stylized economic model to study the decisions of a monopolist durable good producer under EPR-based take-back regulation with (1) collection targets, which can be met by collecting both end-of-life or used products, (2) requirements on collection infrastructure, which will be reflected in the unit collection cost of end-of-life products, and (3) recycling standards, which will be reflected in the unit cost of recycling every product. Their analysis shows that the decision of the producer on interfering with the secondary market is indeed influenced by the regulation. This is evident by the fact that retiring used products can be purely induced by the need to fulfill the regulative collection target and will not exist in the absence of regulation. When such interference occurs, it can lead to a lower reuse level and a higher new production volume, both commonly associated with unfavorable environmental consequences.

In this case, the effectiveness of take-back regulation is weakened by the fact that there are two types of collection channels that a durable good producer can strategically use for compliance: In addition to collecting end-of-life products, the producer can also acquire used products from consumers in the secondary market for recycling. Since the existence of this alternative collection channel is unique to durable products, regulators and producers of durable products should pay particular attention to the environmental and supply chain implications of take-back regulation.

From a regulator perspective, the results in Alev et al. (2014a) suggest the following: First, recycling standards remain effective. Higher recycling standards help ensure the producer collect and recycle end-of-life products. Consequently, premature retirement of used products decreases. Second, collection infrastructure requirements bring in similar benefits as the recycling standards, but only up to a certain stringency, beyond which their effect negates and leads to increased producer interference with the secondary market. Finally, the effect of the collection target is not always positive. To be specific, when the collection target increases within a low value range, it may incentivize the producer to interfere with the secondary market, and hence adversely results in increase in new production and decrease in reuse levels. These results suggest that the take-back regulation for durable goods, while achieving the objective of increasing the level of collection for recycling, may compromise other environmentally sound objectives such as reuse and consumption reduction. This outcome appears undesirable from the perspective of the well-established Waste Management Hierarchy, which prioritizes reduce over reuse, and reuse over recycling.

From the supply chain perspective, these observations once again highlight the importance of the reverse supply chain manager's role in compliance. In particular, the reverse supply chain manager who observes the costs of compliance and different product recovery options can help resolve such dilemmas for the firm. For instance, the reverse supply chain manager can bridge the connections between compliance and marketing departments to manage the acquisition of used products through trade-in programs and direct such flows towards take-back regulation, which appears to be the essence of Apple's recent Recycling and Reuse program (Apple 2015).

10.5   Durability or Recyclability?

The durability embedded in products raises complexities in regulation in regards to not only how it influences the collection decisions for producers by providing an additional collection channel as discussed above, but also how it influences the design decisions. Recall that incentivizing environmentally sound product designs is one of the basic goals of take-back regulation. When regulation on recycling is enforced, one expects that it should induce producers to make recycling cheaper by improving product recyclability (e.g., incorporating easier disassembly features) in the design. This assumption is also popular among regulators as reflected in regulative statements. One example is the E-waste Recycling Law in Washington State, which spells out that "The legislature further finds that the system must encourage the design of electronic products that are less toxic and more recyclable" (New Section, Sec 1, SB4628). However, for durable products, enhancing recyclability to reduce the unit cost of recycling is not the only option for producers to alleviate the total economic burden associated with the recycling obligation. Producers can also improve the product durability to lower the recycling volume. The underlying rationale is that making products more durable enables the producers to set a higher price for new products and sell less, leading to a smaller amount of end-of-life products and hence a lower total cost of recycling. As such, when recyclability and durability are both available design options for producers, it may be of interest to review the design implications of regulation. In particular, one would like to understand how the producer's design choices and the regulatory efficiency change in the presence of these alternative design options, especially when they are interdependent. This problem is examined by Huang et al. (2014).

Huang et al. (2014) consider a monopolist producer selling a single durable product and facing take-back regulation that imposes a collection target and a recycling target for end-of-life products. The producer, in response to take-back regulation, can choose both the product recyclability and durability in the design stage to deal with the cost associated with the regulation. The authors find that when the product recyclability and durability are independent or complementary attributes, increasing the recycling target helps induce the desired outcome with improvements on both the product attributes. However, when recyclability and durability are substitutes, the design trade-off between them can result in non-monotonic effects of the recycling target, which is in sharp contrast to common expectations: As the recycling target goes up, it first leads to recyclability improvements (while the durability may decrease) and then leads to durability improvements (while the recyclability may decrease). Note that increasing recyclability in product design encourages recycling by bringing down the unit recycling cost, while increasing durability promotes waste reduction by leading to a lower production volume. Therefore, when recyclability compromises durability, the design trade-off suggests that recycling comes at the expense of waste reduction. Finally, contrary to the non-monotonic effects of the recycling target, the collection target always favors recyclability when recycling can generate value since a tighter collection target results in an increase in recyclability while durability may be compromised due to the recyclability-durability trade-off.

These conclusions send an important message to regulators: Design alternatives for the producer to deal with the costs associated with the EPR obligation are critical operational factors that influence the outcomes of take-back regulation. As demonstrated by Huang et al. (2014), the existence of durability as an alternative design option to recyclability may not necessarily expand the effective scope of regulation (i.e., enhance both product attributes). On the contrary, the possible trade-off between design choices may diminish or even negate the effectiveness of regulation (see Plambeck and Wang 2009, Krass et al. 2015 for similar observations in the context of new product introduction frequency and technology choices, respectively).

From the supply chain perspective, these results once again suggest that effective compliance with take-back regulation will require coordination between the reverse supply chain manager, the compliance department and the design/engineering department. Consider photovoltaic panel (PVP) producers for instance, who face a clear trade-off between designing products for durability and recyclability (see Huang et al. 2014 for details). The 2012 Recast of the WEEE Directive has recently added PVPs into the regulated product categories. Even though compliance with such regulation may not be a concern for the producers today because the lifespans of PVPs are estimated to be 25 years, it will be critical for the producers to prepare for future liabilities take-back regulation will impose on them. In this case, it is important for PVP producers to plan for a reverse supply chain infrastructure that will be able to accommodate different design profiles and help reduce future liabilities associated with PVP recycling.

10.6   Durable or Consumable Products?

While our discussion so far has been centered around durable products, EPR-based take-back regulation has also extended to consumable products in recent years, with examples being the announcements of the Pharmaceutical Stewardship Act of 2011 (H.R. 2939 (112th) 2011) and the Alameda County Safe Drug Disposal Ordinance (Alameda County, CA 2012) in the US.

In the context of take-back regulation for consumables, leveraging experiences from durable product markets may appear ideal. However, producers and regulators must be aware of the implementation differences stemming from the consumable and perishable nature of consumable products and adjust accordingly. In particular, contrary to durable products, the volume of end-of-life waste does not equal to the volume of production for consumables. Moreover, recovery options for consumables are limited because reuse and recycle are usually not applicable. Therefore, regulation for consumables needs to focus more on reducing the volume of unused items that are not disposed in an environmentally friendly way. In doing so, there exist two prevalent implementation approaches. The first is Source Reduction (SR), which aims to lower production by charging a fee based on production volume. The second is End-of-pipe Control (EC), which mandates the producer to organize or finance proper waste treatment. Given the product nature of consumables, further exploration is needed in order to determine how one can choose between the SR and the EC approaches to effectively improve the environmental and economic impacts of regulation. Alev et al. (2014b) pioneer in this area and their findings depart considerably from the existing results for durable products.

The products considered in Alev et al. (2014b) are consumable pharmaceuticals. The decision makers in the pharmaceutical chain include a social planner, a producer, a doctor and a patient, whose interactions are captured by a sequential game model. The doctor acts as an intermediary between the producer and the consumer (the patient). Therefore, the sales volume of pharmaceuticals is not directly determined by the consumer behavior, but by the doctor's prescription instead. The prescription amount that exceeds the actual consumption by the patient (overprescription) constitutes the main source of pharmaceutical waste. The doctor makes the prescription decision based on not only the cost of treatment and the impacts of the prescription on patient's health, but also the doctor's own utility from the prescription. The producer influences the sales volume by deciding the market price, as well as setting the promotion efforts on both the doctor and the patient. The social planner chooses between the two implementation approaches of regulation from below and sets the respective policy parameter.

(1) EC: Requires the producer to collect a certain fraction of unused pharmaceuticals. The producer also bears the associated collection cost. This implementation resembles a typical producer-operated collection and recycling system observed in prevalent EPR implementations.
(2) SR: Imposes a fee on every unit of sales. After obtaining the fee payments, the regulator manages the collection (e.g., chooses the collection level) and the costs incurred. SR resembles a typical state-operated system observed in prevalent EPR implementations.

The analysis finds that for pharmaceuticals that are consumable in nature and have a different demand structure with the doctor acting as an intermediary between production and actual consumption, the comparison between the two implementation approaches is very different from that for the durable products. The paper shows that a producer-operated system (under EC) can be preferred by a social planner when the following conditions are met: (i) the cost of collection is high, (ii) the use-phase impact (i.e., the health condition improvement for the patient) is less significant, and (iii) the impacts on the society (e.g., medicine abuses) and the environment (e.g., chemical contamination in the ecology) are high. Notably, (iii) is in direct contrast to the conclusion for durables, which suggests that under similar condition the state-operated system should work more efficiently (Atasu et al. 2013).

This study, although solely focuses on pharmaceuticals, delivers an insightful lesson that may be generalized for other consumables. The product nature is the operational detail that matters. While take-back regulation is devoted to dealing with products that are at the end of their useful life, the definition of useful life can vary substantially depending on the product nature. For a durable product, the end-of-life item has lost its functionality and will not be demanded by consumers. For a consumable, on the other hand, reaching the end of its useful life means it no longer provides the original designated usage, but it may still be in a functional state and may be consumed by others. This difference can significantly affect the efficiency and implications of different regulation implementation choices as demonstrated by Alev et al. (2014b).

Therefore, the product nature must be carefully accounted for by regulators and producers in order to avoid implementation choices that would compromise operational or regulatory efficiency. It is especially important that the reverse supply chain manager understands these implementation issues. In particular, Alev et al. (2014b) show that which implementation model will be preferred by a regulator depends on the unused pharmaceutical collection infrastructure the producer has access to. For instance, while leveraging existing pharmacies or municipal collection systems may appear a low-cost option for the producer, in those circumstances the regulator may favor a SR approach with higher taxes, eventually leading to a lower profit for the producer. In turn, the reverse supply chain design that serves take-back compliance needs not be the most cost efficient one in the context of consumables.

Our discussion so far has demonstrated that the proper evaluation and development of policy instruments must be based on correct and thorough understanding of the detailed operational characteristics of the target industries, including the commodity market dynamics, the alternative strategic responses available to producers, and the nature of products. Beyond that, the devil in the details also matters in the implementation stage, in which regulators and producers translate the regulation into a working system. We illustrate this phenomenon in what follows.

10.7 Collective or Individual Producer Responsibility?

Although EPR-based take-back regulation sets a unified principle of assigning producer responsibility, it leaves discretion for regulators to choose the operationalization of product collection and recycling. Typically, two models of implementation can be observed: Individual, and Collective Producer Responsibility (abbreviated as IPR and CPR respectively, see Plambeck and Wang 2009 for a similar discussion). Under IPR, each producer deals with only its own products. A somewhat similar model is adopted by the Personal Computer Recycling Law in Japan, where products are separated by brands after collection and then become the responsibility of the corresponding producers. Under CPR, all participating producers jointly conduct end-of-life product treatment and share the total costs. Examples of this model can be seen in the WEEE Directive implementations in several EU member states.

Both IPR and CPR models have certain pros and cons, and neither of them is dominantly better than the other. On one hand, CPR is commonly considered superior in cost-efficiency because it realizes economies of scale by aggregating the collection and recycling of a large volume of products and also saves on the costs associated with brand identification and separation. However, CPR is criticized for significantly undermining the eco-design incentives. Under CPR where costs are shared, the benefits (such as recycling cost reduction) from the individual design efforts spill over to other producers or even competitors, and hence producers may be less motivated to improve the product design for recyclability. The IPR model, on the other hand, overcomes this weakness of CPR and creates stronger design incentives because the independence of processing costs among producers under IPR enables each producer to retain the returns from the investment on product design improvements. Therefore, the choice between IPR and CPR is largely driven by the trade-off between design incentives and cost-efficiency. At the same time, the impacts of these two factors also depend on the dynamics in the market. As such, it is a useful exercise to compare the two models following Atasu and Subramanian (2012) and Esenduran and Kemahlioglu-Ziya (2015).

Atasu and Subramanian (2012) build a single-period model with a duopoly sales market in which high-end and low-end products are sold respectively by two producers. Consumers make purchasing decisions based on their heterogeneous product valuations for the differentiated products. The regulation mandates producer responsibility by imposing a binding recovery target for end-of-life products on both producers. The regulation can adopt either the IPR or the CPR model. Under IPR, each producer only pays the cost associated with its own products. Under CPR, the two producers share the total processing cost. The cost-sharing can be set endogenously (i.e., according to the return shares, which also reflect the market shares in this context) or exogenously (which will be predetermined and fixed). In response to the regulatory obligation, each producer can invest in improving the product recovery attributes to reduce the cost of end-of-life recovery treatment of its products.

By comparing the outcomes under IPR and CPR, the paper shows that incentives to design more recoverable products exist under both models, but the incentives are always weaker under CPR than under IPR. The reason is that CPR allows for one of the producers to free-ride on the other's design efforts. Under CPR, although the existence of free-riding is less surprising, the detail as to who free-rides can be counterintuitive. When the cost-sharing is endogenous, the bigger contributor (whose processing cost has a higher weight in determining the final shared unit cost) may suffer from being free-ridden just as expected. However, when the cost-sharing is determined exogenously, the bigger contributor can become the free-rider. This reversal of the outcome is caused by the competitive structure in the primary market. Under IPR, however, the market competition does not have direct influences on the design incentives. In return, the free-riding under CPR also has feedback effects on the primary market because the producer who benefits from free-riding can lower the price more aggressively and hence provides a higher surplus to its consumers, while its competitor only offers a lower consumer surplus. Note that these observations are nicely aligned with perspectives from different fields such as industrial ecology (Lifset and Lindhqvist 2008) and practitioners (Atasu et al. 2015).

This analysis draws our attention to another operational aspect that matters in implementing take-back regulation: The scope of responsibility, shared under CPR versus independent under IPR, may have different influences on product design. Furthermore, the strategic dynamics including competition and integration of the compliance-related considerations into the design and pricing decisions for producers are key drivers of take-back regulation efficiency.

Interestingly, while also looking at the comparison between IPR and CPR, Esenduran and Kemahlioglu-Ziya (2015) take a very different perspective: They analyze how the coalition structure under the collective model matters. The composition of a coalition is a non-trivial factor because it can vary dramatically in reality. For example, the European Recycling Platform (ERP) that is set up in response to the WEEE Directive mainly consists of large (in terms of market/return share) firms including Braun, Electrolux, HP and Sony. On the contrary, the collective systems set up by the local government authorities such as the one in Washington State covers a much wider range of both big and small firms. The authors argue that the coalition structure in a collective system may have important implications as to the efficiency of the take-back regulation implementation. Esenduran and Kemahlioglu-Ziya (2015) look at n firms with distinct market shares in a collective system. All firms are subject to the same regulation that mandates a collection target. In response, each firm can choose the recyclability of its products. A higher recyclability helps reduce the unit cost of recycling, but it also incurs the cost of increased recyclability because it makes production more expensive. To stay focused on the take-back context, the paper focuses on compliance-related costs that include collection and recycling costs, as well as the cost of increased recyclability. Compliance schemes can be of two types. Under IPR, each firm sets the actual collection rate to minimize its own overall cost. Under CPR, the central entity of the collective system determines the actual collection rate to minimize the total cost of collection and recycling incurred to the entire system, which will then be split among all producers by market shares. Note that the option of overcompliance for producers, i.e., the actual collection being higher than the regulation target, is also considered. Economies of scale are reflected in the marginal recycling cost that is decreasing in the total recycling volume.

Esenduran and Kemahlioglu-Ziya (2015) show that under CPR, the equilibrium recyclability level is lower for smaller firms, which is somewhat consistent with the free-riding result in Atasu and Subramanian (2012). In addition, the paper also reveals some unexpected conclusions. One result shows that the equilibrium recyclability level can be higher under CPR than under IPR, which is in direct contrast to Atasu and Subramanian (2012). The recyclability being higher under CPR tends to happen when the collective system is formed by big firms. The underlying rationale is that under CPR, free-riding issues are less severe for the partnership with big firms. Moreover, producers benefit from higher economies of scale. Therefore, the equilibrium collection rate is higher, which then drives up the total return of the recyclability investment (reduced processing cost for more units) and hence encourages better design. Another conclusion points out that although CPR appears to facilitate economies of scale and hence should always lead to a higher collection rate (i.e., higher degree of overcompliance), it is in fact possible to have a higher collection rate under IPR than under CPR, especially when the collective system consists of small firms. The reason is that in addition to economies of scale, better designs can also induce more collection because when products are more recyclable they become cheaper to process. However, when a firm is in a collective system with other small firms, it bares the risk of being free-ridden and cannot retain the full benefit of design enhancements. As a result, it has lower design incentives than when it acts alone. The negative effects of diminished design incentives can even dominate the positive effects of processing at bulk and therefore results in a lower overall collection rate under CPR.

Another insightful finding is that a firm may incur a higher cost when it joins a collective system with other relatively smaller firms compared to when it collects and recycles individually. In that case, if the firm pulls out of the collective system and if the firm is big enough, then the compliance cost of the collective system goes up. Note that these observations have important implications for supply chain managers. In particular, these results suggest that the reverse supply chain manager needs to consider take-back compliance collaboration with other firms very strategically. Depending on the type of compliance partners, a reverse supply chain manager may increase or decrease the reach of its collection programs and inform the design/engineering department regarding the extent of take-back compliance cost savings that can be achieved by improved designs.

The take-away from this study is that the coalition structure in a collective system is another operational detail that makes a difference in implementation. Specifically, compliance behaviors of a producer in collection or product design can vary significantly depending on the relative size of the producer and those of the other participants in the coalition.

In sum, Atasu and Subramanian (2012) and Esenduran and Kemahlioglu-Ziya (2015) collectively provide a comprehensive understanding of collective and individual models of producer responsibility in implementation. Their results reveal certain weaknesses associated with each model, and motivate the need for research towards more powerful regulative tools for efficient implementation. One natural direction for such pursuit is to explore the possibility of integrating the most prominent advantages of the two models, namely, generating superior design incentives and achieving cost-efficiency.

As such, we start with the collective model as a base to seek potential improvements. First and foremost, note that the consolidation of end-of-life products, while facilitating economies of scale, does not exclude the potential of a collective model to properly internalize the associated processing costs for incentivizing eco-design. Rather, the root of the problem actually resides in the cost allocation mechanism, which is usually based on return share or market share. Such proportional cost allocations gain popularity among both scholars and regulators mainly due to their simplicity and transparency. However, they are not ideal solutions because they give rise to the first weakness of the collective model, which involves fairness and stability concerns. Producers who feel overcharged by a collective system may be driven to break away and operate in an individual system instead. This jeopardizes the stability of the collective system, which is a prerequisite to sustain the scale advantage. This outcome is indeed observed in practice. One recent example is that in Washington State, where a centrally run standard plan is in place with a statewide collective system, some producers file requests for switching to self-operated independent plans with the belief that their stand alone cost will be lower. This is because the proportional cost allocation model employed by the collective system in Washington State falls short of accounting for recycling cost heterogeneity across producers. Note also that responsibility allocation problems are not unique to the take-back regulation context. See Caro et al. (2013) and Sunar (2015) for similar discussions in the emissions regulation context.

As such, a first step towards building a more robust collective system starts with a search for a cost allocation mechanism that accounts for product-specific metrics to help achieve fairness in cost allocation and guarantee stability. Meanwhile, the concrete operations of collection and recycling in a collective system are likely to be conducted in a network where the end-of-life items from numerous producers are processed by the aggregation of different recycling capacities. Consequently, the cost allocation model to guarantee fairness and stability should also properly incorporate network effects in a collective system. Gui et al. (2014a) present a fruitful attempt in this direction.

10.8   The Individual or the Network?

Gui et al. (2014a) study a set of producers that are faced with recycling standards imposed by regulation. A collection and recycling network (CRN), which effectively is a collaborative reverse supply chain, collectively handles all the end-of-life products from producers. The network comprises of three sets of nodes that represent the collection points, the consolidators, and the processors respectively. All items go through one of each set of these nodes in sequence. The edges in the network stand for costly processes of collection, consolidation, processing, and the transportation in-between. Product heterogeneity in the model is reflected by different costs of processing the products of different producers. The collective system is stable when a grand-coalition is formed and all producers choose to voluntarily stay in the system. The system stability requires a fair cost allocation, which is defined as one that ensures each producer to be better off by remaining in the grand-coalition. If a producer can achieve lower cost outside the collective system, it will leave the grand-coalition to operate individually or to form a sub-coalition with some of the other producers.

The processing capacities in the network consist of capacities that are privately owned (or contracted) by producers and capacities that are contracted by the central authority who runs the grand-coalition. While the former type of capacities can be used by any (grand- or sub-) coalition the owner producer belongs to, the latter can only be used by the grand-coalition at no additional cost. The total cost incurred by the collective system is calculated based on the socially optimal routing (i.e., the cost minimizing solution to the network flow problem) and will be shared by the members in the system.

The paper develops a fair cost allocation model based on the prevalent return share heuristic: The cost-corrected return share with capacity adjustment (hereafter referred to as the dual-based cost allocation) makes two adjustments to the return share-based cost allocation. The first is that in deriving the return share, each producer's return volume at every collection point is weighted by the marginal cost of processing its products. This adjustment reflects the product heterogeneity in the network. The second adjustment is to grant a reward to each producer for the valuable capacities it contributes to the network, at a properly set unit reward price.

The study further shows that this cost allocation can be widely applicable and retain fairness even when economies of scale enter the model, or when the central authority-contracted capacities are open at a fee to producers outside the grand-coalition. These findings are validated using the actual EPR implementation data from Washington State.

This research once more highlights the importance of operational angle, this time in the form of network effects under the collective model. Since the key characteristic of operations in a network is the pooling of available capacities for better utilization, the critical operational angle here is how resource sharing can be reflected in the cost allocation. Notably, the dual-based cost allocation, in addition to maintaining system stability, also shows potential to make up for another deficiency of the prevalent return share-based allocation. To be specific, the dual-based allocation can help enhance the undermined design incentives in collective take-back regulation implementations because it rewards the ease of recycling of products by accounting for the product heterogeneity. Gui et al. (2014b) dive into exploring this possibility, and the result shows that not only the product design choices, but also the process technology matters in a network setting.

In Gui et al. (2014b), end-of-life product treatment is conducted collectively in a network with a similar setting to the one in Gui et al. (2014a). One crucial aspect of the network configuration highlighted in this paper is the differentiation in both cost-efficiency (i.e., process technology) and capacity of processors. When there are sufficient low-cost capabilities, cost synergy in the collective network is high because the resource sharing in collection and recycling has a higher potential for cost savings. In the network, product design improvements are also related to the characteristics of the processors, because the benefits of design are mostly realized through influencing the processing cost. Specifically, product design is a substitute (complement) for process technology when the enhancement of recyclability leads to higher (lower) cost reduction at the less efficient processors. The paper focuses on a collective system under a stable cost allocation, such as the dual-based cost allocation that ensures the grand-coalition stability, and concludes the following: Under certain conditions, a collective implementation, while having a cost advantage, can stimulate design incentives that are comparable or even superior to those under an individual implementation. The conditions to achieve this environmentally and economically desirable outcome are to have low (high) cost synergy when the product design and the process technology are substitutes (complements).

When these conditions are not met, the tension between achieving cost-efficiency and creating design incentives is irreconcilable under a collective system. That is, a collective system may not be both coalitionally stable (which facilitates economies of scale) and strong in motivating product recyclable design at the same time.

This paper points out the importance of another operational detail: Understanding the level of cost efficient technology in a collective system network and its relation to the product design is key to constructing effective regulation and successfully coping with it. It also suggests that the reverse supply chain manager needs to weigh the value of collection and recycling capacity investments or product design improvements it may make for take-back compliance in the light of the existing collection and recycling infrastructures. Such systems operated by other producers or statewide compliance schemes and the availability of the technologies they leverage can significantly influence the value-added from capacity investments or product design improvements.

10.9   Local Regulation or Global Goals?

Another major concern in dealing with end-of-life products is their leakage from the regulated work management systems due to exports: As end-of-life product waste is costly to process, exporting the waste to developing areas such as Africa and Asia may become an attractive option to producers. The processing costs in these areas are typically much lower due to the lack of stringent processing requirements and the availability of cheap labor. Obviously, this is bad news for the exporting area because when the waste leakage is not properly handled, the effectiveness of regulation in meeting the environmental objectives is seriously undermined. On the other hand, mishandled waste poses an acute hazard to the health and environment in the destination areas of waste export. Note also that such global leakages of environmental externalities are not unique to the take-back context. Similar observations have been made for emissions leakage as well (see Sunar 2015; Drake and Just 2015; Islegen et al. 2015).

In view of this real threat that has already been observed in the practice of electronics recycling (e.g., documented in BAN 2005), the European Union has ratified the Basel Convention, which is an export restriction that prohibits export of end-of-life products. Nevertheless, although dumping waste is unacceptable, the export of used but still functioning products to developing countries may be allowed. The rationale is that exporting functional used products can be a win–win solution. It helps manage the unwanted items in the developed country and provides people in a developing country with affordable access to used products. This forms the foundation for what we call partial export restrictions, under which used products in working condition are permitted for export while end-of-life products are not. A similar example is the introduction of the Responsible Electronics Recycling Act in US Congress in 2011 (Kyle 2011).

Some NGOs, such as the Basel Action Network, however, argue that it may be beneficial to ban exports of even used products, i.e., a full export restriction. As we compare the partial export restriction to the full export restriction, we have to keep in mind that producers may utilize the used products pulled off the secondary market along with the end-of-life products to fulfill the recovery obligation as aforementioned. Then allowing used products with remaining lifespans to be exported may accentuate this type of secondary interference that has been shown to be environmentally unfavorable. Therefore, the problem becomes of concern that how do different stringencies in export regulation (none, partial or full restriction) differ in terms of environmental performance. This problem is addressed in Alev et al. (2014a).

In Alev et al. (2014a), the setup and assumptions for this problem are the same as in the main model exhibited earlier. When products are exported from the developed country to a developing country, the associated unit recycling cost is reduced to reflect the lower cost in the developing country due to cheaper labor or lower processing stringency requirements. The authors then compare the partial and the full export restrictions, while the former forbids the export of end-of-life products, the latter forbids the export of both end-of-life and used products.

The first finding in Alev et al. (2014a) is that when compared to the case with no export restriction, under a full export restriction, the reuse level is higher and the new production volume is smaller in the developed country. This result substantiates the need for closing the door for the export of products from the developed country's perspective, because preventing the export of both used or end-of-life items reduces a producer's incentive for secondary market interference. The result of a partial export restriction, on the other hand, is surprising. Intuitively, we expect that the partial export restriction should partially attain the benefits of a full restriction. However, a partial restriction may lead to even worse outcomes. To be specific, with a partial export restriction, the reuse level may be lower and the total production may increase in the developed country. Moreover, the developing country that receives exports may suffer from the environmental consequences of a higher export volume.

These results once more show that the lack of understanding the operational mechanisms that underlie producer incentives can compromise the regulation effectiveness; not only in the developed economies where take-back regulation is enacted, but also in developing economies importing used products. The detail that critically matters in this case is that reverse supply chains for compliance can in fact have two destinations for recycling, namely, domestic and international. Overlooking the international export as a way to deal with end-of-life obligation can create loopholes in export restriction mechanisms.

10.10 Conclusion: The Devil in the Details

In this chapter, we reviewed a series of operations management papers dealing with take-back regulation implementations to discuss a broad spectrum of possible issues that may arise in crafting of and complying with environmental regulation. This review suggests that the supply chain challenges associated with environmental regulation may particularly be driven by policy implementation decisions, often because of certain assumptions based on abstraction of environmental problems and industrial dynamics: Even basic assumptions that are intuitive, sound and applicable in general circumstances may in fact not hold due to various reasons. These may include technology or commodity market dynamics, differences across the regulated industries, nature of the products of interest, or less obvious but valid alternative responses for producers under regulation.

In turn, these observations suggest that successful design of and compliance with environmental regulation can only be possible with careful implementation choices that account for the devil in the details. This insight emphasizes the merits and importance of taking a supply chain perspective in the context of environmental regulation. We posit that for environmental regulation to achieve its goals, it must account for its influence on the operational decisions of all stakeholders involved, especially those who are directly targeted by the regulation, e.g., producers and their supply chains. In other words, an operational lens appears to be a key instrument in defining appropriate implementation structures for environmental regulations and responding to the ground rules they impose. It is critical that supply chain managers understand the details of take-back policies as they are often not what they appear to be on the surface.

As environmental regulation gains momentum, it will inevitably have to deal with more problems emerging from a wider scope of fields. To triumph in these new challenges calls for more supply chain research in different directions. Looking again at the take-back regulation, although extensive work already exists as discussed, its continuous development may still give rise to new questions to be answered. One instance is that, as recycling activities flourish, encouraged by the more stringent recovery targets, an increasing number of entities are entering the recycling industries to share the pie and make profit. To ensure regulatory effectiveness in promoting environmentally superior treatment of end-of-life products, current regulation on recycling standards may need to be modified and extended to also cover these recyclers. As demonstrated by research studies considered in this chapter, crafting more efficient regulation will require a thorough understanding of the operational details involved. The same is also true for other forms of environmental regulation, such as the RoHS and the REACH (Registration, Evaluation, Authorization and Restriction of Chemicals) Directives of the European Union that regulate the use of certain substances and chemicals, and the variety of emission regulations around the globe. In particular, the emission issues have a wide range of influence because pollutants can transport to other areas easily. As a result, dealing with emission problems may involve extensive collaboration and coordination between various supply chain stakeholders and lead to different operational problems.

References

Alameda County, CA (2012) Alameda county safe drug disposal ordinance. https://www.acgov.org/aceh/safedisposal/documents/SDD_Ordinance.pdf. Accessed Dec 2014

Alev I, Agrawal V, Atasu A (2014a) Extended producer responsibility, secondary market, and export restrictions. Georgia Institute of Technology, Working Paper

Alev I, Atasu A, Ergun O, Toktay LB (2014b) Extended producer responsibility for pharmaceuticals. Georgia Institute of Technology, Working Paper

Apple (2015) Apple reuse and recycling program. http://store.apple.com/us/browse/reuse_and_recycle. Accessed Dec 2014

Ata B, Lee D, Tongarlak MH (2010) Optimizing organic waste to energy operations. Manuf Ser Oper Manag 14(2):231–244

Atasu A, Lifset R, Linnell J, Perry J, Sundberg V, Mayers CK, Dempsey M, Van Wassenhove LN, Van Rossem C, Gregory J, Sverkman A, Therkelsen M, Kalimo H (2015) Individual producer responsibility: a review of practical approaches to implementing individual producer responsibility for the WEEE directive. http://papers.ssrn.com/sol3/papers.cfm?abstractid=1698695. Accessed Dec 2014

Atasu A, Ozdemir O, Van Wassenhove LN (2013) Stakeholder perspectives on E-waste take-back legislation. Prod Oper Manag 22(2):382–396

Atasu A, Subramanian R (2012) Extended producer responsibility for e-waste: individual or collective producer responsibility? Prod Oper Manag 21(6):1042–1059

Basel Action Network (BAN) (2005) The digital dump: exporting reuse and abuse to Africa. http://ban.org/library/TheDigitalDump.pdf. Accessed Dec 2014

Caro F, Corbett CJ, Tan T, Zuidwijk R (2013) Double counting in supply chain carbon footprinting. Manuf Ser Oper Manag 15(4):545–558

Dhanorkar S, Donohue K, Linderman K (2015) Repurposing materials and waste through online exchanges: overcoming the last hurdle. Prod Oper Manag 24(9):1473–1493

Drake D, Just R (2015) What drives firm responses to environmental regulation. In: Atasu A (ed) Environmentally responsible supply chains. Springer, New York

Electronics Take Back Coalition (ETBC) (2013) Brief comparison of state laws on electronics recycling. http://www.electronicstakeback.com/wp-content/uploads/Compare_state_laws_chart. Accessed Dec 2014

EPA (2011) Electronics waste management in the United States through 2009, EPA 530-R-11-002. http://www.epa.gov/wastes/conserve/materials/ecycling/docs/fullbaselinereport2011.pdf. Accessed Dec 2014

EPA (2015) Summary of the clean water act. http://www2.epa.gov/laws-regulations/summary-clean-water-act. Accessed Dec 2014

Esenduran G, Atasu A, Van Wassenhove LN (2014) Valuable E-waste: implications for extended producer responsibility. Ohio State University, Working Paper

Esenduran G, Kemahlioglu-Ziya E (2015) A comparison of product take-back compliance schemes. Prod Oper Manag 24(1):71–88

Europa-Environment (2000) On end-of-life vehicles (ELV). http://eur-lex.europa.eu/LexUriServ/LexUriServ.do?uri=CONSLEG:2000L0053:20050701:EN:PDF. Accessed Dec 2014

Europa-Environment (2002) On the restriction of the use of certain hazardous substances in electrical and electronic equipment (RoHS). http://eur-lex.europa.eu/legal-content/EN/TXT/PDF/?uri=CELEX:32002L0095&from=EN. Accessed Dec 2014

Europa-Environment (2003) On waste electrical and electronic equipment (WEEE). http://eur-lex.europa.eu/resource.html?uri=cellar:ac89e64f-a4a5-4c13-8d96-1fd1d6bcaa49.0004.02/DOC1&format=PDF. Accessed Dec 2014

Fullerton D (2001) A framework to compare environmental policies. National Bureau of Economic Research, Working Paper (No. w8420)

Greenpeace (2010) The E-waste problem. http://www.greenpeace.org/international/en/campaigns/toxics/electronics/the-e-waste-problem/. Accessed Dec 2014

Gui L, Atasu A, Ergun O, Toktay LB (2014a) Efficient implementation of collective extended producer responsibility legislation. Manag Sci

Gui L, Atasu A, Ergun O, Toktay LB (2014b) Design incentives under collective extended producer responsibility: a network perspective. Georgia Institute of Technology, Working Paper

H.R. 2939 (112th) (2011) Pharmaceutical stewardship act of 2011. https://www.govtrack.us/congress/bills/112/hr2939. Accessed Dec 2014

Huang X, Atasu A, Toktay LB (2014) Design implications of extended producer responsibility: durable or recyclable products? Georgia Institute of Technology, Working Paper

Islegen O, Plambeck E, Taylor T (2015) The impacts of climate policy on facility location, production and shipping. In: Atasu A (ed) Environmentally responsible supply chains. Springer, New York

Kalkanci B, Ang E, Plambeck E (2015) Strategic disclosure of social and environmental impacts in a supply chain. In: Atasu A (ed) Environmentally responsible supply chains. Springer, New York

Krass D, Nedorezov T, Ovchinnikov A (2015) Environmental Taxes and the choice of green technology. Prod Oper Manag 22(5):1035–1055

Kyle B (2011) E-waste export legislation is the most important action the federal government can take on E-waste problem. http://www.electronicstakeback.com/2011/06/23/e-waste-export-legislation/. Accessed Dec 2014

Lifset R, Lindhqvist T (2008) Producer responsibility at a turning point. J Ind Ecol 12(2):144–147

Organization for Economic Cooperation and Development (OECD) (2001) Extended producer responsibility: a guidance manual for governments. OECD, Paris

Plambeck E, Wang Q (2009) Effects of E-waste regulation on new product introduction. Manag Sci 55(3):333–347

Regional Greenhouse Gas Initiative (RGGI) (2013) Model rule. http://www.rggi.org/docs/ProgramReview/FinalProgramReviewMaterials/ModelRule FINAL.pdf. Accessed Dec 2014

Richards KR (1999) Framing environmental policy instrument choice. Duke Environ Law Policy Forum 10:221–282

State Council of China (2008) Regulation on the take-back and treatment of waste electrical and electronic equipment. http://www.chinarohs.com/chinaweee-decree551.pdf. Accessed Dec 2014

Sunar N (2015) Emissions allocations under climate policy. In: Atasu A (ed) Environmentally responsible supply chains. Springer, New York

US Geological Survey (USGS) (2001) Obsolete computers, "Gold Mine," or High-Tech Trash? http://pubs.usgs.gov/fs/fs060-01/fs060-01.pdf. Accessed Dec 2014

Walls M (2006) Extended producer responsibility and product design. Resources for the future. Discussion Paper 03–11

Chapter 11
Responsible Purchasing: Moving from Compliance to Value Creation in Supplier Relationships[1]

Arjan van Weele and Kristine van Tubergen

11.1 Introduction

11.1.1 Why Responsible Purchasing?

An increasing number of companies are intertwined with a large number of suppliers. Suppliers are increasingly important for the competitive advantage of the buying company, as the latter is relying on the innovative and quality-enhancing capabilities of its suppliers to reduce costs and improve time to market (Matthyssens and Faes 2013). However, this relationship creates a high dependency of the buying company on its business critical suppliers, making buying companies extremely vulnerable for irregularities in their supply chain.

Boeing's Dreamliner may serve here as an example. The first Dreamliner was delivered in September 2011 to All Nippon Airways, 3.5 years behind schedule. There were many reasons for this significant delay. First, the large number of new technologies (e.g., new composites for body parts, new electronics for customer entertainment and climate control) resulted in many problems. Next, Boeing's complex global supply chain design represented an even greater challenge (Tang et al. 2009). Parts were sourced from specialized suppliers worldwide. The orchestration of the parts among the supply partners and Boeing seemed an impossible job. Next, it was no surprise that the first planes showed significant failures

[1] The authors are grateful to Dr. Regien Sumo's comments on earlier versions of this text.

A. van Weele, Ph.D. (✉)
TU Eindhoven, Eindhoven, Netherlands
e-mail: A.J.v.Weele@tue.nl

K. van Tubergen, M.Sc.
Department of Business-Society Management, Rotterdam School of Management,
Erasmus University, Rotterdam, The Netherlands
e-mail: vantubergen@rsm.nl

Y. Bouchery et al. (eds.), *Sustainable Supply Chains*, Springer Series in Supply
Chain Management 4, DOI 10.1007/978-3-319-29791-0_11

257

(ranging from cockpit windshield crack, to overheated batteries and even interior fires). When mismanagement takes place in a wrong supply chain design involving monopolistic and specialized business critical suppliers, the consequences will both hit the supplier, the buying company, and the end-consumer. In addition, sustainability risks arise with these global supply chain complexities following from unforeseen supplier malpractices. This results in supply chain interruptions and reputation damage.

Supplier relationships clearly pose new challenges in terms of transparency and traceability. Therefore, it is time for companies to address these challenges and take sustainability criteria into account in their purchasing practices. Principles regarding ethics, safety, and diversity should be supported in order to benefit the firm, supply chain, and society. Support for these principles should be demanded from the suppliers' suppliers as well. However, demanding compliance is one challenge, creating shared value in the supply chain is quite another challenge. The latter requires an orientation towards responsible purchasing, i.e., a (governance) process of creating more transparency, education, collaborative partnerships, and of implementing sustainability practices. Doing so effectively will take time and efforts as companies will move through different stages of maturity.

In this chapter, we argue that responsible rather than sustainable purchasing is needed to support the company's overall business strategy. These two concepts are detailed in the following section.

11.1.2 Responsible vs. Sustainable Purchasing[2]

Corporate social responsibility (CSR) relates to an organization's responsibility to meet the present needs of its various stakeholders without jeopardizing the future needs of these stakeholders (Brundtland 1987). Other authors have referred to CSR as the economic, legal, environmental, ethical, and philanthropic expectations that society has of organizations at any given point in time (Carroll 1991). In line with these definitions, we define sustainable purchasing as: "the supply of all goods, services, capabilities and knowledge which are necessary for running, maintaining and managing the organization's primary and support activities secured at the most sustainable conditions." Sustainability refers to economic, legal, ethical, and philanthropic aspects in relationships with suppliers. We differentiate between sustainable purchasing and responsible purchasing, as the latter would require a different mentality and orientation from purchasing professionals. Sustainable purchasing includes designing and implementing procedures and guidelines, based on external standards, aimed at fostering sustainable supplier relationships. Responsible purchasing implies that purchasing professionals take it as their personal, rather than their company's, responsibility to secure that these principles are implemented. Whereas sustainable purchasing refers to the institutional responsibility, i.e., corporate responsibility, responsible purchasing is reflected by the adoption of

---

[2]Responsible Purchasing equals in this chapter Green Purchasing, Environmentally Preferable Sourcing, Green Sourcing.

sustainability in the daily activities of purchasing professionals based upon their own personal, ethical, and professional standards.

Responsible purchasing does not only look at the effects of supplier relationships on company financial results, risks, and reputation. Rather, it also includes designing and implementing supply chain solutions that are beneficial not only for the company, but also for the world around us. This connotation of purchasing is in line with stakeholder theory as suggested by Freeman (1984), who argues that an organization should not only satisfy the interests of their shareholders, but also the interests of other stakeholders such as customers, suppliers, employees, regulatory agencies, competitors, consumer advocacy groups, and media. This connotation also aligns with what Porter and Kramer (2011) referred to as shared value creation. Implementing sustainable purchasing is already a massive task. The step to implement responsible purchasing is even greater.

11.1.3 Objectives and Structure of the Chapter

Our focus in this chapter is on large (multinational) companies that source *products*. The objective of this chapter is to show what it takes to go to difficult and troublesome route to drive CSR in supplier, i.e., supply chain relationships. We discuss some important CSR adoption models for large multinational companies (MNCs). This knowledge will enable companies to design a roadmap towards integrated, responsible supply chain practices. Implementing this roadmap comes with significant challenges. Therefore, we end with some critical issues and questions for companies to reflect on, when taking the journey towards responsible purchasing and supply chain practices. However, before doing so we position our paper by discussing three relevant theoretical perspectives for our discussion.

The rest of the chapter is organized as follows. We start by presenting three different approaches for value creation at the firm level in Sect. 11.2. We show that the traditional resource-based view has been supplemented by the resource dependence theory and the stakeholder theory. In Sect. 11.3, we review several approaches to CSR in the supply chain as well as the programs and methods to drive sustainability in supply chain relationships. Section 11.4 is devoted to the presentation of a time-phased model for responsible purchasing adoption. These concepts are compared to practice in Sect. 11.5 through several examples. Section 11.6 presents some challenges related to sustainable supplier relationships. Finally, Sect. 11.7 is devoted to conclusions and suggestions.

11.2 From the Resource-Based View to Stakeholder Theory[3]

Shareholder value creation has dominated management theory and business practices for decades. The purpose of the firm was to create maximum wealth for its owners, i.e., its shareholders. In doing so, the firm should use and capitalize on its

---

[3]This section is partially derived and rewritten from Kibbeling (2010, pp. 20–24).

resources, i.e., the combination of technology, assets, knowledge, financial resources, and expertise. For a long time, the resource-based view was positioned as the most dominant research paradigm in strategic management (Wernerfelt 1984). The resource-based view suggests that a firm's unique resources, its competences to deploy those resources, and its capabilities that are derived from bundled resources provide a source for growth and competitive advantage (Rumelt 1984; Wernerfelt 1984). Possessing and having access to valuable, rare, inimitable, and non-substitutable resources would provide competitive advantages in itself, according to these researchers. However, other researchers suggest that value is created only when these resources are evaluated, manipulated, and deployed appropriately within the firm's environmental context. Resources thus require a purpose in order to be successfully structured, bundled, and leveraged. Purpose and value is given to a firm's resources through directing them with an external orientation (Sirmon et al. 2007). An external orientation allows firms to leverage capabilities and resources in such a way that they fit to their context and are considered valuable. This approach is called resource management (Sirmon et al. 2007, 2008).

The resource-based view, however, is in essence internally oriented and does only implicitly embed supplier resources and capabilities in the process of structuring, bundling, and leveraging resources to obtain competitiveness. It remains unclear about how to adopt the proposed external orientation, which is necessary to create sufficient "fit" with the firm's environment, i.e., its multiple stakeholders.

Therefore, other researchers have suggested that rather than internal resources, the way the firm needs to deal with its external resources, i.e., its external dependencies, is important in order to achieve competitive advantage. The central proposition in the resource dependence theory is that firms change as well as negotiate with their external environment in order to secure access to the resources, which they need in order to survive (Pfeffer and Salancik 1978). The resource dependency theory thereby typically looks beyond the boundaries of an individual firm. The resource dependence theory advocates that information generation and intelligence on the environment are key for creating firm awareness and firm responsiveness to stakeholder demands (Handfield 1993; Pfeffer and Salancik 1978). Next it argues that firms are not self-contained in fulfilling demands and therefore need to establish effective linkages with suppliers to access resources and capabilities required to deliver value (Pfeffer and Salancik 1978; Ulrich and Barney 1984). Hence, this theory argues that a firm's success is particularly reflected in the *external* evaluation of the firm's performance (Christensen and Bower 1996; Pfeffer and Salancik 1978). The resource dependence theory implies that suppliers are necessary for adapting to and anticipating on the developments in the supply chain's environment. Developing effective relationships with the most qualified suppliers seems to be a prerequisite to secure the external resources, which are required to create customer value creation and, hence, foster the firm's competitiveness (Pfeffer and Salancik 1978).

The resource dependence theory is explicit about the purpose of the firm: satisfying external stakeholders, i.e., customers, investors, and other organizations that are affected by the firm (Christensen and Bower 1996). This idea is acknowledged and elaborated on by stakeholder theory. Stakeholder theory suggests that each stake-holder represents different values that the focal firm should try to realize (Donaldson and Preston 1995; Freeman 1984; Freeman et al. 2007). The aim of stakeholder theory is to satisfy a broad array of stakeholder groups based on their specific demands. Creating value for different stakeholders has an effect on the way firms allocate their resources through adopting different stakeholder orientations; firms may create the proper attitudes and behaviors for satisfying its stakeholders and achieving superior firm performance simultaneously. Stakeholder orientations result in firm competitiveness because focus on stakeholder satisfaction allows a firm to develop trusting relationships with their stakeholders, giving these firms the opportunity to deal better with changes in the environment and consequently spur innovation (Freeman et al. 2007; Harrison et al. 2010).

A stakeholder can be "any group or individual who can affect or is affected by the achievement of the organization's objectives" (Freeman 1984). These include, for instance, employees, communities, customers, political groups, investors, governments, suppliers, and trade associations. Even though it may be difficult to classify stakeholders, it seems that the stakeholder view is especially useful for reflecting resource-based considerations, market considerations, and socio-political considerations simultaneously. When we adopt this perspective, suppliers should not only create value to the firm's markets (customers), but also to society (all stake-holders representing social and environmental concerns) and to those who did invest financial resources in the firm (shareholders, investors).

In conclusion, the resource-based view of the firm, the resource dependence theory, and stakeholder theory each emphasize a different element of how firms may create value through supply chain cooperation. The resource-based view of the firm is more concerned with the management of a firm's internal resources and capabilities that may satisfy external stakeholders of the firm. In the resource depen-dence theory, the firm's dependence on other external parties, such as suppliers, is central. Finally, the stakeholder theory focuses on the diverse stakeholder perspec-tives a firm needs to balance, weigh, and respond to. It argues that for achieving competitive advantage, a firm and its supply chain partners should create in parallel customer value, societal value, and shareholder value (Porter and Kramer 2011). Chapter 21 by Sodhi and Tang (2017) provides further discussion of the stakeholder resource-based view in the context of social responsibility.

11.3 CSR Models and Approaches in Large Companies

There are several approaches to CSR in the supply chain, all having a (slightly) dif-ferent focus. Some CSR models differentiate between companies, on the basis of, for example, sectors (e.g., food, energy, commodities), value chain position (upstream vs. downstream), or size (large enterprises vs. SMEs). In this section, we briefly discuss some important CSR models for large (multinational) companies and show their importance for the supply chain and purchasing function.

Most CSR models for large companies focus on the steps that are needed to integrate sustainability in the different functions. Several models also focus on the practices that are needed outside the company to create a transparent sustainable supply chain. Various CSR models have determined certain stages of maturity in the implementation of sustainability practices in the organization and its value chain. For example, Zadek (2004) has identified five stages organizations typically go through when developing a sense of corporate responsibility, as they move along the learning curve: defensive, compliance, managerial, strategic, and civil. In addition, research from Van Tulder and Van der Zwart (2006) has distinguished between passive, reactive, active, and proactive approaches of organizations to CSR. Also Nidumolu et al. (2009) have established several stages in the adoption process of CSR for organizations. This model is a good representation of the adoption process of CSR. Consequently, we provide more information about this model in Box 11.1.

Box 11.1 Stages in the Adoption of CSR by Organizations

According to Nidumolu et al. (2009), sustainability is the key driver of organizational and technological innovations that create competitive advantage and lower costs in the supply chain. Based on 30 case studies, they have discovered five stages of change that organizations go through on the "march to sustainability," each stage creating opportunities and requiring new capabilities to deal with challenges (see Fig. 11.2).

Stage 1: Viewing compliance as an opportunity—Being the first to adopt emerging laws allows companies more time to experiment with creative solutions and discover new business opportunities. It may also reduce costs as one single chain is required for all markets, rather than having to adapt it to the variations of each set of regulations.

Stage 2: Making value chains sustainable—Once companies have learned to keep pace with regulation, they become more proactive about sustainability and in particular about environmental issues such as resource use. Initially, this helps the company's image, but down the line it also helps to reduce costs and create new businesses.

Stage 3: Designing sustainable products and services—An improved supply chain management allows a company to take a closer look at their product structures and redesign them to meet customer concerns and examine the products' life cycles.

Stage 4: Developing new business—New business models provide alternatives to the current way of doing business while succeeding in the value delivery to the customer. These often materialize in collaborations with other companies like when FedEx integrated their chain over that of Kinko's so that documents would no longer have to be shipped, but could be printed on location.

Stage 5: Creating next-practice platforms—Corporations move from looking for ways to deliver value that are compatible with CSR and sustainability, to make sustainability the main tenant through which business models are created (Fig. 11.1).

(continued)

Box 11.1 (continued)

STAGE 1 Viewing Compliance as Opportunity	STAGE 2 Making Value Chains Sustainable	STAGE 3 Designing Sustainable Products and Services	STAGE 4 Developing New Business Models	STAGE 5 Creating Next-Practice Platforms
CENTRAL CHALLENGE To ensure that compliance with norms becomes an opportunity for innovation.	CENTRAL CHALLENGE To increase efficiencies throughout the value chain.	CENTRAL CHALLENGE To develop sustainable offerings or redesign existing ones to become eco-friendly.	CENTRAL CHALLENGE To find novel ways of delivering and capturing value, which will change the basis of competition.	CENTRAL CHALLENGE To question through the sustainability lens the dominant logic behind business today.
COMPETENCIES NEEDED >> The ability to anticipate and shape regulations. >> The skill to work with other companies, including rivals, to implement creative solutions.	COMPETENCIES NEEDED >> Expertise in techniques such as carbon management and life-cycle assessment. >> The ability to redesign operations to use less energy and water, produce fewer emissions, and generate less waste.	COMPETENCIES NEEDED >> The skills to know which products or services are most unfriendly to the environment. >> The ability to generate real public support for sustainable offerings and not be considered as "greenwashing."	COMPETENCIES NEEDED >> The capacity to understand what consumers want and to figure out different ways to meet those demands. >> The ability to understand how partners can enhance the value of offerings.	COMPETENCIES REQUIRED >> Knowledge of how renewable and nonrenewable resources affect business ecosystems and industries. >> The expertise to synthesize business models, technologies, and regulations in different industries.
INNOVATION OPPORTUNITY >> Using compliance to induce the company and its partners to experiment with sustainable technologies, materials, and processes.	INNOVATION OPPORTUNITIES >> Developing sustainable sources of raw materials and components. >> Increasing the use of clean energy sources such as wind and solar power. >> Finding innovative uses for returned products.	INNOVATION OPPORTUNITIES >> Applying techniques such as biomimicry in product development. >> Developing compact and eco-friendly packaging.	INNOVATION OPPORTUNITIES >> Developing new delivery technologies that change value-chain relationships in significant ways. >> Creating monetization models that relate to services rather than products. >> Devising business models that combine digital and physical infrastructures.	INNOVATION OPPORTUNITIES >> Building business platforms that will enable customers and suppliers to manage energy in radically different ways. >> Developing products that won't need water in categories traditionally associated with it, such as cleaning products. >> Designing technologies that will allow industries to use the energy produced as a by-product.
	>> The capacity to ensure that suppliers and retailers make their operations eco-friendly.	>> The management knowhow to scale both supplies of green materials and the manufacture of products.		

Fig. 11.1 Stages in the adoption of CSR by organizations (*source:* Nidumolu et al. 2009)

These and other CSR models consider sustainability as a key driver of innovation and of benefits in terms of people, planet, and profit. As we have argued, sustainability is increasingly becoming a prerequisite for existing business models to remain competitive. Successful sustainability strategies should integrate ethical, operational, relational, and co-marketing approaches (Matthyssens and Faes 2013). In addition, they require collaboration between different functions, such as research and development (R&D), logistics, purchasing, marketing, and sales. Particularly, purchasing departments should take the lead in driving sustainability through the organization, given the importance of suppliers due to the tremendous outsourcing practices of current MNCs and the inherent carbon footprint of upstream supply chains. In addition, the models show that monitoring and evaluation (M&E) are important aspects for the management of sustainability in large companies. The transparency in sustainability performance resulting from M&E does not only benefit the company's reputation in relation to critical external parties, such as non-governmental organizations (NGOs), consumer action groups, public sector actors, and customers that have called upon the business sector to act more responsibly. It also serves as an internal driver for employees and stakeholders in the supply chain. Transparency and an improved sustainability reputation seem to have a positive effect on the employees' and supply chain partners' motivation (Matthyssens and Faes 2013). Further discussion on how firms can use a "sense and response" framework to improve social and environmental performance in their supply chains is provided by Lee and Rammohan (2017) in Chap. 20.

In order to create transparency in the sustainability domain, large companies report on indicators that are derived from the external indices such as the Dow Jones Sustainability Index and the Global Reporting Initiative.[4] In their reports, these institutions use a wide range of indicators to measure CSR progress and performance. Examples of indicators are the way in which the company is managed (i.e., its corporate governance), risk and crisis management, ethical codes that are present within the organization, the way in which the company tries to improve eco-efficiency and reduce carbon footprint, fuel efficiency, labor conditions, and social reporting.

Large buying corporations could take a leadership role by influencing the CSR policies of their (current) suppliers. More and more MNCs are aware of this so-called "responsibility for sustainability stewardship." They integrate sustainability indicators in the supplier selection process to carefully select suppliers on their current sustainability performance and their potential and willingness to comply with the sustainability policy of the buying company in order to prevent certain suppliers for being excluded, such as smallholders. In addition, companies recognize the value of local sourcing, including small and diverse businesses that can

---

[4] See also Chap. 6 by Bateman et al. (2017) for more on sustainability reporting.

benefit their communities. In addition, large buying corporations can influence sustainability practices through codes of conduct and audits. Box 11.2 provides an overview of the different programs and methods that companies use to drive sustainability in the supply chain relationships (Van Weele and Vivanco 2014).

Box 11.2   Programs and Methods to Drive Sustainability in Supply Chain Relationships

- Stakeholder management

  - Corporate social responsibility committee
  - Stakeholder meetings on creating shared value (in water, nutrition, rule development, energy, environmental stewardship)

- Supply-chain sustainability strategy

  - Programs aimed at value chain carbon emission reduction
  - Support local buying in countries where sales are made
  - Water management plan across the supply chain
  - Secure long-term raw material supply
  - Product recovery programs
  - Increase share of renewable energy

- Supplier relationships

  - Supplier quality assurance programs
  - Supplier traceability programs
  - Supplier compliance to local legal requirements
  - Supplier sustainability audits (self-assessment, external audits)
  - Supplier sustainability and integrity codes

- Competence development

  - Training buyers in responsible procurement practices
  - Supplier development programs
  - Supplier productivity programs

- External standards

  - Global reporting initiative
  - Dow Jones sustainability Index
  - NGO fair labor Association
  - ISO 14 001
  - EICC code of conduct
  - FSC standard (wood, forestation)

(continued)

Box 11.2 (continued)

• Supply-chain sustainability measures

  – Supply chain carbon dashboard
  – Percentage of sustainable suppliers
  – Percentage of sustainable spend
  – Supplier code of conduct violations

Source: (Van Weele & Vivanco 2014)

These programs and methods may be used to create a common approach towards sustainability in the supply chain. In order to increase the compliance and engagement of suppliers, stakeholder meetings and supplier development programs are organized by the buying company. Buyer-imposed standards and practices may foster innovation within the supplier's organization, which will result in a direct benefit for the supply chain, including the buying company, to serve its customers and society.[5] Therefore, an increasing number of sustainability indices also take the supply chain performance into account when assigning a sustainability score to a company. An example is the ISO 26000 guideline that provides indicators for companies to make their supply chain more sustainable.

11.4 Adopting Responsible Purchasing: A Time Phased Model

In the previous section, we discussed programs and methods to drive sustainability in supply chain relationships. These programs and methods are not used by all companies all of the time. On the contrary, as we observe from company practices, companies seem to go through a growth path in adopting these tools and techniques and in developing responsible purchasing. This growth path is in line with the growth path that companies need at corporate levels to adopt sustainability as a concept as discussed in Sect. 11.3 in the model of Nidumolu et al. (Nidumolu et al. 2009). However, as our previous research shows,[6] there seems to be a time lag between the adoption of sustainability at the corporate, i.e., company

---

[5]"Creating value in supply chains: supplier's impact on the value for customers, society and shareholders" Kibbeling, M.I. (2010) Ph.D. dissertation, Eindhoven University of Technology. The reason why CSR drives innovation in supply chain relationships is that imposing CSR requirements on incumbent suppliers reduces their product and process solution space. In order to fit the buyer's smaller solution space new products and process solutions are necessary.

[6] See Van Weele and Vivanco (2014).

level, and at the purchasing, i.e., supply chain level. We suggest that the following stages mark the adoption of sustainability in supply chain relationships:

Stage I: *Denial*—As the company has not integrated sustainability in its business strategy, purchasing is traditionally cost-driven in its supply chain relationships. Suppliers are selected based on the lowest price, i.e., total cost of ownership. Supplier codes of conduct and business integrity codes are usually not present. The dominant view at the board level is that adopting CSR will increase cost and complexity. CSR practices are adopted as long as the balance between extra revenues and extra costs incurred is positive.

Stage II: *Opportunism*—Here the company expresses sustainability as a prime concern in its public advertising and marketing. However, it is not integrated in its business strategy and operations. Hence, ideas and concepts covering sustainability are not cascaded down to the purchasing department and supply relationships. Hence, there is little difference with the previous stage. The board starts to think about CSR as a concept to foster its customer reputation and to counterattack assaults from external parties. Individual ad hoc CSR initiatives are highlighted and overexposed in company advertising and brochures.

Stage III: *Compliance to the law*—As the company has faced some difficulties on sustainability issues with the external world, the board of directors has become sensitive to the company's risk profile. Hence, business managers are instructed not to violate any social laws or environmental laws in the areas in which they operate. The first training and awareness programs are designed at a corporate level, following a typical top-down approach. These programs, however, have not trickled down to the purchasing and supply operations yet. Occasionally, purchasing may have introduced an integrity code to its suppliers. At this stage, purchasing is still passive, traditional, and cost-driven.

Stage IV: *Sustainability as a driver for lower cost*—At this stage, due to a number of consulting assignments and studies within the company, the board of directors has become aware that pursuing sustainability in its operations might drive down the costs, fostering internal motivation for sustainability. When energy consumption is decreased overall, the company's carbon footprint will go down resulting in lower energy bills. Internally, energy saving programs show great results and new solutions. As the company is aware of its high external cost, initiatives trickle down to the purchasing department to pursue similar programs in supply chain relationships. This leads to specific sourcing programs aimed at reducing energy costs and carbon footprint at suppliers. In addition, procurement managers start to set up supplier sustainability audits to make suppliers comply with social and environmental regulations.

Stage V: *Sustainability as a driver for product and business innovation*—At this stage, the company has experienced that driving sustainability in its company operations leads to new products, processes, and customer solutions. Imposing CSR requirements on incumbent suppliers changes their product and process solution space. In order to fit the buyer's smaller solution space, new products and process solutions are necessary. Suppliers are invited to discover better sustainable solutions to enable less energy consuming products and processes. As a result, supplier relationships change from being competitive to more collaborative. Suppliers are urged to transfer sustainability requirements to their next-level suppliers. The board monitors progress on specific supply chain sustainability initiatives. CSR performance measures, next to traditional cost and savings measures, make up the procurement organization's dashboard.

Stage VI: From corporate social responsibility to creating shared value—At this stage, sustainability is fully integrated into the company's business and supply chain strategy and operations. Over time, the change of the company's philosophy has led to a reduction of the number of supply chain relationships and towards more transparent and collaborative partnerships with suppliers. There is an active exchange of ideas and best practices between both the company and its key business-critical suppliers about how to grow profitable and even more sustainable business in the future, while at the same time reducing carbon footprint and creating value for all stakeholders. Procurement specialists engage with local and smaller suppliers, after thorough pre-qualification, to support them in adopting CSR practices and upgrading their sustainability performance. At this stage, the company pursues a truly responsible purchasing strategy.

As companies move from Stage 1–6, purchasing as a business function becomes more integrated and its focus shifts from traditional cost-driven transactional purchasing to value-driven, supplier development (a theme also emphasized in Lee and Rammohan (2017), Chap. 20).

In the next section, we provide some examples of how companies handle responsible purchasing as well as a discussion on how the examples relate to the theoretical concepts presented above.

11.5   Examples[7]

11.5.1   Mattel: How Bad Practices at the Suppliers May Affect the Entire Supply Chain?

Violation of human rights or environmental unfriendly practices by suppliers do harm to the entire supply chain. In 2007, Mattel, the global leader in children's toys, became front-page news due to its problems with Chinese suppliers. A few suppliers had replaced certified paint with cheaper paints to reduce cost. Unfortunately, the new paint contained lead, which is generally considered to be harmful to children's health and safety. By bringing these products to consumers, Mattel apparently was violating US regulations on health and safety. Mattel was not informed by its contract manufacturers of the change of paint. The company received the news when a European retailer discovered lead paint on a toy. Due to extensive press exposure, Mattel's senior management had to recall 1.5 million Chinese-made products. Later, another 436,000 products had to be recalled. Because of this incident, Mattel found itself in the center of a debate over sustainable sourcing and more particularly about the safety of products made in China.

---

[7] Parts of this section are derived from Van Weele (2014), Chapter 14.

Apparently, during the many years that Mattel sourced its products from China, the company had become overconfident about its ability to operate in China without major problems. Initially, it seemed that the problem was limited to only one supplier. However, when Mattel's safety lab at Shenzhen investigated the contents of their toys, other products with similar failures surfaced. That was the moment that the management recognized it probably had to deal with a more systemic problem, rather than the isolated case of one bad paint supplier. Earlier, Mattel was involved in another affair when it had to recall millions of toys with tiny magnets that had harmed some children who swallowed them. Mattel found out that some of its preferred suppliers, in order to save costs, used cheaper suppliers themselves. One of these low-cost suppliers was the paint supplier who was not listed on Mattel's approved supplier list.

Mattel has been manufacturing in Asia far longer than many other companies. The first Barbie was made there in 1959. Other products, like its Fisher Price toys, Matchbox cars, and Pixar toys, followed. It developed long-term relationships with certain Chinese contractors, some of which spanned decades. Paradoxically, this might have worked against the company. The longer it outsourced to a factory supplier with good results, the more lax its controls became. Two contractors that caused the recalls were among the most trusted. Lee Der, the supplier involved in the first recall, worked with Mattel for 15 years. Early Light Industrial, which made the Sarge cars, supplied toys for more than 20 years. The latter supplier caused the recall of 436,000 Pixar car toys, which was also caused by yet another contractor, as Early Light had subcontracted production of the cars' roof and tires to a subcontractor called Hong Li Da. In all cases, Mattel's contract manufacturers violated the company's rules on what paint they were allowed to use. Mattel had certified only eight paint suppliers. Mattel realized that it was not monitoring its contract manufacturers closely enough. It appeared that a number of companies were part of Mattel's supply chain that were never visited by Mattel's sourcing professionals and quality inspectors. As a result, Mattel's board of management decided on a three-point action plan which included: (1) tightening control of production, (2) investigating unauthorized use of subcontractors by contract manufacturers, and (3) bringing back in-house testing of all purchased products. Based on its investigations, Mattel fired four contractors and they enforced the rule upon their contract manufacturers that they cannot hire two or three layers of suppliers below them. In order to restore its reputation, global advertising campaigns were set up to inform consumers about the measures that were taken. Part of the campaign was the statement that Mattel is less dependent on Chinese suppliers than most of its competitors.

11.5.2   *Philips: How to Engage Suppliers in Promoting Sustainability Principles?*

Suppliers are an important source for a company's competitive advantage. However, as the examples of Boeing and Mattel have shown, suppliers can also be an important source of unforeseen problems and risk. How should companies deal with these sustainability problems and risks in supply chain relationships? How and what principles should companies put in place with regard to people, planet, and profit in supplier relationships? How should companies convince suppliers to promote sustainability principles in their operational processes? Companies that know how to deal with these issues are still rare. Some companies are leading the way. Philips is one of them.

In 2002, Philips started a worldwide sustainability program for its global procurement organization. For this purpose, in 2003 a standard was developed with regard to the requirements that suppliers should meet in the area of sustainability. The standard was implemented in 2004. This is no small thing, if one realizes that more than 50,000 suppliers worldwide were involved in the program. All suppliers were invited to participate in the program through a formal letter sent by Philips' CEO. The letter encouraged suppliers to conduct a "self-assessment" and to report the outcome of this self-assessment to Philips. Next, Philips would conduct a similar audit by its own internal auditors. For this program, more than 400 associates were trained and instructed. Next, the results of the Philips' audit were compared with the results from the supplier's self-assessments. Variances between both audits were discussed and suppliers were invited to come up with an action plan to take corrective measures, which were periodically followed up by Philips' procurement organization. In its audits, Philips focuses on sustainability and the way in which suppliers deal with issues such as environmental protection, labor conditions, safety, child labor, discrimination and diversity, the number of labor hours, and compliance with local labor laws. Apart from this, the auditors focus on the presence of banned substances. Attention is paid also to the suppliers' relationships with unions. Just asking suppliers to sign a declaration in which they declare to comply with Philips' environmental policies, like in the past, was not enough anymore. In the past, suppliers were, with their eye on future business, very much willing to put their signature without actually checking their operations against Philips CSR guidelines. For Philips' CEO, this was no longer sufficient. The company wanted to ensure that suppliers were meeting its CSR requirements. Suppliers that did not meet these requirements were dropped from Philips' suppliers list. As a result, the number of suppliers worldwide was reduced from 50,000 to about 30,000, most of whom are now in line with Philips' environmental policies. Environmental regulations become increasingly tighter, especially for European firms. The list of banned substances for European firms is consistently growing. Next, European consumer laws require firms to offer a full traceability of their products and product components. After some incidents, where products that were imported from Asian manufacturing facilities contained hazardous materials, Philips started its BOMCheck program that would require suppliers to keep record in a web-enabled Philips-controlled database of their product constituents and origins. This database would secure Philips from future claims from consumers and NGOs based on banned substances.

Is the approach sufficient for the future? The answer, clearly, is "no." Philips, at this moment, has aligned its first-tier suppliers with its environmental policies.

Today, Philips urges its suppliers to transfer their CSR policies to their (second-tier) suppliers and raw materials producers. In this area, the company still has a long way to go.

11.5.3   Unilever: How to Improve the Sustainability of the Supply Chain?

Another company that gives priority to sustainability in the supply chain is Unilever. In 2010, Unilever launched its Sustainable Living Plan. This plan was aimed at achieving three major objectives before 2020: (1) to help more than 1 billion people improve their health and well-being, (2) to halve the environmental footprint of Unilever's products, and (3) to source 100 % of all agricultural raw materials sustainably and enhance the livelihoods of people across the entire value chain. The Sustainable Living Plan was based upon a thorough analysis of Unilever's carbon footprint across its value chain, from its raw materials suppliers up to its retailers and end consumers. The results of this analysis are shown in Fig. 11.2.

This figure shows that only 3 % of Unilever's carbon footprint is caused by its factories. Around 2 % is caused by its distribution and transport network. However, its supplier network is responsible for 26 %, which represents a significant challenge for its sourcing specialists. In addition, the majority of its carbon footprint is caused by the consumer at the point of consumption. This analysis explains why Unilever has put great emphasis on new product development and innovation in order to stimulate sustainable behavior from their consumers.

New detergents, allowing for less water consumption and lower temperatures, have been introduced. Another example is body care products, such as shampoos that allow faster rinsing when taking a shower. Sourcing strategies have been aimed at improving farmer productivity, less use of pesticides, and increasing the use of renewable energy. Unilever's Sustainable Living Plan has changed its international sourcing strategies significantly. Unilever is not unique in taking supply chain sustainability initiatives. Other frontrunners in the food business are Nestlé and Mars, who embarked on similar programs.

OUR FOOTPRINT

Fig. 11.2   Carbon footprint of Unilever's Value Chain (*source*: www.unilever.com)

11.5.4 Nestlé: How to Adopt Responsible Purchasing? [8]

Nestlé's Nespresso division may serve as an example of the time-phased model presented in Sect. 11.4. Until 2003, Nespresso was a growing coffee roaster focused on the premium consumer segment. It sourced its high-quality coffee through global commodity traders such as ECOM and Expocafe. In 2003, it had to rethink its sourcing model. The reason was threefold.

On the one hand, its sourcing strategy was felt to be too much supply-driven. Until the beginning of the 1990s, the coffee market was a controlled market regulated internationally through the International Coffee Agreement (ICA). However, in 1999, the International Coffee Organization failed to set new export quotas and as a result it collapsed. Oversupply in many coffee markets led to price erosion, which had terrible social, economic, and political consequences. Nespresso, being a high-quality coffee brand, was confronted with flawing and ever-changing coffee quality grades. Moreover, the fluctuating raw materials prices were a direct threat to a consistent consumer pricing policy and the company's profitability. On the other hand, global coffee consumption went through a period of significant growth creating a high demand. The company constantly had to struggle to find high-quality coffee at the right volumes and the right prices. In addition, oversupply in the coffee markets led to low and unfavorable prices that had a detrimental effect on farmer incomes. Grassroots and NGOs, such as Greenpeace and the Fair Trade movement, joined forces in promoting the welfare of small producers in developing countries (Alvarez 2008), accusing MNCs such as Nestlé of unethical and unsustainable practices in their supply chain relationships. Multinationals were, rightly or wrongly, accused of violating local labor laws, ignoring issues of climate change, and performing unethical practices in their supplier relationships. More specifically, NGOs took aim at the unjustified profits that were reported by these companies, accusing them of unfair distribution of profitability within the coffee supply chain. Nespresso had to increasingly deal with the pressure of these three forces.

Mr. Lopez, Chief Procurement Officer (CPO) of Nespresso, was asked to look into this changing context, as it had direct consequences for his global sourcing organization. The challenges he and his team had to deal with were as follows: How could Nespresso secure its supply of high-quality coffee in such unstable market conditions? How could Nespresso avoid bad publicity, when they operated at such a large distance from the coffee growers? How could or should Nespresso improve the conditions in the supply chain? Would it be possible to conceive of a sourcing model that would incorporate all of these factors? And how should such a sourcing model look like?

Mr. Lopez and his colleagues pondered about designing a new sourcing model for Nespresso. Here, companies like Toyota and IKEA, who had long-term and strong sourcing relationships with their suppliers, served as a source of inspiration. They decided to change Nespresso's mediated sourcing model and go for a model allowing

---

[8] The following text is derived from: Van Weele and Van Tubergen (2013), p. 18.

Nespresso to deal directly with the coffee growers. This would mean that gradually most intermediate organizations that Nespresso had dealt with for such a long time needed to be bypassed. The basic idea underlying this plan was that if Nespresso was able to select its suppliers itself, it could build a strong personalized relationship with them and transfer knowledge to improve farmer practices and secure the supply of coffee. Nespresso would motivate its coffee growers by paying them a premium over the market price. This direct sourcing model would allow Nespresso to have a much larger control over its supply chain, which was felt necessary to improve farmer productivity and quality and increase supply chain transparency and sustainability.

In order to implement the direct sourcing model—changing the entire way of working with suppliers—Nespresso needed to change its business model. Therefore, Mr. Lopez and his staff initiated a companywide program, i.e., Nespresso's AAA Sustainable Quality Program in 2003. The aim of this program was to foster both quality and sustainability in all supply chain relationships. Several tools, such as an innovative farm assessment and support program, were developed to select and involve coffee suppliers in the program (Goodbrand.com). Core elements of the program were:

1. *Certificates*: Nespresso developed a proprietary standard to assess social and environmental standards on coffee farms. This was done in close collaboration with Rainforest Alliance.
2. *Premiums*: Nespresso paid 30–40 % above the standard coffee market price; this would amount to about 10–15 % above the coffees of the same quality.
3. *Partnering*: Nespresso aimed at developing long-term relationships with coffee farmers to improve farmer productivity and decrease crop diseases.

The growth path in adopting sustainability and responsible practices in its supply chain relationships took Nespresso almost 10 years. However, today its global program for coffee supply is unique, representing a firm basis for Nespresso's market success. It has built some strong supplier relationships, although these have to be continuously adapted to challenges in the world, such as climate change, poverty, or changing regulating environments.

11.5.5 Shared Value Creation in the Examples

As the examples of Mattel, Philips, Unilever, and Nestlé show, the relationship with suppliers is an important topic to foster supply chain value creation. In order to unleash the innovative capacity and create shared value in the supply chain, extensive (green) collaboration is needed between supply chain partners. This list of examples could have been much longer. Other companies operating in retail and fast-moving consumer goods have made CSR a cornerstone in their sourcing policies and supply chain relationships.[9] Value creation is not only aimed at creating

---

[9] See for other examples Walmart (http://goo.gl/U8wzHT) and IKEA (http://goo.gl/flXzdM).

shareholder value; rather, as companies interact with their environment, it is aimed at meeting demands and requirements of other important stakeholders such as customers, society, NGOs, and suppliers. Creating shared value seems to be the key.

Nespresso's example also shows that driving sustainability in supply chain relationships results in an unexpected source of productivity and human well-being, if and only if sustainability is well-integrated in the business model. However, it is important that the sustainable business model remains adaptable to the ever-changing context in which buyers and suppliers operate. Meanwhile, the example, set by Nespresso, has now been followed by many food producers including Unilever, Danone, Mars, Pepsico, Royal FrieslandCampina, and Nutreco.

11.6 Challenges in Creating Sustainable Supplier Relationships

The examples in this chapter have subscribed the view that driving sustainability through the supply chain is a source of innovation and cost reduction. A growing number of scholars and practitioners state that including sustainability has become a prerequisite for a business model to be competitive these days. Responsible Purchasing (RP) is one of the key elements of a sustainable business model, although it is not always easy to integrate it in an (existing) business model. It requires (long term) commitment not only from the buying company, but also from its (business critical) suppliers. Previous research has shown that four important issues hamper the implementation of RP, i.e., a complex context, the lack of internal commitment, the difficulty in obtaining supplier involvement, and the evaluation of sustainable practices. It is important for purchasing to take these challenges into account from the very first phase of an RP implementation strategy. Here, we discuss each of these issues in more detail.

Complex context: Since companies are increasingly sourcing on a global scale, they are operating in differing national and international institutional contexts; thereby they are coping with a lot of (heterogeneous) suppliers. Major differences exist among suppliers (e.g., firm size and business model orientation) and in the (institutional) environments of suppliers (e.g., in public policy, national labor law, environmental standards, and poverty levels). The sustainability practices of a supply chain can be compliant with the law in one country, yet they may not meet the minimum standard of another country's law. In addition, there is an abundance of local and global sustainability standards and benchmarks for supply chains that are not always compatible. Section 11.3 has listed some well-known general standards. However, this list is far from complete, as also many sector-specific sustainable supply chain standards exist. This abundance makes it easy for companies to get lost in the details of the standards. Thus, which standards and certificates should organizations choose and comply with? In addition, which standards will survive in the future?

Internal commitment: Another challenge is the internal commitment to RP within the buying company. As the shift towards sustainable supply chain management, particularly RP, requires a sustained business model, top management commitment is an issue, especially when the urgency for sustainability has not reached the boardroom yet. Several studies have shown the importance of top management commitment for responsible purchasing and supply practices in the organization (Walker and Brammer 2013). The purchasing function should be able to present the strategic value of RP, clearly showing the social, environmental, and financial benefits of RP. In addition, they have to create commitment from other departments within the organization as well, such as the marketing and R&D function. This requires collaboration and integration among multiple levels of the organization and the supply chain. It also requires a frontrunner mentality within those who lead the purchasing function.

Supplier involvement: In order to benefit from sustainability initiatives in the supply chain, all business critical supply partners should comply with the sustainability policy. However, how do suppliers benefit from complying with the sustainability policy? How should organizations deal with suppliers that do not want or are not able to comply with the sustainability standards and the combined risks for excluding certain qualifying suppliers, for example, smallholders? What are the effects of imposing rules and guidelines on supplier operations and innovativeness? How should organizations deal with the suppliers of the suppliers, what are the boundaries of the corporate responsibility of the buying company? These issues could be addressed by integrating (key) suppliers in the design and development of the sustainability standards within the supply chain by means of stakeholder meetings and co-creation sessions. In this way, a certain platform among the supply chain partners is created, increasing the chances that suppliers transfer these sustainability practices to their own supply chain partners as well.

Monitoring and evaluation: Companies are using several techniques to measure and report the level of progress in sustainability practices of their suppliers. However, monitoring is one thing, acting upon it is another. Based on extensive multinational company research, it turns out that companies measure many (intermediate) results, but they do not always show them against actual targets set in the supply chain (Van Weele and Vivanco 2014). In addition, it is unclear what initiatives, i.e., actions, deliver the best results in terms of corporate advantage and shared value in the supply chain. Sustainability practices should be evaluated just like any other business practice instead of within a separate CSR department with separate KPIs and performance measures. Organizations should try to map the business impact from particular sustainability initiatives and make a selection on the profitable initiatives (profitable in the broadest sense of the word, i.e., people, planet, profit (PPP)). However, many researchers state that the current tools are not able to measure the impact in all three PPP dimensions accurately. Especially, direct and indirect social impact, both on the value chain members and on their communities, is difficult to measure. This requires further development of current M&E sustainability performance tools.

11.7   Conclusions and Suggestions

What should companies do to foster RP and build responsible supply chain relationships? Here, we present some suggestions:

- Conduct a full Value Chain Analysis, revealing your company's carbon footprint (see also Chap. 3 by Boukherroub et al. (2017)) and CSR risk exposure. Every CSR policy starts with a thorough fact-finding. Every value chain is different. When the company conducts such an analysis, it will realize that significant part of its total carbon footprint is related to actual product used by customers and its suppliers. In addition, the value chain analysis should also focus on other elements regarding responsibility such as compliance to social laws and human labor conditions. Hence, new product development for less energy intensive products is needed. This should be followed by a sustainable sourcing policy aimed at reducing the carbon footprint in the upstream supply chain; preferably with suppliers that have a sound and well-implemented CSR policy. Procurement and supply chain management without doubt will appear to be the key drivers of initiatives to drive down the supply chain carbon footprint, water usage, and waste and improve social conditions at supplier worksites.
- Formulate ambitious goals and objectives to drive down upstream supply chain carbon footprint and other CSR impacts. Ambitious goals like reducing both water consumption and energy consumption with 50 % in 5 years time in the upstream supply chain are necessary to create a sense of urgency and drive innovative solutions. More importantly, these goals and objectives need to be followed up both by the supply chain management and the board.
- Partner with suppliers. The formulated goals and objectives cannot be achieved by the company in isolation. They need to seek support from their supply base. Auditing suppliers on implementation of sustainability practices (see Box 11.2 of this chapter) is the first step. Inviting suppliers to come up with ideas and solutions to meet the predetermined sustainability goals and objectives is the second step. When selecting suppliers for future business, having a sustainability policy in place is recommended as a qualifying criterion.
- Supplier development. As meeting these predetermined sustainability goals and objectives is to be seen as the joint responsibility between the buyer and his suppliers, buyers need to be intimately familiar with the best practices within the suppliers' industries. Rather than deal-making, the buyer will spend his time setting up supplier development programs. Part of his/her job will be discussing and suggesting ideas for productivity improvement and shop floor efficiency. This would call for a new generation of buyers, who need to be technically qualified, commercially skilled, and sensitive to dealing with different cultures.
- Value- and revenue-driven, rather than cost-driven. When adopting these practices, purchasing will change in nature from a traditional cost-driven activity, to a value- and revenue-driven activity that is much better aligned with business management. Next to cost savings, the percentage of spend that is sourced sustainably, the number of suppliers that work according to the sustainability

guidelines, and energy consumption, CO_2 emissions, and water consumption KPIs will make up the purchasing managers' performance dashboards. This will enable them to share best practices within and across sectors and to effectively team up with (non)governmental institutions.

It must be noted, however, that companies will take different pace through different levels of maturity on their path to supply chain sustainability. The path will be different depending on whether companies operate upstream or downstream of their value chain. Companies operating downstream in the value chain in general are more visible to the public and the press and will therefore be pressed to adopt sustainability practices in general, and more particularly, in their supply chain relationships. This will be less true for companies operating more upstream in their value chains. Nevertheless, business experiences show that adopting CSR practices in many cases is sound business, leads to more controlled supply chain relationships and better collaboration, and therefore often results in a better long-term profitability. It should therefore be a prime concern to all purchasing and supply chain managers.

References

Alvarez G (2008) Sustainable agriculture and value networks: an opportunity for small growers to export successfully? International Trade Center. Retrieved from www.intracen.org/WorkArea/DownloadAsset.aspx?id=51770

Bateman AH, Blanco EE, Sheffi Y (2017) Disclosing and reporting environmental sustainability of supply chains. In: Bouchery Y, Corbett CJ, Fransoo J, Tan T (eds) Sustainable supply chains: a research-based textbook on operations and strategy. Springer, New York

Boukherroub T, Bouchery Y, Corbett CJ, Fransoo J, Tan T (2017) Carbon footprinting in supply chains. In: Bouchery Y, Corbett CJ, Fransoo J, Tan T (eds) Sustainable supply chains: a research-based textbook on operations and strategy. Springer, New York

Brundtland (1987) Our common future, Report of the World Commission on Environment and Development, United Nations. Oxford University Press, Oxford

Carroll AB (1991) The pyramid of corporate social responsibility: toward the moral management of organizational stakeholders. Bus Horiz 34(4):39–48

Christensen CM, Bower JL (1996) Customer power, strategic investment, and the failure of leading firms. Strategic Management Journal 17(3):197–218

Donaldson T, Preston LE (1995) The stakeholder theory of the corporation: concepts, evidence, and implications. Acad Manage Rev 20(1):65–91

Freeman RE (1984) Strategic management: a stakeholder approach. Englewood Cliffs, Prentice Hall

Freeman RE, Harrison JS, Wicks AC (2007) Managing for stakeholders: survival, reputation, and success. Yale University Press, New Haven

Handfield RB (1993) A resource dependence perspective of just-in-time purchasing. J Oper Manage 11(3):289–311

Harrison JS, Bosse D, Phillips R (2010) Managing for stakeholders, stakeholder utility functions, and competitive advantage. Strategic Management Journal 31(1):58–74

Kibbeling MI (2010) Creating value in supply chains: suppliers' impact on value for customers, society and shsreholders, Ph.D. dissertation. BETA Research School for Operations Management and Logistics, Eindhoven University of Technology, Eindhoven, p 187

Lee HL, Rammohan SV (2017) Improving social and environmental performance in global supply chains. In: Bouchery Y, Corbett CJ, Fransoo J, Tan T (eds) Sustainable supply chains: a research-based textbook on operations and strategy. Springer, New York

Matthyssens P, Faes W (2013) Green offerings and buyer-supplier collaboration in value chains. In: Lindgreen A, Maon F, Vanhamme J, Sen S (eds) Sustainable value chain management: a research anthology. Gower, Aldershot

Nidumolu R, Prahalad CK, Rangaswami MR (2009) Why sustainability is now a key driver of innovation. Harv Bus Rev 87(9):57–64

Pfeffer J, Salancik GJ (1978) The external control of organizations: a resource dependence perspective. Harper & Row, New York

Porter ME, Kramer MT (2011) Creating shared value: hot to reinvent capitalism and unleash a wave of innovation and growth. Harv Bus Rev 62–77, January/February

Rumelt RP (1984) Towards a strategic theory of the firm. In: Lamb R (ed) Competitive strategic management. Prentice-Hall, Englewood Cliffs, pp 556–570

Sirmon DG, Hitt MA, Ireland RD (2007) Managing firm resources in dynamic environments to create value: looking inside the black box. Acad Manage Rev 32(1):273–292

Sirmon DG, Gove S, Hitt MA (2008) Resource management in dyadic competitive rivalry: the effects of resource bundling and deployment. Acad Manage J 51(5):919–935

Sodhi MMS, Tang CS (2017) Social responsibility in supply chains. In: Bouchery Y, Corbett CJ, Fransoo J, Tan T (eds) Sustainable supply chains: a research-based textbook on operations and strategy. Springer, New York

Tang CS, Zimmerman JD, Nelson JI (2009) Managing new product development and supply chain risks: The Boeing 787 case. Supply Chain Forum 10(2):74–86

Ulrich D, Barney JB (1984) Perspectives in organizations: resource dependence, efficiency, and population. Acad Manage Rev 9(3):471–481

Van Tulder R, Van der Zwart A (2006) International business-society management: linking corporate responsibility and globalisation. Routledge, London

Van Weele AJ (2014) Purchasing and supply chain management, 6th edn. Cengage, London, p 438

Van Weele AJ, Van Tubergen KPJ (2013) Nespresso: creating shared value in the global coffee. Value chain, unpublished case study. Eindhoven University of Technology, Eindhoven, p 18

Van Weele, A.J., Vivanco, L. (2014). Corporate social responsibility : moving from compliance to value creation in value chain relationships, Chapter 7, pp. 123-137 published in Cordon, C. and Ferreiro, T. (2014). The value chain shift : seven future challenges facing top executives. Lausanne: IMD Global Value Chain Center, p. 137.

Walker H, Brammer S (2013) Sustainable procurement, institutional context and top management commitment: an international public sector study. In: Lindgreen A, Maon F, Vanhamme J, Sen S (eds) Sustainable value chain management: a research anthology. Gower, Aldershot, pp 19–38

Wernerfelt B (1984) A resource-based view of the firm. Strat Manage J 5(2):171–180

Zadek S (2004) The path to corporate responsibility. Harv Bus Rev. December, 1–8

Chapter 12
Green Technology Choice

Anton Ovchinnikov

12.1   Introduction

In late 2000s, Wells Fargo, a large US bank, asked themselves a profoundly important, yet very simple, question: "If our clients find it profitable to borrow money from us to install solar panels on their roofs, shouldn't we find it profitable too?"

The reason this question is important is because Wells Fargo has over 6000 branches (called "stores" within the bank), which are primarily concentrated along the US "sunbelt." Covering even a small portion of these branches roofs with solar panels would make the bank a large renewable energy producer. The reason this question is simple is because the answer seems to be obvious. And yet, as this chapter describes, the decision to install the photovoltaic, PV, system (solar panels)—the "green technology" in this case—was far from straightforward, with many caveats and sub-questions, which open a variety of opportunities for research in sustainable operations.

The author was fortunate to advise a bank executive who was responsible for this project; see the two-case series by Ovchinnikov and Hvaleva (2012). The chapter therefore starts by using this example to highlight some of the key questions faced when working on this decision; other examples will be drawn upon as well, as the chapter progresses. The chapter is structured around eight key questions related to green technology choices:

1. What exactly does the "green technology choice" imply?
2. What are the different components of costs and revenues (cost savings) that factor into a green technology choice decision?

A. Ovchinnikov (✉)
Smith School of Business, Queens University, Kingston, ON, Canada
e-mail: anton.ovchinnikov@queensu.ca

© Yann Bouchery, Charles J. Corbett, Jan C. Fransoo, and Tarkan Tan 2017
Y. Bouchery et al. (eds.), *Sustainable Supply Chains*, Springer Series in Supply Chain Management 4, DOI 10.1007/978-3-319-29791-0_12

3. What are the impacts of (government) incentives on green technology choice decisions?
4. How does performance uncertainty impact the decision to invest in renewable energy technologies?
5. What is the impact of pricing models on "green" technology choice?
6. Do consumers reward firms that chose "green" technologies?
7. How to motivate and ensure adoption of "green" technologies across supply chains?
8. How governmental regulations may lead to the leakage of unsustainable practices to areas with low enforcement?

In this chapter, we will review the existing operations management literature on each of these questions, describe the main findings, and comment on the open questions. We start by providing a high-level taxonomy of what exactly the "green technology choice" implies?

12.2 A Taxonomy of Green Technology Choices Along a Firm's Supply Chain

Quite generally, sustainable operations consider some "base-line" production system that converts various inputs (materials, energy, labor, time) into outputs. As a byproduct, this system also generates pollutants. A by-far most typical assumption in the economics literature as well as in operations is that pollution is linear in output. In other words, x units of output generate some $x \times w$ units of pollutants.

A green technology i could then be viewed as a set of activities and processes that remove $r_i\%$ of pollutants, so that the resultant emissions become $x \times w \times (1 - r_i)$.

As became common in the literature and practice, this chapter will differentiate these activities by the place in a supply chain where they are undertaken. Scope 1 activities (technologies, emissions, etc.) correspond to those made within the immediate boundary of a focal firm. Scope 2 activities correspond to the union of the firm and its energy sources. Scope 3 includes the upstream supply chain partners of the firm, as well as downstream emissions; we only focus primarily on the upstream part here. See the schematic presented in Fig. 12.1 (and see Chap. 3 by Boukherroub et al. (2017) for more detail):

The majority of research in sustainable operations considered energy-related technologies, and therefore, correspond to Scope 2; the Wells Fargo example is in the same category as well. The number of studies that considered Scope 1 and 3 activities is approximately the same. The chapter will therefore include substantial discussion of energy-related research, but will also consider the decisions within the focal firm and its suppliers. Naturally, those decisions are largely identical as which firm along the supply chain is "focal" depends on the viewpoint.

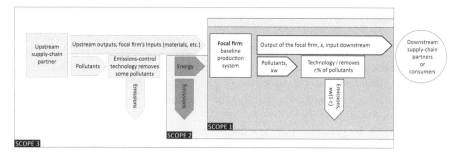

Fig. 12.1 Scope 1, Scope 2, and Scope 3 in supply chains

In that regard, within Scope 1, there are three somewhat different approaches to framing the technology choice problem. First, as is done in Krass et al. (2013), one can consider a problem of changing one technology ("dirty") with another ("clean"), so that after the change all production occurs with the new/clean technology. In the case-study "c-Energy's Red Hill plant: Meeting the SO_2 challenge," Ovchinnikov (2008) illustrates this framing on the example of deciding to install a scrubber at a power plant. In this case, the management of an old power plant faces a decision to operate "as-is," which will require purchasing emissions allowances or invest in either a wet scrubber (with medium efficiency, low fixed cost, but high variable cost) or a dry scrubber (with high efficiency, high fixed and low variable costs). The case provides data to evaluate the economics and risks of each option and the question is that of the choice: the plant management needs to decide which option to adopt. The numbers work out such that the wet scrubber has marginally lower cost, but the dry scrubber removes much more pollutants; hence most decision makers lean toward suggesting that the company should adopt a somewhat costlier but environmentally much better dry scrubber.

A second approach is to consider "how much" of clean technology to invest in. Implicitly, this is the problem Wells Fargo faced (although they always considered the maximum size permitted on a roof). Hu, Souza, Ferguson and Wang (2014), and Kok et al. (2014) consider this question explicitly: the amount of renewable capacity is a decision variable in their papers.

Finally, a third approach is to suppose that a firm already has two types of technologies at its disposal, for example, plants with and without scrubbers, and is deciding on the allocation of production between the different kinds of plants, which have different economic and operational characteristics. This approach has been implemented both in the economics literature, e.g., see Carraro and A. Soubeyran (1996), and in operations, e.g., Drake, Kleindorfer, and Van Wassenhove (2010).

Before proceeding with the insights of these papers, we need to discuss the profit functions.

12.3   Cost Components of Green Technology Choice

As the "economics 101" wisdom states: profit = revenues — costs. In regards to the green technology choice decisions, the revenue component is sometimes disregarded. This can be done with little loss of generality whenever the firm is a price taker, or consumers are not responding to the "greenness" of the firm's technology (see more on this in Sect. 7).

In the Wells Fargo case, although there clearly was a public relations benefit from solar panels, which might have translated into revenue, it was decided to focus solely on cost savings. Hence, the problem became one of cost minimization. In some other cases, for example, in the settings of Krass et al. (2013) or Raz and Ovchinnikov (2015), the firms are price setters, hence they consider the revenue given by the number of units sold × price. An important modeling difference between these two papers (and how they account for revenues) is whether the supply equals demand.

In deterministic demand scenarios, as in Krass et al., demand = sales = quantity produced in equilibrium. This implies that there is a one-to-one relationship between the price, p, and the production quantity, $q \equiv D(p)$, for some demand function, D, and hence one only needs to consider a single decision that characterizes revenue. Then Revenue = $p \times D(p)$. In stochastic demand scenarios, demand < > sales < > quantity produced. This implies that one needs to separately consider price and production quantity, q, decisions. Then Revenue = $p \times \min [q, D(p)]$. An intermediate case is when the price of the product is selected after the uncertain demand is realized. This results in an outcome that supply = demand whenever profitable.

A final consideration for the revenue component is it's stability over time. Intermittency that is inherent, for example, in the renewable energy technologies will be considered separately (see Section 5). But even without intermittency, the performance of some kinds of green technologies tends to degrade over time. As reported in Ovchinnikov and Hvaleva (2013), PV systems' energy output degrades at a rate of 0.5 % per year. Since many technologies could have long lifetimes (25 years for a PV system), this gradual degradation could play an important role.

On the costs side, one generally considers fixed and variable costs. Fixed costs correspond to the cost of procurement and installation of the equipment, retrofitting the machinery, etc. In the Wells Fargo example, the fixed cost is straightforward: it's a one-time outlay of cash to install the system. The caveat with solar is that the cost of solar panels is steadily declining, hence the installation decision has the time dimension: this is the topic of my (B) case on Wells Fargo. In the c-Energy example, the fixed costs also corresponded to installation of the equipment.

For the variable costs, in most cases there is a cost to operate the "green" equipment. In the c-Energy's case with the dry scrubber, there was a small energy that was diverted from the boiler to run the scrubber, and with the wet scrubber, there also was a cost of the reagent and its transportation. Even in the Wells Fargo example, where it is generally believed that renewable energy technologies have a zero variable cost, in reality there was a cost for insuring the additional property and to replace the AC/DC inverters every 10 years.

Two more points are worth mentioning in the elements of the profit function. First is the time dimension. The demand and variable cost numbers are often per year, while fixed costs are one-time. Hence, either a proper net present value analysis must be considered, or annualized costs must be used. Second, the "do-nothing" option, i.e., the option of not investing in green technology, should be carefully analyzed. Specifically, while one might assume that that option involves zero cost, in many cases that is not so: in the c-Energy example, for instance, doing nothing involved purchasing emission allowances, which had an net present value (NPV) of negative USD60 million. As straightforward as these two points are, I saw many students who were making mistakes with these issues.

Hu et al. (2015) present a comprehensive analysis that combines the revenues and costs of investing in a renewable ("green") energy source, as well as accounts for their variability and correlation over time. Their main finding is about the granularity of the analysis. Indeed, if the lifespan of a PV system is 25 years (their paper uses my Wells Fargo case as an example), what time intervals are needed to analyze the problem? The initial analysis of Ovchinnikov and Hvaleva assumed a yearly time increments and average system efficiency of 18 % (meaning that on average over a year the system produces 18 % of its nominal generation capacity, this includes the number of hours of sunlight, location of the sun over the horizon, etc.). With this efficiency and the size of Wells Fargo roof that allowed for a 15 kW system, it will not provide enough power for the branch, hence additional power would have to be purchased from the grid. Hu and coauthors obtained detailed generation and demand data from Wells Fargo and showed that nearly 9 % of the time the PV system generated more power than was consumed by the branch. Figure 12.2 presents a typical summer week's generation (dashed line) and consumption (solid line) and such cases are clearly visible.

These 9 % are very important, because the excess power is sold through net metering, at a rate that is nearly 3 times higher than the cost of buying the power

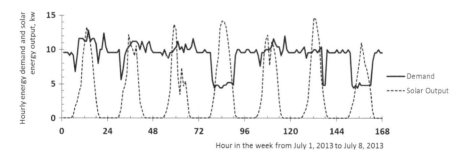

Fig. 12.2 Hourly electricity demand and solar system output at a Wells Fargo branch from July 1, 2013 until July 8, 2013 based on the data from Hu et al. (2015)

from the grid. The yearly granularity masks this effect and, as Hu and coauthors show, results in a major impact on the cost assessment and the optimal size of installed system. Based on their data Figure 12.3 suggests that 15-min or 1-h increments are virtually indistinguishable, but even a 24 h increment already results in nearly 15 % error in assessing the profitability of the system and in over 200 % error in the optimal system size. In other words, granularity really matters: the renewable energy project could be more profitable than the simplified analysis suggest, and smaller installations may be required: both of these findings are critical in promoting green technology choice.

An additional, technical contribution of Hu et al.'s paper is in demonstrating how to implement granular analysis in practice. Indeed, a 25-year cash flow statement implemented, for example, in Excel with 15 min granularity will have $25 \times 365 \times 24 \times 4 = 876{,}000$ columns — an undoable task for most managers and their computers. The authors present a simpler approach stemming from the observation that since all that matters is the NPV of the system, many entries in this massive calculation could have identical NPVs and hence can be collapsed into a single number (e.g., with a discount rate of 10 %, a payment of 1000 in year 0 and a payment of 1100 in year 1 will both have NPV of 1000). This greatly simplifies calculations.

Kleindorfer et al. (2012) present another detailed examination of the costs and benefits of investing in a green technology, now based on the example of fleet renewal at La Poste (French postal service). La Poste currently operates a fleet of over 40,000 diesel (internal combustion engine ICE) delivery vehicles and is evaluating an option of replacing some of them with electric vehicles (EV). ICEs have low(er) fixed costs, but high operating costs, which is also uncertain due to fuel price fluctuations. EVs have a high(er) fixed costs, but lower variable costs: no fuel and 30 % less maintenance. EVs also result in a much lower carbon emissions because nearly 80 % of electricity in France is generated with Nuclear power plants. Referring to the above discussion about the importance of fixed costs, the

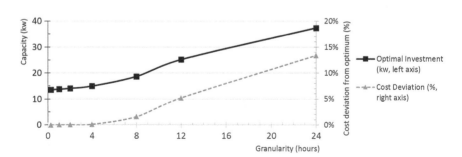

Fig. 12.3 Impact of the granularity on cost and capacity assessments, based on the data from Hu et al. (2015)

authors explicitly account for them and further consider that the EV fixed costs are expected to decline. This creates a strategic delay in adopting the green technology; the next Section will discuss this in further detail. Overall, for each technology they consider the total cost of ownership—the NPV analysis conceptually identical to the Wells Fargo approach. The authors report a pilot test resulting from their model and the plan to significantly expand the EV fleet as a result of that pilot test and their work.

The final element of the profit function: one that was crucial in the Wells Fargo case: government incentives. The reason governments around the world provide incentives for the adoption of green technologies is because of the effect of externality—a situation where the production and consumption of the good impose indirect involuntary benefits or costs on other economic agents who are outside the market place for that good. Generating electricity with a PV system installed on the roof of a building affects the building's owner who pay less for electricity as well as other people, who have nothing to do with the building, by reducing emissions as compared to the fossil fuel sources. Similarly, driving an EV versus an ICE vehicle lowers emissions which benefit the drivers of EVs, the drivers of ICUs, and even those who do not drive at all. Incentives are therefore provided so that the owner of the building would properly factor (the economics term, "internalize") this indirect, "external," benefit to others. See the Introduction to Raz and Ovchinnikov (2015) for a more detailed discussion of this issue.

Overall, while one might think that accounting for the benefits and costs of investing in green technology is rather straightforward, the above studies show that there are numerous detail that must be carefully incorporated. These studies provide excellent examples and a solid starting point for the researchers and practitioners.

With this progress, however, I would identify two open research possibilities. First is the impact of the ownership structures on the technology choice. For example, Wells Fargo's initial approach only considered the 12-year time horizon (as opposed to the PV system 25-year useful life) because an average lease of their building is 12 years. Since a PV system is not easily detachable from the property on which it is installed, the lack of clear agreements between the property owners (who benefit from the residual value of the technology) and the tenants (who benefit from operational savings but incur the initial cost) could be a deterring factor in adoption. A similar deterrent plays a role with many other green technologies that have long lifetimes and relatively long payback periods. A manufacturing firm will not invest in energy-efficient technology if it expects to relocate its production to a lower-cost country in future. Another example of the ownership structure challenges is present in a global shipping industry, where the ship owner selects the energy-efficient technology and bears the capital costs of installing it, but the current contractual agreements are such that the charterer of the ship is incurring the fuel costs which are passed on to the shippers. Hence, despite the existence of multiple green technologies, e.g., see www.theicct.org/reducing-ghg-emissions-ships, with positive NPVs their adoption is lagging. Aligning the incentives of the property owners and users is therefore an interesting avenue for the green technology choice research and practice.

The second opportunity is in expanding the scope of the operational impact of the green technology. In the La Poste example, for instance, the authors note that, with ICEs, the delivery routes and drivers' behavior were optimized so as to minimize fuel consumption. But with EVs, this objective is no longer valid, and rather the objective should be to maximize the average daily kilometers driven per vehicle (so as to leave fewer kilometers to be driven in a fuel-consuming ICEs). The delivery routes re-optimization presents a downstream operational change following the adoption of green technologies. Expanding on this opportunity—what are the other operational decisions (routing, lot sizing, scheduling, etc.) that are affected by the change in the fixed versus variable costs structure following the adoption? And consequently, how should these changes be incorporated upstream to the profitability (total cost) analysis of green technologies? These questions also offer interesting research opportunities.

12.4 Impact of Government Incentives in Green Technology Choice Decisions?

Government incentives generally come in three different forms. First are the incentives provided to consumers who buy the firm's product, for example, the USD7500 tax credit provided to buyers of electric vehicles (EV) in the US; I prefer to call them "rebates"; see Krass et al. (2013), Raz et al. (2014), and their case study of Chevy Volt, a popular EV in North America. In some other papers, these are referred to as subsidies with the implications that those are "consumer subsidies," e.g., see Lobel and Perakis (2011) and Cohen, Lobel, and Perakis (2014).

A form of rebate considered in Alizamir et al. (2014) and implicitly in Hu et al. (2014) is a feed-in-tariff (FIT). FIT is linked to the concept of net metering and refers to a price that is paid by the electric utility to the owner of the renewable energy system should the supply of power generated by the system exceed what had been used by the building. It is as is the energy meter will roll backwards, and the consumer will receive the money for selling power rather than pay for using it.

The second form are the incentives provided to firms who use the green technologies to manufacture their products. These forms of incentives are common in the healthcare industry and somewhat less common in sustainability arena. I prefer to call such incentives "variable cost subsidies." A negative subsidy can be viewed as a tax; note that a rescaling may be required if tax is levied on units of emissions rather than production.

The third form are the incentives provided for the fact of adopting the green technology. As an example, consider the 38 % profit tax credit that Wells Fargo obtained on its investment right in the year when the cost was incurred. I prefer to call them "fixed cost subsidies."

Table 12.1 The four different forms of government incentives

	Firm's price	Consumer price	Firm's cost (variable, fixed)	Units action applies to	Government cost/revenue
Rebate, r	p	$p-r$	c,Θ	$\text{Min}[x, D(p-r)]$	$r\text{Min}[x, D(p)]$
Variable cost subsidy, s	p	P	$c-s,\Theta$	x	$s \times x$
Tax, t	p	P	$c+w(1-r)t,\Theta$	x	$w(1-r)t \times x$
Fixed cost subsidy, FC	p	P	$c,\Theta-FC$	0/1 if the corresponding technology is chosen	FC

These different forms of incentives are summarized in Table 12.1. With these rebate and subsidy incentive tools, researchers considered different mechanisms for incentivizing the adoption of green technologies.

Raz and Ovchinnikov (2015) considered a price-setting newsvendor firm that decides on price and production quantity of a "green product" in response to the policy set by the government regulator. The regulator, in turn, anticipates this response and set the policy so as to maximize societal welfare, accounting for the firm's profit, consumer surplus, externality, and the government cost. Their key analytical finding is that, with a combination of rebate and subsidy, it is possible to achieve the socially optimal (first-best) welfare, but the optimal subsidy is often negative, i.e., is actually a tax. That is, to incentivize the firm, produce the right amount of the green product and price it correctly; the government provides very large rebates to consumers, which generates a windfall of profit to the firm that is then taxed to recover the cost of providing rebates. The intuition for why this approach is optimal is in its impact on the service level: high rebate implies high selling margin, which in turn implies a higher critical fractile. Consumers therefore face less stock-out risk while the government saves because rebates only apply to units sold (as opposed to subsidy that applies to units made, including those not sold).

Raz et al. (2014) further consider an extended example of Chevy Volt (discussed in even further detail in their case study) and show that the current rebate-only incentive of $7500, although structurally suboptimal, has a very small welfare loss. Overall, their work provides a direct support for the use of tax as an incentive mechanism, but does not explicitly deal with the technology choice problem.

Krass et al. (2013) consider the impact of tax specifically in the technology choice problem. In their paper, the firm is considering whether to invest in one of k "green" technologies, where, as discussed above, technologies differ in fixed and variable costs as well as in their environmental efficiency. The regulator taxes the firm for pollution, and investing in an efficient technology is a way to reduce tax obligations. Their main result is that the environmental tax has a non-monotone impact on the green technology adoption: while as expected, small taxes motivate the firm adopt a green technology, large taxes do not. This is driven by the fixed cost effect: subject to a large tax the firm has to raise prices, which reduces the sales quantity, and so the total additional revenue with green technology may not be sufficient to offset its higher installation cost.

They further consider the regulator's problem, and specifically, the efficiency of using tax and the need to support it with fixed cost subsidies and rebates. They find that tax is efficient for medium level of externality parameter (referred to as "environmental concerns" in their paper), but for both small and large externality pollutants a combined approach with taxes, rebates, and fixed costs subsidies is needed. The only case when the combined approach cannot reach the first-best welfare is when the externality is very small and the socially optimal technology choice is actually "dirty," while the firm selects "clean."

In the abovementioned papers, the regulation is modeled through the goal of maximizing the social welfare. A different approach with the goal of achieving an exogenously given adoption target is studied in Lobel and Perakis (2011), Cohen, Lobel, and Perakis (2014), and in Chemama et al. (2014), Cohen, Lobel, and Perakis (2014). These papers consider what I call rebates, although refer to them as "subsidies." Alizamir et al. (2014) consider both an exogenously given target and a welfare maximization problem and use the feed-in-tariff, which is a form of rebate as well, as discussed above.

Lobel and Perakis study a problem of designing the dynamic path for the value of rebate for PV systems in order to achieve (in expectation) the target number of installation by the end of the incentive period. This framing of the problem is motivated by the government programs in Europe, see Jager-Waldau (2012). A consumer's decision to install a system is modeled with a random utility logit model. They fit their model to the date from Germany and show that rather than being constant, the rebate should initially be high, but then gradually decrease as more people adopted the green technology and those who have not yet adopted it are due to self-selection less sensitive to rebates.

This finding echoes what happened in the (B) part of my Wells Fargo case, where the utility company in Los Angeles (LADWP) decided to abandon the flat rebate and introduced a tiered structure, where the more solar capacity has been installed, the smaller the rebate would be. Exhibit 1 in the case reflects the status as of 2013, and the current rebate levels can be found on the LADWP Solar Incentive Program website. For Wells Fargo and others who were deciding whether to install solar system or not, this meant that the decision gained the strategic timing dimension: should they install now, when the rebates are high but the chance of getting them is uncertain, or wait, then the chances will be higher, but the rebates will be lower, yet the cost will be lower to. In Wells Fargo's case, it was more profitable to wait for a year, which is what they actually did. The question of such a strategic behavior impacting green technology adoption is a subject of Chemama et al. (2014). They show that the flat rebate policy is often less expensive on average, but the flexible rebate policy results in a lower variance of the rebate program cost for the government.

Alizamir et al. (2014) explicitly study the question of whether there exists a rebate (feed-in-tariff) schedule that would result in no strategic delay. They show that for some parameter ranges this is indeed the case, and most such cases involve a variable rebate. When the parameters, however, fall outside of this automatic "no delay" region, then should the government decide to design a rebate policy that would result in no delays, then such a policy would have a constant rebate.

Finally, Cohen et al. (2014) study the impact of demand uncertainty on the green technology adoption in more detail. Specifically, they show that ignoring the uncertainty in demand (and optimizing rebates as if demand was deterministic) could lead to significantly missing the adoption target. Additionally, they investigate whether consumer surplus could increase as a result of demand uncertainty—an observation also made by Raz and Ovchinnikov. They show that the situation is somewhat nuanced as there exists a tradeoff between lower prices and possibility to underserve consumers with high valuations (who will receive the highest surplus loss if the product is stocked out).

A third approach to modeling the impact of regulation on the technology choice decision is through capacity allocation among a portfolio of technologies, e.g., see Drake et al. (2014). Wang et al. (2014) and Hu et al. (2014) also implicitly consider portfolios of two technologies, but not from the perspective of incentives and regulation.

Drake et al. compare the impacts of tax (fixed emissions cost) versus cap-and-trade (variable emissions cost) and show that emissions price uncertainty under cap-and-trade results in greater expected profit than a constant emissions price under an emissions tax, which contradicts common logic. They attribute that to two operational drivers: the firm's option not to operate, which effectively right-censors the uncertain emissions price; and dispatch flexibility, which effectively allows the firm to arbitrage on the variability of the emissions cost under the cap-and-trade. They also explore policy implications: they show that variable cost subsidies have little impact on the total capacity, but fixed cost subsidies increase capacity. This happens because the firm benefits from a variable cost subsidy only when the corresponding capacity is utilized (as opposed to the fixed cost subsidy that acts even when the capacity is temporarily not utilized, e.g., if the carbon price is too low).

Islegen and Reichelstein (2011) consider the impact of the cost of emissions on the adoption of a specific green technology—carbon capture and storage (CCS) at fossil-fuel power plants. Krass et al. (2013) also use CCS in cement industry as one of their motivating examples. A distinctive feature of Islegen and Reichelstein's work is that they present a result calibrated on the empirical data (as opposed to stylized models considered by other authors). They account for numerous real-life complications and operational details, and by doing so provide practically relevant estimates. They find that in a typical US scenario, the cost of carbon must be approximately USD$31 for CCS to be a break-even choice for a newly built coal power plant and USD$60 for a natural gas-powered power plant. Their calculations provide insights into how big the effective carbon tax (emissions price if a cap-and-trade is used) should be for CCS to become viable in a practical (operational) power generation setting.

Overall, there has been a significant amount of work done to understand how operational characteristics of green technology choice impact the design of government incentive for their adoption, and a short conclusion is that those characteristics matter a lot.

A curious observation is that all abovementioned papers consider monopolistic firms. Hence, an immediate and very important research opportunity is to understand the impact of competition between firms onto the efficiency of incentives, and the reverse impact of incentives on the competition. To the best of my knowledge, the teams of Cohen&Perakis and Krass&Ovchinnikov are currently working on such competitive analysis, but there likely is more to be done than their papers will accomplish. A related observation is that from sustainability perspective competition happens both in the output markets (e.g., between GM and Nissan, who both sell EVs) and in the inputs markets (e.g., between GM and Samsung, who both buy rare-earth metals for their batteries). Perhaps, incentivizing the adoption of green technologies could be even more efficient if instead of promoting outputs (EVs) the government programs will target inputs, relying on the market forces to do the rest.

12.5   Impact of Performance Uncertainty on "Green" Technology Investment Decisions

An inherent feature of many green technologies is that their performance varies due to a variety of external factors. For example, in regards to renewable energy, wind does not always blow (and when it does the speed varies), sun does not always shine (and when it shines there can be more or less of it depending on the clouds), etc. Even well-established technologies could have varying performance; in the example of cEnergy, the efficiency of "wet" SO_2 scrubbing at power plants depends significantly on the coal being burned. Some of these variations are predictable and can be planned for (e.g., sun does not shine at night), but in many cases the performance of the green technology is truly uncertain in a sense of a random event. This uncertainty is referred to as "intermittency."

Because operations management traditionally enriched economic models with the ways to counter uncertainty, it is natural that several authors considered the impact of intermittency and related challenges and opportunities on the green technology choice. For obvious reasons, much of this research is focused on renewable energy technologies, and I will therefore focus on this application as well.

Intermittency has a dramatically different impact on operations depending on whether the party performing the analysis is a buyer of energy or a seller.

For a buyer of power (such as Wells Fargo), the problem effectively is about correctly taking the expectation over the nonlinearity introduced by the cases when supply is less than demand and power must be purchased from the grid, and the opposite cases when power is sold back to the grid. As discussed earlier, because of net-metering the feed-in-tariffs for the latter are usually significantly higher than the costs of the former, hence this nonlinearity matters. See the paper by Hu et al. (2014) for the treatment of this problem. Technically, the intermittency in their paper is modeled as a discrete random variable with 20 mass points on a [0,1] support.

For the seller of power (such as the utility from which Wells Fargo purchases energy when its PV system does not generate enough for what is demanded), the problem is considerably more difficult. This is because of two factors. Consider a power utility that operates a portfolio of technologies: intermittent renewable capacity, inflexible base-load generation (e.g., coal, nuclear, or hydro power plants), and flexible reactive capacity (such as natural gas turbines). The current dispatch rules favor utilizing the capacity with the lowest marginal cost first, and only after their supply is exceeded, then dispatching the second-highest costs, etc. This suggests that renewal capacity, which has zero marginal cost, is dispatched first; this requirement is also imposed politically in some countries, e.g., in Germany.

The challenge comes from overlaying this dispatch priority with an extremely high service level guarantee that is either implicit, or in many cases, also legislatively mandated, in many jurisdictions: 99.9% or more. Basically, the supply of power must be available whenever a user turns on a switch (or an automated system, such as air conditioning units power up). This means that whenever the intermittent supply drops, e.g., because the wind slows or a cloud covers the sun, some other source of power must become immediately available. This in turn implies that along-side the investments in renewable but intermittent capacity, the sellers of power must also invest in non-renewable, power-on-demand capacity to offset for possible intermissions.

The paper by Aflaki and Netessine (2011) considers strategic investments in renewable energy in the light of intermittency and service guarantee. In their model, intermittency is represented as a two-point distribution (i.e., the energy from the renewable source is either available with full capacity, or completely unavailable) and the service guarantee is assumed at 100% (that is, an equal amount of renewable and non-renewable capacity must be installed to offset intermittence). Their main question is about the impact of carbon pricing (tax, specifically, see previous Section) on the intermittent renewable energy investments.

Their main result is that the impact consists of two counter-acting forces. The first force is the decreased carbon tax obligations from a cleaner renewable technology, and this positively affects installed renewable capacity. But the second force is that the more clean renewable capacity is installed, the more "dirty" backup capacity is needed. Hence, if the tax is low, or the clean technology is rarely not producing, the former effect dominates which motivates higher capacity investments, but if the tax is high or the technology is often down, the latter effect dominates. This finding is qualitatively similar to the non-monotone response to the environmental tax in Krass et al. (2013), but is driven by the increased tax burden of intermittency as opposed to the tradeoff between shrinking demand and fixed costs.

Intermittency is also modeled as a two-point distribution in Kok et al. (2014), but the main focus of their paper is different, and I will discuss it further in this chapter. Such a simplified approach, however, downplays the importance of curtailing—a practice that gains popularity in the industry. Curtailing refers to purposely reducing the output of the intermittent power source; in practice, this can be done, for example, by tilting the blades of a wind turbine to capture more or less wind.

Wu and Kapuschinski (2013) highlight a fundamental importance of curtailing. Contrary to a naïve belief, they show that the operating cost reduction from curtailing can be significant and may exceed the marginal production cost of conventional sources. They further show that minimizing the system operating cost with the curtailment option often reduces emissions. Thus, curtailment can be both economically and environmentally beneficial. This happens because curtailing allows operating the conventional inflexible sources in a more operationally efficient mode.

Another natural solution to the intermittent supply from clean energy sources is storage, and consequently industry players considered the problem of adding storage to the renewable energy generation facilities. General Electric (GE), for example, developed a suite of hardware and software solutions for integrated management of wind turbines, batteries, and consumer applications, see the Fig.12.4 for how such systems work.

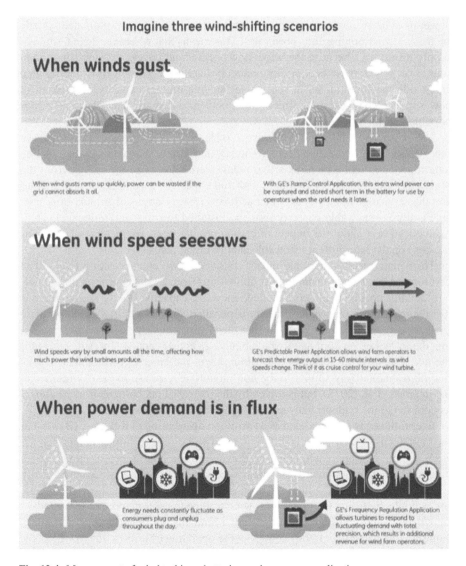

Fig. 12.4 Management of wind turbines, batteries, and consumer applications

Zhou et al. (2014a) consider the problem of operating a wind power generating facility with storage. They also consider transmission constraint, which, in fact, is an additional reason for why such technical curtailing is practiced (in contrast with economic curtailing analyzed by Wu and Kapuschinski 2013). Zhou et al. find that adding storage can substantially increase the value of wind power generation, typically by 30 % or more.

They also point to another source of value from a storage capacity. Since the base-load supply of power (from nuclear, coal, or hydro plants) is very inflexible, when such supply exceeds demand, electricity markets occasionally observe negative prices; this happens up to 5 % of the time (see Fig. 12.5).

In this context, energy storage also provides arbitrage opportunities: buy power when the price is negative and store it until the price becomes positive again. Combining curtailing (i.e., the ability to not produce power when the price is negative) with storage provides an additional 5 % profit gain from the system. In isolation, however, storage operations reduce the benefit from economic curtailment, but increase the overall cost savings (this is also shown by Wu and Kapuschinski 2013).

Zhou et al. (2014b) further analyze storage operation in the presence of (occasionally) negative prices in light of yet another technological possibility: disposal of power. The disposal systems, also known as load banks (see Fig. 12.6), operate at

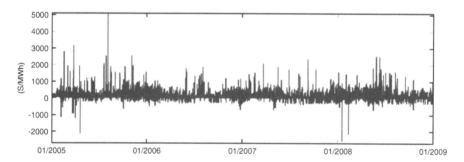

Fig. 12.5 Variations in electricity price, from Zhou et al. (2014a)

Fig. 12.6 Electricity disposal system (*Source*: http://www.emersonnetworkpower.com/en-US/Products/Load-Banks/Permanent-Load-Banks/Pages/default.aspx)

the actual output voltage and are effectively gigantic low-efficiency heaters designed to consume power without heating much.

Zhou et al. (2014b) find that in the presence of negative prices, the optimal storage policy could be significantly different than when prices are always nonnegative; for example, they show that it can be optimal to empty an almost empty storage facility and fill up an almost full one. They also show that the value of disposal is positive, but lower than the value of storage. Their analysis, however, does not directly account for the fixed cost of installing disposal or storage capacity.

Summarizing the research in this category, I would like to make two observations. First, nearly all aforementioned papers are solidly grounded in industry practice and data. The presented analytical models are calibrated with the real operation in mind and the conclusions are drawn in "hard dollars." This is certainly positive. Second, however, these papers focus nearly exclusively on a narrow operational problem of energy producer,without taking the broader demand response into account. Arguably, the existence of negative prices in the grid is an artifact of the current (suboptimal and simplified) demand management practices. This naturally motivates the next Section of this chapter and the respective research opportunity.

12.6   Demand Management and Green Technology Choice

Many view operations management as a science, art, and practice of matching supply with demand. From this perspective, the classical "supply chain management" assumes that demand is given and rigid and devises methods for adjusting supply to meet demand. To the contrary, "revenue management" assumes that capacity is inflexible and therefore considers methods for adjusting demand, most commonly through pricing. A decision to adopt a green technology offers opportunities for both supply-side and demand-side management.

On the supply side, the opportunities and challenges are evident, as discussed in the preceding section, and perhaps for that reason they attracted more attention from researchers.

On the demand side, there are fewer studies, but pricing was nevertheless incorporated in two different ways: static/single price change and dynamic price changes.

Since adoption of a green technology changes the balance between firms' fixed and variable costs, it is natural that the resultant optimal prices change. For example, in Krass et al. (2013) adopting a green technology reduces environmental tax payments, which reduces marginal cost, which in turn increases margin, and consequently lowers the equilibrium price. An increase in tax increases the cost, reduces the margin, and raises the price; an increase in rebate lowers the effective price, etc. In contrast, the fixed cost subsidy does not impact price under a given technology choice, but impacts which technology is chosen. Similar dependencies between the government incentives for green technology adoption and the price charged by the firm are modeled in other studies on regulation, such as Cohen et al. (2014) or Raz and Ovchinnikov (2015). In these studies, price is a decision variable in the firm's optimization problem. Those are static price changes, which are reasonable for the cases of deterministic demand (as in Krass et al study) or newsvendor-like situations (as in Cohen et al. 2014, or Raz and Ovchinnikov 2015).

In the cases with cyclical supply and demand variability, however, a single price approach is suboptimal. Indeed, if there is more demand for electricity for air-conditioning during the day, then shouldn't the electricity price be higher? Similarly, since the sun is not shining at night, the electric utility must use non-renewable power generation, with a positive variable cost, and that should push the prices up as well. Consumers, in turn, could factor such price fluctuations into account and reallocate their consumption patterns so as to maximize their utility.

Kok et al. (2014) consider the impact of such cyclical dynamic pricing on investments in renewable power generation and the resultant carbon emissions. Specifically, they consider two pricing policies: static pricing (that they call "flat") and two-period dynamic pricing (e.g., one price during the day, another price during the night, that they call "peak" pricing). Under the dynamic policy, they do not explicitly consider the utility-maximizing consumer behavior, and instead, use an exogenously given demand function to describe how consumers relocate some of the high-price demand to low-price time periods as a function of the two prices.

They then consider how these two pricing models impact the amount of renewable capacity installed by a household ("distributed generator"), independent renewable energy producer (that only has renewable capacity), and vertically integrated power utility (that has both renewable and non-renewable sources). Their main result is that the same pricing policy leads to distinctively different outcomes for different investors and technologies.

For solar technologies, peak pricing leads to more investment by households, but less by commercial investors. This is because solar energy production is positively correlated with demand, hence peak pricing consumers have more to gain by substituting the expensive (high-demand, peak) power with free solar without changing their consumption habits. But for the commercial investors, the ability of households to shift consumption habits in response to peak pricing implies that the benefit of substituting costly fossil fuel generation with free solar is less than under the flat pricing (when no demand shifts occur). For wind technologies, this logic does not always hold, because the correlation is mostly negative: that is, there are more/stronger winds at night when the demand for power is actually lower. Because of this effect, flat pricing could also lead to substantially lower emissions.

I believe that there are numerous research opportunities in connecting demand management with green technologies. The emergence of smart grid and the "internet of things" would allow for managing various consumer devices and consequently make the use of scarce resources more efficient. Predicting the use patterns and consumer response and designing innovative business models and policies to motivate desired behaviors—all are interesting research opportunities.

An implicit assumption in all the papers surveyed in this section is that consumers are not willing to pay more as a result of green technology choices made by the firms. I discuss this issue in more detail next.

12.7 Green Technology Choices and Consumers' Willingness-to-Pay

When addressing the connection between the green technology choice and consumer willingness-to-pay (WTP), it is very important to differentiate between two seemingly similar questions. First, do consumer wish to pay more for greener products? Despite considerable research, the answer to this question is not unambiguous. Laroche et al. (2001) mention that throughout 1990s, both the percentage of American consumers who are willing to pay more for green products increased to 67 % and how much more they are willing to pay increased to nearly 20 %. They further mention that in UK a survey of female consumers' perceptions of environmental claims on the packaging of clothes detergents found that 79 % agreed to pay up to 40 % more for a product, which was identical in every respect to their own brand and which had been proven to be green. The spread of eco-labeling allowed to test these predictions on sales data, and the report by Carbon Trust (2012) states that 67 % of UK consumers were more likely to buy a product with low carbon footprint and 44 % would switch to a lower carbon product even if it is not their first-choice brand. Motivated by these promising results, marketers went on to identify which consumers were willing to pay more for environmentally friendly products. Roberts (1996) and Straughan and Roberts (1999) are classical studies in this domain with hundreds of citations.

The questions regarding the efficiency of eco-labels also raised significant research interest. For example, with respect to wood and paper products and the Forest Stewardship Council (FSC), several authors examined whether consumers are aware of FSC and are willing to pay more for FSC-certified products. Elliott and Vincent (2014) show that only 3 % of consumers are aware of FSC and nearly half never heard about it. Regarding willingness-to-pay, they list multiple studies which suggest that while consumers state that they might pay more, observing actual behaviors (e.g., Anderson and Hansen 2004 monitored actual purchases of plywood at Home Depot) reveals that consumers are not willing to pay more for certified plywood.

But the above questions are somewhat misleading for the purpose of this Section. Indeed, when Wells Fargo installed solar panels on its roofs, Coca Cola (Wang et al. 2013) or La Poste (Kleindorfer et al. 2012) started using electric delivery trucks, or energy producer added renewable power to its portfolio, the respective products—banking services, drinks, mail and air-conditioning—did not change. Thus, the second question is whether consumers wish to pay more for the same product that are manufactured/delivered/etc. in a "greener" way?

The direct answer to this question is elusive. Intuitively, however, the answer would seem to be "No": for example, would you be willing to pay more for a taxi ride in a hybrid car versus a regular car? Or are you even aware what kind of vehicle delivers your mail?

But the indirect connection between the consumer willingness to pay and the firms' corporate social responsibility (CSR) actions, including technologies they choose, has been studied extensively. Sen and Bhattacharya (2001) found that CSR initiatives have positive effects on consumers' perceptions of the "Self-Company" congruence, i.e., affect consumers' evaluations via their bond with the firms, which depend on consumers' own attributes. Specifically, this evaluation is more sensitive to negative CSR information than to positive one. Similarly, Brown and Dacin (1997) found that CSR affects consumers via overall evaluation of the firm, and this knowledge of the firm in turn affects their evaluation of the product. These two papers are just a small sample of the vast body of literature on CRS and consumer perceptions.

The general conclusion therefore is: while there is no direct evidence that consumers are willing to pay more as a result of green technology choices, indirectly, though, there exists a halo effect: such choices impact consumers' perceptions of firms and consequently their products. This suggests an interesting research question: can firm operations be used to make the otherwise invisible green technology choice more salient in the minds of consumers, and thus enhance the indirect link identified above?

The frequent invisibility of "green" (or not) behavior is an issue not only on the consumer side, but also with supply chain partners. This motivates the next two sections of the chapter.

12.8   Motivating and Ensuring Sustainable Behavior Across Supply Chains

For many large firms in the developed economies, the "technology choice" question is rather indirect. Apple, Disney, Nike, and the likes are outsourcing most of their production, typically to suppliers in Asia. Hence, it is the technology choice of the suppliers that truly matters. Unfortunately, the legal systems and environmental standards in suppliers' jurisdictions are often rather loose and fragile, so that socially and environmentally responsible behaviors cannot be guaranteed locally. At the same time, as described in the previous Section, should those irresponsible behaviors be discovered by the developed-world consumers, the respective firms would suffer through a loss in consumer perception of the firms and their products.

Therefore, a growing body of literature examines non-contractual relationships between the buyers (in the developed world) and suppliers (in the developing world) that could lead to better social and environmental practices/"technologies."

Guo et al. (2015) consider a sourcing decision of a buyer who has two kinds of suppliers: responsible (who charge high price but adhere to strict standards) and risky (who charge lower prices but may have a violation: leak, spill, etc.) The authors consider all-risky, all-responsible, or mixed strategies and show how the optimality of a given strategy is connected to consumers' socially conscious behavior. They show that efforts to improve supply chain responsibility via consumers (e.g., by increasing the number of consumers who are socially conscious or their willingness-to-pay for responsibility) may lead to unintended consequences—"backfire," e.g., increase risky sourcing. In contrast, efforts that focus on enforcement and penalizing the buyer never backfire and always lead to more responsible sourcing. Chen and Lee (2014) apply mechanism design approach to help buyers select responsible suppliers, and Izhutov and Lee (2014) consider the supplier's problem of investing in order to qualify as responsible.

None of these papers, however, directly address the incentives problem: how can buyers motivate suppliers to become more responsible? This question is the topic of Plambeck and Taylor (2014). They note that the most common approach to monitor supplier are inspections. Such inspections are costly, and hence can only be performed occasionally. Should one have a regularly scheduled inspections or rather perform them at random? Intuitively, random inspections should be more efficient. But the authors point out that, in practice, inspections are also imperfect: there are many ways to deceive inspectors: falsify records of maintenance and training, show only exemplar parts of factories, train workers to lie, bribe inspectors, etc. In this situation, they derive a "backfiring" condition, under which random inspections motivate less effort than scheduled, and so do more frequent inspections. They further show that squeezing the margins is also more efficient than increasing them as a common logic might suggest. Kim (2015) also presents a conceptually similar result, but in a context of a regulator that is monitoring a potential violator (polluter). In both cases, even though the focus is on inspections for social conditions, the same logic would apply to auditing firms to verify whether they are in fact using greener technologies. Further discussion of how firms can work with suppliers to enhance sustainability in the supply chain is provided in Chap. 11 by van Weele and van Tubergen (2017) and Chap. 20 by Lee and Rammohan (2017).

Extending the issues of green technology choice from a single firm to a supply chain is certainly an interesting research direction with multiple questions related to international trade (tariffs and export/import restrictions), accounting (allocation of emissions), etc.—the subject is too broad for this chapter. But one immediate research opportunity is in deeper understanding the total impact of green choices throughout the value chains. For example, while incentives may be offered to a focal firm to adopt a greener technology to convert its inputs into outputs, could there perhaps be a "greener" way to process inputs by a supplier that would, even by keeping the focal firm "dirty," still result in a larger environmental/societal impact? Similarly, are there ways to motivate consumers to use the products in a "greener" way?

12.9 Leakage of Unsustainable Practices to Areas with Low Enforcement

When regulations in one geographic area are tightened, firms can either adopt a greener technology in that region, or they can relocate production to a region with less stringent regulation. In this context, "leakage" (e.g., carbon leakage) refers to a situation when a dirty process is relocated from a region in which emissions control is enabled and enforced to a region where it is not. For example, with carbon pricing in the European Union, some cement manufacturers may move their production to Northern Africa (Drake 2012).

In the economics literature, this problem received a significant attention, with some studies arguing that the resultant emissions after the relocation could exceed those prior to relocation, e.g., see Babiker (2005) who report an up to 30 % increase. This is due to the fact that a stringent emission regulation in one region could decrease the global demand for a particular product, hence decreasing it's global price and as a result increasing consumption in other regions (Felder and Rutherford 1993). At the same time, other researchers pointed out that emissions regulation would affect incentives to innovate and such an "induced-technology effect" would counterbalance the negative impact of the leakage (Di Maria and van der Werf 2008).

Various mechanisms have been proposed to minimize the negative impact of leakage. Drake (2012) considers border adjustments: a form of an import tax levied on a good produced in an un-regulated region that is being imported into a region with emissions regulation. He shows that a symmetric border adjustment does not fully eliminate leakage, but could lead to a situation where it induces the firm in the unregulated region to adopt a cleaner technology than one in the regulated region (this happens if the former has a cost advantage). As a result, the total emissions are shown to decrease.

Sunar and Plambeck (2014) study the interaction between border adjustments and allocation of emissions among co-products. They show that the way emissions are allocated (such as based on products' prices or weights) may have a significant impact on the effectiveness of border adjustments, and under some conditions, increase rather than reduce the overall emissions.

Alev et al. (2014) consider another mechanism: the export ban. In a closed-loop supply chain context, it is sometimes more profitable to export used products from one market into another market, rather than remanufacture them. They show that, under some conditions, such export bans may exacerbate the negative consequences of extended producer responsibility regulations by providing manufacturers with an incentive to interfere in the secondary markets and, by doing so, shorten the effective useful life of their products.

As the leakage problems show, the question of green technology choice along a supply chain is a complicated, multi-faceted issue that inevitably embeds all the complications of real supply chains: that they consist of independent agents, in different geographies, with different regulations, etc. This clearly expands the set of challenges, but also the set of opportunities. Same as with the several preceding sections, the most operationally efficient opportunities for addressing sustainability issues through technology choices may lie outside of the focal firm's scope of operations. Returning back to the Scope 1-2-3 taxonomy outlined at the beginning of the chapter, the researchers should consider broader sets of opportunities and questions for technology choices at all the links in a supply chain.

12.10   Conclusions: Rethinking "Technology Choice," Behaviors, and Lifestyle

This chapter surveys the research questions, approaches, and results surrounding a broadly defined notion of green technology choice. Since the notion of "technology choice" is very broad (e.g., one might argue that the location of the firm could be viewed as a "technology"), the chapter focuses on the supply-chain view of the firm, borrowing the well-known Scope 1-2-3 taxonomy pioneered by the Greenhouse Gas protocol.

Starting with the economics and accounting aspects and the associated incentives provided for green technologies, the chapter discussed the operational issues of demand and supply variability and intermittency, as well as consumer reactions and supply chain behaviors. Each of these sub-areas has excellent research studies and open questions. But in the conclusion of the chapter, I would like to post a higher-level, overarching question: are localized technology decisions globally optimal? Specifically, shouldn't we (businesses, consumers, governments—society) move from making pieces of our lives "greener" toward rethinking how to make the entire life "greener"?

Returning back to the Wells Fargo example: it is of course laudable that they installed solar panels and power their branches with renewable energy. But if their employees or customers drive many miles to work every day, then these efforts are a drop in a bigger "sea" of opportunities. The many research studies and examples discussed in this chapter provide a roadmap for making sustainable choices, but I believe that the next step is for people, rather than businesses to rethink day-to-day behaviors. Academics could study innovative business models and incentives, businesses could provide such innovative products and services, and governments could provide incentive structures that would make the costs and benefits of using those products more transparent. But my firm belief is that the biggest "technology choice" opportunities are in rethinking lifestyles, in designing products and services, and in government policies, which would help people make more sustainable choices.

References

Aflaki S, Netessine S (2011) Strategic investment in renewable energy sources. Working paper. INSEAD, Fontainebleau

Alev I, Agrawal V, Atasu A (2014) Extended producer responsibility, secondary markets, and export restrictions. Working paper. Georgia Tech, Atlanta

Alizamir S, de Vericourt F, Sun P (2014) Efficient feed-in-tariff policies for renewable energy technologies. Working paper. Yale University, New Haven

Anderson RC, Hansen EN (2004) Determining consumer preferences for ecolabeled forest products: an experimental approach. J Forest 102(4):28–32

Babiker MH (2005) Climate change policy, market structure, and carbon leakage. J Int Econ 65:421–445

Boukherroub T, Bouchery Y, Corbett CJ, Fransoo J, Tan T (2017) Carbon footprinting in supply chains. In: Bouchery Y, Corbett CJ, Fransoo J, Tan T (eds) Sustainable supply chains: a research-based textbook on operations and strategy. Springer, New York

Brown TJ, Dacin PA (1997) The company and the product: corporate associations and consumer product responses. J Market 61(1):68–84

Carbon Foot Printing (2012) Report by Carbon Trust. https://www.carbontrust.com/media/44869/j7912_ctv043_carbon_footprinting_aw_interactive.pdf

Carraro C, Soubeyran A (1996) Environmental policy and the choice of production technology. In: Carraro C, Katsoulacos Y, Zepapadeas A (eds) Environmental policy and market structure. Kluwer, Dordrecht, pp 151–180

Chemama J, Cohen MC, Lobel R, Perakis G (2014) Consumer subsidies with a strategic supplier: commitment vs flexibility Working paper. MIT, Cambridge

Chen L, Lee HL (2014) Mitigate supplier responsibility risk in emerging economies: an ethical sourcing framework. Working paper. Duke University, Durham

Cohen MC, Lobel R, Perakis G (2014) The impact of demand uncertainty on consumer subsidies for green technology adoption. Management Science (Forthcoming)

Di Maria C, van der Werf E (2008) Carbon leakage revisited: unilateral climate policy with directed technical change. Environ Res Econ 39:55–74

Drake DF (2012) Carbon tariffs: effects in settings with technology choice and foreign comparative advantage. Working paper. Harvard Business School, Boston

Drake DF, Kleindorfer PR, Van Wassenhove LN (2014) Technology choice and capacity portfolios under emissions regulation. Working paper. Harvard University, Cambridge

Elliott J, Vincent J (2014) An analysis of willingness to pay and reasons for purchasing certified forest products. Master's thesis. Nicholas School of the Environment, Duke University, Durham

Felder S, Rutherford TF (1993) Unilateral CO$_2$ reductions and carbon leakage: the consequences of international trade in oil and basic materials. J Environ Econ Manage 25:162–176

Guo R, Lee HL, Swinney R (2015) Responsible sourcing in supply chains. Working paper. Duke University, Durham

Hu S, Souza GC, Ferguson ME, Wang W (2015) Capacity investment in renewable energy technology with supply intermittency. Manuf Serv Oper Manage (Forthcoming)

Islegen O, Reichelstein S (2011) Carbon capture by fossil fuel power plants: an economic analysis. Manage Sci 57(1):21–39

Izhutov PA, Lee HL (2014) Dynamics of a responsible business relationship. Working paper. Stanford University, Stanford

Jager-Waldau A (2012) PV status report 2012. European Commission report EUR 25749 EN

Kim S-H (2015) Time to come clean? Disclosure and inspection policies for green production. Oper Res (Forthcoming)

Kleindorfer PR, Neboian A, Roset A, Spinler S (2012) Fleet renewal with electric vehicles at La Poste. Interfaces 42(5):465–477

Kok AG, Shang K, Yucel S (2014) Impact of electricity pricing policy on renewable energy investments and carbon emissions. Working paper. Duke University, Durham

Krass D, Nedorezov T, Ovchinnikov A (2013) Environmental taxes and the choice of green technology. Product Oper Manage 22(5):1035–1055

Laroche M, Bergeron J, Barbaro-Forleo G (2001) Targeting consumers who are willing to pay more for environmentally friendly products". J Consum Market 18(6):503–520

Lee HL, Rammohan SV (2017) Improving social and environmental performance in global supply chains. In: Bouchery Y, Corbett CJ, Fransoo J, Tan T (eds) Sustainable supply chains: a research-based textbook on operations and strategy. Springer, New York

Lobel E, Perakis G (2011) Consumer choice model for forecasting demand and designing incentives for solar technology. Working paper. MIT, Cambridge

Ovchinnikov A (2008) c-Energy's Red Hill plant: meeting the SO$_2$ challenge, UVA-QA-0726. Darden Business, Charlottesville

Ovchinnikov A, Hvaleva A (2012) Wells fargo: solar energy for Los Angeles branches" (A) and (B), UVA-QA-800, 801. Darden Business, Charlottesville, VA

Plambeck EL, Taylor TA (2014) Supplier evasion of a buyer's audit: implications for motivating supplier social and environmental responsibility. Working paper. Stanford University, Stanford

Raz G, Ovchinnikov A (2015) Coordinating pricing and supply of public interest goods using government rebates and subsidies. IEEE Trans Eng Manage 62(1):65–79

Raz G, Ovchinnikov AS, Elias A (2014) Chevy Volt: pricing and capacity decisions in response to government incentives for the electric vehicle industry. Darden Business, Charlottesville

Roberts JA (1996) Green consumers in the 1990s: profile and implications for advertising. J Bus Res 36(3):217–231

Sen S, Bhattacharya CB (2001) Does doing good always lead to doing better? Consumer reactions to corporate social responsibility. J Market Res 38(2):225–243

Straughan RD, Roberts JA (1999) Environmental segmentation alternatives: a look at green consumer behavior in the new millennium. J Consum Market 16(6):558–575

Sunar N, Plambeck EL (2014) Allocating emissions among co-products: implications for procurement, offsetting & border adjustment. Working paper. University of North Carolina, Chapel Hill

van Weele A, van Tubergen K (2017) Responsible purchasing: moving from compliance to value creation in supplier relationships. In: Bouchery Y, Corbett CJ, Fransoo J, Tan T (eds) Sustainable supply chains: a research-based textbook on operations and strategy. Springer, New York

Wang W, Ferguson ME, Hu S, Souza GC (2013) Dynamic capacity investment with two competing technologies. Manuf Serv Oper Manage 15(4):616–629

Wu OQ, Kapuschinski R (2013) Curtailing intermittent generation in electrical systems. Manuf Serv Oper Manage 15(4):578–595

Zhou Y, Scheller-Wolf A, Secomandi N, Smith S (2014a) Electricity trading and negative prices: storage vs. disposal. Working paper. Carnegie Mellon University, Pittsburgh

Zhou Y, Scheller-Wolf A, Secomandi N, Smith S (2014b) Managing wind-based electricity generation in the presence of storage and transmission capacity. Working paper. Carnegie Mellon University, Pittsburgh

Chapter 13
Principles of EcoDesign in Sustainable Supply Chains

Conrad Luttropp

13.1 Introduction

It is often said that the majority of environmental impacts of products occur during the design stage, so efforts to make supply chains more sustainable should inevitably include the product design process. In this chapter, we put EcoDesign in the broader product design context and discuss some aspects of implementing EcoDesign in companies. We then introduce ten "Golden Principles" (10GP) of EcoDesign and provide an illustration of how they can be used to analyze and redesign a product.

How does EcoDesign fit in the context of sustainable supply chains? If we simplify the concept of supply chain management (SCM), it is a matter of flows: flow of money, goods, and information throughout the life cycle, from extraction of materials via manufacturing, sales, use, and recycling.

Today, information might be the most important element in SCM in order to achieve a true eco-effective product. Figures 13.1 and 13.2 illustrate the shift. Some 50 years ago, the products were made in a physical plant. Material was imported, the products were made from start to finish within the plant, and in the end the full product was delivered out through the factory gates. Today, companies are not characterized so much by fixed physical locations as by moving activities where material, components, and money meet in different locations; what keeps things together is information.

This shift puts strong demands on information in order to achieve sustainable SCM (or eco-SCM). It is then necessary to understand the nature of "eco" in the industrial environment. Figure 13.3 shows all the necessary elements of a product design project and it is important to understand that "eco" is not the dominant part

C. Luttropp (✉)
Machine Design KTH, 10044 Stockholm, Sweden
e-mail: luttropp@kth.se

© Yann Bouchery, Charles J. Corbett, Jan C. Fransoo, and Tarkan Tan 2017   303
Y. Bouchery et al. (eds.), *Sustainable Supply Chains*, Springer Series in Supply
Chain Management 4, DOI 10.1007/978-3-319-29791-0_13

-manufacturing

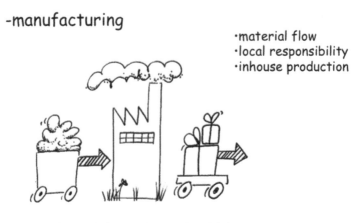

· material flow
· local responsibility
· inhouse production

Ownership of material and products!

Fig. 13.1 Yesterday products were made in a plant and ownership of material, manufacturing resources, and products was strongly connected to the company (Luttropp 1998)

-delivery

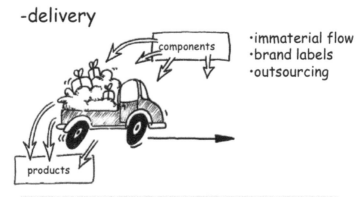

· immaterial flow
· brand labels
· outsourcing

Immaterial ownership of material and products!

Fig. 13.2 Today, extraction of materials, manufacturing of components, and assembly of product altogether is a moving activity. Ownership of material and products are more of a virtual element (Luttropp 1998)

but still a major one. However, there must always be a compromise between all the demands placed on the forthcoming product. Pugh (1991, p. 5) refers to this as the "Design Core":

> Total design may be construed as having a central core of activities, all of which are imperative for any design, irrespective of domain. Briefly, this core, the design core, consists of market (user need), product design specification, conceptual design, detail design, manufacture and sales. All design starts, or should start, with a need that, when satisfied, will fit into an existing market or create a market of its own.

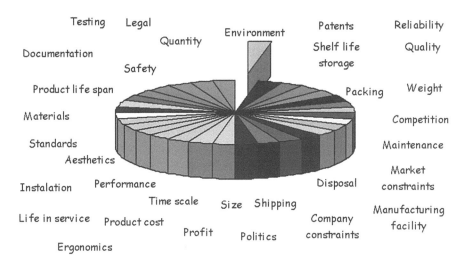

Fig. 13.3 An illustration of all the necessary elements in product development (PD). Entering environmental concern into this compromise makes it also EcoDesign (Luttropp 1999)

The circle diagram in Fig. 13.3 illustrates all these demands connected to the forthcoming product.

Even if environmental demands are important and crucial, there are a lot of other demands to be considered as well.

This means that Eco-performance, as defined by Züst (1996), is one of several very important elements, which has to be balanced in the design core against other functional and economic requirements. Environmental considerations have to be incorporated into the design core without taking over (Züst 1996).

Recycling and other environmentally imposed actions have to be related to all the other elements in the design core without taking over, since environmental demands will rarely have top priority. Functionality of the product and profit to the company are examples of two aspects which always have very high priority, almost always higher than environmental demands. Without customers buying a function and companies making profit, there will be no business, no matter the environmental issue. Consequently, EcoDesign (also referred to as Design for environment) may be defined as a practice by which environmental considerations are integrated into product and process engineering design procedures, while maintaining product, price, performance, and quality standards (Graedel and Allenby 2003). EcoDesign has been extensively studied in the academic literature. We refer to Hatcher et al. (2011), Ilgin and Gupta (2010), and Ramani et al. (2010) for some reviews. The readers may also refer to Bovea and Pérez-Belis (2012) for a review of the main EcoDesign tools. The importance of EcoDesign is also recognized among companies, although there may be confusion about the terminology. Short et al. (2012) ask firms in Sweden and the UK whether design for sustainability should be part of their product development process, and the vast majority of firms responding (97 % of large firms in Sweden and 89 % of large firms in the UK) agree that it should. When asked whether they practice a design for sustainability approach, the proportion who said "yes" dropped, while even less confirmed that they use an EcoDesign approach. The conclusion is clear that there is widespread agreement about the need to incorporate sustainability in product design, but less understanding of the corresponding approaches and terminology. This conclusion is in line with Karlsson and Luttropp (2006) who highlight that answering to why we do EcoDesign is more basic than how.

This chapter mainly focuses on this latter question by discussing some aspects of implementing EcoDesign practices in companies. We organize the rest of the chapter as follows. Sect. 13.1 discusses the importance of design knowledge as a basis for successful implementation of EcoDesign. Section 13.2 presents the key actors to include in the EcoDesign process. Section 13.3 presents the 10GP of EcoDesign and discusses these principles in the context of sustainable SCM. In Sect. 13.4, we show how to apply the 10GP for analyzing and Eco-redesigning two products. Finally, Sect. 13.5 presents some conclusions. Design knowledge—a base for sustainable SCM.

Education and experience are two main elements in design knowledge. Many designers have a basic practical experience from youth by disassembling family goods like toys, clocks, radios, vacuum cleaners, etc. and mending bicycles, schoolbags, sports equipment, etc. This gives a natural sense for gravity, strength, and motion. Later, this practice is combined with formal education in engineering matters. Most machine engineering educations are based on classical technical elements like mechanics, materials, thermodynamics, etc.

This is visualized in Fig. 13.4 by the expression $(1+1=2)$: one plus one is two and nothing else! On this level, "law and order" is predominant and technical students with a new diploma have a preference for facts and correct answers rather than tricky questions. After a few years of practical work, engineers come to amplify their technical knowledge with experience and their real competence improves as a combination of education and experience. Questions have been raised that don't have a single correct answer. This is visualized in Fig. 13.4 with the statement "$1+1=(1:3)$". One plus one equals something between one and three, rather than a single number (Luttropp 1998).

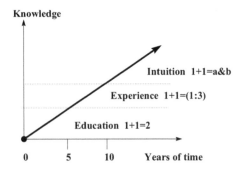

Fig. 13.4 The transformation of education and experience into intuition, the highest form of knowledge (Luttropp 1998)

Later, technical experience and education merge into intuition, reflected by "1 + 1 = a&b". Design knowledge is, at this point, more experienced as "feeling" than a set of technical laws and physical conditions. Technical competence is transformed into technical "wisdom". This status is monitored by Bragd in her study of the development of the Volvo XC90 car and expressed as "Tinkering" (Bragd 2002).

13.2 Managing the EcoDesign process

To succeed with EcoDesigning, integration of environmental competence into the product design process is essential, and early integration is the most effective. The nature of competence varies between persons involved in EcoDesign and four different competencies can be observed: consumers, designers, managers, and environmental specialists.

Designers need basic knowledge in environmental design and a network with environmental specialists. Research carried out by Ehrenfeld and Lenox (1997) shows that a good network including environmental specialists is essential for success in designing environmentally friendly products. Designers should not be the specialist on environmental matters since the design core (see Fig. 13.3) contains a lot of demands apart from environmental requests. There is an obvious risk that being an environmental specialist makes the designer less skilled in other areas.

Consumers ideally need a good basic knowledge of environmental matters in order to be a "good" customer. Choices by ordinary people often determine where on the agenda environmental issues will appear (if at all).

Managers need basic knowledge about environmental matters concerning acquisition, design, legislation, etc. Managers are the key to EcoDesign since designers cannot decide on environmental improvements on their own; it must be agreed on by management as a part of broader decisions about product economics and development.

Environmental specialists need deep knowledge of the environmental field and a good competence in current environmental analysis tools. Life Cycle Assessment (LCA) is well-known (see also Chap. 2 by Guinée and Heijungs (2017)), but many others exist. A specialist should also be well-trained in relevant Eco-design guidelines and checklists, standards such as ISO 14000, and should have a good view of current research related to EcoDesign. A basic task for the specialist is to transform environmental demands into operational design requirements with a connection to economy, legislation, acquisition, etc. One of the best ways to get competence in, for example, LCA is to actually perform a full LCA as a part of the learning process. Every product has one or two main functions, which are the reason why the product is on the market. Environmental aspects can therefore rarely be higher than second or third priority. A vacuum cleaner that does not suck up dust is of no use no matter how environmentally friendly it is. Every designer has to fulfil the main functions first and environmental demands second. An environmental dialogue must be present in the company, and environmental specialists are a major resource in these actions.

13.3 The Ten Golden Principles of EcoDesign in the context of Sustainable Supply Chains

The 10GP by Luttropp and Brohammer (2014) are a tool developed to foster cooperation by uncovering the intuitive design knowledge present in a product design group. The 10GP is an enhanced version of the Ten Golden Rules (10GR) that has been used in the EcoDesign education at KTH (Royal Institute of Technology) in Stockholm by the author since the early 2000s. The Ten Golden Rules were developed by Luttropp as the "lowest common denominator" of ten of the most common issues that must be addressed in EcoDesign (Luttropp and Lagerstedt 2006, p. 1400). Each of the Ten Golden Rules is generic and needs to be customized to the context; the same is true for the 10GP. For instance, the first Golden Rule is "Do not use toxic substances and utilize closed loops for necessary but toxic ones." As Luttropp and Lagerstedt (2006, p. 1402) point out, this could be customized to:

- Identify which toxic substances are currently used in the product with which you are working;
- Try to find a nontoxic substitute that fulfills functional and economic requirements of the product;
- Ascertain if closed loops are already established or can be developed and utilized for recycling the materials including the toxic substances.

Luttropp and Lagerstedt (2006) provide a detailed discussion of how the rules were adopted and customized at Bombardier, using an iterative and participative process. The 10GP, discussed next, are an enhanced version of these Ten Golden Rules.

In this section, we discuss the 10GP of EcoDesign in the context of sustainable SCM. For each of the Golden Principles, we explain how it applies to EcoDesign, and why it is important in the context of EcoDesign. After introducing the Golden Principles, we provide an illustrative example of how a keyboard and a cordless drill were analyzed and redesigned using this approach.

GP1: Clarify product characteristics, functional and immaterial.
How: Identify which functions of the product are important and determine which are directly linked to particular materials or material streams. The material stream is then effectively a function of the function of the product.
Why: In redesigning a product, it is important to find a balance between the functions the product (and hence the embedded materials) aims to provide and the corresponding environmental impact of those materials.

GP2: Manage human resources in a responsible manner without consuming them.
How: Keep track of and note how human resources are used throughout the life cycle, both inside and outside the company. For example, designers can avoid using FeNdB magnets when ordinary magnets are sufficient for the current application since the extraction of neodym (Nd) is creating problems for the work environment.
Why: Even when employees may not be perceived as the top priority in a supply chain, the firm must ensure that the human resources along the life cycle are healthy, as otherwise the market will perceive claims of sustainable SCM as being hollow and thus potentially counterproductive.

GP 3: Minimize hazardous substances and arrange closed-loop systems for the present ones.

How: Ask suppliers for a bill of materials (BOM), which is necessary for any attempt to remanufacture the product. In practice, it is often hard to get a complete BOM since with semi-virtual products that are manufactured in accordance with Fig. 13.2 no single entity has the entire BOM.

Why: Firms may face questions about RoHS compliance as well as REACH reporting or possible toxic content of their product. Just asking and continuing to do so starts a process towards a more visible knowledge of the total material stream.

GP 4: Ensure efficient use of material resources with little generation of waste and efficient transportation.

How: Use recycled materials in manufacturing and measure/report how much goes into the process.

One element in LEAN is effective transportation of materials and in this sense a part of SSCM. Another LEAN element is low waste, which is eco-effective. From an EcoDesign perspective, it is important to use recycled materials in products if possible. Many companies claim use of recycled materials. With a less effective production process, it is then possible to compensate by bragging that recycled material is used when it is in fact production spills. The challenge is to find materials that have been in use and then returning into new products

GP 5: Ensure that GP-related costs are offset by an increase in GP-related income.

How: Firms should try to keep account of both the additional costs and income that is related to EcoDesign. (This is analogous to the requirement in Six Sigma to quantify costs and benefits of individual projects.)

Why: Products designed following EcoDesign principles can provide various benefits to firms, including enhanced brand, which can carry over to the broader portfolio of the firm. Without careful accounting, those benefits will not be attributed to the EcoDesign process, making eco products appear more costly than is appropriate.

GP 6: Minimize energy consumption in use, especially for active products.

How. Ask what types of energy and how much energy is used throughout the life cycle; in the production of raw materials, manufacturing, transportation, power in use, recycling, etc. Questions on these matters result in awareness and in turn often act as a driver towards smaller/more efficient use of resources.

Why. Active products are products with power consumption in use phase as most significant environmental impact. Typical active products are refrigerators and classical cars. For these products, a lot is to be gained by lowering the power consumption in use phase. Furniture are mostly inactive with most significant environmental aspect out of use phase. So, it is gainful to keep this product in the use phase as long as possible.

GP 7: Avoid mixing materials and adopt a clear and obvious structure of attachment joints and fraction borders.

How: Simplify the material composition of products and implement recycling-friendly features in products (sometimes referred to as Design for Environment, Design for Disassembly, etc.). Plan from the start of a product development process for a supply chain for recycled material at the same time as the classical forward supply chain for virgin materials.

Why: The recycling of materials is a critical issue in sustainable supply chains. An improved so-called material hygiene (MH) (a pedagogical concept aimed at managing compromises to optimize materials use in products) leads to cleaner, more efficient and useful material streams.

GP 8: Optimize the usage lifetime of products and promote repair and upgrading.

How: Firms should ensure that there is a system that takes care of discarded products. They should try to maintain relationships with the product owner so that recovery rates can be maintained at a level as high as possible.

Why: The shorter and shorter lifetime of products is perhaps the most important challenge in EcoDesign. Doubling the useful lifetime will reduce the need for recycling processes by 50 %.

GP 9: The product must be surrounded by a corresponding environmental culture.

How: Make sure that everyone involved also acts in an environmentally correct manner. Details such as reusable packaging may circulate backwards in the value chain with discarded products or spillage.

Why: Environment is often seen as a somewhat ethical issue, which means that in a sustainable supply chain one must also secure that the company culture is supporting the sustainability. It is important to "walk the talk". If the company is not supporting sustainability and just the products, the company can easily be perceived as hypocrite.

GP 10: Ensure that the information IN the product, ON the product, and FOR the product is correct and sufficient.

How: Make sure that the information on the product clearly displays how to use it in an energy-efficient manner. Try to publish as much information as possible on bills of material, transportation routes, etc.

Why: This will be regarded as respectful to the concerned eco-consumer and drive towards more sustainable supply chains.

13.4 Golden Principle Analysis

One might be concerned that these EcoDesign principles are difficult to implement in practice, especially when firms are facing many competing priorities. That is not the case. To illustrate that, we provide two examples below of projects conducted by graduate students in the EcoDesign course at KTH Stockholm. The students analyzed and Eco-redesigned a keyboard (Alm et al. 2014) and a cordless drill

Table 13.1 Product characteristics for each of the 10 Golden Principles for the reference product; a keyboard

Golden principle	Reference product characteristics
1. *Function*—Clarify the product characteristics	Mainly functional value. Price motivates purchase. Some immaterial value in terms of brand perception
2. *Human resources*—Manage human resources in a sustainable way	The company has low-wage workers in China, but also have an outspoken agenda for Supply Chain Responsibility where procurement receives responsibility training, direct employment of migrant workers, limited weekly working hours, etc.
3. *Toxic*—Minimize hazardous substances and arrange closed-loop systems for the present	The keyboard contains a small WEEE-core. Otherwise little toxic substances is used
4. *Material resources*—Ensure lean production and efficient transport	The production in this company is highly optimized. Transport is mainly by ship which is relatively effective
5. *Economy*—Ensure that GP-related costs are offset by an increase in GP-related income	The product is profitable today
6. *Energy*—Minimize energy consumption in use, especially for active products	The energy consumption during use is very low relative to the other stages of the life cycle
7. *Material hygiene*—Avoid mixing materials and adopt a clear and obvious structure of attachment joints and fraction borders	The reference keyboard has a relatively low level of material mix
8. *Lifetime*—Optimize the usage time of products and promote repair and upgrading	The reference keyboard is assumed to be used during half its lifetime
9. *Context*—The product must be surrounded by a corresponding environmental culture	The company has a clearly stated agenda for sustainable operations
10. *Information*—Ensure that information IN the product, ON the product, and FOR the product is correct and sufficient	The reference product is labelled with energy consumption and some plastic parts have material labels

(Andren et al. 2014). The products were analyzed according to the 10GP to identify relevant areas of improvement. Tables 13.1 and 13.2 and Figs. 13.5 and 13.6 describe the reference product characteristics for keyboard and the drill is present in Table 13.3 and Fig. 13.7.

13.4.1 Keyboard

The product's performance for every Golden Principle is illustrated in Fig. 13.5. The green rings indicate the areas that are mainly targeted for improvements by the suggested redesigns that follow in Table 13.2.

Table 13.2 Possible improvements of the reference product keyboard

Golden principle	Redesign implications
1. *Function*—Clarify the product characteristics	Connecting a take-back program with component reuse to the product
2. *Human resources*—Manage human resources in a sustainable way	No improvements by redesign
3. *Toxic*—Minimize hazardous substances and arrange closed-loop systems for the present	The circuit board is reused. This should have positive effects since it is the most toxic part
4. *Material* resources—Ensure lean production and efficient transport	Reusing circuit board reduces the amount of material that is used
5. *Economy*—Ensure that GP-related costs are offset by an increase in GP-related income	The cost might increase slightly but the increase can be offset by a reduction in the environmental footprint due to reuse
6. *Energy*—Minimize energy consumption in use, especially for active products	No improvements by redesign
7. *Material hygiene*—Avoid mixing materials and adopt a clear and obvious structure of attachment joints and fraction borders	The number of materials that is used is reduced when the metal plate is removed. The detachable circuit board and break point makes the fraction borders more obvious
8. *Lifetime*—Optimize the usage time of products and promote repair and upgrading	The lifetime is not extended but the detachable circuit board facilitates repair and upgrades without changing the entire product
9. *Context*—The product must be surrounded by a corresponding environmental culture	No improvements by redesign
10. *Information*—Ensure that information IN the product, ON the product, and FOR the product is correct and sufficient	Adding labels for detachable circuit board, the break point, and all plastic parts can simplify recycling. HP can also market the redesigned keyboard as partly reusable

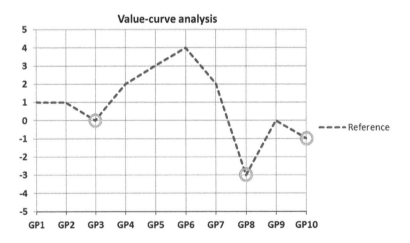

Fig. 13.5 GP value-curve for reference product

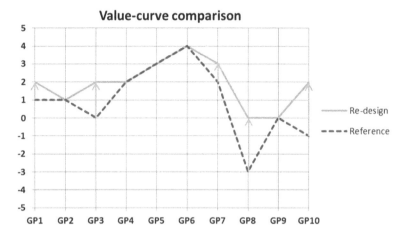

Fig. 13.6 GP value-curve for improved product

After implementing the redesigns, the value-curve analysis is redone. The GPs that have improved are indicated by yellow arrows in Fig. 13.6.

13.4.2   Cordless Drill

The main goal with the improvements of the drill was to lengthen the lifetime and make the disposal and recycling as simple as possible.

When analyzing the 10GP potential, improvements could be identified. By summing up the good and bad qualities of each golden principle, a clearer picture was made and major problem areas could be recognized. In the diagram illustrated in Fig. 13.7, four areas are marked as the major problem areas; the toxic substances, the material hygiene, the lifetime of the product, and the lack of information.

All of the big problem areas seemed to consist of similar suggested improvements. Changing the rechargeable battery to disposable batteries could solve problems in several of the principles. The existing battery in the cordless drill is a rechargeable 12 V NiMH-battery. The disadvantage using that type of battery is that it has to be maintained in order to not deteriorate. The customer, being a regular household-member, will, as mentioned earlier, only use the product a couple of times a year. This means that the user probably won't charge the battery as often as it should be charged or maintain it as it should be maintained, and there could be a problem of the battery deteriorating. By changing the battery to disposable batteries, either several AA batteries, or other standard type batteries of higher voltage, the problem may be solved. Another improvement that could be seen in several of the principles is the change of the plastic materials in the construction. The polystyrene used in the majority of the parts today has the disadvantage of being weak and easily crack, despite having addi-

Table 13.3 This table show possible improvements for the reference product drill

Golden principle	Description	Suggested improvements
1. Function	+ The main function, drill and screwdriver meets the expected qualities	Add more value to the product by adding special properties
	+ Equipped with a special property, a holder for drills	
2. Human resource	− Production mostly located in China, poor working conditions assumed	Move the production or ensure human resource treatment
3. Toxic substances	− If not frequently charged the battery loses potential	Possibly change to disposable batteries
	− Waste electric and electronic equipment (*WEEE*), high demands on recycling	Information about waste treatment
	− Additives in plastics	Change to plastic materials without additives
4. Production resources	− − Long distances	Move the production
	+ Easy to package	Change the design to contain less parts
	− Production of unnecessary parts	
5. Economy	++ Cheaper than most drills on the market	Possibly a higher price if justified
	+ Cheap materials	
	− Could be more expensive in order to live up to the 10G	
6. Energy	+/− Rechargeable battery	Possibly change to disposable batteries
	+ Battery using low wattage	
	− Battery has to be maintained	
7. Material hygiene	− − The chuck is made out of different materials but not separable for recycling	Redesign the chuck
	+/− Low mix of materials though two types of polymers are used	If possible, decrease the number of plastics
	− Difficult to disassemble due to many attachment joints	Decrease the number of parts and joints
8. Lifetime	− If not maintained the battery will deteriorate	Change to disposable batteries
	− Polystyrene, weak plastic	Change plastic material
9. Context	− Assumed poor environmental awareness	Move the production or ensure an environmental policy
	− No services available	Allow service
10. Information	− No material labels	Label the materials (especially the polymers)
	− No eco labels	Label WEEE-waste

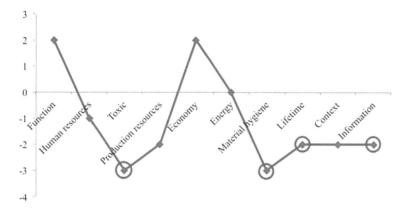

Fig. 13.7 The product's performance for every Golden Principle is illustrated with this graph. The red rings indicate the areas that are mainly targeted for improvements by the suggested redesigns that is given in table 13.3.

tives, which itself is a drawback in a recycling perspective. An improvement in this case could be a material change, to use a polymer with better material properties and better recycling potential. Another disadvantage of the product today is that it's difficult to disassemble. To simplify the recycling process, the design should be changed to consist of less parts and joints. The chuck was identified as a problem-part and should either be redesigned or delivered with better recycling information. The plastic materials and WEEE-cores should also have material and recycling labels.

13.5 Summary and Conclusion

The products business feasibility is basic and implies that environmental design research and developed methods never will get acceptance from designers without taking these elements into account.

The level of EcoDesign is set by the competence of the product developers. It is therefore necessary to understand the nature of EcoDesign knowledge and to launch EcoDesign tools that make it possible for designers to communicate on intuitive level.

Designers and managers have to cooperate in balancing environmental aspects, market opportunities, technical possibilities, and economics.

The situation can be described in four points.

- Environmental aspects must be integrated with technical possibilities, market, and economics
- Designers and managers have to keep up an environmental dialogue
- Environmental demands must be transformed into operational design requirements
- Environmental subjects are fairly new, time and education will do a part of the trick

References

Alm R, Ericson P, Karelfelt E, Ellert W (2014) Ecodesigned keyboard, studyreport in EcoDesign course MF2032 at KTH, Stockholm

Andren A, Hansen J, Sejdic E, Slade M (2014) Analysis and improvements of a cordless drill, studyreport EcoDesign course M2032 at KTH, Stockholm

Bovea M, Pérez-Belis V (2012) A taxonomy of ecodesign tools for integrating environmental requirements into the product design process. J Cleaner Prod 20(1):61–71

Bragd A (2002) Knowing management: an ethnographic study of tinkering with a new car. BAS, Gutenberg

Ehrenfeld J, Lenox M (1997) The development and implementation of DFE programs. J Sustain Prod Des 8:17–27

Graedel TE, Allenby BR (2003) Industrial ecology, 2nd edn. Prentice Hall, New York

Guinée J, Heijungs R (2017) Introduction to life cycle assessment. In: Bouchery Y, Corbett CJ, Fransoo J, Tan T (eds) Sustainable supply chains: a research-based textbook on operations and strategy. Springer, New York

Hatcher GD, Ijomah WL, Windmill JFC (2011) Design for remanufacture: a literature review and future research needs. J Cleaner Prod 19(17):2004–2014

Ilgin MA, Gupta SM (2010) Environmentally conscious manufacturing and product recovery (ECMPRO): a review of the state of the art. J Environ Manage 91(3):563–591

Karlsson R, Luttropp C (2006) EcoDesign: what's happening? An overview of the subject area of EcoDesign and of the papers in this special issue. J Cleaner Prod 14(15):1291–1298

Luttropp C (1998) Education in life cycle design. In: CIRP 5th international seminar on life cycle engineering. KTH, Stockholm

Luttropp C (1999), Eco-design in early product development, World Conference R99, Geneva

Luttropp C, Brohammer G (2014) EcoDesign roadmap. Studentlitteratur, Lund. ISBN 978-91-44-10100-2

Luttropp C, Lagerstedt J (2006) EcoDesign and the ten golden rules: generic advice for merging environmental aspects into product development. J Cleaner Prod 14(15–16):1396–408

Pugh S (1991) Total design. Addison-Wesley, Harlow. ISBN 0-201-41639-5

Ramani K, Ramanujan D, Bernstein WZ, Zhao F, Sutherland J, Handwerker C, Thurston D (2010) Integrated sustainable life cycle design: a review. J Mech Des 132(9):091004

Short T, Lee-Mortimer A, Luttropp C, Johansson G (2012) Manufacturing, sustainability, ecodesign and risk: lessons learned from a study of Swedish and English companies. J Cleaner Prod 37:342–352

Züst R (1996) Sustainable products and processes. In: Proceedings of CIRP 3rd Int. Sem. on Life Cycle Engineering, Zürich, Switzerland, ISBN3-85743-985-8

Part III
Business Models and Strategy in Sustainable Supply Chains

Chapter 14
Market Value Implications of Voluntary Corporate Environmental Initiatives (CEIs)

Brian Jacobs, Ravi Subramanian, Manpreet Hora, and Vinod Singhal

Firms engage in a variety of practices to manage their internal environmental performance as well as those of their supply chains, and they promote those efforts to concerned stakeholders (e.g., employees, suppliers, consumers, NGOs, and shareholders). Montabon et al. (2007) categorize such practices at the operational, tactical, and strategic levels. Examples of operational practices include recycling, waste reduction, returnable packaging, etc. At the tactical level, practices include applying environmental standards to supplier selection, participating in environmental awards programs, and employing life cycle analyses. Strategic practices include incorporating environmental impacts into the corporate mission and strategic planning process.

In addition to improving performance in the environmental dimension, environmental initiatives can result in increased sales, reduced costs, and mitigated risks, thereby improving the market value of a firm and/or its supply chain partners. However, the empirical evidence in the academic literature regarding the effects of environmental initiatives is mixed. In this chapter, we address the following questions:

- Do environmental initiatives of the firm improve its market value?
- Does the impact on market value depend upon the specific type of environmental initiative?
- Does the impact on market value depend upon the context or conditions surrounding the environmental initiative?

B. Jacobs (✉)
Michigan State University, East Lansing, MI, USA
e-mail: jacobsb@broad.msu.edu

R. Subramanian • M. Hora • V. Singhal
Georgia Tech, Atlanta, GA, USA
e-mail: ravi.subramanian@scheller.gatech.edu; manpreet.hora@scheller.gatech.edu;
vinod.singhal@scheller.gatech.edu

© Yann Bouchery, Charles J. Corbett, Jan C. Fransoo, and Tarkan Tan 2017
Y. Bouchery et al. (eds.), *Sustainable Supply Chains*, Springer Series in Supply
Chain Management 4, DOI 10.1007/978-3-319-29791-0_14

For managers, these are key questions to consider not only when deciding whether to undertake environmental initiatives, but also how to manage them and communicate their progress.

14.1   Relationship Between Environmental Initiatives and Market Value

The relationship between environmental initiatives and financial performance or market value is under debate in both the business and academic communities. For example, Skapinker (2008) highlighted the proactive sustainability initiatives of Unilever and Wal-Mart to frame the ongoing debate over whether such initiatives are merely window dressing. Even though Wal-Mart's energy conservation and recycling initiatives, and Unilever's forays into low-cost water purification and eco-friendly detergents, were well-received by the popular press, the question remains as to whether the market perceives the returns on such initiatives to be as attractive as returns on alternative investment opportunities. In other words, can a firm increase market value through its environmental initiatives? Proponents claim that direct economic benefits from environmental initiatives improve return on investment and market value. Benefits include energy, raw material, and abatement cost reductions, as well as intangible advantages of improved consumer perception, community relations, employee morale, and access to new markets. Skepticism remains, however, due to the perceived high costs of improving environmental performance and the uncertain and longer-term payoffs from such efforts (Engardio et al. 2007).

Academics have studied the relationship between environmental performance and financial performance, both theoretically (Walley and Whitehead 1994; Hart 1995; Porter and van der Linde 1995) and empirically (Ullman 1985; King and Lenox 2002; Margolis and Walsh 2003). Friedman (1970) argued that any environmental expenses beyond those required for regulatory compliance were not in the best interest of shareholders and would result in degradation of firm performance and value. However, Barnett and Salomon (2006, 2012) suggested that good corporate social performance, of which environmental performance is a subset, attracted resources to the firm, including better quality employees and expanded market opportunities. Also, since proactive approaches to environmental performance require greater intangible skills (e.g., cross-disciplinary activity and problem solving) than do reactive approaches, related efforts created more valuable resources and could be a source of competitive advantage (Hart 1995; Russo and Fouts 1997). In contrast, Walley and Whitehead (1994) proposed that instances where environmental initiatives can improve firm performance were rare.

Although the dominant view today is that good environmental performance results in improved financial performance and market value, empirical results have been inconclusive and even conflicting, which highlights the complex nature of the link between environmental and financial performance (Corbett and Klassen 2006).

Related empirical studies that use secondary data are of three types: portfolio studies, regression studies, and event studies (King and Lenox 2001; Guenster et al. 2006). Portfolio studies determine whether the return on a portfolio of firms with comparatively better environmental performance outperforms the market. Regression analyses determine the long-term relationships between environmental performance and accounting-based measures of firm performance. These two types of studies require careful matching of the firms under study with control firms to estimate any departures from "normal" financial performance during the study period. Due to the relatively long time periods over which such studies are conducted, they are sensitive to the host of other possible explanatory factors of firm performance.

Event studies estimate market value impacts of firms using announcements of environmental events. A statistically significant market reaction to announcements of environmental events would indicate a causal link. Event studies have been used in the literature to determine the impacts of both positive and negative environmental events, e.g., product and process-related initiatives (Gilley et al. 2000), environmental awards and crises (Klassen and McLaughlin 1996), and lawsuits (Karpoff et al. 2005). Klassen and McLaughlin (1996) documented the market reaction to independent, third-party awards for environmental performance. Using a sample of 140 announcements during the period 1986–1991, they found that environmental awards were associated with a statistically significant average market reaction of 0.63 %. Gilley et al. (2000) studied the market reaction to environmental activities that improve processes and products. Based on a sample of 71 announcements from *The Wall Street Journal* during 1983–1996, they found that process-related announcements resulted in a statistically significant average market reaction of −0.45 %, but the market did not react significantly to product-related announcements.

We use the framework in Fig. 14.1 to consider the impact of environmental initiatives on financial performance and market value. Researchers have proposed different mechanisms by which environmental initiatives influence revenue gains and cost reductions. An examination of these mechanisms illustrates how environmental initiatives can impact market value.

14.1.1   Revenue Effects

Revenue growth can be achieved either through gains in existing markets or access to new markets. Klassen and McLaughlin (1996) proposed that gains in existing markets could be realized through the reputational benefits of positive environmental performance. They argued that demonstration of reduced environmental impacts of products and processes and the establishment of an environmental management system (EMS) improved brand reputation. Dowell et al. (2000) also noted that the development and maintenance of stringent environmental management standards could have positive reputational effects. Corbett and Muthulingam (2007) proposed that a primary reason for firms to pursue Leadership in Energy

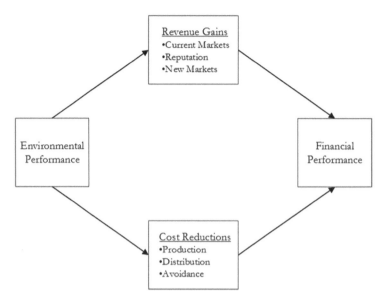

Fig. 14.1 Conceptual model linking environmental performance and financial performance

and Environmental Design (LEED) certification for building construction was to signal environmental concern to regulators, employees, and the public. Brand recognition and corporate reputation can also be enhanced through "strategic philanthropy" to support environmental causes (Seifert et al. 2003). Similarly, other environmentally conscious initiatives, such as alternative energy purchases or investments to reduce emissions below regulatory requirements, can signal a firm's concern for the environment and can have a positive impact on corporate reputation. For example, Cummins Inc. received a high ranking in the inaugural Newsweek "green" survey due to its GHG reduction efforts (*Business Wire*, 2009). Khanna and Damon (1999) found that desire for public recognition was a significant motivator for firms to voluntarily join the EPA Industrial Toxics Project aimed at reducing hazardous chemical emissions. Improved recognition and reputation could potentially lead to increased sales. In support, McGuire et al. (1988) demonstrated that sales growth was positively and significantly related to corporate reputations for corporate social performance.

Improved environmental performance can also provide access to new markets. Evolving environmentally conscious markets with their increasing desire for eco-friendly products can lead to new sales opportunities (Porter and van der Linde 1995). Examples range from high-fashion clothing produced with organic materials (Binkley 2007), to hybrid vehicles and data centers that consume less energy (Bulkeley 2007). US federal agencies, with $350 billion in annual purchases, are mandated to consider environmental criteria in their purchasing decisions (EPA 2008).

14.1.2   Cost Effects

In addition to its effects on revenues, environmental initiatives can impact costs in a variety of ways. Environmental practices reduce the amount of waste, the consumption of various production inputs including energy and materials (Rothenberg et al. 2001; Sroufe 2003), and the number of components in products (Ashley 1993). Given that emissions could represent inefficiencies and waste of material or energy, their reduction can also save input material and energy costs (Porter and van der Linde 1995). For example, Union Pacific's 15 % reduction in diesel emissions from 2000 to 2005 at their Davis, California, rail yard was achieved by reducing fuel usage (*PR Newswire*, 2005). From a supply chain perspective, both inbound and outbound logistics benefit from reduced product weights and packaging (Rao and Holt 2005). Dowell et al. (2000) note that stringent environmental standards can lower the cost to develop, maintain, and enforce policies and procedures, thus allowing easy transfer of accrued knowledge and increasing employee morale and productivity. Similarly, von Paumgartten (2003) argues that LEED-certified buildings can improve worker productivity and retention. Of course, not all environmental improvements are cost-saving. If substitute input materials are more expensive, costs would increase. As evidence, Kroes et al. (2012) find that sulfur dioxide emission reductions in utilities result in decreased financial performance due to the use of lower-sulfur but higher-cost coal. Further, if pollution prevention methods have been exhausted and abatement must additionally be employed, costs will likely increase.

Pollution prevention may not only reduce disposal and mitigation costs, but may also avoid the cost of installing and operating pollution control devices (Hart 1995; Hart and Ahuja 1996). Such pollution control devices can be costly, as evidenced by Reliant Energy's $50 million investment to reduce mercury emissions at its Pennsylvania coal-fired power plants (*Business Wire*, 2008). Other cost avoidance benefits of effective environmental management include mitigation of risks of losses from crises or regulation (Reinhardt 1999) and preventing expenses associated with lawsuits and legal settlements (Karpoff et al. 2005). Risks of adverse events can be decreased either by lowering the probability of occurrence, lessening the cost impact of an event, or shifting responsibility to another party, usually via insurance. By reducing or eliminating emissions, firms reduce the probability of environmental crises such as spills, leaks, or contamination. As an example, after suffering several expensive settlements and fines, DuPont pledged to eliminate the use of perfluorooctanoic acid (*Dow Jones News Service*, 2007).

14.1.3   Competitive Effects

Researchers argue that firm resources employed to achieve environmental initiatives exhibit value, rarity, inimitability, or non-substitutability, the so-called "VRIN" characteristics of the Resource Based View (RBV) outlined by Barney (1991). As such, environmental initiatives can potentially create competitive advantage.

Researchers have often attributed imperfect imitability to resources required for improved environmental performance (e.g., Hart 1995; Russo and Fouts 1997). Environmental initiatives resemble Total Quality Management (TQM) efforts in that they are often accomplished via people-intensive, continuous improvement processes. These resources are causally ambiguous and consistent with inimitability. Russo and Fouts (1997) argued that the culture and organization required for environmental performance were also socially complex. New processes or technologies often required for initiatives either might not be available to other firms due to their proprietary nature, or they might require special skills to effectively implement. A firm's announcement of an environmental initiative could be perceived as evidence that it possesses such valuable resources, helping it outperform its competition.

14.2 Empirical Approach to Test the Relationship Between Environmental Initiatives and Market Value

We employed event study methodology to estimate the market value impacts to announcements of environmental initiatives. This methodology offers an approach to estimate stock market returns associated with specific events, while controlling for market-wide influences on stock prices (see Brown and Warner 1985, for a review of this methodology). The "adjusted" or "abnormal" returns provide an estimate of the percent change in stock price associated with an event. In an efficient market, the stock market reaction immediately reflects the effects of any new information, including the announcement of an environmental initiative, on both current and future financial performance. Thus, an estimate of financial performance impact can be obtained from changes in market value (stock prices) over a relatively short interval of time.

14.2.1 Data and Categorization of Environmental Practices

To develop a comprehensive list of environmental practices commonly employed in business, we searched the business press for announcements related to Corporate environmental initiatives (CEIs) and empirically determined the most frequently occurring types. To generate our sample, we used a preliminary set of keywords to collect a small set of announcements concerning environmental practices from different publications. We read these announcements to identify additional phrases and words that are commonly used in announcements of environmental initiatives. We then used those keywords to search the headlines and lead paragraphs of announcements in the three major business wire services, the ten most widely circulated US daily newspapers, and the leading European business daily during the period 2004–2006. We preserved all announcements that met the search criteria in these publications and read the full text of each announcement. We excluded announcements that were very minor in nature or duplicates of the same activity.

Our final sample comprised 780 announcements spanning 340 unique firms. The sample had variation in firm characteristics, but was generally weighted toward larger firms. The sample included firms from 63 unique three-digit NAICS codes, thus representing a wide range of industries.

The first obvious categorization was to separate out the self-reported corporate efforts to avoid, mitigate, or offset the environmental impacts of the firm's products, services, or processes. We refer to such announcements as Corporate environmental initiatives (CEIs) (CEIs). The remaining second category is announcements about recognition granted by third parties specifically for environmental performance. We refer to such announcements as Environmental Awards and Certifications (EACs).

14.2.2 Corporate Environmental Initiatives (CEIs): Subcategories

Considering our CEI sample more deeply, we identified the following seven subcategories based on announcement content:

- *Environmental Business Strategies*: Acquisitions of environmental-friendly capabilities, joint ventures or alliances, and new corporate environmental policies or standards.
- *Environmental Philanthropy*: Substantial gifts for environmental causes, such as conservation efforts; the majority of such announcements are cash gifts although some are in kind.
- *Voluntary Emission Reductions*: Pledges, investments, or achievements related to reducing emissions levels beyond those required by regulation.
- *Eco-Friendly Products*: Introductions of eco-friendly products, environmental enhancements to existing products, or the incorporation of future regulatory requirements into existing products.
- *Renewable Energy*: Supply or purchase of power from alternative energy sources.
- *Recycling*: Recycling of post-consumer waste and recycling to reduce raw material consumption.
- *Miscellaneous*: All remaining CEI announcements, including joining environmental groups or councils, engaging in energy conservation efforts, and developing eco-friendly technologies.

14.2.3 Environmental Awards and Certifications: Subcategories

We separated our EAC announcements into two certification subcategories, namely, ISO 14001 and LEED, and three award subcategories, namely, federal, state or local government, and non-government. The awards mentioned in EAC announcements

Table 14.1 Examples of press announcements

Panel A: Examples of CEI Announcements
"Caterpillar Sets Aggressive Greenhouse Gas Reduction Target, Goal is Part of EPA's Climate Leaders program", PR Newswire (US), 18 January 2005. Caterpillar pledged to reduce its greenhouse gas emissions by 20 % from 2002 levels, by 2010
"Liz Claiborne Inc. Adopts prAna Natural Power Initiative", PR Newswire (US), 3 November 2005. Liz Claiborne Inc. announced that it would purchase only wind power for its New Jersey headquarters
"Abitibi-Consolidated Launches its largest Recycling Expansion; Paper Retriever begins collection in seven additional US markets", PR Newswire (US), 15 November 2005. Abitibi announced an expansion of its paper recycling program from 16 to 23 US cities
Panel B: Examples of EAC Announcements
"Smithfield Achieves International 'Gold Standard' for its Environmental Management Practices", PR Newswire (US), 27 April 2005. Smithfield attained ISO 14001 certification for the EMS used at its US-based hog production and processing facilities
"Corning's Wilmington, N.C., Optical Fiber Manufacturing Facility To Be Recognized as an Environmental Steward", Business Wire, 2 March 2005. A Corning plant was recognized as an "Environmental Steward" by the North Carolina Department of Environment and Natural Resources for its environmental performance

are specifically those given to recognize environmental performance, including pollution prevention, energy conservation, and habitat conservation. Table 14.1 presents some examples of CEI and EAC announcements.

14.2.4 *Relevance to Operations and Supply Chain Management*

Our analyses of the text of CEI and EAC announcements clearly highlighted the operations and supply chain issues involved in implementing environmental initiatives and improving environmental performance. Using words from the text of the announcements, we recorded phrases representative of the issues being faced. We grouped these issues into 13 operations and supply chain-related categories; we note that an announcement may have multiple issues falling into different categories. Table 14.2 lists the operations and supply chain-related categories. Supply chain-related categories include forward and reverse logistics, designing incentives and contracts for supply chain alignment, and managing supply and demand. The table also indicates the number of CEI and EAC announcements that fall into a particular issue category.

14.3 Findings

For the full sample of 417 CEI announcements, we examined the abnormal stock market returns for the day preceding the announcement, the day of the announcement, and the 2 days combined. The results indicated that the market reaction to

Table 14.2 Operations and supply chain-related issues for CEIs and EACs

Category	Number of announcements			Description
	CEIs	EACs	Total	
Implementing Environmental Management Systems and Practices	52	139	191	Developing and Implementing Environmental Management Systems (including ISO 14001), Practices, and Policies
Product Design and Development	101	57	158	Product or Service Design and Development (Improvements, Testing, and Commercialization)
R&D and Technology Management	92	58	150	R&D and Technology Assessment, Adoption, Development, and Transfer
Improving Resource Efficiency	63	83	146	Reduction, Reuse, and Recycling of Materials or Energy through Improvements in Products, Processes, or Practices
Facilities Management	53	87	140	Facilities Location, Design, and Management
Process Design and Management	57	64	121	Process Design, Improvement, and Testing; Process Metrics and Process Control
Forward and Reverse Logistics and Transportation	90	45	135	Materials Handling, Transportation, and Logistics; Reverse Logistics Network Design and Management
Pollution Prevention and Control	63	44	107	Pollution Prevention, Control, and Offsetting
Improving Operational Performance	27	46	73	Improving Cost, Efficiency, Productivity, Quality, Delivery, and Reliability
Designing Incentives and Contracts	51	8	59	Incentive Alignment and Design (across Employees, Suppliers, and Customers); Contracts and Vertical Integration
Input Choice	40	10	50	Input Choice or Mix (based on Availability, Cost, Regulatory Incentives, Risk, and Constraints)
Managing Supply and Demand	37	11	48	Increasing or Sustaining Supply, Reducing Demand, Managing Capacity (Utilization, Expansion, and Shut-Downs)
Operations Financing and Project Management	26	13	39	Financing Operations, Projects, and Suppliers; Project Management

CEI announcements is marginally positive but insignificant. Similarly, for the full sample of 363 EAC announcements, the evidence suggested that the market does not react significantly to the entire category of EAC announcements. We also analyzed the post-announcement abnormal returns of our sample firms to determine whether a significant market reaction occurred subsequent to our announcement date. We estimated abnormal returns over a 3-month period after the announcement.

Again, the results indicate that the market reaction to announcements of environmental initiatives is marginally positive but insignificant.

It appears that, as a broad and general category, environmental initiatives do not necessarily translate into improved market performance. While the lack of a significantly positive result might be disappointing to environmental advocates, it is worth noting that the result is not significantly negative. In other words, decisions to undertake environmental initiatives do not harm market value as some naysayers may claim. Further, it is plausible that the market may not perceive all types of environmental initiatives to be equally value creating. The market might react positively, or not at all, depending on the initiative type. By aggregating environmental initiatives of different types, the average reaction could well be insignificant. Accordingly, we next examined the relationship between specific types of environmental initiatives and market performance.

14.3.1 Relationships Between Specific CEI Types and Market Value

We subdivided our CEI and EAC samples into the specific initiative types outlined in Sects. 14.2.2 and 14.2.3. We provide results for each of the seven CEI types in Table 14.3 Panel A. For the environmental business strategies type, the mean abnormal return was positive and statistically significant. However, the median and percent positive abnormal returns were insignificant. Taken together, the evidence suggests that the market did not significantly react to environmental business strategy announcements.

Our review of the literature suggests that the empirical evidence on the impact of corporate philanthropy on financial performance is mixed. Orlitzky et al. (2003) found that corporate philanthropy had a positive relationship with accounting-based measures of financial performance, while Wang et al. (2008) found that financial performance and market value were increasing in only low-to-moderate levels of philanthropy. In contrast, Griffin and Mahon (1997), Berman et al. (1999), and Seifert et al. (2004) did not find a significant relationship between the two. In our analyses, we found that the mean, median, and percent positive abnormal returns for environmental philanthropy were all positive and statistically significant. The positive market reaction to environmental philanthropy could be because such actions involve modest investments, but generate significant customer goodwill and enhance corporate reputation, thus contributing to future profitability.

With regard to announcements of voluntary emission reductions, we found that the mean, median, and percent positive abnormal returns were all *negative* and statistically significant. In other words, announcements of voluntary emission reductions were viewed negatively by the market. This finding has some support in the literature. In addition to the theoretical arguments of Friedman (1970) discussed earlier, Hart and Ahuja (1996) suggested that while initial emission reductions

Table 14.3 Stock market abnormal returns for CEI and EAC types for the day preceding and the day of the announcement

	N	Mean abnormal return (%)	t Statistic	Median abnormal return (%)	Wilcoxon signed-rank Z	% Positive	Generalized sign Z
Panel A: CEI type results							
Environmental Business Strategies	53	0.63	2.77***	−0.01	0.36	49.10	0.44
Environmental Philanthropy	30	0.46	1.41*	0.36	1.74**	66.70	2.07**
Voluntary Emission Reductions	39	−0.95	−2.96***	−0.72	−2.63***	30.80	−2.17**
Eco-Friendly Products	60	0.01	0.04	0.07	0.05	5.17	0.48
Renewable Energy	40	0.13	0.28	0.07	0.86	55.00	0.94
Recycling	64	0.33	1.14	0.05	0.46	51.60	0.54
Miscellaneous	131	0.05	0.13	0.07	0.09	52.70	1.02
Panel A: EAC type results							
ISO 14001 Certifications	50	0.35	0.84	0.77	1.56*	60.00	1.80**
LEED Certifications	21	0.02	0.62	0.39	0.84	61.90	1.26
Federal Awards	96	−0.03	−0.07	−0.11	−0.17	44.80	−0.60
State/Local Government Awards	65	−0.21	−0.59	−0.10	−0.66	49.20	0.11
Non-Government Awards	131	−0.26	−1.51*	−0.21	−1.59*	39.70	−1.97**

Note: All tests are one-tailed: *p ≤ 0.10; **p ≤ 0.05; ***p ≤ 0.01

might improve financial performance, subsequent reductions were more likely to result from costly pollution control. Fisher-Vanden and Thorburn (2011) found that membership in the EPA Climate Leaders program yielded a negative abnormal return of −0.90 %; the negative abnormal returns were even stronger when specific pledges are made for greenhouse gas reductions. The Climate Leaders program was referred to in 12 of the 39 announcements in our voluntary emissions reductions subcategory; the remainder of the announcements within the subcategory related to other air emissions or hazardous waste reductions. To further explore this negative market reaction, we conducted additional analyses as described in Sect. 14.3.4.

The market reactions for the four remaining CEI subcategories—eco-friendly products, renewable energy, recycling, and miscellaneous—were statistically insignificant.

14.3.2 Relationships Between Specific EAC Types and Market Value

As seen from the results for each of the five EAC types in Table 14.3 Panel B, the market reaction was moderately positive to announcements of ISO 14001 certifications. The median and percent positive abnormal returns were significantly positive. The literature offers some support for the positive impact of ISO 14001 in particular and EMSs in general on firm performance, using survey data (Delmas 2001; Melnyk et al. 2003).

Although our three measures of market reaction to LEED certifications were all positive, they were statistically insignificant. Thus, despite the benefits of LEED certification cited in the literature (e.g., von Paumgartten 2003; Corbett and Muthulingam 2007), the market reaction was insignificant. We conjecture that since LEED certifications are awarded for individual buildings, their relatively narrow scope may contribute to the lack of market reaction, particularly when compared with ISO 14001 certifications that typically span different geographic locations or even the entire firm.

While the average market reactions for both federal and state/local government awards were statistically insignificant, the market reacted somewhat negatively to non-government awards. The mean, median, and percent positive abnormal returns were all significantly negative. We found no substantive differences in the types of behavior recognized by government versus non-government awards. Our findings of negative abnormal returns for non-government awards compared to government awards seem consistent with findings in the literature that less prestigious and potentially less objective awards were valued less positively (Klassen and McLaughlin 1996; Hendricks and Singhal 1996). An online search for award criteria provided information for federal awards, but not for non-government awards, suggesting that non-government award criteria are perhaps less transparent and less formal. The negative market reaction could be because the market may perceive the efforts associated with such awards as unnecessary relative to the value they provide.

14.3.3   Managerial Implications of Findings

Our findings have a number of interesting managerial implications. First, the market was selective in reacting to types of environmental initiatives. Of the seven CEI types considered in our analyses, the stock market reaction was largely insignificant for the following four categories: environmental business strategies, eco-friendly products, renewable energy, and recycling. The evidence suggests that while the majority of CEI types were value-neutral, there were certain types for which the market reaction was positive and certain types for which it was negative, at least in the short term. Our results for CEIs are important as managers often face pressures from various stakeholders to give consideration for environmental issues. Managers responding to such pressures can benefit from empirical evidence of what types of CEIs improve or at least do not negatively impact market value.

Second, environmental philanthropy was viewed positively by the market. Such philanthropy can generate positive publicity and goodwill among various stakeholders and can also create value through more loyal customers and highly motivated employees. Referring to Fig. 14.1, environmental philanthropy is likely to improve financial performance via the revenue gains from enhanced reputation. Given that the median value of philanthropic contributions by firms in our sample is $2.0 million, the positive market reaction to environmental philanthropy suggests that such initiatives can yield high returns.

Third, the market reacted negatively to voluntary emission reductions. These results are consistent with earlier results that membership in the EPA Climate Leaders program was associated with negative market reaction (Fisher-Vanden and Thorburn 2011). Despite the benefit in terms of mitigating future regulatory risks or positively impacting reputation, the market remains concerned about announcements of voluntary emissions reductions. Referring to Fig. 14.1, it is possible that the market negatively values voluntary efforts at reducing emissions because of the visibility of direct, assignable costs, while the revenue impacts of such efforts are uncertain. Therefore, announcements of voluntary emissions reductions efforts should be accompanied by formal justifications as to why these efforts are being conducted (for example, preparing for future legislation, competitive lobbying, or anticipated carbon trading) and what the expected value from these efforts is likely to be. We discuss this finding further in Sect. 14.3.4.

Fourth, with respect to EACs, we found that ISO 14001 certifications were associated with positive market reaction. This is validation of the value in achieving a level of environmental commitment that is based on a widely recognized and accepted international standard, and more so when the standard is sometimes considered as a prerequisite for trade. Thus, our results suggest that managers could potentially use the ISO 14001 framework for developing an EMS.

Finally, the market reaction to environmental awards in our study is different than in Klassen and McLaughlin (1996), who found significant and positive market reaction. Given that our sample is not an exact replication of Klassen and McLaughlin (1996), the difference in results could be due to sampling variances and/or the different time periods. Our evidence indicates that LEED certifications and government awards are value-neutral, but non-governmental awards have a negative market reaction. While awards and certifications can serve as catalysts for organizational change and innovative business practices, a key implication for managers seeking to influence shareholder value through awards and certifications is to be judicious in pursuing them.

In summary, although we find that the market does not react to announcements in the broad, aggregate categories of CEIs and EACs, we do find significant market reactions for certain initiative types. Thus, it is important for managers to appropriately implement and communicate environmental strategies, as the effects on shareholder value can vary by type. Together with the communication of a sound, economic rationale based on cost reductions, revenue gains, or reputational benefits, certain environmental initiative types can positively impact shareholder value.

14.3.4 Contingencies Affecting the Relationship Between Environmental Initiatives and Market Value

In this section, we consider whether the contexts or conditions surrounding the environmental initiative impacted the corresponding changes in market value. As previously discussed, the literature reports mixed impacts of environmental initiatives on financial performance and market value. The mixed empirical evidence motivates us to examine specific contingency factors that might be causing this ambiguity.

14.3.4.1 Achievements Versus Intents

Since self-disclosed initiatives may not necessarily serve as measures of actual environmental performance, we considered whether the market reacts differently to environmental initiatives that are "achievements" as opposed to "intents". Since announcements of environmental initiatives are signals of firms' environmental concerns, we consider their impact through the lens of signaling theory. A basic tenet is that signal cost is an important influence on efficacy; costly signals decrease the likelihood of false signaling (Connelly et al. 2011). Since announcements of achievement are actual realizations rather than plans, they are a higher cost signal and, hence, more likely to be true and of greater reputational benefit than announcements of intent. Hart and Ahuja (1996), King and Lenox (2001, 2002), and

Matsumara et al. (2014), among others, use actual emissions data (i.e., achievements) to demonstrate mostly positive effects of emissions reduction on financial performance and market value. However, Fisher-Vanden and Thorburn (2011) examine pledges made (i.e., intents) when joining EPA Climate Leaders or the Coalition for Environmentally Responsible Economies (CERES) and find a negative stock market reaction.

We note that EACs are recognitions of achievement by definition. Hence, the comparison between achievements and intents is not pertinent to EACs. Accordingly, we only considered our CEI sample. We read the text of each CEI announcement to separate out achievements of environmental performance from intents. For example, the launch of an eco-friendly product is an achievement, whereas a plan to design or produce such a product is an intent. We compared the mean and median abnormal stock market returns for achievements and intents. The results showed a moderately significant and positive market reaction to achievements, but the reaction to intents was insignificant. Since achievements may more clearly signal either realized or future cost reductions and/or revenue gains as compared to intents, a greater focus in outward communications on achievements as opposed to intents may be warranted.

As we saw in Sects. 14.3 and 14.4, the market value impacts of CEIs can vary substantially by specific initiative type. Accordingly, we consider one specific type of CEI, voluntary emission reductions, to further examine the effects of achievements versus intents. Recall that overall market reaction to voluntary emission reductions was significantly negative. Thus, if achievements are indeed clearer signals, an achievement of voluntary emission reduction should have a greater *negative* impact than an intent to reduce emissions. Using the same process described in Sect. 14.1, we greatly expanded the sample of voluntary emission reduction announcements by collecting data over a 20-year period (1990–2009). The resulting sample comprised 450 announcements. As we found in our initial analysis (see Table 14.3), our analysis of the expanded sample indicated that announcements were again valued negatively. However, and as predicted by signaling theory, announcements of intent were valued more positively than announcements of achievement.

14.3.4.2   Time Dependence

Given that researchers using data from the 1980s and 1990s (e.g., Hart and Ahuja 1996; King and Lenox 2002) found mostly positive effects of environmental performance on accounting-based measures of financial performance, and that researchers using data from the 2000s (e.g., Jacobs et al. 2010; Fisher-Vanden and Thorburn 2011) found more mixed results, we were prompted to consider whether the magnitude and/or direction of financial performance effects of environmental initiatives have changed over time, contributing to the equivocal findings in the literature. To do so, we used the 20-year sample of voluntary emission reduction announcements described above.

Hart (1995) noted that during initial stages of emissions reduction, much "low hanging fruit"—emissions that can be reduced easily and inexpensively—are generally available but further reductions are subject to diminishing returns. Given that firms have been reducing toxic emissions steadily since the initial release of TRI data in 1986 and continuing through the 2000s (EPA 2011), much of the low hanging fruit has probably already been harvested. More recent environmental initiatives are likely accomplished at increased marginal costs since advanced stages of emissions reduction often require more costly control or abatement techniques rather than prevention. In support, the EPA (2008, p. 5) found that the greatest barrier to voluntary emission reductions was "the perceived cost of emission reduction."

In addition to fewer cost opportunities to exploit, emission reduction might have also changed in value as a risk management strategy. If the regulatory environment for emissions is toughening, the expectation of future liabilities associated with emissions taxes, cap and trade systems, and/or stringent enforcement should increase along with the risk management value of reducing emissions. However, as per the World Economic Forum, the stringency of US environmental regulations trended downward during the 2001–2008 period (Wijen and van Tulder 2011). Marcus et al. (2011) argued that regulatory uncertainty continues to grow, increasing difficulties in appropriate corporate planning. Such continued regulatory ambivalence in the US with respect to emissions has likely reduced the risk management value of emission reduction.

Using abnormal stock market reactions to announcements of voluntary emission reductions as our dependent variable, we employed stepwise WLS regressions to assess the effects of time. The statistical tests demonstrate that stock market reaction to voluntary emission reduction is negatively associated with time (see Fig. 14.2). As depicted in Fig. 14.2, this effect applies similarly to GHG and non-GHG emissions, and it persists despite controlling for energy prices and other factors.

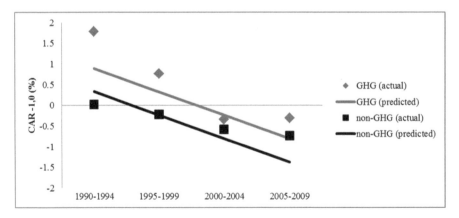

Fig. 14.2 Stock market reaction to voluntary emission reduction of GHG emissions and non-GHG emissions from 1990 through 2009; lines represent predictions of WLS regression model and markers represent actual mean cumulative abnormal returns aggregated over 5-year periods

This evidence is important to both researchers and managers as it highlights the impacts of time-dependent characteristics of emissions reduction in particular.

In this study, we did not determine the precise time-related factors driving the downward trend in shareholder value effects of firms announcing emission reductions. As discussed above, the potential factors include diminishing availability of easily reduced emissions (low hanging fruit), continued regulatory ambiguity in the US, and diffusion of continuous improvement capabilities, among others. Given the number of economic, environmental, and social factors that trend with time, the specific causes of the negative time trend in abnormal returns are indeterminate and require further study.

We note that the results presented here are valid only for the sample frame studied and should not be extrapolated into the future. Just as economic, environmental, and social conditions changed 1980–2009, they will continue to change, impacting the market value impacts of emissions reductions (and other environmental initiatives) to firms. For example, regulatory remedies such as limits or taxes on emissions, or market-based incentives such as cap-and-trade programs, could substantially change the value proposition of environmental initiatives. Similarly, increasing social demand for improved environmental performance could lead to increased brand equity and revenues for environmentally conscious firms. Indeed, as seen in Fig. 14.2, the stock market reaction, although trending downward, appears to be leveling out in recent years.

14.4 Future Research

There exist several avenues for fruitful future research. First, the very nature and definition of environmental initiatives is continually evolving. The emergence of new technologies, scientific discoveries, societal concerns, and the ever-changing state of our natural environment all influence the adoption, growth, or diminishment of specific environmental types. The core sample used in our analyses was collected during 2004–2006. While all samples are time-limited by definition, this can be especially problematic in the fast-changing world of sustainability. As illustrated by the example of emission reductions announced over a 20-year period that we discussed above, the market value impacts of those environmental initiatives are dynamic and time-sensitive. Statistical evidence across time will inform managers as to the changing nature of the market's assessment of environmental efforts.

Second, many environmental initiatives impact not only the focal firm, but also its supply chain partners. For example, incorporating environmental performance criteria in supplier selection might boost both environmental and financial performance for the entire supply chain. Such impacts are challenging to accurately define and measure across multiple firms, but are grounds for interesting future research.

Third, in this chapter we employed the stock market reaction as a proxy for the financial performance impacts of environmental initiatives. Although widely employed and well-established in the academic literature, the effectiveness of this proxy is dependent on the generally accepted notion of market efficiency. Accounting-based measures of financial performance such as ROA, ROE, or sales growth can yield additional information on the specific mechanisms by which environmental initiatives impact financial performance and are not dependent on market efficiency.

Fourth, beyond the value captured in the stock market reaction, it is plausible that environmental initiatives may create value in other, intangible ways including increased customer loyalty (measured as customer satisfaction, retention rate, or word-of-mouth publicity), higher employee satisfaction, reputation within the community, and long-term survivability, which are perhaps not fully reflected in the market's reaction to announcements. Consideration of the impacts of environmental initiatives using a triple-bottom-line perspective could result in greater assigned value to environmental initiatives and is another interesting direction for future research.

In summary, this chapter examines the relationships between firm-level environmental initiatives and market value. We also outline the implications of our results for researchers and managers and suggest avenues for future research. Research that examines the effects, nuances, and limitations of firms' environmental initiatives will continue to be pertinent as society's demands on the natural environment continue to grow.

Acknowledgment The authors wish to acknowledge the publishers of our earlier works for their permission to partially replicate some of the information in this chapter. The two works that we draw upon are Jacobs et al. (2010) and Jacobs (2014).

References

Ashley S (1993) Designing for the environment. Mech Eng 115(3):52–56

Barnett ML, Salomon RM (2006) Beyond dichotomy: the curvilinear relationship between social responsibility and financial performance. Strat Manage J 27(11):1101–1122

Barnett ML, Salomon RM (2012) Does it pay to be really good? Addressing the shape of the relationship between social and financial performance. Strat Manage J 33(11):1304–1320

Barney J (1991) Firm resources and sustained competitive advantage. J Manage 17(1):99–120

Berman SL, Wicks AC, Kotha S, Jones TM (1999) Does stakeholder orientation matter? The relationship between stakeholder management models and firm financial performance. Acad Manage J 42(5):488–506

Binkley C (2007) Green fashion: beyond T-shirts. Wall Street J D8

Brown SJ, Warner JB (1985) Using daily stock returns: the case of event studies. J Financ Econ 14(1):3–31

Bulkeley WM (2007) IBM to launch push for green—new business to address cutting energy thirst of computer centers. Wall Street J B4

Business Wire (2008) Reliant energy invests in emission controls for Pennsylvania generating plants

Business Wire (2009) Cummins recognized for environmental practices by Newsweek magazine

Connelly BL, Certo ST, Ireland RD, Reutzel CR (2011) Signaling theory: a review and assessment. J Manage 37(1):39–67

Corbett CJ, Klassen RD (2006) Extending the horizons: environmental excellence as key to improving operations. Manuf Serv Oper Manage 8(1):5–22

Corbett CJ, Muthulingam S (2007) Adoption of voluntary environmental standards: the role of signaling and intrinsic benefits in the diffusion of the LEED green building standards. UCLA Working Paper, California

Delmas M (2001) Stakeholders and competitive advantage: the case of ISO 14001. Prod Oper Manage 10(3):343–358

Dow Jones News Service (2007) DuPont sets goal of eliminating use of teflon chemical

Dowell GA, Hart SL, Yeung B (2000) Do corporate global environmental standards create or destroy market value? Manage Sci 46(8):1059–1074

Engardio P, Capell K, Carey J, Hall K (2007) Beyond the green corporation. Bus Week 50

EPA (2008) Environmentally preferable purchasing. http://www.epa.gov/epp/index.htm. Accessed 18 Dec 2008

EPA (2011) 2010 TRI national analysis overview. http://www.epa.gov/tri/tridata/tri10/nationalanalysis/overview. Accessed 15 July 2012

Fisher-Vanden K, Thorburn KS (2011) Voluntary corporate environmental initiatives and shareholder wealth. J Environ Econ Manage 62(3):430–445

Friedman M (1970) The social responsibility of business is to increase profits. New York Times Magazine

Gilley KM, Worrell DL, Davidson WN, El-Jelly A (2000) Corporate environmental initiatives and anticipated firm performance. J Manage 26(6):1199–1216

Griffin JJ, Mahon JF (1997) The corporate social performance and corporate financial performance debate. Bus Soc 36(1):5–31

Guenster N, Derwall J, Bauer R, Koedijk K (2006) The economic value of corporate eco-efficiency. http://ssrn.com/abstract=675628

Hart SL (1995) A natural-resource-based view of the firm. Acad Manage Rev 20(4):986–1014

Hart SL, Ahuja G (1996) Does it pay to be green? An empirical examination of the relationship between emission reduction and firm performance. Bus Strat Environ 5(1):30–37

Hendricks KB, Singhal VR (1996) Quality awards and the market value of the firm: an empirical investigation. Manage Sci 42(3):415–436

Jacobs BW (2014) Shareholder value effects of voluntary emissions reduction. Prod Oper Manage 23(11):1859–1874

Jacobs BW, Singhal VR, Subramanian R (2010) An empirical investigation of environmental performance and the market value of the firm. J Oper Manage 28(5):430–441

Karpoff JM, Lott JR, Wehrly E (2005) The reputational penalties for environmental violations: empirical evidence. J Law Econ 48(2):653–675

Khanna M, Damon LA (1999) Voluntary 33/50 program: impact on toxic releases and economic performance of firms. J Environ Econ Manage 37(1):1–25

King AA, Lenox MJ (2001) Does it really pay to be green? An empirical study of firm environmental and financial performance. J Ind Ecol 5(1):105–116

King AA, Lenox MJ (2002) Exploring the locus of profitable pollution reduction. Manage Sci 48(2):289–299

Klassen RD, McLaughlin CP (1996) The impact of environmental management on firm performance. Manage Sci 42(8):1199–1214

Kroes J, Subramanian R, Subramanyam R (2012) Operational compliance levers, environmental performance, and firm performance under cap and trade regulation. Manuf Serv Oper Manage 14(2):186–201

Marcus A, Aragón-Correa JA, Pinske J (2011) Firms, regulatory uncertainty, and the natural environment. Calif Manage Rev 54(1):5–16

Margolis JD, Walsh JP (2003) Misery loves company: rethinking social initiatives by business. Adm Sci Q 48(2):268–305

Matsumara EM, Prakash R, Vera-Muñoz SC (2014) Firm-value effects of carbon emissions and carbon disclosures. Account Rev 89(2):695–724

McGuire JB, Sundgren A, Schneeweis T (1988) Corporate social responsibility and financial performance. Acad Manage J 31(4):854–872

Melnyk SA, Sroufe RP, Calantone R (2003) Assessing the impact of environmental management systems on corporate and environmental performance. J Oper Manage 21(3):329–351

Montabon F, Sroufe RP, Narasimhan R (2007) An examination of corporate reporting, environmental management practices, and firm performance. J Oper Manage 25(5):998–1014

PR Newswire (2005) Union Pacific announces emissions reduction program in cooperation with the California Air Resources Board

Orlitzky M, Schmidt FL, Rynes SL (2003) Corporate social and financial performance: a meta-analysis. Org Stud 24(3):403–441

Porter M, van der Linde C (1995) Green and competitive: ending the stalemate. Harv Bus Rev 73(5):120–134

Rao P, Holt D (2005) Do green supply chains lead to competitiveness and economic performance? Int J Oper Prod Manage 25(9):898–916

Reinhardt F (1999) Market failure and the environmental policies of firms. J Ind Ecol 3(1):9–21

Rothenberg S, Pil FK, Maxwell J (2001) Lean, green, and the quest for superior environmental performance. Prod Oper Manage 10(3):228–243

Russo MV, Fouts PA (1997) A resource-based perspective on corporate environmental performance and profitability. Acad Manage J 40(3):534–559

Seifert B, Morris SA, Bartkus BR (2003) Comparing big givers and small givers: financial correlates of corporate philanthropy. J Bus Ethics 45(3):195–211

Seifert B, Morris SA, Bartkus BR (2004) Having, giving, and getting: slack resources, corporate philanthropy, and firm financial performance. Bus Soc 43(2):135–161

Skapinker M (2008) Virtue's reward? Companies make the business case for ethical initiatives. Financial Times 8

Sroufe R (2003) Effects of environmental management systems on environmental management practices and operations. Prod Oper Manage 12(3):416–431

Ullman AE (1985) Data in search of a theory: a critical examination of the relationships among social performance, social disclosure, and economic performance of US firms. Acad Manage Rev 10(3):540–557

von Paumgartten P (2003) The business case for high-performance green buildings: sustainability and its financial impact. J Facil Manage 2(1):26–34

Walley N, Whitehead B (1994) It's not easy being green. Harv Bus Rev 72(3):46–52

Wang H, Choi J, Li J (2008) Too little or too much? Untangling the relationship between corporate philanthropy and firm financial performance. Org Sci 19(1):143–159

Wijen F, van Tulder R (2011) Integrating environmental and international strategies in a world of regulatory turbulence. Calif Manage Rev 53(4):23–46

Chapter 15
Business Implications of Sustainability Practices in Supply Chains

Mark Pagell and Zhaohui Wu

15.1 Introduction

This chapter uses a number of examples to detail how a series of path-dependent decisions underpins the strategic trajectory of today's leaders in sustainable supply chain management. A truly sustainable supply chain, could customers willing, operate forever (Pagell and Wu 2009). Such a chain would at a minimum create no harm and might even have positive or regenerative impacts on social and environmental systems while maintaining economic viability (Pagell and Shevchenko 2014). True sustainability is the end goal of SSCM, a goal which few, if any, supply chains, especially those with tangible flows, presently meet.

The examples presented in this chapter are then leaders when compared to the norms in their industry, but they are not truly sustainable. The first key question even these leaders need to answer is *what has to change in our supply chain to reach true sustainability*. This chapter offers insight, but the leaders of tomorrow will need to build on these examples and those in the rest of the book if they are to survive for multiple generations.

The awareness that today's leaders are far from the end goal of harm free production and distribution is one of two guiding assumptions for this chapter. The second assumption is that the decisions managers make are path-dependent. At its simplest path, dependency means that previous decisions create constraints for decisions made today (for more information see Pierson 2000). The assumption of path dependency indicates that the further a supply chain travels along a strategic path or trajectory, the more likely it is to stay on that trajectory because the costs of

M. Pagell (✉)
University College Dublin, Belfield, Dublin, Ireland
e-mail: mark.pagell@ucd.ie

Z. Wu
Oregon State University, Corvallis, OR 97331, USA
e-mail: zhaohui.wu@bus.oregonstate.edu

© Yann Bouchery, Charles J. Corbett, Jan C. Fransoo, and Tarkan Tan 2017
Y. Bouchery et al. (eds.), *Sustainable Supply Chains*, Springer Series in Supply
Chain Management 4, DOI 10.1007/978-3-319-29791-0_15

switching to a different trajectory become ever higher. For example, a supply chain that decides to outsource production has made path-dependent decision because it will be difficult, if not impossible, to bring production back in house in the future. Hence, the initial drivers and values that lead a supply chain to pursue sustainability also create future constraints (Wu and Pagell 2011) and limit future strategic options.

This path dependency also raises questions. For managers in supply chains that have already started to evolve and change to meet the needs of the future, the question becomes *how have previous decisions enhanced or limited our options*? For the managers of supply chains just starting on their path to sustainability, the question should be *how will the decisions we make today limit our options in the future*? To answer these questions, the chapter will cover what we know about how supply chains pursue sustainability, and then detail the three path-dependent trajectories that supply chains follow when addressing sustainability; the balanced trajectory, the focused trajectory, and the opportunity-first trajectory.

15.2 What is Known: *The How and Why of Sustainability*

Regardless of a supply chain's trajectory, managerial efforts to create a more sustainable supply chain typically support three main operational goals; increased efficiency, risk reduction, and innovation. Exemplar firms tend to try and achieve all of these goals, and the goals are not mutually exclusive. This section details each of these goals using examples.

One of the main goals of supply chain managers has always been to use resources efficiently to minimize the costs of providing goods and services. This mind-set has proven useful in some sustainability-related initiatives as well; especially initiatives that attempt to reduce the amount of environmental harm created by the supply chain. Environmental harm tends to come either from using a non-renewable resource or from pollutions that is created in the production, delivery, use, or disposal of the chain's goods and services. So when supply chain managers can reduce the amount of an input needed for production, they reduce the costs of production and the impact on the environment. Similarly, pollution is in essence wasted resources. For instance, when a firm sends material to the landfill it means it has bought materials that have not been used in production and may even pay a second time for them to be disposed of. Preventing or reducing pollution is often achieved by making more complete use of inputs or by changing inputs, again reducing waste and environmental impacts. This simultaneous achievement of reduced environmental harm and reduced costs is referred to as *eco-efficiency* (Sharma and Henriques 2005).

One of the more visible and successful eco-efficiency efforts is 3M's Pollution Prevention Pays program (3M 2014). This program is aimed at preventing pollution at the source, rather than paying to clean it up after it is created and was started in 1975. Since then the company estimates that they have eliminated nearly 4 billion pounds of pollution and saved nearly USD1.7 billion.

The second way supply chains address sustainability is via *risk reduction* or elimination. Many environmental and social impacts can be viewed as risks, for instance, the risk of an industrial accident harming the environment or workers and disrupting the supply chain. Similarly, many supply chains decisions are made to codify, understand, or reduce risk.

For instance, many firms have codes of conduct for their suppliers. These codes are a form of non-governmental regulation in that they set standards and rules as to what behaviours are unacceptable for suppliers, regardless of local laws. For example, many clothing and footwear supply chains have suffered because of customer boycotts due to the way suppliers treat the environment or their workers (USAS 2014). In response, organizations like Nike (2014) and Levis (2014) have created codes of conduct. In doing so, they are trying to mitigate the risks associated with unsustainable actions in the supply chain (see also Chap. 11 by van Weele and van Tubergen (2017) and Chap. 20 by Lee and Rammohan (2017)).

Finally, efforts to become truly sustainable require changing both products and processes. These changes are a form of *innovation* and innovation can also be a source of competitive advantage. For some firms, attempts to make the supply chain sustainable have positive spill over benefits in that the same innovations that reduce environmental and social harm also differentiate the chain from its competitors. For instance, the Broad Group (Broad 2014) has developed innovative products for cooling buildings that do not rely on electricity as well as a complete system for creating more sustainable buildings. The firm differentiates itself by having unique, more sustainable, products and services.

These three interrelated goals; eco-efficiency, risk reduction, and innovation are what supply chain managers pursue when making their chains more sustainable. In the next section, we detail how the decisions made to improve the chain in one or more of these areas, overtime, create unique path-dependent trajectories.

15.3 Findings and Practical Implications: *The Three Trajectories*

One of the guiding assumptions of this chapter is that it is the series of decisions managers make that determine the supply chain's sustainability trajectory. Every new process, decision to switch to less harmful materials, or redesign of products will not only have operational implications in terms of waste, risk, and innovation, but will also effect and be affected by the chain's strategic trajectory.

A supply chain's sustainability strategy can be examined from many perspectives. For instance, the Shared Value perspective (Porter and Kramer 2011) focuses on how goods and services are tailored to meet the needs of customers while reducing the harm from production and distribution. For example, when Pepsi works to reduce the amount of water used in creating food and beverages, especially in parts of the world where water is becoming scarce (Pepsi 2014), they are creating shared value by allowing customers to continue to enjoy their products while making sure

The balanced trajectory – The Collins Companies (http://www.collinsco.com) (*Source*: https://www.linkedin.com/company/the-collins-companies)

that water is available for more pressing needs. (Sodhi and Tang (2017), Chap. 21, discuss how the stakeholder resource-based view can help make the concept of "shared value" more tangible.)

The strategic perspective taken in this chapter is different, in that we are not focusing on any one decision, product, or process. Instead, the focus is on how sustainability was initially operationalized/introduced into the supply chain and how the series of decisions managers make will, overtime, determine how/if true sustainability would develop in that specific supply chain. The decisions managers make create a path-dependent trajectory that has implications for priorities and capabilities while also setting some limitations on future actions and outcomes.

There are three main trajectories or archetypes of sustainable supply chain management; opportunity-first, balanced, and focused. The trajectories are in essence the way that sustainability is woven into the strategy and culture of the focal firm and its supply chain.

In supply chains on a *balanced* trajectory, sustainable behaviour is the way of going about one's business day in and day out; and it positively and directly benefits the employees, suppliers, and local communities. As a result, environmental and social issues are highly integrated and equally important in these supply chains.

Strategically, these supply chains set limits on growth based on access to both environmental and social resources. Typically, these chains would have much more stable patterns of sales than their overall industry. In times of soaring demand, they will not increase production beyond what their natural and human resources could maintain in a downturn. This means they miss out on some sales in times of plenty, but they do not deplete natural resources nor do they have to fire people in downturns. Hence, they miss some profit and growth opportunities, at least in the short term that the other chains would likely capitalize on. Supply chains on a balanced trajectory are willing to internalize some of the environmental costs that are not presently mandated by existing regulations to provide long-term benefits to employees, suppliers, and the communities in which they operate.

Operationally, the balanced approach means that these chains are well placed to be both eco-efficient and innovative. The stability they foster means that workers are a long-term investment. These workers are highly trained and motivated to make both continuous improvements in operations as well as to support innovations when needed. Critically they are willing and able to share their knowledge through the supply chain. Balanced firms can significantly reduce the impact of production processes (theirs and suppliers), while increasing efficiency and offering better working conditions for employees and overseas suppliers. These organizations are able to attain resource efficiency in many areas of their supply chains.

A leading company on a balanced trajectory is The Collins Companies, a forest products enterprise headquartered in Wilsonville, Oregon. It owns and manages 307,000 acres of timberland in Pennsylvania, Oregon, and California. While most other wood product companies maximize yield by clear-cutting, Collins lets its forests grow naturally and uses selective harvesting. Since its creation in 1855, it has maintained ethical forestry practices that have allowed the forests to thrive—and provide lumber—for over 150 years. Their overriding operating principle is never log more than the forest grows.

Collins was the first privately owned wood-products company in the US to be certified by the Forest Stewardship Council (FSC), an international organization with membership that includes NGOs, logging and wood-product companies, and environmental groups. Throughout its operations, Collins is committed to maintain the forest ecosystem and support social and economic benefits for its employees and the surrounding communities.

The company's strong stance on environmental and social priorities subjects it to risks and trade-offs. Collins will never use all their resources—there will always be trees in reserve, but they may not always be able to meet demand. And while FSC certification raises their profile, it is expensive to maintain those standards and it may not repay those costs: lumber and building supplies are considered commodity items, and most builders buy based on price, not environmental ideals. The company's balanced approach to profit, people, and planet may limit growth, but the company factors its environmental and social involvement into its business plan. Although the industry has declined in recent years, Collins has maintained a steady workforce.

The steady workforce is critical to Collins and the communities they operate in. Forestry is by nature a highly cyclical business with frequent downturns. Many of their facilities are in rural settings where Collins may be the only major employer. If Collins laid off people in every downturn, some towns would not survive. Stable work then keeps people employed and allows small rural towns to survive industry downturns. Balance allows Collins to protect their workers and the communities they operate in and is a key to their ability to leverage the workforce.

Collins has leveraged the workforce to address sustainability mainly from an eco-efficiency and innovation standpoint, which is exemplified in the journey their Klamath Falls facility (Oregon, US) has made since the mid-1990s. Collins purchased the facility from Weyerhaeuser. Until that point, Collins had concentrated its sustainability efforts on forest stewardship. However, in 1996, they implemented a program they called Journey to Sustainability (JTS) to bring sustainability to their manufacturing operations. By the next year, employees had begun sustainability training. Morale at Klamath Falls had dropped before the purchase by Collins, and the company used JTS to boost the mood in the plant while improving operations. Supervisors received training in the principles of sustainability and sustainable manufacturing. The company implemented a plan to train all the workers within 3 months. The company solicited suggestions while assessing improvements to its capital equipment.

One of the first suggestions to arise was to adopt European standards for off-gassing of formaldehyde from finished products (three times as stringent as US requirements.) The company believes this has enhanced its position among "enlightened" architects, as well as opening potential new markets for its products.

The company stopped using water from the local river to improve resource efficiency and address regional water shortages. Their initial decision was to treat water and reuse it. They leased a nearby farm and built a wetland to store and treat the discharge, but it was too small to hold all of the treated water, forcing them to find a way to use some of it immediately. They realized that they could cut electricity use by modifying their heat exchange and cooling systems to use the extra water. The initial decision to stop taking water forced them to re-engineer production. The new process not only uses less water, but also requires less energy to run, freeing up capital. The experience also bolstered morale as workers saw immediate benefits in terms of efficiency and in their community's water supply.

A capital project at the plant significantly reduced power use: they replaced six old electric motors, saving $118,000 annually. It paid for itself in 2 years. Other projects were similarly eco-efficient. Condensate from a veneer dryer was used to heat water, saving $152,000 per year. Maintenance and repair to steam traps saved $25,000 per year. New equipment allowed sander dust to be incorporated into the finished particleboard. The process saves $563,000 per year—and using the dust not only improves the appearance of the board, but reduces air emissions.

The Klamath Falls facility not only cut water and energy consumption, it reduced waste, as well. A contest to promote water conservation prompted discovery and repair of a leak, saving over 500,000 gal per year. The plant no longer discharges warm water into the river. The Journey to Sustainability has now been incorporated into operations throughout the company.

In its first year, Journey To Sustainability projects saved The Collins Companies almost $1,000,000. Within 3 years, annual savings were $1,370,000—totalling over $3 million. Capital purchases, salary increases, seminars, and travel came to about $50,000—6% of the overall savings. The environmental benefits come from reduced use of resources, especially water in a community that faces water shortages. This is also a social benefit in that it will allow them to continue production without putting other water uses in the community at risk.

The path-dependent decisions that Collins has made over the last 150 years allow them to compete by being more sustainable, but these decisions also create constraints. For instance, the stability of their forestry practices combined with the investments in workers and communities means that operationally they are innovative and productive, but not very flexible. Their supply chain is not able to deal with large fluctuations in demand. And given the investments in workers, practices, and communities, any attempt to alter where work is done or who does it will have to be

The Focused Trajectory – Kettle Foods (http://www.kettlebrand.com) (*Source*: http://www.kettlebrand.com/about_us/sustainability/)

viewed through the lens of protecting the existing workforce and community. Intuitively, this means they never want to close a plant in small town, even if there are no legal constraints on doing so. Instead, the constraint is the intangible. To close a plant in a small town means breaking the bound with the workers and community and undermining their entire philosophy.

A balanced trajectory focuses on conserving social, environmental, and economic resources. Decisions to behave in this way often mean higher short-term costs, weather they be investments in FSC or in training the workforce. However, the payoff is the ability to continue to operate over very long timeframes. Collins is not going to run out of inputs with their present business model, nor do they have to worry about a dip in their demand causing an entire community to collapse.

Supply chains on a focused trajectory have capitalized on either environmental or social issues to create a viable business. For them, business success is contingent on the accomplishment of environmental or social objectives. In supply chains on an *environmentally focused* trajectory, the founders and managers will have strong environmental values that have been imprinted on the organization. For instance, Patagonia, a privately owned apparel company whose founders are self-proclaimed climbers and surfers, has a mission statement to "*Build the best product, cause no unnecessary harm, use business to inspire and implement solutions to the environmental crisis*" (http://www.patagonia.com/eu/enSK/patagonia.go?assetid=8952). These supply chains are a means to carry out a particular environmental agenda. While these companies are engaged in community service and do discuss social issues, tackling environmental issues is an essential part of business operations; dealing with social issues is secondary.

The *socially focused* trajectory is similar, but in these supply chains the values are socially oriented. Supply chains that have adopted Fairtrade certification (http://www.fairtrade.org.uk/en) as a primary means of certifying themselves or for selecting suppliers would be on this trajectory since the primary objective of Fairtrade is to improve the lives of farmers and farm workers. Socially focused organizations take environmental action when the environmental impact of their business on people becomes a concern. In socially focused organizations, environmental initiatives are adopted as a reaction to protect the organization, while in environmentally focused organizations social initiatives will be adoptee reactively.

The major risk from these trajectories is then the lack of balance, but this can also be a source of strategic strength. The environmental features of the products and services offerings from environmentally focused supply chains communicate certain environmental messages; energy efficiency, reduced carbon footprint via local food, and reductions in pollution associated with chemical fertilizers. Meanwhile, their innovative solutions to environmental challenges benefit the customers directly via reduced energy consumption, a healthy living environment, and high-quality products. Similarly, socially focused firms communicate messages such as those associated with fair trade (Fairtrade 2014) or conflict free (CFSI 2014) and are innovating in ways that benefit society in multiple ways such as better working or living conditions. Thus, the companies with a focused trajectory can charge a price premium.

Since the price premiums can offset the higher costs associated with social/environmental practices, managers are emboldened to take on more difficult tasks. From the triple bottom-line perspective of performance, while all show a concern for all elements of the triple bottom line, environmentally focused firms are primarily motivated by a concern for the environment while socially focused firms are primarily motivated by a concern for society.

A leading company with an environmentally focused trajectory is Kettle Foods; a multinational producer and distributor of organic and all-natural snack foods. Kettle began in 1978 as the N.S. Khalsa Company, a small wholesaler of natural snacks in Salem, Oregon. The company started producing its Kettle brand potato chips in 1982. By the time the product line was a year old, the company had grown to $3 million in annual sales. Founder Cameron Healy started the business in an effort to earn a living that fit with his spiritual values; those values dictated the "all-natural" approach that still distinguishes the brand and underlies the company's strong environmental policies. By 1987, the Khalsa Company was growing at a 15 % annual rate, with sales doubling every year. The following year, it changed its name to Kettle Foods and established a UK branch in a converted factory in Norwich.

Kettle adopted an overarching operating principle that guides every decision the company makes: the product has to be all natural and must contain what the label says it contains. The company equates this principle with maintaining a strong environmental policy, so it influences how the company designs products, selects suppliers, and tracks ingredients in its supply chain. Strategically, they address sustainability from an innovation perspective because their environmental focus allows them to sell innovative/differentiated products at a price premium.

Kettle's environmental focus also involves trade-offs. Some of their organic ingredients are seasonal, but most grocery retailers do not stock products on a seasonal basis. Therefore, perishable ingredients have to be stored in refrigerated warehouses to maintain a steady supply. The company's environmental decisions have to be pragmatic, keeping sight of the fact that they must be both economically and environmentally sustainable. This often means putting profits first, at least in the short term. Nonetheless, Kettle addressed environmental issues in their initial business plan, so their business and environmental agendas reinforce each other.

The environmental focus plays out operationally via efforts at creating eco-efficiency and at reducing risk. Kettle has a supplier certification program that demands extensive information from suppliers to ensure ingredients meet their standards. This is explicitly a risk reduction activity since ingredients that do not meet these standards would put their competitive advantage at risk. They do not trace money through the supply chain or determine other practices (labour conditions, for example) that are not directly related to a product's all-natural status. They choose to focus on environmental issues and concerns.

The environmental ethos extends to their downstream and upstream supply chains. As part of the commitment, Kettle uses sunflower and safflower oils. When the oil is spent, it is converted into biodiesel. By using the fuel in its delivery fleet, the company reduces its CO_2 emissions by 8 t every year and does not have to purchase fuel, which is a classic example of eco-efficiency. Kettle has taken other steps to reduce emissions. In September 2003, they partnered with the Energy Trust of Oregon and Portland General Electric to install one of the largest grid-tied solar photovoltaic arrays in the Pacific Northwest. Six hundred rooftop solar panels generate more than 120,000 kilowatt hours (kWh) of electricity per year, enough to reduce annual CO_2 emissions by 65 t. The company offsets the rest of its electricity use in the US by purchasing wind energy credits, preventing more than 13,000 t of emissions. Citing these achievements, the EPA presented its Green Power Partnership award to Kettle in 2012. The Salem plant has also restored surrounding wetlands, clearing invasive plants and reintroducing native species. As birds and other wildlife returned, the company installed pathways and benches to encourage the public's use and enjoyment of the land.

In 2007, Kettle opened the first LEED® Gold certified food manufacturing plant in the US in Beloit, Wisconsin. The "green building" reduces energy use by 20 % compared to conventional construction, saving $110,000 on natural gas and $51,000 on electricity. By reclaiming and reusing water, the plant saves over 3.4 million gallons of water a year. The facility also converts 3200 gal of waste oil to biodiesel each month. Finally, elimination of shipping lines between Oregon and the Midwest further cut the company's CO_2 emissions by more than 3 million pounds per year.

The decision to protect the firm's environmental values via the all-natural principle has allowed Kettle to grow while selling products at a price premium. But this same path-dependent decision also creates serious constraints. At its simplest, Kettle cannot use some ingredients even if they are less expensive or have a smaller carbon footprint. It also means that to sell into markets where customers expect a product to be available year round, Kettle ends up storing ingredients, often in temperature-controlled settings with large costs and environmental footprints. These actions are antithetical to the firm's environmental ethos, so it is no surprise that they work hard to mitigate all of their environmental impacts. However, their resources like most firms are not unlimited. The efforts they have put into their operations have created a unique environmental management capability. But every investment in this environmental capability is also a decision not to make a similar-sized investment in social sustainability capabilities. The decision to embrace an all-natural principal to protect the environmental values leads to the creation of a proactive environmental management capability, which they use to create and maintain their competitive advantage. However, every investment in the all-natural path also makes it harder to embrace/invest in other areas due to resource constraints and knowledge gaps.

Kettle exemplifies the focused trajectory. The organization was founded to meet an environmental objective which translates into their all-natural strategy; a strategy which allows them to charge a price premium which helps to pay for their range of eco-innovations. And over time, they have become very adept at recognizing opportunities to make environmental innovations, be it converting a waste stream into fuel or harnessing renewable energy. Similarly, their risk reduction efforts are aimed mainly at protecting their trajectory. This focus has been profitable and allowed them to grow, but it is not balanced. They do address social issues, but this is not their strategic advantage. Over time, their focus on the environmental impacts of the supply chain has made the chain an exemplar in reducing its environmental impact, but this focus requires resources, resources that are not applied to social issues in the same manner.

The Opportunity First Trajectory – Walmart (http://www.walmart.com) (*Source*: http://news.walmart.com/news-archive/2010/11/16/walmart-canada-opens-its-first-sustainable-distribution-centre)

The *opportunity-first* trajectory is largely driven by an economic opportunity. Unlike the previous two trajectories, where environmental or social values play a leading role in shaping the supply chain's operations, here the causality is reversed. Opportunity-first trajectories occur when a business motive pushes an existing chain to adopt additional initiatives that will inculcate environmental or social values into the organization.

For existing supply chains, this is the most common trajectory. Organizations such as Coca-Cola, Unilever, and GE, which existed for generations with a profit maximizing ethos mainly, have made business decisions to become more sustainable that have put them onto the opportunity-first trajectory. The opportunity-first trajectory enjoys many of the marketing and branding benefits of the focused trajectory, but these supply chains are not able to charge the same price premiums.

The opportunity-first trajectory is different on three main accounts, all of which exemplify the path-dependent nature of decisions surrounding sustainability. First, the sustainability values in this trajectory are recent, which suggests that when faced with decisions where being more sustainable is expensive or risky, these supply chains are less likely to make the investment. This is buttressed by a second key difference: the opportunity-first supply chain was already in the market place as a traditional (not sustainable) competitor. Customers already associate the organization's products and services with specific attributes including prices, and these customer expectations will be slow to change, which can limit the ability to charge a price premium, especially in the short term. Prior decisions create dependencies that influence both how current investments are viewed and interestingly how customers view the supply chain.

Finally, over time, customers, employees, and other stakeholders of the opportunity-first trajectory will come to expect more responsible behaviour. What starts as a business opportunity will have to evolve to something more because stakeholders expect that a supply chain that claims to be more responsible is truly responsible in all of its actions. By announcing their intentions to take advantage of a sustainable business opportunity, supply chains are opening themselves up to much greater scrutiny and higher expectations. Taking the first step towards becoming more sustainable creates a path dependency where the supply chain will have to take many more such steps to maintain support from their stakeholders.

Workers in a company or chain tend to be motivated when the chain becomes more responsible, but they also begin to question why social or environmental issues that make the firm money are addressed while other negative impacts are not. Similarly, customers who respond to a more sustainable message will begin to ask deeper questions about other practices, demanding ever more change. Protecting and growing the brand effectively means that chains on an opportunity-first trajectory will likely have to migrate toward the *balanced trajectory*, otherwise they may fail. This is a critical point since the opportunity-first trajectory is the one on which most existing firms will address sustainability.

Walmart exemplifies the opportunity-first trajectory. With over 11,000 stores in 71 countries and a global workforce of 2.2 million, Walmart is the largest retailer in the world. When Walmart undertakes a change that affects its supply chain(s), that change influences industry sectors globally. So it is with the company's sustainability policies. In 2005, CEO Lee Scott announced the company's new business sustainability strategy, designed to meet three sweeping environmental goals: to be powered by 100 % renewable energy, to create zero waste, and to sell products that "sustain people and the environment." While these were "aspirational" rather than concrete goals with definite timelines, their achievement would require major changes in how Walmart managed its global supply chains.

The first two goals (renewable energy and zero waste) are very much about eco-efficiency and innovations in supply chain operations, which align well with Walmart's existing low price strategy that is based on supply chain efficiencies. Walmart closely tracks numbers across its supply and distribution channels as well as in its retail centres, so it has statistics on its progress toward its measurable goals. At the beginning of 2014, it had over 300 renewable energy projects underway worldwide, providing 2.2 billion kWh a year. Additional purchases of renewable power bring the company to 24.2 % of its energy goal. In the US, more than 81 % of their waste is now diverted from landfills. In Japan and the UK, the number is over 90 %. The company offers electronics recycling at its US stores, along with smartphone and tablet trade-in programs. While all these projects benefit the environment, they also cut operating costs in terms of energy expenditures and landfill fees. In addition, recycled materials provide new revenue streams—including 56 million pounds of recovered cooking oil used in biodiesel or animal feed.

Energy and waste issues are business opportunities where innovative processes allow them to become more eco-efficient and these initiatives extend to the entire supply chain. In 2008, Scott announced a drive to bring suppliers into compliance with fair labour practices and cut energy consumption by 20 % throughout the supply chain. He also stated that the company would drop suppliers who did not meet these goals.

Walmart offers a range of educational and training programs to suppliers to help them to meet these targets. Violation Correction Training requires a factory representative to attend classes where approaches to social and environmental issues and compliance methodologies are explained. The suppliers are expected to choose and implement the procedures that fit them. Orange School provides hands-on training to select factories and suppliers. By focusing on the fundamentals of root cause analysis and procedures, Walmart teaches suppliers to identify noncompliance issues proactively and develop systematic approaches to continuous improvement. Walmart has invested heavily in these training programs, but the onus remains on the suppliers to comply.

Walmart provides a good example of both positives and limits of the opportunity-first trajectory. As Walmart becomes more eco-efficient, other issues become more not less pertinent to external stakeholders. The company would of course like to focus on positives like their reduced footprint, decreased reliance on non-renewable energy, and everyday low prices. But external stakeholders have raised a litany of serious complaints about the firm; some of which have resulted in legal action.

For instance, Walmart is Mexico's largest private employer, with over 220,000 workers and 2200 locations. Walmart has more than once resorted to bribery to obtain building permits in Mexico—in one case, to open a store just a mile from a culturally significant site: Teotihuacán, an ancient Aztec that contains a temple complex and two pyramids (Bloomberg 2014; NYT 2012, 2014). And in the United States, the company is harshly criticized for its anti-union policies, poor working conditions, inadequate healthcare, and low wages (Berfield 2012). In addition, some of Walmart's recent expansion plans have been greeted by protesters who were concerned that Walmart would ruin, not enhance their community (e.g. LA Times 2012). Some of these issues arose long before Walmart started on their path to becoming more sustainable, but these issues become more pertinent as the organization tries to capitalize on its sustainability progress.

Walmart has made significant progress and somewhat paradoxically now faces even more pressure to change. They can't have it both ways—if they are truly trying to reduce the impact of their supply chain, they will have to evolve into one of the other trajectories; or lose trust from multiple stakeholders (suppliers, customers, regulators, etc.) as well as sales. In a sense, Walmart will soon face a crossroad; they have been very successful at making their existing unsustainable business model more resource efficient, but in doing so they have actually increased their exposure. To be truly sustainable, they will have to continue to learn and respond to pressures to make changes that may not create shared value.

The path-dependent nature of sustainability decision is most apparent in the opportunity-first supply chains. By capitalizing on an opportunity, Walmart, like all supply chains on an opportunity-first trajectory, has also created new constraints and expectations. By signalling their progress, they have in essence increased the external pressure on the chain. This is the fundamental paradox of the opportunity-first supply chain, the more they do and the more transparent they become, the more that will be expected.

Supply chains on an opportunity-first trajectory will be indispensable in sustainability for two reasons. First, sustainability has to make sense for companies with such scale to have a significant impact. Second, this is the way the vast majority of existing, presently unsustainable, supply chains will first address sustainability. But, opportunity-first organizations also need to recognize that, over time, they will have to do more than embrace the business opportunity; they will have to fundamentally change.

15.4 Conclusions

This chapter explored the various ways in which supply chains are or could approach sustainability. It starts with two critical pieces of knowledge. First, that no firm has yet created a truly sustainable supply chain, and second, that the choices made to reduce a chain's impacts will create path dependencies.

This starting point leads to a pair of questions all managers will need to ask. The first is "*what has to change in our supply chain to reach true sustainability*". Supply chain managers answering this question focus on three interrelated means to reducing impacts; eco-efficiency, risk reduction, and innovation. As the chapter has shown, many firms are making significant progress in these areas and these examples offer starting points for managers looking for inspiration.

However, managers looking to begin the journey toward sustainability or those looking to make further progress in their supply chains need to remain aware of the way past decisions limit future options. The chapter explores the three main paths or trajectories in which sustainability is embedded into a supply chain, and the trade-offs inherent in each. Balanced chains are just that, but by focusing equally on all aspects of the triple bottom line, they risk not having the market advantages of focused chains, which are truly leaders at something, even if focused chains are also laggards in other areas. Similarly, chains that use a market opportunity as the initial spur to become more sustainable will, somewhat paradoxically, need to be aware that as they make progress more, not less will be demanded of them.

References

3M (2014) http://solutions.3m.com/wps/portal/3M/en_US/3M-Sustainability/Global/Environment/3P/. Accessed December 20, 2014

Berfield S (2012) http://www.businessweek.com/articles/2012-12-13/walmart-vs-dot-union-backed-our-walmart. Accessed December 20, 2014

Bloomberg (2014) http://www.bloomberg.com/news/2014-03-26/wal-mart-says-bribery-probe--cost-439-million-in-past-two-years.html. Accessed December 20, 2014

Broad (2014) http://www.broadusa.com/index.php. Accessed December 20, 2014

CFSI (2014) http://www.conflictfreesourcing.org. Accessed December 20, 2014

Fairtrade (2014) http://www.fairtrade.net. Accessed December 20, 2014

Lee HL, Rammohan SV (2017) Improving social and environmental performance in global supply chains. In: Bouchery Y, Corbett CJ, Fransoo J, Tan T (eds) Sustainable supply chains: a research-based textbook on operations and strategy. Springer, New York

Levi (2014) http://www.levistrauss.com/sustainability/innovative-practices/suppliers-operations/product-suppliers/. Accessed December 20, 2014

Nike (2014) http://nikeinc.com/system/assets/2806/Nike_Code_of_Conduct_original.pdf ?1317156854. Accessed December 20, 2014

NYT (2012) http://www.nytimes.com/2012/12/18/business/walmart-bribes-teotihuacan.html?pagewanted=all. Accessed December 20, 2014

NYT (2014) http://www.nytimes.com/2014/06/05/business/after-walmart-bribery-scandals-a--pattern-of-quiet-departures.html?_r=0. Accessed December 20, 2014

Pagell M, Shevchenko A (2014) Why research in sustainable supply chain management should have no future. J Supply Chain Manage 50(1):44–55

Pagell M, Wu Z (2009) Building a more complete theory of sustainable supply chain management using case studies of 10 exemplars. J Supply Chain Manage 45(2):37–56

Pepsi (2014) http://www.pepsico.com/Purpose/Environmental-Sustainability/Water. Accessed December 20, 2014

Pierson P (2000) Increasing returns, path dependence, and the study of politics. Am Polit Sci Rev 94(02):251–267

Porter ME, Kramer MR (2011) Creating shared value. Harv Bus Rev 89(1/2):62–77

Sharma S, Henriques I (2005) Stakeholder influences on sustainability practices in the Canadian forest products industry. Strat Manage J 26(2):159–180

Sodhi MMS, Tang CS (2017) Social responsibility in supply chains. In: Bouchery Y, Corbett CJ, Fransoo J, Tan T (eds) Sustainable supply chains: a research-based textbook on operations and strategy. Springer, New York

LA Times (2012) http://articles.latimes.com/2012/jul/01/local/la-me-0701-walmart-protest-20120701. Accessed December 20, 2014

USAS (2014) http://usas.org. Accessed December 20, 2014

van Weele A, van Tubergen K (2017) Responsible purchasing: moving from compliance to value creation in supplier relationships. In: Bouchery Y, Corbett CJ, Fransoo J, Tan T (eds) Sustainable supply chains: a research-based textbook on operations and strategy. Springer, New York

Wu Z, Pagell M (2011) Balancing priorities: decision-making in sustainable supply chain management. J Oper Manage 29(6):577–590

Chapter 16
Moving from a Product-Based Economy to a Service-Based Economy for a More Sustainable Future

Ioannis Bellos and Mark Ferguson

16.1   Introduction

Traditionally, economic growth and prosperity have been linked with the availability, production, and distribution of tangible goods as well as the ability of consumers to acquire such goods. Early evidence regarding this connection dates back to Adam Smith's *Wealth of Nations* (1776), in which any activity not resulting in the production of a tangible good is characterized as "unproductive of any value." Since then, this coupling of economic value and material production has been prevalent in both developed and developing economies throughout the world.

One unintended consequence of this coupling has been the exponential increase in the amount of solid waste being generated. The reason is that any production and consumption of material goods eventually generates the equivalent amount of (or even more) waste. Exacerbating this problem is the fact that, with today's manufacturing and supply chain management technologies, it has become cheaper to dispose and replace most products rather than to repair and reuse them. This has given rise to what some call a "disposable society."

To put things in perspective: In 2012, households in the UK generated approximately 22 kt of waste, which amounted to 411 kg of waste generated per person (Department for Environment, Food & Rural Affairs 2015). During the same time period, households in the US generated 251 megatons of waste, which is equivalent to a person generating approximately 2 kg of waste every day (U.S. Environmental

I. Bellos (✉)
School of Business, George Mason University, Fairfax, VA 22030, USA
e-mail: ibellos@gmu.edu

M. Ferguson
Moore School of Business, University of South Carolina, Columbia, SC 29208, USA
e-mail: mark.ferguson@moore.sc.edu

© Yann Bouchery, Charles J. Corbett, Jan C. Fransoo, and Tarkan Tan 2017
Y. Bouchery et al. (eds.), *Sustainable Supply Chains*, Springer Series in Supply
Chain Management 4, DOI 10.1007/978-3-319-29791-0_16

Protection Agency 2012). Out of these 251 Mt of total waste generated, approximately 20 % of the discarded items were categorized as durable goods. The disposal of durable goods is particularly worrisome because they are typically produced using material from non-renewable resources such as iron, minerals, and petroleum-based raw materials.

It is clear that any business model that relies on a disposable society cannot be sustainable long-term model. For this reason, recent efforts have been made by policy makers to enable the creation of a "circular economy," which minimizes waste by re-using, repairing, refurbishing, and recycling materials and products (European Commission 2014). While doing so can minimize the amount of waste produced and promote a more efficient and ecofriendly use of overall resources, the creation of a circular economy does not really address the source of the problem—it is consumption that is the source of most wastes. Thus, reducing consumption can result in decreased production and less waste.

One solution to the disposable-society problem, proposed by the U.S. Environmental Protection Agency's Office of Resource Conservation and Recovery (see U.S. Environmental Protection Agency 2009), is for traditional product-based firms to move towards more service-based business models that do not focus on selling products but rather on selling the solutions that the products can deliver. A potential benefit of such models is that a firm can always maintain the ownership of the products it manufactures, thus reducing the incentive to increase revenue by simply selling more products. Moreover, switching the base of the transaction, from the product level to the use level, can restructure the economics of consumption and encourage more sustainable level of product use. In this chapter, we examine the potential of such a solution from both an economic and environmental perspectives.

The rest of this chapter is organized as follows. In Sect. 16.2, we first provide examples of firms that have transitioned from a product-based state to a service-based state and then we introduce the concept of servicizing. In Sect. 16.3, we discuss some reasons why traditional product-based firms may be interested in transitioning to a more service-based delivery strategy and how this transition may impact a firm's sustainability metrics. In Sect. 16.4, we discuss some of the challenges firms may face when making this transition and some of the key decisions that are required for doing so. We conclude in Sect. 16.5 and provide some possible directions for future research.

16.2 From Products to Services: The Transition Through Servicizing

In this section, we describe how certain companies have made the transition from being product-based to being service-based. We also link such a transition to what has recently become known as servicizing strategies.

16.2.1 Leaving the "Product Comfort Zone"

The service sector has been an integral part of economic activity in both developed and developing economies. In 2013, services accounted for approximately 80 % of GDP in the US (The World Bank 2013). During the same period, in China the service sector continued to grow to 46.9 % of GDP, a dynamic that may indicate the move to a new stage in China's economic growth (Businessweek 2014).

Although such statistics are commonly used in texts describing the role of services in today's economy, another observation may help put a more interesting "face" on these numbers. In particular, for many years organizations that are (or were) typically recognized as manufacturing/product firms have been increasing the service component of their offerings. Examples include GM's successful creation of the OnStar subscription service or its expansion to financial services through the acquisition of AmeriCredit Corp. in 2010 to create what is known today as GM Financial. Similarly, SKF, the Swedish manufacturer of ball and roller bearings, now offers subscription-based diagnostic and predictive maintenance services (SKF 2014). Dell and Hewlett-Packard created Dell Services and HP Enterprise Services, respectively, in order to provide IT and business services. These moves came in response to earlier moves by IBM, who has almost entirely transformed itself from a product-based company into a services company by selling its personal computers and servers business to Lenovo (2004; IBM 2014).

But why do manufacturers choose to go out of their "product comfort zone" to engage and invest in the creation of services? In the face of product commoditization and increasing competitive pressure, services can offer a stable and recurring revenue stream stemming from activities such as support, maintenance, and repair, which can extend well beyond the useful life of a product and generate lucrative profit margins. This can also increase the chances of cross-selling or alleviate customers' hesitation in upgrading to new products and equipment. Additionally, by offering after-sales support services, manufacturers can eliminate the need for third parties, who can erode brand perception, to perform these services. Furthermore, services are more difficult to reverse-engineer (i.e., to be imitated) and can facilitate longer and deeper relationships with customers due to longer contractual agreements. Manufacturers can also obtain a better idea about the customers' needs and the conditions under which the products operate and possibly customize their offerings accordingly. Finally, by offering services the manufacturers can acquire more accurate feedback about the performance of their products in the field, which can lead to product improvements and redesigns.

16.2.2 The Strategy of Servicizing

In the aforementioned examples, regardless of whether the manufacturers offer a support (e.g., maintenance) or an "add-on" (e.g., OnStar) service, the base of the transaction remains at the product level. This is because the service is contingent on the customers purchasing a product. However, in recent years we have observed a

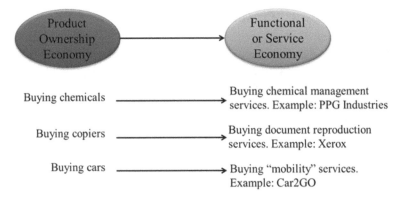

Fig. 16.1 The transition from a product-ownership economy to a functional economy (adapted from White et al. 1999)

trend where manufacturers from various industries have started switching their focus from selling products to actually selling the solutions that their products offer. In most of the cases, manufacturers maintain the ownership of the products; therefore, the base of the transaction no longer seems to be the product per se, but rather the use of the product. This trend, also known as "servicizing,"[1] indicates the transition from a product-based economy to a functional or solutions economy (Stahel 1994). In such an economy, instead of buying chemicals, for example, customers now have the option to buy chemical management services; instead of buying copiers, they can buy document reproduction services; and instead of buying cars, they can buy mobility services (see Fig. 16.1). Such options can be particularly attractive to customers because they free them from the administrative hassles and the operating risks (e.g., maintenance, repair) as well as the financial risks (e.g., depreciation of a product's market value) associated with product ownership.

The strategy of servicizing involves the transition from an existing business model to one where the focus is on the service or, better put, the solution provided to the end-customer. In fact, most business models can be thought of as comprising a combination of a product and a service component (see Fig. 16.2). A newly formed definition in the academic literature describes these models under the general term Product Service Systems (PSS). The definition of PSS varies throughout the literature, but most authors agree that there exist three different PSS types (U.S. Environmental Protection Agency 2009): (1) product-oriented PSS in which a manufacturer, in addition to selling a product, includes extra services (e.g., after-sales service), (2) use-oriented PSS in which the manufacturer maintains ownership of the product and sells the use or availability of it (e.g., leasing, rentals, car sharing), and (3) result-oriented PSS in which the manufacturer and the customer agree on a certain result or performance level (e.g., engine up-time).

---

[1] There is an abundance of similar terms like "servicization" or "servitization." We have chosen to use the term "servicizing" like many before us, without making any claims about its superiority or grammatical correctness!

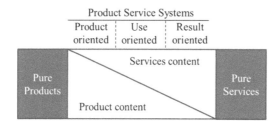

Fig. 16.2 Product-services spectrum and the different types of Product Service Systems (adapted from Tukker 2004)

The above typology is by no means exhaustive, and some business models may fall under more than one type. For instance, the business model of fractional ownership (often found in the private jet industry; NetJets was among the first to offer such a model), where customers own only a fraction of an asset that entitles them to a certain amount of use, can be thought of as a combination of product-oriented and use-oriented PSS. In this chapter, we avoid possible categorization conundrums and simply describe models in which the use, rather than the ownership, of the products governs the relationship between manufacturers and customers. To avoid an overly cumbersome use of terminology and unnecessary confusion, we refer to such models as servicizing business models.

One of the most celebrated examples of a successful servicizing business model in the academic literature is Xerox's document management services (Xerox 2015), where customers are charged on a per-use (per-page-printed) basis (see Fischer et al. 2012). In the automotive sector, servicizing has emerged through the business model of car sharing. Under car sharing, customers obtain access to a fleet of vehicles after paying a small annual fee. Upon joining the service, customers can check the availability of the vehicles and make reservations online. After using a vehicle, they pay only for the reserved amount of time. Although the most well-known car sharing provider is Zipcar, several auto manufacturers such as BMW, Peugeot, and Ford have entered the car sharing arena through small, pilot programs across the world. The most prominent and fastest-growing car sharing program offered by an auto manufacturer is Car2Go, a subsidiary of Daimler AG, which operates in several cities across the US and Europe.

An example of a servicizing model in the aviation sector is offered by Rolls-Royce, who pioneered Power-by the-Hour maintenance agreements under which it charges customers based only on the actual flying hours of the engines.[2] For more examples of servicizing business models, we refer the reader to Rothenberg (2007), U.S. Environmental Protection Agency (2009), and Fischer et al. (2012).

Researchers have argued that servicizing business models can lead to higher profitability. In particular, they have proposed that by focusing on the final customer needs and delivering integrated solutions fulfilling these needs, companies can

---

[2]The term performance-based contracting is also used to describe agreements that are similar in spirit.

improve their positions in the value chain, enhance the value of their offerings, and improve their innovation potentials (Wise and Baumgartner 1999; Sawhney et al. 2003). Such arguments are in line with our previous mention of the economic benefits of more service-oriented business practices. Besides the potential economic benefits that more service-oriented business models may hold, recently researchers and environmental groups have argued that servicizing business models may also be associated with environmental benefits and, therefore, can be positioned to support the objective of sustainable development (Rothenberg 2007). Throughout the rest of this chapter, we explore some of the rationale for this claim.

In this section, we formally introduced the concept of servicizing and presented some of its most successful implementations in practice. We concluded by mentioning the support that servicizing has received as a potentially win-win (i.e., economically and environmentally superior) business strategy. In the next section, we further explore some of the arguments regarding the economic and environmental potential of servicizing business models.

16.3 The Economic and Environmental Impact of Servicizing Models

In this section, we provide details regarding the economic and environmental appeal of servicizing models and, more specifically, their potential to support the three pillars of sustainability: people, profit, and planet.

16.3.1 Servicizing: The "Triple-Threat Business Model?"

The decoupling of customer value from product ownership seems to be at the heart of the arguments in support of the environmental potential of servicizing. The reason is that this decoupling can contribute to the dematerialization of the economy (Heiskanen and Jalas 2000) by requiring less energy or material to generate the same (or even more) customer value. This can sometimes be achieved simply through using novel contractual mechanisms. For instance, in the context of chemical management solutions, shared-savings contracts are sometimes used between suppliers and buyers instead of the typical price-quantity contracts. Under such contracts, a supplier is not rewarded based on the material sold to the buyer, but, rather, based on the savings that the buyer enjoys due to a reduction in the consumption of such materials (Corbett and DeCroix 2001; Corbett et al. 2005).

For another context in which dematerialization may also occur, consider the business model of car sharing. By the very nature of this model, car sharing providers like Car2Go can benefit from a pooling effect and satisfy customers' needs through a smaller number of vehicles because a single vehicle can be used by many customers at different periods of time. This results in better fleet utilization and overall lower production volume, which directly benefits the environment by reducing the production-related emissions and use of raw material. This is true under several servicizing models, the providers of which do not need to dedicate one product to each customer.

The arguments for the environmental superiority of servicizing are also supported by the fact that, in the majority of the business models, customers are charged on a per-use basis (e.g., per-page-printed, per-mile-driven, etc.). Directly linking payment to product usage may incentivize customers to reduce their use of the product, resulting in a lower environment burden. The decrease in usage due to pay-per-use pricing is attributed to what is known as the taxi-meter effect (or flat rate bias; see Lambrecht and Skiera 2006), which postulates that customers enjoy their product usage more at a flat rate and tend to use it less when they are charged for each unit of usage.

Finally, in most of the servicizing business models, the manufacturer maintains the ownership of the products. This may incentivize manufacturers to design and produce products of higher reliability (Guajardo et al. 2012) or with longer useful life, so as to maximize the revenue extracted from each product per unit of time. This can also be achieved through better maintenance, which can typically be accomplished more productively by the manufacturer than the customer. Such practices also affect the end-of-life management of the products since a manufacturer is more likely to choose a more environmentally friendly way to dispose of a product than a customer and may even reduce the number of units that are disposed of in any given period of time by prolonging the useful lifecycles through remanufacturing or harvesting spare parts (see also Chap. 17 by Abbey and Guide (2017)).

Do the above-mentioned arguments imply that servicizing is the "triple-threat business model," that is, a business model that excels simultaneously in all three pillars of sustainability: people, profit, and planet? Recent research (Bellos et al. 2016; Agrawal and Bellos 2015) shows that this may not always be the case. But why not? Before we answer this question, we need to understand how the three pillars of sustainability relate to each other and how the performance of a business model with respect to these dimensions is assessed.

16.3.2 Assessing Business Model Performance Against the Triple Bottom Line

With respect to the profit dimension, it is straightforward to argue that, for a given (pay-per-use) price, profit increases as the number of customers who use the firm's products increases and/or the amount of use that each customer extracts from the product increases (i.e., as customers drive more or print more pages).

With respect to the people dimension, one way to estimate the impact of a new business model is to measure the overall consumer surplus. Assuming that every customer derives a positive utility from using a product, for a given (pay-per-use) price higher product usage increases an individual consumer's surplus. Similarly, the overall consumer surplus increases as the number of customers who adopt and use a product increases.

This brings us to the third dimension: that of environmental performance (i.e., the planet). To assess the environmental performance of a business model, a life-cycle approach can be adopted (see Chap. 2 by Guinée and Heijungs (2017)) and the environmental burden created at the phases of production, use, and disposal can be calculated (Agrawal et al. 2012). The environmental burden during the production and disposal phases depends on the total number of products manufactured and disposed of during each time period, while during the use phase it depends on the amount of the overall use that customers extract from the products (it may already be apparent that what increases profit or consumer surplus may also increase the environmental burden). Each phase may also be characterized by a different per-unit environmental impact. For instance, a certain type of product may cause a higher environmental burden during the use phase as opposed to the production or disposal phase.

16.3.3   Servicizing: Possible Environmental Issues

From an environmental point of view, the implementation of servicizing, as opposed to a traditional sales-only business model, can backfire from a few angles. As an example, consider again the business model of car sharing. It is true that customers may choose to relinquish car ownership and decide to cover their transportation needs by joining a car sharing program, something that would constitute an environmental win. However, at the same time, car sharing may make car usage more attractive to customers who typically use more sustainable modes of transportation (e.g., biking and/or public transportation). While the pooling effect may cause the overall number of vehicles produced to decrease, a larger number of customers adopting car sharing may imply that the overall level of vehicle usage increases (see Bellos et al. 2016). Despite the fact that such an increase in usage may lead to a higher profit and higher consumer surplus, it can also be environmentally problematic because several studies (Sullivan and Cobas-Flores 2001; MacLean and Lave 2003) have shown that the majority of the environmental impact of an automobile occurs during the use phase of its lifecycle. This issue may not be unique to car sharing, as many other types of products are characterized by higher use rather than production impact.

Even the pooling effect, which can be directly linked to the concept of demateri-alization, may also be responsible for some unintended environmental drawbacks. The reason is that a smaller production volume due to pooling results in a smaller overall production cost, which may allow the manufacturer to: (1) lower the prices and/or (2) invest in improving the product efficiency (the manufacturer may be particularly interested in improving product efficiency because, under most servicizing business models, the manufacturer is responsible for the operating cost of the product). Since lower prices and improved efficiencies may further increase adoption and overall product usage (and therefore profitability), the well-known Jevons paradox[3] may occur and result in higher environmental burden.

In this section, we provided a brief summary of the economic and environmental implications associated with the implementation of a servicizing business model. For an analysis of the environmental performance of servicizing, we refer the reader to Agrawal and Bellos (2015). In what follows, we provide more details on how firms may implement a servicizing strategy and some of the major challenges inherent in doing so.

16.4 Implementing a Servicizing Strategy

Having discussed some of the multiple benefits that a servicizing strategy can provide, we now outline some of the possible implementation challenges that an organization may face during the transformation of its business model from a product-based one to a solutions-based one. In addition, we describe the close relationship of an even newer class of business models, known as collaborative consumption models, to servicizing business models. Finally, we provide information about a design technique that is widely used in practice and which can facilitate the implementation of a servicizing strategy.

16.4.1 Possible Transition and Implementation Challenges from Adopting Servicizing

From an economic point of view, the transition to services has not always been successful, as there have been several cases where increasing the service component of a product-based organization decreased the overall firm performance (Gebauer et al. 2005). Interestingly, recent research (Suarez et al. 2013) has identified a nonlinear effect between firm profitability and the extent of the service involvement. Specifically, services appear to have a positive effect on profitability after they reach a critical point of contribution to the firm's overall revenue. This may indicate a strategy where firms initially provide their services at a low price in order to attract customers into buying their products. As the number of customers reaches a critical mass, the firms may tend to focus on service delivery and to streamline the relevant processes, resulting in improved profitability.

---

[3]According to the Jevons paradox (also referred to as the rebound effect; Greening et al. 2000), the overall rate of consumption of a resource increases as the efficiency of the resource improves. That is, as we make the usage of something cheaper, we tend to use more of it.

One may argue that the inability of some product organizations to reap the benefits of providing services relates to the hurdles they face trying to transition from a product-based mentality to a service-based one. These hurdles can be attributed to the inherent differences[4] between managing products and managing services. For instance, in product-based environments, centralization, efficiency, economies of scale, and standardization share a common underpinning, that of eliminating variability, which is almost always considered to be a necessary condition for successful operational and financial performance. Now compare this with the unique characteristics (Zeithaml et al. 1985) that services are known to hold: (1) intangibility (i.e., lack of specifications), (2) heterogeneity in the customer requests and/or the service outcome, (3) perishability (i.e., inability to inventory service performance/outcome), and (4) co-production (i.e., the need for both the provider and the customer to be engaged to deliver the service outcome). If anything, these characteristics imply an exposure to higher variability. Therefore, the tension between the two worlds immediately becomes apparent. Moving from one mindset to another may arguably require extensive organizational "rewiring."

Certain implementation challenges, however, may be unique to (or at least more pronounced under) a servicizing business model that attempts to decouple product ownership from customer value. Such challenges may pertain to:

- Internal resistance from employees, especially salespeople, who under a product regime are typically compensated based on commissions tied to the quantity of products or material sold. Under servicizing, the base of the transaction is the solution that the product offers, not the product per se. For this reason, incentive mechanisms will have to be redesigned so that they do not depend on the quantity of products sold. New incentives may be focused on customer retention, increases in revenue, expansion of the customer base, etc. This can be a rocky transition because the differences in the magnitude of the dollar amount per transaction can be vast. For instance, 60–70 % of the maintenance cost of a jet engine is attributed to the cost of materials. Replaceable parts include airfoils, blades, and guide vanes. Replaceable parts include airfoils, blades, and guide vanes. A turbine blade may cost as much as $8,000. Given that an engine may comprise 60–80 blades, this can bring the value of a potential sale up to $700,000 for the maintenance of a single engine (information and numbers based on Ackert 2011). Without proactively addressing the compensation schemes, a company may realize a loss of talent during the early stages of the transition to servicizing. Toffel (2008) provides a thorough discussion on the agency issues in servicizing business models.
- The complexity of the new contractual agreements. This can be the case especially when such agreements are based on (uncertain) product performance (e.g., engine up-time). The cost of implementing such contracts may be more difficult

---

[4] Some of these differences are probably hard-coded due to differences in the training of key stakeholders. Such differences typically fortify silos within organizations. For instance, think of the eternal clash of the "hard" engineering/operations with the "soft" marketing side of the house.

to estimate since it depends on performance that is unrealized at the time of the agreement. Because of this, manufacturers may be tempted to overpromise on key performance metrics. However, failure to deliver on these promises may impose steep penalties, either by financially compensating the customer or by making last minute arrangements (e.g., through third-party providers) to ensure that customer needs are met. Of course, such problems may subside over time due to the manufacturer obtaining better data about the performance of the products or the client's operating needs and conditions. The manufacturer may even use this feedback to invest in products with higher reliability (Guajardo et al. 2012).

Changing the base of the transaction from the product to the service and solution level can be challenging for the customers too. The reason is that such a change also affects the basis of the cost-benefit analysis. Assessing the benefit requires a good estimation of the product usage needs (e.g., how many pages we print per year and what we gain from that), whereas assessing the cost requires the holistic estimation of expenses related to functions such as purchasing, operation, maintenance, and disposal, which for most organizations are decentralized (i.e., different parts of the organization are responsible for each function).

For instance, consider the failed attempt of Interface to transition from selling carpets to offering "floorcovering services." Specifically, through what was known as Evergreen™ Services Agreement (EVA), instead of selling carpets, Interface began offering long-term carpet leases that required the purchase of additional support services such as maintenance and selective tiles replacement. However, several years after launch and despite the strong support from top-management, the EVA's market acceptance remained weak. One of the main reasons was that customers rarely understood how much they currently were spending on cleaning and maintaining their carpets since these expenses were often buried under more general maintenance and cleaning budgets. For this reason, the EVA option often appeared to be uneconomical compared with the perceived status quo (Oliva and Quinn 2003; for a more detailed discussion of the reasons EVA failed, see Toktay et al. 2006 and Ferguson and Plambeck 2008).

- Behavioral effects such as the endowment effect, which postulates that customers tend to place more value on objects that they own than on those that they do not (Thaler 1980; Kahneman et al. 1991) and, for that reason, may not find servicizing as appealing as direct ownership. Although there is already evidence (The Economist 2012) that customers (especially of younger age) now exhibit a more utilitarian attitude towards consumption that is not influenced as much by behavioral effects, this is a cultural/generational change that may require time to fully occur. Also, the lack of product ownership may induce availability or accessibility anxieties, similar to the range of anxieties observed among drivers of electric vehicles (Avci et al. 2015; Lim et al. 2015).
- Faster deterioration due to heavier use or more frequent repairs of the products due to customers' careless use, or even abuse, of the equipment. For instance, car-sharing customers may be less mindful of road hazards or may be less conservative with their driving behavior when they are not financially responsible

for the maintenance of the vehicle they use. Such behavior can also diminish possible environmental benefits because it may either decrease the efficiency of the products (i.e., products may require more energy to deliver the same amount of use) and/or may require the provider to replace the products more often (i.e., it may increase the number of products required per unit of time). As another example, theft, damages, and vandalism are among the most challenging problems that Vélib, the French bike-sharing provider, has been facing since it started operating in Paris in 2007 (The New York Times 2009; France24 2013). Extra security measures, monitoring mechanisms, product redesigns, and more frequent maintenance, however, can partially address such issues, albeit at an increased cost.

- Customer-induced negative externalities. Specifically, the fact that under servicizing customers do not maintain product ownership implies a loss of control over the product and that the value each customer derives, to a certain extent, depends on decisions made and actions taken (even inadvertently) by other customers. For instance, in a car sharing model, a late return of a vehicle can interfere with the reservations of other customers. Similarly, failure of one customer to refuel or maintain a vehicle's cleanliness can negatively affect the experience of the other users. To counter such negative experiences, the provider may be required to install monitoring mechanisms along with a penalty structure to dissuade such behaviors. However, such "instrumental controls" (Frei 2005) may be perceived as a license to break the rules (e.g., license to be late in the case of car sharing) because it quantifies the implications of doing so and, therefore, a customer can engage in a cost-benefit analysis, ignoring how their actions will affect other customers. According to Levitt and Dubner (2005), this was the case when some daycare centers in Israel imposed penalties on parents who were late in picking-up their kids. After announcing the fees, the centers observed an increase in the parents' tardiness (the original experiment can be found in Gneezy and Rustichini 2000). On the contrary, "normative controls" rely on subjective measures such as shame, guilt, embarrassment, and a sense of community or sense of duty. A provider's task is thus to devise mechanisms that can deter unacceptable behavior by eliciting such reactions and feelings. For instance, Zipcar always tries to create a sense of community by referring to its members as "Zipsters" or by featuring stories of its members and employees on its online magazine Ziptopia. For an excellent discussion of instrumental vs. normative controls, see Frei (2005).

16.4.2   From an Economy Based on Products to Services and Now, to Collaborative Consumption?

Recently, a new type of business model has been gaining traction by building on what is known as collaborative consumption. The concept of collaborative consumption refers to the type of consumption that takes place through (peer-to-peer) sharing, swapping, lending, or other similar activities (Botsman and Rogers 2011). Such activities may or may not involve monetary exchange. For instance, other than maybe some gestures of appreciation (e.g., cooking dinner), members of Couchsurfing do not typically exchange money in return for the hospitality provided. On the other hand, in the more well-known business models of Airbnb and Uber, participating members (i.e., qualified hosts and drivers) contribute their properties by listing their apartments/houses and driving services, respectively, to the greater pool in return for monetary compensation, which is typically based on the amount of time the property was used by other customers. Similar to servicizing,[5] the importance of product ownership is diminished in the sense that no ownership rights are transferred to each end-user and payment is linked to product usage.

Business models that rely on collaborative consumption may alleviate some of the economic issues identified earlier for the servicizing models by achieving a middle ground. For instance, drivers of Uber can still maintain the pride of ownership of their vehicles and, at the same time, improve the utilization for a fair compensation. Essentially, such models achieve a more efficient matching of supply with demand by: (1) increasing both the availability and accessibility of capacity, (2) encouraging efficient allocation of the supply through centralized and dynamic pricing, and (3) removing information asymmetries regarding the quality of the product/service through online review systems.

From an environmental point of view, however, it is not clear whether such new business models will have a positive impact. For instance, one may argue that Uber may be actually contributing to a higher environmental burden because, to a certain extent, it makes vehicle ownership more affordable by creating another source of revenue through which drivers can cover car ownership-related expenses (i.e., gas, maintenance, insurance, etc.). On the other hand, it can also be argued that it contributes to creating a more developed and interconnected network of transportation. As an example, it may make it easier for a traveler to hire an Uber cab to head to a Metro station and then use public transportation to travel to the final destination (e.g., the airport). Therefore, there may be segments of the market that find it more economical to cover their transportation needs through Uber (and public transportation) and, for that reason, choose to relinquish car ownership, thus contributing to the dematerialization of the economy.

Future research is needed to shed more light on the economic and environmental implications of collaborative consumption models. One promising direction can be the identification of the profile of customers (e.g., in terms of income or usage needs, etc.) who would benefit most from choosing to cover their needs through such models.

---

[5] It has been suggested that PSS can be thought of as a special category of collaborative consumption business model (Botsman and Rogers 2011). However, we should point out that most collaborative consumption models are found in B2C contexts and are typically offered by third-party providers. In contrast, servicizing models are observed in both B2C and B2B settings and often are offered by manufacturers and/or third party providers.

16.4.3 Design Tools That Can Facilitate Servicizing

Implementing a servicizing strategy to transform from a product organization to a solutions organization will probably come along with an array of critical decisions. For instance, the firm may need to determine: the pricing structure (e.g., how much to charge and whether to include a fixed fee in addition to a pay-per-use fee), the capacity (e.g., in the context of car sharing, the size of the fleet; see Bellos et al. 2016), the efficiency/reliability/durability of its products (see Guajardo et al. 2012 and Agrawal and Bellos 2015), or to what extent (if any at all) the "business-as-usual" model of selling products should be abandoned (e.g., the firm may decide to focus entirely on selling products, offering solutions, or offering both solutions and selling products; see Agrawal and Bellos 2015).

However, before a firm starts tackling such issues, certain aspects of which it may have addressed in its existing business model (e.g., pricing issues are not unique to servicizing business models), it is important to identify the key differentiator between the practice of selling products and the practice of selling solutions. To do so, it could attempt to answer the question of whether moving from the product business to the solutions business requires a materially different perspective. Namely, does the firm need to use different lenses to look at its offerings, or does it suffice to focus on the aforementioned operational and marketing issues (e.g., determining the capacity and the pricing, respectively)?

To answer these questions requires going through the task of rephrasing and reframing everything in terms of solutions. This can be a revealing exercise. For instance, thinking in terms of selling mobility solutions (as opposed to selling cars) may uncover that the order winners no longer have to do with certain product specifications (e.g., time to increase speed from 0 to 60 mph) and features (e.g., whether a specific car model comes with dual climate control and electronically adjustable seats). This first step can eliminate the product-related tunnel vision and enable the firm to start thinking along the lines of how to best assist their customers in meeting their basic needs.

This implies a holistic perspective that extends before and after the transaction point (i.e., the point where payment occurs) between a customer and a firm. For instance, the satisfaction that customers derive from meeting their mobility needs through a car sharing program is also determined by the ease with which they navigate through the website to find available vehicles and make reservations, make changes in their reservations, find the designated parking lot and the reserved car, address unforeseen situations (e.g., having a flat tire), and finally, make payments and manage their accounts. The challenge in this case for the firm is to identify the different elements that shape the overall customer experience.

Towards this end, design thinking can be of great value. Design thinking (Brown 2008) refers to a human-centered design approach that relies on direct observation and rapid prototyping (indeed, services can be prototyped; see Thomke 2003) to create solutions that holistically address customer needs. It goes beyond traditional marketing techniques (e.g., focus groups) because it allows customers to be in their natural environment where they may use a product or receive a service. This is typically achieved through empathic techniques (Leonard and Rayport 1997) such as shadowing, which allow researchers to have a customer-centric view of the firm's offering. One of the most insightful and practical outcomes of these techniques is the creation of the customer journey[6] map. The customer journey map delineates the series of different steps/stages that customers go through every time they satisfy a need (e.g., mobility need). These different stages are known as touch-points (or moments of truth; see Bitner et al. 2008) because they indicate points/moments at which customers possibly interact with some aspect of the firm's offering (e.g., interact with the online reservation system) and derive an experience.

The value of the customer journey rests on the fact that it enables the firm to identify all the different elements that positively contribute to the customer experience along with the points of failure in which the firm needs to improve on. Essentially, it delineates the process through which customers interact with the firms. This process-based view is indicative of the role that the operations management discipline can play in the development of such methods. In addition to the process, the people (i.e., user) dimension is in support of the expansion of the celebrated "4P's" of the marketing mix to "6P's" that define the service mix (Teboul 2006). The customer journey represents a method that is conducive to collaborations among disciplines that can break the silos we mentioned before. IDEO, the innovation and design consulting firm, has pioneered its use as a design method in the domain of both products and services (Bhavnani and Sosa 2006) through the use of diverse and interdisciplinary teams. For an analytical treatment and discussion on the use of the customer journey as a service design framework, we refer the reader to Bellos and Kavadias (2014).

Admittedly, we have presented two sides of the same coin. On one side, the transition to servicizing can be a challenging one as there are many difficulties that an organization may have to tackle. On the other (brighter) side, there are multiple benefits such as a growing demand for innovative business models that depart from conventional product/ownership-based models and the existence of established design methods that can be used to make the implementation of servicizing models easier. In the next section, we conclude this chapter by offering some thoughts on what remains to be done.

16.5 Conclusion

The increasing number of manufacturing companies that transition to more service- and solution-oriented business models indicates that Theodore Levitt's quote that "People don't want to buy a quarter-inch drill. They want a quarter-inch hole!"

---

[6] The concept of the customer journey relates to the service blueprints first mentioned in the seminal work of Shostack (1987). For a more recent discussion on the application of service blueprint see Bitner et al. (2008). Stickdorn and Schneider (2010) describe additional design thinking methods applied on services.

(Christensen et al. 2006) is more true and relevant than ever. Done correctly, this transition will be associated with environmental as well as economic benefits. In this chapter, we explored some potential advantages and disadvantages, from both the economic and environmental perspectives, associated with this transition. Identifying these advantages and disadvantages is an important step closer to a service-based economy. However, there is more work that needs to be done both from researchers and practitioners to help overcome the hurdles that firms may face when making this transition. For instance,

- From an academic/research point of view: existing assessment methodologies such as Lifecycle Analysis (LCA) may have to be further developed and applied in servicizing settings to account for usage patterns, which may differ significantly compared with when customers own the product. Along these lines, it is not clear whether offering certain types of products through servicizing may result in more frequent replacement (due to increased wear and tear) and overall larger production quantity than other types of products. Furthermore, more light needs to be shed on the major drivers that determine customers' decisions to forego product ownership. When is the lack of ownership more acceptable to customers, and what kind of technologies need to be developed to alleviate "anxieties" about product unavailability (i.e., the concern about not having access to a product when needed)? Can offering an increased variety of products (e.g., under a car sharing program this would imply offering an increased variety of brands and trims) make servicizing models more appealing as customers get to experience a broader range of products?
- From a managerial point of view: perhaps the greatest challenge is a cultural one. Manufacturers need to realize that they are in the solutions business and act on this realization. Ford has already started its transition to a "mobility company" (Fortune 2015) and hopefully more manufacturers will be encouraged to follow this example. Of course, such a transition cannot and should not happen overnight. As highlighted by several successful cases (Ford 2015; Peugeot 2015), constant experimentation through small-scale pilot programs is likely the safest approach that manufacturers can use to gain momentum and make the transition.

Overall, we hope that our discussion in this chapter will motivate further interest in the exciting topic of servicizing as an alternative business model for product-centric firms.

References

Abbey JD, Daniel V, Guide R Jr (2017) Closed-loop supply chains: a strategic overview. In: Bouchery Y, Corbett CJ, Fransoo J, Tan T (eds) Sustainable supply chains: a research-based textbook on operations and strategy. Springer, New York

Ackert S (2011) Engine maintenance concepts for financiers. Elements of turbofan shop maintenance costs. http://www.aircraftmonitor.com/uploads/1/5/9/9/15993320/engine_mx_concepts_for_financiers___v2.pdf

Agrawal V, Bellos I (2015) The potential of servicizing as a green business model. Forthcoming in Manag Sci. http://papers.ssrn.com/sol3/papers.cfm?abstract_id=2325218

Agrawal V, Ferguson M, Toktay B, Thomas V (2012) Is leasing greener than selling? Manag Sci 58(3):523–533

Avci B, Girotra K, Netessine S (2015) Electric vehicles with a switching station: adoption and environmental impact. Manag Sci 61(4):772–794

Bellos I, Kavadias S (2014) A framework for service design, Working Paper. http://papers.ssrn.com/sol3/papers.cfm?abstract_id=2476072

Bellos I, Ferguson M, Toktay B (2016) To sell and to provide? The economic and environmental implications of the auto manufacturer's involvement in the car sharing. Business, Working Paper. http://papers.ssrn.com/sol3/papers.cfm?abstract_id=2372406

Bhavnani R, Sosa M (2006) IDEO: service design (A&B). INSEAD case study 11/2006-5276.

Bitner M, Ostrom A, Morgan F (2008) Service blueprinting: a practical technique for service innovation. Calif Manage Rev 50(3):66

Botsman R, Rogers R (2011) What's mine is yours: how collaborative consumption is changing the way we live. Collins, London

Brown T (2008) Design thinking. Harv Bus Rev 86(6):84

Businessweek (2014) China's revised GDP shows rebalancing success with bigger service sector. http://www.businessweek.com/articles/2014-12-19/china-adds-the-equivalent-of-malaysia-to-its-output

Christensen C, Cook S, Hal T (2006) What customers want from your products. Harvard Business School Newsletter, Working Knowledge. 16 Jan

Corbett C, DeCroix G (2001) Shared-savings contracts for indirect materials in supply chains: channel profits and environmental impacts. Manag Sci 47(7):881–893

Corbett C, DeCroix G, Ha A (2005) Optimal shared-savings contracts in supply chains: linear contracts and double moral hazard. Eur J Oper Res 163(3):653–667

Department for Environment, Food & Rural Affairs (2015) Digest of waste and resource statistics. https://www.gov.uk/government/statistics/digest-of-waste-and-resource-statistics-2015-edition

U.S. Environmental Protection Agency (2009) Green servicizing for a more sustainable us economy: key concepts, tools and analyses to inform policy engagement. http://www.epa.gov/epa-waste/conserve/tools/stewardship/docs/green-service.pdf

U.S. Environmental Protection Agency (2012) Municipal solid waste generation, recycling, and disposal in the United States: Facts and Figures for 2012. http://www.epa.gov/osw/nonhaz/municipal/pubs/2012_msw_fs.pdf

European Commission (2014) Towards a circular economy: a zero waste programme for Europe. http://eur-lex.europa.eu/legal-content/EN/TXT/?qid=1415352499863&uri=CELEX:52014DC0398R%2801%29

Ferguson M, Plambeck E (2008) Teaching note for interfaces' Evergreen Services Agreement. Harvard Business School, Cambridge

Fischer S, Steger S, Jordan N, OBrien M, Schepelmann P (2012) Leasing Society, Policy Department A: Economic and Scientific Policy, Committee on Environment, Public Health and Food Safety, European Parliament

Ford (2015) Mobility experiment: Ford carsharing. Germany. https://media.ford.com/content/ford-media/fna/us/en/news/2015/01/06/mobility-experiment-ford-charsharing-germany.html

Fortune (2015) How Ford's chief became a tech CEO. http://fortune.com/2015/04/24/mark-fields-ford-ceo/

France24 (2013) Theft and vandalism blight Paris bike-share system. http://www.france24.com/en/20130920-france-theft-vandalism-paris-bike-share-system-velib/

Frei FX (2005) Zipcar: influencing customer behavior. Harvard Business School Case Study 9-605-054. Harvard University, Cambridge

Gebauer H, Fleisch E, Friedli T (2005) Overcoming the service paradox in manufacturing companies. Eur Manage J 23(1):14–26

Gneezy U, Rustichini A (2000) A fine is a price. J Legal Stud 29(1):1–17

Greening L, Greene D, Difiglio C (2000) Energy efficiency and consumption-the rebound effect- a survey. Energ Policy 28(6):389–401

Guajardo J, Cohen M, Kim S, Netessine S (2012) Impact of performance-based contracting on product reliability: an empirical analysis. Manag Sci 58(5):961–979

Guinée J, Heijungs R (2017) Introduction to life cycle assessment. In: Bouchery Y, Corbett CJ, Fransoo J, Tan T (eds) Sustainable supply chains: a research-based textbook on operations and strategy. Springer, New York

Heiskanen E, Jalas M (2000) Dematerialization through services: a review and evaluation of the debate., Ministry of Environment

IBM (2014) IBM issues statement on U.S. Government regulatory approval of x86-based server divestiture to Lenovo. https://www-03.ibm.com/press/us/en/pressrelease/44588.wss

Kahneman D, Knetsch J, Thaler R (1991) Anomalies: the endowment effect, loss aversion, and status quo bias. J Econ Perspect 5(1):193–206

Lambrecht A, Skiera B (2006) Paying too much and being happy about it: existence, causes, and consequences of tariff-choice biases. J Marketing Res 43(2):212–223

Lenovo (2004) Lenovo to acquire IBM personal computing division. http://www.lenovo.com/news/us/en/2005/04/ibm_lenovo.html

Leonard D, Rayport J (1997) Spark innovation through empathic design. Harv Bus Rev 75:102–115

Levitt S, Dubner S (2005) Freakonomics: a rogue economist explores the hidden side of everything. William Morrow, New York

Lim M, Mak H, Rong Y (2015) Toward mass adoption of electric vehicles: impacts of the range and resale anxieties. Manufact Serv Oper Management 58(3):523–533

MacLean HL, Lave LB (2003) Life cycle assessment of automobile/fuel options. Environ Sci Technol 37(23):5445–5452

Oliva R, Quinn J (2003) Interfaces Evergreen™ Services Agreement. Harvard Business School Case Study 9-603-112, Harvard University

Peugeot (2015) Mu by Peugeot. http://www.peugeot.com/en/products-services/services/mu-by-peugeot

Rothenberg S (2007) Sustainability through servicizing. MIT Sloan Manage Rev 48(2):83–91

Sawhney M, Balasubramanian S, Krishnan V (2003) Creating growth with services. MIT Sloan Manage Rev 45(2):34–44

Shostack G (1987) Service positioning through structural change. J Marketing 51(1):34–43

SKF (2014) Asset diagnostic services. http://www.skf.com/group/services/asset-management-services/asset-diagnostic-services/index.html

Stahel W (1994) The utilization-focused service economy: resource efficiency and product-life extension. National Academy Press, Washington. DC

Stickdorn M, Schneider J (2010) This is service design thinking: basics-tools-cases. BIS, Amsterdam

Suarez F, Cusumano M, Kahl S (2013) Services and the business models of product firms: an empirical analysis of the software industry. Manag Sci 59(2):420–435

Sullivan J, Cobas-Flores E (2001) Full vehicle LCAs: a review. Tech. rep, SAE Technical Paper

Teboul J (2006) Service is front stage: positioning services for value advantage. Palgrave Macmillan, New York

Thaler R (1980) Toward a positive theory of consumer choice. J Econ Behav Org 1(1):39–60

The Economist (2012) Seeing the back of the car. http://www.economist.com/node/21563280

The New York Times (2009) French Ideal of bicycle-sharing meets reality. http://www.nytimes.com/2009/10/31/world/europe/31bikes.html?pagewanted=all&_r=1&amp

The World Bank (2013) Indicators. http://data.worldbank.org/indicator/NV.SRV.TETC.ZS

Thomke S (2003) R&D comes to services. Bank of America's path breaking experiments. Harvard Bus Rev 81(4):70–79

Toffel M (2008) Contracting for servicizing. Working Paper, Harvard Business School. http://papers.ssrn.com/sol3/papers.cfm?abstract_id=1090237

Toktay B, Selhat L, Anderson R (2006) Doing well by doing good: interface's vision of being the first industrial company in the world to attain sustainability. In: Rouse W (ed) Enterprise transformation: understanding and enabling fundamental change. Wiley, New York

Tukker A (2004) Eight types of product-service system: eight ways to sustainability? Experiences from SusProNet. Business Strat Environ 13(4):246–260

White A, Stoughton M, Feng L (1999) Servicizing: the quiet transition to extended producer responsibility. Tech. Rep. U. S. Environmental Protection Agency, Office of Solid Waste

Wise R, Baumgartner P (1999) Go downstream. Harvard Bus Rev 77(5):133–141

Xerox (2015) Managed print services. http://www.services.xerox.com/xerox-managed-print-services/enus.html

Zeithaml V, Parasuraman A, Berry L (1985) Problems and strategies in services marketing. J Marketing 49(2):33–46

Chapter 17
Closed-Loop Supply Chains: A Strategic Overview

James D. Abbey and V. Daniel R. Guide Jr.

Managers who consider a closed-loop supply chain just another environmental initiative need to update their thinking. Modern firms that use closed-loop supply chains as a competitive strategy receive many benefits—particularly higher profitability and control over a product's entire lifecycle. In fact, the market for multiple lifecycle products continues to grow, with current estimates holding that remanufactured product sales exceed \$100 billion per year.[1] As a result of analyzing the ever-growing remanufacturing sector through years of working with managers in numerous industries, various levers and themes surrounding effective closed-loop supply chain strategies became apparent. This chapter presents these findings and shows how firms in multiple industries experienced both successes and failures of their closed-loop supply chain strategies.

---

[1] Current estimates of the remanufactured products market in the US come from the United States International Trade Commission (USITC) report on remanufactured goods. See USITC. 2012. Remanufactured goods: an overview of the US and global industries, markets, and trade. Public report, U.S. International Trade Commission accessible at http://www.usitc.gov/publications/332/pub4356.pdf.

J.D. Abbey (✉)
Mays Business School, Texas A&M University,
4217 TAMU, College Station, TX 77843-4217, USA
e-mail: jabbey@mays.tamu.edu

V.D.R. Guide Jr.
Smeal College of Business, Pennsylvania State University,
480 Business Building, University Park, PA 16802, USA
e-mail: dguide@psu.edu

© Yann Bouchery, Charles J. Corbett, Jan C. Fransoo, and Tarkan Tan 2017
Y. Bouchery et al. (eds.), *Sustainable Supply Chains*, Springer Series in Supply Chain Management 4, DOI 10.1007/978-3-319-29791-0_17

17.1   Understanding a Closed-Loop Supply Chain

Over the past few decades, environmental initiatives moved from tertiary goals to integral parts of corporate strategy. The environmental transformation manifested for multiple reasons, ranging from corporate social responsibility initiatives (see also Chap. 20 by Lee and Rammohan, in this volume) to increasing levels of legislative mandates (see also Chap. 10 by Huang and Atasu, in this volume).[2] Whatever the reason for the shift toward environmental initiatives, the outcome is clear: managers need innovative ways to reduce environmental impact while simultaneously improving profitability. Though common wisdom holds that environmental constraints will inevitably reduce profits, numerous counterpoints exist as manifested in firms that successfully implemented closed-loop supply chain (CLSC) strategies.[3] This chapter provides a current look at the ever-evolving body of CLSC knowledge. Through looking at the body of knowledge, the chapter provides strategies to help managers understand the challenges and opportunities of CLSCs in various types of industries under differing strategic forces.

---

[2] Corporate social responsibility continues to generate much debate about the role of a corporation as a good citizen. For an excellent discussion of such issues, see Carroll, A. B. 1999. Corporate social responsibility evolution of a definitional construct. Business & Society 38(3): 268–295.

Additionally, for firms less interested in internally promoting environmental initiatives, legislative mandates regarding environmental performance and impact are particularly prevalent in the European Union with the waste electrical and electronic equipment (WEEE: http://ec.europa.eu/environment/waste/weee/legis_en.htm) and reduction of hazardous substances (RoHS: http://ec.europa.eu/environment/waste/rohs_eee/index_en.htm). Both laws seek to control environmental impact. Though the E.U. was among the first to enact such laws, Japan (http://www.env.go.jp/en/policy/) and Australia (http://www.environment.gov.au/about-us/legislation) have followed with similar legislation aimed at curbing environmental impact.

Though much of the strict recycling mandates legislation has not occurred within the US, multinational firms already maintain product portfolios that meet the ambitious requirements. Should the legislative programs continue to expand throughout the world, firms holding such product portfolios may hold a competitive advantage over competitors who currently do not meet the requirements of such legislation. Various recent works address the issue of environmental legislation and product take-back. For two such works, see Atasu, A. and L.N. Van Wassenhove. 2010. "Environmental Legislation Regarding Product Take-Back and Recovery" in 'Closed-Loop Supply Chains,' Eds. M. Ferguson, G. Souza. Taylor and Francis. and a work tailored to the extended producer responsibility for electronics waste Atasu, A., R. Subramanian. 2012. Extended Producer Responsibility for E-Waste: Individual or Collective Responsibility? *Production and Operations Management* 21(6): 1042–1059.

[3] If the concept of a closed-loop supply chain is unfamiliar, multiple resources can provide guidance and insights. For example, see Guide, V.D.R. Jr., and Van Wassenhove, L.N. 2003. "Business Aspects of Closed-Loop Supply Chains" in Guide, V.D.R. Jr., and Van Wassenhove, L.N. (eds.), Business Aspects of Closed-Loop Supply Chains Exploring the Issues. Pittsburgh: Carnegie Mellon University Press. Also, see Ferguson, M.E. and Souza, G.C. 2010. "Closed-Loop Supply Chains New Developments to Improve the Sustainability of Business Practices. Boca Raton: CRC Press."

17.2   The Core of a Closed-Loop Supply Chain

At the core, a closed-loop supply chain represents a series of processes and flows aimed at some form of reuse or reclamation of products and materials. Specifically, a closed-loop supply chain incorporates design, control, and operation of a system to maximize value creation over the entire lifecycle of a product with dynamic recovery of value from different types and volumes of returns over time.[4] As the definition states, a CLSC must be dynamic and evolve over time to handle changing market conditions. Such evolution makes managing a closed-loop supply chain an ever-evolving set of processes, which can take on many different forms depending on the product and industry in which a firm operates. Though a CLSC requires decisions at every macro decision level—operation, tactical, and strategic—this chapter focuses heavily on the broad strategic issues facing a manager considering a CLSC. As will become clear, the decision to operate a CLSC should be based on seeking increased profit—not just reducing costs—and improving corporate social responsibility through improved environmental performance.

Of course, before a CLSC can start a second lifecycle for a product, a first life-cycle must occur followed by the accompanying return of the product into a reuse market. On one extreme, the return of the product into a reuse market can be in the form of an end-of-use product that received considerable use by a prior owner, which is typical in the business-to-business markets for large industrial equipment (e.g., Caterpillar earth moving equipment and Xerox high-speed imaging equipment). On the other extreme, unlike the end-of-use returns that have often experienced extensive use, consumer product returns are often convenience returns—returns due to the customer simply deciding that the product does not suit their needs.[5] These convenience returns, also called false failures, usually require minimal processing before returning to the market. Staggeringly, consumer product returns in the United States now exceed $260 billion in 2013 alone.[6] In either extreme case, a CLSC using remanufacturing provides a direct form of reuse that converts returned products into like new condition for resale. Remanufacturing entails disassembling the returned product, replacing any worn or broken components, repairing any remaining defects, and repackaging the product for sale as a remanufactured item.[7]

---

[4] For a recent discussion of the continuing challenges in closed-loop supply chains, see Guide, V. D. R. and L.N. Van Wassenhove. 2009. The evolution of closed-loop supply chain research. Operations Research 57(1): 10–18.

[5] The rate of false failure returns can vary widely by the nature of the product and industry. As a prime example in the consumer electronics industry, Hewlett-Packard experienced false failure returns rates as high as 80% of all inkjet printer returns. On the other hand, Bosch false failure return rates at a vastly lower 2% of all power drill returns. For more information, see Ferguson, M., V.D.R. Guide, Jr., G.C. Souza. 2006. Supply chain coordination for false failure returns. Manufacturing & Service Operations Management 8(4): 376–393.

[6] The National Retail Federation offers free, detailed reports on returns. For recent reports, such as the 2013 report noted, see http://www.theretailequation.com/retailers/IndustryReports.

[7] The Remanufacturing Institute's (http://www.reman.org) gives an in-depth look at remanufacturing from various industry perspectives. In particular, the website provides details about remanufacturing processes and the resulting environmental benefits.

17.2.1 Overview of Closed-Loop Supply Chain Activities

Before moving into a detailed discussion of the process flows of a CLSC, a high level view at the three major CLSC activities provides context for readers who are not yet familiar with the nature of closed-loop supply chain. Figure 17.1 provides a high level view of the front-end, engine, and back-end of a closed-loop supply chain.

The front-end activities entail collecting returned products through product acquisition management. As noted previously, some products will be heavily used, while others may have seen minimal if any use. Such diversity in the nature of returns makes product acquisition management a critical activity for any manager considering a CLSC strategy. If acquisition of returned product cores is relatively simple, engaging in CLSC operations can be a fairly straightforward endeavor. Conversely, if acquiring returned product cores is difficult or widely dispersed, even the first step of collecting returned products can prove to be a challenge. After returns are collected, the engine activities allow remanufacturing of the returned product to a like new condition.[8] Though this chapter does not delve into the operational details, the topic of the engineering feasibility and technical constraints in a CLSC has

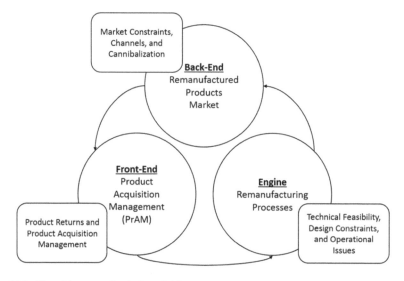

Fig. 17.1 Closed-loop supply chain activities

---

[8] For an examination of issues in production planning and control in the engine portion of remanufacturing, see Guide, V.D.R., Jr. 2000. Production planning and control for remanufacturing: industry practice and research needs. *Journal of Operations Management* 18(4): 467–483. For detailed information about the issues related to grading the quality of cores acquired through the front-end processes of product acquisition management, see Ferguson, M., V.D.R. Guide, Jr., E. Koca, and G.S. Souza. 2009. The value of quality grading in remanufacturing. *Production and Operations Management* 18(3): 300–314.

received much attention over the past decades (see Footnote 3). After the product has been brought back to a marketable condition, the back-end activities entail putting the product back into the market for another lifecycle. Until recently, the nature of the market for reused products has received little attention. Fortunately, recent research has started to define the similarities and contrasts with the typical new product market.[9] As will be discussed at length later in this chapter, the three major CLSC activities all work in unison and can be done in-house or as outsourced operations.

17.2.2 Examining Closed-Loop Supply Chain Flows

The primary function of a CLSC is to employ some form of reuse at the product, component, or materials level. Each of these choices comes with differing degrees of constraints, both in terms of recovery strategy and remarketing of the multiple lifecycle product. Understanding how these constraints vary by the nature of the industry is critical for managers investigating means to implement or improve their firm's CLSC strategy. Figure 17.2 displays various flows at the product, component, and materials levels.[10] (Chap. 5 by Blass et al., in this volume provides more detail on analyzing and managing material flows.) Each of these flows offers firms

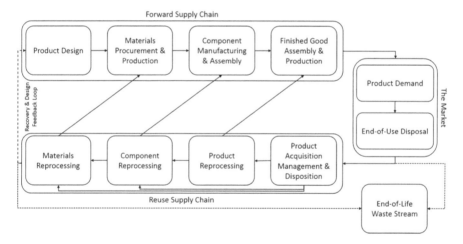

Fig. 17.2 Closed-loop supply chain flows and functions

---

[9] For an overview of the current state of market based literature for remanufactured products and pricing structures, and market segments, see, Abbey, J.D., M.G. Meloy, V.D.R. Guide, Jr., and J.D. Blackburn. 2015. Barriers and Strategies for Product Reuse in Consumer Markets. Under review at *California Management Review*.

[10] This figure is adapted from, Abbey, J.D., V.D.R. Guide Jr. 2012. "Closed-Loop Supply Chains" in T. Bansal, A. Hoffman, (eds.), Oxford Handbook on Business and the Natural Environment. New York: Oxford University Press, 290–309.

different opportunities for recovery and reuse strategies, which are directly influenced by the original product design. In particular, materials reprocessing would typically fall in the realm of recycling. For example, recycled plastics may be used as either like-to-like (e.g., water bottles) or down-cycling (e.g., tires to rubber mulch) materials. The component and product reprocessing, typically called refurbishing or remanufacturing, generally require far less energy intensity than materials recycling. As such, product and component reuse are generally preferable over the more energy-intensive recycling, which is the least preferred of the options from an environmental standpoint.[11]

As shown in Fig. 17.2, some form of a waste stream is inevitable. Simply put, some products, components, and materials have a limited number of lifecycles or only a single use. The goal of a manager trying to implement environmental initiatives through a CLSC is to convert what was previously a stream of waste into profitable reuse. Though this sounds like an ideal win–win scenario—environmental benefits and higher profits—many pitfalls prevent firms from committing to a CLSC strategy. In the consumer products arena, one of the highest hurdles is the challenge of cannibalization of new product sales with the sale of lower-priced remanufactured offerings. As discussed just a few years ago, managers should handle this challenge from a total profitability, portfolio perspective.[12] For most firms considering a CLSC, the problem of reacquiring previously sold products, product acquisition management (PrAM), can be daunting as the reverse supply chain flows may not be a current competence.[13] In particular, for firms in the technology sector that face a high marginal value of time—a rapid decline in a product's value during a lifecycle—acquiring, testing, inspecting, and returning the product to market quickly are imperative. On the flip side, for firms facing lesser marginal value of time pressures—minimal decline in the product's value during a lifecycle—the acquisition and resulting remanufacturing activities are not as time-sensitive or asset-intensive.[14]

Other related research has shown that there is no one-size-fits-all strategy for a closed-loop supply chain. For some firms, such as the Xerox Corporation, product

---

[11] For further information on the reduce, reuse, and recycle (3R) hierarchy, see the Environmental Protection Agency's website at http://www2.epa.gov/recycle.

[12] See Atasu, A., V.D.R. Guide, Jr., L.N. Van Wassenhove. 2009. So what if remanufacturing cannibalizes new product sales? *California Management Review* 52: 56-76.

[13] For additional insights into how to operate in a competitive core acquisition market, see Guide, V. D. R., R.H. Teunter, and L.N. Van Wassenhove. 2003. Matching demand and supply to maximize profits from remanufacturing. *Manufacturing & Service Operations Management* 5: 303–316.

[14] For a detailed look at the nature of such challenges related to marginal value of time in fast moving industries such as consumer electronics, see Guide, V. D. R., G.C. Souza, L.N. Van Wassenhove, and J.D. Blackburn. 2006. Time value of commercial product returns. *Management Science* 52: 1200–1214. For potential solutions to maximize profits based on the nature of the industry's marginal value of time, see Blackburn, J.D., V.D.R. Guide, G.C. Souza, and L.N. Van Wassenhove. 2004. Reverse Supply Chains for Commercial Returns. *California Management Review* 46: 6–22.

acquisition is quite simple as customers often lease large printing equipment, but life-cycle management and design issues represent major challenges.[15] Conversely, many consumer product firms have had great difficulty managing the core acquisition process and reverse supply chain as the consumer products typically have a short, single lifecycle.[16] To shed light on the differences in strategy by the nature of the industry, this chapter delves into two major dimensions that help a firm match their CLSC strategy with the nature of their market — product design and core competencies.

17.3   A Framework for Matching Product Design and Core Competencies

Product design is a highly complex topic in its own right. Thus, adding yet another layer of complexity in the form of designing for more than one lifecycle may seem daunting. Fortunately, designing for multiple lifecycles tends to have many positive effects, such as reduced return rates, easier reparability, and faster turnaround for warranty claims and returns.[17] Of course, when market pressures are high to get an innovative product to the market, speed and efficiency of production often take predominant roles as is often the case in the consumer technology industry. Due to such market-based pressures, many firms have naturally evolved core competencies based on the nature of their industries' competitive layout. However, as a product line matures and technological innovation slows, the move toward CLSC operations

---

[15] The Xerox Corporation has been a world leader in remanufacturing systems at their Webster, New York manufacturing/remanufacturing hybrid facilities. In both popular press and academic research, Xerox stands out as an exemplar of environmentally friendly closed-loop supply chain systems. Xerox works diligently from the design phase forward to recycle and remanufacture their equipment with great success in energy, materials, and waste reduction. For instance, in 2011, Xerox's remanufacturing operations diverted over 13 million pounds of waste from landfills. See a recent corporate sustainability report at http://www.xerox.com/corporate-citizenship/2012/sustainability/product-design/enus.html.

[16] Reverse supply chain design for consumer products remains a persistent issue for many firms. For a detailed discussion of viable solutions in consumer product industries, see the *California Management Review* article, Blackburn, J.D., V.D.R. Guide, G.C. Souza, and L.N. Van Wassenhove. 2004. Reverse Supply Chains for Commercial Returns. *California Management Review* 46: 6–22.

[17] Much recent research focuses on the need for better understanding of design for remanufacturing and reuse. Many resources exist for those interested in the engineering side of design such as the Rochester Institute of Technology's Center for Remanufacturing (http://www.rit.edu/gis/remanufacturing/). For an excellent summary of recent research on the topic of product design in a CLSC, see Bras, B. 2010. "Product Design Issues" in Ferguson, M.E. and Souza, G.C. (eds.), Closed-Loop Supply Chains New Developments to Improve the Sustainability of Business Practices. Boca Raton: CRC Press. Finally, for general resources on remanufacturing, see The Remanufacturing Institute website at http://www.reman.org/ and the Remanufacturing Industries Council website at http://remancouncil.org/.

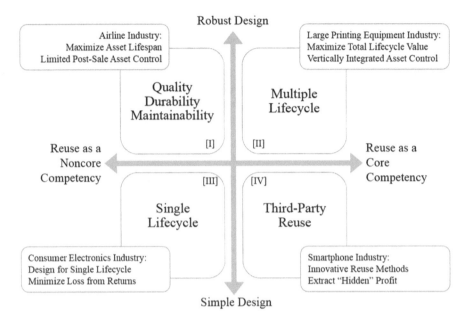

Fig. 17.3 Design and core competence for product reuse in a CLSC

as a core competency may offer increased profit opportunities. Figure 17.3 shows how design and core competencies interact with four resulting strategies.[18]

Breaking down each quadrant in the manager's matrix of Fig. 17.3 provides insights into the influence that product design has on product acquisition management, reverse logistics, reuse processes, and the nature of the reused product market. First, as shown in Fig. 17.3, product design plays a key role in dictating recoverable value, particularly at the product and component levels. Even at the materials level, product design plays a significant role. For example, recovering heavy metals from smartphones and many other small electronic devices is no easy task as the devices are integral by design.[19] Second, reverse logistics both entails product acquisition management—the means to reacquire end-of-use returned products—and requires either ownership or outsourcing the transportation network for moving the end-of-use products. Third, the core operational reuse processes,

---

[18] The major impetus for this chapter and framework for understanding strategies for reuse through remanufacturing comes from ongoing research found in the manuscript, Abbey, J.D. and V.D.R. Guide. 2016. A typology of remanufacturing in a closed-loop supply chain. *Working Paper*, Texas A&M University and The Pennsylvania State University. Relatedly, see Abbey, J.D. and V.D.R. Guide. 2016. Remanufacturing Strategies in a Circular Economy. *Working Paper*, Texas A&M University and The Pennsylvania State University.

[19] Reclaiming rare earth and other precious metals from electronics products has been an issue for decades. For a review of issues related to such reclamation, see Cui, J., and E. Forssberg. 2003. Mechanical recycling of waste electric and electronic equipment: a review. *Journal of Hazardous Materials* 99: 243–263.

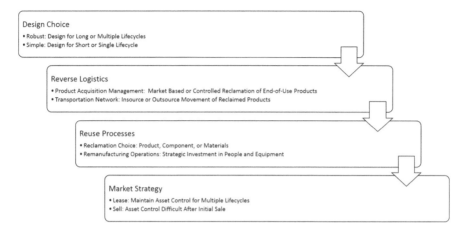

Fig. 17.4 Strategic levers in a closed-loop supply chain

such as the choice of the recovery level (i.e., product, component, or materials), require decisions regarding investment in remanufacturing capabilities in both capital equipment and people. Finally, the fourth lever describes the means of remarketing products going through more than one lifecycle. If a market for such products does exist, then deciding whether to lease or sell the products has major implications on the CLSC strategy. As will become clear throughout this chapter, a decision in any one of the levers can have significant impacts on all other decisions. Figure 17.4 summarizes the four key levers that either derive from or drive a closed-loop supply chain strategy (see Footnote 18).

17.3.1   Quadrant I: Quality, Durability, and Maintainability

In this quadrant of Fig. 17.3, the original manufacturer of the assets tends to focus on selling with limited post-sale support. As a prime example, consider the airline industry. In many cases, airlines prefer to buy the multi-billion dollar fleets of airplanes from the aircraft manufacturers. As such, the aircraft manufacturers accommodate by going through intensive new product design processes focused on quality, reliability, and maintainability in the field. These traits actually mesh with the multiple lifecycle design traits of other industries that do maintain asset control (e.g., Xerox) and lend themselves well to product reuse in a CLSC. However, the loss of asset control post-sale has significant downsides. The most obvious downside is that reacquiring a used product may be difficult if not infeasible. The airplane manufacturers simply have no interest in reacquiring the assets after a sale occurs. Such lack of asset control opened up an entire third-party industry centered on overhauling and remanufacturing products ranging from full airliners to engines to small components of airplanes.[20] In other words, the airplane manufacturers have ceded profits to third-party remanufacturers due to their robust designs combined with a lack of access to the assets after the initial sale.

Another downside is that investing in a reverse logistics network for components/parts is often prohibitive when third-party entrants, such as Delta and Lufthansa, already have a strong presence in the market. Additionally, the airplane manufacturers (e.g., Boeing and Airbus) generally lack both tacit and explicit knowledge of the testing, inspecting, and disposition processes as well as the appropriate asset base for intensive remanufacturing of the assets. Finally, without a strong market presence as a remanufacturing original equipment manufacturer, the airplane manufacturers lack the market cache from which to capitalize. Overall, in this quadrant, firms maintain minimal control over product reacquisition, reverse logistics, and little to no market presence in the multiple lifecycle product market. However, the firms do not need to invest heavily in capital-intensive remanufacturing systems.

17.3.2   Quadrant II: Multiple Lifecycle

In this quadrant, the original equipment manufacturer focuses on designing the product for multiple lifecycles from the inception of a product's design. The intention for such products is to extract as many lifecycles as possible to maximize total lifecycle profits. Such designs require strong vertical integration of both the initial sales and end-of-use product reacquisition channels. If such integration of the initial sale and reacquisition are not present, then third-party remanufacturers will gladly enter the market to extract the additional lifecycle value missed by the original equipment manufacturer as seen in the airline industry. Firms playing in this vertically integrated multiple lifecycle design quadrant also need to invest heavily in the reverse logistics systems to maintain appropriate transportation to the asset-intensive remanufacturing facilities. At the remanufacturing facilities, the product design naturally leads to rapid testing, inspecting, and disposition of the products for reentry into the market. As exemplified by the Xerox Corporation, markets for such multiple lifecycle products are highly segmented based on the dimensions of product performance and price. The Xerox sales force actively markets the right package of "newly manufactured" (i.e., blended new and remanufactured products) and completely new products to suit any customer type. In fact, at the time of end-of-use for a product at a

---

[20] Delta Airlines and Lufthansa continue to generate significant cost savings and profits through repair and refurbishment of both their own equipment and equipment for other airlines. For details on Delta Airlines' continued strategy of extending lifecycles of aircraft, see Carry, Susan. 2012. "Delta Flies New Route to Profits: Older Jets," The Wall Street Journal November 16, 2012. Lufthansa Technik AG actively markets their commercial airline refurbishment services for all levels of maintenance, overhaul, engines, components, aircraft systems, and more. For details, see Lufthansa website at http://www.lufthansagroup.com/en/company/business-segments/maintenance-repair-overhaul.html.

customer site, Xerox uses their sales expertise to provide higher performing, remanu-factured machines as a means to maintain a strong competitive foothold against their non-remanufacturing competitors who cannot compete at the same price-perfor-mance thresholds. In sum, this quadrant represents the pinnacle in maximizing both environmental benefits and profitability through tight control over asset reacquisi-tion, reverse logistics networks, heavy investment in remanufacturing capabilities, and a deep understanding of market segments for the multiple lifecycle products.

17.3.3   Quadrant III: Single Lifecycle

The astute reader might have noticed that the prior two quadrants largely focus on high value, business-to-business products. Though some firms still design such high-value equipment for a single lifecycle, the most common examples of such single lifecycle products come from the consumer products industries. Consumer tastes and preferences often change rapidly, particularly in fast moving product seg-ments such as consumer electronics. Such fast moving industries can make extract-ing value from returned products extraordinarily difficult (see Footnote 14). In response, many firms have abandoned the idea of designing products for anything beyond a single lifecycle. Instead, such firms focus on extracting maximum profit through efficient design and manufacturing systems with an accompanying focus on preventing returns. Such a strategy has been successful for many companies with the side effect of a massive resulting waste stream. Such a copious waste stream represents a continuing force for increasing legislative mandates to prevent elec-tronics waste even in the United States.[21] In effect, though companies found the strategy sustainable for making profits and meeting consumer needs, legislative forces view the strategy as unsustainable from a societal and environmental stand-point. Though little has changed on the design front, the single lifecycle product design may diminish in the coming years.

In sum, firms operating with the single lifecycle design strategy may soon find themselves seeking ways to improve reacquisition of the products through reverse logistics networks at least at the materials level. Without a move away from the sin-gle lifecycle philosophy, investment in testing, inspection, and disposition technolo-gies and related remanufacturing systems will be a moot point. Interestingly, there is recent evidence that select product types should be designed for a single lifecycle or easy materials reclamation, as a sizeable portion of the consumer market holds no interest in purchasing a multiple lifecycle product.[22]

---

[21] As noted before, the E.U., Japan, and Australia have all moved toward increasing legislative mandates for recycling and waste stream reduction. This increasing legislative pressure has also come to the US in the form of California's recycling laws aimed to curbing electronics and other waste (http://www.calrecycle.ca.gov/recycle/).

[22] Two recent studies shed light on the nature of consumer perceptions of multiple lifecycle prod-ucts. The first study delves into the various factors that influence how consumers perceive multiple

17.3.4   Quadrant IV: Third-Party Reuse

The final quadrant represents a simple fact: lost profit opportunities on the part of the original equipment manufacturer. As a case in point, ReCellular started their business by refurbishing Motorola cellular phones when Motorola proclaimed that no one could make money off such a venture. Of course, if the third-party reuse occurs at the materials reclamation (i.e., recycling of plastics) level, the original equipment manufacturer may simply cede such markets for a lack of interest in entering a non-core competence market. However, when the third-party reuse occurs at the component or particularly product level, the original equipment manufacturer has inadvertently created a competitor in their own market space—a competitor using the original equipment manufacturer's own product. The common excuse for allowing such third-party entry comes straight from Fig. 17.3: the original equipment manufacturer views the product or component reuse as a non-core competence region. As such, the original equipment manufacturers argue that reacquisition is simply too expensive or difficult, that reverse logistics systems are too hard to manage, and that investment in remanufacturing equipment as well as the related testing, inspection, and disposition processes is simply too risky. Finally, such original equipment manufacturers may also view internal remanufacturing as a source of new sales cannibalization—a fear shown to be questionable at best.[23] Yet, all these arguments seem to be mythical from the third-party remanufacturer's perspective as thousands of third-party remanufacturers make billions in profits every year.

17.3.5   Contrasting the Quadrants

Table 17.1 provides an accessible summary of the criticality of each major CLSC function available to a manager deciding which quadrant best fits with their design-competence status (see Footnote 18).

Table 17.1 shows that each quadrant has varying functional dimensions for the closed-loop supply chain. In particular, the Quality, Durability, and Maintainability

---

lifecycle (e.g., remanufactured) products (see Abbey, J. D., et al. 2015. Remanufactured Products in Closed-Loop Supply Chains for Consumer Goods. *Production and Operations Management* 24(3): 488–503.). An even more recent work examines how various consumer segments emerge with a sizeable portion—upwards of 35 %—of consumers refusing to consider a remanufactured product of any kind (see Abbey, J.D., J.D. Blackburn, V.D.R. Guide Jr. 2015. "Optimal Pricing for New and Remanufactured Products." *Journal of Operations Management* 36: 130–146.). For a managerially-oriented discussion of these and expanded topics, see Abbey, J.D., M.G. Meloy, J.D. Blackburn, and V.D.R. Guide. 2015. Consumer Markets for Remanufactured and Refurbished Products. *California Management Review* 57(4): 26–4.

[23] Fear of new product sales cannibalization when offering a remanufactured product has been a long-standing source of opposition for remanufacturing at many firms. For a nice discussion of such opposition and strategies to handle common issues with potential cannibalization, see Atasu, A., V.D.R. Guide, Jr., L.N. Van Wassenhove. 2009. So what if remanufacturing cannibalizes new product sales? *California Management Review* 52: 56–76.

Table 17.1 Summary of CLSC process intensity by quadrant

Quadrant	Product design	Reverse logistics	Reuse processes	Marketability
Quality and durability (I)	Maximal lifespan	Minimal	Minimal	Minimal
Multiple lifecycle (II)	Intentional reuse	Simple	Intensive	Simple
Single lifecycle (III)	Maximal efficiency	Minimal (outsourced)	Simple to intensive	Challenging
Third-party (IV)	Profit extraction	Intensive	Intensive	Challenging

quadrant has little to no CLSC functions as a result of the sales of products and little if any direct interaction with the product post-sale. Conversely, the multiple lifecycle quadrant has relatively simple reverse logistics and marketability by the very nature of the typically vertically integrated system. Nonetheless, the multiple lifecycle quadrant also requires intensive resource investment to remanufacture and extract value from the returned end-of-use products. The single lifecycle (i.e., consumer products) quadrant usually focuses on minimizing costs related to returned or end-of-use products. As such, third parties provide most logistics needs to minimize cost, though such a strategy can be a severe mistake for firms that face a high marginal value of time market (see Footnote 14). Additionally, the single lifecycle products typically have highly varied reusability due to both the initial design intentions and lack of investment in remanufacturing technologies by the original manufacturer. Further, the marketability of remanufactured single lifecycle products can be questionable due to varying forces from rapid depreciation, quality concerns, and more.

In general, the third party's core business is finding innovative ways to extract profit that the original equipment manufacturers either ignored or missed completely. The third parties typically lack easy access to the returned or end-of-use products, which makes reacquiring the products an intensive endeavor. The remanufacturing and reuse processes must be retrofitted to the decision made by the external entity—the original manufacturer. Finally, as the third party rarely has the same market power or existing forward supply chain channels as the original manufacturer, remarketing the products can also be an intensive challenge. Yet, in spite of all these challenges, third-party remanufacturers are plentiful, and more importantly, profitable.

17.4   Design and Core Competence: One Size Does Not Fit All

The above discussion demonstrates that implementing a true, fully closed-loop supply chain requires the vertically integrated, multiple lifecycle design strategy. However, many firms may find that complete vertical integration combined with a multiple lifecycle design is both technically infeasible due to the nature of the product and financially infeasible due to requisite investment in reverse logistics and remanufacturing facilities. Moreover, a sizeable reuse market may not even exist for products that have a short market lifecycle. As such, to maximize profitability and environmental benefits under the various constraints, the original equipment manufacturer should take an active role in establishing the appropriate level of third party involvement. Recent research describes just such trade-offs with three major strategies that sit on a continuum from pure outsourcing to pure insourcing. Between these two extreme points sit various levels of hybrid strategies, which are often the best choice for a remanufacturing original equipment manufacturer. Even Xerox, which represents one of the best remanufacturing firms in the world, only maintains a limited reverse logistics fleet with a preference for using third-party logistics carriers to haul end-of-use products back to the centralized remanufacturing facilities. Figure 17.5, adapted from work by Pinar Martin, provides the basic process flow decisions for the vertically integrated remanufacturing, hybrid remanufacturing, and outsourced remanufacturing strategies.[24]

The primary difference among the strategies is the intensity of remanufacturing operations. Even in the vertically integrated CLSC, both initial manufacturing and remanufacturing still source some components from an external entity (e.g., microprocessors or memory cells). Such components are not part of the core-competence

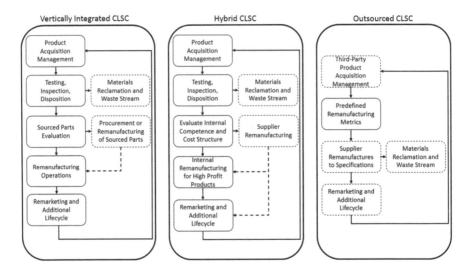

Fig. 17.5 Vertical, Hybrid, and outsourced CLSC strategies

---

[24] Pinar Martin has recently released a book on the various levels of remanufacturing strategy as well as a scholarly paper on the topic. For those interested in the more managerially oriented materials, see Martin, P. 2010. Remanufacturing as a Supply Chain Strategy: Business Models and Case Studies. Dusseldorf, Germany: VDM Verlag. For those interested in the technical details, see Martin, P., V.D.R. Guide, and C.W. Craighead. 2010. Supply chain sourcing in remanufacturing operations: an empirical investigation of remake versus buy. *Decision Sciences* 41: 301–324.

of the manufacturer and are often either replaced with new components or tested for viability in the remanufactured product. In the hybrid strategy, firms handle some products internally, while third parties handle less complex or less profitable products. Finally, in the outsourced CLSC, the original manufacturer exerts only minimal control in the form of performance specifications or other inputs. Note that in all cases, the original manufacturer plays some role to prevent an unauthorized third party from entering the market. Obviously, each of the various choices holds significant tradeoffs. Thus, a quick breakdown of the implications for each choice follows starting with the endpoints of vertical integration and outsourcing.

17.4.1   Vertically Integrated CLSC Strategy

Control represents a major impetus for the vertically integrated strategy. Under vertical integration, a firm retains control over the brand name, customer service, intellectual property, product acquisition, and even the forward and reverse supply chains. However, control creates challenges. For instance, forward supply chain procurement can represent a major hurdle for the remanufacturing operations. If the procurement division has to acquire additional new parts to support the production of new machines but remanufacturing decreases order quantities for new parts, the bulk rate economies of scale in both purchasing and transportation may disappear. Other issues stemming from metrics decisions can also play a significant role. For example, labor and equipment utilization may actually look better with remanufacturing, but variability in production times may increase. Additionally, overhead allocation to both new and remanufactured product production can be a tricky balancing act. Too much or too little allocation to either new or remanufactured products can create major problems for the manufacturing division profitability.

17.4.2   Outsourcing CLSC Strategy

If the forward supply chain is largely outsourced, then the reverse supply chain and reuse operations will be outsourced as well. Simply put, if a firm does not manufacture, they cannot easily remanufacture. This issue became manifest for Dell. As Dell outsourced more of their forward supply chain production, reuse operations became increasingly more difficult. In the end, Dell eventually outsourced of the previously profitable remanufacturing operations.[25] Many other problems emerge when trying to manage a closed-loop supply chain in an outsourced system. Visibility of design flaws and improvements all but vanish as returned products are

---

[25] For a detailed look at Dell's outsourced remanufacturing/refurbishing strategy, see Vitasek, K., Ledyard, M., & Manrodt, K. 2013. *Vested outsourcing: five rules that will transform outsourcing.* Palgrave Macmillan. pp. 185–198.

not highly accessible for designers to garner feedback. Contractual obligations become vastly more complex as contracting parties must consider both the forward and reverse supply chain contingencies. Moving products that lose value rapidly (i.e., high marginal value of time products) represents a major challenge as the contracted reverse logistics and reuse partners typically do not possess great competence in moving products back to market. In sum, with only a few exceptions, a fully outsourced CLSC rarely achieves the same profitability and environmental benefits as a vertically integrated or hybrid strategy.

17.4.3 Hybrid CLSC Strategy

In a hybrid strategy, a firm ideally chooses remanufacturing functions that best mesh with core competencies. However, such hedging can be a double-edged sword as firms may dismiss profit opportunities due to lack of a *current* core competence — one that could easily be developed to generate additional profit. Further, if too many functions are outsourced, the firm loses control over design specifications, which all but assures difficulty for remanufacturing. Other issues include intellectual property, pricing contracts, lack of visibility across the supply chain, and loss of control over both the forward and reverse supply chains. Overall, the hybrid strategy is the most common strategy but always represents a balancing act — in many cases, the hybrid strategy can create cross-divisional conflict as different stakeholders fight for shares of profit.

In the end, there is no single solution for deciding the right level of insourcing or outsourcing. The next section provides some basic guidance and a decision tool when considering the various choices involved in implementing a closed-loop supply chain.

17.5 Choosing a Closed-Loop Supply Chain Strategy

The one clear message so far is that choosing a CLSC strategy is no easy task. As with most decisions, multiple tradeoffs exist when choosing how to compete for more than just maximum profit. In some industries, such as the earth moving and mining equipment, the decision to remanufacture previously produced machinery is a simple matter of materials availability and obvious profitability.[26] Unfortunately, the lines

---

[26] Caterpillar is proud of their industry-leading remanufacturing and reuse systems. To say that remanufacturing and reuse is a core competence of Caterpillar would be an understatement. In any given year, Caterpillar reuses more than 120 million pounds of iron alone. For a detailed look at Caterpillar's remanufacturing operations, see their website at http://www.caterpillar.com/en/company/sustainability/remanufacturing.html.

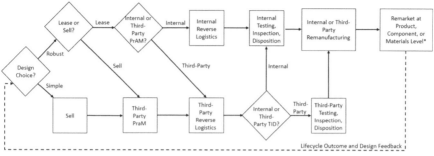

PrAM stands for Product Acquisition Management | TID stands for Testing, Inspection and Disposition

Fig. 17.6 Decision process for major closed-loop supply chain activities

blur as the products become less expensive and more widely distributed. The problems compound when the product has a relatively short lifecycle in the market.

Figure 17.6 puts the pieces, originally outlined in Table 17.1, together with a decision flow process for managers considering particular levels of reuse. In some cases, the decision flow outlined in Fig. 17.5 might have exceptions. However, based on observations from dozens of companies over dozens of years, the decision flow is largely in line with successful CLSC strategies.

Figure 17.6 summarizes the major levers that all managers must consider when contemplating a CLSC strategy: the product design; product (re)acquisition management; reverse logistics; the testing, inspection, and disposition process as well as the remanufacturing processes; and finally the remarketing of the reused product, components, or materials. As the figure displays, third parties typically play a role—often significant—in managing at least some elements of a CLSC. The question managers face is choosing the right level of third-party involvement.

17.5.1 The Role of Third Parties Revisited: When and How to Maintain Control

As noted in the previous section, the choice between internal and third-party activities largely sits on a continuum (see Fig. 17.5). In only a very few cases does a firm do all CLSC activities internally. Xerox and Caterpillar represent uncommon examples of firms that maintained a significant, vertical control over both the forward and reverse supply chains. For both firms, such control has been invaluable in providing improved profitability, design feedback, and environmental benefits. However, such cases of vertically integrated CLSCs are largely the exception.

As outsourcing the forward supply chain gained popularity, insourced remanufacturing became increasingly difficult. Facilities that used to serve for dual new and remanufacturing production were economically unsustainable for only remanufacturing operations. As a case in point, Dell moved nearly all remanufacturing activities to a third party on a contractual basis as the forward supply chain evolved toward outsourced contract manufacturing (see Footnote 25). However, Dell still maintains contractual control over the third party, which is significantly superior to the all too common strategy of simply ignoring the activity of third parties that will enter the market with or without the original manufacturer's consent. In other words, a complete omission of a remanufacturing strategy opens the door for third parties to extract profit that could have been controlled by the original manufacturer, which can have significant implications on the original brand's reputation.[27]

The automotive industry serves as a case in point for ceding control over remanufacturing. The remanufactured automotive parts industry has a long-standing tradition of heavy third-party involvement. Though Ford and other major automotive manufacturers have tried to make inroads into reuse of parts, third-party players (e.g., Cardone Industries) have maintained a strong control on the automotive parts product acquisition market.[28] During a meeting of original equipment automotive manufacturers and their third-party remanufacturing competitors, an interesting argument emerged: the original equipment manufacturer accused the third party of "stealing parts" to which the third party responded "stop me." Though the original manufacturer may felt entitled to "their parts", the original manufacturer had taken no steps to maintain any vertical control after the time of the initial sale. The automotive industry provides a cautionary message: once an industry cedes control over remanufacturing to third parties, regaining control over the remanufacturing market can be a difficult and costly proposition.

17.6   Closing the Loop

This chapter provides high-level guidance on the structure of closed-loop supply chain strategies with an overriding theme: third parties will play a role in nearly all closed-loop supply chain systems. As such, manufacturers in the forward supply chain need to make a conscious decision on their closed-loop supply chain strategy: that decision needs to ask when and how third parties should play a role. If the forward supply chain original manufacturer does not make such conscious decisions, an *unauthorized* third party will make the decision for them by entering the market as a competitor. Even if the prospect of investing in resources—capital equipment, skilled labor, and reverse logistics networks—is beyond the core competencies of an original equipment manufacturer, forethought in developing and contracting with third parties can prove valuable. The value of such contracts comes from

---

[27] For a fascinating look at the adverse and even beneficial consequences of third-party remanufacturing, see Agrawal, V., A. Atasu, K. van Ittersum. 2015. Remanufacturing, third party competition, and the perceived value of new products. *Management Science* 61(1): 60–72.

[28] For a look at the broad range of products—some of which are only available in remanufactured form—that Cardone Industries remanufacturers, see their website at https://www.cardone.com/.

improved control over all aspects of the reverse supply chain including product design feedback, environmental reuse opportunities, hedging against future legislative pressures, increased opportunity to reach additional markets, and greater control over brand image. In the end, if the forward supply chain manufacturer does not have a closed-loop supply chain strategy, a third-party remanufacturer will.

Chapter 18
Sustainable Food Supply Chain Design

Jacqueline M. Bloemhof and Mehmet Soysal

18.1 Introduction

Supply Chain Management (SCM) has become part of the c-management agenda in Western countries since the 1990s, particularly in the manufacturing and retail industries (Chopra and Meindl 2012). More recently, interest in SCM has also been growing in the agrifood industry, both in developed and developing countries. Executives of agrifood companies are aware that successful coordination, integration, and management of key business processes in the supply chain will determine their competitive success. Sustainable Food Supply Chain Management (SFSCM) refers to all forward processes in the food chain, like procurement of materials, production and distribution, as well as the reverse processes to collect and process returned used or unused products and/or parts of products in order to ensure a *socioeconomically* and *ecologically* sustainable recovery (Bloemhof and van Nunen 2008).

Companies—and supply chains—nowadays have to obtain a "license to produce and deliver", that is, society has to accept the way they produce and deliver their goods (Bloemhof and van der Vorst 2015). If this is done by using questionable methods (think of child labor, environmental pollution, and so on), their products become less acceptable. Western-European consumers have become more demanding on food attributes such as quality, integrity, safety, diversity, and sustainability

J.M. Bloemhof (✉)
Operations Research and Logistics, Wageningen University, Wageningen, The Netherlands
e-mail: Jacqueline.Bloemhof@wur.nl

M. Soysal
Operations Research and Logistics, Wageningen University, Wageningen, The Netherlands

Department of Business Administration, Hacettepe University,
Beytepe, Ankara 06532, Turkey
e-mail: Mehmet.soysal@wur.nl; mehmetsoysal@hacettepe.edu.tr

© Yann Bouchery, Charles J. Corbett, Jan C. Fransoo, and Tarkan Tan 2017
Y. Bouchery et al. (eds.), *Sustainable Supply Chains*, Springer Series in Supply
Chain Management 4, DOI 10.1007/978-3-319-29791-0_18

(Van der Vorst et al. 2009). Global consumption of food has significantly increased due to population growth, alterations in overall nutritional needs and rising economic incomes. This increased consumption has increased the demand for production and distribution of food worldwide leading to severe global economic, social, and environmental problems (Tilman et al. 2002). The Food and Agriculture Organization of the United Nations (FAO) states that food sectors have to increase their production and decrease the negative impact of production and distribution simultaneously (FAO 2012).

This chapter discusses the design of sustainable food supply chains. In Sect. 18.1, we discuss the key questions related to the concept of a Sustainable Food Supply Chain, which have to do with (1) the typicality of food supply chains, (2) the issue on how to measure sustainability and (3) the impact of food supply chains to improve sustainability. In Sect. 18.2, we provide a brief literature review on these issues, whereas Sect. 18.3 discusses the trends related to these questions, showing future needs in the field of sustainable food supply chains (puzzles that researchers and practitioners need to work on).

18.2   What Is a Sustainable Food Supply Chain Design?

In this section, we discuss the following key questions:

1. What makes food supply chains different from other supply chains when it comes to sustainability?
2. What are the key performance indicators for sustainability in food supply chains?
3. How to redesign food supply chains to improve sustainability?

18.2.1   What Makes Food Supply Chains Different Than Other Supply Chains When It Comes to Sustainability?

Food supply chains consist of organizations that produce and distribute vegetable or animal-based products to consume. Nowadays, Western-European consumers have become more aware of the origin and nutritional value of their food and expect food in retail stores to be of good quality, to have a decent shelf life and to be fit for purpose (Smith and Sparks 2004). Consumers' requirements especially refer to product availability, product quality, and an acceptable price. These requirements need to be taken into account when (re-)designing Food Supply Chains, next to traditional efficiency and responsiveness requirements (Soysal et al. 2012).

A number of recent trends such as globalization, urbanization and agro-industrialization make the organization of agrifood chains and networks more complex, as these networks are rapidly moving towards globally interconnected systems with a large variety of relationships. This is also affecting the ways in which food is produced, processed and delivered at the market. Perishable food products can nowadays be shipped from halfway around the world at fairly competitive prices. Demand and supply are no longer restricted to nations or regions but have also become international processes. The market exerts a dual pressure on agrifood chains, forcing improved coordination among buyers and sellers and continuous innovation.

Food Supply Chains are different from other product supply chains. The fundamental difference is the continuous and significant change in the quality of food products throughout the entire supply chain until the point of final consumption. Investments in network design should be aimed at both improving logistic performance and at the preservation of food quality.

A Food Supply Chain comprises organizations responsible for the production and distribution of vegetable or animal-based products. These products can be fresh (such as vegetables, flowers, fruit) or processed (such as portioned meats, snacks, desserts, canned food products). In general, these chains may comprise growers, auctions, wholesalers, importers and exporters, retailers and specialty shops and their input and service suppliers. In fresh supply chains, the main processes are the handling, conditioned storing, packing, transportation, and especially trading of goods. Basically, all these supply chain steps leave the intrinsic characteristics of the product grown or produced in the countryside untouched. In processed food supply chains, agricultural products are used as raw materials for producing consumer products with higher added value. In most cases, conservation and conditioning processes extend the shelf life of the agricultural and consumer products.

18.2.2 What Are the Key Performance Indicators for Sustainability in Food Supply Chains?

Traditional performance indicators such as costs, throughput time or technical quality of products are insufficient to find the best sustainable configuration of the supply chain. To help decision makers to assess the sustainability of their supply chain design, a comprehensive assessment regarding the Triple Bottom Line (TBL) performance is needed. This TBL concept was first used by Elkington (2004) and relates to a simultaneous consideration and balance of economic, environmental, and social goals from a business point of view (also known as the Triple P philosophy of People, Planet, and Profit).

Performance measurement tools estimate sustainability throughout indicators. Sustainability indicators are an essential part of the process of assessment, benchmarking, and decision making. Indicators play an important role in sustainability assessment to value the current situation. Moreover, indicators help to benchmark the current sustainability performance with that of competitive companies or the required performance to obtain membership in a certificate scheme (such as Lean and Green) or the performance required by legislation. Indicators also support performance evaluation of management policies and improvement practices. Indicators make visible every change in the social, economic, and environmental dimensions of sustainability.

Within the context of Food Supply Chains, the sustainability discussion focuses on the reduction of product waste (products not used for human consumption because the quality is not suitable anymore), number of miles a product has travelled before it reaches the customer's plate (Food Miles) and all greenhouse gas emissions related to the business processes in the supply chain network (Carbon Footprint, see also Chap. 3 by Boukherroub et al. (2017)).

18.2.3 How to Improve Sustainability in Food Supply Chain Design?

Van Gogh et al. (2013) show that about 40 % of food waste relates to supply chain activities. The top four of the causes of this spoilage are related to the cold chain storage (conditioned transport and storage of perishable products), handling and packaging. Also the Food and Agricultural Organization acknowledges that substantial food loss takes place in the supply chain, during postharvesting, processing, and distribution (Fig. 18.1).

Sustainability of supply chains does imply improvements of a combination of different and sometimes conflicting factors. How to combine economic, social, and environmental indicators? Literature on performance indicators for sustainable logistics shows no consensus. Some authors describe indicators as separate entities, whereas others acknowledge that factors related to sustainable logistics can influence more than one dimension and create several impacts. This change evokes the need for an integrated approach that links food supply chain network decisions to the three dimensions of sustainability (economic, environmental, and social).

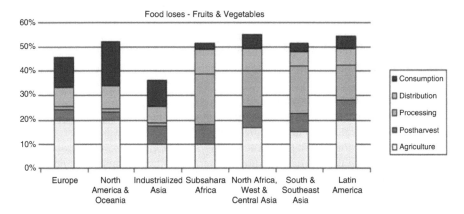

Fig. 18.1 Food losses in the chains of fruits and vegetables (FAO 2013)

Sustainability in itself is not a new research area, but the implication of sustainability in food supply chain networks is quite new. Food Supply Chain Networks are complex, comprising a wide diversity of products with different characteristics and quality requirements, dynamic interactions, and markets (Soysal et al. 2012).

18.3 State-of-the-Art in Sustainable Food Supply Chain Design

This section describes the state-of-the-art in Sustainable Food Supply Chain Design. First, the literature on Food Supply Chain is discussed; resulting in lessons learned why food logistics is not easy. Second, the latest state-of-the-art on sustainability performance assessment is shown, followed by a literature review of papers discussing quantitative models for sustainable food logistics management.

18.3.1 Lessons on Food Supply Chains

Bourlakis and Weightman (2004) discuss a list of specific process and product characteristics of Food Supply Chain Networks that impact the (re)design process for an FSCN, including the following:

- Seasonality in production, requiring global sourcing.
- Variable process yields in quantity and quality due to biological variations, seasonality, and random factors connected with weather, pests, and other biological hazards.
- Keeping quality constraints for raw materials, intermediates and finished products, and quality decay while products pass through the supply chain. As a result there is a chance of product shrinkage and stock-outs in retail outlets when product's best-before-dates have passed and/or product quality level has declined too much.
- Requirement for conditioned transportation and storage means (e.g., cooling).
- Necessity for lot traceability of work in process due to quality and environmental requirements and product responsibility.

Due to these specific characteristics of food products, the partnership thoughts of SCM in FSCs have already received much attention over the past years. These characteristics have an impact on the supply chain design process (see a.o. Lutke Entrup 2006):

- In the overall supply chain, it is important to include shelf life constraints for products and changes in product quality level while a product is progressing through the supply chain (e.g., quality decay or ripening).

- In the supply part of the supply chain, agrifood industries need to contract suppliers that can guarantee the supply of raw materials in the right volume, with the right quality at the right place and time. Agrifood supply has long production throughput times (harvesting only 1 or few times a year), there is seasonality in the production, and quality and quantity have a high variability.
- Apart from the suppliers, also the logistic service providers (LSPs) play an important role as the quality of food products depends heavily on the conditions in all steps of the supply chain. For example, exposing products like fresh milk or meat to high temperatures for sometime will significantly reduce the shelf life of these products. The same is true for disturbances in the supply chain that result in long waiting times at customs or in the airports or harbors. Especially for products with a small shelf life (fresh tropical fruits), disturbances cause a significant percentage of food spoilage.
- For the food industry, process yields are variable in quantity and quality. Alternative process routes and recipes exist for producing the same product. Cleaning and processing times are product-dependent and lot traceability is very important.
- Supply chain coordination is essential to take appropriate decisions on conditioned transport. For retailers, the seasonal supply of products requires often global sourcing.

18.3.2 Lessons on Sustainability Key Performance Indicators for Food Chains

In 1992, in the context of the Rio Declaration on Environment and Development, the Earth Summit recognized in chapter 40 of its proceedings called Agenda 21, the urge for clear and universal metrics of sustainable development. In the opinion of the committee, the need for reliable and pertinent indicators that are able to guide the shift towards sustainability arises from the incapability of current measurement systems to evaluate this aspect. The new standards are required to illustrate both policy makers and the general public the linkages and trade-offs between economic, environmental, and social values as well as to evaluate and monitor the long-term implications of current decisions and behaviors, from the double-edged perspective of institutions and businesses.

According to the FAO report in 2012, more than one hundred countries have established national strategies for sustainable development, including sustainability targets and indicators. In spite of the abundant attempts for making food and agriculture sectors sustainable, no internationally accepted standard defines what "sustainable food production" essentially requires (FAO 2012). "Neither a commonly accepted set of indicators that have to be taken into account when measuring sustainability performance, nor widely accepted definitions of the minimum requirements that would allow a company to qualify as 'sustainable,' exist" (FAO 2012: 9).

Table 18.1 Sustainability indicators for food chains

Environmental indicators	Social Indicators	Economic indicators
SAFA Sustainability indicators for food chains (FAO 2012)		
Energy efficiency	Human rights	Profitability
Climate change (GHG emissions)	Equity	Vulnerability
Emission of air pollutants	Occupational health and safety	Local economy
Water quantity	Food and nutrition security	Decent livelihood
Land use	Product quality	Resilience to Economic
Soil degradation		Risk
Material cycle		
Waste (weight and volume)		
Biodiversity		
Animal welfare		
Sustainability indicators for food logistics (Baldwin 2009)		
Food miles	Ethical transport	Percent of food lost in mishandling
Environmental monitoring system	Health and safety incidents	Type of distribution
Hazard substance exposure	Distance between grower and distributor	Retail access
Environmental reporting	Profit between farmer, processor, retailer	Labor productivity
	Quality of life and working satisfaction	Diversity of market
	Average wage	Transport efficiency
		Imported vs. domestic products

The FAO developed the guidelines for Sustainability Assessment of Food and Agriculture systems (SAFA). SAFA suggest a comprehensive list of sustainability indicators in different categories including both qualitative and quantitative indicators. These indicators relate mainly to production processes at farm level. Baldwin (2009) evaluates the sustainability indicators especially in the logistic part of food chains. Table 18.1 summarizes these indicators, where the first block relates more to production processes and the second block to the logistics processes.

The supply chain processes (e.g., transport and storage) have a significant impact on global warming because food is often shipped long distances. Although the impact of transportation is important, lifecycle analyses (LCAs) indicate that for most foods, transportation does not have the largest environmental impact (see Chap. 2, Guinée and Heijungs (2017) for more on LCA). However, as many options are available for delivering food to consumers, these supply chain configurations have vastly differing energy and emissions profiles, and therefore evaluating trade-offs and opportunities is necessary for a significant improvement in sustainability for food supply chains (Wakeland et al. 2012).

The UK Sustainable Development Commission formulates the following characteristics referred to the sustainable supply chains: safe and healthy production support the existence of the rural communities, elimination of the overusage of natural resources, reaching high environmental performance throughout less consumption of energy and of resource inputs as well as throughout exploiting more renewable energy. Providing safe and hygienic working environment for the employees, establishing high standards of animal health and welfare, sustaining the level of available resources for meeting the needs of the society are also part of the characteristics of the sustainable supply chains.

The main hotspots that relate to sustainability are the impact on energy (emissions, carbon footprint) and materials (spoilage and waste). Researchers have proposed mathematical optimization models to (re-)design the Food Supply Chain taking into account the aforementioned sustainability KPIs. The following part presents a review of these models.

18.3.2.1   Lessons on Sustainable Food Supply Chain Design Models

Food supply chain network design coordinates a variety of activities such as transportation, inventory management, facility location, or production planning. These activities require several decisions to be made, which can be related to strategic (e.g., determining location and sizes of facilities in a supply chain), tactical (e.g., determining inventory replenishment times) and operational (e.g., determining resulting routes to deliver products to the final destinations) levels of planning and execution. Food supply chain network design, therefore, determines the structure of a food chain and has the potential to affect supply chain KPIs such as cost and responsiveness.

While managing the supply chain activities, sustainable food supply chain network design takes environmental and social externalities of operations into account besides traditional cost concerns. The introduced indicators in the previous subsections are used to assess the performance of a supply chain in terms of managing these externalities.

Operations Research literature presents various decision support tools to better manage (sustainable) food supply chain network design problems. We conducted a literature review on quantitative studies to analyze the currently available quantitative models and point out modelling challenges in sustainable food supply chain network design problems. Literature search is carried out within well-known databases, Thomson Reuters (formerly ISI) Web of Knowledge, Google Scholar, EBSCO, and followed by reference and citation analyses to find related contributions. The following search criteria are employed: food supply chain distribution planning, food supply chain quantitative models, food supply chain network design, sustainable food supply chains, network design for perishable products, location and allocation models, and green network design.

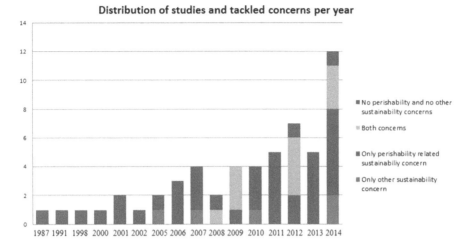

Fig. 18.2 Distribution of food supply chain studies in literature

Analyzing the used indicators, we observe that perishability-related sustainability concerns such as food waste and quality decay have received more attention than other sustainability concerns such as emissions and energy use.

Figure 18.2 shows the distribution of 55 studies between 1987 and 2014. We consider four groups in the literature on food supply chains: (1) no perishability and no other sustainability issues taken into account, (2) both concerns: perishability and at least one other sustainability concern have been taken into account (i.e., emissions, water, accrued jobs), (3) Only perishability-related sustainability concern has been considered, and (4) Only other sustainability concern: has at least one other sustainability concern which is not directly related with perishability. Note that all of these groups have cost or profit concerns, which relate to the economic dimension of sustainability.

The reviewed studies along with regarded sustainability aspects in food supply chain network design models are presented in Table 18.2. According to the results, the number of studies on food supply chain network design has been increasing in the last years. Moreover, incorporating perishability-related sustainability concerns and the other sustainability considerations into the developed food supply chain network design models is becoming trendy. The main reasons for the increased interest to the sustainability are (1) pressures from various stakeholders such as customers and nongovernmental organizations, (2) global competition and economic concerns, and (3) legislation.

The review of the literature shows that most studies assume that products have fixed shelf lives and deteriorate based on time (e.g., Ekşioğlu and Jin 2006; Soysal et al. 2014; Ahuja et al. 2007). In these studies, product quality decays occur either in a linear way (e.g., Ahumada and Villalobos 2009) or in other ways such as exponential (e.g., Blackburn and Scudder 2009). While managing product perishability, some

Table 18.2 Literature review on sustainability aspects in food supply chain network models

#	Studies	Sustainability concerns not related to perishability	Perishability-related sustainability concern
1	Van der Vorst et al. (1998)		√
2	Van der Vorst et al. (2000)		√
3	Apaiah and Hendrix (2005)	√	
4	Kanchanasuntorn and Techanitisawad (2006)		√
5	Ekşioğlu and Jin (2006)		√
6	Gong et al. (2007)		√
7	Ahuja et al. (2007)		√
8	Bilgen and Ozkarahan (2007)	√	
9	Zanoni and Zavanella (2007)		√
10	Dabbene et al. (2008)	√	√
11	Akkerman et al. (2009)	√	√
12	Van der Vorst et al. (2009)	√	√
13	Ahumada and Villalobos (2009)	√	√
14	Blackburn and Scudder (2009)		√
15	Oglethorpe (2010)	√	
16	Rong and Grunow (2010)		√
17	Wang et al. (2010)		√
18	Hsu and Liu (2011)		√
19	Ahumada and Villalobos (2011)	√	√
20	Bosona and Gebresenbet (2011)		√
21	Yan et al. (2011)		√
22	Hasani et al. (2012)		√
23	Rong et al. (2011)		√
24	Zanoni and Zavanella (2012)	√	√
25	Amorim et al. (2012)	√	√
26	Ahumada et al. (2012)	√	√
27	You et al. (2012)	√	√
28	Yu and Nagurney (2013)		√
29	Tsao (2013)		√
30	Piramuthu et al. (2013)		√
31	Grunow and Piramuthu (2013)		√
32	Khalili-Damghani et al. (2014)		√
33	Soysal et al. (2014)	√	√
34	Validi et al. (2014)	√	
35	Pan et al. (2014)	√	
36	Firoozi et al. (2014)		√
37	Chen et al. (2014)		√
38	Kim et al. (2014)		√
39	Seyedhosseini and Ghoreyshi (2014)		√
40	Meneghetti and Monti (2015)	√	√
41	Linnemann et al. (2014)	√	√
42	Liu et al. (2014)		√

studies take also other parameters into account such as temperature, enthalpy, and color through specific quality decay models (e.g., Linnemann et al. 2014; Ahumada et al. 2012; Gong et al. 2007).

Another finding is that the developed models do not always allow product wastes. In some cases, products have to be used within the limited time period and waste cannot occur (e.g., Soysal et al. 2014; Seyedhosseini and Ghoreyshi 2014). In other cases, it is not always possible to use products before they are spoiled (e.g., Wang et al. 2010).

Lastly, some researchers do not focus on quality decay during only storage, but also have addressed temperature tracking during transportation through temperature-controlled trucks or multi-temperature logistics (e.g., Bosona and Gebresenbet 2011; Hsu and Liu 2011).

Regarding sustainability indicators which are not related to perishability, it has been observed from the literature that energy use and emissions are the most acknowledged indicators in the reviewed models (e.g., Validi et al. 2014; Van der Vorst et al. 2009; Pan et al. 2014). The other issues addressed in the studies are the following: nutritional content of products (e.g., Oglethorpe 2010), water use (e.g., Ahumada and Villalobos 2009), number of accrued jobs (e.g., Ahumada et al. 2012), and energy levels of operations (e.g., Linnemann et al. 2014).

As discussed above, researchers rely on several assumptions while managing sustainability in food supply chain network design problems. These assumptions obviously affect the developed decision support models and therefore the resultant food supply chain network design plans. Concluding, while modelling sustainable food supply designs, the following issues have to be taken into account:

1. The main factors affecting **shelf life of products** have to be determined. Food science literature can be consulted to have a better insight in the perishability nature of food products. If a specific quality decay model exists for the studied problem, this model or its simplification can be employed to tackle with the perishability of the product. The existing models can be too complex to simplify or they may require many parameters which are difficult to obtain. Otherwise, generic models which are proposed for food products can be used. For instance, the generic model used in Rong et al. (2011) to estimate product shelf life could be an option. The model is dependent on various parameters such as storage time, temperature, activation energy, etc.

2. **Product waste risk** should not be ignored in food supply chain network design problems. Due to several reasons such as service level requirements and demand uncertainty, it could be inevitable to have zero product waste. As shown in Soysal et al. (2015), the ignorance of product perishability in a quantitative model for a special supply chain problem might lead to higher product wastes, infeasible solutions, and unsatisfied service level targets. Therefore, decision support models for food supply chain problems should take potential product waste into account.

3. Product quality decays do not occur only during storage. Products start to deteriorate even before they are completely produced or ready for the consumption.

This fact requires tracking product quality throughout the whole chain starting from production to the point of consumption. The interested reader is referred to the study of van der Vorst et al. (2011). They claim that a **quality controlled chain** could bring the benefits of higher product availability, constant quality, and less product losses by the help of controlling goods in a proactive manner and having better established supply chain designs.

4. Most of the sustainability indicators for food supply chains introduced in Table 18.1 have not been incorporated in food supply chain network design models. However, social awareness on these sustainability indicators has been growing in practice. It might be thus expected that future OR models can comprise an **extended set of sustainability indicators** to better aid decision makers in sustainable food supply chain management.

5. Researchers often use simple models or approaches to estimate sustainability indicators, which results in rough calculations of e.g., water consumption or energy use. More interdisciplinary research is required to advance our understanding of sustainability-related KPIs. Quantitative approaches which are proposed in other research fields to estimate performance of sustainability indicators can be incorporated into the decision support models in Operations Research.

6. Most studies put boundaries to the sustainability considerations, i.e., taking energy use from transportation into account but ignoring energy used for stocking, which restricts the assessment of environmental or social impacts associated with all the stages of a product's life. These limited views can affect the trade-off relationships among KPIs and therefore the resulting plans in network management. Lifecycle Analysis (LCA) models can be combined with OR models to better estimate the externalities of products from cradle-to-grave (see also Chap. 2 by Guinée and Heijungs (2017)).

To conclude: the research on food supply chain network design is still developing considering the extension of the traditional approaches through taking environmental and social considerations of the supply chain operations into account. These enhanced models can better capture current food supply chain dynamics and improve food quality and safety, availability of food, and create sustainable and efficient business networks, which are the main issues faced by stakeholders in food supply chains (Soysal et al. 2012).

18.4 Practical Implications: Trends in Sustainable Food Supply Chains

Here, we discuss the impact of trends in the coming years on the agrifood sector. We discuss the impact of urbanization and the upcoming of sustainable modalities. Further, we discuss the development of Sustainability Dashboards.

18.4.1 Impact of Urbanization

First, the demographic developments are such that more people live on the planet, but less people live in Western-Europe. More people live in urban areas in an individualized society. In 2015, already 60 % of the world population lives in cities. This results in an increase of demand for meat, fish, and dairy, while the employment rate for farming activities in the countryside drops. The carbon footprint of meat and fish is on average much higher than that of vegetables and grains. Therefore, land, material, and energy use will increase as well as the amount of food spoilage and waste. Secondly, climate change will result in a decrease in the variety of species. Nowadays, only 150 different crops are harvested worldwide resulting in a drop of biodiversity. Only 12 crops are responsible for 75 % of the world food production, making this system very vulnerable. One of the practical implications of sustainability in food supply chains is the shift in production activities. Agrifood production will move to cheap countries, but there will be also a focus on locally produced products (e.g., urban farming).

Urban farming gives an opportunity to operate more independently from global threats related to climate, prices, and political stability. Urban farming can lead to a variety of meaningful social functions. However, urban farming also asks for a new way of short-distance logistics to ensure that processed and unprocessed products are distributed fast and safe to the places in the city where consumers need them. Metropolitan food clusters and logistic lines around the major global cities will provide residents with sufficient food.

As distribution is one of the main sources of food waste and carbon emissions in the food lifecycle, this is another motivation to a shift in food production activities. Geographically local supply chains are considered to be more sustainable due to the encouragement of the rural enterprising and the opposition against the agriculture monopolies (Smith and Sparks 2004).

In the future, we expect a combination of global low-cost agrifood production with local sustainable high-quality agrifood production.

18.4.2 Emission Driven Transportation

At the moment, initiatives start all over the world. In California, USA, sustainable freight pathways to zero and near-zero emissions are explored. Zero-emission drive-train technologies have been developed for on-road heavy-duty freight vehicles and 100 % solar-powered and wind-powered cargo ships make their way through the seas (e.g., the Turanor Planet Solar, Eco Marine Power, Green Marine, and the Dutch Ecoliners). Low Emission Zones in cities (such as London) do not allow entrance to vehicles that do not satisfy the emission requirements. Electric vehicles could be a solution for entering these zones, but requires extra handling at the borders of the city (Blanco and Sheffi (2017) discuss green logistics in greater detail in Chap. 7).

18.4.2.1 Sustainability Dashboards

Sustainability assessment aims to facilitate the decision making process related to actions which are needed to provide sustainability in short-term or long-term perspective for global or local systems. At the moment, most Business Dashboards focus only on numerical economic results and do not take into account the numerical visualization of social and environmental indicators.

One tool for visualizing sustainability results is the Dashboard of Sustainability. The Dashboard of Sustainability is elaborated by the Consultative Group on Sustainable Development Indices and the Joint Research Centre. It dates from the end of the 1990 and measures the economic, social, and environmental dimensions of sustainability. The Sustainability Dashboard allows comparing different scenarios taking into account the economic, social, and institutional trends. The information which needs to be measured is organized in three levels:

1. Individual indicators for sustainability evaluation
2. Synthetic indexes which integrate multiple indicators into one single indicator (Environment, Economy, Society)
3. Index of overall sustainability (Sustainability Development Index or Policy Performance Index) which averages the synthetic indexes

The information is presented in a numerical and graphical way. The individual indicators are assigned to segments. The achievements of the indicators for all different contexts are revealed by the color of the segment. Usually the color varies from dark green (excellent) to dark red (very bad).

Bloemhof et al. (2015) collected primary and secondary data on sustainability KPIs from food and logistics companies in the Netherlands. Results show that energy and water use as well as emissions have most attention from food industry; carbon footprints are central to LSPs (Chapter 4 by Hoekstra (2017) focuses on water footprinting).

18.5 Future Needs

For a more sustainable food supply chain, a redesign of the food supply chain network is necessary. To meet the future challenges on sustainability and efficiency, biomass materials must be converted into valuable products. Future food supply chains are not only challenged to increase productivity, but also to supply energy and other biobased products without compromising on resources availability and resource efficiency. This requires a biobased circular economy, i.e., encompassing the sustainable production of biomass and its conversion into food, feed, biobased materials, and bioenergy. So far, optimization models have only been used to find the optimal route for the production of food products or biofuels (Zondervan et al. 2011). This needs to be extended to a multiproduct optimization to create food, feed, fuel, chemicals, and materials from biomass.

Research will be necessary in the field of time-dependent environmental conditions, under which products are (re)packed (e.g., using modified atmosphere packaging), stored, and transported (e.g., using reefer containers), in order to improve on food quality. This will result in longer shelf lives, and therefore, less spoilage. Furthermore, emphasis should be put on redesigning processes in order to reduce greenhouse gas emissions and energy consumption. The transition towards a sustainable food chain is a challenge for the food sector. Future food chains should operate in synergy with environmental, social, and economic aspects leading to the following targets:

1. *Improve resource efficiency and effectiveness in the food chain:* prevent food spoilage and shrinkage, optimal valorization of by-products and waste streams, extending shelf life of food products.
2. *Efficient supply chain networks:* reduction of CO_2 emissions in food logistics reducing transport kilometers improves mobility.
3. *Reduces environmental impact of packaging,* reduces carbon emissions related to plastic packaging materials and improve recycling rates.

References

Ahuja RK, Huang W, Romeijn HE, Morales DR (2007) A heuristic approach to the multi-period single-sourcing problem with production and inventory capacities and perishability constraints. INFORMS J Comput 19(1):14–26

Ahumada O, Villalobos JR (2009) Operational model for planning the harvest and distribution of perishable agricultural products. Int J Prod Econ 133(2):677–687

Ahumada O, Villalobos JR (2011) A tactical model for planning the production and distribution of fresh produce. Ann Oper Res 190(1):339–358

Ahumada O, Rene Villalobos J, Nicholas Mason A (2012) Tactical planning of the production and distribution of fresh agricultural products under uncertainty. Agr Syst 112:17–26

Akkerman R, Wang Y, Grunow M (2009, July) MILP approaches to sustainable production and distribution of meal elements. In: Computers and Industrial Engineering, 2009. CIE 2009. International Conference on, IEEE, pp 973–978

Amorim P, Günther HO, Almada-Lobo B (2012) Multi-objective integrated production and distribution planning of perishable products. Int J Prod Econ 138(1):89–101

Apaiah RK, Hendrix EM (2005) Design of a supply chain network for pea-based novel protein foods. J Food Eng 70(3):383–391

Baldwin CJ (2009) Sustainability in the food industry. Wiley-Blackwell, Chichester

Bilgen B, Ozkarahan I (2007) A mixed-integer linear programming model for bulk grain blending and shipping. Int J Prod Econ 107(2):555–571

Blackburn J, Scudder G (2009) Supply chain strategies for perishable products: the case of fresh produce. Prod Oper Manag 18(2):129–137

Blanco EE, Sheffi Y (2017) Green logistics. In: Bouchery Y, Corbett CJ, Fransoo J, Tan T (eds) Sustainable supply chains: a research-based textbook on operations and strategy. Springer, New York, Chapter 7

Bloemhof JM, Nunen JAEE (2008) Integration of environmental management and SCM. In: Ghose A (ed) Green marketing strategies. The ICFAI University Press, India, pp 49–68, Chapter 4

Bloemhof J, van der Vorst J (2015) Sustainable food supply chain networks. In: Vlachos I, Malindretos G (eds) Markets, business, and sustainability. Bentham Books, The Netherlands, pp 99–122, Chapter 5

Bloemhof JM, van der Vorst JGAJ, Bastl M, Allaoui H (2015) Sustainability assessment of food chain logistics. Int J Logist Res Appl 18(2):101–117

Bosona TG, Gebresenbet G (2011) Cluster building and logistics network integration of local food supply chain. Biosyst Eng 108(4):293–302

Boukherroub T, Bouchery Y, Corbett CJ, Fransoo J, Tan T (2017) Carbon footprinting in supply chains. In: Bouchery Y, Corbett CJ, Fransoo J, Tan T (eds) Sustainable supply chains: a research-based textbook on operations and strategy. Springer, New York, Chapter 3

Bourlakis MA, Weightman PWH (2004) Food supply chain management. Blackwell, Oxford

Chen C, Zhang J, Delaurentis T (2014) Quality control in food supply chain management: an analytical model and case study of the adulterated milk incident in China. Int J Prod Econ 152:188–199

Chopra S, Meindl P (2012) Supply chain drivers and metrics. In: Supply chain management, strategy, planning and operation, 5th edn. Pearson, Upper Saddle River, Chapter 3

Dabbene F, Gay P, Sacco N (2008) Optimisation of fresh-food supply chains in uncertain environments, Part II: A case study. Biosyst Eng 99(3):360–371

Ekşioğlu SD, Jin M (2006) Cross-facility production and transportation planning problem with perishable inventory. In: Computational science and its applications-ICCSA 2006. Springer, Berlin, pp 708–717

Elkington J (2004) Enter the triple bottom line. In: Henriques A, Richardson J (eds) The triple bottom line: does it all add up? Earthscan, London, pp 11–16

FAO (2012) FAO Statistical Yearbook, Food and Agriculture Organization of the United Nations. FAO, Rome

FAO (2013) Toolkit, reducing the food waste footprint. Food and Agriculture Organisation of the United Nations, Rome

Firoozi Z, Ismail N, Ariafar S, Tang SH, Ariffin MKMA, Memariani A (2014) Effects of integration on the cost reduction in distribution network design for perishable products. Math Probl Eng 2014

Gogh B, Aramyan L van, Sluis AVD, Soethoudt H, Scheer F-P (2013) Feasibility of a network of excellence postharvest food losses, combining knowledge and competences to reduce food losses in developing and emerging economies, Report 1402, Wageningen UR Food and Biobased Research

Gong W, Li D, Liu X, Yue J, Fu Z (2007) Improved two-grade delayed particle swarm optimisation (TGDPSO) for inventory facility location for perishable food distribution centres in Beijing. N Z J Agric Res 50(5):771–779

Grunow M, Piramuthu S (2013) RFID in highly perishable food supply chains–Remaining shelf life to supplant expiry date? Int J Prod Econ 146(2):717–727

Guinée J, Heijungs R (2017) Introduction to life cycle assessment. In: Bouchery Y, Corbett CJ, Fransoo J, Tan T (eds) Sustainable supply chains: a research-based textbook on operations and strategy. Springer, New York, Chapter 2

Hasani A, Zegordi SH, Nikbakhsh E (2012) Robust closed-loop supply chain network design for perishable goods in agile manufacturing under uncertainty. Int J Prod Res 50(16):4649–4669

Hoekstra AY (2017) Water footprint assessment in supply chains. In: Bouchery Y, Corbett CJ, Fransoo J, Tan T (eds) Sustainable supply chains: a research-based textbook on operations and strategy. Springer, New York, Chapter 4

Hsu CI, Liu KP (2011) A model for facilities planning for multi-temperature joint distribution system. Food Control 22(12):1873–1882

Kanchanasuntorn K, Techanitisawad A (2006) An approximate periodic model for fixed-life perishable products in a two-echelon inventory–distribution system. Int J Prod Econ 100(1):101–115

Khalili-Damghani K, Tavana M, Amirkhan M (2014) A fuzzy bi-objective mixed-integer programming method for solving supply chain network design problems under ambiguous and vague conditions. Int J Adv Manuf Technol 73(9/12):1567–1595

Kim T, Glock CH, Kwon Y (2014) A closed-loop supply chain for deteriorating products under stochastic container return times. Omega 43:30–40

Linnemann AR, Hendrix EM, Apaiah R, van Boekel TA (2014) Food chain design using multi criteria decision making, an approach to complex design issues. NJAS-Wageningen J Life Sci 72–73:13–21

Liu W, Tang W, Feng L, Zhang J (2014) Dynamic pricing under temperature control for perishable foods. J Syst Sci Syst Eng 23(3):252–265

Lutke Entrup M (2006) Advanced planning in Fresh Food Industries. Physica-Verlag, Heidelberg

Meneghetti A, Monti L (2015) Greening the food supply chain: an optimisation model for sustainable design of refrigerated automated warehouses. Int J Prod Res 53(21):6567–6587

Oglethorpe D (2010) Optimising economic, environmental, and social objectives: a goal-programming approach in the food sector. Environ Plan A 42(5):1239–1254

Pan S, Ballot E, Fontane F, Hakimi D (2014) Environmental and economic issues arising from the pooling of smes' supply chains: case study of the food industry in western France. Flex Serv Manuf J 26(1–2):92–118

Piramuthu S, Farahani P, Grunow M (2013) RFID-generated traceability for contaminated product recall in perishable food supply networks. Eur J Oper Res 225(2):253–262

Rong A, Grunow M (2010) A methodology for controlling dispersion in food production and distribution. OR Spectr 32(4):957–978

Rong A, Akkerman R, Grunow M (2011) An optimization approach for managing fresh food quality throughout the supply chain. Int J Prod Econ 131(1):421–429

Seyedhosseini SM, Ghoreyshi SM (2014) An integrated model for production and distribution planning of perishable products with inventory and routing considerations. Math Probl Eng 2014

Smith DLG, Sparks L (2004) Logistics and Tesco: past, present and future. In: Ferne J, Sparks L (eds) Logistics and Retail Management, 2nd edn. Kogan Page, London, pp 101–120

Soysal M, Bloemhof-Ruwaard JM, Meuwissen MP, van der Vorst JG (2012) A review on quantitative models for sustainable food logistics management. Int J Food Syst Dyn 3(2):136–155

Soysal M, Bloemhof-Ruwaard JM, van der Vorst JGAJ (2014) Modelling food logistics networks with emission considerations: the case of an international beef supply chain. Int J Prod Econ 152:57–70

Soysal M, Bloemhof-Ruwaard JM, Haijema R, van der Vorst JGAJ (2015) Modeling an inventory routing problem for perishable products with environmental considerations and demand uncertainty. Int J Prod Econ 164:118–133

Tilman D, Cassman KG, Matson PA, Naylor R, Polasky S (2002) Agricultural sustainability and intensive production practices. Nature 418:671–677

Tsao YC (2013) Designing a fresh food supply chain network: an application of nonlinear programming. J Appl Math 2013

Validi S, Bhattacharya A, Byrne PJ (2014) A case analysis of a sustainable food supply chain distribution system—a multi-objective approach. Int J Prod Econ 152:71–87

Van der Vorst JGAJ, Beulens AJ, Wit WD, van Beek P (1998) Supply chain management in food chains: improving performance by reducing uncertainty. Int Trans Oper Res 5(6):487–499

Van der Vorst JGAJ, Beulens AJ, van Beek P (2000) Modelling and simulating multi-echelon food systems. Eur J Oper Res 122(2):354–366

Van der Vorst JGAJ, Tromp S-O, Van der Zee D-J (2009) Simulation modelling for food supply chain redesign; integrated decision making on product quality, sustainability and logistics. Int J Prod Res 47(23):6611–6631

Van der Vorst JGAJ, van Kooten O, Luning P (2011) Toward a diagnostic instrument to identify improvement opportunities for quality controlled logistics in agrifood supply chain networks. Int J Food Syst Dyn 2:94–105

Wakeland W, Cholette S, Kumar V (2012) Food transportation issues and reducing carbon footprint. In: Boye J, Arcand Y (eds) Green technologies in food production and processing, Food engineering series. Springer, New York, pp 211–235, Chapter 9

Wang X, Li D, O'brien C, Li Y (2010) A production planning model to reduce risk and improve operations management. Int J Prod Econ 124(2):463–474

Yan C, Banerjee A, Yang L (2011) An integrated production–distribution model for a deteriorating inventory item. Int J Prod Econ 133(1):228–232

You F, Tao L, Graziano DJ, Snyder SW (2012) Optimal design of sustainable cellulosic biofuel supply chains: Multiobjective optimization coupled with life cycle assessment and input–output analysis. AIChE J 58(4):1157–1180

Yu M, Nagurney A (2013) Competitive food supply chain networks with application to fresh produce. Eur J Oper Res 224(2):273–282

Zanoni S, Zavanella L (2007) Single-vendor single-buyer with integrated transport-inventory system: Models and heuristics in the case of perishable goods. Comput Ind Eng 52(1):107–123

Zanoni S, Zavanella L (2012) Chilled or frozen? decision strategies for sustainable food supply chains. Int J Prod Econ 140:731–736

Zondervan E, Nawaz M, De Haan AB, Woodley JM, Gani R (2011) Optimal design of a multiproduct biorefinery system. Comput Chem Eng 35:1752–1766

Chapter 19
Risk and Uncertainty Management for Sustainable Supply Chains

Kirstin Scholten and Brian Fynes

19.1 Introduction

Supply chains are the backbone of the global economy as well as a major influence on the social and natural business environment (van der Vegt et al. 2015). In today's globalized world, every organization is part of at least one supply chain. Furthermore, the majority of everyday transactions - withdrawing money, eating in a restaurant, shopping for food or clothes, ordering something online - involves participation in a supply chain. As such, supply chains are the channels via which resources, services, and information flow from the originating supplier to the end user. A company's relationships across their supply chains combined with increasing globalization have facilitated worldwide operations, better communication, and the ability to integrate enlarged product variety and greater consumer choice. Simultaneously, the emergence of longer and more complex supply chains and relationships, shorter product lifecycles, increased competitive pressure, and environmental uncertainty (Mentzer et al. 2001) have exposed every business to the risk of unexpected disturbances that can lead to financial losses and in some cases firm closures (Skipper and Hanna 2009). Our world is increasingly uncertain (Tang 2006) and our supply chains more vulnerable than ever (Wagner and Bode 2008).

Vulnerability in the supply chain centers around the disruption of information, product, service, knowledge, control coordination, or monetary flows between organizations (Jüttner 2005; Narasimhan and Talluri 2009) and as a result exposes organizations to risks (Craighead et al. 2007). On a daily basis, newspaper headlines

K. Scholten (✉)
Faculty of Economics and Business, University of Groningen, Groningen, The Netherlands
e-mail: k.scholten@rug.nl

B. Fynes
Smurfit School of Business, University College Dublin, Belfield, Dublin, Ireland
e-mail: brian.fynes@ucd.ie

© Yann Bouchery, Charles J. Corbett, Jan C. Fransoo, and Tarkan Tan 2017   413
Y. Bouchery et al. (eds.), *Sustainable Supply Chains*, Springer Series in Supply
Chain Management 4, DOI 10.1007/978-3-319-29791-0_19

highlight the consequences of risks: Toyota's product recalls in 2012, the horse meat scandal in 2013, industrial action at airports in France, Germany, and Belgium in 2014, the Rana Plaza factory collapse in Bangladesh in 2012, the volcanic ash eruption in Iceland in 2010 are only some of many examples that caused disruptions to supply chains globally. Each year 75 % of companies experience at least one supply chain disruption adding up to more than €1 M in costs for a single incident for 21 % of them; causes range from workforce strikes to adverse weather conditions, currency exchange rates, energy scarcity, service provision failures, and IT breakdowns (Business Continuity Institute 2013). Even a relatively minor problem within a supply chain can have significant consequences: a late delivery of raw materials can affect operations, with knock-on effects to company reputation, perception of brands, ability to win orders, quality, prices, profit margins, and lead times (Waters 2011). At worst, these contingencies can threaten the continuity and hence sustainability of organizations as has been shown in the past (van der Vegt et al. 2015). Hendricks and Singhal (2005) found that companies facing supply chain disruptions experience 33–40 % lower stock returns relative to their industry benchmarks over a 3-year period (one year before and two years after the disruption announcement date). At the same time, this might affect society as a downturn in financial performance often results in labor redundancies. Other disruptions have impacted severely on the environment e.g., the Deep Water Horizon Spill in the Gulf of Mexico in 2010 with subsequent long-term consequences for society in terms of water cleanness and the oil and gas industry in terms of policies. As the examples above illustrate, disruptions can affect any of the three dimensions of sustainability.

While the possibility of a disruption to a single facility or supplier may be relatively small, the probability in the end-to-end collective supply chain is much greater (Knemeyer et al. 2009). The network architecture of a supply chain is structured around a chain of decision nodes, where each node plays a role in adding value to final products and/or services. At the same time, each node also contributes to the risk profile in a positive or negative way (Ritchie and Brindley 2007a). For those reasons, firms are required to pay attention to factors such as labor conditions (social), financial stability (economic), and emissions (environmental) of their supply chain members. Yet, organizations frequently overlook such critical exposure to risk along their supply chains (Jüttner et al. 2003). Customers, however, are less concerned about why or where a disruption occurred; they expect the final product or service to be available to them at the right time and price (Elkins et al. 2005). Therefore, managers must delicately balance inventory, capacity, and other elements at appropriate levels across the entire supply chain in a dynamic, fast-changing environment (Chopra and Sodhi 2004).

Supply chain risk management and supply chain uncertainty management via resilience are the managerial counterparts of the concept of supply chain vulnerability (Jüttner 2005). This relationship is depicted in Fig. 19.1. The ultimate objective is to ensure that supply chains continue to work as planned, with smooth and uninterrupted flows of materials, information, and money from initial suppliers through to the final customers (Waters 2011). Hence, risk and uncertainty management contribute to business survival by limiting vulnerabilities and are therefore recognized

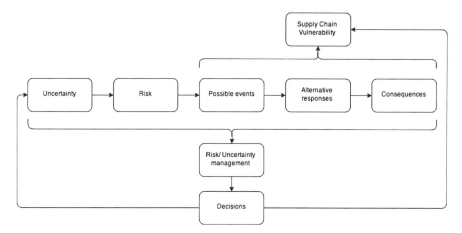

Fig. 19.1 Relationship uncertainty, risk, and vulnerability (adapted from Waters 2011)

by many organizations as an essential contributor to sustainable operations (Carter and Rogers 2008). While risk and uncertainty are intimately linked, they are not the same: risk is something measurable in the sense that estimates can be made of the probabilities of outcomes; uncertainty is not quantifiable and hence probabilities of possible outcomes are unknown (Khan and Burnes 2007). As such, risk is the expected outcome of an uncertain event (Manuj and Mentzer 2008b), whereas vulnerability is the exposure to serious disturbance arising from supply chain risks (Jüttner 2005).

This chapter sets out to examine how supply chain risk and uncertainty management practices support organizations and their supply chains in achieving long-term sustainability, whether it is in relation to economic, environmental, or societal factors. Firstly, we examine the process of *supply chain risk management* including *risk identification, risk assessment, and analysis* as well as *risk management strategies* and how these enable decisions; we then show how *uncertainty management* extends traditional supply chain risk management and how supply chain resilience enables organizations and their supply chains to also deal with unforeseeable events. Furthermore, we will discuss *disaster management* from a humanitarian perspective as a source of learning for uncertainty management in commercial supply chains. We conclude with a summary and a reflection.

19.2 Supply Chain Risk Management

While a crisis in a supply chain may be unpredictable, it may not be unexpected. To deal with and reduce the impact of global supply chain risk, existing theory suggests that businesses follow a course of action from risk identification to strategies specifically aimed at managing risk (Manuj and Mentzer 2008a). Effective supply chain risk management tries to do exactly that: identifying and managing risks in the supply chain through a synchronized approach among supply chain members, to lessen supply chain vulnerability as a whole (Faisal et al. 2006; Jüttner 2005). Proactively identifying where and when vulnerability is present creates the potential to avoid risks, prevent them from actually happening and reduce or mitigate their impact (Waters 2011). Stages in the risk management processes (labels differ among authors although the steps are similar see e.g., Manuj and Mentzer (2008a) or Jüttner et al. (2003)) include risk identification (or estimation), risk assessment (or analysis), evaluation to make a choice between strategies to manage risk as well as ongoing monitoring (Norrman and Jansson 2004). To be able to conduct the risk management process effectively, top management support is required so that a shared, supply chain-wide understanding and awareness of risks is created (Chopra and Sodhi 2004; Sheffi and Rice 2005). Only then can ongoing monitoring and control be conducted successfully as an essential part of the risk management processes. The stages of the risk management process will be further outlined in the following sections.

19.3   Risk Identification

The identification of risk sources is an important step in the risk management process as decision-makers become aware of events that may cause disturbances (Norrman and Jansson 2004). It encompasses a comprehensive and structured determination of potential supply chain risks (Tummala and Schoenherr 2011). Risks to the supply chain consist of anything that may interrupt the normal flows of the chain and as a consequence expose organizations within the supply chain to economic, environmental, and societal consequences (Craighead et al. 2007). Hence, there are a huge number of possible risks that can appear in almost endless variety (Waters 2011): sources of risk can be organizational, supply chain or environmental-related factors that affect the supply chain performance (Faisal et al. 2006; Peck et al. 2003; Jüttner 2005) - see Fig. 19.2. Taken together these risks define the vulnerability of a supply chain (Waters 2011).

- *Organizational risk sources:* Organizational sources of risk affect the operational side of an organization (Manuj and Mentzer 2008a). Hence, they are internal to any organization and relate to processes and controls (Peck et al. 2003; Jüttner 2005). Processes facilitate the management and production of value in an organization in the form of products and services for the end consumer (Christopher 1998). Risk inherent in processes can relate to accidents, the reliability of equipment, loss of an information technology system and quality issues (Waters 2011). Variability in processes can be managed via controls, which are assumptions, rules, systems, and procedures such as order quantities, batch sizes, and safety stocks (Christopher and Peck 2004). Therefore, risks in relation to controls arise more directly from human decision making via the application or misapplication of these assumptions, rules, systems, or procedures (Peck et al. 2003).

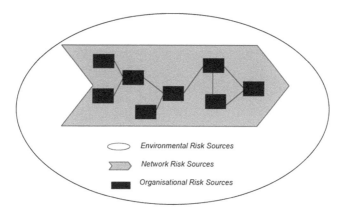

Fig. 19.2 Risk sources in supply chains (Jüttner et al. 2003)

- *Network risk sources:* Network risks are internal to the supply network but external to an organization (Jüttner et al. 2003). As such, these sources are prone to affect a number of interdependent parties in a supply chain (Jüttner 2005). Network risk sources refer to the possibility and impact of a mismatch between supply and demand (Jüttner et al. 2003). Therefore, network risks have been categorized as originating from the demand or the supply side. Demand and supply risks occur from the interactions between members of the supply chain and are often caused by inadequate coordination between members and lack of visibility (Waters 2011).

  Demand risk relates to vulnerabilities associated with the outbound logistics flows and product demand (Jüttner 2005). It can be any potential or actual disturbance within the network to the supply chain flows downstream (Christopher and Peck 2004) such as variable demand, payments, problem with order processing, or customized requirements (Waters 2011). Demand risks vary with the nature of the product, with functional products generally less exposed to risks than innovative products (Fisher 1997; Manuj and Mentzer 2008a). Similarly, on the supply side, risks are associated with possible events that may affect the inbound flows (Manuj and Mentzer 2008a). Hence, supply risks are related to supplier actions or supplier relationships (Jüttner 2005). Consequently, the risk manifests itself upstream in potential or actual supply chain disturbances (Peck et al. 2003) caused by variability in the availability of materials, lead times, delivery problems, industrial action, or reliability of a supplier (Waters 2011).
- *Environmental risk sources:* As environmental risk is associated with disruption external to the focal organization and supply chain network (Jüttner 2005; Peck et al. 2003; Christopher and Peck 2004), it represents a level of risk that is often beyond the direct control of supply chain operators (Peck 2005). Factors influencing the level of environmental risk can be summarized as political, environmental, social, technological, economic, or legal aspects (PESTEL).

Table 19.1 Examples of classifications of risk sources in literature

Author (Year)	Risk sources
Mason-Jones and Towill (1998)	Environmental risk
	Demand and supply risk
	Process risk
	Control risk
Jüttner et al. (2003)	Environmental risk
	Organizational risk
	Network risk
Chopra and Sodhi (2004)	Disruption risk
	Delay risk
	System risk
	Forecast risk
	Intellectual property risk
	Procurement risk
	Receivables risk
	Inventory risk
	Capacity risk
Christopher and Lee (2004)	Financial risk
	Chaos risk
	Decision risk
	Market risk
Wagner and Bode (2006)	Demand side risk
	Supply side risk
	Catastrophic risk
Manuj and Mentzer (2008a)	Supply risk
	Operational risk
	Demand risk
	Security risk
Wagner and Bode (2008)	Demand side risk
	Supply side risk
	Regulatory, legal, and bureaucratic risk
	Infrastructure risk
	Catastrophic risk
Rao and Goldsby (2009)	Environmental risk
	Industry risk
	Organizational risk
	Problem-specific risk
	Decision-maker risk

Other categorizations of sources of risk, rather than organizational, network, and environmental are also reported in the literature (see Table 19.1). Whatever categorization one prefers, identifying risks related to such categories is critical so that consequences can be understood and assessed (Tummala and Schoenherr 2011).

There are many methods for the identification of specific risks (Norrman and Jansson 2004). "Five whys," cause-and-effect diagrams, Pareto analysis, checklists, interviews, process charts and controls supply chain even management and supply chain risk mapping (for further details see Waters 2011), are only some of the methods that can be used by managers to identify possible risk sources. Care needs to be taken in the identification as risk sources can never be seen in isolation: they are linked to each other in complex patterns with one risk source leading to another, or influencing the outcome of other risks (Manuj and Mentzer 2008b; Miller 1992) e.g., environmental risks can cause supply or demand risks (Jüttner 2005; Manuj and Mentzer 2008a). Furthermore, as a result of complex supply chain designs, there is the risk of additional chaos resulting from overreactions, unnecessary interventions, second guessing, mistrust, and distorted information throughout the supply chain (Christopher and Lee 2004) which could potentially lead to e.g., the bullwhip effect (for further details see Lee et al. 1997).

Irrespective of the source of the risk, the profile and nature of risk can be highly divergent: the financial default of a supplier (network risk) and a natural disaster destroying production capacity (environmental risk) are situations with completely different attributes in terms of incubation period, probability, predictability, and severity (Wagner and Bode 2006). As such, classifying risks into categories simply indicates the source of the risks and does not indicate the nature, scale, or manageability (Ritchie and Brindley 2007b). Hence, the identification and classification of risk sources on its own is meaningless as each risk effects the supply chain differently; at the same time, risk identification is of great importance (Jüttner et al. 2003) providing the basis for risk quantification, assessment, and evaluation that can be used in deriving risk mitigation strategies (Narasimhan and Talluri 2009). This will be further discussed in the following section.

19.4   Risk Assessment and Analysis

The main focus of supply chain risk assessment is to recognize and analyze future uncertainties to enable proactive management of risk-related issues (Norrman and Jansson 2004). This involves the determination of the consequences of all identified, potential supply chain risks, together with their magnitudes of impact (Tummala and Schoenherr 2011). Impact refers to the significance of the loss to the organization and/or supply chain(s) (Zsidisin et al. 2004). Adverse risk consequences can become manifested in any outcome measure such as loss of or damage to assets, income, service levels, or schedules. Supply chain design characteristics such as density, complexity, and node critically have been shown to increase the severity of possible risks (Craighead et al. 2007). Some further examples have been given in the introduction already. Accordingly, supply chain risk assessment should be a formal part of the decision-making process at every level from product design to component availability and lead time determination (Christopher and Peck 2004).

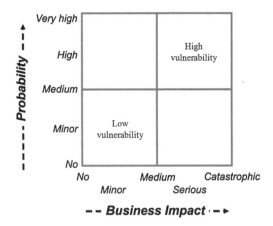

Fig. 19.3 Risk matrix (adapted from Norrman and Jansson 2004)

Nonetheless, the consequences of risk do not necessarily need to be negative as the essence of risk-taking is the potential opportunity to produce positive outcomes (Ritchie and Brindley 2007a) although in the context of this chapter, we define risk outcomes as negative.

In addition to the severity and impact, organizations need to understand that supply chain disruptions can be frequent or infrequent and short- or long-term (Chopra and Sodhi 2004). Risk is perceived to exist if there is a relatively high likelihood that an event occurs and that the event has a significant associated impact or cost (Zsidisin et al. 2004). Therefore, as some risks will have severe consequences and others not, it is important for organization to assess the probability of the risk occurrences alongside the possible impact (Cohen and Kunreuther 2007). The likelihood of occurrence, typically expressed as a probability, can be articulated in objective (absolute values) or subjective terms (ranges) (Ritchie and Brindley 2007a). In this context, probability is a measure of the likelihood of occurrence of a negative event.

Combining the assessment of impact (consequences) and probability allows organizations to classify their supply chain vulnerability as shown in Fig. 19.3. This is calculated by multiplying the value of the impact of risk by its probability of occurrence (giving the expected value of the impact) or by Monte Carlo simulation, scenario analysis, failure modes, and effects analysis or network models (Waters 2011). The most important consideration for a risk manager is to have an advanced plan that indicates a suitable response to any possible event (Spekman and Davis 2004) that has first been identified and then quantified as shown in the section via considerations of impact and probability (vulnerability). Hence, following these steps in the risk management process, different possible risk management strategies need to be considered to derive at a decision of what to do. Consequently, in the next section, we will describe possible risk management strategies.

19.5   Risk Management Strategies

While it is impossible to completely eliminate risks and consequent vulnerabilities from a supply chain, they can be reduced if an organization is proactive and prepared (Faisal et al. 2006). Risk management is the process in which decisions are made to accept a known or assessed risk and strategies are developed that reduce the probabilities and impact of negative events and/or their consequences in case they occur (Cohen and Kunreuther 2007; Manuj and Mentzer 2008b). Depending on the assessment of risks, different strategies can be deployed to manage the risks: risk reduction or mitigation, risk avoidance, risk-taking or acceptance and risk sharing or transfer (Norrman and Jansson 2004) (see Fig. 19.4). There is no one best strategy for protecting supply chains against risks, instead, managers need to know which strategy works best against which given risk (Chopra and Sodhi 2004).

Notwithstanding the level of vulnerability, managers have two choices, either they can ignore (or accept) the risk and do nothing, or they can respond and do something (Waters 2011). Since it is not feasible nor practical to develop mitigation and sharing/transfer strategies for every risk identified, risk management begins with the examination of the costs required to implement each preventative action to contain and manage the identified supply chain risks (Tummala and Schoenherr 2011). Often a cost-benefit analysis of low-probability low-impact risks shows that the cost to mitigate the risk is higher than the cost to bear the risk; e.g., in the case of a stationery supply chain for a food processing company, the risk to the stationery supply chain can be accepted without further action, but needs to be monitored closely to ensure that the impact remains low in case the risk should manifest itself in a disruption.

Companies typically focus on managing risks with the greatest impact and the greatest probability. Accordingly, Kleindorfer and Saad (2005) suggest that *risk avoidance*, the strategy used for high-probability high-impact risks, should precede risk reduction and mitigation. An avoidance strategy is used when the risks

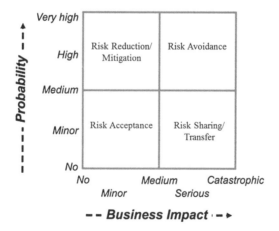

Fig. 19.4   Risk management matrix (adapted from Norrman and Jansson 2004)

Table 19.2 Supply chain risk mitigation strategies (Tang 2006)

Risk mitigation strategy	Benefit(s) under normal circumstances	Benefits after a major disruption
Strategic stock	Improves capability to manage supply	Enables a firm to respond to market demand quickly during a major disruption
Postponement	Improves capability to manage supply	Enables a firm to change the configurations of different products quickly
Flexible supply base	Improves capability to manage supply	Enables a firm to shift production among suppliers promptly
Make and buy	Improves capability to manage supply	Enables a firm to shift production between in-house production facility and suppliers rapidly
Economic supply incentives	Improves capability to manage supply	Enables a firm to adjust order quantities quickly
Flexible transportation	Improves capability to manage supply	Enables a firm to change the mode of transportation rapidly
Revenue management	Improves capability to manage demand	Enables a firm to influence the customer product selection dynamically
Assortment planning	Improves capability to manage demand	Enables a firm to influence the demands of different products quickly
Silent product rollover	Improves capability to manage supply and demand	Enables a firm to manage the demands of different products swiftly

associated with operating in a given market (environmental risk) or working with particular suppliers or customers (network risk) is considered unacceptable (Manuj and Mentzer 2008a). To avoid is to eliminate the types of event that could trigger the risk by either driving overall probabilities associated with risk events to zero or by reducing the frequency and probability of a risk (Manuj and Mentzer 2008b). Being attacked by pirates for example is a high risk for cargo ship operators in some parts of the world; to reduce the risk other routes that avoid the most dangerous seas that can be used (Waters 2011). Another option for an organization is to drop specific products, suppliers, or geographical markets if supply is seen to be highly vulnerable (Jüttner et al. 2003).

Similarly, *risk reduction and mitigation*, aim to reduce both the probability and consequence of the possible risk event (Manuj and Mentzer 2008b). Mitigation tactics are those by which an organization takes some action in advance of a disruption (Tomlin 2006) with the aim of achieving robustness. Table 19.2 gives an overview of risk management strategies that aim to achieve robustness for supply network risks rather than organizational risks only (for further details on each strategy see Tang 2006). Furthermore, information sharing, aligning incentives, risk sharing, and corporate social responsibility are required to successfully implement risk mitigation strategies (Chopra and Sodhi 2004; Faisal et al. 2006; Spekman and Davis 2004).

As illustrated in Table 19.2, supply chain risk mitigation strategies can be beneficial under normal circumstances as well as during a major disruption (Tang 2006).

However, at the same time, they can create challenges: every decision that mitigates one risk can end up intensifying another (Chopra and Sodhi 2004). As slack is taken out of supply chains with the aim to reduce costs, the chance that events in one link will affect other links considerably increases. Hence, typical supply chain risk management solutions such as the maintenance of buffer stocks, built in slack in delivery lead times, excess profit margins to cover returns are becoming less viable in a world of outsourcing, just in time (JIT) and materials requirement planning (MRP). As a result, trade-offs between the robustness (benefit) of a supply chain to disruptions and the overall efficiency (cost) of the supply chain under normal operations have to be made. (Kleindorfer and Saad 2005). For example, having additional inventory that might buffer a supply failure can at the same time significantly increase inventory holding costs and in some cases risk of obsolescence.

Risk sharing or transfer move some of the risks from one organization in the supply chain to another (typically more able or willing to handle it) (Waters 2011) via outsourcing, offshoring, or contracting (Manuj and Mentzer 2008a). Risk could for example be transferred to insurance companies or supply chain partners by moving inventory liability, changing delivery times of suppliers (just-in-time deliveries), dealing with customer uncertainty (make-to-order manufacturing), or by deciding to move a part of the production to an outside party (Manuj and Mentzer 2008b). However, sharing or transferring risk neither eliminates nor reduces the probability or impact of a possible risk event. So while insurance can cover the costs of disruption, the disruption nonetheless can occur.

Generally, organizations take decisions and plan to protect themselves against recurrent, low-impact risks in their supply chains by making use of one of the strategies above but ignore high-impact, low-likelihood ones (Faisal et al. 2006) simply because of the low probability of occurrence (Waters 2011). Yet the exacerbating frequency, magnitude, and impact of disasters present an increasing threat to the sustainability of communities, supply chains, businesses, and their resources. The impact of local or regional events can transcend globally: for example, the earthquake in Japan 2012 not only affected the Japanese and Asian economies but led to shortages in the automobile and technology industry globally. However, such low probability supply chain disruptions are hard to identify, hence cannot be assessed and analyzed which limits the possibilities of deriving risk management strategies and decisions. Hence, they cannot be managed via the risk management process so far; they have to be managed in a different way. In the following section, we examine how to manage the unknown: supply chain uncertainty. We will do so by reflecting on practices from an extreme case context: humanitarian disaster management.

19.6 Supply Chain Uncertainty Management via Resilience

Uncertainty management is no longer about if, but when a disruption is going to happen. In its extreme form, uncertainty relates to the situation in which there is a total absence of information, knowledge, understanding, or awareness of a potential event occurrence (Ritchie and Brindley 2007a). Hence, it is difficult if not impossible to follow the risk management process from risk identification to risk assessment and management. By accepting that not all risks can be foreseen, controlled, or eliminated (Jüttner and Maklan 2011) supply chain resilience enhances the traditional risk management process as it enables an organization to deal with uncertain factors that can only be identified and predicted to a limited extent (Scholten and Schilder 2015). Whereas risk management tries to decrease the vulnerability (probability and impact) of a certain risk, resilience focuses on the ability to absorb the impact of a disturbance that might stem from any risk by enabling the supply chain to return to stable conditions faster (Peck 2005). The aim is not to analyze risks and find the best strategy to respond, but to consider each part of the supply chain, see what happens when the part is disrupted and set up mechanisms that enable quick recovery of operations (Waters 2011).

Resilience has been defined in supply chain terms as "the adaptive capability of the supply chain to prepare for unexpected events, respond to disruption and recover from them by maintaining continuity of operations at the desired level of connectedness and control over structures and function" (Ponomarov and Holcomb 2009:131). An often-cited example in the context of supply chain resilience is a fire at a Philips Electronics plant in Albuquerque, New Mexico in March 2000 which simultaneously affected Nokia and Ericsson (see e.g., Norrman and Jansson 2004; Sheffi and Rice 2005), who accounted for 40 % of the plant's shipments (Mukherjee 2008). Both competitors were solely dependent on Philips for the chips they produced (Sheffi and Rice 2005). The two companies reacted differently to the supply chain disruptions. Nokia was better able to deal with the disruption than Ericsson, displaying the adaptive capabilities that allowed the organization to quickly discover and efficiently recover from the disruptive event (Blackhurst et al. 2011; Pettit et al. 2010). Ericsson on the other hand, had to quit the mobile-phone business as a result of the disruption, leaving Nokia to reinforce its position as the European market leader. But what made the adaptive capability of Nokia better than the one of Ericsson?

While there are few conceptual differences in how supply chain resilience is defined (see e.g., Brandon-Jones et al. 2014; Peck et al. 2003; Ponomarov and Holcomb 2009; Sheffi and Rice 2005) the formative elements needed to secure the adaptive capability of resilience are presented with significant disparity in literature (Jüttner and Maklan 2011; Scholten et al. 2014). Formative elements of the adaptive capabilities of a supply chain have, for example, been conceptualized as collaboration, supply chain design principles, risk awareness, visibility, flexibility, security and velocity (Blackhurst et al. 2011; Christopher and Peck 2004; Jüttner and Maklan 2011; Sheffi and Rice 2005) - see Table 19.3 for an overview. On their own, all of these elements display good SCM practices based on integrating and coordinating resources (Jüttner and Maklan 2011). The example of Nokia and Ericsson further illustrates this: Nokia acted quickly after hearing about the fire and moved to tie up spare capacity at other Philips plants and every other supplier they could find (Mukherjee 2008). The company sent 30 employees to work with Philips and other suppliers to restore supply (Sheffi and Rice 2005). Furthermore, they

Table 19.3 Supply chain resilience overview (Excerpt from Scholten et al. 2014)

System level resilience capabilities	Resilience elements	Christopher and Peck (2004)	Sheffi (2005), Sheffi and Rice (2005)	Ponomarov and Holcomb (2009)	Pettit et al. (2010, 2013)	Zsidisin and Wagner (2010)	Jüttner and Maklan (2011)	Wieland and Wallenburg (2012, 2013)
Supply chain (re-)engineering:								
The conceptualization, design, implementation, operation, and re-engineering of the supply chain (Naim et al. 2000)	*Efficiency:* The ability to produce outputs with minimum resource requirements (Pettit et al. 2010)	X	X	X	X			
	Redundancy: Limiting or mitigating the negative consequences of change by keeping resources in reserve, such as having safety stock, maintaining multiple supplier and running operations at a low-capacity utilization rates (Blackhurst et al. 2005; Sheffi and Rice 2005)	X	X	X	X	X		
	Robustness: The ability of a supply chain to resist change without adapting its initial stable configuration (Wieland and Wallenburg 2012)							X

(continued)

Table 19.3 (continued)

System level resilience capabilities	Resilience elements	Christopher and Peck (2004)	Sheffi (2005), Sheffi and Rice (2005)	Ponomarov and Holcomb (2009)	Pettit et al. (2010, 2013)	Zsidisin and Wagner (2010)	Jüttner and Maklan (2011)	Wieland and Wallenburg (2012, 2013)
Collaboration:		X	X	X	X	X	X	X
The level of joined decision making and working together at a tactical, operational, or strategic level between two or more supply chain members (horizontal or vertical). Scalable through the magnitude of relationship strength, quality, and closeness. (Jüttner and Maklan 2011)	*Visibility:* The identity, location, and status of entities transiting the supply chain, captured in timely messages about events, along with the planned and actual dates/times for these events (Francis 2008)	X	X	X	X	X	X	X
Agility (Flexibility):		X	X	X	X	X	X	X
The ability to rapidly respond to change by adapting its initial stable configuration (Wieland and Wallenburg 2012)	*Velocity:* The speed in which a supply chain can react to changes in demand, upwards or downwards (Christopher and Peck 2004)	X	X	X	X	X	X	X
	Visibility: see above	X	X	X	X		X	X
Risk Awareness: Making supply chain risk assessment a formal part of the decision making process at every level (Christopher and Peck 2004)		X	X	X	X			
Knowledge Management: Knowledge and understanding of supply chain structures—both physical and informational and its ability to learn from changes (Adapted from Ponomarov and Holcomb 2009)		X	X	X	X			

changed some of the product specifications so that they could take chips from other Japanese and American suppliers (Mukherjee 2008). The company's culture (risk awareness) together with the deep relationships with suppliers (collaboration) enabled the company to recognize the severity of the situation quickly (visibility and velocity), disseminate the news and take immediate action at various levels of the organization (agility and knowledge management) (Sheffi and Rice 2005). Hence, they displayed all system level adaptive supply chain resilience capabilities: supply chain re-engineering, collaboration, agility, risk awareness and knowledge management. Therefore, Nokia had the adaptive capabilities that supported its supply chain to overcome the disruption by continually adapting and altering itself to meet required changes, that would let the company deal with the situation (Scholten et al. 2014).

Ericsson on the other hand was not proactive and did not realize the seriousness of the disruption until weeks later (Sheffi and Rice 2005). It took too long before higher management was aware of the incident and the company had neither alternative sources of supply nor was it prepared for this kind of accident (Mukherjee 2008). In fact, by the time Ericsson took action for recovery, the worldwide supply of the chips in question, was committed to Nokia (Sheffi and Rice 2005). Ericsson employed sharing and transfer of risk via insurance: business interruption costs were calculated and compensated as approximately $200 million (Norrman and Jansson 2004). However, the insurance was not able to eliminate the consequences of the manifested risk. As Waters (2011) argues, low probability high-impact risks should not be managed with regular supply chain risk management tools and strategies. Instead, holistic mechanisms considering the system level adaptive supply chain resilience capabilities of supply chain re-engineering, collaboration, agility, risk awareness and knowledge management need to be put in place. Hence, the incident made Ericsson realize the importance of not only understanding and managing risks internally—but also trying to manage *uncertainty* along the supply chain (Norrman and Jansson 2004) in a way that operations can continue during any emergency.

While the importance of uncertainty management is evident in both theory and practice, the literature has moved little beyond basic conceptual frameworks to assess the resilience of a *supply chain* rather than a single organization (Blackhurst et al. 2011; Jüttner and Maklan 2011; Pettit et al. 2013). Hence, there is hardly any management guidance on the implementation and operationalization of the concept of supply chain resilience (Scholten et al. 2014). Recent supply chain studies suggest that commercial supply chain operations can benefit from research into disaster SCM (Christopher and Tatham 2011) especially in relation to risk and uncertainty management practices (Day et al. 2012): private sector businesses can learn about vulnerability assessment, preparation, and response to disasters from humanitarian organizations (Van Wassenhove 2006). As breakdowns and interruptions in material and information flow (Blecken 2010) occur frequently in emergency situations, organizations that are active in disaster management are experts in working with uncertainty and risk - for them experiencing unpredictability is the norm (Scholten et al. 2014). As such, the disaster management sector has the potential to create a hothouse of information for risk and uncertainty management practices in addition to the traditional practices described in this chapter so far, thereby providing critical insights applicable to private sector SCM. This has been shown by recent research from Scholten et al. (2014) and will be further outlined in the following section.

19.7 Disaster Management

The disaster management context represents an ideal opportunity to examine supply chain risk and uncertainty given the exacerbating frequency, magnitude, and impact of disasters threatening the sustainability of communities, businesses, and their resources around the globe (Scholten et al. 2014). Disasters seriously disrupt the functioning of society, and cause widespread human, material, or environmental loss or damage, which is often of such magnitude that the affected areas cannot rely just on their own resources to manage their situations (United Nations 1992). Hence, they test the resilience of affected local supply networks which integrate government agencies, non-governmental organizations, for-profit organizations, the military and community organizations into relief efforts (Day 2014). The aim of humanitarian relief is to quickly provide assistance and alleviate suffering either long term or during and after a disaster in affected areas with the aim of saving and sustaining lives as well as (re)creating self-sufficiency (Thévenaz and Resodihardjo 2010). According to van Wassenhove (2006) SCM is a crucial function in disaster management for the following reasons:

- The performance of relief operations in terms of effectiveness and speed of current and future operations and programs.
- Serving as a bridge between disaster preparedness and response, between procurement and distribution and between headquarters and the field.
- Providing a rich source of data in terms of tracking of goods, which could be used to analyze post-event effectiveness.
- Representing 80 % of relief operations (and their costs) and therefore being the element that can make the difference between a successful or failed operation.

Both private sector and disaster, not-for-profit SCM not only have a lot in common (Ernst 2003), but humanitarian supply chains may be somewhat commercial in the way that private sector companies might undertake production and some of the transport and logistical activities (Jahre et al. 2009). However, at the same time disaster relief chain management differs on various levels (Beamon and Balcik 2008) as shown in Table 19.4. As a result of the unpredictability and uncertainties around disasters, humanitarian relief operations are faced with unique characteristics: zero lead times affecting inventory, procurement and distribution, high stakes at risk, unreliable supply and transportation information (Beamon 2004).

While nobody can identify exactly when or where a low-probability high-impact disaster, such as an earthquake or tsunami, is going to happen, identifying vulnerable areas that are at risk (Peck 2005, 2006) creates opportunities to put in place

Table 19.4   Comparison of private sector vs. humanitarian logistics (Mizushima 2008)

	Private sector	Humanitarian
Situations	Fairly predictable	Unpredictable: emergencies
		Fairly predictable: development
Execution time	Varies due to market conditions	Extremely compressed
Demand	Relatively stable, predictable	Determined by random events, relatively unpredictable location/type/size
Distribution network configuration	Methodology to determine structure and locations	Challenging; Location/type/size unknown
Universal language	English	Depends on location
Technology	State-of-the-art systems, well-defined processes	Lack of standardized systems, Information unreliable, incomplete or non-existent
Strategic objectives	Maximize profit; Improve shareholder value	Save lives, alleviate suffering
Personnel	Skilled, specific logistics education	Little or no education in logistics
Stakes	Customer satisfaction, profitability	Human life
Infrastructure	Modern, well-maintained	Primitive, poor, sometimes totally destroyed
Environment	Stable, conducive to business, and transportation	Problematic, often extremely dangerous

practices and resources that minimize the impact of disasters before they occur (Dilley 2006; Scholten et al. 2014). This echoes similarities to the traditional risk management process described earlier. However, sustainable relief operations and their management involve a continuum of interlinked activities (Pettit and Beresford 2005) across the four disaster phases: preparedness, immediate response, recovery, and mitigation. The disaster management cycle depicted in Fig. 19.5 indicates that effective and efficient disaster management is about the application of a strategic focus to the processes of making *proactive* decisions to lessen disaster impact (during mitigation and preparation) and *reactive* decisions in overcoming the impact (during response and recovery) (Natarajarathinam et al. 2009) comparable to definitions of supply chain resilience in academic research:

- *Mitigation* concerns the application of measures that will either prevent the onset of a disaster or reduce the impact should one occur (Altay and Green 2006; Tomlin 2006).
- *Preparedness* includes activities that prepare for an effective and efficient response (Altay and Green 2006; Tomlin 2006).
- *Response* processes include the employment of resources to preserve life, property, the environment, and the social, economic, and political structures (Altay and Green 2006).

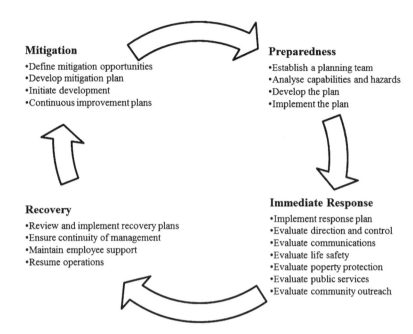

Mitigation
•Define mitigation opportunities
•Develop mitigation plan
•Initiate development
•Continuous improvement plans

Preparedness
•Establish a planning team
•Analyse capabilities and hazards
•Develop the plan
•Implement the plan

Recovery
•Review and implement recovery plans
•Ensure continuity of management
•Maintain employee support
•Resume operations

Immediate Response
•Implement response plan
•Evaluate direction and control
•Evaluate communications
•Evaluate life safety
•Evaluate poperty protection
•Evaluate public services
•Evaluate community outreach

Fig. 19.5 Disaster management processes (adapted from Helferich and Cook 2003)

• During *recovery*, actions are taken in the long term after the immediate impact has passed to stabilize and restore some semblance of normalcy in structures (Altay and Green 2006).

As with the Ponomarov and Holcomb's (2009) definition of supply chain resilience, resilience in the context of humanitarian aid has been defined as "a process linking a set of adaptive capabilities to a positive trajectory of functioning and adaptation after a disturbance" (Norris et al. 2008:130). In an empirical study, Scholten et al. (2014) establish a link between the conceptual supply chain resilience adaptive capabilities and practical disaster management processes part of the disaster management cycle (Fig. 19.5). The results depicted in Fig. 19.6 show that mitigation processes are of paramount importance as they are the antecedents to building supply chain resilience capabilities which in turn enable the execution of the necessary processes during preparedness, response, and recovery. The authors emphasize that there is no "one-size-fits-all" model for supply chain resilience as each organization will have idiosyncratic requirements (van Vactor 2011) in terms of time, human, physical, and organizational resources. Christopher and Peck (2004) highlight that determining the appropriate practices to manage supply chain vulnerabilities and risk appears to be context-specific, dependent amongst other things on the supply chain's response to the need for operational excellence. Hence, the framework by Scholten et al. (2014) depicted in Fig. 19.6 is not to be seen as a specific defined route to supply chain resilience but more as a road map that can guide individual,

Disaster Management Processes		Supply Chain Resilience Capabilities				
		Horizontal & Vertical Collaboration	Supply Chain (Re-)engineering	Agility	Risk Awareness	Knowledge Management
Mitigation	Establish a cross-functional planning team	√	√		√	√
	Analyze supply chain capabilities and hazards	√			√	√
	Develop and communicate plan for preparedness, response and recovery	√	√		√	√
	Agree measurements and metrics for preparedness, response and recovery	√	√		√	√
	Develop continuous improvement and supply chain risk mitigation plans	√	(√)		**√**	**√**
Preparedness	Implement preparedness plan: Translate strategic agreements into operational matters	√	(√)	(√)		√
	Evaluate based on measurements and metrics	√		(√)		√
	Establish routines through training and simulation	√	√	(√)		√
Response	Implement response plan, measurements and metrics	√	(√)	√		√
	Evaluate direction and control	√		(√)		(√)
	Evaluate communications throughout the supply chain	√		(√)		(√)
	Evaluate supply chain disruption outreach	√	(√)	√		(√)
Recovery	Review and implement recovery plans	√	(√)			√
	Ensure continuity of risk and resilience management	√			√	
	Maintain employee support	√			√	
	Resume operations	√		(√)		√

(√) =   possibly required
√ =   required

Fig. 19.6 Integrative framework for building supply chain resilience (Scholten et al. 2014)

context-specific supply chains (commercial and disaster management businesses) in improving and building their supply chain resilience and disruption management capabilities. Furthermore, their framework contributes to the development of an awareness of the value of the strategic capabilities involved in the different disruption phases and of how they interact with each other through specific processes.

However, supply chain resilience is only one aspect contributing to sustainability in the humanitarian context. Often humanitarian organizations are still years behind their private sector counterparts who realized the importance of using efficient supply chains at an earlier stage. Academic literature has highlighted the lack of recognition for the supply chain function within humanitarian organizations (see e.g., Pettit and Beresford 2005; Van Wassenhove 2006). Modest progress is evidenced as some of the bigger humanitarian organizations' senior management has recognized the importance of SCM to the performance of relief operations. Nevertheless, things are often different in the field. Even where proven SCM practices and strategies are used, acceptable response and recovery performance has remained elusive (Day 2014). The pipeline of publications in general SCM journals on humanitarian aid, and the establishment of a specialized journal demonstrate the growing acknowledgement of the value, importance, and potential of this research field. Nevertheless, advancements in humanitarian SCM remain necessary for the prompt alleviation of a disaster's impact and overall sustainable operations: "What is lacking, is a body of theory that can help explain why some approaches manage to create effective disaster supply chains, whereas so many disasters suffer the lack of effective disaster supply chains" (Boin et al. 2010:4). This highlights the possibilities for cross learning between commercial and disaster management organizations: commercial companies can learn about supply chain risk and resilience management from disaster management organizations (effectiveness) while at the same time passing on their general knowledge on supply chain management (effectiveness and efficiency). Balaisyte et al. (2017) discuss such cross-sector partnerships in more detail in Chap. 22.

19.8   Conclusion

Today more than ever, managers need to be aware of risk and uncertainty that might negatively impact the organizational sustainability due to suboptimal supply chain performance. Adopting supply chain risk management practices cannot only yield continuous improvement of supply chain operations (Elkins et al. 2005), but also be the key to business survival and sustainability. While there is a large body of knowledge and research on risk management and how to try and prevent supply chain disruptions via the supply, chain risk management process (identification, assessment and analysis, strategies and decisions), in today's global and complex world it is not a question of if a disruption is going to happen but when. Therefore, we need to know how they can be dealt with in an effective and efficient way. Yet, research on supply chain resilience, a concept that extends supply chain risk management to deal with uncertainties, is for a large part conceptual; more empirical research and practical insights, particularly beyond a single company perspective, are required to help organizations and their supply chains to become more sustainable.

One area for potential insights on supply chain resilience is the humanitarian aid sector. On the one hand, humanitarian SCM, while particularly rich and exciting, could be treated as just another research context for applying theories developed in the mainstream commercial SCM. On the other hand, this approach overlooks the potential opportunities for reverse learning as the dynamic and unpredictable environment of humanitarian SCM may provide unique insights for building mainstream theory. Humanitarian SCM shows many similarities and faces many of the challenges of commercial SCM, except in a more extreme context. Existing research on humanitarian SCM highlights the possibilities of cross learning and integration between humanitarian and commercial operations. However, more bridges need to be built for two-way learning.

Bibliography

Altay N, Green WG (2006) OR/MS research in disaster operations management. Eur J Oper Res 175(1):475–493

Balaisyte J, Besiou M, Van Wassenhove LN (2017) Cross-sector partnerships for sustainable supply chains. In: Bouchery Y, Corbett CJ, Fransoo J, Tan T (eds) Sustainable supply chains: a research-based textbook on operations and strategy. Springer, New York

Beamon BM (2004) Humanitarian relief chains: Issues and challenges. In: Proceedings of the 34th international conference on computers and industrial engineering, 34th international conference on computers and industrial engineering, San Francisco, pp 77–82

Beamon BM, Balcik B (2008) Performance measurement in humanitarian relief chains. Int J Public Sector Manag 31(1):4–25

Blackhurst J, Craighead CW, Elkins D., Handfield RB (2005) An empirically derived agenda of critical research issues for managing supply-chain disruptions. Int J Prod Res 43(19): 4067–4081

Blackhurst J, Dunn KS, Craighead CW (2011) An empirically derived framework of global supply resiliency. J Bus Logist 32(4):374–391

Blecken A (2010) Supply chain process modelling for humanitarian organizations. Int J Phys Distrib Logist Manag 40(8):675–692

Boin A, Kelle P, Whybark DC (2010) Resilient supply chains for extreme situations: outlining a new field of study. Int J Prod Econ 126(1):1–6

Brandon-Jones E, Squire B, Autry CW, Petersen KJ (2014) A contingent resource-based perspective of supply chain resilience and robustness. J Supply Chain Manag 50(3):55–73

Business Continuity Institute (2013) Supply chain resilience 2013. 5th annual survey. http://www.bcifiles.com/131029SupplyChainSurveyReportfinallowres.pdf. Accessed 24 March 2014

Carter CR, Rogers DS (2008) A framework of sustainable supply chain management: moving towards new theory. Int J Phys Distrib Logist Manag 38(5):360–387

Chopra S, Sodhi MS (2004) Managing risk to avoid supply-chain breakdown. MIT Sloan Manag Rev 46(1):53–62

Christopher M (1998) Logistics and supply chain management. Financial Times, London

Christopher M, Lee H (2004) Mitigating supply chain risk through improved confidence. Int J Phys Distrib Logist Manag 34(5):388–396

Christopher M, Peck H (2004) Building the resilient supply chain. Int J Logist Manag 15(2):1–13

Christopher M, Tatham P (2011) Humanitarian logistics: meeting the challenge of preparing for and responding to disasters. Kogan Page, London

Cohen MA, Kunreuther H (2007) Operations risk management: overview of Paul Kleindorfer's contributions. Prod Oper Manag 16(5):525–541

Craighead CW, Blackhurst J, Rungtusanatham MJ, Handfield RB (2007) The severity of supply chain disruptions: design characteristics and mitigation capabilities. Decis Sci 38(1):131–156

Day JM (2014) Fostering emergent resilience: the complex adaptive supply network of disaster relief. Int J Prod Res 52(7):1970–1988

Day JM, Melnyk SA, Larson PD, Davis EW, Whybark DC (2012) Humanitarian disaster relief supply chains: a matter of life and death. J Supply Chain Manag 48(2):21–36

Dilley M (2006) Setting priorities: global patterns for disaster risk. Philos Trans Royal Soc 364(1845):2217–2229

Elkins D, Handfield RB, Blackhurst J, Craighead CW (2005) 18 ways to guard against disruption. Supply Chain Manag Rev 9(1):46–53

Ernst R (2003) The academic side of commercial logistics and the importance of this special issue. Forced Migr Rev 18:5

Faisal MN, Banwet DK, Shankar R (2006) Supply chain risk mitigation: modeling the enablers. Bus Process Manag 12(4):535–552

Fisher ML (1997) What is the right supply chain for your product? Harv Bus Rev 75(2):105–116

Francis V. (2008) Supply chain visibility: lost in translation? Supply Chain Manag 13(3): 180–184

Helferich OK, Cook RL (2003) Securing the supply chain: management report. CLM Publications, Oak Brook

Hendricks KB, Singhal VR (2005) An empirical analysis of the effect of supply chain disruptions on long-run stock price performance and equity risk of the firm. Prod Oper Manag 14(1): 35–52

Jahre M, Jensen L-M, Listou T (2009) Theory development in humanitarian logistics: a framework and three cases. Manag Res News 32(11):1008–1023

Jüttner U (2005) Supply chain risk management: understanding the business requirements from a practitioner perspective. Int J Logist Manag 16(1):120–141

Jüttner U, Maklan S (2011) Supply chain resilience in the global financial crisis: an empirical study. Supply Chain Manag 16(4):246–259

Jüttner U, Peck H, Christopher M (2003) Supply chain risk management: outlining an agenda for future research. Int J Logist 6(4):197–210

Khan O, Burnes B (2007) Risk and supply chain management: creating a research agenda. Int J Logist Manag 18(2):197–216

Kleindorfer PR, Saad GH (2005) Managing disruption risks in supply chains. Prod Oper Manag 14(1):53–68

Knemeyer AM, Zinn W, Eroglu C (2009) Proactive planning for catastrophic events in supply chains. J Oper Manag 27(2):141–153

Lee HL, Padmanabhan V, Whang S (1997) The bullwhip effect in supply chains. Sloan Manage Rev 38(3):93–102

Manuj I, Mentzer JT (2008a) Global supply chain risk management. J Bus Logist 29(1):133–155

Manuj I, Mentzer JT (2008b) Global supply chain risk management strategies. Int J Phys Distrib Logist Manag 38(3):192–223

Mason-Jones R, Towill DR (1998) Shrinking the supply chain uncertainty circle. Inst Oper Manag Control J 24(7):17–23

Mentzer JT, DeWitt W, Keebler JS, Soonhoong M, Nix NW, Smith CD, Zacharia ZG et al (2001) Defining supply chain management. J Bus Logist 22(2):1–25

Miller KD (1992) A framework for integrated risk management in international business. J Int Bus Stud 23:311–331

Mizushima M (2008) Presentation given at Stanford University, Fritz Institute

Mukherjeea AS (2008) The fire that changed an industry: a case study on thriving in a networked world. FT Press, Upper Saddle River

Naim M, Lalwani C, Fortuin L, Schmidt T, Taylor J, Aronsson H (2000) A model for logistics systems engineering management education in Europe. Eur J Eng Edud 25(1):65–82

Narasimhan R, Talluri S (2009) Perspectives on risk management in supply chains. J Oper Manag 27(2):114–118

Natarajarathinam M, Capar I, Narayanan A (2009) Managing supply chains in times of crises: a review of literature and insights. Int J Phys Distrib Logist Manag 39(7):535–573

Norris FH, Stevens SP, Pfefferbaum B, Wyche KF, Pfefferbaum RL (2008) Community resilience as a metaphor, theory, set of capacities, and strategy for disaster readiness. Am J Community Psychol 4(1/2):127–150

Norrman A, Jansson U (2004) Ericsson's proactive supply chain risk management approach after a serious sub-supplier accident. Int J Phys Distrib Logist Manag 34(5):434–456

Peck H (2005) Drivers of supply chain vulnerability: an integrated framework. Int J Phys Distrib Logist Manag 35(4):210–232

Peck H (2006) Reconciling supply chain vulnerability, risk and supply chain management. Int J Logist 9(2):127–142

Peck H, Abley J, Christopher M, Haywood M, Saw R, Rutherford C, Strathern M. (2003) Creating resilient supply chains: A practical guide. University Cranfield, Bedford

Pettit SJ, Beresford AKC (2005) Emergency relief logistics: an evaluation of military, non-military and composite response models. Int J Logist 8(4):313–331

Pettit TJ, Fiksel J, Croxton KL (2010) Ensuring supply chain resilience: development of a conceptual framework. J Bus Logist 31(1):1–21

Pettit TJ, Croxton KL, Fiksel J (2013) Ensuring supply chain resilience: development and implementation of an assessment tool. J Bus Logist 34(1):46–76

Ponomarov SY, Holcomb MC (2009) Understanding the concept of supply chain resilience. Int J Logist Manag 20(1):124–143

Rao S, Goldsby TJ (2009) Supply chain risks: a review and typology. Int J Logist Manag 20(1):97–123

Ritchie B, Brindley C (2007a) Supply chain risk management and performance: a guiding framework for future development. Int J Oper Prod Manag 27(3):303–322

Ritchie B, Brindley C (2007b) An emergent framework for supply chain risk management and performance measurement. J Oper Res Soc 58:1398–1411

Scholten K, Schilder S (2015) The role of collaboration in supply chain resilience. Supply Chain Manag 20(4):471–484

Scholten K, Sharkey-Scott P, Fynes B (2014) Mitigation processes—antecedents for building supply chain resilience. Supply Chain Manag 19(2):211–228

Sheffi Y (2005) Supply chain strategy—building a resilient supply chain. Harv Bus Rev 1(8):1–4

Sheffi Y, Rice JB (2005) A supply chain view of the resilient enterprise. MIT Sloan Manag Rev 47(1):41–48

Skipper, JB, Hanna, JB (2009) Minimizing supply chain disruption risk through enhanced flexibility. Int J Phys Distrib Logist Manag 39(5):404–427

Spekman RE, Davis EW (2004) Risky business: expanding the discussion on risk and the extended enterprise. Int J Phys Distrib Logist Manag 34(5):414–433

Tang CS (2006) Robust strategies for mitigating supply chain disruptions. Int J Logist 9(1):33–45

Thévenaza C, Resodihardjob SL (2010) All the best laid plans…conditions impeding proper emergency response. In J Prod Econ 126(1):7–21

Tomlin B (2006) On the value of mitigation and contingency strategies for managing supply chain disruption risks. Manag Sci 52(5):639–657

Tummala R, Schoenherr T (2011) Assessing and managing risks using the Supply Chain Risk Management Process (SCRMP). Supply Chain Manag 16(6):474–483

United Nations (UN) (1992) Glossary: internationally agreed glossary of basic terms related to disaster management. UN, Geneva

Van der Vegt GS, Essens P, Wahlström M, George G (2015) From the editors: managing risk and resilience. Acad Manage J 58(4):971–980

Van Vactor JD (2011) Cognizant healthcare logistics management: ensuring resilience during crisis. Int J Disaster Resilience Built Environ 2(3):245–255

Van Wassenhove LN (2006) Blackett Memorial Lecture Humanitarian aid logistics: supply chain management in high gear. J Oper Res Soc 57(5):475–489

Wagner SM, Bode C (2006) An empirical investigation into supply chain vulnerability. J Purch Supply Manag 12(6):301–312

Wagner SM, Bode C (2008) An empirical examination of supply chain performance along several dimensions of risk. J Bus Logist 29(1):307–325

Waters D (2011) Supply chain risk management: vulnerability and resilience in logistics. Kogan Page, London

Wieland A, Wallenburg CM (2012) Dealing with supply chain risks: linking risk management practices and strategies to performance. Int J Phys Distrib Logist Manag 42(10):887–905

Wieland A, Wallenburg CM (2013) The influence of relational competencies on supply chain resilience: a relational view. Int J Phys Distrib Logist Manag 43(4):300–320

Zsidisin GA, Wagner SM (2010) Do perceptions become reality? The moderating role of supply chain resiliency on disruption occurrence. J Bus Logist 31(2):1–20

Zsidisin GA, Ellram LM, Carter JR, Cavinato JL (2004) An analysis of supply risk assessment techniques. Int J Phys Distrib Logist Manag 34(5):397–413

Part IV
The Social Dimension of Sustainable Supply Chains

Chapter 20
Improving Social and Environmental Performance in Global Supply Chains

Hau L. Lee and Sonali V. Rammohan

20.1 Introduction: Social and Environmental Problems in Global Supply Chains

In his best seller, *The World Is Flat: a brief history of the twenty-first century,* T.L. Friedman (2005) described how emerging economies like China and India have risen as major manufacturing and service centers for the global economy. Over the last few decades, as production shifted from the West to emerging economies, global enterprises were able to leverage cost and other advantages which outweighed factors such as loss of control, increases in lead time, inventory, and other risks. This globalization of production has delivered benefits to corporations and to consumers in the form of more affordable products and services.

However, with these benefits have come significant costs. O'Rourke (2014) highlights the fact that current levels of global production and consumption are using 50 % more natural resources and services than ecosystems generate. Weaker law enforcement, corruption, cultural, and other factors in developing countries have led to myriad social, environmental, and ethical problems at factories which directly or indirectly supply goods and services (called suppliers in this chapter) to global corporations (called buyers in this chapter). When factory workers exceed working hour limits and incur excessive overtime, their health can be impacted along with product quality. Excessive factory carbon emissions have climate impacts, and ethical breakdowns such as intellectual property theft can affect company sales. In addition to the obvious human and environmental costs associated with these problems, such issues can impact both the reputation and profits of global brands.

H.L. Lee (✉) • S.V. Rammohan
Graduate School of Business, Stanford University, Stanford, CA 94305, USA
e-mail: haulee@stanford.edu; sonalir@stanford.edu

© Yann Bouchery, Charles J. Corbett, Jan C. Fransoo, and Tarkan Tan 2017
Y. Bouchery et al. (eds.), *Sustainable Supply Chains*, Springer Series in Supply
Chain Management 4, DOI 10.1007/978-3-319-29791-0_20

To combat the social, environmental, and ethical problems in global supply chains, governments have increased the level of regulation placed on buyers and suppliers (Westervelt 2012). Consumers, activists, and investors are also increasingly vocal about improving supplier responsibility. This has caused global firms to pay closer attention to the issue, and, in many cases, use self-regulation such as supplier codes of conduct to compensate for weak law enforcement.

Despite the push for multinational corporations to develop and enforce supplier codes of conduct to address employee safety, labor, and environmental issues at their suppliers, violations of these codes of conduct remain problematic in many industries, and vary in nature. The tragic collapse of the apparel factory building, Rana Plaza in Bangladesh in April 2013, killing over 1000 people, is an example of a major lapse in building safety codes. The building housed suppliers for apparel brands including Benetton, Walmart, Matalan, and Primark. The problem of excessive overtime in factories is widespread with 90 % of factories audited by the Fair Labor Association in 2011 committing overtime violations (2011 FLA Annual Report). It is estimated that 21 million workers are trapped in modern slavery, many of whom are part of global supply chains (Economist 2015). On the environmental side, the Institute of Public and Environmental Affairs, a prominent NGO which maintains an air and water pollution database of factory environmental violations in China, recorded over 100,000 violations between 2006 and 2012. It made public evidence that suppliers of world-renowned brands such as Apple (Mozur and Dou 2013) and Marks & Spencer (IPE 2012) polluted rivers and air in China.

Buyers have many motivations for improving supply chain responsibility, including adherence to regulations, avoidance of supply side disruptions (e.g., a factory closure resulting from a health and safety violation), negative media coverage, and pressure from external stakeholders (Cousins et al. 2004; Newman and Breeden 1992). Additionally, consumers are becoming increasingly aware of and concerned about responsible supply chain practices, thus influencing demand for responsibly made products. Cotte and Trudel (2009) reviewed 13 studies with consumer willingness-to-pay data, and found an average premium paid for a product manufactured with sustainable practices is 10 %, and consumers demand a discount for "unsustainability." They found consumers willing to pay a premium are more willing when the premium is small relative to product cost, and that willingness to pay a premium drops off sharply at higher premium levels.

Lee et al. (2012) found that, among 1281 supply chain executives surveyed, 49 % were somewhat or very concerned about unsatisfactory social and environmental standards at suppliers, and the corresponding percentage on breach of intellectual property rights was at 53 %. An even higher percentage, 58 %, worried about counterfeit products from the supply network. As discussed in Chap. 1, improving supply chain responsibility is not only seen as a way to mitigate a variety of risks and meet regulations, but also as a means to increase profits, either by saving costs, growing revenues via brand image, or doing both.

Corporations, governmental, and nongovernmental organizations, consumers and other groups have made progress in recent years to understand the activities in global supply chains and implement strategies aimed at making an impact. Still, O'Rourke (2014) calls for better data, decision-support tools, and ultimately incentives to move from policing supply chains to predicting and preventing unsustainable practices.

Research suggests that various supplier management strategies aimed at improving social and environmental performance can also improve economic performance (Rao and Holt 2005; Vachon and Klassen 2006; Lewis et al. 2012; Gimenez and Tachizawa 2012). This complements evidence that socially responsible firms yield higher returns (Derwall et al. 2005) and that social and environmental incidents and noncompliances can lead to subsequent financial losses (Klassen and McLaughlin 1996; PwC 2010). Rao and Holt (2005) empirically find significant positive relationships between "green" supply chain management across the entire supply chain and economic performance measures. Wu and Pagell (2011) find their sample of firms maintains business viability while pushing for improved environmental performance. Cousins et al. (2004) look at actions that can be taken by a buying firm to manage the environmental performance of its suppliers, comparing the resources available and perceived losses from environmental noncompliances. They suggest that incentives and supplier-monitoring schemes typically require more resources but are adopted by proactive companies who wish to gain competitive advantage through improved environmental supply chain performance.

Still, debate exists on the link between responsible supplier management practices and the resulting economic benefits (Corbett and Klassen 2006). We will examine the relationship between responsible supplier management practices and social, environmental, and when possible, economic performance using a "sense" and "response" framework. To do this, we will examine research as well as case studies.

20.2 A Framework for Continuous Improvement: Sense and Response

Seuring and Müller (2008) define sustainability in supply chain management as the "management of material, information, and capital flows as well as cooperation among companies along the supply chain while taking goals from all three dimensions of sustainable management, i.e., economic, environmental, and social into account which are derived from customer and stakeholder requirements." Similarly, in operations management literature, Bowen et al. (2001) and Handfield et al. (1997) discuss "green supply" and "green value chain practices" respectively, "which are used to characterize environmental aspects of supplier arrangements; all of these implicitly or explicitly focus on improved environmental performance through better supplier management" (Corbett and Klassen 2006).

A useful guide to address responsible supply chain management is the sense and response framework. Haeckel (1992) described the sense and response framework

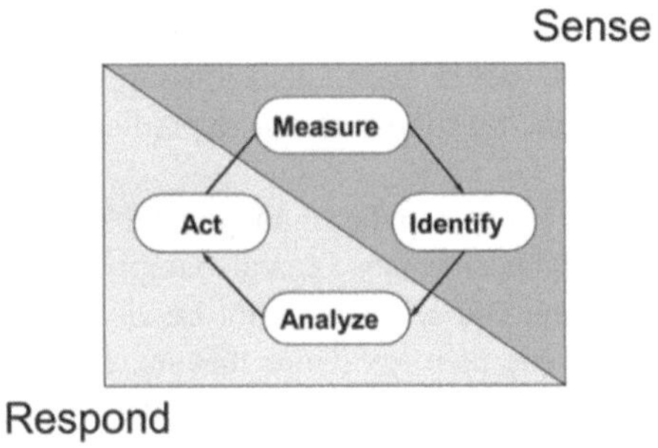

Fig. 20.1 Sense and respond framework

as a system for companies to respond to rapidly changing customer needs. In larger firms, this can mean that networks of skills, assets, cross-functional processes, information, and knowledge are linked into capabilities, which are in turn linked into processes for creating product and service responses to customer needs. The framework can be applied to continually evolving social, environmental, and ethical issues in global supply chains, such as human trafficking, pollution, and intellectual property protection, as argued by Gillai et al. (2015). Kapoor et al. (2005) discuss the sense and response model as a management tool for managing risk and unpredictability in operations. These dimensions mirror the structure adopted by Gimenez and Tachizawa (2012), who define assessment and collaboration as the two governance structures for management of supplier responsibility, and include a further dimension of managerial and external "enablers" that influence the implementation and success of responsible supply chain practices. A buyer must first gain visibility, or "sense," into issues in the supply chain. After understanding the present state by measuring and identifying problems, a buyer can then "respond" by analyzing the problem and taking action. This process can be repeated for continuous improvement. The framework mimics [the familiar] Six Sigma management cycle for eliminating defects and minimizing variability in manufacturing and business processes (Fig. 20.1).[1]

Buyers can gain a "sense" of activities and impacts on the supply chain through practices including:

- Traceability: the ability to trace the points of origin of materials used in a product
- Visibility: knowledge of social, environmental, and ethical performance of suppliers
- Monitoring: the action of examining supplier performance

Once buyers have a "sense" of the supplier's behavior, there are various ways to "respond." The following are typical practices commonly used in industry:

---

[1] Originally based on Motorola's work to eliminate quality defects, the Six Sigma process is a management process used by many companies such as Motorola, GE, and others. For an introduction to Six Sigma, see Harry and Schroeder 2000.

- Reactions to violations once they have occurred (e.g., root cause analysis, and penalties such as fines, supplier warning, reduced business, contract termination)
- Incentives (e.g., preferred supplier status, increased business, price premium)
- Supplier capacity building (e.g., productivity improvement and capability expansion)
- Proactive product and/or process design (e.g., design for the environment)
- Shared value chain strategies (e.g., extended value creation through community development)
- Cascading responsible practices to the supplier network (e.g., training and motivating the suppliers to adopt incentives, capacity building, and design principles to improve the sustainability of their own supply network)

20.3 Sense and Respond Practices

How can companies improve the sustainability of their supply chain through initiatives in "sense" and "respond"? In this section, we describe some such examples.

20.3.1 Sense

20.3.1.1 Traceability

Buyers cannot effectively control the sustainability of the supply network if they do not even know exactly where the materials in products come from. Being able to trace the points of origin of materials used in the product is a crucial step in being able to "sense" the sustainability status of a supply chain.

Early in 2008, Levi Strauss & Co. (2014) faced pressure from external stakeholders—media, worker-rights, and environmental nongovernmental organizations, socially responsible investment firms and retailers—about the cotton used in their products, as there were reports that forced child labor had been used to harvest cotton in Uzbekistan. This prompted the company into action. Tracing the exact origin of a commodity like cotton is difficult; the company had to reach out to the textile mills that supply the cotton fabric. Textile suppliers and licensees were informed that, unless there was clear evidence that the use of forced child labor had been eliminated, Uzbek cotton would be forbidden in the production of branded products of Levi Strauss. But, as cotton went through the apparel supply chain, there was little transparency into its country's origins. In order to trace the country of origin of the cotton in their products, the company had to partner with external organizations with expertise in supply chain traceability to implement a tracking system from the level of the yarn spinner to the product manufacturer. This provided confidence that Uzbek cotton was not being used in the Levi Strauss supply chain. At the same time, the company joined NGOs, the socially responsible investment community, major US apparel and retail trade associations and the US Department of State in engaging the Uzbek government to address the problem.

A similar traceability challenge applies to "conflict minerals," such as cassiterite (for tin), wolframite (for tungsten), coltan (for tantalum), and gold ore. These minerals are mined in various regions of the world, and then passed through many intermediaries before they are used by electronic companies to produce consumer electronics such as mobile phones and laptop computers. Many of these minerals are mined in Eastern Congo, a region dominated by conflicts and human rights violations. Various international efforts have been made to reduce trading of conflict resources. A prominent effort is the 2010 Dodd–Frank Act that requires manufacturers to audit their supply chains and report conflict minerals usage (SEC 2012).

20.3.1.2   Visibility

As discussed above, traceability refers to knowing which suppliers are providing materials to a firm. While knowing a firm's supplier is important, it is also critical to understand what those suppliers are doing. Visibility refers to having knowledge of a supplier's sustainability performance. While efforts to gain visibility into the supply chain can be associated with improved social and environmental performances (Awaysheh and Klassen 2010); it can be a challenge for buyers to obtain this visibility. In a survey by Lee et al. (2012), supply chain executives reported having fairly limited visibility of environmental and social sustainability violations at various levels in the supply network. For example, 39 % of respondents reported having visibility of environmental violations only within internal operations. The percentage declined when considering operations outside of the firm, with 28 % of respondents reporting having visibility of immediate suppliers, and 25 % reporting having visibility of the extended supply network. Finally, 8 % reported having no visibility at all. The degree of visibility on social sustainability violations was similar, as seen in Fig. 20.2.

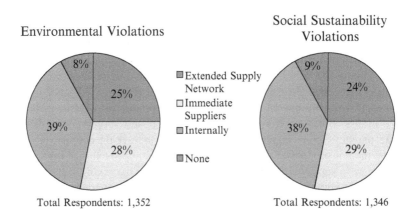

Fig. 20.2 Percentage of respondents reporting they have visibility of violations at various levels in the supply network. *Source*: The Chief Supply Chain Officer Report 2012, SCM World

Gaining visibility of violations or improved sustainability performance requires firms to carefully establish mechanisms to detect them. Such mechanisms can include (1) suppliers sharing data with the buyer, which requires a high degree of trust and a collaborative relationship; (2) direct monitoring by buyers, and (3) reporting from interested parties. One example of the latter is the nongovernmental group called the Institute of Public and Environmental Affairs, or IPE (Shao and Yatsko 2010), which uses a vast volunteer network to collect extensive data and report environmental violations throughout China on a public website. Another example of reporting from interested parties is the effort of groups such as Labor Link (Schwartz 2013) and Labor Voices (Lahiri 2012) which utilize information technologies such as mobile phones for workers to directly report to global brand violations and information about working conditions, well-being, job satisfaction, and more.

20.3.1.3   Monitoring

While there are myriad regulations in developing countries addressing labor rights, employee health and safety, environmental standards and other issues, there also exists many private sector supply chain interventions which can act as complements or substitutes, depending on the context and factors such as regional governance (Locke et al. 2013). Before a buyer enters into a contract with a supplier, there is typically a supplier certification process which involves examining the supplier's product quality, ability to deliver the product, pricing, financial status, communication capabilities, and other factors. Increasingly, companies are also assessing supplier social and environmental practices as part of this certification process. Once a contract is established, the supplier may be asked to provide self-assessments of its social and environmental practices. The buyer may also choose to conduct internal audits to verify that the supplier is conforming to the buyer's code of conduct and/or contract with a third-party to obtain this assurance.

While it is common industry practice to conduct audits to understand a supplier's conformance to a code of conduct, research suggests the effectiveness of using audits (a "sense" tool) alone is limited. In a study of 763 factories that served as suppliers to Nike, Locke et al. (2007) examined whether audits had affected compliance ratings of factories between 2001/2002 and 2004/2005. The observation was that about 42 % did not have any rating change despite audits, while more factories had their ratings downgraded. This resulted in the authors calling for more proactive actions to make an impact on sustainability.

20.3.2   Response

Given weak enforcement mechanisms in many developing countries and the fact that monitoring alone can have limited effectiveness, many buyers have adopted additional practices to motivate suppliers to improve social and environmental practices. Some companies use penalties and/or incentives tied to social and environmental performance in supplier contracts (Porteous et al. 2015). Some collaborate with suppliers to increase their awareness of issues and provide them with tools needed to address social and environmental challenges. Another growing practice is to collaborate with various actors in the value chain to create shared value. We examine key response methods and the research regarding their effectiveness below.

20.3.2.1 Reactions to Violations

Once a violation has occurred, buyers can react with consequences such as root cause analysis, and penalties such as fines, supplier warning, reduced business, contract termination. Chen and Lee (2015) modeled supplier behavior under the premise that noncompliance is a result of unexpected and uncertain costs faced by a supplier. The uncertain costs can be due to fluctuating input material costs, unexpected external disruptions, or internal manufacturing operational problems that may result in more frequent breakdowns or lower yields. Hence, a supplier may engage in noncompliant activities to save money when faced with unexpected and uncertain cost increases that threaten profits. The propensity of a supplier to do so is a function of the ethical standard of the supplier, which may or may not act as a deterrent to his/her urge to violate. Accordingly, penalties could discourage violations by "increasing the stakes" to suppliers. One form of monetary penalty is the use of contingencies. A buyer can withhold a portion of payment, which is subject to forfeiture if a supplier violation is found through an audit (the base payment can be paid to the supplier either upfront or at the end of the contract). Alternatively, the withheld payment can also be construed as a bonus, i.e., the supplier would receive an additional payment if no violation is found through an audit. The authors reported that, according to a supplier manual, a major European retailer charged 10 % of order payment as a penalty for any social responsibility audit problems.

Lee et al. (2012) found that companies are becoming increasingly intolerant of sustainability violations. Examples of penalties enacted for violations include monetary fines, reduced business or termination of business relationships (with and without an initial warning). Those surveyed reported that monetary fines were not as common as reducing or terminating business relationships. Many companies have a "zero tolerance" policy for serious issues such as child labor, and will terminate business relationships if such issues are detected (Fig. 20.3).

20.3.2.2 Incentives

In contrast to penalties, incentives are increasingly being used to motivate suppliers to invest in social and environmental improvements. As we shall see in the case study of Starbucks' "C.A.F.E. Practices" scheme (Lee 2008), Starbucks has used positive incentives like preferred supplier status as well as price premiums to reward coffee farmers that achieve high sustainability standards. Motivated by Starbuck's

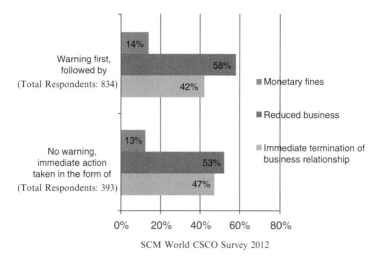

Fig. 20.3 Reactions to violations

"C.A.F.E. Practices" scheme, Lewis et al. (2012) show that supply contracts can facilitate the long-term commitment of supply chain partners to collaborate with a firm to achieve social and environmental performance. Klassen and McLaughlin (1996) find that public recognition environmental awards and environmental crises for a firm can signal good and poor financial performance respectively.

Lee et al. (2012) find that companies have used various incentive schemes to induce suppliers to be sustainable. Very few companies used price premiums as a reward. Instead, giving suppliers special status, increased businesses, recognition and better terms and conditions are more commonly used. Of these companies, 42 % also invested in training and education of suppliers (Fig. 20.4).

20.3.2.3 Supplier Collaboration and Capacity Building

Since suppliers may not have the means and know-how to improve sustainability on their own, buyers often find they must implement collaborations with their suppliers. Such collaboration often takes the form of education and training, capability enhancement, and the introduction of better production methods for productivity improvement. Research has shown the effectiveness of certain collaborative mechanisms to encourage improved supplier performance (Distelhorst, Hainmueller et al. 2015; Vachon and Klassen 2006; Locke and Romis 2006; Bowen et al. 2001). Gimenez and Tachizawa (2012) find the implementation of both supplier assessment and collaboration with suppliers improves environmental and social performance. Furthermore, Krause et al. (1998) investigate firms' supplier development processes (not specific to SER) comparing reactive approaches to strategic efforts to increase supplier capabilities, and thus a firm's competitive advantage. The development

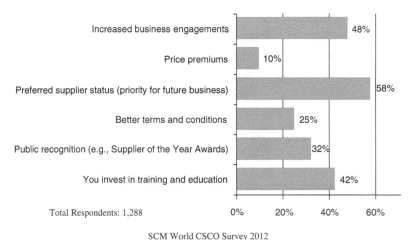

SCM World CSCO Survey 2012

Fig. 20.4 Incentives used

process includes identifying suppliers, issues and opportunities, and also collaborative efforts to increase capabilities, training, rewards and recognition, and continuous improvement programs. Krause et al. (2000) find direct involvement of a firm, including providing supplier incentives, is a key enabler of supplier development.

Chen and Lee (2015) find that a supplier can be vulnerable to noncompliant activities when faced with unexpectedly high costs that threaten its profit margins. One strategy is to invest in improving the productivity of suppliers, so that it can "weather the storm" and maintain margins despite cost hikes. Based on a study of 25 Indian textile plants from 2009 to 2011, Bloom et al. (2013) examined the effect of training and support of suppliers. The plants were separated into experimental and control groups, with experimental groups receiving diagnosis, training and consultation on factory operations, quality control, inventory, human resource, and sales, and order management. The experimental groups were found to have significant improvements in quality, inventory performance, and finally productivity. This study suggests that collaborating with and training factory management can influence a factory's performance. Related to this, Distelhorst, Hainmueller et al. (2015) found that, by introducing Lean[2] production practices to factories supplying to Nike, labor compliance significantly improved. The study, based on labor compliance data from 2009 to 2013 at 300 factories 2 years prior and 2 years after the introduction of Lean practices, suggests that stronger performance can enable a factory to be more compliant. Chapter 11, by van Weele and van Tubergen (2017), discusses the phases that supplier relationships often go through in making this transition.

---

[2] The Lean production process was championed by Toyota, and has been widely adopted by companies as a way to eliminate waste, improve productivity, and increase the efficiency of production systems.

20.3.2.4   Proactive Product and Process Design

In quality management, it is well-known that product and process design, in addition to product inspection and testing, can be an effective way to assure quality. Motorola's Six Sigma process (Pande et al. 2000) was based on the premise that, by improving product or process design and management approaches, the variability of processes could be reduced and quality control assured, thereby reducing the reliance on inspection. Similarly, by improving the design of products or processes, a supplier's manufacturing, farming or other processes can be made less vulnerable to cost shocks and other external disturbances, resulting in a lower risk of sustainability breaches. In Chap. 19, Scholten and Fynes (2017) provide a framework for identifying and managing risks in supply chains.

In the textile industry, Esquel (Pelleg and Lee 2013) invested in R&D on the scientific development of cotton seeds that are more pest-resistant, so that cotton farmers could use fewer pesticides and insecticides. The company also conducted research on ways in which fabrics could be dyed with less chemicals and water, so that the fabric mills could reduce pollution. Similar "design for the environment" techniques are now being used by firms to reduce the use of water, waste, and energy at various parts of a product's lifecycle. In the agriculture sector, McDonald's (Rammohan 2013) worked with its major supplier in India to experiment with the right types of potato seeds and growing methods that would achieve an optimal quality and texture, and increase productivity of potato farmers.

20.3.2.5   Shared Value: Extended Value Creation and Community Development

The previous sections described how buyer "response" strategies such as positive incentives and investments in suppliers could improve productivity, reduce noncompliances, improve sustainability performance, and in some cases, increase the incomes of suppliers. Increasingly, firms such as Johnson & Johnson, Walmart, Coca-Cola, Unilever, and others are also using shared value strategies to address issues in the supply chain. Shared value is a management strategy focused on companies creating measurable business value by identifying and addressing social problems that intersect with their business (Porter and Kramer 2011). One aspect of this concept involves increasing productivity of the company or its suppliers by addressing the social and environmental constraints in its value chain. Li & Fung (Melvin 2015) is a consumer goods management firm using a shared value approach with the goal of increasing the long-term income of factory workers in addition to factory owners, which in turn, is intended to lead to economic development in regions where suppliers are based. Sometimes, its buyers have also invested in community development such as building infrastructure, engaging in education activities, and creating other income-generating activities in supplier communities. Such shared value creation—delivering value to buyers, to suppliers, to workers, and ultimately, to communities—can be considered the highest level of sustainability, and a growing goal of leading firms. Sodhi and Tang (2017), in Chap. 21, go deeper into how the stakeholder resource-based view can make concepts such as shared value more tangible.

20.3.2.6 Cascading Responsible Practices to the Extended Supply Network

In 2007, Mattel had a massive recall of its toys due to the tainting of toys by lead paint (Hoyt et al. 2008). The root of the problem turned out to be a pigment supplier using pigment-containing lead. The tainted pigments were provided to a paint supplier, whose paint was then supplied to a contract manufacturer who manufactured the toys for Mattel. The violation occurred at the third tier of Mattel's supplier network. As seen by this example, it is often a daunting job for a buyer to effectively check so many layers of a supply chain. This problem points to the need to cascade responsible practices to each supplier tier.

Cascading practices to the extended supply network refers to transforming suppliers to be as vigilant as the buying firm in managing and assuring sustainability. If suppliers recognize the value and importance of maintaining the sustainability of its own supply network, and are motivated to engage in similar types of "respond" strategies as the buyer, then it will increase the chances of the whole supply network being able to effectively address sustainability problems. In other words, the accountability of sustainability must be cascaded to the next level, which in turn should cascade to another level, and so on. As illustrated in the Hewlett-Packard example later in this chapter (Rammohan 2008), the company engaged intensively with its key suppliers, with the intent of guiding them in being equally focused on sustainability improvements with their own supply networks.

By using a cascading approach, Intel has worked to permeate socially and environmentally responsible practices throughout its supply network (Intel and BSR 2013). The company advocates the concept of supplier ownership of issues, so that suppliers will take a proactive approach in determining their own sustainability strategies and objectives. The company has experienced positive results when key suppliers such as Murata and Schneider Electric were able to take on the role of sustainability advocates in managing their own supply network.

20.4 Research Highlight on "Response": Carrots or Sticks—Improving Supplier Social and Environmental Compliance[3]

As described earlier, a growing number of companies are responding to social and environmental risks by implementing supplier incentive schemes for good performance in addition to having strict penalties in place for noncompliance. Starbucks,

---

[3] Materials for this section based on research by Porteous et al. 2015.

Nike, and HP, for example, incorporate both penalties and incentives into supplier evaluations (Lewis et al. 2012; Porteous and Rammohan 2013; Rammohan 2008). What is the impact of these practices on social, environmental, and economic performance? Porteous et al. (2015) developed a model of the relationship between the incentives and penalties buyers issue to suppliers for social and environmental performance and two outcomes—improved supplier compliance (measured by a reduction in violations of laws or corporate codes of conduct) and buyer-operating costs (used as a measure of a firm's economic performance). This model was empirically tested by analyzing opinion-based survey responses from supply chain executives at 334 companies across 17 industries.

The study did not find a significant relationship between visibility and monitoring efforts (sensing) and reduced violations or reduced operating costs. This aligns with research that finds traditional monitoring for violations through supplier audits, when not complemented with supplier collaboration, can be ineffective in addressing persistent supplier violations (Locke et al. 2007). Instead, the study suggests that incentives and penalties have a stronger influence. The strongest predictors of reduced violations were found to be the penalty of contract termination after a warning, and the incentives of supplier training, increased business and public recognition. This suggests that firms can improve supply chain social and environmental performance by ceasing business with continually violating suppliers, while using specific incentives to motivate and further build capabilities of higher-performing suppliers.

Some incentives, such as offering suppliers training and increased business for strong SER performance, were associated both with reduction in SER violations and reduced buyer operating costs. These incentives may motivate suppliers to take more ownership of SER in order to benefit from the rewards on offer. For example, environmental compliance can reduce costs if fewer resources are wasted in the production process, and higher productivity may be realized from efforts to improve worker skills and empowerment (Bloom et al. 2013). This research supports evidence that select supplier incentives can improve social, environmental, and economic performance.

20.5   Case Examples

Many companies employ the sense strategies of traceability, visibility, and monitoring discussed above. While corporate innovators are using novel means to get a "sense" of social and environmental performance, there is less variation in these practices when compared to "response" practices. For example, most companies employ some means of auditing to monitor their suppliers, and conduct traceability to detect hazardous or outlawed materials. Given the many "response" strategies available to a firm, we have chosen to highlight a few case examples of global companies using innovative "response" practices with positive results. These cases have been selected to demonstrate that responsible supply chain issues and practices have commonalities across geographies and industries. The cases illustrate that a combination of "response" practices is often required to effect change.

20.5.1   Starbucks C.A.F.E. Practices[4]

Starbucks is the world's largest coffee retailer, and sources from all over the world, including developing regions such as East Africa, Central America, and Indonesia. Coffee farmers in these regions, many of whom live in poverty, are vulnerable to the highly fluctuating prices on the world coffee market. While Starbucks seeks a stable supply of high-quality coffee, the company has always been focused on ensuring that coffee farmers avoid bankruptcy when coffee prices are low, grow coffee in environmentally sound ways, and that farm owners avoid unsafe or exploitative labor practices. In the early 2000s, Starbucks initiated a program called C.A.F.E. (Coffee and Farmer Equity) Practices to develop a sustainable coffee supply chain.

The C.A.F.E. Practices initiative (C.A.F.E) was developed to build mutually beneficial relationships with coffee farmers and their communities. C.A.F.E. aimed to (1) increase the economic, social, and environmental sustainability in the specialty coffee industry, including conservation of biodiversity; (2) encourage suppliers to implement C.A.F.E. Practices through economic incentives and preferential buying status; (3) ultimately purchase coffee under C.A.F.E. guidelines; (4) build mutually beneficial and increasingly direct relationships with suppliers, with long-term contracts to support Starbucks' growth; and (5) promote transparency and economic fairness within the coffee supply chain.

C.A.F.E. included a set of guidelines designed to support coffee buyers and farmers, ensure high-quality coffee, promote equitable relationships with farmers, workers, and communities and protect the environment. It was not a code of conduct or compliance program. The guidelines consisted of a set of supplier prerequisites that had to be met to be considered for C.A.F.E. These standards included coffee quality and economic transparency (suppliers were expected to disclose the amount of money that was ultimately paid to farmers).

After the prerequisites were met, suppliers were graded based on a set of environmental and social criteria. They were evaluated not just on performance, but also on their farm supply networks. Farmers were rewarded for coffee growing and processing practices that contributed positively to the conservation of soil, water, energy, and biological diversity, and had minimal impact on the environment. Workers' wages needed to meet or exceed the minimum requirements under local and national laws. Effective measures needed to be taken to ensure workers' health and safety and to provide them with adequate living conditions. Farms, mills, and suppliers also needed to illustrate equitable payments to those who worked for them or sold to them. They had to demonstrate economic accountability and document their hiring and employment practices. Based on their performance on these criteria, suppliers could earn up to 100 percentage points in C.A.F.E. Practices. Scores were audited by an independent verifier, and licensed by Scientific Certification Systems. Since the verifier was independent of Starbucks, the cost of the verification had to

---

[4]The materials in the case were drawn from Lee (2008).

be negotiated between the supplier and the verifier. However, there was no cost to the supplier to submit a C.A.F.E. application to Starbucks.

Starbucks invested in capacity building of coffee farmers by setting up farmer support centers in coffee growing regions. These gave technical support and training to improve the farmers' cultivation and production methods, and provided microfinancing loans to help farmers in making the necessary investments in tools. Moreover, the company used a set of positive incentives. For example, when a supplier was found to score at least 60 % of the available points in the certification process, the supplier would qualify as a preferred supplier and gain preferential treatment in future purchases (i.e., Starbucks would buy from the supplier first and offer preferential contract terms). Additionally, suppliers who earned scores above 80 % would qualify as strategic suppliers and would earn a sustainability conversion premium of $0.05 per pound of coffee for 1 year.[5] To encourage continuous improvement, the company also offered an additional sustainability performance premium of $0.05 per pound of coffee to suppliers who were able to achieve a 10-point increase above 80 % over the course of a year.

C.A.F.E. delivered benefits to both Starbucks and suppliers. The company enjoyed a more stable supply base, and gained more direct access to farmers. The farmers benefited in several ways. Based on a study in Costa Rica by Earthwatch (2007), C.A.F.E. implementation resulted in annual cost savings of $243 per hectare, which translated to an increase of $1200 in the annual income of a small farmer; there was a 25 % increase in yield, which is equivalent to an average annual revenue increase of $2875 per farmer; and coffee quality improved as a result of stronger plant health and increased farm productivity.

20.5.2 Case Example: Supplier Collaboration by McDonald's India[6]

By the time McDonald's opened its first store in India in 1996, its efforts to source locally had mostly been successful. However, MacFries, as McDonald's French fries were known, were particularly tough to source locally—and importing fries was undesirable for both cost and availability reasons. While India was the third largest producer of potatoes in the world, less than 1 % were of processed grade, with the necessary high solids, low sugars, large, oblong shape, disease resistance, and long dormancy needed for McDonald's fries. Ideal potato growing season was 120–150 days, compared to the typical 90–100 days in India. Outdated farming and irrigation practices limited yields as well.

---

[5] On average, Starbucks pays about $1.20 per pound of coffee (FY04 CSR Report).
[6] The materials for this case were drawn from Rammohan (2013).

McDonald's faced many challenges in finding cold storage, growing the right type of potatoes locally, and scaling up operations to meet fast-growing demand. Furthermore, the Indian government encouraged small-scale farming, which made it difficult to gain economies of scale. It was common to have 50–100 farms across a 100-acre region, compared to the United States, where the average farm size was 418 acres in 2007. Still, sourcing from within the country was particularly important in India, given steep import duties.

McDonald's approached one of its suppliers, Canada-based McCain, to import frozen fries. However, duties and lead time were high, making it clear that imports would not be a long-term solution. The company decided to try growing potatoes in India with McCain's help. McCain understood that growing the right potato was the key. In India, the import of raw potatoes was not allowed, so McCain had to bring in the potato germplasm (a collection of genetic resources that could be used to grow potatoes). McCain learned that cultivating potato seeds at high elevations was ideal because seeds grown at high altitude had high vigor, enabling a commercial crop planted with those seeds to have higher yield and larger-sized potatoes. So it instituted a Shepody potato seed multiplication program in the 13,000-ft high Lahaul Spiti Valley, part of the Himalayan mountain range in Northern India.

McDonald's helped McCain get access to excess capacity at Vista Foods, another supplier. McCain produced potato wedges to build up some business with local farmers and convince them to try growing potatoes. Knowing they would have McDonald's commitment to buy fries, McCain built a $25 million (Canadian) manufacturing facility dedicated to processing French fries, with capacity to process 40,000 potatoes. Seeds were planted in farms in the central state of Gujarat in September and October, and potatoes were harvested in February and March. Once processed, fries were frozen and sent to third-party logistics storage facilities or to McDonald's distribution centers. From here, they were shipped to restaurants.

McCain established a one-acre demonstration farm in Gujarat for farmers to learn how to grow this new crop. McCain showed farmers the best seeds to use, how to improve yields through more efficient sowing, drip irrigation, and harvesting techniques. The company transformed storage practices by applying a potato sprout suppressant in combination with using controlled temperature storage. The local Gujarat government had a scheme to subsidize farmers' drip/sprinkler irrigation system purchases. Key agricultural breakthroughs were demonstrated to farmers, such as converting from traditional row planting to mechanical field preparation, shifting from hand picking of potatoes to mechanical picking, and planting in double rows to utilize space better and reduce water consumption.

By 2008, 30 % of McDonald's India's supply was being manufactured locally. By 2010, that number grew to 75 %. The benefits to McDonald's from using local fries were a 30 % lower cost structure and no exposure to the fluctuating exchange rate. With local fries, inventory levels were reduced from an average holding of 15 days for imported fries to 6 days for local fries. The reduction in shipping time (60 days from the US to less than a day for getting local product) also had a significant benefit for risk management and contingency planning. In addition, McCain's close relationships with farmers helped ensure a secure supply. There were benefits to farmers as well. Traditionally, farmers sold produce at the local "mandi," or village market, where sales and prices could fluctuate dramatically. With McCain, farmers were guaranteed sales of farm output, while seeing an increase in yields of 30–40 % compared with "regular" potatoes, reduced operating costs, increased and predictable farm income, and reduced consumption of natural resources like water. Another benefit was trust. By avoiding selling to a middle man at the mandi, many farmers reported making more money.

McDonald's India and McCain India had come a long way, not least because they had discovered that close collaboration with farmers was essential to their collective success and to achieving their goal of local sourcing.

20.5.3 Case Example: Supplier Collaboration at Hewlett-Packard in China[7]

With the fast-paced growth of the electronics industry in recent decades arose problems such as excessive overtime, child labor, environmental pollution, unsafe working conditions, and more disadvantages to workers. By 2008, the industry had made important improvements in social and environmental responsibility (SER) compliance among first-tier suppliers, due in part to the standardization of SER practices set forth in the Electronics Industry Code of Conduct (EICC). Hewlett-Packard (HP), the first company in the industry to implement a supplier code of conduct, had taken a comprehensive approach by educating suppliers on how to achieve compliance, conducting individual audits and third-party joint audits, and emphasizing continuous improvement. This approach was continually being cascaded to sub-tier suppliers, with the goal of improving standards throughout HP's supply chain. Distelhorst, Locke et al. (2015) described how results from one HP capability program were not strong. Still the practice of capability building is worth describing here given the growing use of such programs by buyers.

What motivated suppliers to strive for full SER compliance? Were there business benefits to meeting and exceeding standards? In 2009 we explored the business case for SER by examining three HP suppliers with significant operations in China—Flextronics, ΛU Optronics (ΛUO), and Delta Electronics.

HP's SER program focused on integrating social and environmental requirements into sourcing operations. The company conducted audits on suppliers deemed to be "high risk" given their location, process, relationships, and/or company information. In 2008, over 400,000 people worked at manufacturing sites audited by HP for SER. In the information technology industry, since the number of suppliers for specific components could be limited, HP focused heavily on working with existing

---

[7]The materials on this case were drawn from Rammohan (2008).

suppliers to improve SER activities. Through self-assessments in 2008, HP identified around 200 "high-risk" suppliers around the world.

At HP suppliers Flextronics and AUO, executives reported that SER activities generated several business benefits. Both suppliers improved environmental, labor, and health and safety performance from 2005 to 2008. While formal supplier SER programs at both companies were only 2–3 years old at the time of the case, certain short-term business benefits had already been realized. Delta began SER work in 2002 at HP's request but did not report seeing concrete business benefits from 2002 to 2008. Later, HP began to increase the importance of SER ratings in its supplier evaluation process, providing suppliers with more of an incentive to perform well. Below are the key SER benefits suppliers reported in 2008:

- SER can help a company become a supplier of choice. Flextronics and AUO executives felt that SER could enhance their reputation with many stakeholders.
- Certain environmental investments can have short-term payoffs. In 2007, AUO implemented several environmental projects that delivered financial benefits. Investment costs related to water recycling and reduction projects, dormitory solar panels, and exhaust recycling were outweighed by savings from most of these projects in the first year alone. In the years preceding 2008, AUO's energy, water, and waste per substrate (a standard unit of glass used to manufacture computer panels) significantly decreased. Meanwhile, overall energy, water, and waste increased due to higher production output.
- Health and safety programs can reduce accident rates. Both AUO and Flextronics made improvements to their health and safety programs. They found that strengthening safety training, improving/installing machine guards, and improving/providing protective gear such as masks and gloves for workers resulted in lower accident rates. This saved costs by reducing the time a worker is unproductive, and was believed by some to reduce healthcare costs.
- There is potential for beneficial labor practices such as limiting overtime, paying fair wages, and providing employee welfare activities, good dormitories, canteens, and other amenities to reduce or limit attrition in the future.

This case highlights benefits suppliers achieved when collaborating closely with HP. In addition to the short-term gains realized, suppliers recognized the potential for longer term benefits from SER activities.

20.5.4   Case Example: Comprehensive Sustainability at Li and Fung[8]

Li & Fung Limited is a Hong Kong-based global leader in consumer goods design, development, sourcing, and distribution. It serves retailers and brands around the world by managing a network of over 15,000 supplier companies in more than

---

[8]The materials in this case were drawn from Melvin (2015).

40 countries in Asia, Europe, Africa, and the Americas. In 2013 this sourcing and trading activity accounted for more than $16 billion of revenue. Sustainability is of great importance to Li & Fung, since its brand owner customers expect the company to manage the sustainability of the supply network for them, and because former chairman Dr. Victor Fung held a personal passion for sustainability. The company recognized that factory audits were not sufficient to ensure a sustainable supply network, and that suppliers, many of them located in developing economies, might not have the capability and resources to develop sustainable practices. The company identified that one of the impediments to sustainability was supplier productivity.

In January 2014, Li & Fung announced the creation of a new business unit called Vendor Support Services (VSS). The new unit provided services to a vast supply network on safety and compliance training, audits, trade credit services, product development, and technical and operations support. VSS would build on the company's knowledge about the supply chain and access to best practices and emerging trends to create a stronger vendor ecosystem that was economically vibrant and socially and environmentally sustainable. Instead of just auditing, Li & Fung became a coach, providing capacity building, skills, knowledge support, training, technology, financial assistance, and connections. VSS manufacturers improve environmental performance by educating them on energy efficiency, carbon emissions management, waste and water management, and then helping suppliers implement improvements.

While production costs and compliance standards were rising, suppliers were also faced with shorter turnaround times, driven by trends such as fast fashion and advancements in retail technologies and e-commerce. Thus, VSS also offered supply chain productivity services like Lean training, industrial engineering, and productivity consulting.

Li & Fung's sustainability efforts were also intended to benefit the communities in which its many vendors were located by creating better economic, environmental, and social ecosystems. This concept is related to "shared value," described in the previous section. The company had long viewed itself as "an essential hub in the wheel of economic development that starts by enabling job creation in emerging markets and supporting employers (factories) to keep moving up the value chain." Improvements in factory productivity could directly benefit workers. At one factory in India, for example, a significant increase in productivity over a 6-month period in turn helped raise the monthly wage of workers paid by the piece from 1000 to 4000 rupees and led to a steep drop in absenteeism (Melvin 2015). Factories that produced sustainably and provided safe, steady employment were of critical importance in developing stronger communities and better-off families, and in enabling social mobility.

Just as improved productivity and standards can benefit workers through better conditions and higher salaries, investing in worker well-being can also create tangible benefits for factories. Since 2010 Li & Fung has supported certain customers in implementing the HER Project (Health Enables Returns), training largely female workforces about personal and reproductive health and hygiene issues over 18 months as a way to reduce absenteeism, increase productivity, and build loyalty amongst factory employees.

20.5.5 Case Example: Investing in Cotton Suppliers at Esquel[9]

Esquel Corporation is the largest cotton-shirt manufacturer in the world. Its major cotton supply comes from Xinjiang, a developing province in northwestern China. Esquel has been focused on environmental protection and sustainable development in its supply bases. The company has hosted conferences to educate communities on the importance of protecting the environment and deployed an Eco Mobile Lab—a classroom on wheels—to bring the message of environmental protection to primary schoolchildren in hard-to-reach areas. The lab visited remote areas in Xinjiang, educating children on conservation through interactive and entertaining activities. During seven tours of the Xinjiang province, the Eco Mobile Lab reached 146 schools and over 138,000 students and teachers. As part of the activities, over 22,000 trees were planted.

Through the Esquel-Y.L. Yang Education Foundation, the company supported local education in Xinjiang, financing the rebuilding of decrepit schools and donating mini-libraries for rural communities. Over the years, Esquel had rebuilt 12 schools in various rural locations, and set up around 800 mini-libraries throughout Xinjiang. Esquel employees participated directly in projects in less fortunate communities. With employee and company contributions, Esquel provided thousands of needy children with financial support for basic education expenses such as tutorial and exercise books. Finally, Esquel sponsored college students to study science, and provided scholarships to outstanding high school graduates to attend university.

Esquel was focused on developing the local agricultural economy in Xinjiang, and on protecting farmers. To improve the quality of the cotton and minimize impurities, Esquel provided farmers free pure cotton garments as a benefit. It also offered farmers workshops on cotton farming, and invited them to visit its spinning mills to demonstrate the impact of cotton quality on the quality of the yarn, and eventually, the garments. A research team in Xinjiang looked for ways to modify the cottonseeds to achieve higher-quality cotton, with better strength and fiber length. The research team also studied irrigation methods in order to conserve water, a scarce resource in Xinjiang. A dedicated team worked with local farmers in Xinjiang on sustainable farming techniques, and advised them on ways to grow and collect the cotton so as to improve quality while at the same time increasing the farmers' income. These efforts also enabled farmers to grow organic

---

[9]The materials of this case were drawn from Pelleg and Lee (2013).

cotton with high productivity. In addition, Esquel placed orders with the farmers in advance, when the cotton was planted, and guaranteed them a minimum price, with the maximum set by the market. Both Esquel and the farmers benefited from this arrangement: farmers were not wiped out if prices went extremely low, and Esquel secured its cotton supply and also had better rapport with the farmers, who were wary of dealing with foreign capitalists after decades of selling only to the government.

20.5.6 Case Example: Creating Shared Value at Nestlé—Rural Development Initiatives[10]

Nestlé is the world's largest food and nutrition company, and procures agricultural commodities from many emerging economies (Africa, South America, and South East Asia). Creating Shared Value (CSV) has been the basic way Nestlé conducted its business to create long-term value for shareholders and for society. CSV involved compliance with laws, Nestlé business principles, and codes of conduct developed by Nestlé. CSV also ensured sustainable development that meets the needs of the present without compromising the ability of future generations to meet their own evolving needs.

Nestlé identified rural development as one of the areas that they would focus on for their CSV initiatives. To create value for its suppliers, Nestlé developed CSV initiatives intended to help the poor farmers to break the vicious circle of poverty:

In many developing countries, the farming business is fragmented and most farmers run their operations on small lots of farmland (average 1.5 ha). Scale is low and small farmers are spread over wide geographies, and thus often have to sell through layers of middlemen, who sell to wholesalers, who sell to brand owners. This long and inefficient supply chain creates a lose–lose situation: (a) farmers get a low selling price; and (b) the brand owner such as Nestlé pays a high purchasing price for crops that may not be fresh (due to delays in handling and transportation). In China, Nestlé worked with over 40,000 fresh milk suppliers (farmers) by adapting the "Swiss Milk District System" which involved: (1) disintermediation: cut the middlemen by developing transportation and infrastructure to collect milk directly from farmers; (2) aggregation: group famers into "districts" to reduce logistics costs for the farmers who deliver their milk to the milk collection centers; (3) quality: establish milk collection centers with quality controls and cooling tanks to reduce spoilage and improve quality; (4) productivity: provide free veterinary services and animal husbandry to improve the quality and productivity of milk production; and (5) financial assistance.

---

[10]The materials of this case were drawn from Lee et al. (2015).

There are two fundamental ways to help farmers reduce production costs: (a) improve yield and quality; and (b) increase productivity. Nestlé provides technical assistance to farmers so that they can produce milk and crops more effectively and efficiently.

Nestlé built its own "cold chain" due to lack of infrastructure in many low-income countries. This involved collecting milk directly from farmers using Nestlé containers, processing collected milk, storing pasteurized milk safely, and transporting finished products to markets. In many developing countries, Nestlé built food processing facilities (e.g., coffee roasting facilities, milk pasteurizing facilities) in rural areas of low-income countries. In 2010, 60 % of Nestlé's 422 factories were located in rural areas, thus creating new nonfarm employment opportunities. By expanding the local pool of skilled workers, Nestlé made the area more attractive to other potential employers, which is essential for rural development. Not only can these job opportunities generate higher income, but these facilities create an efficient supply chain (lower cost, higher quality, and higher volume) for Nestlé.

20.5.6.1   Summary of Case Examples

By understanding supplier management practices such as visibility and monitoring methods, incentives and penalties, supplier collaboration and other practices associated with improved compliance and improved business performance, firms can better target investments in responsible supplier management. In Table 20.1, we summarize the "response" strategies used by the firms highlighted in the cases above, along with the benefits achieved. As mentioned earlier, we focus on "response" strategies due to the greater variation in corporate practices compared to "sense" practices.

20.6   Summary

There is a need for more research on the impact of various sense and response sustainability strategies on social, environmental, and economic performance. As responsible supply chain management continues to evolve and incorporate practices that go beyond monitoring efforts, there is an opportunity to better integrate management into core supply chain operations in order to have a stronger impact on conditions in global supply chains. For firms which engage the entire supply chain in the search for breakthroughs and risk reduction, there are opportunities to gain competitive advantage (Lee 2010). Calls for increased collaboration with suppliers and stronger incentives (Plambeck et al. 2012) will likely continue to grow, as will the call to improve monitoring methods, seek opportunities to build shared value, and ultimately cascade these practices to suppliers throughout a firm's network in order to create lasting change.

Table 20.1 Response strategies and results: Summary of case examples

Company	"Response" strategies						Results
	1 Reactions (e.g., root cause analysis, penalties)	2 Incentives	3 Capacity building	4 Proactive product and process design	5 Shared value	6 Cascading practices to the supply network	
Starbucks	X	X	X		X		Starbucks gained secure, high-quality, added supply
							Farmer income increased
McDonald's	X		X	X		X	McDonald's obtained secure, high-quality, added supply for its growing demand
							Supplier McCain cascaded practices to farmers
							Farmer income increased
HP	X	X	X			X	Supplier reported water, energy waste cost reductions
							Supplier reported lower accident rates
							Supplier reputation was enhanced by becoming a "supplier of choice"
Li & Fung	X		X		X	X	Li & Fung gained from higher worker productivity
							Suppliers saw higher incomes through higher productivity, women obtained health services
Esquel	X		X	X	X		Esquel obtained high-quality supply
							Farmers received benefits and higher income
							Community members received education support and environmental awareness training
Nestlé	X		X		X		Disintermediation and other strategies improved yield, quality, and productivity
							Community saw growth of nonfarm jobs

The purpose of this table is to highlight key practices discussed in the case studies, rather than capture all practices employed by these companies. The one exception is column 1. Since all of these companies use certain reactive methods when violations are detected (e.g., penalties for using child labor), they have all been marked with an "X" even if those practices were not covered in the case

Acknowledgements We thank Angharad Porteous for her significant contribution to the paper cited in Sect. 20.4. Elements of the paper were used throughout this chapter.

References

Awaysheh A, Klassen RD (2010) The impact of supply chain structure on the use of supplier socially responsible practices. Int J Opera Prod Manag 30(12):1246–1268

Bloom N, Eifert B, Mahajan A, McKenzie D, Roberts J (2013) Does management matter? Evidence from India. Q J Econ 128(1):1–51

Bowen FE, Cousins PD, Lamming RC, Faruk AC (2001) The role of supply chain management capabilities in green supply. Prod Oper Manag 10(2):174–189

Chen L, Lee HL (2015) Sourcing under supplier responsibility risk: the effects of certification, audit and contingency payment (December 2, 2015). Stanford University Graduate School of Business Research Paper No. 15–61.

Corbett CJ, Klassen RD (2006) Extending the horizons: environmental excellence as key to improving operations. Manuf Service Oper Manag 8(1):5–22

Cotte J, Trudel R (2009) Socially conscious consumerism: a systematic review of the body of knowledge. Network Bus Sustain. http://nbs.net/wp-content/uploads/NBS_Consumerism_SR_Researcher.pdf

Cousins PD, Lamming RC, Bowen F (2004) The role of risk in environment-related supplier initiatives. Int J Oper Prod Manag 24(6):554–565

Derwall J, Guenster N, Bauer R, Koedijk K (2005) The eco-efficiency premium puzzle. Finan Analyst J 61(2):51–63

Distelhorst G, Hainmueller J, Locke RM (2015) Does lean improve labor standards? Management and social performance in the Nike supply chain. Watson Institute for International Studies Research Paper No. 2013–09; Management Science, Forthcoming; Watson Institute for International Studies Research Paper No. 2013–09; Rotman School of Management Working Paper No. 2337601

Distelhorst G, Locke RM, Pal T, and Samel HM (2015) Production goes global, compliance stays local: private regulation in the global electronics industry (June 8, 2015). MIT Political Science Department Research Paper No. 2012-1; Regulation & Governance. 9(3): 224–242.; MIT Political Science Department Research Paper No. 2012-1; Watson Institute for International Studies Research Paper No. 2014–13.

Earthwatch Research Report (2007). http://earthwatch.org/corporate-partnerships/corporate-partnership-case-studies/starbucks. Accessed 13 June 2015

Economist (2015) Modern slavery (everywhere) in supply chains. http://www.economist.com/news/international/21646199-how-reduce-bonded-labour-and-human-trafficking-everywhere-supply-chains. Accessed 18 June 2015 (March 14, 2015)

Fair Labor Association (2011) Annual public report. http://www.fairlabor.org/sites/default/files/documents/reports/2011_annual_report.pdf. Accessed March 27, 2016

Friedman TL (2005) The world is flat: a brief history of the twenty-first century. Farrar, Straus and Giroux, New York

Gillai B, Rammohan SV, Lee HL (2015) Supply chain's new role in protecting your IP. Supply Chain Manag Rev:34–39 (January/February 2015)

Gimenez C, Tachizawa EM (2012) Extending sustainability to suppliers: a systematic literature review. Supply Chain Manag 17(5):531–543

Haeckel SH (1992) From "Make and Sell" to "Sense and Respond.". Manag Rev 81(10):3–9

Handfield RB, Walton SV, Seeger LK, Melnyk SA (1997) Green value chain practices in the furniture industry. J Oper Manag 15(4):293–315

Harry M, Schroeder R (2000) Six sigma. Random House, New York

Hoyt D, Lee HL, Tseng M (2008), Not safe for children: Mattel's toy recalls and supply chain management. Stanford Business School case GS-63. https://cb.hbsp.harvard.edu/cbmp/product/GS63-PDF-ENG. Accessed March 27, 2016

Intel and BSR (2013) Accelerating supplier sustainability: from compliance to maturity and collaboration

IPE (Institute of Public and Environmental Affairs) (2012) Sustainable apparel's critical blindspot. http://www.ipe.org.cn/en/about/notice_de_1.aspx?id=10860

Kapoor S, Bhattacharya K, Buckley S (2005) A technical framework for sense-and-respond business management. IBM Syst 44(1):5–24

Klassen RD, McLaughlin CP (1996) The impact of environmental management on firm performance. Manag Sci 42(8):1199–1214

Krause DR, Handfield RB, Scannell TV (1998) An empirical investigation of supplier development: reactive and strategic processes. J Oper Manag 17(20):39–58

Krause DR, Calantone RJ, Handfield RB (2000) A structural analysis of the effectiveness of buying firms' strategies to improve supplier performance. Decis Sci 31(1):33–55

Lahiri T (2012) Can mobile phones improve factory safety? Wall Street J Ind (24 Dec 2012)

Lee HL (2008) Embedding sustainability: lessons from the front line. Int Commerce Rev 8(1):10–20

Lee HL (2010) Don't tweak your supply chain—rethink it end to end. Harvard Bus Rev 88(1):62–69

Lee HL, O'Marah K, John G (2012) The chief supply chain officer report - 2012. SCM World :1–52

Lee HL, Over K, Tang C (2015) Creating shared value at Nestle, Stanford University and UCLA Case

Levi Strauss & Co. (2014). http://www.levistrauss.com/wp-content/uploads/2014/01/Addressing-Forced-Child-Labor-in-Cotton-Harvesting_Uzbekistan.pdf

Lewis TR, Fang L, Song JS (2012) A dynamic mechanism for achieving sustainable quality supply. Fuqua School of Business, Duke University, Durham

Locke RM, Romis M (2006) Improving work conditions in a global supply chain. MIT Sloan Manag Rev 48(2):54–62

Locke RM, Qin F, Brause A (2007) Does monitoring improve labor standards? Lessons from Nike. Ind Labor Relat Rev 61:3–31

Locke RM, Rissing BA, Pal T (2013) Complements or substitutes? Private codes, state regulation and the enforcement of labor standards in global supply chains. Br J Ind Relat 51(3):519–552

Melvin S (2015) Everything is connected: a new era of sustainability at Li & Fung. Stanford University Case, GS-87

Mozur P, Dou E (2013) Chinese activist accuses apple supplier of polluting. Wall Street J, August 2, 2013

Newman JC, Breeden KM (1992) Managing in the environmental era: lessons from environmental leaders. Columbia J World Bus 27:210–221

O'Rourke D (2014) The science of sustainable supply chains. Science 344(6188):1124–1127

Pande P, Neuman R, Cavanagh R (2000) The six sigma way: how GE, Motorola and other top companies are honing their performance. McGraw Hill, New York

Pelleg B, Lee HL (2013) Esquel Group: a vertically integrated apparel manufacturer, Stanford University case

Plambeck E, Lee HL, Yatsko P (2012) Improving environmental performance in your Chinese supply chain. Sloan Manage Rev 53(2):43–51

Porteous AH, Rammohan SV (2013) Integration, incentives and innovation: Nike's strategy to improve social and environmental conditions in its global supply chain. Stanford University Global Management Supply Chain Forum

Porteous AH, Rammohan SV, Lee HL (2015) Carrots or sticks? Improving supplier social and environmental compliance through incentives and penalties. POM 24(9):1402–1413

Porter ME, Kramer M (2011) Creating shared value. Harvard Bus Rev 89(1):62–77

PwC (2010) Value of sustainable procurement practices, PwC, EcoVadis, INSEAD Social Innovation Centre. http://www.pwc.com

Rammohan S (2008) Business benefits to Hewlett-Packard suppliers from socially and environmentally responsible (SER) practices in China—a case study. Stanford Global Supply Chain Management Forum

Rammohan S (2013) McDonald's India: optimizing the french fries supply chain. Stanford University Graduate School of Business Case, GS-79

Rao P, Holt D (2005) Do green supply chains lead to competitiveness and economic performance? Int J Oper Prod Manag 25(9):898–916

Scholten K, Fynes B (2017) Risk and uncertainty management for sustainable supply chains. In: Bouchery Y, Corbett CJ, Fransoo J, Tan T (eds) Sustainable supply chains: a research-based textbook on operations and strategy. Springer, New York (Chapter 19)

Schwartz A (2013) Can mobile phones prevent more factory deaths? Fast Company (9 Jan 2013)

Securities and Exchange Commission (2012). http://www.sec.gov/rules/final/2012/34-67716.pdf

Seuring S, Muller M (2008) From a literature review to a conceptual framework for sustainable supply chain management. J Cleaner Prod 16(15):1699–1710

Shao M, Yatsko P (2010) Ma Jun and IPE: using information to improve China's environment. Stanford University Graduate School of Business Case, SI-115

Sodhi MS, Tang CS (2017) Social responsibility in supply chains. In: Bouchery Y, Corbett CJ, Fransoo J, Tan T (eds) Sustainable supply chains: a research-based textbook on operations and strategy. Springer, New York (Chapter 21)

Vachon S, Klassen RD (2006) Extending green practices across the supply chain: the impact of upstream and downstream integration. Int J Oper Prod Manag 26(7):795–821

van Weele A, van Tubergen K (2017) Responsible purchasing: moving from compliance to value creation in supplier relationships. In: Bouchery Y, Corbett CJ, Fransoo J, Tan T (eds) Sustainable supply chains: a research-based textbook on operations and strategy. Springer, New York (Chapter 11)

Westervelt A (2012) How international regulations are changing american supply chains. Forbes. http://www.forbes.com/sites/amywestervelt/2012/05/10/how-international-regulations-are-changing-american-supply-chains/. Accessed 18 June 2015 (May 10, 2012)

Wu Z, Pagell M (2011) Balancing priorities: decision-making in sustainable supply chain management. J Oper Manag 29(6):577–590

Chapter 21
Social Responsibility in Supply Chains

ManMohan S. Sodhi and Christopher S. Tang

21.1   Introduction

Companies are increasingly confronted with social responsibility questions in the media along the entirety of the supply chain they are seen to control and they find it particularly challenging. We look at how companies can design and operate supply chains to fulfil their social responsibility and aim to address four key questions that face managers and researchers.

One question is about the choice of the level and scope of supply chain operations to take into account. Supply chain operations comprise coupled processes that in turn comprise coupled sub-processes and so on, whether within a department or across many companies. Moreover, for social responsibility, the context of analysis is typically a large company. Such a company would typically have a global supply chain entailing many other large and small companies so the context for any analysis or application has to be chosen carefully. Finally, the observed operations may be considered 'socially responsible' at one level and in one context but not so at another level or in another context. An example is the 2014 spat between Oxfam and American actress Scarlett Johanssen, then brand ambassador for the charity. Johanssen also became the brand ambassador for SodaStream, an Israeli company manufacturing in the occupied West Bank, claiming the company contributed to peace by giving jobs to Palestinian people under occupation. At another level, Oxfam maintained that "businesses, such as SodaStream, that operate in settlements further the ongoing poverty and denial of rights of the Palestinian communities that we work to support." (BBC 2014)

M.S. Sodhi (✉)
Cass Business School, City University London, London, UK
e-mail: mohansodhi@gmail.com

C.S. Tang
UCLA Anderson School, University of California, Los Angeles, CA, USA
e-mail: chris.tang@anderson.ucla.edu

© Yann Bouchery, Charles J. Corbett, Jan C. Fransoo, and Tarkan Tan 2017   465
Y. Bouchery et al. (eds.), *Sustainable Supply Chains*, Springer Series in Supply
Chain Management 4, DOI 10.1007/978-3-319-29791-0_21

A second question pertains to the large number of alternative definitions as well as the huge and diverse objectives of social responsibility. Dahlsrud (2008) has identified 37 definitions of CSR from various researchers and industry bodies (mostly in the period 1998–2003). In the operations literature, Carter and Jennings (2004) take CSR to include business ethics, philanthropy, community, workplace diversity, safety, human rights, and environment. Lists of objectives tend to be rather long—see for instance Carroll (1979, 1999) and Bowen (1953:8–12) although Friedman (1970) advocates the single-objective view that 'the social responsibility of business is to increase its profits'. Dealing with multiple objectives raises the question of Pareto efficiency (how to trade off one objective against another) as well as maximizing versus *satisficing* (meeting some threshold value of) these objectives (Ackoff 1970). Shareholders may also content themselves with satisficing share-holder value (Monsen and Downs 1965).

A third question is how companies can be socially responsible by working directly with the weaker members of society, the 'poor', who comprise the majority in every society. Social responsibility refers to the responsibility of business to society. In the business-and-society discourse, 'business' really means large compa-nies (corporations) because "the powerful are given closer scrutiny" (Carroll and Buchholtz 2012:6; see also Bowen 1953:6), narrowing further on the senior manag-ers who make strategic decisions at these companies (cf. Bowen 1953). Equally, while 'society' is a broad concept, political, media and research attention is focused on those at the other end of the power spectrum, i.e., groups of people without eco-nomic or political power: employees, small suppliers, and local communities. So the question is: can companies with economic power run supply chains to meet the needs of the weakest in society, the poor, not just by selling to them but also by employing them or buying from them to improve their economic level?

A final question for managers and OM researchers is to decide whether to or how to develop overarching frameworks to guide a company's strategy to incorporate social responsibility. An overarching framework requires consistency with theoreti-cal frameworks already in use in the strategy, the OM and the social responsibility literature and practice. For instance, strategists may use resource-based view, OM modelling may entail utility theory and the social responsibility practitioners may draw on stakeholder theory. The alternative would be either to develop an entirely new framework or to separate social responsibility efforts from its operations by, for instance, relying solely on philanthropy.

21.2 Literature Review

21.2.1 Corporate Social Responsibility

The social obligations of business are generally codified as corporate social respon-sibility (CSR). Rangan et al. (2015) describe two other 'theatres' for a company doing CSR besides philanthropy: operational improvement, and new business models. In the OM literature, there is interest in how CSR initiatives impact purchasing and supply chain management (Cruz 2009) and how supply chain managers incorporate or implement CSR (Carter and Jennings 2004; Carter 2005; Maloni and Brown 2006). London et al. (2010) examine value creation with social enterprises, while Sodhi and Tang (2011) take a supply-chain perspective on these enterprises.

In general, there remains considerable scepticism about whether a modern corporation can or does fulfil its social obligations (Banerjee 2007; Devinney 2009). Such scepticism may explain why research in 'socially responsible operations' tends to focus on social enterprises, small farmers, foundations, etc. Only a handful of papers in the operations or supply chain literature focus on large company initiatives such as ITC's e-choupal, an electronic platform to provide farmers the company's purchase price one day in advance, or Unilever's Shakti Amma, training women in rural areas to sell Unilever's products with financial help from microfinance NGOs. Some additional examples are provided by Lee and Rammohan (2017) in Chap. 20.

21.2.2 Sustainability

'Sustainability' has become an instrument for large companies to subsume diverse company initiatives pertaining to CSR, environment, and profitability. It provides companies a way to align their CSR and environmental efforts with profitability. Originally, the concept was conceived as being broader in scope (cf. Elkinton 1998): The Brundtland Commission defined it "as development that meets the needs of the present without compromising the ability of future generations to meet their needs" (Carter and Rogers 2008).

Elkinton (1998) presents sustainability as having three 'pillars'—economic, environmental and social—with overlapping zones. Such overlapping zones are helpful for a company because it can report initiatives as serving the environmental (or social) cause even when these are economically motivated. Indeed, the most commonly reported initiatives in companies' sustainability reports are about the reduction in energy consumption. However, the focus on overlaps avoids the awkward question of how to make trade-offs between profitability and social objectives—see Pagell and Shevchenko (2014) in this regard. There are also trade-offs between environmental and economic sustainability: shutting down coalmines (to reduce pollution) adversely affects the economic and social sustainability of mining communities.

The OM literature has considered sustainability from an environmental perspective without explicit incorporation of the social aspects (Carter and Rogers 2008). Sustainability has entered the OM literature as 'sustainable operations management' (Kleindorfer et al. 2005), or more commonly as, 'sustainable supply chain management' (cf. Linton et al. 2007; Seuring and Müller 2008; Pagell and Wu 2009; Carter and Easton 2011). Pagell and Shevchenko (2014) argue that sustainability should be entrenched in all aspects of supply chains.

21.2.3   The 'Poor', the Bottom of the Pyramid and Shared Value

The 'bottom-of-the-pyramid' (Prahalad 2006) approach entails large companies seeking to increase profits by selling goods and services to the 'poor' and possibly using them as suppliers or distributors while doing so. Such operations can require redesigning goods and packaging such as Unilever selling shampoo or its skin-colour-lightening product in small sachets to poor consumers in developing countries (Karamchandani et al. 2011). However, Karnani (2007) provides economic arguments against such marketing of consumer goods to the bottom-of-the-pyramid poor. A broader approach is the 'base-of-the-pyramid' (cf. London and Hart 2011) where 'shared value' is highlighted. An example is the German company Bayer selling agricultural chemicals in small packets to smallholder farmers in developing countries (Karamchandani et al. 2011) creating profits for itself and the farmers. The redesign of modes of production and delivery using the poor as suppliers and distributors *can* make help them in becoming economically better off (Sodhi and Tang 2014).

Engagement with the 'base' of the pyramid requires new business models to engage with the 'poor' as customers or suppliers. Karamchandani et al. (2011) discuss challenges for companies wishing to engage profitably with the bottom of the pyramid: (1) uncertainty of cash flows given the large number of low-margin and low-value transactions, (2) gauging demand and working in 'informal' markets, (3) sales and distribution, (4) providers being neither aggregated nor capable enough to provide quality or volume, (5) business ecosystems not being able to support initiatives.

Although sustainable development has been studied extensively in the development economics literature (Ray 1998; Lal 2000; Hayami 2005), *operational* issues in this context have not been explored much yet. Sodhi and Tang (2011) have looked at social enterprises from a supply chain perspective: These are not large companies but the work of social enterprises has practical implications for what large companies can do. They explore this idea further by looking at the poor as suppliers or distributors in supply chain rather than as consumers (Sodhi and Tang 2014).

The relationship between the company and those at the bottom of the pyramid can create 'shared value' (Porter and Kramer 2006), which recalls the overlaps between the pillars of sustainability "by reconceiving the intersection between society and corporate performance". However, they avoid discussing how to divide the 'shared' value (Coff 1999); Crane et al. (2014) provide some more limitations of the 'shared value' concept.

21.2.4   Stakeholder Resource-Based View

To better understand how to incorporate social responsibility in supply chain operations, Sodhi (2015) outlines 'stakeholder resource-based view' (SRBV) building on resource-based view, utility theory and stakeholder theory.

One model for companies to build lasting competitive advantage is the **resource-based view** (RBV) or its extensions (cf. Hart 1995; Lavie 2006), whereby part of the resources are bundled as firm-specific 'capabilities' that the firm develops in a static economic setting (cf. Wernerfelt 1984; Barney 2001). The resources must raise barriers to entry to others if a competitive advantage is to be durable (Rumelt 1984). In a dynamic economic setting with high uncertainty, resources have to be changed using 'dynamic capabilities' as the firm seeks competitive *survival* in a rapidly changing environment (cf. Teece et al. 1997). Dynamic capabilities "are the organizational and strategic routines by which firms achieve new resource reconfigurations as markets emerge, collide, split, evolve, and die" (Eisenhardt and Martin 2000) although there are many other definitions (Ambrosini and Bowman 2009). 'Dynamic' refers to the external environment rather than to the capabilities, which are built around 'routines' that are the organization's processes. Being able to deliver on social responsibility could be a firm's capability or dynamic capability. But dynamic capability, say, with the company moving facilities from one low-cost country to another lower-cost one continually, could also be tied to social *irresponsibility*.

Garriga and Melé (2004) classify theories in the social responsibility literature as: (1) *instrumental theories* with the corporation solely as an instrument for wealth creation so any social responsibility activity only serves to further that aim; (2) *political theories* about the responsible use power of corporations in society and the politics; (3) *integrative theories* on how business integrates social demands based on the assumption that business depends on society for its existence, continuity and growth; and (4) *ethical theories* based on ethical responsibilities of corporations to society. These can overlap: integrative theories can potentially be reconciled with instrumental theories if a company can meet some social demands only to make more profits in the long run, then it is trying to be integrate society into its decisions. If political power, such as that exerted by large companies on governments, from this perspective is for increasing wealth then an instrumental view can subsume political views as well.

One integrative theory is **stakeholder theory** (Freeman 2010). The assumption is that managers have fiduciary duties to the corporation, not just to the shareholders, and the stakeholders are all the people and groups with an interest in the corporation. According to Donaldson and Preston (1995), the interests of all stakeholders are of intrinsic value and "each group of stakeholders merits consideration for its own sake and not merely because of its ability to further the interests of some other group, such as the shareowners".

In the analytical operations and supply chain literature, **utility theory** is used in the economics of decision-making. Here, the assumption is that we have rational players who seek to maximize their utility—their preference for goods and services—given the possible/actual moves of the other players. Utility theory is consistent with the corporation as an instrument for wealth creation for wealth-maximizing shareholders. And if the concept of utility can extend to the *means* for acquiring goods and services, we have a broad concept maximizing which can cover both resources (as in the resource-based view) under known conditions and dynamic capabilities under uncertainty.

Building on RBV, utility theory and stakeholder theory, Sodhi (2015) proposes **stakeholder resource-based view** (SRBV), defined as

> SRBV is a model to guide the decision-making of managers towards maximizing their utility by developing their organization's capabilities—dynamic capabilities, resources and routines—while recognizing the need to improve the respective utilities of other groups of the organization's stakeholders, possibly by helping them develop their respective capabilities as extensions of the company's own capabilities. Under SRBV, stakeholders for the organization are those whose utility is significantly dependent on these managers' decisions.

SRBV helps managers recognize, whether for a company or for particular operations within a company or across companies, that *there are different groups of stakeholders with their respective resources, routines and dynamic capabilities, seeking to maximize their respective utilities under uncertainty and over their respective time horizons.* Stakeholders for a large corporate include those involved in operations: *suppliers* such as smallholder farmers and contract labourers, *employees*, *mid-level managers*, *senior managers*, and *distributors/wholesalers/franchisees*. *Shareholders*, *government*, *communities* in which facilities are located, and *consumers* are also stakeholders. Note that the 'company' or 'corporation' is not a monolith—instead, we have senior managers, mid-level managers and shareholders of companies although our focus is on senior managers as decision makers. Under SRBV, each stakeholder (individually or as a group) is treated on a par with other stakeholders from a research perspective.

SRBV allows the manager as well as the researcher to tackle the four key questions listed in Sect. 21.1:

The first question was about the choice of the level and scope of supply chain operations to take into account. Under SRBV, there is no explicit restriction. The manager could consider any subset of stakeholders as long as the utility and capabilities of each (type of) stakeholder is fully accounted for. In the Johanssen-Oxfam example, both sides could agree on the utility of Palestinians obtained from gainful employment at Israeli companies operating in the occupied territories. But equally, they could agree that there are other (non-working) Palestinians whose utility is affected by living conditions under occupation, which is only solidified through the operations of Israeli companies. Under SRBV, the manager (or researcher) has to treat all stakeholders of interest on a par with each other to understand them at an economic level. Different managers may select different subsets of stakeholder groups but they can agree on any stakeholder's utility derived from the operations in scope. Furthermore, the unit of observation is the "operation", whatever its scope. A particular manager researcher will have to scope out the breadth and level of the operations over which he or she can make decisions.

The second question pertained to the large number of alternative definitions as well as the huge and diverse objectives of social responsibility. Under SRBV, we have a broad conceptual view of utility and managers have to recognize that other stakeholders have their own objectives underlying their respective utility. Under SRBV, the different *objectives* that the broad CSR literature considers are split up across the different stakeholders and the manager should recognize other stakeholders' objectives into their respective utility. Understanding utility by stakeholder allows the manager to focus on and differentiate stakeholder-specific drivers of utility-maximizing effort.

The third question was how companies can be socially responsible by working directly with the weaker members of society, the 'poor', who comprise the majority in every society. The poor, if part of the company's supply chain as suppliers, distributors, or consumers or even as members of communities where the company has supply chain operations may be stakeholders. If their utility (or disutility) is affected by the company's operations—indirectly by the managers' decisions—then the poor are stakeholders. Developing their capabilities may be part of or get aligned with the managers' efforts to develop their company's capabilities. However, philanthropic efforts unrelated to the company's operations are not included in SRBV. This is because the intended beneficiaries of philanthropic may not be stakeholders whose utility depends significantly on a company's operations. Still, there is a grey area if the philanthropic effort is considered useful for marketing purpose.

The last question for managers was deciding whether to or how to develop overarching frameworks to guide a company's strategy to incorporate social responsibility. SRBV provides such a framework that enables decision-making consistent with utility theory, resource-based view and stakeholder theory. Concepts like 'shared value' are rendered more tangible under SRBV in terms of increasing utility for the managers themselves, their shareholders, and their suppliers or the communities in which these suppliers have operations. Using SRBV, a manager can have a long-term view focusing on developing his/her company's capabilities (dynamic capabilities, resources and routines) as well as those of the company's stakeholders by extension.

21.3 Related Findings and Practical Implications

We find many operations and supply chain configurations being tried by different organizations mainly targeting economic improvement of the poor. These organizations are mostly social enterprises rather than large companies. As such, we discuss our findings specifically for social enterprises first in Sect. 21.3.1. Next, we discuss our findings related to the poor as suppliers (Sect. 21.3.2), as distributors (Sect. 21.3.3), and as borrowers of working capital lending specifically targeting them (Sect. 21.3.4). This sets the stage for us to discuss implications for large companies in Sect. 21.3.5.

21.3.1 Social Enterprises

Sodhi and Tang (2011) view social enterprises as enabling the supply chains of micro-entrepreneurs with the supply-chain perspective of material, information and cashflows. Here are some examples of social enterprises: To lend to the poor,

Grameen Bank relies on group lending, SKS is a for-profit organization that utilizes capital markets to scale up its operations quickly, and Kiva is a person-to-person online lending organization.

Then there are the enterprises that consider the poor as suppliers. For instance, Arzu sells custom designed rugs made by Afghan women weavers. Thamel is an online portal that allows diasporas to send gifts and money to their loved ones who live in Nepal. Coconut World sells coconut sugar produced by the farmers in the Philippines. Another example of a social enterprise is Ecomaximus that produces and sells elephant dung paper that is co-produced by the villagers and their elephants in Sri Lanka, and Men-on-the-Side-of-the-Road (MSR)—serves as an agent to help the day laborers in South Africa to find jobs in a safe and humane environment.

VisionSpring uses the poor as distributors. It procures cheap reading eyeglasses and sells them through micro-entrepreneurs, thus providing affordable reading glasses for low-income individuals with presbyopia.

Other social enterprises seek to help micro-entrepreneurs become more productive. KickStart develops and sells mechanical irrigation pumps and cooking oil presses so that the farmers can improve productivity. Solar Cooker allows villagers to start bakery businesses in areas that do not have easy access to energy.

21.3.2   The Poor as Suppliers

A company may be able to buy goods from the poor directly at good prices and, at the same time, be seen as contributing towards poverty alleviation. In developing countries, social enterprises and companies can help the poor as suppliers by using three basic models:

1. *Reducing intermediate echelons to obtain higher selling prices*: Farmers and other small producers in developing countries typically sell their output through layers of middlemen and consequently get low prices for their product. This creates an opportunity for social enterprises or companies to help the poor by purchasing their output directly. For example, Coconut World purchases coconut sugar made by small farmers in the Philippines directly, and then sells directly to consumers through its online store and to other retailers in the US (Cameranesi et al. 2010). Walmart purchases the crops directly from farmers in China to reduce its costs; the farmers also benefit by getting a higher price (An et al. 2012). The social enterprise Arzu purchases wool rugs directly from Afghan women and sells these in the US. Organizations such as Fairtrade certify such direct purchase from the farmer by manufacturers and retailers. Doing so enables these manufacturers and retailers to advertise to (largely) western consumers that the company is working to ensure the farmer gets a higher price than he would get from middlemen.

2. *Reducing search cost:* The poor as suppliers do not have an easy way to search for customers for their products or services. In South Africa, Men-on-the-Side-of-the-Road (MSR) developed an online portal as a marketplace for day laborers

(micro-entrepreneurs) and homeowners, which helps laborers and potential customers find each other (Sodhi and Tang 2011). Likewise, truck owners in India or South Africa are typically micro-entrepreneurs with a single vehicle, private enterprises have created websites offering to match loads from shippers with trucks to help reduce the problem of trucks heading back home empty after delivery, e.g., LoadJunction.com in India or 123LoadBoard in South Africa. Chipchase et al. (2006) reports that customer demand information available on the mobile phones has helped taxi drivers to increase their earnings in Pakistan and Thailand. The same has been reported for fishermen in Kerala seeking markets for fish, a perishable product because of the fishermen's lack of access to cold chain facilities (Jensen 2007). A broader question is that of the value of information. For instance, Chen and Tang (2015) analytically obtain conditions under which use of (free) public or (costly) private information can be beneficial to a smallholder farmer or not.

3. *Improving productivity*: The poor, especially small farmers, often lack relevant information to improve productivity and to increase selling opportunities. In India, IFFCO disseminates information about weather forecasts and crop advisory information (what to cultivate, when to harvest, and how to improve yield and quality) to farmers via mobile phones so that they can plan their farming activities accordingly (Ghosal and Parbat 2012). Also, Reuters Market Light (RML) tracks the prices of 50 commodities over 1000 markets and the weather conditions of 2000 locations and disseminates crop- and location-specific information to subscribed farmers in India using SMS text messages so that farmers can sell their products at a higher price (Preethi 2009).

21.3.3 The Poor as Distributors

In developing countries, the distribution infrastructure is inadequate. A social enterprise or a company can help reducing distribution cost by using micro-entrepreneurs as distributors. For example, Mozambique-based VidaGas uses micro-entrepreneurs to sell propane gas to food-stall owners, fishermen, health clinics, etc. (Watson and Kraiselburd 2009). Vision Spring sells affordable reading glasses to low-income individuals through a network of micro-entrepreneurs in developing countries (Bhattacharya et al. 2010). Social enterprises like Living Goods and Solar Sisters, both operating in Uganda, also use women micro-entrepreneurs to do last-mile distribution of household necessities and solar lamps respectively thus emulating the model of the famed Avon Ladies (Economist 2012).

The basic distribution strategy entailing the poor as distributors is a **hub-and-spoke** strategy. An enterprise can set up a center in a larger village as a "hub" from which micro-entrepreneurs (or employees) can travel to the more remote rural areas as "spokes" to sell goods or provide services. Such a distribution network can further benefit from (a) using existing commercial/non-commercial networks for moving goods to the micro-entrepreneurs or (b) providing additional services at the hub or sell more products or services to create more supply chain surplus.

Providing additional services is a **piggyback** strategy. Gramin Suvidha Kendra, a private–public partnership between MCX and Indian Post Office established in 2006, distributes seeds, fertilizers, water purifiers, micronutrients and solar lanterns to farmers via the ubiquitous post offices in India (Vachani and Smith 2008). In Africa, Cola Life, an independent UK charity, has used a wedge-shaped container that fits between the Coca Cola bottles in their crates to reduce distribution costs (see www.colalife.org).

21.3.4 Working Capital Lending for the Poor as Suppliers or Distributors

Micro-entrepreneurs have very little access to credit from traditional banks not only because of lack of credit history or collateral but also because of the small amounts of money involved relative to the transaction cost for the bank for screening and collection. Therefore, social enterprises and companies can find ways to finance the working capital if they are to engage the poor as suppliers or distributors. For example, as already noted, Vision Spring provides each micro-entrepreneur in its supply chain with $75 worth of eye charts, brochures, and a stock of reading glasses. In general, there are different types of microfinance models for micro-entrepreneurs to obtain micro-loans:

1. *Self-help groups (SHG)/Rotating Savings and Credits Associations (ROSCAs).* A community of the poor can form self-help groups, where all members bring savings to weekly (or monthly) meetings, and one of the members can take a loan from these savings (Ardener 1995; Snow 1999). While this approach cannot be used for working capital funding, it might be useful for a micro-entrepreneur to purchase capital goods like a bicycle.
2. *Community banks.* These banks seek to stimulate economic development (in terms of business and job creation) for their communities. Grameen Bank uses "group lending" to reduce its screening, monitoring and collection costs: all members in a group are responsible to provide the repayment when one of the members is behind (Foroohar 2010). Benefits of group lending can be extended for working capital funding if all members of the group are suppliers or distributors in the same supply chain and both materials and cash flows can be aggregated at the group level.
3. *Peer-to-Peer Networks.* Kiva is a person-to-person online lending organization that enables people in developed countries to provide micro-loans (Flannery 2007). So this could be used for funding micro-entrepreneurs wishing to be suppliers or distributors, but more for investment in capital goods rather than working capital.
4. *Commercial MFIs*: SKS is a for-profit, publicly traded microfinance organization in India that uses capital markets to scale up its operations quickly and uses information technology to reduce operating cost (Akula 2008). Such a system could also be useful for working capital funding if micro-entrepreneurs can keep rotating balances.

21.3.5   Practical Implications for Large Companies

Large companies seeking for ways to discharge their social responsibility can learn from social responsibility can learn from social enterprises. Indeed, a company can offer all three types of benefits to the poor as suppliers—reducing the number of intermediate echelons, reducing search costs for selling products/services and improving their productivity—by exploiting both supply chain structure and information technology.

Consider Indian consumer-goods giant ITC's e-Choupal initiative: ITC provides farmers the historical selling prices of different crops at different locations on its web portal, and ITC pre-announces its own price for purchasing the crops directly from the farmers before the market opens the next day. These smallholder farmers are least aware of a floor price when bringing their produce to ITC or to a commodity marketplace (Anupindi and Sivakumar 2006, 2007; Goyal 2010).

Companies can also use the poor as distributors. One example is Coca Cola in East Africa, where bottlers deliver over $500 million worth of product to 1800 "manual" distribution centers operated by 7500 micro-entrepreneurs. There micro-entrepreneurs use push carts or even bicycles to distribute the product to small retailers (who are also micro-entrepreneurs) in congested areas, making frequent but small deliveries to these cash-strapped micro-retailers. Another examples is Hindustan Unilever, a subsidiary of Unilever in India, that started Project Shakti in 50 villages in 2000 with woman-entrepreneurs receiving training and stocks of consumer-packaged goods from Unilever's rural distributor to sell the goods to consumers and micro-retailers in 6–10 villages (Rangan and Rajan 2007).

Finally, companies can offer microfinance as working capital for the poor as suppliers or distributors, e.g., by pre-paying for supplies from the poor. Collection costs are also reduced because collection can piggyback on the transfer of goods. Lending transaction costs are greatly reduced if we tie micro-lending to the actual transaction. Moreover, aggregation of suppliers or distributors can fit the group-lending model well as we already noted. A practical way would be to provide micro-retailers inventory on credit till the end of the day: the micro-retailer would effectively get credit for the day and the company would limit its risk to the value of 1 day's inventory (Sodhi and Tang 2014). Or, a company like ITC could lend to farmers before the sowing season and then gets its money back by receiving the produce when the farmer brings produce to ITC directly or receiving cash when he sells his produce on the Mandi.

21.4   Future Research

Integrating social responsibility into operations and supply chain management practice using SRBV provides many opportunities for socially responsible operations and for future research. This is because, as SRBV makes explicit, the researcher can choose any subset of stakeholders for study and suggest norms for their choices rather than take the viewpoint of only a company's managers. Below are some of these opportunities.

21.4.1 Developing Case Studies

There is shortage of well-researched case studies or even descriptions of different operation settings detailing how different groups of stakeholders became better off (or not) because of the operations. One research question can be about the type of operations and how these operations are being economically sustained: What's the business model and where's the money? Implicitly, this research question can include research objectives tied to *value creation* and *value delivery* (London et al. 2010) and *value sharing* (say between micro-entrepreneurs and the corporation as between farmers and ITC in the latter's e-Choupal project). Sodhi and Tang (2012) attempt to understand how the supply chains of individual micro-entrepreneurs can be strengthened by social enterprises, and examine the economic sustenance of such operation. Phenomenological investigation by way of field study and ethnography would be quite useful as a foundation for further research.

One aspect of such studies could lead to better understanding of the multi-way partnership and factors behind success/failure for particular operations by way of, say, local communities, NGOs and the regional government working or not working together. Unanticipated *side effects* of seemingly socially responsible operations would stem from studying a wider set of stakeholders. For instance, donated clothes can have a detrimental impact on the local apparel and retail industry, as seen in Africa. Looking at a wider set of stakeholders, as with SRBV, can help anticipate 'side effects'.

Research in social irresponsibility beyond excellent journalism is limited. The problem of large companies setting up elaborate operations to avoid taxes is not new (Christensen and Murphy 2004) and may even be considered desirable by managers rather than being 'socially irresponsible'. But there are other instances of well-documented irresponsible behaviour by corporations. Armstrong (1977), using behavioural experiments, suggests the problem of *irresponsible* behaviour among managers may be widespread and is possibly linked to 'stockholder' perspective such as that advocated by Friedman (1970).

21.4.2 Social Enterprise

Social entrepreneurship offers an appealing proposition—making money by doing good. There are several topics that merit further study such as appropriate supply chain and other performance measures for social enterprises working with micro-entrepreneurs; supply chain coordination and collaboration between social enterprises and other organizations; how mutually created value is shared between the social enterprise and its micro-entrepreneurs; and support of government policy for social enterprises.

21.4.3 Better Understanding of the Poor

There are plenty of opportunities to research the decision making of the poor in emerging markets. For instance, as feature mobile phone penetration rate exceeds 90 % in India, companies such as Reuters Market Light (RML) and Nokia are offering information services to farmers (cf. Chen and Tang 2015). Some key issues to investigate include identifying the key drivers for farmers as regards paying for subscription, how farmers use the information in practice to make farming decisions, and whether or not such market information actually helps farmers earn more.

Mobile-based finance has been considered as a major breakthrough to help the poor-conduct financial transactions (savings, loans, remittances, loan repayments, payments) over the mobile phones (Lee and Tang 2012). One area of study could be how mobile finance services with instant access change the spending and savings habits of the poor.

21.4.4 Impact Studies

Measuring the alleviation of the targeted social problem across different time frames and scopes requires field study by way of so-called 'impact' studies. Current studies do not have consistent results. For instance, Mittal et al. (2010) finds that farmers subscribing to market information via mobile phones enjoyed higher income, while Fafchamps and Minten (2012) find no evidence supporting this claim. There is room for analytical models here too: Chen and Tang (2015) show that that more accurate market information can have a detrimental effect to prices and therefore to farmers' wellbeing. Incidentally, studies of stock performance are not uncommon. Frooman (1997) does a meta-analysis of event studies to examine the impact of socially responsible announcements on the stock performance of a firm—similar work could be done with not only companies' but also other stakeholders' performance.

21.4.5 Monitoring Suppliers

Companies that face consumers directly do not wish to be associated in the media with such problems at their suppliers as child labour or poor work conditions of workers. How should companies monitor and motivate their suppliers? Porteous et al. (2015) analyse the responses from practitioners at 334 companies and report that incentives for suppliers rather than penalties are strongly associated with a reduction in the company's violations and operating costs.

21.4.6 Understanding the Role of Markets and Government in Improving Social Welfare

As groundwater or other natural resources get depleted, trading on the market is considered as the best possible solution. But does it actually work? Murali et al. (2015) show that exporting water through a water market with exogenous price is detrimental to both society and the environment within the community if we consider 'triple bottom line benefits'. Their work generalizes to other commodities as well: consider for instance, India's ban on export of cotton in 2012 and a 30 % tax to discourage export of iron ore in 2011. Also, different parties may not actually participate in the market. For instance, a significant amount of waste currently going to landfill or incinerators could potentially be re-purposed. Dhanorkar et al. (2015) consider why such exchanges have had limited take-up. Their work has implications beyond such exchanges to those of manpower such as Men-on-the-Side-of-the-Road in S. Africa and freight-boards for truck transportation in Africa or Asia as there may be similar factors affecting lack of take-up.

How should government balance different interests? This is an important research topic. Park et al. (2015) consider social welfare stemming from optimal application of carbon taxes with retailers seeking to maximize profit and consumers seeking to maximize utility and show that the government will find carbon taxes more effective as the competition becomes higher.

21.4.7 Improving the Lot of Smallholder Farmers in Developing Countries

Tang and Zhou (2012), Chen et al. (2013), Devalkar et al. (2011) and McCoy (2012) provide welcome first steps for further research in this area. Aggregating smallholder farmers via cooperative or other aggregations has attracted the attention of policymakers, those interested in social development and certainly many OM researchers (Chen et al. 2015). But are these always beneficial for farmers? An et al. (2015) find that cooperatives (or other aggregations) of smallholder farmers are not necessarily a silver bullet relative to farmers who choose not to join the cooperative.

One way to develop resources for smallholder farmers is online or telephone forums. But how should such forums be designed and operated? For a forum with experts and (some) knowledgeable farmers, Chen et al. (2015) use game-theoretic analysis to show that knowledgeable farmers never provide answers that are more informative than the experts in equilibrium. Chen and Tang (2015) show that the value of private information providers such as RML in India decreases as public information services improve.

In this context, studying how to optimize different types of supply contracts (e.g., wholesale price, revenue sharing, or profit sharing) with a view to poverty alleviation as well as profits for the enterprise would be useful. These contracts would include supporting the micro-entrepreneurs' need for capital, say, farmers having to buy equipment, seed, or fertilizer. The role of the wholesale auction markets in India called *mandis* also needs to be better understood as to how the government can achieve its objectives optimally.

21.4.8 Distribution Models Using the Poor

Efficient distribution strategies for enabling micro-entrepreneurs in developing countries to buy, distribute, and sell products have not been studied much. Moreover, for *piggyback distribution*, it is not clear how the value created should be shared between the network owner and the enterprise or micro-entrepreneurs. For example, how much should Coca Cola charge Cola Life for distributing its AidPods? How much should India Post charge Gramin Suvidha Kendra? Inventory issues arising from a hub-and-spoke system with many micro-entrepreneurs as spokes provide interesting research opportunities. For example, a hub-based inventory at a centralized warehouse reduces the inventory due to the "pooling" effect, but makes it costly for the micro-entrepreneurs to replenish their inventories especially if they have to do so frequently owing to limited purchasing power. Involving local entrepreneurs as informal sales force in developing countries creates new research opportunities to extend the existing marketing and the OM literature in the area of sales force planning, sales territory design, and incentive design (Lilien et al. 1992).

21.4.9 Working Capital Lending to the Poor

Economists have studied microfinance since the early 1990s (cf. Armendáriz and Morduch 2007) and there are different economic theories on group lending—see and for comprehensive reviews. One research opportunity lies in testing the assumption of risk reduction in group-lending. The same could be applied to micro-entrepreneurs as distributors when provided with goods on inventory on a credit basis. Another research opportunity deals with optimal loan repayment: frequent repayment schedule reduces the amount of defaulted loans but it increases the lenders' cost of collection. A third research opportunity is screening micro-entrepreneurs for lending to reduce the cost associated with default loans. Developing effective way to develop new credit scoring methods by analyzing the data captured by the financial transactions (remittances, loan repayments, payments) conducted over the mobile phones (Lee and Tang 2012) may be a practical way to carry out such research. Researchers have also used Kiva's online portal to examine how this information on financial transactions would affect lending behaviour among online lenders (Hartley et al. 2010). This can be specialized to screening for distributors especially when the goods are being provided on credit.

References

Ackoff R (1970) A concept of corporate planning. Long Range Plann 3(1):2–8

Akula V (2008) Business basics at the base of the pyramid. Harvard Bus Rev 86(6):53 (June, 2008)

Ambrosini V, Bowman C (2009) What are dynamic capabilities and are they a useful construct in strategic management? Int J Manag Rev 11(1):29–49

An, J., S.-H. Cho, C. S. Tang. 2015. Aggregating smallholder farm- ers in emerging economies. Prod. Oper. Manag.. 24(9), 1414–1429.

Anupindi R, Sivakumar S (2006) Supply chain re-engineering in agri-business—a case study of ITC's e-Choupal. In: Lee HL, Lee CY (eds) Supply chain issues in emerging economies. Springer, New York, pp 265–307

Anupindi R, Sivakumar S (2007) ITC's e-Choupal: a platform strategy for rural transformation. In: Rangan VK, Quelch JA, Herroro G, Barton B (eds) Business solutions for the global poor: creating social and economic value. Jossey Bass, San Francisco

Ardener S (1995) Women making money go round: ROSCAs revisited. In: Ardener S, Burman S (eds) Money-go-rounds: the importance of rotating savings and credit associations for women. Berg Publishers, Oxford

Armendáriz B, Morduch J (2007) The economics of microfinance. The MIT Press, Cambridge

Armstrong JS (1977) Social irresponsibility in management. J Bus Res 5(3):185–213

Banerjee SB (2007) Corporate social responsibility: the good, bad and the ugly. Edgar Elger, Cheltenham

Barney JB (2001) Resource-based theories of competitive advantage: a ten-year retrospective on the resource-based view. J Manag 27(6):643–650

BBC (2014) Scarlett Johansson quits Oxfam role over SodaStream row. Downloaded from http://www.bbc.co.uk/news/world-us-canada-25958176 (30 Jan)

Bhattacharya O, Khor S, McGahan A, Dunne D, Daar AS, Singer PA (2010) Innovative health service delivery models in low and middle income countries—what can we learn from the private sector? Health Res Policy Syst 8(24):1–11

Bowen HR (1953) The social responsibilities of the businessman. Harper, New York, Reprinted 2013, University of Iowa Press, Iowa City

Cameranesi S, Huang Y, Tang CS (2010)Coconut world: a sweetener from the heart, UCLA Anderson School Teaching Case

Carroll AB (1979) A three-dimensional conceptual model of corporate performance. Acad Manage Rev 4(4):497–505

Carroll AB (1999) Corporate social responsibility evolution of a definitional construct. Bus Soc 38(3):268–295

Carroll A, Buchholtz A (2012) Business and society: ethics, sustainability, and stakeholder man- agement, 9th edn. Cengage Learning, Stamford

Carter CR (2005) Purchasing social responsibility and firm performance: the key mediating roles of organizational learning and supplier performance. IJPDLM 35(3):177–194

Carter CR, Jennings MM (2004) The role of purchasing in corporate social responsibility: a struc- tural equation analysis. J Bus Logist 25(1):145–186

Carter CR, Rogers DS (2008) A framework of sustainable supply chain management: moving toward new theory. IJPDLM 38(5):360–387

Carter, C. R., P. L. Easton. 2011. Sustainable supply chain man- agement: evolution and future directions. Int. J. Phys. Distrib. Logisti. Manag. 41(1): 46–62.

Chen Y-J, Tang CS (2015) The economic value of market information for farmers in developing economies. POM 24(9):1441–1452

Chen YJ, Shantikumar G, Shen ZJ (2013) Training, production and channel separation in ITC's e-Choupal Network. POM 22(2):348–364

Chen Y-J, Shantikumar JG, Shen Z-J (2015) Incentive for peer-to-peer knowledge sharing among farmers in developing economies. POM 24(9):1430–1440

Chipchase J (2006) Mobile phone practices and the design of mobile money services for emerging markets. http://www.janchipchase.com

Christensen J, Murphy R (2004) The social irresponsibility of corporate tax avoidance: taking CSR to the bottom line. Development 47(3):37–44

Coff RW (1999) When competitive advantage doesn't lead to performance: the resource-based view and stakeholder bargaining power. Organ Sci 10(2):119–133

Crane A, Palazzo G, Spence LJ, Matten D (2014) Contesting the value of the shared value concept. Calif Manage Rev 56:2

Cruz JM (2009) The impact of corporate social responsibility in supply chain management: multi-criteria decision-making approach. Decis Support Syst 48(1):224–236

Dahlsrud A (2008) How corporate social responsibility is defined: an analysis of 37 definitions. Corp Soc Responsib Environ Manag 15(1):1–13

Devalkar SK, Anupindi R, Sinha A (2011) Integrated optimization of procurement, processing, and trade of commodities. Oper Res 59(6):1369–1381

Devinney TM (2009) Is the socially responsible corporation a myth? The good, the bad, and the ugly of corporate social responsibility. Acad Manag Perspect 23(2):44–56

Dhanorkar S, Donohue K, Linderman K (2015) Repurposing materials and waste through online exchanges: overcoming the last hurdle. POM 24(9):1473–1493

Donaldson T, Preston LE (1995) The stakeholder theory of the corporation: concepts, evidence, and implications. Acad Manage Rev 20(1):65–91

Economist (2012) Selling sisters. Econ. http://www.economist.com/blogs/schumpeter/2012/11/retail-developing-countries. Accessed on May 24, 2013 (November 29)

Eisenhardt KM, Martin JA (2000) Dynamic capabilities: what are they? Strateg Manag J 21(10–11):1105–1121

Elkinton J (1998) Cannibals with forks: the triple bottom line of 21st century business. Capstone Publishing Ltd (Wiley), Oxford

Fafchamps M, Minten B (2012) Impact of SMS-based agricultural information on Indian farmers. World Bank Econ Rev 26(3):383–414

Flannery M (2007) Kiva and the birth of person-to-person microfinance. Innovations 2:31–56

Foroohar R (2010) The poor always pay. Newsweek :44–45 (July 12)

Freeman, R. E. 2010. Strategic Management: A Stakeholder Approach. Cambridge University Press, Cambridge, UK.

Friedman M (1970) The social responsibility of business is to increase its profits. N Y Times Mag :211–227 (September 13)

Frooman J (1997) Socially irresponsible and illegal behavior and shareholder wealth a meta-analysis of event studies. Bus Soc 36(3):221–249

Garriga E, Melé D (2004) Corporate social responsibility theories: mapping the territory. J Bus Ethics 53(1–2):51–71

Ghosal S, Parbat K (2012) Farmers bet on mobile advisory for crop sowing. EconTimes (August 11, 2012)

Goyal A (2010) Information, direct access to farmers, and rural market performance in Central India. Am Econ J Appl Econ 2(3):22–45

Hart SL (1995) A natural-resource-based view of the firm. Acad Manage Rev 20(4):986–1014

Hartley SE (2010) Kiva.org: crowd-sourced microfinance and cooperation in group lending. Working paper, Columbia Business School, Columbia University

Hayami Y (2005) Development economics: from the poverty to the wealth of nations. Oxford University Press, Oxford

Jensen R (2007) The digital provide: information (technology), market performance and welfare in the South Indian fisheries sector. Q J Econ 122(3):879–924

Karamchandani A, Kubzansky M, Lalwani N (2011) Is the bottom of the pyramid really for you? Harv Bus Rev 89(3):107–111

Karnani A (2007) The mirage of marketing to the bottom of the pyramid. Calif Manage Rev 49(4):90–111

Kleindorfer PR, Singhal K, Van Wassenhove LN (2005) Sustainable operations management. POM 14(4):482–492

Lal D (2000) The poverty of "development economics". MIT Press, Cambridge

Lavie D (2006) The competitive advantage of interconnected firms: an extension of the resource-based view. Acad Manage Rev 31(3):638–658

Lee HL, Rammohan SV (2017) Improving social and environmental performance in global supply chains. In: Bouchery Y, Corbett CJ, Fransoo J, Tan T (eds) Sustainable supply chains: a research-based textbook on operations and strategy. Springer, New York

Lee HL, Tang CS (2012) Experian microanalytics: accelerating the development of mobile financial services in developing market. Teaching case, UCLA Anderson School

Lilien GL, Kotler P, Moorthy KS (1992) Marketing models. Prentice Hall, Upper Saddle River

Linton JD, Klassen R, Jayaraman V (2007) Sustainable supply chains: an introduction. J Oper Manag 25(6):1075–1082

London T, Hart SL (2011) Next generation strategies for the base of the pyramid: new approaches for building mutual value. FT Press, Pearson Education, Upper Saddle River

London T, Anupindi R, Sheth S (2010) Creating mutual value: lessons learned from ventures serving base of the pyramid producers. J Bus Res 63(4):582–594

Maloni MJ, Brown ME (2006) Corporate social responsibility in the supply chain: an application in the food industry. J Bus Ethics 68(1):35–52

McCoy J (2012) Overcoming the challenges of the last mile: a model of riders for health, Healthcare operations management handbook. Springer, New York

Mittal S, Gandhi S, Tripathi G (2010) Socio-economic impact of mobile phones on Indian agriculture. Working paper 246, Indian Council for Research and International Economic Relations

Monsen RJ, Downs A (1965) A theory of large managerial firms. J Polit Econ 73(3):221–236

Murali K, Lim M, Petruzzi N (2015) Municipal groundwater management: optimal allocation and control of a renewable natural resource. POM 24(9):1453–1472

Pagell M, Shevchenko A (2014) Why research in sustainable supply chain management should have no future. J Supply Chain Manag 50(1):44–55

Pagell M, Wu Z (2009) Building a more complete theory of sustainable supply chain management using case studies of 10 exemplars. J Supply Chain Manag 45(2):37–56

Park SJ, Cachon GP, Lai G, Seshadri S (2015) Supply chain design and carbon penalty: Monopoly vs. Monopolistic Competition. POM 24(9):1494–1508

Porteous A, Rammohan SV, Lee H (2015) Carrots or sticks? Improving social and environmental compliance at suppliers through incentives and penalties. POM 24(9):1402–1413

Porter ME, Kramer MR (2006) The link between competitive advantage and corporate social responsibility. Harv Bus Rev 84(12):78–92

Prahalad CK (2006) The fortune at the bottom of the pyramid: eradicating poverty through profits. Wharton School Publishing, Pearson, Upper Saddle River

Preethi J (2009) Reuters market light goes to Himachal: Pan-India with Nokia; Txt vs. GRPS vs. Voice. News and Analysis of Digital Media in India, Medianama

Rangan VK, Rajan R (2007) "Unilever in India: Hindustan lever's project shakti—marketing FMCG to the rural consumer," Harvard Business School Case #9-505-056. Harvard Business School Publishing, Cambridge

Rangan K, Chase L, Karim S (2015) The truth about CSR. Harvard Business Review 93(1/2):41–49

Ray D (1998) Development economics. Princeton University Press, Princeton

Rumelt RP (1984) Towards a strategic theory of the firm. Competitive Strat Manag 26:556–570

Seuring S, Müller M (2008) From a literature review to a conceptual framework for sustainable supply chain management. J Clean Prod 16(15):1699–1710

Snow D (1999) Microcredit: an institutional development opportunity. Int J Econ Dev 1:65–79

Sodhi MS (2015) Conceptualizing social responsibility in operations via stakeholder resource-based view. POM 24(9):1375–1389

Sodhi MS, Tang CS (2011) Social enterprises as supply-chain enablers for the poor, Socioecon Plann Sci 45(4):146–153

Sodhi, M. S., C. S. Tang. 2011. Social enterprises as supply-chain enablers for the poor". Socio-Econ. Plann. Sci. 45(4): 146–153.

Tang CS, Zhou S (2012) Research advances in environmentally and socially sustainable operations. EJOR 223(3):585–594

Teece DJ, Pisano G, Shuen A (1997) Dynamic capabilities and strategic management. Strateg Manag J 18(7):509–533

Vachani S, Smith NC (2008) Socially responsible distribution: distribution strategies for reaching the bottom of the pyramid. Calif Manage Rev 50:52–84

Watson N, Kraiselburd S (2009) VidaGas: VillageReach—the mozambican foundation for community development joint venture. Harvard Business School case # 609107

Wernerfelt B (1984) The resource-based view of the firm. Strateg Manag J 5(2):171–180

Chapter 22
Cross-Sector Partnerships for Sustainable Supply Chains

J. Balaisyte, M. Besiou, and L.N. Van Wassenhove

22.1 Introduction

Sustainability issues are so immense that no single organization can face them alone. Global business, in order to deal with the pressure coming from governments and society, seeks to better manage their supply chains with regard to social and environmental impacts, and contribute to society. They often work with multiple stakeholders such as NGOs, through cross-sector partnerships. Many examples of cross-sector partnership-based initiatives exist such as the TNT and World Food Program partnership, or the partnership between the humanitarian Logistics Cluster and logistics companies (Stadtler and Van Wassenhove 2013).

This chapter focuses on how supply chains can be used to create sustainable value through cross-sector collaboration. The objective of this chapter is twofold. First, we conduct a case study research by using three examples of cross-sector partnerships to identify challenges that arise in the process of value creation. Second, we discuss how these challenges could be addressed by using Operations Management (OM)/Supply Chain Management (SCM) research.

To achieve the first objective, we select three examples of cross-sector partnerships between pharmaceutical companies and healthcare focused NGOs, since we had the opportunity to follow their development over more than 1 year and they provide good illustrative examples of typical challenges. The pharmaceutical industry has been growing rapidly for the past decades, saturating developed markets, and exploring growth opportunities in emerging markets. Health supply chains in emerging markets face a number of challenges that require local market knowledge

J. Balaisyte • L.N. Van Wassenhove
INSEAD, Fontainebleau, France
e-mail: jurgita.balaisyte@gmail.com; luk.van-wassenhove@insead.edu

M. Besiou (✉)
Kühne Logistics University, Hamburg, Germany
e-mail: maria.besiou@the-klu.org

like retail distribution and pricing. Collaboration with NGOs can help pharmaceutical companies improve their corporate social responsibility (CSR) performance and close their local knowledge gap, while at the same time support healthcare systems in developing countries. From a supply chain management perspective, the private partners may engage in cross-sector partnerships in order to assess the potential of developing markets, build their reputation and motivate their employees.

The first case involves the Janssen Pharmaceutica haematology department unit of Johnson & Johnson, a multinational medical devices, pharmaceutical, and consumer packaged goods manufacturer. The other two of our three cases involve Tibotec, a pharmaceutical company belonging to the Johnson & Johnson group, with a focus on research and development for treatment of infectious diseases. The first partnership was built between Johnson & Johnson and International HIV/AIDS Alliance in Zambia, the second between Tibotec and International HIV/AIDS Alliance in Ukraine, and the third between Tibotec and International HIV/AIDS Alliance in Uganda. International HIV/AIDS Alliance[1] is a global partnership of nationally based governmental and non-governmental organizations that support community organizations in addressing HIV/AIDS issues in developing countries.

All three cases were part of an Executive Development Programme (EDP) run by INSEAD, a global business school and PEPAL, a global foundation that fosters partnerships between businesses and nonprofit organizations to achieve scalable and sustainable social change in developing and emerging markets[2]. Hence the NGOs participated in the EDP, together with business executives, in order to get exposed to supply chain and other management-related tools that would help them improve their skills. This program was implemented in collaboration with the International HIV/AIDS Alliance (IHAA) headquarters and its regional partner organizations that took part in the program. The EDP involved two 1-week sessions of executive training at INSEAD, one at the beginning and the other at the end of the program and a 1-year project in-between aiming to address challenges identified by NGO participants.

The chapter is organized as follows. In Sect. 22.2, we present an overview of literature on supply chain, cross-sector partnerships and introduce a theoretical framework depicting factors that affect partnership success. Section 22.3 describes the three cases. Section 22.4 uses the framework to analyze the case studies, summarizes the main findings and practical implications and discusses possible avenues for value creation using OM/SCM research. Finally, Sect. 22.5 presents our conclusions.

22.2   Literature Review

In order to address our question—what are the challenges affecting the success of cross-sector partnerships in value creation for the partners—we first consider the supply chain partnership literature. According to the Supply Chain Management

---

[1] http://www.aidsalliance.org

[2] http://PEPAL.org

Institute "supply chain management is the management of relationships in the network of organizations, from end customers through original suppliers, using key cross-functional business processes to create value for customers and other stakeholders" (Lambert 2014).

Supply chain partnerships develop through different levels (Lambert 2014). At the first level, the partners articulate their objectives. At the second level, the partners need to align their expectations by setting the partnership's objectives and then at the third level they develop the action plan and assign responsibilities. When the action plan is implemented, the partners review performance (fourth level) against expectations in order to decide how to proceed with the partnership.

In the case of cross-sector partnerships, private companies typically engage in such collaborations in order to improve their reputation, motivate their employees, and develop or assess potential markets (Maon et al. 2009), while the NGOs' drivers are the opportunity to increase their resources and the exposure to SCM and management-related tools (Van Wassenhove 2006). Cross-sector partnerships refer to the partnerships that involve government, business, nonprofits and philanthropies, communities, and/or the public as a whole (Bryson et al. 2006; Cooper et al. 2006; Austin and Seitanidi 2012a, b). Figure 22.1 presents the cross-sector supply chain partnership.

The supply chain partnership model was originally built to describe business-to-business collaborations. While partnerships between private companies face multiple challenges, like incentive misalignment or information asymmetry, these challenges are even more complex in the case of cross-sector supply chain partnerships. Health management in developing countries faces a lot of uncertainty due to constraints in funding and skills of the people employed (Thomas 2005; Gustavsson 2003). Hence, NGOs often do not have the necessary resources to acknowledge the importance of supply chain management, regarding it as an auxiliary function (Arminas 2005). While the partnership model provides a good understanding of the private supply chain partnership, it ignores the complex environment of cross-sector collaboration. For this reason, we consult literature on cross-sector collaboration between business and nonprofit organizations.

A clear difference between the typical partnership model, described by Lambert (2014), and a cross-sector partnership is that private partnerships are seen as static while Austin (2000a, b) argues there are three stages of collaboration in cross-sector partnerships: philanthropic (unilateral transfer of resources), transactional (reciprocal exchange of resources), and integrative (based on a very close organizational

Fig. 22.1 Cross-sector supply chain partnership

coordination and co-creation of value). Austin and Seitanidi (2012b) build on the work of Austin (2000a, b) and suggest collaboration may evolve to a fourth trans-formative stage (aimed to co-create change at the societal level). This implies that cross-sector partnerships are dynamically evolving over time based on the nature, intensity, and form of interaction.

No matter at which stage partners commence their collaboration, they go through several phases. Selsky and Parker (2005) distinguish three phases of partnership lifecycle: (1) formation, (2) implementation and (3) outcomes, looking at project-based cross-sector partnerships to address social issues. Austin and Seitanidi (2012b) divide partnership lifecycle into the following phases: (1) partnership selection and formation, and (2) partnership implementation and post-formation management. Similarly, Kale and Singh (2009) suggest three phases of alliance: (1) partner selection and alliance formation, (2) alliance governance and design and (3) post-formation alliance management. The expected benefits should be articulated to the partners and society (Austin et al. 2000) and, eventually, decide if the partner-ship should be continued or terminated. The processes describe how the actions and the dynamics take place during the phases. Finally, the outcomes reflect the value created as the impact of the partnership. Measurement systems and key performance indicators (KPIs) could be of help in achieving this.

Austin and Seitanidi (2012a, b) argue that value of partnering originates from resource complementarity, resource nature, resource directionality and use, and linked interests. It eventually materializes into one of the following types of values: associational, transferred resource, interaction, and synergetic. Associational value is a consequent benefit accruing to a partner from having a collaborative relation-ship with the other one. Transferred resource value arises by receiving a resource from the other partner. Interaction value depicts the intangibles that derive from the collaboration like communication or leadership skills. Synergistic value reflects the value that arises by combining partners' resources; this value is higher than the one that would be accomplished if they would have acted separately.

We use the literature on cross-sector partnerships and supply chain partnerships to build a framework that will help us identify factors leading to successful cross-sector partnerships. Specifically, we look into the literature for factors that influence partnership formation and selection management, partnership implementation man-agement and outcomes. We also examine the managerial challenges and complex environment in which these partnerships occur.

In Sects. 22.2.1 and 22.2.2 we focus on the two phases of partner selection and for-mation, and partnership implementation and post-formation management, respectively.

22.2.1 Partner Selection and Partnership Formation

Decisions at the partner selection and formation phase influence partnership's future potential to evolve and create value. This phase allows partners to align expecta-tions and determine if a potential relationship is worth time and investment. It includes a range of activities such as problem-setting processes (Gray 1989; McCann 1983), initial conditions of the partners, for example resources they possess (Bryson et al. 2006), and assessments indicating benefits likely to be produced by the collaboration (Clarke and Fuller 2010; Gourville and Rangan 2004). As identi-fied by Lambert (2014) it is also crucial for the supply chain partnership to set objectives and match expectations.

Austin and Seitanidi (2012b) show that initial articulation of the problem, linked interests and resources, partners' motives (Seitanidi and Crane 2009) and missions, history of past interactions and visibility fit are key measures of partnership forma-tion and fit potential. Visibility fit reflects the desire to gain visibility (Gourville and Rangan 2004) that may enhance reputation (Tully 2004), and public image (Alsop 2004; Heap 1998; Rondinelli and London 2003), which are benefits that can be attributed to associational value. Visibility fit is a very important aspect in Corporate Social Responsibility (CSR)-based relationships.

One indicator of the potential for value creation is the identification of linked interests through the initial articulation of a social problem relevant to both partners (Bryson et al. 2006; Gray 1989; Waddock 1986). Addressing the social problem often becomes the key objective for the partnership itself. The process of articula-tion can be challenging and show the incompatibilities between partners signalling the need for realignment (Austin and Seitanidi 2012b). Moreover, when the social problem is linked to the interests of the partners, the probability that they will ben-efit from the partnership is higher (Le Ber and Branzei 2010). So matching the interests of the partners shows that they better fit with one another and may increase partnership success.

Partners' motives and missions reveal possible linked interests and expected benefits (Seitanidi 2010). According to Kale and Singh (2009), partner complemen-tarity shows how partners contribute non-overlapping resources to the partnership and it may include both tangible and intangible (knowledge, capabilities, manage-ment practices, and skills) resources. It also refers to the fit between partner working styles and cultures (Austin and Seitanidi 2012b). Corporations willing to enter developing regions have to understand the unique conditions of this environment and try to fit culturally (Dahan et al. 2010). Checking for compatibility and comple-mentarity early on, by verifying the past history of interactions and visibility fit (Austin and Seitanidi 2012b), can reduce the probability of misunderstandings, misallocation of costs and benefits, mismatches of power, lack of complementary skills, and mistrust (Berger et al. 2004). Social partnerships are inherently fragile also because of individuals involved in the collaboration for whom partnerships may be of secondary concern when compared to their daily jobs (Waddock 1988).

Once the formation measures are set, the next step concerns the partner selection using predefined partnership criteria and the measures of partnership formation and fit the potential discussed above. Specific criteria may involve factors such as the industry of interest, resource availability, and scope of operations and may facilitate the process of assessing potential partners. There are cases where some organiza-tions may not agree with all of the activities involved in the partnership formation and selection process or some activities may overlap.

22.2.2   Partnership Implementation and Post-Formation Management

The implementation of the partnership commences when the needs and problems of the partners are clear and the partnership is formed. At the beginning of this phase, the partnership is designed and then the operations follow. Partnership design processes include setting objectives and structures (Austin 2000b; Bryson et al. 2006; Googins and Rochlin 2000), rules and regulations (Das and Teng 1998; Gray 1989), leadership positions (Austin 2000a; Waddock 1986) and agreements on partnership management (Seitanidi and Crane 2009). Moving from design to operations is often followed by experimentation, adaption (Austin 2000a; Gray 1989), operationalization, and institutionalization of processes as partners improve and readjust their coordination mechanisms and structural arrangements (Austin and Seitanidi 2012b). This process is facilitated by frequency in communication, professional leadership, evaluation of progress, and the ability to set objectives (Googins and Rochlin 2000; Austin and Seitanidi 2012b).

While setting the objectives is an important factor for partnership success (Googins and Rochlin 2000), rules and regulations can also emerge as partnership evolves (Austin and Seitanidi 2012b). Informal communication is more likely to be effective in dealing with tensions between the partners and harmonizing different organizational cultures (Orlitzky et al. 2003). Austin and Seitanidi (2012b) find by conducting a literature review that harmonizing two different organizational cultures, leadership, forms of communication that enable trust, mutual respect, openness, constructive criticism, and open dialogue play an important role in cross-sector partnerships. Shah and Swaminathan (2008) emphasize that commitment is crucial for partnership success especially when partners have clear expectations from the partnership but vague processes regarding how to achieve them. In this case, partners should be willing to dedicate more resources to the relationship and pledge to work with each other even when they realize that some adaptation might be required.

The value created by partnerships should then be measured. For example, a group of companies, including pharmaceutical companies like, Abbott, AbbVie, Astra Zeneca, GlaxoSmithKline, uses a framework to assess the real value and impact of their community investment to both business and society.[3] Other practitioner studies, such as IFC, Community Investment Guidelines[4] and TPI, Current Practice Evaluation[5], provide guidelines on how to measure and communicate community investment for strategic advantage. In this respect, Googins and

---

[3] LBG Model: http://www.lbg-online.net/about-lbg/the-lbg-model.aspx

[4] Strategic Community Investment: A Good Practice Handbook for Companies Doing Business in Emerging Markets: http://www.ifc.org/wps/wcm/connect/60a5be8048855226aab4fa6a6515bb18/12014chapter8-.pdf?MOD=AJPERES&CACHEID=60a5be8048855226aab4fa6a6515bb18

[5] The Partnering Initiative: Current practice in the evaluation of cross-sector partnerships for sustainable development http://thepartneringinitiative.org/wp-content/uploads/2014/08/WP1_Evaluation.pdf

Rochlin (2000) raise a question that is common among practitioners: how partners can measure results of their partnerships. On an organizational level, by reviewing best practices of social programmes, Sept et al. (2011) proposes four methods for evaluation: impact evaluation, performance monitoring, process evaluation, and social return on investment evaluation. Koza and Lewin (2000) discuss the importance of monitoring performance outcomes. Specifically, they find that in partnerships with less well-defined objectives such as exploration alliances, monitoring progress and performance outcomes, and setting clear partnership goals is greatly complicated and requires the design and execution of process controls. This often happens because the performance goals are generally stated in much less specific, causally ambiguous, open-ended terms such as acquiring new capabilities and learning new technologies. Key performance indicators (KPIs) can also be used to show whether the partnership is moving towards its objectives. At that point, the partners need to decide if they should exit the partnership or develop a continuation strategy.

The key processes of the post-formation management and implementation phase described above are used in our framework, presented in Fig. 22.2. These processes highlight also the challenges that partners may face at every phase, like lack of commitment, trust and an open relationship. The two phases are followed by the decision to assess value created and to exit or continue the partnership (continuation strategy). Hence the framework presented in Fig. 22.2 captures the factors that according to the literature affect partnership success. In Sect. 22.3 we use this framework to analyze our three cases.

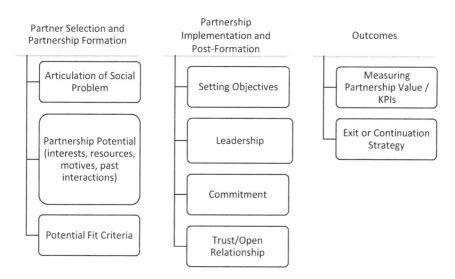

Fig. 22.2 Framework depicting potential factors affecting cross-sector partnership success

22.3 Empirical Study: Case Description

In this section we present three case studies of partnerships between pharmaceutical companies (headquartered in Belgium) and healthcare focused nonprofit organizations operating in developing countries. The three partnerships were built and implemented in 2009–2010, during the 12 months Executive Development Program (EDP) commissioned by PEPAL, a social enterprise and carried out by the INSEAD Humanitarian Research Group. Using the framework, (Fig. 22.2) developed in the previous section, we identify main challenges that arise in the process of building and implementing the cross-sector partnerships and then we compare the three partnerships.

Partnerships underwent several phases (Austin and Seitanidi 2012b). First, a partnership formation and selection phase took place during which, with assistance of PEPAL, potential candidates were identified and matched. PEPAL following discussions with both NGO and private partners built a list of criteria to match the partners. Thus the three partnerships were formed based on the skills of the private partners, their previous collaboration experience, the mutual interests of both partners and the chemistry developed between the individuals forming the partnership. Table 22.1 presents the partner selection criteria.

Second, partnership implementation and post-formation management followed, throughout which partners carried out partnership management activities as part of the 1-year program. Our three partnerships had no formal governance structure. The collaboration was based on mutual trust and informal relationships. Lastly, the

Table 22.1 Partner selection criteria for the three cases

Criterion	Partnership in Zambia	Partnership in Ukraine	Partnership in Uganda
Industry of interest	Previous experiences of both partners in healthcare	Previous experiences of both partners in healthcare	Previous experiences of both partners in healthcare
Previous collaboration experience	No previous cross-sector collaboration experience of either partner	No previous cross-sector collaboration experience of either partner	Previous experience of private partner in healthcare and developing countries
Interests	Mutual interest: healthcare in developing regions	Mutual interests: healthcare in developing regions, cost effective relationship (money/time/investment vs. outcomes)	Mutual interest: healthcare in developing regions
Personal factor	Personal chemistry with some people across the two organizations	Personal chemistry between the core people of the two organizations	

outcomes of the partnerships are also discussed looking at them as the result of the collaboration rather than a separate phase. After 1 year, partners evaluated their progress and outcomes, and made decisions with regard to the future of their collaboration [the full cases can be found in Balaisyte and Van Wassenhove (2011)].

The structure of the mini-cases is as follows. We first describe how the partnership was formed. Then we briefly discuss the evolution of the partnership. Finally we summarize the challenges encountered and outcomes achieved by the partnership.

22.3.1   Case 1: Partnership in Zambia

Around 68 % of Zambians live below the recognized national poverty line (United Nations Statistics Division 2014). The country is experiencing a generalized HIV/AIDS epidemic, with a national HIV prevalence rate of 17 % among adults, with the NGO sector being a crucial player in providing health services to the community. Lack of resources, capacity and training in the public sector for the healthcare services create demand for NGO services.

22.3.1.1   Formation of the Partnership

International HIV/AIDS Alliance in Zambia, established in 1999, has been a partner organization for the Zambia Integrated Health Program (ZIHPCOMM)[6]. Since it was founded, International HIV/AIDS Alliance in Zambia was challenged by decentralization since it has grown with a need to make the transition from a country office of the International HIV/AIDS Alliance to a fully independent Zambian NGO. Change management and capacity were required to handle this transition. International HIV/AIDS Alliance in Zambia joined this EDP while seeking to benefit from marketing expertise to build the image of the evolving organization, to increase the available resources of its supply chain, and gain benefits through the associational value (by improving its image) and interaction value (acquiring marketing skills from interaction).

At the same time, the private partner, backed by its organization, was looking for a 1-year engagement within an NGO operating in the healthcare sector. The private partner had worked in the pharmaceutical industry for the past 10 years, mostly in developed countries, and had extensive experience in the domains required by the NGO. So the private partner could help the NGO improve the management skills of employees and the NGO's operations and hence no longer regard their supply chain as an auxiliary function (Arminas 2005). The private partner was interested to build an understanding of how the healthcare system functions in a less developed context and how the pharmaceutical industry could contribute. Thus the expected benefits of the private partner through this partnership included interaction value

---

[6] http://bixby.berkeley.edu/bixby-internship-zambia-2003/

(learning how a nonprofit organization operates) and satisfy his interest in learning how to operate in a developing country. With the support of PEPAL, the two partners were matched and introduced to each other based on the objectives of the partners and potential fit criteria. For example for the NGO the skillset that the private partner possessed, industry (healthcare) expertise, and interest in developing regions were important criteria.

22.3.1.2 Evolution of the Partnership

The private partner joined Alliance Zambia as an advisor to the senior management team, which allowed him to take a leadership position. Partnership management tools and performance metrics initiated by the private partner through the form of semi-annual surveys were used. Partners established trust, compatibility, complementarity and commitment-based relationships. The relationships were straight, equal, and built on trust. With the private partner being on the ground for the 1-year period, partners had an opportunity to build close relations through daily communication. For example, the private partner supported Alliance Zambia team to prepare for one of the largest events, the National Prevention Convention by supporting and empowering its employees to take on new roles such as public speaking and succeed during the event. This is an example of how with the help of the private partner, the skills of the NGO's employees can be improved and their knowledge gap of business practices can be addressed (Samii and Van Wassenhove 2003).

22.3.1.3 Challenges and Outcomes

Unfortunately, in the midsummer the NGO experienced funding challenges. As a result, there was a change in management and the new Executive Director had different priorities. This is a common phenomenon in NGO supply chains which often face difficulties to attract and retain employees with management experience because of funding issues (Thomas 2005; Gustavsson 2003). The financial difficulties the International HIV/AIDS Alliance in Zambia faced jeopardized project goals. Taking the limited available resources into account, the partners decided not to continue with the collaboration and terminate it at the end of the programme at INSEAD.

22.3.2 Case 2: Partnership in Ukraine

Ukraine's major developmental challenges include underdeveloped infrastructure, unstable political environment, corruption, and excessive bureaucracy. The country has one of the highest HIV/AIDS prevalence rates in Europe, an area in which the NGO community is very active. The primary issues faced by the supply chains of most NGOs operating in the area, including International HIV/AIDS Alliance in Ukraine, were limited resources and strong competition for funding.

22.3.2.1 Formation of the Partnership

Five years after its foundation, Alliance Ukraine expanded by establishing a subsidiary that hosts the Regional Technical Support Hub (TS Hub) for the Eastern Europe and Central Asia region. The TS Hub provides technical support services to a wide range of NGOs, acting in this way as a new product that Alliance Ukraine can offer to other NGOs, and serves as a mechanism for the International HIV/AIDS Alliance to obtain additional funding for their operations.

Before joining the EDP, the Alliance Ukraine team was struggling to turn the hub into a sustainable business entity. Alliance Ukraine easily identified the TS Hub as the project for this partnership. The potential benefits of engaging in the partnership were of resource nature (to increase their funding) and interaction value (acquiring marketing skills and project development from interaction).

The private partner Tibotec has a strong CSR culture. It was a good match for Alliance Ukraine's needs in terms of skillset and expertise, as they had extensive experience in marketing and project development. Tibotec was interested in the partnership as a career development opportunity for its senior staff. Moreover, the corporate partners saw this partnership as an opportunity for improving their understanding of the epidemic in Ukraine which may facilitate their future operations in this new market as well as collaboration with the NGO sector. Tibotec partners supported Alliance Ukraine with market growth strategy expertise by sharing market analysis and its strategic planning knowledge. The potential benefit for the private partner was interaction value (learning how a nonprofit organization operates, employees' personal interest and motivation).

22.3.2.2 Evolution of the Partnership

With the support of PEPAL, the two partners were matched and introduced to each other based on their objectives and potential fit criteria. For example for the NGO the skillset that the private partner possessed, their social mission and the interest of the private partner in developing regions were important fit criteria. Table 22.1 presents the partner selection criteria for this partnership.

During the kick-off week at INSEAD, the project team divided roles, leadership and responsibilities, and also agreed on the interaction patterns. The project team had established a routine of bi-weekly telephone conferences that helped partners build a strong relationship and confront all issues openly. After the first 2 months of the partnership, the hub manager left the organization and a temporary manager from the International HIV/AIDS Alliance in Ukraine was assigned.

After the new TS Hub manager joined the HIV/AIDS Alliance in Ukraine, the private partners came to Ukraine and spent 1 week working with the new TS Hub manager and her team in order to readjust project goals. The project team developed good relationships. The partners shared the leadership of the project, with the private partner taking the lead on communication and mentoring, and the NGO partner leading the direction of the project.

22.3.2.3 Challenges and Outcomes

The first 2 months of the project were challenging since the International HIV/
AIDS Alliance team in Ukraine did not have a clear direction regarding the hub, a
typical characteristic of NGO supply chains (Maon et al. 2009). However, partners
managed to overcome this challenge by developing their strategic direction. One
year later, the partnership proved to be very collaborative with strong commitment
and trust coming from both sides. The TS Hub became a fully functional and revenue generating unit and partners maintained good relationships.

22.3.3 Case 3: Partnership in Uganda

Uganda is a landlocked country in East Africa with more than 35 % of its population living on less than $1.25 a day[7]. Currently, 7.2 % of Uganda's population is
suffering from HIV/AIDS[8]. The high poverty of the population combined with the
lack of public resources spent on health services, increases the demand for NGO
services.

22.3.3.1 Formation of the Partnership

The International HIV/AIDS Alliance in Uganda has been present in the country
since 2005 with an objective to improve access to HIV/AIDS prevention means,
care treatment and support services to orphans and vulnerable children. Being a
young organization, the International HIV/AIDS Alliance in Uganda suffered from
their staff lacking project and program implementation skills, a common characteristic of NGO supply chains (Thomas 2005; Gustavsson 2003). Therefore, a partnership with the private sector was considered a good opportunity to improve project
management skills and acquire a commercial sector perspective. Tibotec was ready
to offer these capabilities and welcomed the project as an opportunity to engage in
a meaningful CSR initiative. Through this partnership, Alliance Uganda was seeking to acquire increased resource base (in order to improve the skills of their
employees). The benefit for the private partner was associational value (through the
CSR initiative).

    With the support of PEPAL, the two partners were matched and introduced to
each other based on the potential fit criteria and their interests. Past experience of
the private partner in working with NGOs and in developing regions was considered an advantage. Table 22.1 presents the partner selection criteria.

---

[7] http://data.worldbank.org/indicator/SI.POV.DDAY

[8] http://www.avert.org/hiv-aids-uganda.htm#footnote3_we9dl36

22.3.3.2 Evolution of the Partnership

The partnership evolved through several phases. Partnership formation occurred during the EDP at INSEAD where partners agreed to work on the project through frequent communication over the phone and e-mails. At the beginning of the project, private partners made a first visit to Uganda, which was an eye-opening experience. They realized that defining clear goals was not an easy task. The first 4 months of the project were spent on discussions about how Tibotec could help Alliance Uganda. Then financial challenges arose for the NGO. The International HIV/AIDs Alliance in Uganda office was downsized, including management. The executive director left the NGO, leaving Tibotec without a leadership partner on the ground.

Following 2 months of struggle, a temporary project manager from the headquarters of International HIV/AIDS Alliance stepped in to support the partnership and Alliance in Uganda while the headquarters of the HIV/AIDS Alliance was supporting the hiring of the new executive director and project manager for the partnership. Because of this change, the partners were forced to redefine the goals of the supply chain partnership. Due to the financial challenges, International HIV/AIDS Alliance in Uganda decided to develop a Technical Support Hub (TS Hub), designed to generate revenues as an additional service that Alliance in Uganda could offer to other NGOs. Preparing a business plan and conducting market research became the new partnership objectives. Nine months after the beginning of the project, a new manager arrived at the NGO. The partners had to go through the whole adjustment and relationship-building cycle again, which negatively affected the project development dynamics, as described in the next section.

22.3.3.3 Challenges and Outcomes

To sum-up, despite a number of adjustments, it was hard for both sides to work on the project with no leadership support coming from the Alliance Uganda side. There was a lack of clarity in responsibilities and understanding by the Alliance Uganda team on how to accomplish the goals of the supply chain partnership, and misalignment of expectations on both sides. When the new executive director was hired, due to financial challenges and other priorities, he was not in a position to engage in the partnership to the full extent. Therefore, without active leadership, commitment, and support from the executive director, the project was not able to make progress.

After 1-year of not being able to find a common ground for collaboration, the partners re-evaluated their efforts and decided to terminate the partnership. They used the Programme's final training week at INSEAD to meet face-to-face and take this decision.

22.4   Propositions and Research Implications

Four stages of collaboration in cross-sector partnerships are identified by Austin (2000a, b): philanthropic, transactional, integrative, and transformative. Our three cross-sector partnerships are based on transfer of resources to one another. However, our partnerships are not yet so advanced in order to co-create value or to make changes at the societal level, even if these are their future goals. So our three partnerships fall into the transactional stage. The forms of value identified in our partnerships are associational, transferred resource, interaction and synergetic value as presented by Austin and Seitanidi (2012b, 2010a).

In this Section the three cases are analyzed using the findings from the literature. Section 22.4.1 presents the propositions that arise, while Sect. 22.4.2 discusses the research implications.

22.4.1   Propositions

In this Section we use the framework developed in Sect. 22.2 (Fig. 22.2), which depicts potential factors affecting the success of the cross-sector partnerships, and the case studies conducted to identify the factors that affected the outcomes of the three cross-sector partnerships.

Our analysis of the three cases revealed that during the partnership selection and formation phase setting clear objectives for the supply chain partnership (relevant to all cases), and having compatible and complementary partners regarding skills and available resources (relevant to all cases) improves chances to achieve partnership goals (Fig. 22.3). These findings are supported by the literature on the

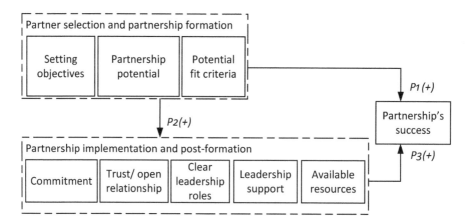

Fig. 22.3 Factors affecting success of cross-sector partnerships. Positive signs (+) indicate that the factor/-s at the beginning of the arrow and the variable at the end change in the same direction; for example if the partners put more effort on setting clear objectives for the partnership, then there is higher probability that the partnership will be successful

importance of cultural fit (Dahan et al. 2010), compatibility and complementarity of skills (Austin and Seitanidi 2012a, b; Berger et al. 2004) and resources (Kale and Singh 2009). Taking into account these findings, we form our Proposition 1.

Proposition 1 (P1) During the partner selection and partnership formation phase, improving

- *Setting objectives*
- *Identifying the partnership potential (clear benefits to all partners)*
- *Identifying fit criteria (between partner working styles and cultures, and clear understanding of the skills and weaknesses on both sides)*

will have a positive impact on the success of cross-sector supply chain partnership

In all three case studies we found a link between the success of the partner selection and partnership formation, and the partnership implementation and post-formation management. For example, we find that if the partnership potential is not adequate during the partner selection and partnership formation phase (e.g., regarding available resources of the supply chain partnership) then the partnership during the implementation and post-formation management phase faces challenges (all three cases) and objectives, processes and responsibilities may need to be readjusted. These results are in accordance with the findings of Kale and Singh (2009), Austin and Seitanidi (2012b) and Le Ber and Branzei (2010).

Taking into account these findings, we form our Proposition 2.

Proposition 2 (P2) Improving the planning of the partner selection and partnership formation phase will have a positive impact on the partnership implementation and post-formation phase of the supply chain partnership.

The success of the three cross-sector partnerships depends on factors linked to the partnership implementation and post-formation management phase. In all three cases we find that sustaining the commitment (evident in the Zambia and Ukraine cases) (Shah and Swaminathan 2008), building trust and open relationship (as was the case for all three partnerships) (Austin and Seitanidi 2012b), having a detailed map of leadership roles and responsibilities (evident in the Ukraine case) (Googins and Rochlin 2000; Austin 2000b; Bryson et al. 2006), establishing leadership support (as in the Ukraine case) (Austin 2000a and Waddock 1986), and having available resources for the partnership implementation (which was a barrier for all three cases) (Kale and Singh 2009) has a positive effect on achieving partnership objectives. Based on these observations, we form our Proposition 3.

Proposition 3 (P3) During the partnership implementation and post-formation phase, improving

- *Commitment*
- *Trust and open relationship*
- *Having a detailed map of leadership roles and responsibilities*
- *Establishing leadership support*
- *Having available resources for the partnership*

will have a positive impact on the success of the cross-sector supply chain partnership

<u>B</u>y comparing the literature findings (Fig. 22.2) with our three case study propositions (Fig. 22.3), we observe that articulation of the social problem did not challenge the partnership's success; perhaps this is due to the set-up of the EDP that allowed clarifying the social problem early in the program. However, there was a difference in the timing of the objectives. The partnership objectives were instrumental for the partner selection and were set before the partnership implementation started. On the contrary, the literature suggests that objectives are typically set later.

Finally, all three partnerships were challenged to measure the success of their supply chain partnerships, both on an organization and partnership level. Corporate partners did not establish any specific measures to track partnership impacts on their organizations. For the NGOs, the positive impacts of the collaboration were attributed to the success of the partnership in general. Observing our partnerships we found that the main challenge for setting KPIs and monitoring performance was related to the combination of several factors: partners' inability of setting objectives, and constantly changing available resources and engagement of senior management. Partners often were not sure about their ultimate objectives or these objectives were too broad or ill-defined. Initially all partnerships had very ambitious goals such as creating a new marketing strategy or designing a new business plan, that often proved difficult to achieve. These factors affected the progress of the partnership, resulted in a need to readjust or change objectives, and affected the ability to track partnership performance.

22.4.2   Research Implications

The analysis of the three cases also revealed that business and nonprofit partnerships are characterized by complexity due to the nature of NGO resource constrained environment, uncertainty, and multiple trade-offs (Besiou and Van Wassenhove 2015). Often NGOs are challenged by the resources that are required in advance for the partnership to function properly. Uncertainty is reflected in fierce competition among NGOs for limited funding, which makes the future of the NGO employees insecure. In our cases the business partners were often left without any support coming from the NGO side. Furthermore, due to the uncertainty of resource availability, the objectives of the partnerships, the support coming from the leadership, the roles of the partners and their commitment change dynamically. There are also time delays in building trust between the partners and improving their skills/capacity. Moreover, the partners need to deal with trade-offs between the short-term losses of investing constrained resources and the long-term benefits of the social cause. In "uneasy" partnerships, like the three cases discussed in this chapter, it may be challenging to capture and monetize the value created by the supply chain partnership. Value is often rather intangible, so setting quantitative KPIs may be hard.

We believe that there is an opportunity for OM/SCM research to dive into the interesting environment of cross-sector partnerships. First, OM/SCM researchers need to go to the field to understand the constraints and the complex environment of these partnerships. After mapping the territory, modeling could be used to better understand the impact of the limited resources (for example lack of funding) on the supply chain partnership.

Then the impact of different decisions and actions could be evaluated to maximize the benefits of working together and building more effective partnerships. Education in OM/SCM could also find research in cross-sector supply chain partnerships beneficial. Examples of cross-sector partnerships could be used contrasting them to examples of commercial partnerships. The students could initially try to explore the impact of constrained resources on the operations of the supply chain partnership at a conceptual level and then capture the right trade-offs with OM/SCM models. From a pedagogical perspective, students could also try to come up with KPIs that could measure the social impact and the success of such partnerships.

Our examples of cross-sector partnerships are characterized by stakeholders with conflicting goals (private companies, NGOs and donors) (Van Wassenhove and Besiou 2013). The private companies engage in such partnerships because of their CSR strategy, while the NGOs use them as means to improve the skills of their employees and improve their funding. Private sector supply chain partnerships also face multiple challenges like incentive misalignment but what makes these issues more challenging in cross-sector environments are limited resources and higher levels of uncertainty. For example NGO supply chains suffer from high turnover due to limited funding (Thomas 2005; Gustavsson 2003). Moreover, as seen in our cases, many of the partners were engaging for their first time in a cross-sector partnership and they had different expectations. So being part of such a partnership may not be straightforward for all the partners, or even desirable for all employees, an unfamiliar context for private supply chains. OM/SCM can also be used to map the stakeholders' dynamic goals and understand this context. For example Stadtler and Van Wassenhove (2013) study the partnership between the humanitarian Logistics Cluster and four logistics companies. Even if the four logistics companies are competitors, when a disaster strikes they activate the supply chain partnership and share resources to optimize the social benefit. Broader issues from a supply chain perspective need to be taken into account, like the strong commitment coming from the partners. Collaborative game theory and system dynamics could be applied in order to study the dynamic changes of the partner roles for different levels of decentralization and competition coming from the funding in an effort to maximize the benefit of the partners.

The complexity and the unfamiliar context of the cross-sector supply chain partnerships can lead to counterintuitive behavior (Besiou and Van Wassenhove 2014). In our cases even if the partners had to face many challenges, their commitment was really strong due to their belief in a social cause. Pedagogical cases in OM/SCM discipline could also be used here in order to study how the objective functions of the supply chain partnership would change under such conditions.

22.5 Conclusions and Practical Implications

Today increasingly more companies are under pressure to engage in corporate social responsibility initiatives like partnerships with non-governmental organizations. In response to increased practitioner interest on the topic, this chapter studies three examples of cross-sector supply chain partnerships between pharmaceutical companies and healthcare focused NGOs. In this study we look at the factors that affect the success of such partnerships, and identify the avenues for future research on cross-sector partnerships for the OM/SCM discipline.

We hope that our findings will be helpful to master-level students, academia, but foremost to the actual practitioners in healthcare sector both on business and NGO sides, who are already managing or planning to engage in cross-sector partnerships.

As observed from the three partnerships, engaging in cross-sector collaboration requires substantial amount of resources and efforts that may not be straightforward to all partners. Our framework and findings can help practitioners manage the value creation process better through cross-sector partnerships and answer the following questions: How different partnering processes and factors (e.g., setting objectives) affect value generation? How these different factors can be most effectively organized during different phases of partnership (e.g., leadership)? How and in what combination can partners use resources designated for partnering (e.g., available resources)? What actions can help partners improve implementation of the partnership internally, externally and between partners (e.g., communication and commitment)? We hope that this study will support their efforts in setting-up partnerships and will provide insights on how to build more efficient collaboration.

To have a successful partnership, the engagement process needs to be supported by the leadership. The benefits for each partner and for the social cause need to be communicated to all employees; unclear communication and lack of commitment can undermine the partnership's success. If the partners due to external constraints, like lack of funding, lose their direct interest in the partnership, then resetting the objectives of the supply chain partnership or changing the leadership roles may be helpful. For example, in the case of the partnership in Uganda the initial goals concerned how to improve business related skills of employees. However, when the NGO faced funding issues, the partners decided to set sustaining the service of the TS Hub in order to increase their financial resources as the new objective.

In addition, given the specifics and challenges presented by these partnerships, characterized by multiple stakeholders with differing objectives, and the complexity of the system in which they operate, we see ample of space for further research. We believe that the trade-off between short-term goals of spending fewer resources and the long-term goal of capacity building offers interesting research opportunities.

This chapter shows that for research on sustainable supply chains we need to take into account all the other broader issues that should go beyond the traditional supply chain perspective. It is in particular relevant in addressing healthcare management issues in developing countries where actors face uncertainty due to capacity constraints such as funding and skills of their employees (Thomas 2005; Gustavsson 2003).

In addition, the cross-sector supply chain partnerships are very different from the ones developed between private partners. In the NGO context, SCM is of increasing importance but it has been undervalued since NGOs often regard it as an auxiliary function (Arminas 2005). In order to overcome this gap, private companies have an opportunity through cross-sector supply chain partnerships to help NGOs increase their resources and the exposure to SCM and management related tools (Van Wassenhove 2006). In this way, the skills of the NGO employees will improve and their knowledge gap will decrease (Samii and Van Wassenhove 2003). At the same time the pharmaceutical companies engaged in such partnerships will acquire valuable experience of operations in developing markets. Interdisciplinary research combining OM/SCM discipline with behavioral, management and strategy topics could be beneficial to optimize the desired impact of the partnership with the existing resources.

This research has some limitations. First, it is limited to three cases. This was necessary to be able to focus only on one specific industry in order for the results to be comparable, but the generalization of the findings is limited. Second, more research is needed to test the propositions.

References

Alsop RJ (2004) The 18 immutable laws of corporate reputation. Free Press, New York

Arminas D (2005) Supply lessons of tsunami aid. Supply Manag 10(2):14

Austin JE (2000a) The collaboration challenge: how nonprofits and businesses succeed through strategic alliances. Jossey-Bass, San Francisco

Austin JE (2000b) Strategic collaboration between nonprofits and businesses. Nonprofit Volunt Sect Q 29(1):69–97

Austin JE, Seitanidi MM (2012a) Collaborative value creation: a review of partnering between nonprofits and businesses. Part 2: partnership processes and outcomes. Nonprofit Volunt Sect Q 41(6):929–968

Austin JE, Seitanidi MM (2012b) Collaborative value creation: a review of partnering between nonprofits and businesses. Part I: value creation spectrum and collaboration stages. Nonprofit Volunt Sect Q 41(5):723–755

Austin JE, Hesselbein F, Whitehead JC (2000) The collaboration challenge: how nonprofits and businesses succeed through strategic alliances. Jossey-Bass, San Francisco

Balaisyte J, Van Wassenhove LN (2011) Partnerships for development, INSEAD Working Paper

Berger IE, Cunningham PH, Drumwright ME (2004) Social alliances: company/nonprofit collaboration. Calif Manage Rev 47(1):58–90

Besiou M, Van Wassenhove LN (2015) Addressing the challenge of modeling for decision-making in socially responsible operations. Prod Oper Manag 24(9)

Bryson JM, Crosby BC, Middleton Stone M (2006) The design and implementation of cross-sector collaborations: propositions from the literature. Public Adm Rev 66:44–55

Clarke A, Fuller M (2010) Collaborative strategic management: strategy formulation and implementation by multi-organizational cross-sector social partnerships. J Bus Ethics 94(1):85–101

Cooper TL, Bryer TA, Meek JW (2006) Citizen-centered collaborative public management. Public Adm Rev 66:76–88

Dahan NM, Doh JP, Oetzel J, Yaziji M (2010) Corporate-NGO collaboration: co-creating new business models for developing markets. Long Range Plann 43(2–3):326–342

Das TK, Teng B (1998) Between trust and control: developing confidence in alliances. Acad Manage Rev 23(3):491–512

Development Indicators Unit, Statistics Division, United Nations (2014) Population below national poverty line, total, percentage. http://mdgs.un.org/unsd/mdg/SeriesDetail.aspx?srid=581. Accessed 6 Oct 2014

Googins BK, Rochlin SA (2000) Creating the partnership society: understanding the rhetoric and reality of cross sector partnerships. Bus Soc Rev 105(1):127–144

Gourville JT, Rangan VK (2004) Valuing the cause marketing relationship. Calif Manage Rev 47(1):38–57

Gray B (1989) Collaborating. Jossey-Bass, San Francisco

Gustavsson L (2003) Humanitarian logistics: context and challenges. Forced Migr Rev 18:6–8

Heap S (1998) NGOs and the private sector: potential for partnerships? (INTRAC Occasional Papers Series, 27). INTRAC, Oxford

Kale P, Singh H (2009) Managing strategic alliances: what do we know now, and where do we go from here? Acad Manag Perspect 23(3):45–62

Koza M, Lewin A (2000) Managing partnerships and strategic alliances: raising the odds of success. Eur Manag J 18(2):146–151

Lambert DM (2014) Supply chain management: processes, partnerships, performance, 4th edn. Supply Chain Management Institute, Sarasota

Le Ber MJ, Branzei O (2010) Towards a critical theory value creation in cross-sector partnerships. Organization 17(5):599–629

Maon F, Lindgreen A, Vanhamme J (2009) Developing supply chains in disaster relief operations through cross-sector socially oriented collaborations: a theoretical model. Supply Chain Manag Int J 14(2):149–164

McCann JE (1983) Design guidelines for social problem-solving interventions. J Appl Behav Sci 19(2):177–189

Orlitzky M, Schmidt FL, Rynes SL (2003) Corporate social and financial performance: a meta-analysis. Organ Stud 24(3):403–441

Rondinelli DA, London T (2003) How corporations and environmental groups cooperate: Assessing cross-sector alliances and collaborations. Acad Manag Exec 17(1):61–76

Samii R, Van Wassenhove L (2003) The United Nations Joint Logistics Centre (UNJLC): the genesis of a humanitarian relief coordination platform. Case Study 02/2003-5093, INSEAD, Fontainebleau

Seitanidi MM (2010) The politics of partnerships. A critical examination of nonprofit-business partnerships. Springer, London

Seitanidi MM, Crane A (2009) Implementing CSR through partnerships: understanding the selection, design and institutionalisation of nonprofit-business partnerships. J Bus Ethics 85:413–429

Selsky JW, Parker B (2005) Cross-sector partnerships to address social issues: challenges to theory and practice. J Manag 31(6):849–873

Sept L, Naylor S, Weston R (2011) Measuring the impact of social programs: a review of best practices. Stanford supply chain management forum, socially and environmentally responsible supply chains forum

Shah R, Swaminathan V (2008) Factors influencing partner selection in strategic alliances: the moderating role of alliance context. Strateg Manag J 29(5):471–494

Stadtler L, Van Wassenhove LN (2013) Coopetition as a paradox: handling coopetitive relationships in multi-company, cross-sector partnerships. Working Paper

Thomas A (2005) Humanitarian logistics: matching recognition with responsibility. Asia-Pacific Develop Rev 21:32–34

Tully S (2004) Corporate-NGO partnerships as a form of civil regulation: Lessons from the energy and biodiversity initiative (Discussion Paper 22, ESRC Centre for Analysis of Risk and Regulation [CARR]). London School of Economics, London

Van Wassenhove L (2006) Humanitarian aid logistics: supply chain management in high gear. J Oper Res Soc 57(5):475–489

Van Wassenhove LN, Besiou M (2013) Complex problems with multiple stakeholders: how to bridge the gap between reality and OR/MS? J Bus Econ 83(1):87–97

Waddock SA (1986) Public-private partnerships as social product and process. Res Corp Soc Perform Policy 8:273–300

Waddock SA (1988) Building successful social partnerships. Sloan Manage Rev 29(4):17

Index

Yann Bouchery, Charles J. Corbett, Jan C. Fransoo, and Tarkan Tan 2017   507
Y. Bouchery et al. (eds.), *Sustainable Supply Chains*, Springer Series in Supply
Chain Management 4, DOI 10.1007/978-3-319-29791-0